The
PC-SIG
LIBRARY
4th EDITION

A Directory of Public Domain
and User-Supported Software for
the IBM-PC, PCjr, and Compatibles

Published by:

PC-SIG, INC.
1030 E. Duane Avenue, Suite D
Sunnyvale, CA 94086

March 1987
January 1988 Second Printing

Trademarks:

dBASE, dBASE II, dBASE III are trademarks of Ashton-Tate.
IBM PC, PC/XT, PCjr, PC/AT and PC-DOS are trademarks of International Business Machines.
Lotus, Symphony, and 1-2-3 are trademarks of Lotus Development Corporation.
MS-DOS and Multiplan are trademarks of Microsoft Corporation.
VisiCalc is a trademark of VisiCorp.
WordStar is a trademark of MicroPro International.

ISBN 0-915835-05-3

"We estimate that PC-SIG has helped us to reach well over half a million computer users. With a bi-monthly magazine and frequent ads in the major computer magazines, PC-SIG reaches a vast number of personal computer users.

In addition, people know that if they want the lastest version of a good piece of software, PC-SIG will have it. PC-SIG has a reputation for providing the latest and greatest software. I am pleased to have ButtonWare software featured in the PC-SIG catalog."

> Jim Button, CEO
> ButtonWare, Inc.
> Author of PC-FILE, PC-CALC,
> PC-STYLE, PC-TYPE, and others

"I was very pleased when PC-SIG began to promote our software products because PC-SIG is the premiere Public Domain and User Supported Software distributor in the United States. I knew that other distributors would follow PC-SIG's lead and our software would get wide exposure.

PC-SIG is different from other software distributors. They are the only company that regularly contacts me by phone and mail. Many other software distributors are simply mail-order business that don't begin to offer the full range of services that PC-SIG does."

> Christopher O. McVicar, Owner
> Image Computer Systems
> Author of IMAGE PRINT

"PC-SIG provides a much needed service, organizing and distributing the vast amount of public domain and user-supported software available for the IBM PC. We are happy to have our user-supported software included in the library; many of our registered users obtained their first copy of PC-Write from PC-SIG."

> Bob Wallace, President
> Quicksoft
> Author of PC-Write

We dedicate this Fourth Edition Directory of the PC-SIG
Library to the authors whose considerable talents fill this book.
Their extraordinary qualities of generosity and creativity have
produced a unique asset for the personal computer community.
As part of that community, we offer this expression of our
thanks and admiration.

We further wish to acknowledge the contribution of all the
end-users of Public Domain and Shareware software. Your
keen interest in quality software and your support of the
authors within the Library make this unique venture a success.

ACKNOWLEDGEMENTS:

Founder   President

Richard Petersen   Hazel Gray

THE DIRECTORY TEAM:

Documentation Manager
Walter L. Hudson

Senior Technical Advisor
Francis M. Juliano

Senior Reviewers:

Peter Lindquist   Steven Opson

PC-SIG Technical Support Team:

Dave Cagle   Mike Shaw

Denise Lindquist   Brian Tuck

Contributing Reviewers:

Penni Alexander   D. A. Crim

Carroll Baker   Trudy Lavar

Ed Bellezza   Michael Saintloud

Barbara Chisolm   Ed Sisler

Table of Contents   *4th Edition Directory*

1.0   Introduction 1

2.0   How to Use This Book 7

3.0   Getting Started 9

4.0   **DESCRIPTION OF DISK CONTENTS** 21
      APPLICATION SOFTWARE
      Artificial Intelligence 22
      Bulletin Board Software 25
      Business Applications 29
      Communication 55
      Computer Education 68
      Databases 74
      Desktop Managers 95
      Education 106
      Entertainment 121
      Financial Applications 139
      Games 149
      Graphics 172
      Home Applications 190
      Languages 205
      Math/Scientific/Statistics 222
      Reference Materials 232
      Special Applications 241
      Spreadsheets and Templates 262
      Word Processors 278
      UTILITIES SOFTWARE
      Copy/Uncopy 294
      DOS Level 299
      Endcode/Decode 323
      General System 327
      Language 344
      Printer 362
      Programmer 375
      Screen 387

5.0   **INDEX** 393
      By Disk Number 393
      By Disk Title 398
      By Subject 405

APPENDIX 415
   Glossary..415

FORMS
   The PC-SIG Library on CD ROM
   Order Forms
   Submission Forms

1.0 Introduction

This, the Fourth Edition of the PC-SIG Directory, is our largest ever
compilation of user-supported and public domain software. The 705 disks
in the Library contain thousands of programs for the IBM Personal
Computer and its compatibles (hereafter referred to collectively as PCs).
Each program has been screened and analyzed by our staff and reviewed
by outside reviewers to insure quality, resulting in the most complete and
up-to-date directory of its kind.

Consider this Directory your personal access tool to a world of inexpensive
yet quality software. from short, specialized subroutines to fully formed,
powerful word processing, spreadsheets, database packages and, of course,
all those neat games!

The Directory is designed to be straight-forward and easy to use.

- This Introduction will tell you about PC-SIG, our software and how
  this Directory is put together.
- Next is How To Use This Book! which gives you a quick overview
  and how the program reviews can be most useful to you.
- For people new to PCs, the Getting Started section describes booting
  your PC, hints on using DOS to your advantage, and tips on how to
  use the programs in this Directory.

Finally, The the Good Stuff: we have arranged our description of The
Library in two alphabetically-ordered categories of software:

- First, an APPLICATIONS SOFTWARE section covering everything
  from Artificial Intelligence to Word Processing;
- Second, an UTILITIES SOFTWARE Section packed with specialized
  programs for such things as maximizing your printer, encoding data
  or constructing the perfect subroutine in Turbo Pascal.

Whether you are a beginner or an "old pro," we are sure that you will
benefit from this edition of the Library. So, Enjoy and Happy Computing!

1.1 About PC-SIG

Consumer demand for high quality, low cost software for PCs has made PC-SIG the world's largest distributor of public domain and user-supported software. Since its inauguration in 1982, the PC-SIG software library has grown in size, quality and stature among computing enthusiasts. We could not have made it to over 700 disks and thousands of supporting members without vigorous and critical support from the personal computing community. We feel our success has come from following the maxim of cooperating with and learning from the grassroots users' skills and needs.

Our goal is to match those needs with the best available public domain and user-supported software. To do this we work closely with the authors, a group of dynamic and cooperative programmers. For them, PC-SIG is a clearinghouse for their unique and beneficial programs, with virtually no distribution costs for the author. This allows specialized programs not normally seen in the retail market place to reach the consumer through the PC-SIG Library. It also provides the author with a financial base unencumbered by middlemen. Developing and refining this three-way partnership — you the users, the authors, and PC-SIG — is the way we aim to continue putting the finest quality software within the reach of all.

More than just a distribution center, PC-SIG offers telephone technical support for all of its products. Your questions and feedback are a major factor in our success. We send a User Response disk with each order; we collect and review your comments on these programs and regularly pass them along to the authors. For this edition of the Directory we have inserted representative user comments in our program reviews. We believe your perceptions are invaluable feedback for the whole computing community.

PC-SIG is moving forward with hardware as well as software innovations. With the advent of our CD-ROM publishing capacity, PC-SIG has placed the entire library on the user's desk. We will continue to promote and develop creative applications in CD-ROM publishing.

1.2 Public Domain and User-Supported Software

The entire PC-SIG Library consists of public domain and user-supported software. While they are mixed here, they are different in several important ways.

Unlike copyrighted material, public domain material was originated by authors who chose not to seek formal rights or royalties; the work is free to be used or altered with few or no restrictions. Our library contains hundreds of such public domain programs.

The user-supported software in our library falls under a different legal category. Rather than sell their programs on the retail market like other copyrighted programs, authors of user-supported programs have elected to market their works directly. You, the buyer, deal directly with the author of a particular program that you decide has lasting value and suits your computing profile. Marketing software in this manner allows you to purchase quality software at a fraction of the price from normal retail channels.

Authors of user-supported programs often request a contribution from satisfied, regular users of their programs. In return for this contribution, such "registered users" are entitled to a wide variety of support, for example, full documentation from the author, telephone-based technical support and notification of updates and upgrades are common means authors use to support their registered users. Your direct contributions compensate the author for his completed work and provide a real incentive to produce further original, quality programs for this unique type of software marketing.

1.3 Disclaimer

PC-SIG distributes its software directly to subscribers from our Sunnyvale headquaters and through Authorized PC-SIG Dealers. Only by dealing directly with PC-SIG or Authorized Dealers can you be assured that you receive the most up-to-date version of the PC-SIG disk. We cannot be responsible for, or support, public domain software obtained from other sources.

1.4 The Design of the Directory

We have spent many years collecting, testing and supporting this Fourth Edition of our Library. Guiding us in this endeavor have been these beliefs about you, the vigorous, curious and adventurous supporters of our Library in particular and the personal computer industry in general:

- You want the highest quality of software available;
- Your input and experiences, not advertising slogans, are crucial to evaluating software;
- Low cost and wide variety are key issues for you;
- You believe in supporting shareware and freeware software, their authors and their audiences.

To put these beliefs into action, we designed a review process for each of the 705 disks in our Library. The distilled and formatted results are in your hands. Here is how they got here:

The description listed for each program on each disk in our catalog was compiled from work done by our commissioned disk-reviewers or extracted from the on-disk documentation. As a final step, a copy of the review was sent to the original author with a request for updating, corrections, etc. There was a surprisingly large response, with many authors sending major updates and new programs. All of this was reviewed, edited and prepared to fit into the following format structure. However, as good as these reviews are, they won't replace your careful study of the on-disk documentation which accompanies each program.

This information was then placed in the following format:

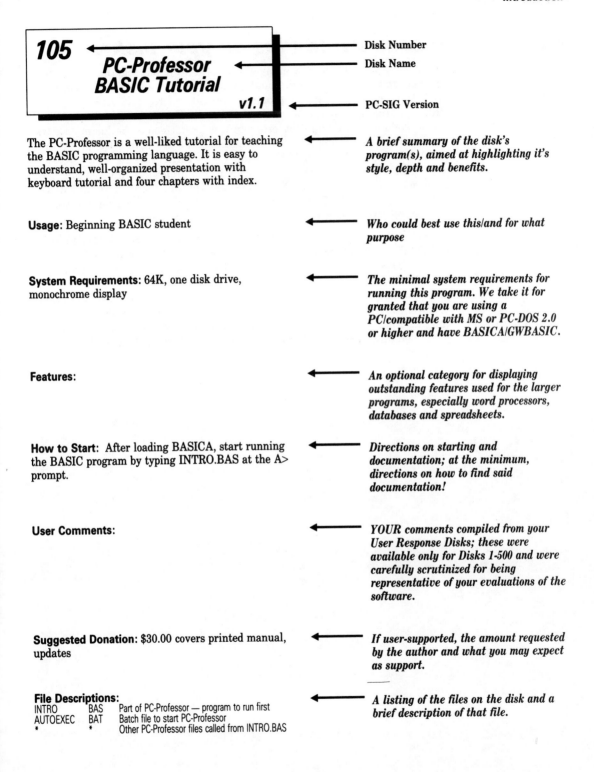

105 ← Disk Number

PC-Professor BASIC Tutorial ← Disk Name

v1.1 ← PC-SIG Version

The PC-Professor is a well-liked tutorial for teaching the BASIC programming language. It is easy to understand, well-organized presentation with keyboard tutorial and four chapters with index.

A brief summary of the disk's program(s), aimed at highlighting it's style, depth and benefits.

Usage: Beginning BASIC student

Who could best use this/and for what purpose

System Requirements: 64K, one disk drive, monochrome display

The minimal system requirements for running this program. We take it for granted that you are using a PC/compatible with MS or PC-DOS 2.0 or higher and have BASICA/GWBASIC.

Features:

An optional category for displaying outstanding features used for the larger programs, especially word processors, databases and spreadsheets.

How to Start: After loading BASICA, start running the BASIC program by typing INTRO.BAS at the A> prompt.

Directions on starting and documentation; at the minimum, directions on how to find said documentation!

User Comments:

YOUR comments compiled from your User Response Disks; these were available only for Disks 1-500 and were carefully scrutinized for being representative of your evaluations of the software.

Suggested Donation: $30.00 covers printed manual, updates

If user-supported, the amount requested by the author and what you may expect as support.

File Descriptions:
INTRO   BAS   Part of PC-Professor — program to run first
AUTOEXEC   BAT   Batch file to start PC-Professor
*   *   Other PC-Professor files called from INTRO.BAS

A listing of the files on the disk and a brief description of that file.

1.5 About those unlisted files on your disks:

In the early years of PC-SIG many of the disks were put together with little or no documentation, just a thorough, functional review by our Technical Staff. In those days we placed a pair of files called CRC.TXT and CRC4.COM as special verifiers for your benefit. The CRC.COM file was a Cyclic Redundancy Computing program that performed a checksum on a file you specified. For example, you have questions as to whether the program FRED.EXE is really "A-OK". You enter CRC4 FRED ENTER. The CRC program computes the total sum of bytes in the program and gives the answer in hexadecimal form. You then compare that to the value in FRED's listing in the CRC.TXT. If it is not the same, contact us for a replacement as a bad/missing sector is there and is sure to give you fits!

As our disk duplication and technical review process improved, this addition of CRC files was dropped, though we still replace any defective disk at no charge. Instead, we add a pair of files called FILES(Disk Number).TXT and NOTES(Disk Number).TXT. FILES gives a descriptive listing of all the program files on the disk, pointing out documentation, batch files and other goodies. NOTES is generally the review done by our outside reviewers, ranging from brief to extensive and enthusiastic. We heartily recommend your spending some time checking these out when you get the disks.

2.0 HOW TO USE THIS BOOK

The Directory to the PC-SIG Library, the very large book you are holding, actually represents an ENORMOUSLY LARGER collection of programs, files and information. That collection, of course, is the PC-SIG Library, an immensely varied selection of the best public domain and user-supported software in almost every imaginable applications category.

YOUR PROBLEM:

How do I get exactly what I want from all this?

OUR SOLUTION:

To assist you in getting what you want from the PC-SIG Directory, we have designed it with several different people and approaches in mind. THE FIRST STEP is easy: Lets find out WHO YOU ARE!

Are you NEW to Personal Computers?

READ the GETTING STARTED sections slowly and carefully. Practice the DOS commands described there and get comfortable with how to run BASIC programs on your particular system.

Are you looking for a TYPE of Program or Application?

GO to the TABLE OF CONTENTS (page iii) to find which of the ALPHABETICALLY LISTED CATEGORIES of programs your particular choice is probably in. Flip to it and have fun browsing through, comparing features, usage, and size of program.

Are you LOOKING for A PARTICULAR PROGRAM?

GO to the INDEXES (SECTION 5.0) where you can search for a program by program name, disk number and category. You might also just go to its category and compare it to what's available.

3.0 Getting Started

If you are new to computing, be sure and read this section carefully. What follows is a brief introduction to some of the commands you will use to run programs on your PC. For those already familiar with DOS commands and running programs, this should serve as a handy reminder.

Simply by purchasing a PC/compatible, you have joined the illustrious group known as 'Users'. Welcome. Many times new users are in awe of their systems and may feel slightly inhibited about using them. You will not damage your computer by typing on the keyboard with anything smaller than a hammer. Make backup copies of your software, especially your DOS disk, then feel free to experiment and to learn at your own pace.

Without you the computer is nothing more than a table ornament. You're in charge, with some limitations. The PC does not evaluate your skill as a user. The computer takes everything literally. It is up to you to insert the periods and spaces in the correct places. To save time and anguish before we begin, plug it in.

3.1 Disk Operating System (DOS)

DOS is the heart of your system. It contains the necessary information for your computer to understand the commands you type in from the various programs. This allows you to retrieve information from a diskette or hard disk. You must start with DOS before using any program from our library.

Below are 5 basic DOS commands you will use:

DIR	Abbreviation for DIRectory. Allows you to view the names of the files on the disk.
DISKCOPY	Allows you to make copies of the entire disk.
FORMAT	Enables you to prepare a blank disk for use by your computer.
COPY	Allows you to copy files from one disk to another or to the printer.
TYPE	Enables you to display the contents of the text on the screen.

Insert your DOS program disk in disk drive A: and turn on your computer. Please refer to your system manual if you are unsure of your disk drive locations. As your machine whirs to life it may display a numerical count of your memory on the screen followed by a beep and a red light appearing over your disk drive A. Lock your DOS diskette in your A drive and you are off. The machine is now reading your DOS disk. You may be asked to fill in a date or a time (all time is in military time with midnight being 2400) or you can just press return each time the questions are asked. Once completed the A> is followed by a blinking cursor. Congratulations, you have just booted your computer. Booted, in this case, having good connotations. You are now ready to run your programs.

Following the A> type (in either lower case or upper case):

DIR   (press ENTER or ◄┘).

All DOS commands require that you depress the ENTER or ◄┘ key to activate the command. Your screen should now show a table of names and numbers similar to the following illustration:

```
Volume in drive A is MSDOS320-01
Directory of A:
ANSI        SYS      1651     7-07-86     12:00P
APPEND      COM      1725     7-07-86     12:00P
ASSIGN      COM      1523     7-07-86     12:00P
ATTRIB      EXE      8234     7-07-86     12:00P
CHKDSK      EXE      9680     7-07-86     12:00P
COMMAND     COM     23612     7-07-86     12:00P
DISKCOMP    EXE      3808     7-07-86     12:00P
DISKCOPY    EXE      4096     7-07-86     12:00P
DRIVER      SYS      1102     7-07-86     12:00P
EDLIN       EXE      7356     7-07-86     12:00P
EXE2BIN     EXE      3050     7-07-86     12:00P
FC          EXE     14558     7-07-86     12:00P
FDISK       EXE     16830     7-07-86     12:00P
FIND        EXE      6403     7-07-86     12:00P
FORMAT      EXE     11005     7-07-86     12:00P
GRAFTABL    EXE      8210     7-07-86     12:00P
GRAPHICS    EXE     13170     7-07-86     12:00P
JOIN        EXE      9012     7-07-86     12:00P
KEYBDV      EXE      2886     7-07-86     12:00P
KEYBFR      EXE      2948     7-07-86     12:00P
KEYBGR      EXE      2940     7-07-86     12:00P
KEYBIT      EXE      2892     7-07-86     12:00P
KEYBSP      EXE      2983     7-07-86     12:00P
KEYBUK      EXE      2886     7-07-86     12:00P
LABEL       EXE      2750     7-07-86     12:00P
MODE        EXE     13928     7-07-86     12:00P
MORE        COM       282     7-07-86     12:00P
PRINT       EXE      8824     7-07-86     12:00P
RAMDRIVE    SYS      6462     7-07-86     12:00P
RECOVER     EXE      4145     7-07-86     12:00P
REPLACE     EXE      4852     7-07-86     12:00P
SORT        EXE      1898     7-07-86     12:00P
SUBST       EXE      9898     7-07-86     12:00P
SYS         COM      4607     7-07-86     12:00P
       34 File(s)   81920 bytes free
```

The first column in the illustration lists the name of the files on the disk. The second column is that file's three-character extension. The remaining columns of numbers represent, in order left to right, the size of the file, creation date and finally the time the file was created.

Please note that the creation date or "time stamp" will change whenever you modify and save a file; one of the available functions of DOS is as a timekeeper. However, you must initiate this by giving the date and or time when you boot the system up. Its up to you!

3.2 Displaying what is on your disk

Now comes the fun part. With the A> and blinking cursor on your screen remove your DOS disk from drive A: and place in your first program. To start some program in the library you simply have to type "GO" and you are off. These disk are marked with a "GO" on the disk. Others will require a little different approach. For example, after the A> on your screen again type:

        DIR   (press ENTER or ◄─┘).

This will show you a listing of the files on the program you are about to run:

```
Volume in drive A is #270 vxx.xx
 Directory of A:
 1-100          UPP      123662    1-27-86         4:12P
 101-200        UPP      117056    1-27-86         4:19P
 DFIND          BAT          85    2-09-86        10:08P
 GO             BAT          20    2-09-86        10:09P
 INDEX          TXT       38338    8-06-86         9:34a
 MORE           COM         384    2-09-86        10:09P
 ORDER          TXT        3465    5-05-86         1:59P
 PC-SIG         TXT         588    5-05-86         1:59P
 Q&A            TXT        5114    5-05-86         1:59P
 README                    2838    2-09-86        10:08P
 SUBMIT         TXT        1758    2-09-86        10:09P
 URESP          TXT         195    2-09-86        10:09P
        14 File(s)   68993 bytes free
```

In order to read the text included on this disk, return to the A> and type:

        TYPE README   (press ENTER or ◄─┘).

This will allow you to see what is on the text file as it scrolls (rolls) up your screen. To stop this rolling depress the CTRL and NUM LOCK keys simultaneously. The scrolling should stop allowing you to read the information at your own pace. To start the scrolling again strike any key. It is suggested that you print the information on your printer thereby allowing you to refer to it at any given time. To accomplish this after the A> type:

        COPY README.TXT LPT1:   (press ENTER or ◄─┘)

or

        COPY README.TXT PRN   (press ENTER or ◄─┘).

LPT1: means line printer #1 which works for most machines. PRN means printer and this works on the remaining machines. Your printer (if it is turned on) should now be merrily printing away.

Most library programs are either written in BASIC or have been compiled into .EXE or .COM files (see listings of file extensions below). Programs written in BASIC can be distinguished by the file extension .BAS after the filename. These require a different method of running the program.

First, these require you to load BASIC (or BASICA, the advanced form of BASIC). On a PC, this can be done by typing BASIC or BASICA and the filename of the program that you choose to run. On a PCjr you will need to load the BASIC ROM cartridge. Because the procedure depends a great deal on your system's configuration, we urge you to read the next section carefully to get comfortable with yours.

3.3 Running BASIC programs

Almost 30% of the programs in the PC-SIG Library are written in the BASIC programming language. It is crucial that you understand how to run them on your system, whether it has one or two drives, whether it is a standard IBM or a compatible configuration. This section is devoted to giving you a clear step-by-step set of directions for these situations.

Please note that in following sections mention of the program BASIC.EXE is replaced by an all-inclusive use of the term BASICA for the program BASICA.EXE, the Advanced form of BASIC introduced with DOS 2.0 and above. Using the command for BASICA will invoke all the earlier forms of BASIC. For systems using MicroSoft's GWBASIC, the BASIC interpreter of the MS-DOS world, or other forms of BASIC, please see your Users Manual.

Why the difference between PC-DOS and MS-DOS? IBM placed part of tis BASIC lanuage into two hardware chips on the systemboard (called ROMs) and the rest is on the PC-DOS disk; hence you need both present to run BASIC/BASICA programs. The BASIC of MS-DOS is on disk. Simply put, for IBM-specific programs, you must have a version of PC-DOS running on your IBM PC.

3.4 Running BASIC with one floppy drive

Method 1:

After loading the DOS, you type BASICA ENTER at the DOS prompt (A>).
After the BASIC screen comes up and greets you with its cheery "OK",
remove the DOS disk and put the program disk in the A: drive. Then you
type LOAD "filename.BAS" and press ENTER. When the OK returns, type
RUN ENTER. Your BASIC program will then "come up" for you.

***** Two Noteworthy Things: *****

First, when you enter the filename in the LOADing process, you do not need
to type the ".BAS." Second, if you examine the disk contents from DOS by
running a DIR, you will find most times that there is a MENU.BAS or a
MAIN.BAS or a INTRO.BAS named file; choosing these brings you to a
selection menu allows you to choose from the entire contents of the
disk/program without having to exit and reselect by the above step-by-step
method. There are easier ways! See Below!

Method 2:

Use the COPY command to put a copy of the BASIC or BASICA.EXE file
from your working DOS disk — don't use the ORIGINAL! -onto your
program disk. PRECAUTION: Run a DIR to be sure there is enough free
space on your floppy disk to add it! When you have loaded the DOS, you can
swap disks and enter BASICA filename ENTER. In one command you will
load BASIC and load and run your BASIC program of choice. Not bad, eh?

A variation on this theme:

Format a disk with the command "FORMAT A: /s", the "/s" telling the DOS
to put the system files onto it. Next, copy COMMAND.COM onto it. With
these there, if you add the BASIC or BASICA to it, you can then copy the
BASIC program(s) of your choice to this disk with two excellent results: One
is that you have a working copy of your PC-SIG program disk, "working"
meaning you can store files on it as well as you can boot your system from
this disk instead of "doing the DOS swap and shuffle" all the time. The
second is that your original PC-SIG is now a MASTER which protects you
against losing your valuable programs and all those records and data
thereon.

3.5 Running BASIC with two floppy drives

First method:

With a two drive system, load DOS and then put the DOS disk in drive B: and the program disk in drive A:; then type the following:

       B: filename   (press ENTER or ⏎)

Second method:

With your DOS disk in drive A: type:

       BASICA   (press ENTER or ⏎)

When your screen displays an "ok" prompt, remove your DOS disk and place your program disk in its place. Then type:

       RUN "MENU"   (press ENTER or ⏎).

Now you are ready to go. This method of running BASIC should work on all computers; however, your computer may have a more efficient way of accomplishing the same task. Because of the many different variations between computers, it is impossible to list the most efficient way to run chain programs. As your knowledge of your machine increases, you will be able to develop your own short-cuts and methods.

3.5.5 Starting EXE, COM, or BAT Files

As mentioned above, many of the Library's programs have been compiled into files which are marked with the file extension .COM or .EXE; some of them end with .BAT and will execute a series of commands in DOS automatically. While different in substance and origin, they all can be run in the same manner.

With .EXE, .COM, or .BAT files, you do not have to load BASIC or any other program to start you application. For example, to run a program named FUNYFACE.EXE (or FUNYFACE.COM or FUNYFACE.BAT) all you have to do is type: FUNYFACE and then press the ENTER key.

3.6 Filename extension conventions

Certain filename extensions have been adopted for specific types of files.
These extensions tell you the user what kind of material is in a file.

The following table shows the extension conventions that are generally
used, although there may be exceptions. "Listable" means that they are text
files that may be typed using the DOS "TYPE" command, copied to a
printer, or viewed using a text editor. Please refer to the Glossary at the
end of this book for any unfamiliar terms used in this table.

.ABS	Abstracts; brief, listable program descriptions
.APL	APL source files
.ASC	Listable ASCII text files
.ASM	Listable assembly language source files
.BAS	BASIC source files
.BAT	Listable batch files
.C	Listable C language source files
.COM	Command files that are directly executed by typing the filename from DOS
.DAT	Data files
.DBF	dBASE II or III data files
.DOC	Listable document files
.EWF	Easywriter text file
.EXE	Executable files by typing the filename directly from DOS
.FOR	Listable Fortran source files
.NDX	dBase II or III index files
.OBJ	Object files (used by a linker)
.PAS	Listable Pascal source files
.PIC	Color graphic screen images
.PRG	Listable dBase II or III program files
.TXT	Listable text files
.UNP	Text files describing how to 'unprotect'
.VC	Visicalc templates
.WKS	Lotus 1-2-3 worksheets
.WRK	Symphony worksheets
.WS	Wordstar text file

3.7 Formatting and Copying

Formatting a blank disc is required before you can copy files to it. Notice the operative word here is "blank". Always make sure the disk you are formatting is blank or you will lose whatever information you had stored on that disk prior to formatting.

To format a blank disk using a two-drive disk system, insert your DOS disk in drive A: (remembering, of course, that you have A> showing on your screen) and type:

FORMAT B: (press ENTER or ⏎).

You will be told to then put a disk in drive B: (in single drive machines you will be told when to switch disks). Place the blank disk in drive B: and press RETURN. You will then be asked on your screen whether you wish to "Format Another?" You then have the option or either formatting another disk or returning to DOS. Your screen should resemble the following:

```
Formatting...Format complete

362496 bytes total disk space
362496 bytes available on disk


Format another (Y/N)?
```

The DISKCOPY command is used to make a copy of an entire program on your freshly formatted disk. Making a backup copy protects you in case the original disk is damaged, lost or erased. To make a copy of a disk, put your DOS disk in drive A:. To get to A> type:

A: (press ENTER or ⏎)

When your A> appears type:

DISKCOPY A: B: (press ENTER or ⏎).

You will then be told to insert your Source (original) disk in drive A and your Target (blank, formatted) disk in drive B. Those will single disk drive machines will be told when to alternate between drives A and B in order to complete the transfer. After you have accomplished this your screen should read:

```
Copy complete
Copy another (Y/N)?
```

If you want to copy another strike Y (yes) or N (no) if you're completed with the copying process; then press ENTER.

Often it is useful to add files to a disk, such as BASICA.COM to a public domain disk, so you can easily run BASIC programs. Or, you can create disk with selected files of your choice. Because of the varying structure, the most common format for copying BASICA·from the disk in drive A to the disk in drive B is to type:

        COPY A:BASICA.* B: (Press ENTER or ◄┘).

Here the wildcard symbol, *, is used to copy multiple files. We used the
wildcard symbol in the above example because compatible systems generally
have more than one BASICA file.

3.8 Compatibility

It is important to note the compatibility requirements in regard to the disks in our library. Even the IBM PC will not run all programs. Some programs, for example, were written to use a color graphics card and will not run without it. In our reviews of the software, these programs are identified with a "+" after the filename extension.

Other factors to take into consideration are the type of computer you own, the options installed in your computer, the amount of memory your computer contains, the requirement for another program to run with it, and the version of DOS that you are using.

DOS is important because it will affect whether a program will operate in your system. Some programs require DOS 1.1, others DOS 2.0 or higher. DOS compatibility primarily affects those programs that access the file directory. The versions of DOS access the directory differently.

Know your machine and it's capabilities. Ask questions and refer to your systems manual whenever possible.

3.9 The PCjr

The PCjr is very close in design to the IBM PC. However, there are several subtle differences that the PCjr owner should be aware of from the start. Most of the software in the PC-SIG library works well on the PCjr, and all the of the programs can be copied or have their directories listed on the PCjr.

Some programs require an 80-column display. When the PCjr is first turned on, your screen display is only 40 columns wide with fairly large type. To convert the PCjr to 80 column display, put your DOS disk in the drive and following the A> type:

MODE CO80   (Press ENTER or ◄┘).

PCjr owners may encounter other difficulties with modem communications. If you are planning to use a modem with your PCjr, be forewarned that the PCjr has different internal communication circuitry from the standard IBM PC. Communication packages written for the IBM PC do not work with the PCjr. It is important that your communications program was written for the PCjr, or that it specifically states it will run on the PCjr.

Graphics programs that were written before the popularity of the PCjr may not make the necessary adjustments for the PCjr to work properly. More recent graphic programs do not seem to have the difficulties of earlier programs. PC-SIG library disks with higher disk numbers are more likely to run on the PCjr.

4.0 Description of Disk Contents

A Word of Introduction to the Fourth Edition Library:

Welcome!

We are delighted to introduce you to the Directory for the PC-SIG Library of public domain and user-supported personal computer software.

Here is the structure of the Directory to the Library:

- The collection is divided into two groups: Applications and Utilities software.
- Applications has been subdivided into nineteen categories; Utilities is sectioned into eight.
- Each of these groups and categories has its own introduction and description.
- The categories are listed in alphabetical order.
- Within each category, disks are listed in numerical order.

APPLICATIONS SOFTWARE:

An Introduction

Applications Software is primarily task-oriented, specific in context and functional.

Even in the amazing variety you will find here, applications means above all the ability to perform/compute/entertain by itself.

Consider the variety represented by the categories themselves!

ARTIFICIAL INTELLIGENCE:

The use of specialized languages and logic structures to define "knowledge bases" and expert systems is one of the most exciting frontiers of computer applications. The concept of giving computers the "ability to think" has long stirred the imagination of ardent scientists and science fiction writers alike. However, in these early stages of "artificial intelligence," the complexity of the task of creating such AI applications certainly makes us marvel at how complex OUR thinking processes are.

Our small but growing library includes representatives of the LISP and PROLOG families, considered by many to be the 4th generation tools for writing the 5th generation languages.

148 XLISP Version 1.7
v3

XLISP is an experimental programming language combining some features of LISP with an object-oriented extension capability. It is written in C and is easily extended with user-written built-in functions and classes. It assumes some knowledge of LISP and object-oriented programming. This version contains both MS-DOS and PC-DOS specific code.

Usage: Artificial intelligence, programming or languages.

System Requirements: 128K of memory, one disk drive and monochrome or color display.

How to Start: As all program, sample and documentation files are in archived form, consult the README.1ST for directions.

User Comments: "Very well done AI programming language. Not for the uninitiated and it would be more useful to the novice if it included a short tutorial on LISP." "A valiant effort! It's a lot of work to write a LISP interpreter and Betz has done a fine job." "Excellent AI language. Well written manual and syntax."

File Descriptions:

README	1ST	Directions on unarchiving
XLISPDOC	ARC	XLISP documentation
XLISPEXE	ARC	XLISP executable files (archive)
XLISPLSP	ARC	Sample XLISP programs (archive)
XLISPSRC	ARC	XLISP source code (archive)
DEARC	COM	File dearchiver program

398
ESIE Expert System Shell
v1

ESIE, the Expert System Inference Engine, is an artificial intelligence shell that allows the user to build a custom knowledge base for assistance in making decisions. It operates by ESIE loading in a knowledge base, and building inferences out of the rules contained therein. This is especially good as an introduction to expert systems as ESIE can build knowledge bases as well as having excellent on-disk documentation for getting you started in KBs. For the advanced, ESIE can handle the normal gamut of expert systems building.

To see how ESIE works without building your own knowledge base, load ESIE and one of the three supplied knowledge bases (ANIMAL, DOCTOR, or GLASS) and see how it works!

Usage: Artificial intelligence, programming or languages.

System Requirements: Monochrome or color/graphics display, 128K, and one disk drive

How to Start: Consult the READ.ME, TUTOR and USER files for instructions for using the system

• To run it, enter ESIE at the DOS prompt. The user manual which explains how to use ESIE to set up a knowledge base is in the MANUAL file.

User Comments: "A little complicated at first, but useful for an introduction on the subject of expert system inference engines." "Overall, I enjoyed the program. The instructions and formatting are simple but effective." "ESIE is an excellent introduction to the concepts of artificial intelligence. The diagnosis demo program is very impressive." "A good introduction to AI, knowledge bases, inference engines and expert systems. I enjoyed the text file on the history of AI."

Suggested Donation: For $75.00 you will receive the most recent version of ESIE; for at least $145: the most recent version of ESIE, fully commented Pascal source code for ESIE, a copy of PC-Write ESIE, and access to a help line.

File Descriptions:

ANIMAL		A sample knowledge base
DOCTOR		A sample knowledge base
ESIE	COM	The main program
FORM		Text file of the form for registering the program
GLASS		A sample knowledge base
HISTORY		Text file containing a short history of the field of AI
MANUAL		Text file containing a user manual of how to use ESIE
READ	ME	Text file containing instructions for use of the system
TUTOR		Text file containing a tutorial to get a working shell
USER		Text file containing a user manual for those using ESIE

417
A.D.A. PROLOG v1.91p
3.1

The PROLOG — "Programming in Logic" — language on this disk is the educational/public domain version from Automata Design Associates (A.D.A.). PROLOG is considered one of the major fifth generation languages and is not for the faint-hearted. Considered the leading edge of most expert systems and artifical intelligence program developments, PROLOG is remarkably good for writing "question answering" systems. It excells at writing programs that perform complicated strategies for computing the best or worst way to accomplish a task, or to avoid an undesirable result.

Besides PROLOG, there are many companion programs here: PROLOGED.COM is a simple screen editor for use within PROLOG; ATN.ARC contains Lou Schumacher's natural language parser; EXPERT.ARC contains expert systems for such fields as medical, rockblasting, fault diagnosis, etc. GAMES.ARC has some simple board games and adventure games, while PUZZLES.ARC demonstrates techniques of translating word problems into unambiguous logic.

PIE.ARC contains Simon Blackwell's "PIE" Truth Maintenance System in revised, debugged, and enlarged form. This system is found in the directory "expert" and augments the strictly deductive capabilities of raw Prolog with additional forms of reasoning.

Usage: Artificial intelligence, programming or languages.

System Requirements: 256K, one disk drive and monochrome display.

How to Start: As all programs and documentation are archived, consult the READ.ME for detailed information about the files on this disk and on how to unsqueeze all the archived files. First one to get is PROLOG.DOC!

User Comments: "Quite intriguing and interesting; now I'm starting to become interested in AI." "Outstanding AI system. Could use additional sample programs. Good experimental language. Nice to have the ability to upgrade to a more complex system." "Prolog is a very powerful language for database applications requiring an intelligent user interface. I recommend this disk for people requiring flexibility in a microcomputer-based knowledge system."

Suggested Donation: $10.00

File Descriptions:

FILES417	TXT	Description of files contents
GO	BAT	Batch file for basic directions
PROLOG	ARC	Squeezed Documention for the PROLOG programs
READ	ME	Detail about the files on this disk and how to unsqueeze
ARC	EXE	Utility to "Unsqueeze" the files on this disk
ARCDOC	EXE	Directions on using the ARC.EXE utility

BULLETIN BOARD SOFTWARE:

Sharing ideas, information, problems and profound thoughts are what electronic bulletin boards are all about. Much like their physical counterparts, electronic bulletin boards can be wide open or highly selective in what gets posted: items for sale, arguments about foreign policy, hardware problems, "lonely hearts," and more. Using the BBS, you can communicate with computing enthusiasts from all parts of the country — the world, if you wish!

Our collection of bulletin board software makes communications easy with easy-to-use systems that vary in size and sophistication. You can initiate a BBS in your own area and meet people with similar interests. BBS's generally get started by a shared/special interest group (SIG). Look around and start getting on-line!

125 HOST-III Public Bulletin Board Package V1.1g
v2

The HOST-III communications package, while designed for private remote-to-host type file transfers, can be used as a public BBS. HOST-III automates the RECEIVE end of any file transfer, allowing unattended operation of the host. HOSTCALL automates unattended file transfers for late-night, low-rate use.

HOSTCALL can also initiate telephone calls to host computers (such as an IBM-PC running HOST-III) and exchange files based on the commands in what is called a Command File. The host computer may or may not be an IBM-PC. You create the Command File which contains the information HOSTCALL needs, such as the time to call a host system, the telephone number, and the names of the files to exchange. A single COMMAND FILE can sequentially access a number of host computers. Both programs support the XMODEM protocol of file transmission.

FORMGEN (another program by the author of HOST-III) is a "Mail-Merge" type program intended to be used in conjunction with PC-FILE or FILE EXPRESS. It interfaces with your datafile manager to produce reports integrating data from your databases. This evaluation package contains version 1.2c, which supports PC-FILE only.

Usage: Anyone needing file transfer programs.

System Requirements: 128K, two disk drives, a monochrome display and a Hayes Smartmodem or equivalent.

How to Start: After loading DOS, read the README file (and the other .DOC files) by entering TYPE A:README

● To run HOSTCALL.EXE, enter HOSTCALL at the DOS prompt and press ENTER.

User Comments: "This program is difficult to get started, but the documentation is extensive. One problem as I see it, is the fact that is HOSTCALLX should cover more AUTODIAL/AUTOANSWER types of features." "EASY TO USE."

Suggested Donation: $35.00 registration

File Descriptions:

HOST-III	DOC	Documentation for HOST-III
HOSTCALL	DOC	Documentation for HOSTCALL
HOST-III	EXE	Program that receives telephone calls
HOSTCALX	EXE	Program that initiates telephone calls...Part 1
HOSTCL2X	EXE	Program that initiates telephone calls...Part 2
HOSTCALL	BAT	Batch file that starts up HOSTCALX
FORMGEN	DOC	Directions for the Forms Generator program
FORMGEN	EXE	Forms Generator program
FORMGSET	FRM	Example form
README		Information about HOST-III use & other programs available
SAMPLE		Sample files for practice setups

150 IBM BBS by Gene Plantz

v1

A simple, straightforward BBS written especially for the IBM PC. The code is compiled BASIC. Both the source and executable versions are provided so you can run it as is or modify it. It is a powerful system with a lot of thought and experience behind its design. An intriguing touch shows some of that thoughtfulness: since the program was originally written apart from the computer destined to run it, a facility is provided for the program to upload a new version of itself!

Usage: Anyone with the desire to operate a BBS.

System Requirements: 192K, two drives, one serial port, a modem.

How to Start: Documentation is spread out in files marked .DOC (for DOCument) and .HLP and plenty of simple text files

● To run, type IBBS and press ENTER.

File Descriptions:

BBSCOMP	BAT	BAT startup file
BBSLOGO	BAS	Logo displayed upon BBS startup
CALLERS		List of each logon, excepting SYSOP
COUNTERS		Workfile containing next message #, next caller, etc.
FLASH		File displayed after WELCOME file
HARDWARE		Information file on hardware prices
HELP	BBS	Help file
IBBS	BAS	Compiler BASIC source code
IBBS	DOC	Limited documentation

IBBS	EXE	Compiler object code for IBBS
MESSAGES		Main messages file
NEWCOM		Message file for first-time callers
RBBSUTIL	BAS	Source code for file cleanup utility
RBBSUTIL	EXE	Compiled object code for file cleanup utility
SOFTWARE		Information file on software prices
SUMMARY		Messages summary file
USERS		List of logon IDs
WELCOME		First file displayed after logon
XFER	HLP	Help file for file transfer function
XFERLIST		List of files that can be transferred

152 RBBS for the IBM PC

v1

This is a really nifty package from the Capital PC Users Group that allows you to set up your own BBS. This was originally a CP/M BBS written in BASIC; many people have built onto it. This one disk is all that is necessary to run and modify a BBS. For a less technical BBS, read the sample bulletin BULLET1.

Usage: Anyone wishing to run a BBS.

System Requirements: 128K RAM, two drives, one serial port, a Hayes Smartmodem or equivalent.

How to Start: After loading DOS, enter A:TYPE -README-.DOC for instructions. For the documentation check RBBS-PC.DOC.

User Comments: "Set up a BBS with this at its base. Learned a lot from this one." "Very powerful. My company uses it quite a bit." "The documentation is great it tells everything that a new sysop needs..." "It's a great Bulletin Board for starting out and it's features are more advanced than a lot of others, plus the graphics make it real nice too."

Suggested Donation: $6.00

File Descriptions:

-README-	DOC	Initial suggestions for starting out
BULLET1		Sample bulletin
BULLETIN		Menu for bulletins
CAPITAL	PC	Capital IBM PC Users Group information
CONFIG	BAS	Sets up RBBS configuration
DIR		Description of file directories
DIR99		Description of most recent file uploads

FIXFILES	BAS	Cleans up caller file
HELP??		User help files (7 files)
MENU1		Menu — SYSOP utilities
MENU1G		Menu — SYSOP utilities — with border
MENU2		Menu — main RBBS menu
MENU2G		Menu — main RBBS menu — with border
MENU3		Menu — RBBS files
MENU3G		Menu — RBBS files — with border
NEWUSER		Welcome message
RBBS-PC	BAS	BASIC version
RBBS-PC	DOC	Documentation
RBBS-PC	EXE	Compiled version
RBBS-PC	REM	Remarks used by RBBS-PC.xxx programs
STARTUP	BAT	Installs RBBS onto two diskettes
USRINIT1	BAS	Clears user download/upload counts
USRINIT2	BAS	Reads callers file & updates
UTSPACE	OBJ	Part of RBBS-PC.xxx programs

212 RBBS Version CPC14.1a (Disk 1 of 4) v6

The RBBS is the bulletin board system of choice for most PC-based boards. It is a LARGE system, here on four disks, but it is even bigger in features and power, with multiple styles for file storage, coding, protection and many others. Whether you are starting a BBS or considering upgrading your present operation, you have to give this one SERIOUS THOUGHT!

The rest of the disks in the set are numbered 334, 621, 622. Disk number 212 has the SYSOP information and bulletin files. Disk 334 contains help and menu files plus BASIC source code for the system. Disk 621 has the system in executable form (compiled BASIC), plus system subroutines written in BASIC. Disk 622 contains the System Documentation — 114 PAGES of it!

Usage: Individuals/groups willing to set up a public or private BBS.

System Requirements: 192K, two disk drives, and a HAYES Smartmodem or compatible.

How to Start: IMMEDIATELY go to disk 622 and review the documentation; then print it with the .BAT file there. Return to 212 and begin reading the BULLET files here; then go on to the .DOC, .HLP, README, NEWUSER, MENU and HELP files. When you are ready, type RBBS and go for it!

User Comments: "Good program...Excellent BBS system." "It works the first time." "If only ALL software was of this same quality- impressive features and first-rate documentation. An awful lot of work has gone into this one, and it shows."

Suggested Donation: $25.00

File Descriptions:

ANSI	ASM	ANSI driver source code
ANSI	OBJ	Linkable ANSI driver
BDRIVEC	OBJ	Driver program
BULLET?		Bulletin text files for system (16 files)
BULLETG		Bulletin graphics file
CONFIG	BAS	Configuration program used to customize the system.
CONFIG	EXE	Configuration program for screens definition files
DTRPATCH	DOC	Documentation on how to fix Basic Compiler DTR
EXITRBBS	BAS	Source code
EXITRBBS	EXE	Allows you to exit RBBS through a "backdoor"

334 RBBS Version CPC14.1a (Disk 2 of 4) V6

File Descriptions:

NEWUSER		New user introductory text file
PC-NET	OBJ	PC-Net driver source code
RBBS-PC	BAS	Source code for main program
HELP*		Help text files (9 files)
MENU?		Menu text files (5 files)
MENU?G		Menu graphics (5 files)

621 RBBS Version CPC14.1a (Disk 3 of 4) V6

File Descriptions:

RBBS-PC	EXE	RBBS-PC main program file
RBBS-SUB	BAS	Source code for system subroutines
RBBS-SUB	OBJ	RBBS subroutines
RBBS-VAR	BAS	Listing of arrays and subroutines system uses
RBBSML	ASM	Multilink interface for system
RBBSML	OBJ	Linkable Multilink Interface

WELCOME		Welcome text file
WELCOMEG		Graphics for WELCOME text file
XMODEM	ASM	XMODEM source code
XMODEM	OBJ	XMODEM object code

622
RBBS Version
CPC14.1a (Disk 4 of 4)
V6

File Descriptions:

| RBBS-PC | DOC | Documentation file (114 pages) |
| GO | BAT | Batch file to print DOC file |

BUSINESS APPLICATIONS:

Our selection of business software is targeted for personal financial and small business applications. This includes:

- Accounting programs (also see FINANCIAL)
- Payroll programs
- Tax reporting
- Personnel management
- Inventory programs
- Cash management
- Mailing lists
- And more!

Tracking personal and small business income and expenditures can be done by category or project using standard accounting line items or user-described categories. The form can be as simple as a check register or as complex as a point-of-sale device that can also establish inventory depletion. The advantage is that you can anticipate your tax problems and opportunities. Personal record keeping keeps you a step ahead of the taxman, but that's where you always want to be, right?

The quality of managing "people information" often turns a struggling business into a growing one. This category includes mailing list managers, mailing list/address book systems and complete sales office prospect trackers. For more in this line, see our DESKTOP MANAGERS category.

62 Inventory Program
v1

These programs are fun to work with, and a great way to become familiar with database programs. All programs are written in BASIC, are menu driven, and use screen inputs for data entries.

Personal Home Inventory lets users add, change, or delete inventory entries. It prints out the completed inventory file to either the screen or printer. The Cash/Checkbook Accounting program lets the user input data, add, delete, edit, and print reports of the transactions. The Mailing List is a database program that lets the user add, change, or delete names. It can do a search via the last name, or the city, or the state. It alphabetizes entries, prints a roster, and can do mailing labels, etc.

Usage: Personal or small business use.

System Requirements: 64K, one disk drive and monochrome display;

How to Start: Consult the INVENTORY.DOC file for documentation about the Home Inventory program; the rest have interior directions.

- To run the BASIC programs, consult the directions in GETTING STARTED.
- To run a program with the suffix .COM or .EXE, just type its name, i.e., for HEBREW.COM, type HEBREW and press ENTER.

File Descriptions:

HEBREW	ASM	Assembly language source for HEBREW character set
HEBREW	COM	Loads HEBREW character set
CHARS2	BAS	Displays ASCII character set with octal, hex or decimal value
LINREGRS	BAS	Calculates multiple linear regression coefficients
WB-UPTLE	BAS	Modification for PC-TALK 2.0 to allow file transmission while
—— —	——	Applications
MAILIST2	BAS	Mailing list program — with search and alphabetic sort
INVENTRY	BAS	Helps to keep list of possessions on computer
INVENTRY	DAT	Data file for INVENTRY.BAS
INVENTRY	DOC	Few notes for INVENTRY.BAS — very short
CASHACC	BAS	Simple cash accounting system
REMCACC	BAS	Remark lines which may be merged with CASHACC.BAS
TESTDATA	ACC	Part of CASHACC.BAS

155
Budget/ Taskplan/Loan
v1.2

Here are five useful programs in BASIC for planning or tracking business projects, expenses and making loan analyses. BUDGETRAK (Budget Track) tracks budgeted disbursements by numbering budgeted items as grouped under any one of eighty projects. It tracks them on three levels: DISBURSEMENTS being the lowest level, ITEMS comprise the middle level and PROJECTS are the highest level.

The three-part LOAN section contains a Loan Savings Solution which prepares schedules of loan payments, with and without extra payments to the principal. Leas-By1 compares automobile purchase (with loan) to closed-in lease. It's an analysis applications package for "private use" autos. Loan Mortgage Solutions prepares schedules of loan payments, both with and without payment to the principal. Rounding out this package is TASKPLAN, an elementary project manager.

Usage: Personal/business financial tools

System Requirements: 64K, one disk drive and monochrome display

How to Start: Consult the DOC files for BudgetTrack and TaskPlan; the other three have interior directions

- To run the BASIC programs, consult the directions in GETTING STARTED for your configuration.

User Comments: "Budget Track does the basics of tracking a budget, but nothing fancy." "Task Plan has poor documentation, but performs well for light to moderate business applications."

File Descriptions:

——	——	BUDGETRK 3.3
BUDGETRK	BAS	Budget tracking program
BUDGETRK	DOC	Documentation for BUDGETRK.BAS (2 pages)
BUDGETRK	MOD	Part of BUDGETRK
——	——	TASKPLAN
TASKPLAN	BAS	Task planning program
DESCRIPT	DOC	Task plan documentation
SAMPLE	TPN	Sample task plan
——	——	LOAN
LEAS-BY1	BAS	Lease — buy analysis for auto purchase or lease
LOAN-MTG	BAS	Loan mortgage schedules, after tax impact
LOANSVGS	BAS	Loan payment solutions

165
Personal General Ledger
v1

Personal General Ledger is a template software package designed to work with the Lotus 1-2-3 spreadsheet program. This program handles cash receipts, disbursements, salary, and general journals. It also offers a full general ledger and chart of accounts.

Usage: Personal/business financial tools

System Requirements: 128K, 1 disk drive, monochrome display and Lotus 1-2-3 version 1 or 1a.

How to Start: Check out the LEDGER.DOC and CHART.DOC files for directions

- To run, enter Lotus 1-2-3 and type: AUTO123 and press ENTER.

User Comments: "Probably will be difficult for someone new to Lotus 1-2-3." "JUST OK" "Probaly useful for some small business. I don't use this disk at all because I don't need the many accounts involved."

Suggested Donation: $50.00

File Descriptions:

RECTJRNL	WKS	Cash receipt journal
DISBJRNL	WKS	Cash disbursements journal
SLRYJRNL	WKS	Salary journal
GENLJRNL	WKS	General journal — everything else
AUTO123	WKS	Sets up automatic menu when first accessing 1-2-3
GENLEDGR	WKS	Full general ledger
LEDGER	DOC	Documentation for Person General Ledger
CHART	DOC	Full chart of accounts

169 Mailing List Programs
v1

This disk contains three mailing list programs and a membership program, all written in BASIC. Mailist1 lets the user add new names and addresses, and sorts files by either the name or zip code. It updates, corrects, deletes, and prints files. It also displays a list of phone numbers and automatically dials selected numbers. It can add, delete, and sort your files to print labels and report lists. The Membership program adds, renews, and reviews memberships and club affiliations.

Usage: Home or small business use.

System Requirements: 64K, two disk drives, BASIC or BASICA

How to Start: Check the MAILIST1.DOC, MEMBER.ASC and EASYMENU.ASC files for directions

- To run the BASIC programs, consult the directions in GETTING STARTED for your configuration.

User Comments: "The programs are well documented and seem to run well. I have encountered a couple of program location problems which required putting the programs onto the Basic/Basica disk." "I especially like the mailist1 program." "Very useful; The programs are pretty good but the documentation is poor."

Suggested Donation: $15.00 for "Mail List"

File Descriptions:

EASYMAIL	ASC	Documentation for EASYMAIL.BAS
EASYMAIL	BAS	Mailing label system
BUILDML	BAS	Part of EASYMAIL.BAS
LAB?????	BAS	Part of EASYMAIL.BAS (3 files)
???MAIL	BAS	Part of EASYMAIL.BAS (4 files)
MAILMENU	BAS	Part of EASYMAIL.BAS
????MAIL	BAS	Part of EASYMAIL (4 files)
MEMBER	ASC	Documentation for MEMBERS.BAS
MEMBERS	BAS	Membership system based on EASYMAIL.BAS
????MEMB	BAS	Part of MEMBERS.BAS (8 files)
MAILIST1	BAS	Another mailing list system
MAILIST1	DOC	Documentation for MAILIST1.BAS
MAILLIST	BAS	Another mailing list system
MAILSORT	BAS	Sort for MAILIST1.BAS

179 Pizza & Check Register Systems
v1

This is a multi-purpose check register accounting system, written for individuals and small businesses that can use a check register for thier accounting. The program writes and prints checks that have been addressed for use with window envelopes. The standard check register can be printed with a running balance, a memo report, and an account distribution summary. A significant feature of this program is the budget analysis and average month report. This report shows how much was expended, the amount budgeted, and computes an average monthly amount for each account. The other programs on this disk are for preparing pizzas, recipes for dough and various toppings.

System Requirements: 64K, one disk drive and monochrome display;

Features:

- Transaction entries
- Reconcile checkbook
- Run alternate accounts
- Begin new year
- Report Menu
- File maintenance menu
- Pizza recipes!

How to Start: At the DOS prompt, enter TYPE MA.DOC and press ENTER. This provides the user with setup and operating instructions.

User Comments: "A good initial program to balance your checkbook, but has limitations." "I get more use out of the Pizza program than most!"

Suggested Donation: $35.00

File Descriptions:

PIZZA	EXE	Pizza recipes — main program
MA	BAS	Micro Accounting check register system
MA	DOC	Documentation for MA.BAS
MACOPY	BAT	Batch file to copy MA files
MADOC	BAT	Batch file to print MA.DOC
SCR*	DOC	Data for PIZZA.EXE

235
Parts Inventory Control
Version 1.1
v1.1

The Parts Inventory Control database program can be used to track inventory of parts and service businesses. It is menu driven and fast. Inventory programs like this one do five things: 1) Decrease the time it takes to record changes in your inventory; 2) Show where your inventory is too large or too small; 3) Provide immediate access to the status of any inventory item; 4) Help you determine your tax liability; and 5) Help you spot sales trends and obsolete parts.

Usage: Inventory control for business use.

System Requirements: 256K, 2 disk drives, 80-column display, 132 column printer

Features:

- Class supplier
- Manufacturer
- Description
- Part number
- Location
- Date
- Counted
- Items
- Reorders
- Costs
- Receipts

How to Start: Before beginning, read the README and other .DOC files for the documentation (Tutorial and a User's Guide). The program runs off INVENT.COM; after that it is menu-driven to get to the other modules.

User Comments: "Very good program." "I've found that it's been an asset in my job." "Seems to be quite complete with good manual and tutorial." "An excellent program for small business inventory!" "Adequate inventory program. Have recommended it to friends. Can be used in small business. Solid addition to my software library."

Suggested Donation: $50.00 includes notification of new releases and technical support

File Descriptions:

INVENT	COM	Program driver, enter INVENT from DOS to load and run program
DISKETTE	COM	Loaded by INVENT.COM — formats and copies disks
FILE	COM	Loaded by INVENT.COM — create inventory records
RECORD	COM	Loaded by INVENT.COM — update inventory records
PRINT	COM	Loaded by INVENT.COM — prints current and history reports
HISTORY	COM	Loaded by INVENT.COM — transfer data to history disks
UTILITY	COM	Loaded by INVENT.COM transfers data to DOS-formatted disks
INVENT	DOC	Tutorial and User's Guide
README	DOC	Notes about files on disk and printing documentation
NOTICE	DOC	Press release
AUTOEXEC	BAT	Loads INVENT.COM at power on

237
PC-General Ledger
Version 1.3a
v1.2

PC-General Ledger, a user-supported program from Charter Software, was written by a financial executive with over 25 years of experience in all areas of accounting, finance, taxes and general management. The program has all of the controls necessary to make sure that everything is kept in balance and that a complete audit trail always exists. The manual and the programs assume you have a working knowledge of bookkeeping, know the difference between debits and credits, and know how to prepare and post entries.

The program is easy to use and can be set up and running in less than 15 minutes. It can handle up to five bank accounts and eight departments or cost centers; it can even print checks!

IMPORTANT NOTE: THE PROGRAMS FOR THIS VERSION ARE NOT COMPATIBLE WITH DATA CREATED BY VERSIONS 1.0 THROUGH 1.2.

System Requirements: 128K, one disk drive or a hard disk, monochrome or color monitor.

How to Start: Read the MANUAL thoroughly!! To install and run, enter GLMENU at the A: or C: prompt. This brings you to the main menu from which everything operates.

User Comments: "Found this to be an excellent general ledger program." "Decent program if you want a double entry bookkeeping system." "Seems to be a sound entry level program for small businesses just beginning to get everything on computer. Monthly reports and year to end a must for preparing records for accountants for tax season." "An excellent program for my needs. Easy to use and understand."

Suggested Donation: $50.00 makes you a registered owner, gets you the most recent manual, telephone support,and updates and enhancements.

File Descriptions:

GL??????	EXE	Parts of PC-General Ledger (7 files)
MANUAL		PC-General Ledger Manual (38K)
MANUAL	BAT	Batch file to print manual
AUTOEXEC	BAT	Part of PC-General Ledger — autostart file

243
Sage
Calendar/Tag
v1

Sage Calendar is an electronic desk calendar. It allows you to create memos, store addresses or record events. The program will display active memos and create calendars for any date you select. Tag was written for a seed company to produce tags. It may be useful to others who need to produce multiple copies of several different tags. Both programs include documentation on disk.

System Requirements: 64K, one disk drive, monochrome monitor

How to Start: Review files marked .HLP and .PRN for directions on use

● To run either program, just type its name, i.e., for CAL.COM, type CAL and press ENTER.

User Comments: "I like its versatility and strength." "Handy programs." "I couldn't live without this one. I'm nominating it for best performer in the Secretaries' Day competition. This is what computers are supposed to do for you!"

Suggested Donation: $25.00

File Descriptions:

– – – –	– –	Sage Calendar
CAL	COM	Sage Calendar main program
SCRN	OVL	On line help for Sage Calendar
CAL	PRN	Documentaion for Sage Calendar
CALINST	BAT	Batch program to make working copy
– – – –	– –	Sage Tag
TAG	COM	Sage Tag main program
TAG	HLP	On line help for Sage Tag
TAG	PRN	Documentation for Sage Tag
TAGINST	BAT	Batch program to make working copy

251
Time and Money
Version 1.5
v1.2

Time and Money is a simple financial record keeping system that also keeps a budget, cash projections, calculates interest, compares rent/buy options, etc. This program will allow you to track your money, create and use budgets, project how certain financial plans will work out for you in the future, and give you an analysis to help with common financial decisions. All of the programs on this disk are designed to be called from the menus that are displayed.

System Requirements: 128K, one floppy or hard drive, color/monochrome monitor

How to Start: After you check the README.TXT file, run it by entering TAMSTART and press ENTER which will bring up the program and put you at the opening menu. From here you can either go directly to the program or start an on-disk Tutorial to acquaint you with the program.

User Comments: "Very good program for tracking checkbook accounts and budgets." "This is a program that is used primarily by my wife. It is just about her only contact with the computer, and she finds that the program is easy to use, and provides an insight to home budjeting that she can make use of." "I have only used it for two weeks and it already saves me money." "Excellent implimentation of financial tools for home use."

Suggested Donation: $50.00

File Descriptions:

BUDCODES	TXT	Expense category data file
README	TXT	Introductory text file
TAMCHN?	EXE	Subprogram files (9 files)
TAMSTART	EXE	Main program file
*		Data files for demonstration (3 files)

261 PC-SIG Business Sampler No 1
v1.1

Here is an organizer for the home and office. A perfect example is The Personal Datebook, a menu driven program that maintains a daily calendar of appointments, birthdays, memos, events and anything else you want to record. The Address Label System is an address data entry system for producing and maintaining customer files, address labels, and mailing lists. It's especially useful for capturing large volumes of names and addresses for direct mail advertising. The combined Cash and Hardcash programs are intended to track cash flow transactions. This is a simple general ledger which provides a convenient method for small businesses to record their cash transactions.

System Requirements: 128K, two disk drives and either a monochrome/graphics or color/graphics setup

How to Start: Consult the .TXT and .DOC files for directions and documentation. NOTE: The Mailing Label program requires BASRUN.EXE.

• To run the BASIC programs, consult the directions in GETTING STARTED for your configuration. For the .EXE and .COM programs, just type its name, i.e., for FILEMAN.COM, type FILEMAN and press ENTER.

User Comments: (Personal Datebook)"Okay program, but could be more useful if had a tickler." "Although I found the Personal Date useful, it is too slow being in BASIC and I thought the documentation was ambiguous." "Ok, but could be better structured." (EIGHTCRV) "One of the best microcomputer programs I have seen on this topic

(curve fitting). Very easy to use!" (FILEMAN) "The best file — copy, delete, etc. program I have seen from PC-SIG." (LABELS) "Because of the intial brochure, we figured this would be a good mailing label program (the only one with labels listed as primary use). However, it is a hopeless lightweight"

Suggested Donation: Personal Datebook $12.95; Flight-Plan $20.00

File Descriptions:

————	——	Cashflow Program by Gregory N. Doudna
CASH	BAS	Data entry, file maintenance, etc.
HARDCASH	BAS	Provides printed records
CASH	DOC	Documentation for Cashflow Programs
————	——	Personal Datebook by Lateral Programming, Inc.
MEMO	BAS	Personal Datebook: Appointments, Addresses, Memos etc.
MEMO	BAT	Runs MEMO.BAS with proper / parms
MANUAL	TXT	Reference Manual for Personal Datebook
MANUAL	EXE	Display or print the reference manual
CONVERT	BAS	Converts address list for use with wordprocessors
CONVERT	BAT	Runs CONVERT.BAS with proper / parms
————	——	Mailing Label Package (BASRUN.EXE required)
LABELS	EXE	Menu shell for Mailing Label Package
NEWLAB	EXE	Generates new mailing label file
LABELINP	EXE	Data entry program for Mailing Label Package
SRTLAB	EXE	Sorts labels by ZIP code
LABRPT	EXE	File listing and Summary reports
LABPRT02	EXE	Label Printing program for Mailing Label Package
LABELS	DOC	Documentation for Mailing Label Package
————	——	File Management System
FILEMAN	COM	File Management System — very neat!
MAKEMEMO	BAS	Write reminders to tickler file
SHOWMEMO	BAS	Brings up reminder notes on proper dates
————	——	FLITEPLN 2.2
FLITEPLN3	2vv	Aids in preparing flight plan (BASIC program)
FLITEPLN3	DOC	Documentation for FLITEPLN.BAS
————	——	EIGHTCRV Package
EIGHTCRV	XXX	This description of the EIGHTCRV programs
EIGHTCRV	SDA	Sample data file
EIGHTCRV	BAS	First eight curves to data
EIGHTCRV	TXT	Documentation for EIGHTCRV.BAS

282
PC-SIG Business Sampler No 2
v1

The Home Financing Analyst is a comprehensive real estate evaluation program written from the perspective of homeowners, potential homeowners, or renters. It can also assist real estate agents, brokers, and developers in forcasting and allocating the cost of home ownership and then comparing ownership, rental, and alternatives. It can be used to determine if mortgage refinancing is worthwhile. The program can not be used to evaluate real estate purchased for investment purposes, as it does not take into account depreciation charges and rental income.

PC-Check has been designed to track one or more home or office checking accounts. It will allow you to create your own code file in which you can store up to 677 two letter codes.

The Checkbook Distribution program provides a quick and easy way to group credit card data or checks into expense catageories, handy for tracking check data entry and editing, balancing, and coding of entries. For example, check data may be abbreviated to just the dollar amount and a short expense code for speedy data entry. However, more complete entries, including dates and check descriptions, may also be used when desired. This flexibility provides fast results for tax, business, or budget purposes.

Usage: Personal finances

System Requirements: 64K, one disk drive and monochrome display; Checkbook Distribution needs 128K

How to Start: Consult the .DOC and README files for directions and documentation

• To run the BASIC programs, consult the directions in GETTING STARTED for your configuration.

User Comments: "The Checkbook program is great." "I'm still trying to figure it out."

Suggested Donation: ANALYST $15.00; PC-CHECK $40.00; the CDB package $20.00

File Descriptions:

————	——	MERGEPLAN V1.00 (Multiplan spreadsheet consolidator)
MERGE	EXE	Main program
————	——	Checkbook distribution by John Stevens
CBD	BAS	Main program
CBD	DAT	Part of CBD.BAS
CBD-READ	ME	Checkbook distribution documentation (39K)
————	——	PC-CHECK
PC-CHECK	BAS	Checkbook management program
PC-CHECK	DOC	PC-CHECK documentation
HELP	BAT	How to print PC-CHECK documentation
REGIS	DOC	User support registration
AUTOEXEC	BAT	Prints registration form
SMPLCODE	CO	Suggested two letter codes
SMPLCHK		More suggested codes
————	——	Stock Analyst
STKANALY	SIS	Stock value analyzer
DATAST		Sample data sheet
STKANAL	DOC	STKANALY.SIS documentation (16K)
————	——	Home Financial Analyst
ANALYST	EXE	Home ownership cost analyzer
SAMPLE	HFA	Example
ANALYST	DOC	Documentation (9K)

313
PC-SIG Business Sampler No 3
v1

Time Management is the theme of this business collection. Highlights include: the PC Yearbook which is a calendar/appointment schedule program written in C; it also includes a notepad. IPM.COM is a (Critical Path Method) project scheduler written in Turbo Pascal. This is a methodology for determining the critical task that, if not accomplished by a certain time, contributes directly to the delay of the whole project. It does not have a calendar function or a project tracking function.

UserLog is a system utility designed to maintain a disk-based file of computer usage, thus eliminating the need for a written log that monitors the business and personal use of a computer. Program Time calculates the amount of computer time used. It allows apportionment of the time between business and non-business use.

Usage: Personal and small business

System Requirements: 64K, one disk drive and monochrome display; IPM requires 128K

How to Start: Consult the .DOC and README files for directions

- To run the BASIC programs, consult the directions in GETTING STARTED for your configuration
- To run a program suffixed .COM or .EXE, just type its name, i.e., for IPM.COM, type IPM and press ENTER.

Suggested Donation: IPM $15.00; USERLOG $25.00

File Descriptions:

ACRS	BAS	Depreciation Calculating Program
ACRS	DOC	Documentation for ACRS
CALCULA	BAS	Large Screen Calculator
IPM	COM	Ivy League Project Manager
IPM	DOC	Documentation for IPM
KEYPAD	BAS	Keypad Practice Typing Program
PCYEARBK	DOC	Day Month and Year Calendar Program
PCYEARBK	EXE	Documentation for PCYEARBK
PERT3	BAS	PERT/Path Critical Scheduling Program
PRGTIM	EXE	Computer Utilization Program
PRGTIM	BAS	Utility Program for PRGTIM
PRGTIM	DOC	Documentation for PRGTIM
RPTUSE	BAS	Utility Program for PRGTIM
TMSTRT	BAS	Utility Program for PRGTIM
TMSTRT	EXE	Utility Program for PRGTIM
USE-TIME	DOC	General Documentation for TMSTRT and PRGTIM
TAXDEDCT	BAS	Income Tax Deduction Recording Program
USERLOG	COM	Maintains Disk-Based File of Computer Usage
USERLOG	DOC	Documentation for USERLOG

330 PC-SIG Business Sampler No 4

v1

While very different, these programs are alike in that this general ledger program, a check register program, and two mail list programs here are all menu-driven and will run on a PCjr with disk drive and sufficient memory.

DataCount is a general ledger program suitable for individuals or small businesses. The Micro Accounting System is a multi-purpose check register accounting system. This software package was

written for individuals and small businesses that can use a check register for their accounting. The MaiListI program allows you to create a file of names and addresses. You can add to this list, change and delete entries. It sorts, displays, prints a hardcopy to labels or reports, and it will automatically dial selected phone numbers with an autodial modem.

System Requirements: 64K, one disk drive and monochrome display;

How to Start: Consult the .DOC and README files for directions.

- To run the BASIC programs, consult the directions in GETTING STARTED for your configuration.
- To run a program suffixed .COM or .EXE, just type its name, i.e., for DATAC.EXE, type DATAC and press ENTER.

User Comments: "Not a lot of frills; it's simple; it works." (DATACOUNT) "As good as a simple ledger program as I've seen, basic and no frills. I'm still evaluating it, but no flaws so far. Put a few frills (color, individual screens, better printout) on it and it would be ideal."

Suggested Donation: MAILIST1 $15.00; DATAC $30.00; MA $35.00

File Descriptions:

— — — —		General ledger program
DAT	DOC	ASCII text file containing documentation for DATAC.EXE
DATAC	EXE	General ledger program
DEMO		Sample data file for DATAC.EXE
DEMOA		Sample data file for DATAC.EXE
DEMON		Sample data file for DATAC.EXE
— — — —	— —	Check register
MA	BAS	Multi-purpose check register accounting system
MA	DOC	ASCII text file containing documentation for MA.BAS
MACOPY	BAT	Batch file for copying this group of files to user disk
MADOC	BAT	Batch file for printing MA.DOC
START	BAT	Batch file for running MA.BAS
— — — —	— —	Maillist program
DATA		Sample data file for MAIL.IST
MAIL	DIR	ASCII text file containing a list of this group of files
MAIL	DOC	ASCII text file containing documentation for MAIL.IST
MAIL	IST	Mail list maintenance program (BASIC language; treat as
— — — —	— —	Another maillist program
AUTODIAL	BAS	Autodial program chained to by MAILIST1.BAS
MAILIST1	BAS	Mail list maintenance program

MAILIST1	DIR	ASCII text file containing a list of this group of files
MAILIST1	DOC	ASCII text file containing documentation for MAILIST1.BAS
MAILSORT	BAS	Sort program chained to by MAILIST1.BAS

File Descriptions:

PC-AR	COM	Accounts receivable and sales analysis package
PC-AR	DOC	Documentation for PC-AR.COM
PC-GL	DOC	Documentation for PC-GL.COM
PC-GL	COM	A double entry accounting program
PC-GL	COA	Standard chart of accounts to use or modify
PC-PR	DOC	Documentation for PC-PR.COM
PC-PR	COM	Payroll package

331
PC-GL
Version 2.9
v3

PC-GL contains three companion accounting packages for full charge accounting. The first and main program, PC-GL, is a double entry accounting program. It can be used by itself or in tandem with with PC-AR (the accounts receivables package). PC-AR is menu-driven, and supports up to 2000 accounts, with up to 1500 charges and payments per period. PC-PR is the payroll writing system. This version includes the 1986 Federal tax tables and registered users also receive the 1987 updates.

PLEASE NOTE: All programs keep data in RAM, so the more RAM you have, the more accounts you will be able to support. For example, PC-GL allows a maximum of 800 items in the chart of accounts and 4000 transactions per accounting period. With 128k of memory the number of transactions is reduced to about 300 per accounting period.

Usage: Accounts management for small business

System Requirements: 128K, two disk drives, monochrome/graphics card and monitor for PC-GL and PC-PR; 256K needed for PC-AR

How to Start: Read the manual carefully; to print it, enter COPY PC-GL.DOC LPT1:

● To run, enter PC-GL and press ENTER.

User Comments: "Good accounts receivable program." "Good little program for small simple business." "Excellent general ledger program for a small (emphasized) business, but it cannot do any number of things that my current commercial G/L program can do. I may use it later as a personal G/L — to keep my own checkbook and savings, etc."

Suggested Donation: PC-GL: $35.00; $95.00 for source code.

332
KLP/DTA/MUA
v1

The Kinetics Linear Programming (KLP) System requires a knowledge with linear (LP) programming. KLP in an integrated software system which can be used to define, solve, review and refine a linear programming problem. Although no other software is necessary, KLP can be used with VisiCalc, Lotus 1-2-3, and SuperCalc 2. KLP is an integrated software system that allows you to solve linear programming problems of considerable complexity. The results can be printed, saved to the disk, or written to a spreadsheet input file.

System Requirements: one disk drive, 128K, an 80 column monitor, DOS 1.1 and above, printer with condensed print capabilities (132 columns).

How to Start: Consult the .DOC and README files for directions and documentation

● To run the BASIC programs, consult the directions in GETTING STARTED for your configuration
● To run any of these programs, just type its name, i.e., for KLP.EXE, type KLP and press ENTER.

Suggested Donation: KLP $45.00

File Descriptions:

————	——	KINETICS LINEAR PROGRAMMING SYSTEM (version 1.9)
KLP	EXE	System can integrate Lotus, SuperCalc or VisiCalc
FURNFAC	DMP	Matrix print file
FURNFAC	MAT	Furniture factory problem
FURNFAC	SSI	Spreadsheet output
FURNFAC	TXT	Results file
KLP	DOC	Documentation (27pp) manual
README	KLP	Documentation (brief introduction)
————	——	DECISION TREE ANALYSIS & MULTIATTRIBUTE UTILITY ANALYSIS
DT	EXE	DECISION TREE ANALYSIS: A technique to analyze

DTDATA	S-1	Sample data file
MESSAGE	KEY	Message file
MESSAGE	TXT	Message file
COBRUN	EXE	Microsoft COBOL Runtime Monitor (Both DT & MU need it)
MU	EXE	MULTIATTRIBUTE UTILITY ANALYSIS
MUMSG	TXT	Message file
MUMSG	KEY	Message file
MUDATA	S-1	Sample data file

388
Form Letters
V1.1

Here is an extensive collection of samples of common business letters that can be tailored to your individual needs. This disk contains 100 boiler-plate business letters. Note: Refer to your word processing manual for information on reading ASCII files. If you want to edit the letter, you can use any standard ASCII word processor. So check out our Word Processing section!

Usage: Business correspondence.

System Requirements: 64K, one disk drive and monochrome display;

How to Start: Consult the AD file for directions and documentation.

● To run, enter PRINTLET and press ENTER.

User Comments: "The program letters were great for me. I hate to write and I found that they cover most of the situations that I have need for in my mail order business." "The form letters should be useful for routine business use. It would be nice to have a brief explanation of each letter."

File Descriptions:

1LTSCHRA	Overdue account letters
1SLPYBS	Overdue account letters
2LTSCHRA	Overdue account letters
2SLPYBS	Overdue account letters
3LTSCHRA	Overdue account letters
3SLPYBS	Overdue account letters
4LTSCHRA	Overdue account letters
4SLPYBS	Overdue account letters
5LTSCHRA	Overdue account letters
5SLPYBS	Overdue account letters
6SLPYBS	Overdue account letters
ABSNTRCD	Attendance notice
ACKNORDR	Acknowledge order

AD	Information about this and other programs
AFTRSLSL	Proposal follow up
APOLOGYC	Apology for incorrect collection letter
BADCHK	Bad check notice
BDBHVR	Bad behavior notice
BDRSK	Bad risk notice
BLLNGMST	Billing error
BNKDPST	Idle bank account inquiry
BSAPPCTN	Credit account denial
BSCLSD	Layoff notice
CHRGACCT	New charge account acceptance
CLAIMS	Response to complaint about employee behavior
CLLCTN	Request for bill due date extension
CMPLNTAD	Product defect and replacement request to supplier
CNCLCNTR	Certified letter canceling the order
COMPLNT	Incomming product variance notice
COND	Sympathy letter for co-workers death
COPLCY	Company policy denial of donation request
CRDTINFR	Request to supplier for a credit account
CRDTRQST	Response from supplier granting credit request
CRDTSTND	Response from supplier turning down credit request
CRDTSUSP	Response from supplier suspending credit
CRVOUCH	Neutral response to credit reference inquiry
CSTMRTHS	Customer thank you letter
DCLDN	Dinner invitation turn down letter
DLVRMTH	Delivery method error refund letter
DLYDCRD	Delayed returned merchandise refund
DTHOTHER	Death sympathy
EMPLMNT	Job inquiry turn down letter
EXPNSVGT	Return of an expensive gift from a client
FLLUPREP	Mailing list follow up letter
FLLWUP	Customer sales visit follow up letter
FNDRSNG	Decline charity sponsorship request
FNDSLMT	Turn down charity donation request
FOLLWUP	Follow up to phone call when customer not in
FURN	Furniture store grand opening
GDCRDTST	Positive response to credit reference inquiry
GVNGLTR	Cancel incorrect service charges
HSPTYGFT	Hospitality gift thank you letter
ILL	Ill employee response letter
ILLHLTH	Ill health resignation letter
INACTVCS	Inactive customer status inquiry
INACTVE	Inactive customer sales inquiry
INCMTXCO	Tax consultant sales mailer
INCOMPL	Letter of sales exchange
INJURY	Injury gift
INTROSLS	Sales introduction
JBDNWL	Christmas rush employee effort commendation letter
JBRSM	Job advertisement inquiry
LFINSRNC	Life insurance policy inquiry
LTDLVY	Late delivery due to engraving
MNRNIMG	Gift return by civil court judge
MSMTNG	Apology for missed meeting
NOINFRMT	Incomplete credit application response
NWCSTMR	New customer thank you
OPNACCT	Request for credit account
ORDRCNFR	Mail order request
ORDRCONF	Mail order request

PERSCRDT		Incomplete credit application response
PERSCRE		Credit account offer mailer
PMPTPMNT		Thank you for prompt credit account payments
POSUNSTE		No position available response to job inquiry
PRCRDIT		Order refusal due to bad credit history
PRCRDT		Negative response to credit reference inquiry
PRINTLET	EXE	Program to print all the letters out to a prnter
PRPY		Credit denial
PRQUOTE		Request for quote
PRSNLCRD		Credit line denial
QUESTNNR		Sample credit questionnaire
RECMMD		Neutral response to company reference inquiry
REFPR		Deny price discount request
REFRNCE		Positive response to company reference inquiry
REFUND		Wrong product refund
RESCHDLO		Request production schedule change
RESIGN		Resignation letter
RETRMNT		Retirement congratulations
RJCTREF		Negative response to employment reference
RSMJOB		Resume cover letter
SECYRCM		Positive response to employment reference
SERVCHRG		Service charge increase announcement
SHRTEPMT		Negative credit application response
SLS		Mail inquiry response letter
SLSGRMTN		Sales agreement cancellation confirmation
SLSLLPRD		Negative response to slow selling product return request
SLSVLM		Salesman congratulation for landing a new account
STATEMNT		Correction for billing error
STMTER		Corrected statement cover letter
THNKYOU		COD shipment denial, holding product for payment
UNSATCRD		Negative response to credit reference inquiry

393
Checkbook Management Version 2.2
v1.2

A complete checkbook management system which is essentially a comprehensive check register. It allows users to: create all needed data files; enter, delete, or correct all forms for checking account transactions (including bank charges, automatic teller deposits and withdrawals, interest for NOW accounts, etc). Output will guide you through bank statement reconciliation.

Reports generated based on this information (can be date specified):

- Listing all transactions
- Transactions in a Category
- List of all current Budget Categories
- List of all automatic teller transactions
- List of all deposits Annual Expenditure Report
- Total Transaction Report

Usage: Total checkbook management

System Requirements: 192K, one disk drive and color/monochrome monitor.

How to Start: Consult the documentation in the four CHECKS files

- To run, enter CHECK and press ENTER.

User Comments: "The program was a pleasure to use. Documentation was complete and clearly written. The program performed as explained (better than expected.) "VERY good program. Could be improved by giving total for any listing of checks." "Very easy to use and the documentation answers all questions. I wish a portion of the program was dedicated to savings and IRA accounts, but after all it is a checking program." "Should be expanded into a complete home finance package."

Suggested Donation: $25.00 includes complete documentation

File Descriptions:

README		TYPE this file out for instructions
CHECKS	EXE	Checkbook Management Program
CHECKS	?	Documentation to be printed out (4 files)

399
Loan Amortization and Prospect List
v1

Both programs on this disk are written in Microsoft Business Basic but have been compiled for superior speed. AMORTIZE provides analysis data for amortizing loans with output either to the screen or printed reports; it is menu-driven and includes quite a bit of online help. The second program maintains a "prospect" mailing list.

Usage: Loan calculations and prospect listings

How to Start: Consult the .DOC files for directions and documentation

- To run, enter AMORTIZE and press ENTER.

User Comments: "Very useful loan amortization program" "Very Good amortization program but a printout can be tricky." "Just what I needed to calculate loan schedules." "The amortization program was my prime reason to purchase this disk. I use it to add data to spreadsheets for budget forecasting. Great for figuring net worth balances."

Suggested Donation: $10.00

File Descriptions:

AMORTIZE	DOC	Text file containing information about AMORTIZE.EXE
AMORTIZE	EXE	The compiled loan amortization program
PLIST	DIS	The menus and screens for use by the PLIST.EXE program
PLIST	DOC	Text file containing information about the PLIST program
PLIST	EXE	The compiled Prospect-list program
PLIST	TRM	The terminal definition file used by the PLIST program

404

EZ-FORMS PACKAGE
Version C.24

v1

EZ-FORMS is a form-generating program that allows you to generate master forms tailored to your individual needs. Using the menu-driven design process, you can create a new one of your own or revise a "master"(one of the supplied forms). All forms can be stored and printed. Direct screeen memory access is used to provide high speed screen updates. EZ-FORMS package supports IBM/Epson/compatible printers as well as daisy-wheel printers. However, only Epson and Pro-Writer compatibles can take advantage of the compressed mode used by FORMS package when printing out larger forms. Extensive and well-written documentation is provided.

Usage: Personal forms creation and production

System Requirements: 256K, two disk drives, monochrome display

How to Start: Start with the OVERVIEW.DOC and then go to the EZF-HLP.TXT for directions and documentation

● To run, enter EZF and press ENTER.

User Comments: "Excellent program. I have used it to generate many pieces for such small organizations as Scouts to generate short one-time use forms: lists for camping trips, permission slips,etc." "This is an excellent program, especially for a small business just starting up. It allows you to produce small quantities of forms as needed. It also lets you test forms before printing large quantities."

Suggested Donation: $49.95 gets a printed manual, latest version and one month technical support; $250.00 for site license

File Descriptions:

BUGREPT	FRM	EZ-FORMS Bug Report Form. Use this to document any bugs.
BUSCARD	FRM	Form consisting of 10 business cards
CALENDAR	FRM	General calendar which can be completed for any month
CUSTBILL	FRM	Customer billing memo: labor, travel expense, desc of work
DATAENTR	FRM	Generalized database entry form: name, DOB, family, phone#s
DAYNOTES	FRM	Broken up by day of week and has area for notes
EO	FRM	Engineering Order. (example of technical form)
EXPENSE2	FRM	Expenses — charge to who, date, purpose, amount, etc
EXPENSES	FRM	Summary of expenses: meals, transportation, expense, misc.
EZ	COM	The executable program for EZ-FORMS
EZ	DOC	Documentation for EZ-FORMS
FILES	DOC	Listing of files on disk.
GO	BAT	Start: Batch file to type READ.ME & then execute EZ.COM
INVOICE	FRM	Invoice listing item, qty, price, total, & other info.
INVOICE2	FRM	Simplified version of above Invoice
LEDGERAS	FRM	Ledger Series — ACCOUNT SUMMARY (Weekly or Monthly)
LEDGERDD	FRM	- DAILY DETAIL
LEDGERPR	FRM	- PAYROLL
LEDGERTR	FRM	- TOTAL RECEIPTS
MEETAGEN	FRM	Meeting Series — MEETING AGENDA
MEETDELG	FRM	- MEETING DELEGATIONS & ASSIGNMENTS
MEETNOTE	FRM	- MEETING NOTES — DECISIONS REACHED
MEETPROG	FRM	- DETAILS OF MEETING & PROJECT PROGRESS
MEETSCHD	FRM	- SCHEDULED MEETINGS & PROGRESS REPORTS
MEMBER	FRM	Form for local PC organization membership application
MEMO	FRM	Simplified memorandum
MEMO2	FRM	Memo — less structured than MEMO.FRM
MEMOLETR	FRM	Memo letter
ORDER	FRM	Order form listing addresses, quan, desc, price, & amount

ORDER2	FRM	Lined version of ORDER.FRM
ORDER3	FRM	Order form similar to ORDER.FRM and ORDER2.FRM
ORDER4	FRM	Lined version of ORDER3.FRM
PHONEDIR	FRM	Address and phone directory
QIKREPLY	FRM	Quick replay form
READ	ME	File containing brief overview of EZ-FORMS Package
RECRDSUB	FRM	Record of substantiation
REGISTER	FRM	Registration form for EZ-FORMS Ver A
RID	FRM	Engineering form example for: Review Item Disposition
SERVICE	FRM	Service form: lists customer, service No., total $, etc.
TELEMSG	FRM	Sheet of 4 telephone message forms — can cut up into 4
TIRF	FRM	Engineering form: Transmittal/Information Request form
WEEKPLAN	FRM	Weekly Plan Sheet, space for schedules
WORKORD	FRM	Work Order listing material, time, & description of work

423 PROJECT MANAGEMENT Version 3.6
v1.1

This disk contains the complete PC Project Management system. PCPM is a system of interactive programs for project management using the Critical Path Method (CPM) to calculate: the critical path, cash-flow, cost reports, Gantt charts, and Precedence networks.

The system is designed to handle all necessary functions internally or allow sophisticated users to build and modify files making use of system editing software. PCPM is almost completely menu-driven and is capable of handling up to 500 tasks, subcontractors, variable start dates, and holidays. A surprisingly sophisticated tool for those in need of a good planning utility.

System Requirements: 64K, one disk drive and monochrome display; a 132 column printer (or a standard printer with compressed mode) is needed for most printout.

How to Start: Consult PCPM.DOC for documentation

● To run this BASIC program, consult the directions in GETTING STARTED for your configuration.

Suggested Donation: $50.00 is requested.

File Descriptions:

PCPM	BAS	Basic language Program Management main program
PCPM	BAT	Batch file for starting the PCPM program from DOS
PCPM	DOC	Documentation/40 page manual for the PCPM system
LLP		Sample data file
LLP	BAR	Sample Gantt chart
LLP	DAY	Sample day numbers
LLP	CFA	Sample cash flow analyst
LLP	CPM	Sample main input file
LLP	LGS	Sample file of data for sorts
LLP	NDS	Sample data file
LLP	OUT	Sample output report
LLP	UPD	Sample updated input data file
CPA???	BAS	Called by PCPM.BAS (16 files)

430 AnalytiCalc System (Disk 1 of 3)
v1.2

AnalytiCalc is a complete Spreadsheet/Database/Graphics/Word Processor program. Written in FORTRAN, it is quite fast and has attractive features. The author's goal is an inexpensive, highly integrated package. The complete system comes on three disks. Disk one is the primary disk for a computer that is limited to 256K memory. Disk two is the supplemental disk with documentation and extra files. Disk three is the primary disk for a computer with more than 320K memory. This is a complex package, and the user should be sure to read the documentation before using it.

ALL THREE DISKS ARE NEEDED TO USE THE SYSTEM.

System Requirements: 256K, two disk drives and monochrome display

Features:

- Number of Columns 18000
- Number of Rows. 18000
- Maximum Length of Formulas (characters).109
- Number of cells that can be full at once . 18000
- Number of simultaneous named areas permitted 300

- Number of scratch cells outside spreadsheet. 60
- Precision of calculations (digits; 8 bytes used)..................................... 16
- Total maximum storage managed (bytes)............................2,113,020
- Maximum depth of document nesting (outline processor)................................. 4
- Maximum number of parameters varying to goal seek 8
- Maximum record size for data files accessed as database............................... 128
- Maximum number of files namable in one sheet...............................18000
- Maximum cell columns displayable on one screen................................... 20
- Maximum number of rows displayable in one display 75
- Maximum simultaneous different cell display formats per sheet (taken from large set) 76
- Length of format specification (characters)... 9

How to Start: Read and print the document files ACSTART.DOC, README.DOC, MANUSQ.HLP, PKGINS.DOC, and ANALY.TUT. MANUSQ.HLP will describe how to unsqueeze the manual file. Unsqueeze it and read it before starting. When you have read the manuals, boot Disk 1 and type ANALY to fire up the spreadsheet system. Then run through the tutorial to get a feel for it.

User Comments: "Good spreadsheet program" "...utilities provided are useful." "The documentation is not too clear" "Very good for technical/professional users who would use it regularly, as command format requires commitment to learn and use to remember." "Program is complex and documentation covers it. Looks like it will do what you get a spreadsheet with useful additions for models. Main drawback — SLOW!!" "Recommend it provided that user has 8087 processor (too slow otherwise) and really needs the advanced features."

Suggested Donation: $49.95 includes update notification, latest version with auxiliary programs and features

File Descriptions:

ANALY	EXE	Main program of Spreadsheet/DB/WP system
ANALY	TQT	Tutorial on use of AnalytiCalc as spreadsheet
ANALYTCL	CRD	Pocket Reference Card summary of cmds, functs
AUTOEXEC	BAT	Demo Autoexec.bat that types AUXKPD.TXT to set up BIGANSI.SYS
AUXKPD	TXT	File of escape sequences to initialize BIGANSI.SYS when typed
BER	PCC	Business expense report template.
BIGANSI	SYS	Modified ANSI.SYS that supports more defs than standard
CONFIG	SYS	CONFIG.SYS that loads BIGANSI.SYS
CPM	EQE	CP/M-86 SSDD disk read/write/etc. under MSDOS. Squeezed.
DIFF	DOC	Intelligent differences between 2 text files (or saved sheets)
DIFF	EQE	Squeezed executable (Use USQ to unsqueeze)
DPATH30	COM	DOS PATH command extension: handy to run ANALY off RAM disk
DPATH30	DQC	Squeezed documentation of above (Use USQ.EXE to unsqueeze)
EDIT	DQC	Editor manual (condensed) for EDIT.EQE on Disk 2. Squeezed.
GRF	BAT	Batch file that goes with GRF.CMD
KEYPAD	DOC	Documentation on function key usage
LSTX	EXE	A very fast text file editor with online help
NOTICE	TXT	Documents new features and distribution policy/price
PCCHELP	HQP	Online direct access HELP file
PIE	BAS	Piechart program for sections of AnalytiCalc spreadsheets
SCRNCOLR	AQM	source code for SCRNCOLR.COM
SCRNCOLR	DOC	Documentation for SCRNCOLR.COM
SCRNCOLR	COM	Program to change screen colors.

431 AnalytiCalc System (Disk 2 of 3)
v1.2

This is the second AnalytiCalc disk. It contains the user manual and auxiliary programs and is not duplicated on either of the other two disks in the AnalytiCalc system. Note: All three disks are necessary for this system.

File Descriptions:

MANUSQ	HLP	Documentation on what's here and how to unsqueeze
USQ	EXE	Unsqueeze utility
DTC	DQC	Desktop Calendar documentaion, squeezed. Handy appointment keeper
DTC	HQP	DeskTop Calendar online HELP screen. Unsqueeze.
DTC	EQE	DeskTop Calendar program. Use for all your timekeeping, appts.
README	1ST	Initial documentation
F1040	PQC	Part of US Federal Income Tax system; saved worksheet, squeezed
PKGINS	DOC	How to install the package
ACSTART	DOC	More startup information
GRF	BQS	Line chart, fitting, and scattergram program.

ANALY	MQN	AnalytiCalc manual file, squeezed. Full reference manual + index.
EDIT	EQE	A screen editor. Simple but fast and handles any size file.
ANALY	TQC	Approximate table of contents for AnalytiCalc manual (squeezed)
LST	COM	Screen lister. Very fast listings to screen of a file.
CPM	EQE	CP/M-86 SSDD disk read/write/etc. under MSDOS. Squeezed.
ZERO	EQE	CP/M-86 SSDD disk initialize CP/M directory structure, squeezed
EDIT	DQC	Brief doc file for EDIT above. Squeezed.
ACGRAF	EXE	Histogram and scatterplot utility for AnalytiCalc.
IDENT	TXT	Identifies the disk.
GRF	CMD	Command file to generate graphs from inside AnalytiCalc
GRF	BAT	BATch file that goes with GRF.CMD
AUXKPD	TXT	BIGANSI.SYS setup that binds Control F2 to @GRF.CMD

432
AnalytiCalc System (Disk 3 of 3)
1.2

The complete AnalytiCalc system comes on three disks of which this is the third. It contains the equivalent program disk to that on Disk No 430 but it is for systems with 320K or more of memory. Please see description under Disk No 430. NOTE: You need all three disks for this system.

File Descriptions:

1040	PCC	Part of US Federal Income Tax spreadsheet template
AKA	CMD	One of the command files executing a keypad command
AKB	CMD	One of the command files executing a keypad command
AKD	CMD	One of the command files executing a keypad command
AKDA	CMD	One of the command files executing a keypad command
ANALY	EXE	Main program of Spreadsheet/DB/WP system
ANALY	TQC	Approximate table of contents for AnalytiCalc manual (squeezed)
AUTOEXEC	BAT	Demo Autoexec.bat that types AUXKPD.TXT to set up BIGANSI.SYS
AUXKPD	TXT	File of escape sequences to initialize BIGANSI.SYS when typed
BIGANSI	SYS	Modified ANSI.SYS that supports more defs than standard
BUF160	AQM	Source to keyboard buffer extender; may be better than BUFEXTEND

BUF160	COM	Keyboard buffer extender
BUFEXTEN	COM	Keyboard buffer extender (allows type ahead of 150 chars)
CCO	CMD	One of the command files executing a keypad command
CONFIG	SYS	CONFIG.SYS that loads BIGANSI.SYS
CPR	CMD	One of the command files executing a keypad command
CRW	CMD	One of the command files executing a keypad command
CRWA	CMD	One of the command files executing a keypad command
DIFF	DOC	Intelligent differences between 2 text files (or saved sheets)
DIFF	EQE	Squeezed executable (Use USQ to unsqueeze)
DIFRDWRT	FQR	sources for DIFRW.EXE, squeezed. Use USQ to unsqueeze.
DIFRW	DOC	Documentation for DIFRW.EXE
DIFRW	EXE	Utility to read or write DIF files from AnalytiCalc saved files.
F1040	CMD	Part of US Federal Income Tax template
F1040	DOC	Documentation on the pieces of US Income Tax template
GRF	CMD	Line chart, fitting, and scattergram program
HTX	CMD	One of the command files executing a keypad command
HTXT	CMD	One of the command files executing a keypad command
INCENT	CMD	One of the command files executing a keypad command
KER	DOC	Documentation for generic Kermit communications program
KER	EQE	Communications program, an old Kermit using IBM BIOS only
LST	COM	Screen lister. Very fast listings to screen of a file.
NOTICE	TXT	Documents new features and distribution policy/price
PCCHELP	HQP	Online direct access HELP file
PIE	BAS	Piechart program for sections of AnalytiCalc spreadsheets
SCHEDA	PCC	Part of US Federal Income Tax template for AnalytiCalc
SCHEDB	PCC	Part of US Federal Income Tax template for AnalytiCalc
SCHEDX	PCC	Part of US Federal Income Tax template for AnalytiCalc
SCHEDY	PCC	Part of US Federal Income Tax template for AnalytiCalc
SETUP	CMD	How to configure ANSI.SYS for aux keypad definitions
SRCH	CMD	One of the command files executing a keypad command
TOEND	CMD	One of the command files executing a keypad command
WND	CMD	One of the command files executing a keypad command

440

Miscellaneous Applications

v1.1

A mixture of BASIC and Pascal programs that perform a variety of personal and business tasks.

The major program here, Disk File, is a simple but complete database program for making disk labels rather than using the labels supplied by the disk manufacturer. It supports IBM/Epson/compatible printers. NOTE: These are ONE-UP gummed labels.

The Printed Circuit Board (PCBD.BAS) assists in estimating the production cost of double-sided printed circuit boards. The Restaurant House Charge Billing System (GBILL) lets you record each of your guest's house charges and produce mail-ready bills and stubs. The bills that the system produces provide your "open account" customers with year-to-date account totals, and helps your account management.

System Requirements: 128K, one disk drive and monochrome display

How to Start: Consult the .DOC and README files for directions and documentation

- To run the BASIC programs, consult the directions in GETTING STARTED for your configuration
- To run a program with the suffix .COM or .EXE, just type its name, i.e., for DISKFILE.EXE, type DISK and press ENTER.

Suggested Donation: $28.00 GBILL; $5.00 DISKFILE

File Descriptions:

READ	ME	Explains the file extensions of some of the Basic programs
————	——	IRA/SPDA
IRA	BAS	Individual Retirement Account / Single Premium Deferred
HOLD	DAT	}
IRA	DAT	} Data files used by IRA.BAS
————	——	AMORTIZATION SCHEDULES
GO	BAT	Batch file to start AMRTMENU.BAS program
AMORT	BAS	Calculates Loan Amortization — results to the printer
AMRTMENU	BAS	Program that selects AMORT.BAS or SCRNAMRT.BAS
SCRNAMRT	BAS	Calculates Loan Amortization — results to the screen
AMRTMENU	ABS	Abstract of the AMRTMENU.BAS program
AMORT	ABS	Abstract of the AMORT.BAS program
SCRNAMRT	ABS	Abstract of the SCRNAMRT.BAS program
————	——	RESTAURANT HOUSE-CHARGE BILLING (v1.0)
GBILL	EXE	The House-charge billing program
CLEAR	EXE	Creates data files for the GBILL.EXE program
SETUP	EXE	Customizes the entire system
READ-ME		Notes for printing documentation and installing system
GBILL	DOC	Documentation (15K)
————	——	PCBD
PCBD	BAS	A program that assists in estimating the production cost
PCBD	DOC	Documentation for PCBD.BAS (4K)
PCBD	ABS	Abstract of the PCBD.BAS program
PCBD	ASC	ASCII text file of the Basic source code
————	——	FILEFIX
FILEFIX	BAS	Prepares ASCII text files with CR/LF delimiters for import
FILEFIX	DOC	Documentation file (2K)
FILEFIX	ABS	Abstract of the FILEFIX.BAS program
FILEFIX	ASC	ASCII text file of the Basic source code
FILEFIX	PAS	Pascal source code
FILEFIX	COM	Compiled version of the FILEFIX.PAS program
————	——	DISKFILE LABEL MAKER
DISK	PRG	dBASE III source code for the Disk-File system
FILELIST	TXT	List of files on this disk
DISK	EXE	Compiled version of Disk-File Disk Label Maker
DISKFILE	DBF	Data base for Disk-File
CAPSLOCK	COM	Program to set Caps Lock to on. Place in Autoexec.bat
COMMENT	MEM	Memory file used in Disk-File

466

CPA-LEDGER Program (Disk 1 of 2)

v2.0

This is disk 1 of CPA-LEDGER; it contains all of CPA-LEDGER's main and practice programs. CPA-LEDGER is a menu-driven general ledger and financial statement program. It's designed for non-manufacturing businesses that offer products or services for sale. You must have a knowledge of double entry bookkeeping to operate this package.

The CPA- LEDGER has plenty of muscle to record your daily transactions. Any one general ledger entry may have up to 30 debits and 30 credits, with total values of up to 999,999,999.99. Also, you may use any combination of 1 to 30 characters to identify the payee of a check. A Very Powerful System!

Be sure to read the user's manual on DISK 468 before you attempt to use the CPA-LEDGER in your business.

System Requirements: 128K, 80-/132-column printer, two disk drives and monochrome display

How to Start: As CPA-LEDGER operates from BASICA make sure it is loaded according to your systems configuration

- To run CPA-LEDGER, type either SETUP or DAILY followed by ENTER.

User Comments: "An excellent accounting program, written with an easy-to-use interface, with an extensive manual in basic english — a real plus!" "The programmers had a very good understanding what an individual needs to know in order to use a general ledger on a computer. Very well written and easy to use and understand." "EXCELLENT DOCUMENTATION."

Suggested Donation: $45.00 includes three financial statement features, up to eight hours of consulting and update notification.

File Descriptions:

ACTDTL	BAS	This program processes the G/L files that are on your data disk
CHKREG	BAS	This program prints transactions that inc or dec bank accts
DAILY	BAS	This program handles most daily operations and transactions
GENLGR	BAS	This program is to be used for establishing a new general ledger
GLACTS	BAS	This program prints a chart of general ledger accounts
NEWACT	BAS	This program allows the user to add new accounts to the g/l
OPNBAL	BAS	This program opens and posts balances to the general ledger
PANDL	BAS	This program handles primary & contra accnts & income statements
POST	BAS	This program allows the user to post entries
PSTCLS	BAS	This program will prepare a Post-closing trial balance
READ	ME	Author supplied documentation file
SELTRA	BAS	This program selects input ranges and dates
SETUP	BAS	This is the User's initial "SETUP" program
STOACT	BAS	This program sets up and stores the accounts
TRIBAL	BAS	This is the Trial Balance program
GENJNL	FIL	This is the general journal file
GENLEG	FIL	This is the general ledger file
INVPRO	FIL	Part of ledger program
PASACT	FIL	Part of ledger program
READ	ME	Author supplied documentation file
TEST1	FIL	Test1 is a practice file
TEST2	FIL	Test2 is a practice file

468 CPA-LEDGER User's Manual (Disk 2 of 2)
2.0

This is the second of a two disk set. It contains CPA-LEDGER's User's Manual (over 150 pages). The manual is subdivided into 15 chapters and Appendix A through Appendix E. They may be printed out using an ASCII word processor or the DOS COPY command. We suggest you start with the README and the PREFACE.TXT; they are excellent introductions.

File Descriptions:

APNDX-A	TXT	CPA-LEDGER and the income statements cost of goods sold section
APNDX-B	TXT	Using CPA-LEDGER with FIXED disk drives
APNDX-C	TXT	Directions if you do not have fixed disk
APNDX-D	TXT	Some comments about an Accounting and Bookkeeping System
APNDX-E	TXT	Contains forms for summarizing data before entering into CPA
CHP1	TXT	CPA-LEDGER overview
CHP2	TXT	Standard messages and reminders
CHP3-5	TXT	Setup Menus — options 1,2 and 3
CHP6-7	TXT	Daily Menus — options 1 and 2
CHP8	TXT	Daily Menu — option 3
CHP9-11	TXT	Daily Menus — options 4,5 and 6
CHP12-15	TXT	Daily Menus — options 7,8,9 and 10 plus Setup Menu -
PREFACE	TXT	Introduction, Table of Contents, disclaimer etc.
READ	ME	Author supplied documentation file

469 Mr. BILL (Disk 1 of 2)
1.1

Mr Bill consists of fourteen (14) separate programs accessed through a main menu. These programs prepare itemized invoices and bills, and reports items billed/credited, ageing reports for clients, audit trail of billing entries, and summary reports. It is a very flexible billing system with many uses. This is disk one of a two disk set.

System Requirements: 64K, one disk drive and monochrome display

How to Start: The documentation in BILL.DOC is formatted with WordStar which means you need that program or get an UNWS program to make it legible for ASCII word processors

● To run, enter BILL and press ENTER.

User Comments: "MR. BILL is an extremely good program for billing. Also, the documentation is geared to the average person trying to set up a billing system." "The documentation was not as helpful as I would have liked. " "Well written, easy to understand." "Seems to assume one already knows about billing practices in general."

Suggested Donation: $30.00 gets the full documentation and update.

File Descriptions:

BILL	EXE	Main billing program
BILLADD	EXE	Sub-program : enter/change/delete/look at name/addresses
BILLIN	EXE	Sub-program : enter billing data
BILLINIT	EXE	Sub-program : initialize system
BILLMERG	EXE	Sub-program : merge data from several small files
BILL	DOC	Documentation/User manual (WordStar document) (20 pgs)
BILLS		Data file — serial number of next bill
BILLSET	EXE	Sub-program : set/change/delete/look at codes/rates
BILLSORT	EXE	Sub-program : sorts billing entries
BILLSUB	EXE	Sub-program : enter/change/delete/look at subtotals
ORD		Blank order data file

470
Mr. BILL
(Disk 2 of 2)
1.1

This is disk two in a two disk set. Please refer to Disk No 469 for the product overview, setup and system requirements.

File Descriptions:

BILL	EXE	Main billing program
BILLAGE	EXE	Sub-program : produces ageing report
BILLDATE	EXE	Sub-program : produces report of billings by date
BILLRPT	EXE	Sub-program : prepares bills

BILLRPTP	EXE	Sub-program : printed report of bills
BILLS		Data file — serial numbers
BILLSORT	EXE	Sub-program : sorts billing entries
BILLTRL	EXE	Sub-program : audit trail
MBINST	EXE	Sub-program : part of installing system
SORT	EXE	Sub-program : used by BILLSORT sub-program

472
Simplified
Business Bookkeeping
1

All of the programs on this disk are menu driven and written in BASIC. However, simplified doesn't mean simple; its powers and features are quite substantial and we urge a careful reading of the documentation. The Simplified Bookkeeping System offers you the following programs: Expenses, Income, Bank Account, Payroll, Accounts Receivable, and Summary of Operations. A quite powerful collection for financial management.

System Requirements: 128K, two disk drives, monochrome display and a printer

How to Start: Consult the BKG.DOC file for documentation

● To run the BASIC programs, consult the directions in GETTING STARTED for your configuration.

User Comments: "Not a bad little program." "Setup on the disk was too cumbersome" "Haven't had a chance to do much with it but so far am relatively pleased. It seems to have everything I need." "Only bad point is assumption of BASICA. After rewriting .BAT files and substituting GWBASIC, BKPG is very excellent."

Suggested Donation: $35.00

File Descriptions:

A	EXE	Information on how to use to *.bat files to backup your data
ACCTREC	BAS	Processes Accounts Receivables
AUTOEXEC	BAT	Request the DATE then loads BASICA BKPG /F:5
BKPG	BAK	Backup file of bookkeeping
BKPG	BAS	This is the bookkeeping program
BKPG	DOC	Author supplied documentation file
C	BAT	COPY PAYEE.FIL, CATEGORY.FIL, INCOME.FIL to B:, CHKDSK A: & B:

CHECKING	BAS	Maintains the checking account
EXPENSE	BAS	Keeps track of expenses
F	BAT	Creates and formats two new disks, for bookkeeping fiscal year
G	BAT	Copies totals to new backup bookkeeping disk, runs bkpg.bas
INCOME	BAS	Keeps track of income
L	BAT	Copies checking.acc to new backup bookkeeping disk, runs bkpg.bas
N	BAT	Creates two disks then loads BASICA & runs Payroll program
PAYROLL	BAS	Processes the payroll
R	BAT	Creates two disks then loads BASICA & runs A/R program
S	BAT	Format 6 disks by responding "Y" first 5 times, for startup
SHELLSRT	BAS	This is a shell sort program for sorting files
STARTUP	BAT	Author supplied User startup procedure batch file
X	BAT	Makes new backup copy of PAYROLL FILE DISK on drive B:

501 SALESEYE (2.3) Program (Disk 1 of 2) v1

The SALESEYE package is ideal for individuals in sales, because it is designed to help users keep track of prospects, leads, and those all important memos. It has a highly developed system of "tickler" files designed to keep track of deadlines, calls to be returned, lunch appointments, etc. There is even a simple word processor, along with commonly used letter formats. This is disk one of a two disk set. The tutorial is on disk 502.

Usage: Sales management and tracking

System Requirements: 256K, two floppies or a hard disk, monochrome display.

How to Start: Read the README.1st file and then begin the Tutorial on Disk #502 by consulting the BEGINNIN.TXT for documentation

• To run, enter SELL and press ENTER.

Suggested Donation: To register this copy of SALESEYE and obtain a printed 240 page manual (includes a full Tutorial Manual, Reference Manual, Appendices, glossary and index), technical support, and upgrade notices, send a check for $89 less the amount you paid PC-SIG for these disks.

File Descriptions:

CONFIG	SYS	Configuration file
????????	MEM	Memory data files used by program
MLEADS	HIS	Followup leads file
MLETTER	MLE	Letter format
MQUAL?	CDF	Leads file — 1-8 & 44
MREPORT	CDF	Leads report
QTS????	SCR	Help details file — 1 thru 5
SAMPLE	???	Sample leads files
SELL	EXE	Main Program
SELL	OV?	Overlay 1 & 2
????????	TIK	Tickler file

502 SALESEYE (2.3) Tutorial (Disk 2 of 2) v1

This is the second of the two disk set. It is the instruction disk for the SALESEYE program. This tutorial is designed to explain the various features of the package. It contains a series of lessons and documentation. This package is ideal for salespersons with significant amounts of detail work.

How to Start: To review on your monitor the documentation compiled here on using SALESEYE enter: TYPE INSTALL.TXT and press ENTER.

• To print the information on using SALESEYE enter: COPY INSTALL.TXT LPT1: and press ENTER.

File Descriptions:

LEADS	DBF	Leads file
LEADS	NDX	Leads instruction file
LEADS	HIS	Leads follow-up file
LEADS	HDX	Leads follow-up instructions
QUAL?	CDF	Qualified leads — 1 thru 7
QUAL?	NDX	Qualified leads index — 1 thru 7
QTMEMFIL	MEM	Memo file
TICKLERS	TIK	Tickler file
TICKLERS	NDX	Tickler instructions
PRINTDEF	MEM	Definitions file
ADDEFS	MEM	Additional definitions
DEFAULTS	MEM	Defaults file
BEGINNIN	TXT	Starting Instructions
LESSON?	TXT	Lessons 1 thru 8
PICS-?	TXT	Draft Letter — 1 thru 3
PUR-LTR1	TXT	Draft Letter — 4

SE-LTR1	TXT	Draft Letter — 5
SURVEY	TXT	Draft Letter — 6
THANKS	TXT	Draft Letter — 7

MAIL	DOC	System documentation
MQUIKREF	DOC	Quick reference documentation
MAIL	INF	General information
MCOMPILE	DOC	Compiling & file information

503 Reliance Mailing List Version 2.01
V1

Reliance Mailing List is a quick and sophisticated mailing list program that should interest many groups, including political parties, charitable organizations and small businesses. It is extremely easy to use; menus show all program functions. You can select the names to print in a variety of formats and sort them by last name or zip code.

It is capable of printing mailing labels 2-across using AVERY 4143 or compatible labels. Groups of people can be selected by specifying up to 8 characteristics. It will even create a Mailmerge file. It maintains two different indexes by name and zip code. The source code is provided along with the package. The documentation is thorough (30 pages) and very good.

System Requirements: 128K, two floppies or a floppy and a hard drive, monochrome/color display, and a printer capable of printing 132 columns across in a compressed mode.

How to Start: Read the MAIL.DOC and MQUIKREF.DOC files for directions and documentation

● To run, enter MAIL and press ENTER.

Suggested Donation: $15.00

File Descriptions:

MAIL	PAS	Main Program — Source code
IO20	INC	Input-Output routines
MPRINT	INC	Print list of names
MADDETC	INC	Add, delete or change a name
MAILGLOB	INC	Global definitions
MINIT	INC	Initialization program
MROOT?	INC	Miscellaneous routines
MSETUP	INC	Set-up menu
MAILMERG	INC	Create Mailmerge file
MAILDATE	INC	Reading & Writing Dates
MAIL	COM	Main program — compiled form
MAIL	000	Main program overlay

533 PDS*QUOTE Version 3.12
v1

This group of programs allows quick and accurate preparation of quotations for projects based on user-prepared databases containing the elements required for the project, e.g., materials, processes, parts, labor rates, markups, etc. If you need quick analysis and production of financial data, this could be of great help. A very professional package for small to medium-sized businesses needing analysis and projections tools.

Usage: Professional estimation for businesses

System Requirements: 256K, 1 disk drive, monochrome/color display

How to Start: After consulting the README.DOC, print out and read the manual in QUOTE.DOC

● To run, enter QUOTE and press ENTER.

Suggested Donation: $35.00

File Descriptions:

VERSION3	12	Version 3.12 trademark
QUOTE	EXE	Main program
DBMANAGE	EXE	Program to create databases
QUOTBASE	DEF	Definition file for database fields
QUOTE	DOC	Registration form and manual
AUTOEXEC	BAT	Autoexecute batch file
HARDAUTO	BAT	Batch file for hard disk
CONFIG	SYS	Sample of CONFIG.SYS file
README	DOC	Installation instructions
QUOTE	HLP	Help screens data file
QUOTE	HTC	Help file Table of Contents
FORMULA	BAS	To test the ROS formula
SETUP	BAT	Batch file to setup working disk

552
PC-SELL
v1

PC-SELL is a Point-Of-Sale System for the retail sales environment. It is written in Microsoft Compiled BASIC which means you must have either Microsoft's or IBM's BASRUN.EXE program to run these programs.

PC-SELL is a totally integrated program designed to assist a wide range of retail stores through: inventory control, accounts receivable and invoice production. Its 17 modules and five databases comprise a networkable point-of-sale system specifically designed for the retail industry. Also, it can be interfaced via DIF to LOTUS 123 and Fast Graphs.

Usage: Retail sales accounting

System Requirements: 256K, two floppies or a floppy and a hard disk, monochrome monitor

How to Start: The extensive documentation is on SELLMAN.PCL which can be screened by entering START or printed using TYPEMAN and press ENTER

• To run, type PC-SELL and press ENTER.

Suggested Donation: $150.00 registers you and entitle you to the following benefits: your company name will print instead of the name on this copy; you will receive a $25 commission each time a copy is registered with your company name on it; hot-line telephone service from the author; access to custom changes, installation and training at reasonable prices.

File Descriptions:

AUTOBACK	BAT	Automatic backup bath file
AUTOEXEC	BAT	Autoexecute file for startup
START	BAT	Another file to print the manual, SELLMAN.PCL
????????	EXE	Subprograms called by PC-SELL.EXE
MASK1	DIF	Data Interchange Format file
PC-SELL	EXE	Main executable program
PC-SHARE		Author's advertising and notice
READ	ME	Directions for startup and printing the manual
SELLMAN	PCL	Documentation
SETUP	EXE	Executable setup program
TYPEMAN	EXE	Executable program to type the manual

559
PC Accounting System (Disk 1 of 2)
v1

PC Accounting is a general purpose business program with modules for processing payroll, calculating depreciation by several methods, tracking contractors, processing 1099's and also managing the general ledger. It is a useful package for small businesses using the single entry accounting method. It uses a process similar to that in the DOME Accounting books, and has several modules spread over two disks.

The payroll section will allow you to calculate paychecks, print W2's, track employee information and payroll liability. Three smaller sections cover tracking automobile expenses, calculating depreciation, and comparing bank statements.

Some of the limits of PC Accounting are that it will only accommodate 99 classes of transactions, 99 employees in a year, 16 tax tables, and a maximum of 99 contractors. The actual number of transactions that can be entered is determined by available disk storage.

Usage: Small business accounting

System Requirements: 256K, two floppies or one floppy & one hard disk; monochrome display

How to Start: Documentation is in file MAN; use PRINTMAN to print it out

• To run, enter MAIN and press ENTER.

Suggested Donation: $49.00

File Descriptions:

BANK		Names of all banks
CARLOG		Details of all car transactions posted
CLASS		Description of different classes
COMPANY		Company information file — name, address, W2 & 1099 Numbers
CONTRACT		Name, Address & Tax numbers of contractors
EMPLOYE		All employee information
GROSSPAY		All gross pay and tax liabilities
INVENTOR		Inventory file
LASTGROS		Last gross pay for each employee
MAIN	EXE	Main Program — Posts transaction, Car Log & 1099s
MAN		System Manual (84k)
PAY	EXE	Third Menu — Post tax liabilities, Paychecks, W2's

PAYCK		Paycheck file
PRINTMAN	EXE	Program to print the manual
SCREEN		Screen for transaction input
SECOND	EXE	Second Menu — Depreciation, Company information
TAXTBL		Taxtable file
TRANSACT		Details of all transactions posted

560 PC Accounting System (Disk 2 of 2)
v1

This is the second of the two disk set called PC Accounting, an excellent single entry accounting system for general ledger, accounts receivable, accounts payable, and inventory. It comes with good documentation. If you are involved with accounting chores for a small business, this could make your job a lot easier.

Usage: Small business accounting

System Requirements: 256K, two floppies or one floppy & one hard disk; monochrome display

How to Start: Documentation is in file MAN; use PRINTMAN to print it out

• To run, enter START and press ENTER.

Suggested Donation: $49.00

File Descriptions:

ACCOUNTS		File of all general ledger accounts
ARAP		Accounts Receivable & Accounts Payable file
BANK		Bank file — used by PC Accounting I
CLASS		Class file — used by PC Accounting I
COMPANY		Company details file
CONTRACT		Contractors master file
DBCR		Debit & Credit transactions
EMPLOYE		Employee master file
ENTRY	EXE	Program to make entries
INITIAL	EXE	Initial startup program
INVENT		Inventory change entries
MAN		System Manual (116k)
OF		Order form file
PRINTMAN	EXE	Program to print the manual
PRODUCTS		Inventory master file
SCREEN		Screen file — used by PC Accounting I
START	EXE	Main Start program
SUMMARY	EXE	The Summary program
TAXTBL		Tax table file
TRANS		Sample transactions file

565 PC-PAYROLL
v1

PC-Payroll is a complete, menu-driven payroll system for moderate sized companies, 80 employees for floppy based systems, 200 employees on hard disk systems. PC-Payroll accepts hourly, salary and tips as well as bonuses and commisions. A full range of reports are included: monthly, quarterly and year-to-date summaries, Federal Tax reports (W2, W3, 941) and a pay period detail. Federal, state and local taxes, FICA, pension/insurance withholding, and user-defined deductions are internally computed. Paychecks and stubs are printed according to several predefined formats.

PC-Loans is well organized, and appears to have as complete a list of facilities as commercial, remote batch processing payroll systems which many small firms commonly use.

System Requirements: 192K, two disk drives, monochrome display

How to Start: Consult the .DOC, .TXT and README files for directions and documentation

• To run, enter PCPR and press ENTER.

Suggested Donation: An annual update service fee of $50.00 is requested. A customizing fee and other telephone support services for PC-PAYROLL is $45.00 per hour.

File Descriptions:

PCPR	EXE	Part of PC-PAYROLL
PCPU	EXE	Part of PC-PAYROLL
PCPC	EXE	Part of PC-PAYROLL
PCPS	EXE	Part of PC-PAYROLL
PCPY	EXE	Part of PC-PAYROLL
PCPW	EXE	Part of PC-PAYROLL
PAY	BAT	Batch file to start PC-PAYROLL
DELXTRA	BAT	Deletes extra files
PRNTDOC	BAT	Batch file to print the documentation
README	BAT	Important information from the author(s)
PCPAY	DOC	Documentation for PC-PAYROLL
MSG?	TXT	Help screens accessed by BATCH files (6 Files)
BUSINESS	DAT	Company information
EMPL	DAT	Employee records
PAY	DAT	Payroll history

593
GANTT
v1

The GANTT package is a group of project management aids that will produce presentation-quality Gantt charts from a list of dates and times on file. The types of displays provided by GANTT are commonly used throughout industry for management presentations of project status and resource utilization. Gantt charts are used as a graphic means of displaying schedules.

This program has four primary applications: It produces Gantt chart transparencies for meeting displays, directly drives a video projector from a personal computer for meeting displays, creates Gantt charts to be inserted into the text files of word processors, and is used directly to view project status.

To get you going, this disk has a DEMO, a TUTOR and a "sister" program SCHEDULE which is a limited working model of another sophisticated project management tool. GANTT and SCHEDULE will run on the entire line of IBM/compatibles including PC, PCjr, Portable PC, PCXT, 3270PC, PCAT.

Usage: Critical task tracking, project managment

System Requirements: 128K, 1 floppy drive, monochrome or color display IBM matrix or graphics printer (for printed output)

How to Start: If the DEMO and TUTOR aren't enough, there is a full manual in GANTT.DOC.

● To run, type GANTT and press ENTER.

File Descriptions:

EASY	BAT	Batch file to start the easy Turorial for Gantt
EASY	L?	Tutorial files (5 files)
EASY	SKB	Tutorial file
EXITCODE	BAT	Batch file listing all possible exit error codes
GANTT	DOC	Documentation file
GANTT	EXE	Main program file
GANTT	GKB	Data file used by program demonstration
GANTT	PRT	Data file used by program demonstration
MENU	BAT	Batch file to print the MENU.DOC file
MENU	DOC	Documentation file
NEW	BAT	Batch file to create a new database
NEW	SKB	Data file used by NEW.BAT
PLAN	BAT	Project planning batch file
PLAN	SKB	Data file used by PLAN.BAT

READ	BAT	Batch file which prints an text introduction
READ	ME?	Text files used by READ.BAT (4 files)
SCHEDULE	EXE	Sister program to Gantt
SCHEDULE	SKB	Data file for SCHEDULE.EXE
STATION	???	Data files (7 files)

637
UNCLE
v1

UNCLE provides analysis of four different possible tax strategies simultaneously. All four alternate form 1040s can be on screen at the same time. This version even has an on-screen RPN calculator! UNCLE was professionally written for annuity and life brokers, and financial planners; they had no method of properly interpreting and illustrating certain obscure sections of the tax code, lacked computer savvy, and couldn't adequately illustrate the concepts of tax planning and pension maximization.

The user projects taxes for the current year (to be prepared NEXT year) using a full 1040 input format and then tries alternative scenarios using four columns on a single screen (inputs need only be entered once). W-4 changes for one or two combined wage earners may be calculated to correspond to whatever part of the tax is targeted for prepayment and what has already been prepaid. Pocket expense of investment and paycheck changes are shown.

Usage: Financial planning through spreadsheet analysis

System Requirements: 256K, two disk drives and a monochrome/graphics display

How to Start: Documentation is found in files PART1, PART2 and CALCKEY; as it is written using PC-WRITE, if possible use that program to print it.

● To run: after loading DOS, enter INTRO or UNCLE and press ENTER.

Suggested Donation: $40.00 (includes full manual, update of Tax Analysis module and telephone support)

File Descriptions:

PART1	DOC	The MANUAL part 1
PART2	DOC	The MANUAL part 2
CALCKEY	DOC	Some information about the calculator
INTRO	EXE	The basic menu and system manager
FEDERAL	EXE	The Fed 1040 analysis module
AUTOEXEC	BAT	Automatic start up, if you want it
UNCLE	BAT	Start up batch file
BRUN10	EXE	BASIC Runtime
SAMPLE	FED	Tax files
AMSTADT	FED	Tax files
ERASEME	FED	Tax files
READ		Some information from the Author.
README	BAT	File to automate READ

671
FREEWAY Payroll System (Disk 1 of 3)
v1.0

This is the first of a three disk payroll management system built expressly for the European businessplace. It contains the first half of the Payroll programs and modules; documentation is on Disk No 672. NOTE: All three disks are necessary to make the system function.

FREEWAY PAYROLL programs can accomodate weekly, fortnightly, four weekly and monthly pay frequencies. The programs provide:

- Payslip stationery (obtainable from FREEWAY)
- Bank Giro's and Payment Lists.
- Cheque Printing.
- Internal Pension Schemes with fixed sum or percentage contributions.
- Additional Voluntary Contributions.
- Up to 99 departments each with a coin analysis and cost of payroll total.

non-taxable additions to pay and post-tax deductions. You may produce lists of deductions under these headings. (Year-end documentation includes P35 and P60 forms, also obtainable from FREEWAY.) The system accomodates statutory sick pay, and password protection. The user may change tax rates and bandwidths, as well as earnings brackets

Each employee may have attached to his record card, in addition to basic pay and hours, any regularly occuring payment — or deduction. During entry of pay data, only these employees will have the variables entered. Calculation of pay and

deductions is very flexible, permitting recalculation if necessary.

Usage: Small to medium sized businesses

System Requirements: 256K, two floppy or one floppy/one hard disk, and a monochrome display

How to Start: Consult the README and the FREEWAY.DOC files on Disk No 672 for full instructions.

- To run, enter "PAYROLL" and press ENTER.

Suggested Donation: $30.00 covers manual, telephone support and upgrade eligibility

File Descriptions:

PAY??	EXE	Sub routine programs for PAYROLL.EXE (25 files)
PAY43	LU	Data file
PAYROLL	EXE	Main program file
PAYSTART	BAT	Batch file to start program running
PRINTERS	DRV	Text file listing printer driver codes
READ	ME	Introductory text file
STATUS	PAY	Data file

672
FREEWAY Payroll System (Disk 2 of 3)
v1.0

This is the second of a three disk payroll management system designed expressly for the European businessplace. It contains the compiler library and documentation.

NOTE: All three disks are necessary to make the system function.

File Descriptions:

????????		Data file (12 files)
FREEWAY	DOC	Documentation file
FREEWAY	SYS	System file
HDINIT	BAT	Hard disk system intializing batch file (part 1)
HDINIT2	BAT	Hard disk system intializing batch file (part 2)
HSTART	BAT	Batch file to start program on hard disk
HSTATUS	PAY	Data file
INIT	BAT	Batch file to install DOS on a working disk
ORDER	DOC	Order form text file
PRICES	DOC	Accessory price list
PRINTMAN	BAT	Batch file to print manual
PRINTORD	BAT	Batch file to print order form
READ	ME	Introductory text file

673 FREEWAY Payroll System (Disk 3 of 3)
v1.0

This is the third of a three disk payroll management system designed expressly for the European businessplace. It contains the second half of the Payroll programs and modules; documentation is on Disk No 672.

NOTE: All three disks are necessary to make the system function.

File Descriptions:

ACCOUNTS	BAT	Batch file to start the program running
BASRUN	EXE	Compiler library
FREEWAY	SYS	System file
HDINIT	BAT	Hard disk system intializing batch file (part 1)
HDINIT2	BAT	Hard disk system intializing batch file (part 2)
HSTART	BAT	Batch file to start program on hard disk
INIT?	BAT	Batch files to install DOS and make a working system (3 files
INVOICE	LU	Data file
NOM?	EXE	Sub-program accessed by PAYROLL.EXE (3 files)
PDBSUMM	TAB	Data file
PRINTERS	DRV	Text file listing printer driver codes
READ	ME	Introductory text file
SAL???	EXE	Sub-program accessed by PAYROLL.EXE (16 files)
SDBSUMM	EXE	Sub-program accessed by START.EXE
SDBSUMM	TAB	Data file
SETUP	EXE	Sub-program accessed by START.EXE
SMENU	EXE	Sub-program accessed by START.EXE
START	EXE	Main program
STATMNT	LU	Data file
STATUS		Data file
VAT1	EXE	Sub-program accessed by PAYROLL.EXE

697 The Front Office (Disk 1 of 3)
v1

THE FRONT OFFICE is a control system for prospecting, sales management, sales order processing, job costing, and profit analysis. It is designed specifically for direct sales buisness but can be easily adapted to many other types of buisness. The system is very easy to setup and operate. TFO is menu-driven wherever possible and uses a single entry system for all data; this means that data entered in one area is automatically used by all other applicable areas. This feature saves time and prevents mistakes in data entry.

This is the first of a three-disk set; it contains the 72 program modules for running this under a Foxbase DBMS which is included. The second disk (698) has the Foxrun program and .DBF files. the third disk (699) contains the system's documentation. The documentation (all 135+ pages) provided is quite thorough. It is organized into tutorial and reference sections.

NOTE: All three disks are needed to run the system.

Usage: Sales office management

System Requirements: 256K, a 10M or greater hard disk, monochrome display

How to Start: Read and print out the six documentation files on disk 699 for instructions on installing and running.

Suggested Donation: $99.00 includes latest version, hardbound manual, one year phone support, and one update (update can be exchanged for a copy of the source code)

File Descriptions:

DISK1		Checks for first disk
????????	FOX	Program modules called by the main program (72 files)
GO	BAT	Starts the main program file
HELP	BAT	Batch file for quick instructions on THE FRONT OFFICE
READ	ME	Instructions for installation
TINSTALL	BAT	Installs 'The Front Office' onto hard disk

698 The Front Office (Disk 2 of 3)

v1

This is the second of the three-disk set for The Front Office. It contains the Foxrun program and .DBF files; the third disk (699) has the system's documentation.

NOTE: All three disks are needed to run the system.

File Descriptions:

DISK2		Checks for second disk
FOXRUN	EXE	Foxbase (runtime version)
IAMCONT	DBF	Data files for 'The Front Office' (9 files)
TFO	BAT	Starts 'the front office'
TFO	FOX	Main program, executed by TFO.BAT
TINSTALL	BAT	Installs 'the front office' on a hard disk

699 The Front Office (Disk 3 of 3)

v1

This is the third of the three-disk set for The Front Office. It contains the the system's documentation. All these files may be printed out by using the command PRINT filename prn ENTER at the DOS prompt.

File Descriptions:

TFO2	PRO	Documentation for 'the front office'
TFO3	PRO	"
TFO4	PRO	"
TFO5	PRO	"
TFO6	PRO	"
TFO1	PRO	"

COMMUNICATIONS:

Computerized communications is far more than "computers talking to computers." Good communications software is judged on two complementary standards: How well does it protect the integrity of the data transferred and how versatile is it in communicating between computers of like and dislike data structures?

Protecting data is the area of communications protocols, the best known, most reliable being XMODEM and KERMIT. These standards allow the precise transfer of crucial information by built-in error checking devices of extreme quality. However, as it takes two to tango, there are more than two dozen variants of these leaders, so your communications software needs to know quite a few dance steps. We have some "Fred Astaires" which can handle six to 15 different protocols.

If you work with other types of computers (mainframes or minis or different makes), you need to emulate the other machine. Emulations provides a "shell" that you can invoke for data transmission or reception between different computers. Accuracy and versatility for your purposes are the keys to getting the right communications software. Many of our packages are targeted at one particular family of computers, such as DEC or TeleVideo, while many packages contain several emulations.

41 Kermit Version 2.29 (Disk 1 of 2)
v2.3

Kermit-MS is a two-disk set which implements the KERMIT file transfer protocol for machines using the same processor family (Intel 8088 or 8086) and MS/PC-DOS operating system family. The package contains a complete program for IBM-speciifc machines as well as generic MS-DOS ones. This first disk contains the Assembly language source code; disk #42 contains the programs and documentation.

Kermit-MS 2.29 performs almost complete emulation of the DEC VT-102 terminal at speeds up to 19,200 baud (lacking only smooth scrolling, 132 column mode, and ANSI printer control). Much of the speed is accomplished via direct writes to screen memory, but this is done in a "TopView" aware manner to allow successful operation in windowing environments like TopView, MS-Windows, and DesqView. Full-speed 9600 baud operation is possible on 4.77Mhz systems.

Kermit-MS 2.29 runs on a wide variety of MS-DOS systems, including the entire IBM PC family (the PC, XT, AT, PCjr, Portable PC, PC Convertible) and compatibles (Compaq, Z150, etc), the DEC Rainbow, NEC APC, Sanyo MBC, Victor 9000, HP-110, HP-150, HP Portable Plus, and many others.

Kermit-MS version 2.29 runs in as little as 60K of memory (about 55K contiguous), but will occupy up to 100K, if it can be found, for extra screen rollback memory.

NOTE: Both disks are required to run the package.

Usage: Communications

System Requirements: Two disk drives, 64K and monochrome display

Features:

- Local operation
- Remote operation
- Binary file transfer
- Filename collision avoidance
- Wildcard sending
- 8th-bit and repeat count prefixing
- Time out

- Alternate block checks
- Terminal emulation
- Session logging
- Local file management
- Advanced commands for servers
- Command/init files
- Command macros

How to Start: From DOS, insert Disk No. 42 and enter TYPE MSKERMIT.HLP to access the Kermit System help file. To read the documentation on Kermit-MS from DOS, enter TYPE MSKERMIT.DOC.

User Comments: "Excellent!" "I use this along with an HP150 version to send disks full of files between machines." "KERMIT is a must for remote mainframe computing."

File Descriptions:

*	ASM	Kermit assembly language source code (12 files)
MSDEFS	H	Kermit assembly language source code
MSKERMIT	INI	Kermit assembly language source code
MSXDMB	HLP	Help file for Kermit
MSBUILD	HLP	Help file for Kermit

42 Kermit Version 2.29 (Disk 2 of 2)
v2.3

This is the second disk of a two disk set. Kermit-MS is a program that implements the KERMIT file transfer protocol for the IBM PC and several other machines using the same processor family (Intel 8088 or 8086) and operating system family (PC-DOS or MS-DOS).

NOTE: Both disks are required to run the package.

Usage: Communications.

System Requirements: Two disk drives, 64K, and monochrome display

Features: see listing above

How to Start: From DOS, insert Disk No. 42 and type MSKERMIT.HLP to access the Kermit System help file. To read the documentation on Kermit-MS from DOS, enter TYPE MSKERMIT.DOC.

File Descriptions:

MSKERMIT	HLP	Part of Kermit system — help file
MSKERMIT	DOC	Part of Kermit system — documentation (104K)
MSXGEN	ASM	Part of Kermit system — assembly source code
MSXSYS	DOC	Part of Kermit system — documentation (13K)
MSXHP150	ASM	Part of Kermit system — assembly source code
MSXRB	ASM	Part of Kermit system — assembly source code
MSXWNG	ASM	Part of Kermit system — assembly source code
MSKERMIT	EXE	Main program for Kermit communications
COMMER	DOC	Part of Kermit system — documentation

54 XMODEM
v1.1

The XMODEM is a communications program that imposes no restrictions on the contents of the data being transmitted. Any kind of data may be sent — binary, ASCII, etc. The IBM Asynchronous Communication Support Program provides software needed to allow the Personal Computer to communicate with a wide variety of computer systems including several IBM mainframe computers. It emphasizes great flexability in communications and provides a protocol for file transfer between Personal Computers. The user must be technically competent in communications protocol to be able to properly set selectable parameters provided through various menus. A user-friendly design has been substantially ignored.

Usage: Communications.

System Requirements: Two disk drives, 64K and monochrome display

Features:

- A 64K version named SHORTERM.BAS, and a 96K version named LONGTERM.BAS
- Automatic selection of screen width and an option to bypass all intermediate menus
- Preselected parameters for Display Selection and Dialing Option for the Hayes Smartmodem
- Download capability, including error trapping, file directory printout, On/Off switching of data recording for open files, and status indicator
- Upload capability, including error trapping, file directory printout, On/Off switching, status indication
- Time/Date/Status line
- Telephone/LOG-ON menu and function

- Automatic enabling of error messages upon terminal startup
- Error trapping routines supported in many areas for printer applications
- Changes to preset terminal parameters, facilitating program initialization in full duplex mode and the bypassing of intermediate menus

How to Start: From DOS, enter TYPE TUTORIAL to access a tutorial on IBM ASYNC COM PROGRAM. To read the documentation on XMODEM, enter TYPE XMODEM.DOC

- To run it, type XMODEM and press ENTER.

File Descriptions:

TUTORIAL		Tutorial for IBM ASYNC COM PROGRAM
PROGRAMN	OTE	Programming notes for IBM ASYNC COM PROGRAM modifications
DESCRIPT	ION	Program description for IBM ASYNC COM PROGRAM modifications
SHORTERM	BAS	64K version — see PROGRAMN.OTE
LONGTERM	BAS	96K version — see PROGRAMN.OTE
PROFEEL		Sony Profeel monitor modifications (Text file)
— — — —	— —	XMODEM
XMODEM	ASM	Source code (52K)
XMODEM	DOC	Documentation for XMODEM.COM
XMODEM	COM	Modem communication program (DOS 1.1)

81 Communication Programs No 1
v1

This disk contains several communications programs as well as programs to help your communications. For instance, .UNWS (UNWordstar) strips the high order bits from WordStar files, making WordStar compatible with many other word processors, communications programs and printers. Another program, SCNMAP.BAS, allows programmers to sketch out the appearance of detailed screen layouts before writing code to print them. The program will print a form on 8- 1/2" X 11" paper to lay out either 40 column or 80 column screens. HOST.BAS allows you to access an IBM PC from a remote location for the purpose of transmitting or receiving an ASCII file.

Usage: Communications or programming.

System Requirements: 64K, one disk drive and monochrome display; HOST.BAS requires ASYNC Communication board, Hayes Smartmodem.

How to Start: To read documentation on any of these files, from DOS level, enter TYPE (FILENAME).DOC and press ENTER.

- To run the BASIC programs, consult the directions in GETTING STARTED for your configuration
- To run MODEM.COM or UNWS.EXE, enter MODEM or UNWS and press ENTER.

User Comments: "I've found this disk very valuable. I occasionally have need to translate a WordStar file into ASCII." "A good program set."

Suggested Donation: $15.00

File Descriptions:

HOST2	BAS	Upgrade of HOST.BAS on Disk No 33
HOST2	DOC	Documentation for HOST2.BAS
MAGDALEN	BAS	Music from Bach
MODEM	ASM	Source for MODEM.COM
MODEM	COM	IBM PC version of Ward Christensen's MODEM.ASM (Version 3.0)
SCNMAP	BAS	Generates screen layout form on Epson with script
SCNMAP	DOC	Documentation for SCNMAP.BAS
SORTS	BAS	Sort routines, various types, times different cases
SORTS	DOC	Documentation for SORTS.BAS (References)
UNWS	ASM	Source for UNWS.EXE
UNWS	EXE	Strips high order bits from WORDSTAR files

129 PC-DIAL
v2.1

PC-DIAL is a modem communications program from Jim Button, the author of PC-FILE III. It has the ability to create autologon scripts but lacks some of the functions of PC-TALK III.

Usage: Communications.

System Requirements: 256K memory ,a serial I/O port with a Modem, a video monitor capable of displaying 80 characters per line. If you want to run the Mini-Editor, you will need 220K.

Features:

- Send and receive electronic mail
- Use any DOS command (like DIR or COPY) without leaving PC-Dial
- Use a built-in Mini-Editor to create or edit logon files
- On line help screens
- Set up Smart Keys to save keystrokes
- On-line timer
- Communicate at speeds from 300 and 1200 all the way up to 9600 baud
- Exchange (send or receive) text or non-text (.EXE or .COM) files with other computers which support the X-Modem (CRC or Checksum) protocol
- Use modems which support auto-dial
- Automatic redial
- Capture incoming data to a disk file.
- Save a "picture" of your screen to disk at any time.

How to Start: To print the documentation in PC-DIAL.DOC, enter DOC for directions

- To run it, enter PC-DIAL and press ENTER.

User Comments: "Good communications software that can easily be used with PC-WRITE for editing. Easy to use and modify for different systems." "Easy to use-ideal starter program." "A good program, but difficult to use."

File Descriptions:

BUTTON7	LOG	A sample logon file for use with (F7)
BUTTON9	LOG	A sample logon file for use with (F9)
DOC	BAT	A batch file that will the documentation on the printer
OAG	LOG	A sample logon file
PC-DIAL	DOC	Documentation for PC-DIAL
PC-DIAL	EXE	The main program
PC-DIAL	PIF	The program information file
PC-DIAL	PRO	A control file used by PC-DIAL
PCLTRO	EXE	The mini text editor
READ	ME	Introduction to PC-DIAL
RESPONSE		The user response form

135 Programmer/ Communications Utilities

v1

This disk contains many utility programs to facilitate modeming in special situations. For instance, included here is LAR, a program to manipulate CP/M LU format libraries. The primary use of LAR is to combine several files together for upload/download to a personal computer. There are also utilities for patches and ways to get around different problems with a BASIC Compiler.

Usage: Communications utilities

System Requirements: 64K, one disk drive and monochrome display

How to Start: Read the files suffixed .DOC or .TXT for directions and documentation

- To run any file suffixed .EXE or .COM, just type its name. ,i.e. for X.COM, type X and press ENTER.

File Descriptions:

APLCHIP	DOC	Where to get an APL character generator chip for IBM APL
BASCOM	PAT	Fixes for BASCOM.COM (See BASCOM.TXT)
BASCOM	TXT	Instructions for program to fix all BASIC Compiler bugs!
BASLIB	PAT	Fixes for BASCOM.LIB
BASRUN	PAT	Fixes for BASRUN.LIB (See BASCOM.TXT)
DOSFTE	PAS	Part of DOSFUN.PAS
DOSFUN	INC	Part of DOSFUN.PAS
DOSFUN	PAS	Procedures for extended DOS file access from Pascal
DRIVER	ASM	Interrupt driven comm I/O driver for Lattice c
DRIVER	OBJ	Linkable module for above
FILKQQ	INC	Part of DOSFUN.PAS
FILUQQ	INC	Part of DOSFUN.PAS
IBMPCTIP	DOC	Tips on using PCDOS
LAR	DOC	Documentation for file library program
LAR	EXE	Program to combine files into libraries to save space
PAD	WKS	123 desktop-type worksheet, lots of useful functions
PATCHER	BAS	Program to apply patches to IBM BASIC (See BASCOM.TXT)
PRTSCRN	ASM	Replacement print screen driver, filters ctrl chars
PRTSCRN	COM	Executable version of above
SCAV2XX	ASM	Program to make diskette with bad sectors useable

| SCAV2XX | COM | Executable version of above |
| SYSCOM | INC | Assembly language includes for DOS functions |

187 Communication Programs No 1

v1

This disk contains various communications programs. Included is AUTODIAL.BAS, an auto telephone dialer; BASECONV.BAS which converts to/from hex, binary, decimal; EZSIG3.HLP which prints out a guide to SIG functions and commands, it is meant to be printed onto six pages and kept handy by your terminal while using the SIG; and HAYSMODM.BAS a Hayes SmartModem demo.

Usage: Communications utilities

System Requirements: 64K, one disk drive, monochrome display, modem

How to Start: To run the BASIC programs, consult the directions in GETTING STARTED for your configuration.

File Descriptions:

AUTODIAL	BAS	Auto telephone dialer
BASECONV	BAS	Converts to/from hex, binary, decimal (Robert West)
CONVERT	BAS	Converts EXE & COM files to BASIC for transmission (Version 1.1)
EZSIG3	HLP	CompuServe IBM SIG instructions (1/84)
HAYSMODM	BAS	Hayes SmartModem demo — nifty!
KILLNULL	BAS	Converts nulls in a file to spaces
PC-SPEAK	BAS	Data communications program by Larry Jordan
TALK450	DOC	Documentation on how to speed up Hayes to 450 baud
TALK450	MRG	BASIC code to program 8250 to run at 450 baud

188 MINITEL Communications Version 1.0

v1

MINITEL is an asynchronous communications program for any MSDOS or PCDOS machine. The program's author calls it a "stripped version of TELINK." MINITEL can receive or transmit files in XMODEM, MODEM7 (batch) or TELINK modes. It is menu-driven, with all commands accessible by two keystrokes. Error handling is simple and straightforward. Documentation is provided on the disk.

Usage: Communications

System Requirements: 64K, one disk drive and monochrome monitor with a serial port, and a modem.

Features:

- MINITEL can receive or transmit files in XMODEM, MODEM7(batch),or TELINK modes
- MINITEL is menu driven, with all commands accessible by two keystrokes
- Most command keys are mnemonic
- Error handling is simple and straightforward
- Error recovery usually consists of some default action
- Illegal baud rate selections result in no change
- All error messages are in plain English, so you don't have to memorize secret codes

How to Start: From DOS, enter TYPE MINITEL.DOC for documentation.

- To run MINITEL, at the system prompt enter MINITEL and press ENTER.

File Descriptions:

IBMMINI	EXE	IBM PC version of MINITEL
MINITEL	ABS	Abstract
MINITEL	DOC	Documentation
MINITEL	DQC	Compressed documentation
MINITEL	LBR	File transfer program

258
Communication Programs No 2
v1

This disk includes an assortment of communications programs and utilities. HC.COM is a Hex File converter which converts to and from HEX format. It can automatically provide a COM or EXE extension. TALK.EXE is a simple terminal emulator. RING.BAS will set up the HAYES to patiently look for an incoming ring, and turn SYSTEM control over to the caller. SCRIPT.DOC is a procedure to set up a menu processing system for Crosstalk. Included are procedures to perform automatic logon and capture to the IBMSIG which may be extracted and used as stand-alone Crosstalk scripts. SERIAL.COM inserts itself into memory below command.com ,and changes the ROM bios interupt vectors for RS232 I/O to use interupt driven I/O.

Usage: Communications utilities

System Requirements: 128K, one disk drive and monochrome display

How to Start: Consult the .DOC files for documentation and directions

- To run the BASIC programs follow the GETTING STARTED instructions for your configuration. Programs suffixed .COM or .EXE type `filename` and press ENTER.

User Comments: "Works great. Lets my PCjr talk to the world." "Some very nice utilities here!" "Performs adequately."

File Descriptions:

HC	COM	Hex Converter, very fast
HC	DOC	Documentation for HC.COM
HC	ASM	Source for HC.COM
TALK	EXE	Simple terminal emulator from December '83 Softalk
TALK	DOC	Documentation for TALK.EXE
TALK	ASM	Source for TALK.EXE
RING	BAS	Turns SYSTEM control over to caller
CTTY	DOC	Discussion of CTTY command and RING.BAS
SCRIPT	DOC	Script files for CROSSTALK XVI
ATO	BAS	CompuServe auto logon and message retrieval
ATO	EXE	Compiled version of ATO.BAS
ATO	DOC	Documentation for ATO.BAS/EXE
QPRINT	OBJ	Link with ATO when compiled

XAPRIN	BAS	Prints files downloaded from Compuserve database
PCT3JR	MRG	Merge file for PC-TALK III to run on PCjr
PCT3JR	DOC	Documentation for PCT3JR.MRG
AT	COM	"AT hhmm" waits until hh:mm (Within 24 hours)
AT	ASM	Source for AT.COM
Z	COM	"Z s" sleeps for s (5 if omitted) seconds
Z	ASM	Source for Z.COM
SERIAL	COM	Makes BIOS serial (COM1) I/O interrupt-driven so
SERIAL	DOC	Documents SERIAL.COM
SERIAL	ASM	Source for SERIAL.COM

286
PC-VT
Version 8.4
v3.1

PC-VT is a software emulator which makes the IBM PC function as a DEC VT102 or a VT100 Video Terminal. PC-VT emulates most VT100/102 functions of the VT100/102. With this package, you can communicate with larger mainframes, or services that would normally only be available to access by a dedicated terminal. It's like having a second computer available to you when you need it! NOTE: PC-VT no longer supports DOS 1.0 or 1.1.

Usage: Terminal emulation and communications

System Requirements: Monochrome or Color/Graphics card, an 80 column screen, 128K and one RS-232 port.

Features:

- Communications support for all of the popular baud rate and data bit/parity bit combinations
- On line HELP by pressing the ALT-H key while in the Communications, Setup, Dialing, or Macro frames
- Fast screen update for PC's with the color graphics display card
- Select either a VMS or UNIX host
- Full duplex with no EIA modem control
- VT52 compatibility mode
- Support for Hayes dialing commands and includes a dialing directory with 10 entries
- Full receive parity checking can be enabled
- Both numeric and application keypad modes
- Full feature upload and download file capability

- Capability to echo all displayed characters to LPT1 or LPT2 as hardcopy record of a terminal session
- Run DOS functions or other programs without terminating PC-VT
- PC-VT supports buffer sizes of 256 and 2048 characters

How to Start: Check the READ.ME for the author's note and for documentation consult the file PC-VT.DOC

- To run enter PC-VT and press ENTER.

User Comments: "The program works and is very useful if you have to communicate with a VAX." "This is one of the best terminal programs I have ever used." "Works like a charm!" "Outstanding implementation of VT-100, better than SMARTERM or POLYCOMTM."

Suggested Donation: $35.00

File Descriptions:

PC-VT	EXE	Main PC-VT program
PC-VT	DOC	Documentation for PC-VT (aprox. 100 pages)
READ	ME	Authors note
KERMIT	COM	Kermit protoccol
*	DAT	Data file for PC-VT (4 files)

310 QMODEM Communications Version 2.0E

v2

An excellent telecommunications program. Written in Turbo Pascal, it is fast and versatile, supports Hayes, Racal Vadic and other modems and runs up to 9600 baud. A noteworthy feature is its Command Language for automating your use of the commercial services through scripted signons, signoffs, etc. Other major features include: windowing, screen color definition, X Y and IMODEM protocols, autodial/redial, a DOS command shell, and even subdirectory support. A "must-have" program!

Usage: Communications

System Requirements: 192K memory, serial port, a color/graphics or monochrome/graphics card and monitor, and a modem.

Features:

- Dialing directory
- Script file execution
- Graphics mode toggle
- Hang-up modem
- Windowing
- Function key menu
- Communication parameter menu
- Redial last number
- Supports DESKview and TopView environments

How to Start: Review the documentation in the QINSTALL.HLP and the QMODEM.DOC files before running their companion program files.

User Comments: "First class program, better than the commercial program I had bought earlier." "The speed of the program, the flexibility and ease of use impress me very much. I use it with a Tandy 1000 and have had no problems with compatibility." " A must for anyone with a modem!" "An outstanding program for anyone needing a communications package."

Suggested Donation: $20.00

File Descriptions:

CIS	SCR	Automatic logon data file for CIS bulletin board.
CNVRTFON	COM	Program to Convert old Qmodem directory files to the new.
COLOSSUS	SCR	Automatic logon data file for Colossus bulletin board.
FIDO-NET	SCR	Automatic logon data file for Fido-Net bulletin board.
GENIE	SCR	Automatic logon data file for Genie bulletin board.
INVOICE	TXT	Order form for Qmodem.
MCI-MAIL	SCR	Automatic logon data file for MCI bulletin board.
NOCHANGE	SCR	Automatic logon data file for No Change bulletin board.
PCBOARD	SCR	Automatic logon data file for PC Board bulletin board.
QINSTALL	COM	Installation program for Qmodem.
QINSTALL	HLP	Help file for QINSTALL.
QMODEM	COM	Main program
QMODEM	DOC	How to use QMODEM
QMODEM	00?	Overlay file for initialization (7 files)
QMODEM	PIF	Overlay file #6 for initialization
RBBS	SCR	Automatic logon data file for RBBS bulletin board.
RBBS13	SCR	Automatic logon data file for RBBS Ver13.1a bulletin board.

README	NOW	Information about qmodem.
SOURCE-T	SCR	Automatic logon data file for the Source via Tradnet.
SOURCE-U	SCR	Automatic logon data file for the Source via Uninet.

316
Communications Utilities No 3
v1

This disk contains a collection of popular, public domain communication utilities and a list of IBM-PC oriented BBS's. Most are oriented to the Hayes Smartmodem command set. HC.COM is a IIex File converter which converts to and from HEX format. It can automatically provide a COM or EXE extension. NUSQ-11.COM is a utility for expanding squeezed files to their original uncompressed state. Two separate versions of NUSQ are available, one for CP/M-86 and one for the MS-DOS operating system. PCTERM.ASM is a simple terminal program which uses interrupt driven buffered communications. The program can thus operated at 9600 baud without losing data.

Usage: Communications utilities

System Requirements: 64K, one disk drive and monochrome display

How to Start: Review documentation in the .DOC and .TXT files

- To run any program with the suffix .COM or .EXE, just type its filename, i.e., for SQPC.EXE type SQPC and press ENTER
- To run the BASIC programs follow the GETTING STARTED instructions for your configuration.

User Comments: "Helps immensely in an area with a poor phone system." "I got this disk for the file squeezing and unsqueezing utilities; but, was disappointed to find that the use of these was only partially covered." "I have used HC and UNWS many times."

File Descriptions:

ADDCRS	BAS	Copies files without carriage returns & adds them
APPLECOM	BAS	Allows keyboard input to flow out to com port & file
AREACODE	EXE	Displays geographic location of telephone area codes

CVTBIN	COM	Converts binary files
FILTER	BAS	Filters non-ASCII characters from a transmitted file
HAYES	TXT	Text file of handy POKES to be used with Hayes Micromodem
HAYESTST	BAS	Tests and reports the switch settings on Hayes Smartmodem
HC	COM	Hex file convertor HEX @ COM or EXE or BIN
HC	DOC	Text file : documentation for HC.COM program
IBMPCBBS	LST	Text file containing directory of IBM-PC bulletin boards
LYNC	COM	Links two computers together; runs DOS-friendly pgms remotely
LYNC	DOC	Brief documentation of LYNC.COM
MODEM7PC	COM	Christensen's XMODEM7 (IBM-PC Main Serial Port version)
NSQ-201	EXE	Advanced file squeezer
NUSQ-11	COM	File un-squeeze utility
NUSQ-11	DOC	Text file documentation of NUSQ-11.COM
PCTERM	ASM	Dumb-terminal program using interupt driven buffered commun.
PCTERM	DOC	Text file description of PCTERM.ASM
SQ	EXE	Advanced file squeezer
SQPC	EXE	File squeezer
TYPESQ	EXE	Type a squeezed file
UNWS	EXE	Remove high-order bits from WORDSTAR files
WARGAMES	BAS	Automatic sequence dialer; seeks carrier signal; Hayes Modem
XMODEM	DOC	Text file of Christensen's Modem Protocol overview

338
SYSCOMM
v1

This is an excellent menu-driven communications package. It comes in three parts:

SYSCOMM is a general purpose comunications package. It can comunicate with other computers, transfer files, and act as your window to the world when connected to one of the information networks. Several features of SYSCOMM make it easy to connect with other systems, including auto-dialing and auto-logon.

ABSCOMM is a special purpose program used for un-attended file transfer. Jobs are submitted to ABSCOMM to place calls at certain times of the day and to send a list of files to the remote computer. The times can be selected to take advantage of the lower phone rates. ABSCOMM is also the un-attended answering software used when another system running SYSCOMM or ABSCOMM wants to send you a file.

EDCOMM is a supplemental program. SYSCOMM and ABSCOMM have data files that contain initialization parameters and phone directories. EDCOMM allows the user to alter the initialization parameters and manage the phone directories. An additional feature is used to create auto-logon sequences for SYSCOMM.

Usage: Communications

System Requirements: 256K, one disk drive and monochrome display

How to Start: From DOS, enter EXPAND for a hard copy of the documentation. All the programs (marked .EXE) run from DOS.

Suggested Donation: $70.00 gets you telephone support, a printed manual, and free updates for two years

File Descriptions:

ABSCOMM	DAT	ABSCOMM parameters and phone directory file
ABSCOMM	EXE	Allows unattended file transfer between systems
EDCOMM	EXE	Alters parameters and phone directories
EXPAND	BAT	Batch file to expand the manual files
MAKEMAN	COM	Expands compressed manual files
MANUAL?	!!!	Manual part 1 compressed (3 files)
MLREAD	ME	How to expand the manual files using EXPAND.BAT
SYSCOMM	DAT	SYSCOMM parameters and phone directory file
SYSCOMM	EXE	General purpose communications program
SYSCOMM?	BAT	Batch file to copy SYSCOMM files to drive B: (3 files)

362 SIMTERM

v2

This package provides Hewlett-Packard terminal simulation to Unix systems; it was last revised 07/28/84. SimTerm creates on an IBM-PC simulation of an H/P like terminal to the UNIX system. It no longer requires the asynchronous communications software supporting package. If you have need of terminal simulation for your communication chores, this disk may be just what you've been looking for.

Usage: Communications, terminal simulation

System Requirements: 128K, one disk drive and monochrome display

How to Start: To read the documentation, enter TYPE README and press ENTER.

● To run, enter SIMTERM and press ENTER.

File Descriptions:

ARCHCOPY	BAT	
ARGLIST	INC	
ARGLIST	PAS	
BOARDS		(BBS #s)
COM	ASM	
COMM	INC	
COMP	PAS	
ESCPAR	PAS	
GETPUT	PAS	
GRAPH	INC	
IBMPR	C	
INFO		(Prologue) terminal
KEYPARSE	PAS	
LOGIN	PAS	
MACTEST	ASM	
MAINSIM	PAS	
MENUIT	PAS	
MENUS		(Clues)
README		Documentation (14 pp) manual
SAVDIS	PAS	
SCANLINE	PAS	
SIMTERM	EXE	Main program execution file
SIMTERM	INC	
SIMTERM	LNK	
SMTERM	LNK	
SMVENTEL	PAS	
STDIO	ASM	
STDIO	INC	
STRUCT	MAC	
TERMCAP	IBM	
TOKEN	PAS	
UPDOWN	PAS	
UTIL	INC	
UTIL	PAS	
VENTEL	PAS	
VERSION	OBJ	
XRECV	C	
XTRANS	C	
XXGRAPH	ASM	

433 KERMIT-MS Compatibles, ASM modules
v1

KERMIT is a communications system that allows different types of computers to exchange information. The files on this disk are used by smaller computers so that they may communicate with an IBM minicomputer or mainframe computer.

Usage: Communications

System Requirements: 128K, one disk drive, and monochrome display

How to Start: To view the documentation for Disks No. 433 and 434, place Disk No. 433 in your disk drive and enter TYPE MSXSYS.DOC

● To run any program file, type its name and press ENTER.

File Descriptions:

MSGENER	EXE	Generic MS-DOS KERMIT.
MSHP150	EXE	Hewlett-Packard 150
MSRB100	EXE	DEC Rainbow 100, 100+
MSXGEN	ASM	Generic MS-DOS KERMIT module.
MSXHP150	ASM	Hewlett-Packard 150 module.
MSXRB	ASM	DEC Rainbow 100, 100+ module.
MSXSYS	DOC	Description of system dependent modules.
MSRBEMAC	INI	EMACS function key setup for Kermit-MS/Rainbow.
MSPCTRAN	BAS	Converts MSKERMIT.BOO to an executable file.
MSPCTRAN	EXE	Compiled version of MSPCTRAN.BAS.
MSPCBOOT	BAS	Used on PC to download KERMIT from mainframe.
MSRBBOO	HLP	Info on MSRBBOO.BAS.
MSRBBOO	BAS	Used on Rainbow to download KERMIT from mainframe.
MSBOOT	FOR	Used on mainframe when downloading KERMIT.
MSMKBOO	C	Four-for-Three encoder, DEC-20 specific.

434 KERMIT-MS Compatibles, ASM modules II
v1

This is the second disk of a two disk set. The KERMIT program is a communications system that allows communication between different types of computers. Refer to the description on Disk #433.

Usage: Communications

System Requirements: 128K, one disk drive and monochrome display

How to Start: To access the documentation for Disks No. 433 and 434, place Disk No. 433 in your disk drive and enter TYPE MSXSYS.DOC.

● To run any program file, type its name and press ENTER.

File Descriptions:

MSRB100	EXE	DEC Rainbow 100, 100+
MSAPC	HLP	Documentation for NEC APC Kermit
MSAPC	EXE	NEC APC
MSXAPC	ASM	NEC APC module
MSXTIPRO	BWR	Documentation for TI Professional Kermit
MSTIPRO	EXE	TI Professional
MSXTIPRO	ASM	TI Pro module
MSXTEK	ASM	TI Pro Tektronix emulation module
MSXTIPRO	BAT	TI Pro assembly/link script
MSWANG	EXE	Wang PC
MSXWNG	ASM	Wang PC module
MSZ100	HLP	Documentation for Heath/Zenith Z-100 Kermit
MSZ100	EXE	Zenith Z-100
MSXZ100	ASM	Zenith Z-100 X-module
MSYZ100	ASM	Zenith Z-100 Y-module

439 Communications Programs

v1

MODEM86 is a communications program for Intel 8086/88 based computers. It runs under both CP/M-86 and MS(PC)-DOS. It provides such features as file copying using XMODEM protocol, terminal emulation, file transfer with all hosts, X-ON/X-OFF flow control, batch mode, optional on-line help and menus, file transfer and conversion utilities, and auto-dialing.

"IT" stands for Intelligent Terminal. IT is an easy-to-use communications program without a complicated setup. It has a clean, uncluttered look, emulates a VT-52 terminal, supports XMODEM protocol yet allows autodial with Hayes compatible modems.

Usage: Communications

System Requirements: 64K, one disk drive, a monochrome monitor and one serial port.

Features:

- Runs under both CP/M-86 and MS(PC)-DOS
- Provides reliable file copying using XMODEM protocol
- Provides terminal emulation
- File transfer with all hosts
- X-ON/X-OFF flow control
- Provides batch mode
- Optional on-line help and menus
- Helpful file transfer utilities
- Auto dialing

How to Start: To view the documentation, enter TYPE MODEM86.DOC. For other documentation, enter TYPE (filename).DOC and press ENTER.

User Comments: "Very nice and easy to use." "Seems to work without a hitch...A good telecommunications program to add to your quiver." "MODEM86 is an effective program."

Suggested Donation: $35.00

File Descriptions:

BIN2HEX	COM	Converts a binary file to a hex file
COM2CMD	COM	Converts MS(PC)-DOS programs to CP/M-86 programs
COM2CMD	CMD	Converts MS(PC)-DOS programs to CP/M-86 programs
CMD2COM	COM	Converts CP/M-86 programs to MS(PC)-DOS programs
DISTMDM	BAT	Copies distribution disk files — for MS(PC)-DOS
DISTMDM	SUB	Copies distribution disk files — for CP/M-86
EXPAND	COM	Replaces tabs with blanks
MODEMSET	COM	Configures MODEM86 for running environment
MODEM86	DOC	Abbreviated user manual
MODEM86	HST	Program's revision history info
MODEM86	SET	Unconfigured MODEM86 program
PATCHES	DOC	Text file containing a history of programming patches
PHONES	DAT	Example phone number directory
REMOVECC	COM	Removes FORTRAN-style carriage controls
SHRINK	COM	Replaces blanks with tabs
SIOBIOS	A86	Source for an example CP/M-86 custom serial I/O BIOS
SIOBIOS	MAC	Source for an example MS(PC)-DOS custom serial I/O BIOS
UNSQZ	COM	Decodes squeezed files
————	——	IT COMMUNICATIONS PROGRAM
IT	DIR	Dialing Directory for Auto-dialing
IT	EXE	Main program
IT	DOC	Documentation (1K)

441 TEKTRONIX 4010 Emulator

v1

The program on this disk emulates a Tektronix 4010 storage tube display terminal, both full text and graphics. The PC's screen may still be faster graphics (320 x 200), but all the detail is still there. Also included is a DEC VT100 mode simulation.

Usage: Communications

System Requirements: 64K, one disk drive and monochome display

How to Start: To run TekTerm use the command TEKTERM2 to call TEKTERM2.EXE. A welcome screen will come up and then the main menu with a notation that no setup has been automatically loaded. Type "L" for load setup and use the TT.CFG.

User Comments: "Emulation fine. The documentation is not too helpful, especially in telling how to toggle parameters." "I was unable to make this program work." "It has some very nice features that one would not expect to find, such as the ability to save graphic images for off-line recall."

File Descriptions:

TEKTERM2	EXE	The main emulation program
TT	CFG	A configuration file
TT	DOC	A brief explanation of how to use the TEKTERM2 program
TT	EXE	A utility overlay
TTUTIL	EXE	A utility overlay
VDAT01	OVL	An overlay to the main program
VDAT02	OVL	An overlay to the main program

499
ProComm
Version 2.42
V1.1

ProComm is a professional communications program written in compiled MicroSoft C and assember. This state-of-the-art program is extremely powerful yet extremely easy to use. It is suitable for the computer hobbyist as well as professional and business uses.

It is packed with features! ProComm supplies terminal emulations modes that include the IBM-3101, DEC VT-52/100, ADM-3, TeleVideo 912/920 and 925/950, and many others! File-transfer and error-checking protocols include Xmodem, Ymodem, ASCII, Kermit among others.

ProComm provides a macro function which allows you to automate your communication needs. Also, communication can be temporarily suspended to go to and from DOS. As a final plus, ProComm has included a nice little text processor that is more than sufficient for most communications needs.

NOTE: Due to the size and complexity of ProComm, it is archived. ARCE.COM is the file archiving and unarchiving program.

Usage: Communications

System Requirements: 128K memory, modem, one disk drive

Features:

- Rotating auto-dial
- Operates at 300, 1200, 2400, 4800, 9600 & 19,200 baud
- Instantly available keyboard macros
- Programmable command files
- Unattended Operation
- Concatenation of screen prints to a named file
- Direct access to the DOS system

How to Start: Read the READ.ME file for directions on unarchiving the documentation and program files.

User Comments: "Great program! I plan to register right away, but the 80K version is useful already." "The best communications program I have used, period!" "An excellent, multi-featured communications program."

Suggested Donation: $10.00 for current version; $25.00 registration entitles you to priority phone support and special BBS; $35.00 has all previous and manual on disk; $50.00 all of the above plus bound, printed manual!

File Descriptions:

PROCOMM	ARC	ProComm executable file;update info;license info
PRCMDOCP	ARC	ProComm reference manual.
PRCMUTIL	ARC	Timed Execution Facility utility;dialing directory utility and sample BBS programs.
ARCE	COM	File archiving/unarchiving program.
READ	ME	Instructions on running ARCE.COM

626
PC-Dial jr
v1

PC-Dial is a modem communications program from Jim Button, the author of PC-File III. It has the ability to create auto-logon scripts but lacks some of the functions of PC-Talk III. With this version the author provides a special communications program just for PCjr owners.

Usage: General purpose computer communications

System Requirements: PC-Dial requires a 64K or larger IBM PC (with PC-DOS 1.0 or 1.1), a 96K or larger IBM PC (with PC-DOS 2.0 or later), one disk drive, and a serial I/O port with a Modem. You must also have a video monitor capable of displaying 80 characters per line. PC-Dial will run on the PCjr, but downloading of files must be done using X-Modem protocol.

How to Start: Use the DOC.BAT file to print out the documentation If your computer is a PCjr, consult the READ.ME file.

● To start the program, enter PC-DIAL at the DOS prompt and press ENTER.

Suggested Donation: $29.00 which includes printer Users Manual

File Descriptions:

DOC	BAT	A file that will print the documentation on the printer
JR-DIAL	COM	Version for the PCjr
PC-DIAL	DOC	Documentation for PC-Dial
PC-DIAL	COM	The main program
PC-DIAL	PRO	A control file used by PC-Dial
READ	ME	Introduction to PC-DIAL

679

IT
(Ideal Terminal)
Version 1

V1

This disk contains the Ideal Terminal (IT), a VT-100 and VT-52 terminal emulator and communications program for the PC/XT/ATs and compatible computers. IT can also communicate via Hayes Smartmodem/compatible modems with a dial-up host. IT can also auto-dial with such modems.

IT is fast. You can use IT at 9600 baud with a host's screen editor such as EDT, EVE, or RAND and enjoy screen updates at the full 9600 baud rate. IT is also small (35K) and it loads fast. IT can do file transfers between the PC and the host using two popular error checking protocols (Xmodem and Kermit). IT can also send and receive ASCII files unchecked to and from hosts that have no XMODEM or KERMIT services.

Usage: General communications and terminal emulation

System Requirements: 64K, one disk drive, monochrome display and modem

Features:

● Simple to operate
● Help display
● Set-up file to override defaults
● Dialing directory for use with modem
● Modem initialization
● Macro keys
● Logging to disk with optional time tagging
● Logging to printer
● Get and put screen images
● Wildcard file specs for Kermit transfers
● Automatic path search for IT data files
● Execute DOS commands from within IT

How to Start: Full documentation in IT.DOC on installing and running.

Suggested Donation: $20.00 covers phone or mail support and next version of IT

File Descriptions:

IT	EXE	The program.
IT	DOC	A 25-page user's guide.
IT	HLP	A File used by IT for on-line help.
IT	SET	Sample set-up file, customize it if you like.
IT	DIR	Sample auto-dial file, you put your own phone numbers in it

COMPUTER EDUCATION:

Surprise! You don't need a degree in Electronic Engineering to get the basics of BASIC or learn how to boss your DOS! Using these computer-based, self-paced instruction packages, you can begin at whatever level you feel comfortable and learn at your own pace.

We concentrate on three categories:

- Learning the Disk Operating System (DOS)
- Learning BASIC (simple to complex introductions)
- Learning Pascal and C programming languages

Start here to begin learning about your PC and the major programming languages. As you build your fluency in "computerese," you'll be delighted how it makes everything about computers and computing start to fall into place. Then pick out particular programs, subroutines, and games from other sections to investigate, to use, maybe even improve!

19 ARCHIE
v1

The title program, ARCHIE, gives you the basic elements for doing structured BASIC programming. ARCHIE is a fun tutorial for beginners in BASIC. RV-EDIT is a simple and sturdy full-screen text editor written in BASIC and PCS is a program control system designed to help take charge of your PC. RV-EDIT and PCS are well documented and invite tinkering!

Usage: Excellent introduction to the design of structured BASIC.

How to Start: To run BASIC programs consult the directions in GETTING STARTED for your configuration. Consult the .DOC files for program documentation.

System Requirements: 128k, two disk drives, some of the programs on this disk require color graphics.

File Descriptions:

MENU	BAS	Menu program for Disk No 19
ARCHIE	BAS	Archie la cucharacha — game, BASIC tutorial & fun program
ARCHIE	DOC	Documentation for ARCHIE
PCS	DOC	Program control system description
CONTROL	BAS	Runs the prime program on a BASIC diskette
CONTROL	PCS	Returns control to Drive "A"
AUTOEXEC	BAT	Requests date & time and gives control to SYSTEM.BAT
SYSTEM	BAT	Loads BASICA, runs TRANSFER.BAS, runs b:CONTROL.BAT
RUN	BAT	Runs the program passed as a parameter
TRANSFER	BAS	Displays disk swap message, waits for keystroke
MENU	PCS	Sample menu file for BASIC programs
COVER	PCS	Mergeable cover page and exit hierarchy
EXIT	PCS	Mergeable exit hierarchy
CONTROLB	PCS	Copy to CONTROL.BAT on BASIC program diskettes
CONTROLD	PCS	Copy to CONTROL.BAT on data diskettes
CONTROLM	PCS	Copy to CONTROL.BAT on machine language program diskettes
RV-EDIT	BAS	Full screen editor (Limited usefulness)
RV-EDIT	DOC	Full screen editor documentation

105 *PC Professor BASIC Tutorial* v1.1

PC-Professor is a well liked tutorial for teaching the BASIC programming language. It has an easy-to-understand, well-organized presentation and a comprehensive keyboard tutorial. It also includes four chapters of indexed documentation for quick-referencing capability.

Usage: Beginning BASIC programmers.

System Requirements: 64K, one disk drive and monochrome display

How to Start: Instructions come within the program

● To run, enter INTRO once you are in BASIC.
● To avoid the musical opening, enter A0.

User Comments: "I enjoyed it. Excellent aid in learning BASIC!" "Rather limited in scope, nonetheless enjoyable in its approach to programming training. Easy to understand and effective in promoting on-line exercises." "Very good basic intro to BASIC. My students refuse to use it because of the music that plays as the program loads. This embarrasses them in the computer room. Couldn't the program offer option of disabling music?"

Suggested Donation: $30-$50.00

File Descriptions:

INTRO	BAS	Part of PC-Professor — program to run first
AUTOEXEC	BAT	Batch file to start PC-Professor
*	*	Other PC-Professor files called from INTRO.BAS

254 *PC-DOS HELP* v1.2

Don't remember what to do? This program gives you an on-line help capability for DOS commands. Just type HELP and the selected command for doing something. Two level explanations plus special batch files demystify learning and using DOS. TYPE plus directory filenames opens additional files, including registration/info form.

Usage: Recommended for all levels

System Requirements: 64K, one disk drive and monochrome display

How to Start: HELP.DOC contains an excellent manual

● To run, enter HELP at the DOS prompt and press ENTER.

User Comments: "This is an excellent disk. As a PCjr owner I especially liked CNV2*.BAT, CNVPCJR.BAT, HELP2*.DIR, and HELPPCJR DIR. I think Microsoft Corp. should hire the guy who made this one because it is far superior to their book on DOS." "Too cumbersome, takes too much space." "I am new to DOS and computers in general and I found the help screens very informative. Much more readable than the DOS manual!...Should be updated to include 3.1. For this price a person could save 30 to 60 dollars on a DOS manual."

Suggested Donation: $15.00

File Descriptions:

HELP	EXE	The HELP Function program
HCONFIG	EXE	HELP Function configuration program
HELP	DOC	Documentation for HELP.EXE (10K)
HELPREG	DOC	Registration form for HELP
MAKEBKUP	BAT	Makes a backup of this disk
CNV2-00	BAT	Convert HELP for DOS 2.0
CNVPCJR	BAT	Convert HELP for the PC jr
CLEANUP	BAT	After HELP is configured, use this one to clean up
*	<DIR>	Directories containing help files

403

TUTOR.COM
(Version 4.3)

v2.1

TUTOR.COM (previously cataloged as Computer Tutor) is an outstanding educational package composed of easy, understandable menu segments for self-programmed learning. Tutorials cover the basics of a first course in computer use from bits and bytes to Winchester technology.

As well as a general introduction and history, the tutorials cover some of the IBM-PC disk operating system from simple commands to batch files. An easy and enjoyable way to find out about computers. Registered users have the opportunity to obtain tools to help them build their own tutorials.

Usage: Beginner or anyone serious about their computer literacy.

System Requirements: 128K, one disk drive and monochrome or color display.

How to Start: Type READ to run the informational files. INSTALL runs the system installation for you

• To run, enter TUTOR and press ENTER.

User Comments: "First rate instructional program for novice (not first- time) users." "Well designed algorithm and comprehensive content." "Computer Tutor [TUTOR.COM] seems to be a good way of introducing people to the PC. It looks like it will allow me to let people learn the basics about the computer with much less hand holding."

Suggested Donation: $12.00 for registered disk; $25.00 for registered disk, manual, screen dumps and tutorial building tools.

File Descriptions:

GO	BAT	Batch file to display "how to start" files
READ	BAT	Batch file to display the following information files
READ	111	Information file
READ	222	Information file
READ	333	Information file
READ	444	Information file
INSTALL	BAT	Displays instructions about installing TUTOR.COM
TINSTALL	DOC	Text file containing installation information
TINSTALL	COM	Program to install TUTOR.COM for different terminals

TINSTALL	DTA	Data file used by TINSTALL.COM
TINSTALL	MSG	Message file used by TINSTALL.COM
INVOICE	BAT	Batch file that prints an invoice for registration
INVOICE	TXT	Text of the invoice
TUTOR	COM	Tutorial reading program
EXPLAIN	TUT	Tutorial that explains TUTOR.COM (menu item #1)
KEYBRD	TUT	Tutorial on IBM-PC keyboard (menu item #2)
HISTORY	TUT	Tutorial on computer history (menu item #3)
TERMS1	TUT	Tutorial on computer hardware (menu item #4)
TERMS2	TUT	Tutorial on computer hardware, continued (menu item #5)
DOS1	TUT	Tutorial on PC-DOS commands (menu item #6)
DOS2	TUT	Tutorial on PC-DOS subdirectories (menu item #7)
BATCH	TUT	Tutorial on PC-DOS batch files (menu item #8)
MENU	TUT	Text file of menu choices used by TUTOR.COM
DESCRIBE		Text file describing the contents of the diskette
REGISTER		Registration info file required for program to run

577

C TUTOR
(Disk 1 of 2)

v1

This is the first disk of the C Tutor system. This is a COMPREHENSIVE introductory tutorial to programming in the C language. This disk contains the textual tutorial material in a series of .TXT files. This series is targeted at the person with at least a modicum of programming experience in other languages.

Usage: Intermediate, experienced programmers

System Requirements: 64K, one disk drive and monochrome display

How to Start: Load up the printer, type LIST and press ENTER.

Suggested Donation: $10.00.

File Descriptions:

— — — —	— —	C Tutor
READ	ME	Short program description and printing instructions
PRINTEXT	BAT	Batch file to print all .TXT files
TABCONT	TXT	Tutorial table of contents
INTRO	TXT	Tutorial introduction
CHAP1	TXT	Tutorial chapter 1
CHAP2	TXT	" " 2
CHAP3	TXT	" " 3
CHAP4	TXT	" " 4

CHAP5	TXT	"	"	5
CHAP6	TXT	"	"	6
CHAP7	TXT	"	"	7
CHAP8	TXT	"	"	8
CHAP9	TXT	"	"	9
CHAP10	TXT	"	"	10
CHAP11	TXT	"	"	11
CHAP12	TXT	"	"	12
CHAP13	TXT	"	"	13
CHAP14	TXT	"	"	14
LIST	COM	Program to print files		

578 C TUTOR (Disk 2 of 2)
v1

This is the second disk of the C Tutor system. It contains the example C programs as discussed in the text portion of the tutorial, as well as a discussion of the various C compilers. Basically a comprehensive text on disk, it also includes an executable visual calculator file program.

Usage: Intermediate, experienced programmers

System Requirements: 64K, one disk drive and monochrome display

How to Start: Load up the printer, type PRINTALL and press ENTER.

Suggested Donation: $10.00.

File Descriptions:

————	—	C Tutor
READ	ME	Short text file to describe program and printing process
COMPILER	DOC	Discussion of various compilers
PRINTALL	BAT	Batch file to print out all source C files
???????	C 76	Source code files for miscellaneous applications
TEST	BAT	
LIST	EXE	program to list source files
STRUCT	DEF	Data file structure definition
VC	EXE	Executable calculator file
VC	DOC	Short documentation about the Calculator program
HELP		Calculations text file
AMORT		Calculations text file
PAYMENT		Calculations text file
TEST		Calcualtions text file

579 PASCAL TUTOR (Disk 1 of 2)
v1

Pascal Tutor is a paper-based introductory tutorial on the use of the Pascal language. The tutorial is distributed on diskette and can be printed conveniently. The second disk contains the Pascal source code for examples used throughout the tutorial.

Usage: Beginning and intermediate level programmers.

System Requirements: One disk drive, monochrome display and 128K; Turbo Pascal 3.0/Standard Pascal compiler if you intend to run the routines.

How to Start: Load up the printer and enter PRINTEXT and press ENTER.

Suggested Donation: $10.00

File Descriptions:

————	——	Pascal Tutor
READ	ME	Text file describing product & printing procedures
PRINTEXT	BAT	Batch file to print all of the .TXT files
TABCONT	TXT	Tutorial table of contents
INTRO	TXT	Tutorial introduction
CHAP1	TXT	Tutorial Chapter 1
CHAP2	TXT	" " 2
CHAP3	TXT	" " 3
CHAP4	TXT	" " 4
CHAP5	TXT	" " 5
CHAP6	TXT	" " 6
CHAP7	TXT	" " 7
CHAP8	TXT	" " 8
CHAP9	TXT	" " 9
CHAP10	TXT	" " 10
CHAP11	TXT	" " 11
CHAP12	TXT	" " 12
CHAP13	TXT	" " 13

580
PASCAL TUTOR
(Disk 2 of 2)
v1

This is the second disk of the Pascal Tutor system. It contains the Pascal source code for all of the examples discussed in the text based tutorial as contained on disk No 579.

Usage: Aspiring programmers who want to go beyond the BASIC's.

System Requirements: One disk drive, monochrome display and 128K; Turbo Pascal 3.0/Standard Pascal compiler if you intend to run the routines.

How to Start: Load up the printer and enter PRINTEXT and press ENTER.

Suggested Donation: $10.00

File Descriptions:

— — — —	— —	Pascal Tutor
READ	ME	Short description of programs and printing process
PRINTALL	BAT	Batch file to print source code files
???????	PAS	67 Source files
REALDATA	TXT	Data file
OT	DOC	Notes on the OT program
OT	PAS	source code for the OT program
OT	COM	Executable OT program
LIST	COM	DOS program to list files

595
BASIC Games &
Programming Intro
v1

This product is a handy and interesting tool for getting acquainted with the micro-computer. It has an easily understood tutorial about the world of computers and does an excellent job on BASIC, introducing the beginner to the elemental concepts of the language. A big plus is that there are a series of practice sessions so the user can acutally see the programs operate!

The set of games which are included are simple, and engage the user with a lot of keyboard interaction.

They include a simple word processor and several number games as well as varying levels of anagrams.

Usage: Advanced beginners.

System Requirements: One disk drive, 64K and monochrome display

How to Start: Once you have BASIC loaded, enter MENU and make your choice!

File Descriptions:

MENU	BAS	Main menu for the system
MATH	BAS	Math program
MISSING	BAS	Missing Word program
PRINT	BAS	Printing Fun program
REPORT	DAT	Report data file
DOC SWAN	BAS	Doc Program
PRINTING	BAS	Printing Program
MPG	BAS	M.P.G. Program
TYPE	BAS	Typing Practice Program
NUMBER	BAS	Number Program
NUMFUN	BAS	Number Fun Program
SPELLING	BAS	Spelling Skill Program
COUNTING	BAS	Counting Program
WURD	BAS	WURD Program
SUPSCRAM	BAS	Superscam Program
GUIDE	BAS	Guide Program
MODES	BAS	Modes Program
BASIC	BAS	BASIC Programming Section
LET	BAS	Command — 1
INPUT	BAS	Command — 2
IFTHEN	BAS	Command — 3
READDATA	BAS	Command — 4
SCRAMBLE	BAS	Command — 5
GR	BAS	Command — 6
BTMENU	BAS	Command — 7
GOTO	BAS	Command — 8
FORNEXT	BAS	Command — 9
GUESS	BAS	Guess My Number Exercise

686
HelpDOS
v1

HelpDOS is a "Help System" for learning and using the commands and functions of DOS version 2.0. HelpDOS consists of menus, detail reference information, a technical dictionary and a cross-reference feature called "Hints." These components work together to show you, quickly and easily, what DOS can do and how to use it. There are three main sections:

From the Main Menu you can select brief or indepth infomation on basic and advanced DOS Commands, special keyboard keys, batch subcommands, and an overview of the DOS facilities.

A Technical Dictionary explains the terms that are frequently used with Overviews of DOS Facilities DOS and personal computers. In addition to defining the terms, the dictionary contains additional reference information and usage notes.

The Hints Menu shows categories of actions you can take with DOS. When you select a Hint category from the menu, HelpDOS will show you a menu of the DOS facilities that pertain to that category. For example, when you select the Hint category "Print," HelpDOS will give you a menu of the ways you can print information with DOS. The Hints feature is a unique and powerful aspect of HelpDOS.

Usage: Learning DOS

System Requirements: 128K, one disk drive, monochrome display

How to Start: Read the HELPDOS.DOC and then start by running the install HELPSET.

• To invoke, type HELP and press ENTER.

Suggested Donation: $20.00 gets you: The next major update on disk upon its release; the commercial HelpDOS User's Guide and diskette; which contains Help files and menus for DOS Versions 2, 3.0, 3.1 and 3.2; telephone support from Help Technologies; Notification of new releases; and Reduced fees for new releases (the fee for the most recent update was $10).

File Descriptions:

HELP	COM	HelpDOS main program
HELPSET	UP	Data file holing system cofiguration info
MENUS	MEN	Data file holding menu
*	MEN	7 menu data files
HINTS	XRF	Cross reference for hints files
BACKUP	HLP	Data files used by HelpDOS
*	HLP	76 help data files
READ	ME	Start up information
HELPDOS	DOC	Documentation text file
HELPSET	COM	Program to specify system configuration

DATABASES:

In our explosively growing "information society," the field of database management is expanding in all directions. For example, to categorize the Library's selection of database managers by structure solely, it would include:

- Flat file managers
- Relational databases
- Hierarchical databases
- Mother/daughter databases
- Integrated spreadsheet/databases

There is even a BASIC "Database of Steel" which contains an Expert System programming structure!

What and how you choose depends a great deal on the kind of data you regularly work with. Before selecting a database, clarify the characteristics of the data and the intended methods for storage and retrieval. Here are some questions to aid your selection:

- Is it simple (addresses, mailing lists, etc.)?
- Is it complex (business or scientific)?
- Is it financial (accounting or inventory)?
- Is it specialized (index card or "free form")?
- Does it have special characteristics you need to identify and track?
- What reporting needs do you have?
- How do you want the data to appear on your screen of in print?

As with any software need, you must examine the advantages and tradeoffs among programs to select the right database for you.

Our collection contains both database managers (the structural programs that you can use to create and build up your database) as well as specialty databases. These are complete programs that may or may not be expandable but include a database structure. Two excellent examples are our VCR and movie databases. The first allows you to build a reference device for your VCR tapes. The second has vital statistics on 1500+ movies, with the capacity for more.

5 PC-FILE III Version 4
v5

This is Jim Buttons' very popular database filing program. PC-File III allows you to quickly retrieve data, change it, resequence it, perform queries, and prepare reports for display, printing or subsequent retrieval by your word-processing program. This is one of the most widely respected programs in the public domain. Try it and you'll see why.

Usage: For any business, professional, or home users who need an inexpensive, useful filing system.

System Requirements: 128K memory, one disk drive and monochrome display

Features:

- Maintain mailing lists and print mailing labels, 1-up or multi-up.
- Address envelopes.
- Maintain price lists.
- Maintain telephone or name and address directories.
- Keep various types of inventory records.
- Build personnel databases.
- Keep customer lists.
- Build and maintain databases to be exported for use by other programs, such as Visicalc™, Multiplan™, 1-2-3™, etc.
- Import files from other programs into the PC-FILE III format.

How to Start: To print documentation, type PCDOC and press ENTER.

- To run, enter PCFILE and press ENTER.

User Comments: "Excellent!" "I wish more programs were as helpful as this one." "It is easy to use and very versatile." "Highly recommended for anyone looking for a small to medium-sized database program."

Suggested Donation: $59.95 includes printed manual, update notification, technical support phone number and special ButtonWare BBS membership.

File Descriptions:

READ-ME		Read Me file on disk
RESPONSE		User Response form
PC-FILE	BAT	File to access PCFILE.EXE (for users of earlier versions)
PCDEF	EXE	PCFILE utility
PCDOC	EXE	Utility to print documentation on disk
PCEXPOR	EXE	PCFILE utility
PCFILE	EXE	PCFILE main program
PCFIX	EXE	Utility to repair damaged index
PCIMPOR	EXE	PCFILE utility
PCLABEL	EXE	PCFILE label utility
PCOVL	EXE	PCFILE utility
PCPRINT	EXE	PCFILE utility
PCSETUP	EXE	Hardware configuration utility
PCSORT	EXE	PCFILE utility
PCUTIL	EXE	PCFILE utility
PCFILE	PIF	Information to run PCFILE in Topview or Windows
PCFILE	PRO	File created from PCSETUP
PCFILE	XXX	Compressed documentation

26 Book Index Builder
v1

BOOK INDEX is a simple and straightforward set of programs and procedures for preparing book indices. They allow the user to easily create a data file that will form the index. This program can be a lifesaver for those aspiring writers whose word processors do not include built-in index abilities.

Usage: For those who wish to index a book.

System Requirements: 128k, two disk drives, monochrome monitor

How to Start: From DOS, enter INFO for documentation and instructions on using the program. With program disk in drive A and working data disk in drive B, enter START to begin program.

User Comments: "If you are indexing a book, Peter Norton [BOOK INDEX author] has developed a simple and clean set of programs." "This program ran and worked well. I was delighted. Happily, it even worked with my word processor." "This little jewel also worked! Made my day, for sure."

File Descriptions:

INFO	BAT	Informational file for Book Indexing programs
START	BAT	Start-up program. Creates empty data file
ENTER	BAT	Begin index entries
COMBINE	BAT	Sort/merge new entries with any previous entries
INDEX	BAT	Format an index from the data
INPUT	EXE	Compiled programs for Book Indexing
SORT	EXE	Compiled programs for Book Indexing
MERGE	EXE	Compiled programs for Book Indexing
BUILD	EXE	Compiled programs for Book Indexing
INPUT	PAS	Pascal source code for Book Indexing Program
SORT	PAS	Pascal source code for Book Indexing Program
MERGE	PAS	Pascal source code for Book Indexing Program
BUILD	PAS	Pascal source code for Book Indexing Program

106 DISKCAT 4.3f
v2.1

DISKCAT keeps track of all of your disk files. It reads eight- or ninesectored, single- or double-sided disks. It will not read fixed disks or high-capacity drives or other non-standard disks. DC4-SORT.EXE compares two catalogs and prints a comparative list. DC4-READ.EXE puts a directory listing on a disk with file descriptions.

Usage: Anyone who wants to catalog their disk library.

System Requirements: One disk drive, 128K memory, 80-column monitor. Recommended: a RAM disk-emulator or hard disk to hold the data, a printer, and a graphics board.

Features:

- Read a disk's directory
- Form a table-of-contents for a disk
- Print a file listing for each disk
- Display the names of all disks in the catalog
- Display the number of sectors and free space remaining on each disk
- Compare two catalog files and print a comparative list
- Create data files in a format that can be read by Lotus 1-2-3
- Search the catalog for a specific file

How to Start: To start, run DC4-READ and edit the program parameters. Change DC4-SAMP to whatever you like and respond Y when asked "Make the changes permanent?" Press the Esc key, as directed, and the file will be created. To read the documentation, enter TYPE DC4-DOC and press ENTER.

User Comments: "A useful utility. Would prefer a version without the commercial." "Too many commands to use to produce a catalog of my disks files." "I really want a good catalog program and this one just isn't it."

Suggested Donation: $50.00 for source code

File Descriptions:

DC4-CAT	EXE	Program to add descriptions to DISKCAT data files
DC4	DOC	Documentation file for DISKCAT (41K)
DC4-CNVT	BAS	Converts pre-DC3 format to current
DC4-DOC	EXE	Prints DISKCAT documentation
DC4-FIND	EXE	Finds a file in DISKCAT catalog
DC4-PGM	DTA	DISKCAT program data file
DC4-READ	EXE	Program to read & catalog disk files
DC4-SAMP	DT2	Sample data file for DISKCAT
DC4-SAMP	DTA	Sample data file for DISKCAT
DC4-SORT	EXE	Program to sort & print DISKCAT catalog
CNVRTDC	COM	Conversion program
INVOICE	DC4	Invoice for your records or to bill your company

119
ABC Database
v1.1

ABC DATABASE is a user-friendly data filing system that accepts up to 1,500 records with up to 12 fields in each record. It handles customer files or mailing lists of 100s to 1000s of records. It will also handle daily schedules or technical article cross references.

Usage: For data filing.

System Requirements: 128K of memory, Epson FX/MX-80 or equivalent.

Features:

- Maintains up to 1,500 records, 12 fields, and 50 characters per field
- Handles customer files or mailing lists of up to 1000s of records
- Handles daily schedules, technical article cross references, recipe files, sales records, parts inventories, student grades, etc.
- Ability to specify character or numeric fields
- Simple calculations on fields

How to Start: Consult the .DOC files for documentation and directions.

- To run the ABCFILE.EXE program, just enter ABCFILE and press ENTER.

User Comments: "A very easy-to-use list manager." "Good — I have been able to use the program; it is comparable to PC-FILE."

Suggested Donation: $30.00

File Descriptions:

ABCFILE	EXE	ABC database main program
ABCFILE	HLP	Help data
ABCFILE	DOC	Documentation
ABCONVRT	BAS	Convert files to ABC format
AUTOEXEC	BAT	Boot start up file
DBII-ABC	EXE	Translate dBASE II files to ABC
NUMSAM	CFG	Sample configuration
NUMSAM	DAT	Sample program data
NUMSAM	NUM	Part of sample program
NUMSAM1	NDX	Sample program
README	1ST	Initial documentation
SAMPLE	CFG	Sample configuration
SAMPLE	DAT	Sample program data
SAMPLE	NUM	Part of sample program
SAMPLE1	NDX	Sample program

147
SDB — A Simple Database System
v1

SDB is a relational database system written in the C programming language. SDB is a simple database manager which was developed to provide a relatively low overhead system for storing data on machines with limited disk and memory resources.

Usage: For database management.

System Requirements: 64K, one disk drive, a monochrome display and a C compiler

How to Start: Read the SDB, MEM and README for documentation notes about the programs on the disk

- To run type SDB and press ENTER.

File Descriptions:

README		Note about programs on this disk
SDB???	BAT	Batch files for generating a Simple Data Base (4 files)
SDB	EXE	Database program
SDB	HLP	Help screen
SDB	MEM	Document file (30 pages)
*	C	C Source files
*	OBJ	Object files
SDBIO	H	Source files

---

214 Data Base of Steel (3.1) (Disk 1 of 4)
v2

This is the first volume of Potomac Engineering's database, spreadsheet and expert system offerings, all grouped under the title "... of Steel". The first two disks contain the Database Management System which includes Accounting, Payroll, Inventory, and A/R Applications Programmable, Relational. The documentation for the whole system is on Disk No 215.

The Spreadsheet (No 267) includes 21 ways to calculate numbers or write your own subroutine. It is written in BASIC for easy modification, and a compiled version is available.

The Expert System (No 268) provides for inference engines, designing your own expert systems, and intelligent search patterns. The entire system is menu driven, so all the options are displayed on the screen.

Usage: For database management, spreadsheet usage, and artifical intelligence applications. Intermediate-Advanced users.

System Requirements: 128K, two disk drives (Hard disk recommended) and a monochrome display

Features:

- Written in BASIC for easy modification
- Compiled version provided (192k)
- Sample checkbook application
- Automatic recalculation
- Bar charts
- Full cursor control
- Report generator
- Customizable screens

- ASCII output
- Tax tables
- Create subfiles
- Sort on 3 fields
- 3 files open simultaneously
- Global field changes
- Transfer data between files
- Inference engine
- Design expert systems
- Assigns probability with rules
- Intellignet search pattern with manual override
- Detects contradictory evidence
- Explanation of reasoning

How to Start: Consult the README file for documentation and directions

- To run the BASIC programs follow the GETTING STARTED instructions for your configuration.

User Comments: "Slow BASIC program. Not written efficiently. In my search for a good DBMS it was only fair." "The documentation is hard to follow!!!" "Powerful, but not easy to use, needs better documentation. Also needs better error checking."

Suggested Donation: $20.00

File Descriptions:

— — — —	— —	Database of Steel — Source Code
MAIN	BAS	Main database program
SCAN	BAS	Database extract and select program
CHANGE	BAS	Global database change and replacement
FORM	BAS	Report format program
TRANSFER	BAS	Transfer data from one file to another
SORT	BAS	Sorts database
CFILE	BAS	Creates (defines) database file
CINPUT	BAS	Sets up new data entry for the file
CTRANSFE	BAS	Customizes transfers between files
CFORM	BAS	Creates print forms
CLIMITS	BAS	Sets range limts for numeric fields
CREAL	BAS	Realtime transfers between files
CSCREEN	BAS	Sets up screen display for record
ASCII	BAS	Convert from random access format to ASCII
TESTASCI	BAS	Reads file created from above and display it
READ	ME	Descriptions of files on disk

215
Data Base of Steel (3.1) (Disk 2 of 4)
v2

This is the second volume of Potomac Engineering's database, spreadsheet and expert system offerings. This is the documentation disk for the data base and spreadsheet applications. The other disks are No. 214, 267, 268.

Usage: For database management, spreadsheet usage, and artificial intelligence applications.

System Requirements: 128K, two disk drives (HARD DISK RECOMMENDED) and a monochrome display

Features: SEE DESCRIPTION OF DISK 214

How to Start: After loading DOS, consult the README file for brief information on the programs; the major documentation is in WordStar format in text file MASTER.TXT.

User Comments: "Slow BASIC program. Not written efficiently. In my search for a good DBMS it was only fair." "The documentation is hard to follow!!!" "Powerful, but not easy to use, needs better documentation. Also needs better error checking."

Suggested Donation: $20.00

File Descriptions:

— — — —	— —	Database of Steel — sample programs and files, documentation
READ	ME	Descriptions of files on disk
MASTER	TXT	Manual (WordStar format — 153K)
PRINTMAN	BAS	Procedure to print the manual
REMARKS1	BAS	Program remarks
REMARKS2	BAS	Program remarks
REMARKS3	BAS	Program remarks
REMARKS4	BAS	Program remarks
????????		Sample programs (58 Files)

218
Address Manager Version 3.0
v1

The Address Manager Program allows one to maintain multiple databases of names, addresses, phone numbers, and useful comments. New entries can be added and current ones deleted or updated with ease. It is especially designed to address envelopes, print out labels or even entire mailing lists.

Its menus are function-key driven. Each command is invoked using a function key. This provides a quick and user-friendly interface, one that is easy to learn and to use. There are three program menus from which all operations are initiated: the database menu for reading and writing databases, the address maintenance menu for database maintenance, and the print menu for printing labels, envelopes, or a whole database.

Usage: For home use — each database can hold 125 to 600 entries — for anyone wanting to organize personal contacts lists, address envelops, print labels.

System Requirements: 128K, one disk drive and monochrome/color display

How to Start: Consult the README.DOC and MANUAL.DOC files for documentation and directions

• To run the Address Manager, at the DOS level, enter ADDRESS and press ENTER.

User Comments: "Good program." "Once figured out it is an excellent mailing list program for non-business purposes." "Good program but the menu needs to state that function keys are used, rather than just the numbers indicated."

Suggested Donation: $20.00

File Descriptions:

ADDRESS	EXE	Executable program file — Address Manager
ADDRESS	MEN	Program menu file
ADDRESS	DAT	Sample data base file
ADDRESS	DOC	Documentation (8 pages)
PAPER	OUT	Disables paper out detector on printer
ADDRESS	BW	Monochrome program menu file
ADDRESS	COL	Color program menu file

CATALOG	DSK	Catalog of Address Manager Files
SCREEN	ASM	Source for SCREEN.COM
SCREEN	COM	Screen utility to change fgd/bkgd colors
COLOR	BAT	.BAT version of screen (Uses prompt cmd)
SCREEN	EXE	Link command output [will not run...only .COM]
READ-ME	DOC	How to use screen & color programs

233

newBASE
Version 3.40

v2.1

newBASE V3.40 is a menu-driven database manager for mailing lists, name and address lists, sales reports, expense account maintenance, budget preparation and maintenance, etc. newBase is a data management system that makes it easy to organize and manage information so it can be ordered, changed, or retrieved and then printed to suit a variety of circumstances. Also, newBase interfaces with many of the most popular word processing systems. Ease of use by non-technical personnel has been the primary design consideration.

Usage: Tracking addresses, mailing lists, or other data.

System Requirements: 128K memory with two floppy disk drives (or a hard disk) and an 80 column monitor.

Features:

- Multi-key sorting
- Searching for less than, greater than, equal, included, not, etc.
- Global update/edit multiple records with a single entry
- Audit trail
- Multi-level file password protection
- Lookup tables
- Macro keys
- Single keystroke entry of repetitive data
- Protected fields
- Date fields
- Numeric accuracy to 16 digits
- Report and form library

How to Start: For instructions on starting, enter TYPE READ-ME.DOC To run, type NB and press ENTER.

User Comments: "Excellent teaching tool. Powerful, yet simple appliction." "Again, one of the best BASIC database programs for the new user." "Very good."

Suggested Donation: $39.00

File Descriptions:

NB1	EXE	Executable program called from NB.EXE
NB	EXE	Main executable program
NB19	EXE	Executable program called from NB.EXE
NB16	EXE	Executable program called from NB.EXE
NB	CFG	Configuration file
NB	HLP	Help file
SAMPLE		Sample database file
READ-ME	DOC	newBASE documentation

253

3X5 CARD
Version 3.0

v2

This program is an information handling system that allows your computer to act like a very efficient 3 by 5 card system, thus it's name. 3 by 5 information management programs offer speed, simplicity and versatility in entering, indexing and retrieving free-text and structured data. This program would be great for keeping track of small pieces of information such as patient listings or a small library's card catalog.

Usage: For quick entry, indexing and retrieval of free-text data.

System Requirements: 256K, two disk drives, and monochrome display

Features:

- Search for incomplete words or phrases.
- Search may be limited to specific fields.
- Edit and search up to five files at a time.
- WordStar and WordPerfect document files may be searched.
- Transfer 3 by 5 records to ASCII, Wordstar, and WordPerfect files.
- Fifteen variable length fields.

- Sort records by one or two fields when copying or printing.
- Underline and bold commands.
- Improved indexing for records greater than 512 bytes.
- Multiple print formats for mailing labels, 3 by 5 cards, etc.
- List files on a disk from within the program.

How to Start: For information on printing the documentation, enter GO. Information on starting the program is in CHAP2.DOC. Type 3BY5 and press ENTER to start.

User Comments: "This is a GOOD database program — the speed of execution is quite admirable." "I love it. Right now using for a card file for magazine articles." "Liked program — good for small database applications."

File Descriptions:

3BY5	EXE	Main 3 by 5 prorgram
ADDRESS	3X5	Used by 3 by 5
ADDRESS	MAP	Used by 3 by 5
CHAP?	DOC	9 Chapters of documentation which can be printed
CHAPIDX	DOC	Index for the documentation
CONFIG	SYS	Configuration file used by DOS
FORM	3X5	Used by 3 by 5
FORM	MAP	Used by 3 by 5
GO	BAT	Start-up file
NOFIELDS	3X5	Used by 3 by 5
NOFIELDS	MAP	Used by 3 by 5
PROGRAMS	3X5	Used by 3 by 5
PROGRAMS	MAP	Used by 3 by 5
README		Brief direction on how to print documentation
REF	3X5	Used by 3 by 5
REF	MAP	Used by 3 by 5

267
Data Base of Steel (3.1) (Disk 3 of 4)
v1

This is disk three of a set of four. It contains the Spreadsheet of Steel; it is designed to interface to the databases generated through the programs on disks No. 214, 215. This is a very complex, powerful set of programs; they pretty much demand a hard disk for best performance. Reading the documentation is a MUST before operating this program series.

Usage: For database management, spreadsheet usage, and artificial intelligence applications.

System Requirements: 256K, two disk drives (HARD DISK RECOMMENDED) and monochrome/graphics display

Features:

- Written in BASIC for easy modification
- Compiled version provided (192K)
- Sample checkbook application
- Automatic recalculation
- Bar charts
- Full cursor control
- Report generator
- Customizable screens
- ASCII output
- Tax tables
- Create subfiles
- Sort on 3 fields
- 3 files open simultaneously
- Global field changes
- Transfer data between files

How to Start: READ THOROUGHLY the documentation on Disk No 215 as well as the README here

- To run, enter SS and press ENTER.

User Comments: "This is a GOOD database program — the speed of execution is quite admirable." "I love it. Right now using for a card file for magazine articles." "Liked program — good for small database applications."

Suggested Donation: $20.00

File Descriptions:

————	——	Spreadsheet of Steel and Compiled Database Program
SORT	BAS	Sort source for database
SORTINT	BAS	Sort source for database
SORTSTR	BAS	Sort source for database
SS	BAS	Spreadsheet source
SSREMARK	BAS	Spreadsheet remarks
SS	EXE	Compiled spreadsheet
TAX		Sample spreadsheet
CHECK		Sample spreadsheet
MAIN	EXE	Compiled database program
REMARKST	BAS	Sort remarks
READ	ME	Description of files on this disk

268
Data Base of Steel (3.1) (Disk 4 of 4)
v1

This is the concluding part of the "of Steel" series. It contains the Expert System which is a specially designed set of programs for evaluating and analyzing the meaning of all the information in your database/spreadsheet.

The whole disk series is required to operate, and reading the documentation is highly recommended before running the programs, especially this one!

Usage: For database management, spreadsheet usage, and artificial intelligence applications.

System Requirements: 256K, two disk drives (HARD DISK RECOMENDED) and a monochrome display

Features:

- Written in BASIC for easy modification
- Compiled version provided (192K)
- Full cursor control
- Customizable screens
- ASCII output
- Form generator
- Transfer data between files
- Inference engine
- Design expert systems
- Assigns probability with rules
- Intellignet search pattern with manual override
- Detects contradictory evidence
- Explanation of reasoning

How to Start: Consult the READ ME and use some sample programs to get the feel of how this Expert System operates.

User Comments: "This is a GOOD database program — the speed of execution is quite admirable." "I love it. Right now using for a card file for magazine articles." "Liked program — good for small database applications."

Suggested Donation: $20.00

File Descriptions:

		Expert System of Steel
READ	ME	Description of files on this disk
REM	BAS	Remarks for source program (33K)
EXPERT	EXE	Compiled program for expert system
EXPERT	BAS	Source code for expert system
FORM	EXE	Compiled program for database
SCAN	EXE	Compiled program for database
CLS	OBJ	Part of expert system disk
TEMP	BAS	Part of expert system disk
*		Sample programs for the expert system (27 files)

287
File Express Version 3.72 (Disk 1 of 2)
v4.1

File Express is a database management system that is menu driven and easy to use. A mailing list and report generator are included in the system. It has a complete and comprehensive manual on Disk No 288. It is quite easy to use, and can make your organizational tasks quite a bit easier. Highly recommended!

Usage: Database management

System Requirements: 192K, two disk drives and a monochrome display

Features:

- Define new databases.
- Easily add, delete, edit and display information from files.
- Generate reports.
- Sort records on up to ten fields.
- Search or sort for specific information within a record.
- Designate certain fields for automatic entry of time and date.
- Define fields within a record to be self-calculating.
- Print mailing labels, up to three across.
- Create new databases from existing ones.
- Create MailMerge-type files from your databases.

How to Start: To get a hard copy of the manual put Disk No 288 in the default drive and enter PRINTDOC

● To run, enter FE and press ENTER.

User Comments: "Excellent — I use this more than any other program." "All programs should be written like this one. It is ideal for casual home use." "Very well-written program."

Suggested Donation: $40.00

File Descriptions:

README		List changes and additions to File Express
FE	EXE	Main File Express program
FE-DEF	EXE	File Express definition file
FE-SORT	EXE	Sort routine for File Express
FE-RPT	EXE	Report generator for File Express
FE-LBL	EXE	Label maker for File Express
FE-SRCH	EXE	Search routine for File Express
FE-EXP	EXE	Import/export routine
FE-OVL	EXE	Program overlay file

288
File Express Version 3.72 (Disk 2 of 2)
v4.1

This is the second of the two disk set for File Express, a database management system that is menu driven and easy to use. A mailing list and report generator are included in the system. It has a complete and comprehensive manual on Disk #288. It is quite easy to use, and can make your organiizational tasks quite a bit easier. Highly recommended.

Usage: Database management

How to Start: To get a hard copy of the manual, type PRINTDOC and press ENTER.

User Comments: See comments for Disk No 287

Suggested Donation: $40.00

File Descriptions:

WHATSNEW	DOC	List of the changes that are in the version.
PRINTDOC	BAT	Batch file to print out documentation
PRINTER	SET	Parameter file to set up printer

EXAMPLE	DTA	Example data file
EXAMPLE	HDR	Example header file
EXAMPLE	INX	Example index file
EXAMPLE	STK	Example
EXAMPLE	RPT	Example report file
EXAMPLE	LAB	Example label file
EXAMPLE	QLB	
FE-?	DOC	Four sections of manual printed by PRINTDOC.BAT
ORDER	BAT	Program to print an order form
ORDERFRM	DOC	Order form document

311
The Movie Database
v1

A database of nearly 2,000 movies which are available on videotape. Each movie entry can be searched by movie title, MPAA rating, major cast members, writer, director, and other information. Find out which movies starred and were directed by Clint Eastwood, or what movies have the word "time" in their titles, and lots more. You can even add information for new movies.

Usage: Movie database management.

System Requirements: 128K, one disk drive, and monochrome display

Features:

● Movie titles
● MPAA ratings
● Dates of release
● Major cast members
● Directors
● Scriptwriters
● Original story author

How to Start: From DOS, enter TYPE MFIND.DOC for documentation. For more information, enter TYPE README.MOV and press ENTER.

User Comments: "Useful and entertaining." "This is a gold mine, and fun to dig in, too." "Delightful program." "Not extensive enough to be really useful."

File Descriptions:

MFIND	C	Source code for database search program
MFIND	DOC	How to locate movies in the database
MFIND	EXE	Locates movies in database using multiple search criteria
README	MOV	Idea behind The Movie Database
SURVEY	DOC	Vote for your favorite movies — stand up and be counted!
??		Text files of movie information

317
Database Programs
v1

A collection of database management programs. The mailing labels program allows sorting by four fields and keying printing of labels by any field. PMB15.BAS provides a way of keeping track of events which occur periodically such as bills, preventive maintenence items, dental appointments, etc. INDXCARD.BAS is intended to make it very easy to create and maintain 3" by 5" card files. By itself, it forms an electronic typewriter with full editing facilities for the 3 by 5 card format. It can be used with the program PC- FILE III.

Usage: Database management

System Requirements: 128K, two disk drives, a Color/Graphics Adapter Card (color not used), Epson MX-80 (or comparable) printer.

Features:

- Forms an electronic typewriter with full editing facilities.
- Uses PC-FILE to sort index cards prior to printing.
- Sorts a mailing list by four fields.
- Prints one across or two across labels.
- Keeps track of bills, preventive maintenence items, dental appointments.
- Writes your appointments or activities for the whole year.
- Schedules your activities from 6 a.m. till 10 p.m.
- Creates a computerized Rolodex.

How to Start: Consult the .DOC files for documentation and directions

- To run the BASIC programs follow the GETTING STARTED instructions for your configuration.

File Descriptions:

ADDRESS	BAS	Random address file and mailing label printing program
ADDRESS1	FIL	Subroutine for the above program
BARRGOLD	FRM	Format of gold prices quotes
BOOKINV	BAS	Menu for book tracking in the library
FILECAB	BAS	BASIC program to create and maintain databases
FRM	BAS	BASIC program to generate blank 3" by 5" index cards
INDXCARD	BAS	BASIC program to generate index cards
INDXCARD	BAT	A DOS batch file to prepare a data disk
INDXCARD	CMP	A BASIC program to compress data
INDXCARD	DOC	Documentation for INDXCARD.BAS
INDXCARD	DTA	Card data entered by INDXCARD.BAS
INDXCARD	FRM	Card format created by INDXCARD.BAS
INDXCARD	HDR	Field definitions used by PC-FILE
INDXCARD	INX	Index file used by PC-FILE
INDXCARD	KEY	Key definitions used by INDXCARD.BAS
INDXCARD	RPT	Used by PC-FILE to clone sorted data
MAIL1	BAS	Mailing list program
MAIL1	DOC	Documentation for MAIL1.BAS
PC˜3LOG	FRM	Format for meeting reminder and log for PC meetings
PMB15	BAS	A preventive maintenance, bills and message program
PMB15	DOC	Documentation for PMB15.BAS
ROLODEX	BAS	A computerized Rolodex
ROLODEX	DOC	Documentation for Rolodex.bas
SCHEDU	BAS	A BASIC program to generate and maintain calendars
SCHEDU	DOC	Documentation for SCHEDU.BAS
TEST	FRM	Format for test pattern
VWREPAIR	FRM	Format for VW Rabbit service log
WEATHER	FRM	Format for weather report
WSJSTOCK	FRM	Format for stock prices

339
Creator
v1

Creator, Reporter and Cheapsort comprise this database management system. Creator provides the principle database functions (record, add, delete etc.); Reporter writes report programs; Cheapsort sorts Creator files as well as files created under other database systems.

Usage: For database management.

System Requirements: 128K, two disk drives, and monochrome display

How to Start: From DOS, enter TYPE CSORT.DOC for documentation.

- To run the BASIC programs consult the GETTING STARTED for your configuration. The Cheapsort programs run from DOS.

User Comments: "Takes much more effort and question/answer routine to establish files and reports as opposed to say PC-FILE...not visually appealing and readable. Seen better." "A good BASIC data base generator package. If you want a quick and not too dirty data base that is very easy to modify, this is it."

File Descriptions:

C451	LIB	Main record management program
C451MIN	LIB	Alternate record management program
CREATOR	BAS	Program that introduces the Creator system
CSORT	DOC	Documentation for Cheapsort
CSORT	EXE	The Cheapsort program
CSORT2	EXE	Cheapsort, version 2
CSORT3	DOC	Documentation for Cheapsort, version 3
CSORT3	EXE	Cheapsort, version 3
MENU	BAS	Menu program for Creator system
R451	LIB	BASIC program shell for custom report programs
REKEY	BAS	Utility program for maintaining Creator key files
REPORTER	BAS	Writes custom report programs

340
Infobase
v1

Infobase is a forms-driven database management system with mailmerge capabilities and is similar in function and capability to Info-Star and Versa Form. Infobase is forms driven; that is you create forms that match preprinted forms (e.g., IRS forms). These forms can then be used to create databases or access databases created by other forms.

Usage: Database management

System Requirements: 128K, two disk drives and monochrome display

Features:

- Comprehensive help messages and instructions displayed on the screen.

- Searching on any field.
- Multiple FORMS per DATABASE.
- Multiple-page FORMS.
- Two DATABASES open concurrently.
- DATA verification.
- DATA entry power to support high volume operators.
- Multiple record formats per DATABASE.
- Mailmerging including full text readjustment.
- Select subsets of records for special processing.
- Sort RECORDS into any order.

How to Start: For documentation, enter TYPE INFOBASE.DOC and press ENTER.

User Comments: "Good program. Excellent on-screen forms preparation." "Too complicated. Poor lead through." "Not bad, but the docs leave a lot to be desired."

File Descriptions:

ATTACH		Documentation and startup information
CLIENT		Text version of a demo form
CLIENT	DBS	Demo database
CLIENT	FOR	Report form
CLIENTD	FOR	Report form
FINAL	FOR	Last form in demonstration
FLETTER		Text version of a demo form
FLETTER	FOR	Demo form for form letter
FLETTERD	FOR	Demo form for form letter
FORMGEN	EXE	Generates forms from text files
FTEXT		Help screens for form generation
IBASE	EXE	Starts Infobase
INFOBASE	DOC	Complete documentation
INSTALL	BAS	BASIC program for color monitor information
INVOICE	DBS	Demonstration database
INVOICE	FOR	Demo invoice form
INVOICED	DBS	Alternate demonstration database
INVOICED	FOR	Alternate demo invoice form
ITEXT		How to get started with Infobase
LABEL		Text version of a demo form
LABEL	FOR	Demo for mailing labels
LABELD	FOR	Demo for mailing labels
NARS		A sample form
NELSON		Introduction letter for Infostar
REPORT		Program to print reports from forms

383 PC-DBMS
Version 1.0
1.1

PC-DBMS is a relational database management system that provides screen-editing functions and on-line help. The data of a database is in named tables that have records and fields. Each table resides in its own file. There may be any number of data files associated with a database.

Usage: For database management.

System Requirements: 192K, two disk drives and monchrome display

Features:

- Dynamically formatted full-screen forms for data entry.
- A query command that can retrieve records.
- Dynamic files.
- A fast-screen editor.
- A menu-based help system.
- Files resemble the data tables.
- Indexing with an automatic index update.

How to Start: From DOS, enter TYPE MANUAL.1 and TYPE MANUAL.2 for documentation

- To run, enter PC-DBMS and press ENTER.

User Comments: "Very good Tutorial-quality program." "Much too complicated." "Difficult for beginners."

Suggested Donation: $35.00

File Descriptions:

MUSIC	DEF	A sample database used in the tutorial
COMPOSER	DAT	A sample database used in the tutorial
OPUS	DAT	A sample database used in the tutorial
MANUAL	1	First half of the manual
MANUAL	2	Second half of the manual
PC-DBMS	EXE	The PC-DBMS program
READ	ME	Printing instructions for the manual
REQUEST	DOC	Payment form and invoice

396 PDS*BASE
Database System
Version 3.23
v1.1

This disk contains a complete hierarchical database system. It is a Master/Detail (or Mother/Daughter) type. It consists of a series of program generators that create both a custom database (with up to 10 files) and BASIC programs to operate against the custom database. The generated programs can be easily modified. The system has excellent documentation (80 pages). This is THE database management system for those who don't want to go to the expense and trouble of learning a whole new language.

Usage: For database management

System Requirements: 256K, two disk drives and monochrome or color display

Features:

- Open ten files at once.
- A calculated record formula determines record location.
- Immediate reading of records in a Master file.
- Very quick random access speeds.
- Can be used for inventory systems, payroll, or job control systems.

How to Start: For the documentation, consult the README.DOC; print the manual by entering TYPE MANUAL.DOC

- To run this BASIC program, follow the GETTING STARTED instructions for your configuration.

User Comments: "Excellent way to construct simple or complex databases." "Very helpful to the hacker to eliminate random file drudgery." "This source provides a lot of very useful subroutines."

Suggested Donation: $39.95

File Descriptions:

AUTO1	BAT	Batch file for starting MENU1.BAS
AUTO2	BAT	Batch file for starting PRTMANUL.BAS
DBCREATE	BAS	Program to create a blank custom database
DBDEF	BAS	Program to define a custom database. It creates a definition file

DBMANAGE	BAS	Program to append a complete main program to add, modify
DBOPSUB	BAS	Program generator that creates the basic operational subroutines
DBREPORT	BAS	Generates report programs (can optionally contain a sort)
DBSORT	BAS	Generates a program to create a key sort file
DBUTIL01	BAS	Creates a file maintenance program
HARDAUTO	BAT	Batch file to start MENU.BAS from hard disk directory \PDS
HARDINST	BAT	Batch file for installing system on hard disk
INVENTRY	DEF	Sample database definition file
MANUAL	DOC	Text file of 80 page user manual
MENU	BAS	Main menu to control entire program generation process
PRIMES	BAS	Part of PDS*Base
PRTMANUL	BAS	Program to print user manual and registration form
README	DOC	Text file containing instructions and hints on using system
REGISTER	DOC	Text file containing registration information and form
SETUP	BAT	Batch file to create working disks
VERSION3	22	Text file containing version number

401
The Address Book
v1

The Address Book is a user-friendly personal or business address book program written in BASIC. With it, you can create your own address book file which can be edited, printed, searched, and sorted. Mailing labels can be routinely prepared. Birthdays and other user-defined notes may be kept. WordStar and WordPerfect mailmerge files also can be created. Sub-directories of the main directory can be routinely created. Function keys are used extensively and a RAM-disk may be used for more speed.

NOTE: This program is set up to run on PC-DOS; clear directions to move to MS-DOS are enclosed. It has been updated recently to assure it will run on compatibles as well as IBM systems.

Usage: Address-book style database management

System Requirements: 64K, one disk drive and monochrome display

How to Start: Read the README.DOC and MANUAL.DOC files before starting

- To run the BASIC programs follow the GETTING STARTED instructions for your configuration.

User Comments: "This program is great for someone too lazy to build their own database address manager." "Program does not have enough flexibility for general purpose address book." "Very useful for small business or club." "Very effective once you get past all the options up front and into the program itself."

Suggested Donation: $25.00

File Descriptions:

AD	BAS	Abreviated ADSTART.BAS without starting graphics
AD	BAT	Batch file for starting ADSTART.BAS
AD	HLP	Text file used by program to provide online help
ADDELETE	BAS	Program to delete entries << doesn't load properly
ADEDIT	BAS	Program to edit entries
ADFILES	BAS	Creates all necessary data files
ADLIST	BAS	Prints address book
ADMAIL	BAS	Prints address labels
ADMAIL	HLP	Help file used by ADMAIL.BAS
ADMAIN	BAS	Main address book program
ADNAME	BAS	Determines name of sub-program to run
ADNOTE	BAS	Program to create notes to records
ADPRINT	BAS	Program to set printer parameters
ADPRT	BAS	Master printing program
ADPRTA	BAS	Supplemental printing program
ADPRTC	BAS	Supplemental printing program
ADREAD	BAS	Program to scan entries
ADRODX	BAS	Program to print Rolodex-type labels
ADSEARCH	BAS	Program to search by criteria
ADSORT	BAS	Program to sort base by criteria
ADSTART	BAS	Set-up and start program — chains to ADMAIN.BAS
ADTRANS	BAS	Program to transfer records
ADWP	BAS	Converts data files for WordPerfect mail-merge
ADWS	BAS	Converts data files for WordStar mail-merge
ADZIP	BAS	Prints labels by zip code
AUTOEXEC	BAT	Auto-start batch file to run ADSTART.BAS
MANUAL	DOC	Text file containing instructions and user manual
SAMPLES	DAT	Sample data file
SAMPLES	ISS	Sample configuration file
SAMPLES	NTE	Data file — note codes
TEMPOR	TEM	Temporary data file (used internally)

| REALTY | PRG | Test program — real estate listing property info |
| WINE | PRG | Sample program showing simple SQL commands — wine cellar |

464
pBASE
Version 1.2
v1

pBASE is a programmable, relational database management system designed for programmers. It provides facilities for querying and manipulating data, as well as report writing. Unlike most database managers, pBASE represents all data as a table. Data may be accessed and revised using interactive commands or through user-written application programs. pBASE is based on the Structured Query Language (SQL).

Usage: Database management.

System Requirements: 256K, two disk drives and monochrome display

Features:

- Select and update data.
- Sort retrieved data in a specified sequence.
- Do calculations using data values.
- Format display of queried data.
- Develop application programs.
- Interface to external hardware devices.
- Commands may be stored in files and executed.

How to Start: For documentation consult README and PBASE1.REF.

- To run, enter TYPE PB and press ENTER.

User Comments: "Found it very useful and I would recommend it to others." "This is just what I've been looking for years!" "Inadequate documentation. Hard to understand."

Suggested Donation: $35.00

File Descriptions:

EDITFORM	PRG	A pBASE program to edit forms
EXPENSE	PRG	Sample pBASE program to track business expenses
INVENTRY	PRG	Test program — inventory control
MAILLIST	PRG	Sample program — keep mailing lists, etc.
PB	EXE	Main pBASE program
PBASE1	REF	Text file containing the documentation/User manual
README		Text file containing 'How to get started', etc.

483
MAIL MONSTER
Version 2.3
V1

The MAIL MONSTER is an extremely flexible program that allows the user to create a mailing label manager for small to large usages. It permits the user to add, edit, sort, and print mailing labels in many different configurations. Users can define the categories that fit their list of people and/or organizations.

MAIL MONSTER organizes the user's mailing list, allowing highly selective printings, for example, only those labels that needed to reach a specific group, by targeted organization, zip code area, etc. It also includes a mailmerge feature to merge-print letters as well as a personal telephone directory. A complete manual is included on disk.

Usage: Small to large business mail list management.

System Requirements: 256K, two disk drives and monochrome display

How to Start: Consult the README.TXT to understand the MM; then read the documentation on how to begin by entering READ ENTER

- To run it, type MM and press ENTER.

User Comments: "Very functional mail list program." "Needs more flexibility in the names for two people." "I haven't put it to a tough test yet, but, it ran well on first try and seems to be well written."

Suggested Donation: $10.00

File Descriptions:

AUTOEXEC	BAT	Starts "MAIL MONSTER" from warm/cold boot
MAIL	DBF	Database file
MAIL	EXE	MAIL MONSTER program
FILES	LBL	Label producing files (one, two, and three up)
TELELIST	FRM	Produces telephone listings as defined
CATLIST	MEM	File containing defined categories
DUPEDATE	MEM	Date last indexed the duplicates routine

INDXDATE	MEM	Date last indexed the add records routine
MACHINE	MEM	File containing defined machine type (floppy/hard)
ZIPFORM	MEM	File containing zip code data entry format
CONFIG	SYS	Required config.sys file to run MAIL.EXE
FILES	NTX	Initialized index files for MAIL.DBF
FILES	TXT	List of files that make up MAIL MONSTER
FILES	BAT	Batch program to display file list
README	TXT	Short explanation of MAIL MONSTER
READ	BAT	Batch program to display README.TXT
FSETUP	BAT	Program to setup your MAIL MONSTER on floppy
HSETUP	BAT	Program to setup your MAIL MONSTER on hard disk
MANUAL	TXT	Manual for MAIL MONSTER
PRINTDOC	BAT	Program to print MANUAL.TXT

493 VCRDBASE

v1

VCRDBASE is an easy and structured way of keeping track of all the movies in a personal video library. Written in Turbo Pascal, it can be used to keep record of a personal video library by the reference of the following data elements:

Movie Name: String of up to 20 characters
Movie Publisher: String of up to 20 characters
Movie Star: String of up to 20 characters
Movie Style (Horror,Comedy,Action,Drama,Misc.)
Movie Sub-Style
(Horror,Comedy,Action,Drama,None)
Tape Number Integer Counter Starter
Integer Counter End
Integer Tape Speed (S,L,E)

Usage: VCR database management.

System Requirements: 64K, one disk drive and monochrome display

How to Start: From DOS, enter TYPE VCRDBASE.DOC for documentation.

- To invoke the program, enter VCRDBASE and press ENTER.

User Comments: "Attractive, nice features like printing labels as well as a good looking list. Seems to be fast, also." "Excellent database for VCR library. Well put together."

Suggested Donation: $10.00

File Descriptions:

VCRDBASE	COM	The runtime module of VCRDBASE.
VCRDBASE	DOC	Complete documentation file for VCRDBASE.
HEADER	DAT	Header file for program storage.
DATAFILE	DAT	Data file containing movie entries.

521 FreeFile Version 1.0

V1

FreeFile is a menu-driven data management system that allows a user with little or no programming experience to determine how files are to be created, enter information, and print reports. It is particularly useful for those interested in maintaining a collection of information with the ability to set up "calculated fields", and import or export data to and from other packages. FreeFile has online help and two tutorials with explanations.

Usage: Database management.

System Requirements: 256K, two disk drives and monochrome or color display.

Features:

- Maximum number of databases opened at any one time is one.
- Maximum number of indexes for any one database is 10.
- Maximum number of records in any one database is 2 billion.
- Maximum record length is 1,000 characters.
- Maximum number of fields in a record is 100.
- Maximum field length is 65 characters.
- Maximum number of sorts for the print or export features is 100.
- Maximum number of computed fields (formulas) is 100.
- Computed fields are similar to formulas used in spreadsheets.
- Supports date fields

How to Start: From DOS, enter TYPE FF.DOC for documentation.

- To run program, type FF and press ENTER.

Suggested Donation: $45.00

File Descriptions:

READ	ME	Introduction to print documentation
FF	EXE	Main Freefile program
FF	HLP	Freefile help text
FF	DOC	Freefile documentation
DEMO1	?	First tutorial with names & addresses
DEMO2	?	Second tutorial with rental business application
COLOR	EXE	Set up color for color monitor
NO-COLOR	FIL	Set up for monochrome graphic monitor

522
INSTANT RECALL
Version 1.64F
V1

Instant Recall is a memory-resident, free-form database program with its own word processor. Data can be entered in whatever form you like without worrying about field sizes, and can be recalled without worrying about keywords. Since it runs at the same time as your other programs, the process is highly interactive — you can quickly get the data you need, or enter new data, and go on working. It lets you cut and paste information from Instant Recall's record right into another document without exiting from either program.

Usage: For database management.

System Requirements: 72K RAM, one disk drive

Features:

- Run Instant Recall as memory resident or standalone
- Instant Recall has a single, heterogeneous database
- Automatic indexing, word by word if specified!
- Re-indexes quickly.
- Records may have up to 60 lines of text.
- The database may be up to 80kbytes.
- No practical limit to the number of records in the database.
- Up to 64 records may be matched in a single retrieval.

How to Start: Typing INSTANT at the DOS prompt loads Instant Recall as standalone. Typing INSTANTR at the DOS prompt loads Instant Recall as memory resident. For documentation, enter TYPE INSTANT.DOC For more information, enter TYPE README or TYPE IR–USES.DOC

Suggested Donation: $69.00 Registration

File Descriptions:

INSTANT	DOC	Documentation for Instant Recall (40 Pages)
INSTANT	EXE	Instant Recall Program
INSTANT	XXT	Instant Recall database file
INSTANT	KEY	Instant Recall database file
README		General Introduction to Instant Recall
IR–USES	DOC	Some possible uses for the Instant Recall Program
IR164F	ARC	Instant Recall archived backup

537
DBS-KAT Version 1.3
V1

DBS-KAT is a diskette cataloging system; it is intended for people using hard disk systems who use floppy disks for backup/archival purposes. Its central database can catalog the contents of 9,999 diskettes containing 16,000,000 files — without sacrificing performance. The DBS-KAT manual claims a savings of 20 to 40 percent on hard disk space because of this capability.

Usage: Database management

System Requirements: 256K memory, two disk drives, (HARD DISK RECOMMENDED); monochrome or color supported

Features:

- Individual diskette password protection
- A system manager's level of password protection
- The ability to track a disk's age
- Backup
- Log files
- Database integrity analysis

How to Start: Documentation is squeezed in files marked *.OQT; follow directions in READ.ME to unsqueeze

• To run, enter KAT and press ENTER.

Suggested Donation: $27.50

File Descriptions:

KAT	EXE	Main Catalog Program
KATAD	BAT	Advertisement about DBS-KAT
KATAD	KP	Text for Advertisement
KATBOOK	BAT	Program to print documentation
KATBOOK2	BAT	Used by KATBOOK.BAT to print the documentation
KATBUG	FRM	Type: KAT -P to print the DAT-DBS problem report form
KATDB	???	The DBS-KAT database comprises these six files
KATDRIVE	EXE	Program to scan directory
KATLOG	BAT	This and KATSTRIP.BAT are used in maintaining and recovering the database
KATSTRIP	BAT	the DBS-KAT program.
KATLOOK	EXE	Program to allow inquiry against DBS-KAT database
KATORDER	FRM	Type: KAT-O to print the KAT-DBS order form
KATSORT	BAT	Program to KAT-DBS database
KPRINT	EXE	Multi-feature print program
READ	ME	Notes on how to install the KAT disk catalog system
*	OQT	Squeezed files containing the documentation
USQ	COM	Program to un-squeeze the documentation (see READ.ME)
VOLSER	COM	Device volume labler

566
Surveysoft Version 3.0
v1

SURVEYSOFT is a series of programs designed for the surveyor with modules including field traverse, entry and storage of coordinates and many more. It is a fairly comprehensive package and has a complete set of documentation.

Usage: Surveyors.

System Requirements: Two disk drives, 128K and monochrome/graphics display

Features:

- Field traverse
- Bearing/bearing intersection
- Close and adjust
- Bearing/distance intersect
- Distance/distance intersect
- Rotate coordinates

- Inverse with curves and areas
- List coordinates
- Data storage
- Data retrieval

How to Start: Read the READ–ME and MANUAL.TXT. Enter GO to start.

Suggested Donation: $75.00

File Descriptions:

DRIVFILE	PAS	Name of drive
PRINTEXT	BAT	Batch file to print manual
GO	BAT	Main system loader
READ–ME	BAT	Instructions file
RUN	BAT	Execution program (Copy of GO.BAT)
FILES	TXT	File with list of package files
MSG?	01	Text printed by batch file
SURVEY?	001	Surveysoft routines
SETDRIVE	COM	Utility to set drive
MANUAL	TXT	Detailed documentation

599
DREAM (Data Retrieval, Entry And Management) 1 of 3
v2

DREAM is a relational database program that comes in three diskettes, all three needed to complete the package. The archiving procedure was used to combine the contents of original five DREAM disks into three.

The first disk contains installation procedures, notes, and two archived files. The first archived file consists of main menu, driver modules of the package, and design modules; the programs on this file are used when DREAM is started. The second archived file contains sample data to illustrate the program's various and powerful functions and the files used for the on-line help. The second disk contains continuation of the installation procedure and two more archived files that comprise data entry and single-file report generators, and programs which handle all of the utility and database administration for DREAM. The last disk contains the final portion of the installation procedure and the archived files which contain programs enabling the relational database processing.

DREAM, produced by PC-Systems, is a relational database system with extreme power and flexiblity. Much like dBASE, it can custom design database applications, which include reports, sorting abilities, query abilities, and data entry and retrieval abilities without writing code. DREAM comes complete with over 200K worth of on-line and manual documentation which lead the user step by step through the program. DREAM can handle over 32,000 records per data file with over 1,500 characters per fixed record length.

Usage: Database management for business applications.

System Requirements: 256K memory, two disk drives, (HARD DISK RECOMMENDED) and monochrome/graphics or color/graphics display

Features:

- Two modes of operation: technical and end user.
- Three levels of data protection.
- Multiple views of data.
- Multiple record updates (batch processing).
- Edit, format, and range tests on input.
- Computations on input/output, including computations with dates.
- Auto-generation and duplication of data fields and records.
- Single data file reports — post or concurrent with data entry.
- Relational operations for multiple files.
- Data restructuring.
- Copying/moving data from one file to another.
- Screen painting for data entry and reports.
- Windowing technique for multiple data files.
- Unique report layout features.
- Four character sizes for reports and labels.
- Multiple look-up and data transfer from outside files.
- On-line help and tutorial.
- Interrupt routines using function keys.
- Color selection.
- ASCII file format and portability of data.
- Five levels of user expertise.
- Electronic note pad.

How to Start: Read the READ-IT.DOC for a picture of the system and read the INSTALL.DOC to install.

Suggested Donation: $35.00

File Descriptions:

INSTALL	DOC	Description of installation procedure.
INSTFLPY	BAT	Installation driver for 2 floppy disk drives
INSTHARD	BAT	Installation driver for a hard disk
NOTES599	TXT	Review of DREAM
PARMFLPY	SYS	DREAM parameters for floppy disk drives
PARMHARD	SYS	DREAM parameters for a hard disk
PKXARC	EXE	Un-archiving program Version 1.1 by Phil Katz
READ-IT	DOC	Short description of DREAM

DREAM1.ARC archived file:

BASRUN	EXE	Compiler library
COMLIST	LST	program commamds file
COMMENU	EXE	Menu module
DESEDIT	EXE	Program module — design edit
DESFORM	EXE	Program module — forms design
DESIGN	EXE	Design program module
DESPROC	EXE	Program module — procedure design
DESREL	EXE	Program module — relations design
DESSUB	EXE	Design program module
DREAM	BAT	Batch file for technical mode, hard disk drive
DREAM1	EXE	Starter program for technical mode, floppy disk drive
EQNR	LST	Program miscellaneous data
HELPRINT	EXE	Standalone module to print DREAM tutorial
PARM	SYS	Parameter system file
PARAMS	EXE	Parameter system program module
SYMBOLW	LOG	Program miscellaneous data
UD	BAT	Batch file for user mode, hard disk drive
UD1	EXE	Starter file for user mode, floppy disk drive

DREAM5.ARC archived file:

FORM	ADM	Forms catalog
SCREEN	ADM	Screens catalog
HELPUSER	DAT	On-line help data
HELPUSER	SCR	On-line help screen
HELPUSER	CTL	On-line help control
HELPUSER	FRM	On-line help print form
HELPUSER	IND	On-line help index

600 DREAM (Data Retrieval, Entry And Management) 2 of 3
V2

DREAM is a relational database program that comes in three disks, all three needed to complete the package. The archiving procedure was used to combine the contents of original five DREAM disks into three.

This is the second disk which contains the continuation of the installation procedure and two more archived files that comprise data entry and single-file report generators; these are the modular programs which handle all of the utility and database administration for DREAM.

DREAM, produced by PC-Systems, is a relational database system with extreme power and flexiblity. Much like dBASE, it can custom design database applications, which include reports, sorting abilities, query abilities, and data entry and retrieval abilities without writing code. DREAM comes complete with over 200K worth of on-line and manual documentation which lead the user step by step through the program. DREAM can handle over 32,000 records per data file with over 1500 characters per fixed record length.

File Descriptions:

INSTFLPY	BAT	Installation driver for 2 floppy disk drives (cont.)
INSTHARD	BAT	Installation driver for a hard disk (cont)
PKXARC	EXE	Un-archiving program Version 1.1 by Phil Katz
		DREAM2.ARC archived file:
COMMENU	EXE	Menu module
INSTFLPY	BAT	Installation driver for 2 floppy disk drives (ending)
MULTUPDT	EXE	Program module — multi record update
SELQRY	EXE	Program module — select query options
SYMBOLW	LOG	Misc program data
VIEWDATA	EXE	Program module — data entry module
VIEWUPDT	EXE	Program module — view data updates
VIEWMAIN	EXE	Program module — data entry/report setup
VIEWFORM	EXE	Program module — print/display report
VIEWQRY	EXE	Program module — user selection options
VIEWSORT	EXE	Program module — sort data
VINDEX	EXE	Program module — process index data
		DREAM4.ARC archived file:
ADMIN	EXE	Program module — administrative options
COMMENU	EXE	Program module — menu module
HELP	EXE	On-line help and tutorial program (27k)
PROFILE	EXE	Program module — display application profile
REORG	EXE	Program module — reorganize report format
SELQRY	EXE	Program module — select query
SYMBOLW	LOG	Misc program data
VIEWFORM	EXE	Program module — form generator
VIEWQRY	EXE	Query program module — user selections
VIEWSORT	EXE	Program module — sort options
VIEWUTIL	EXE	Program module — export data

601

DREAM
(Data Retrieval, Entry And Management) 3 of 3

DREAM is a relational database program that comes on three disks, all three needed to complete the package. The archiving procedure was used to combine the contents of original five DREAM disks into three.

This is the third disk which contains the final portion of the installation procedure and the last archived file that contains programs enabling the ability for relational database processing.

DREAM, produced by PC-Systems, is a relational database system with extreme power and flexiblity. Much like dBASE, it can custom design database applications, which include reports, sorting abilities, query abilities, and data entry and retrieval abilities without writing code. DREAM comes complete with over 200k worth of on-line and manual documentation which leads the user step by step through the program. DREAM can handle over 32,000 records per data file with over 1500 characters per fixed record length.

File Descriptions:

INSTFLPY	BAT	Installation driver for 2 floppy disk drives(cont.)
INSTHARD	BAT	Installation driver for a hard disk (cont)
PKXARC	EXE	Un-archiving program Version 1.1 by Phil Katz
		DREAM3.ARC archived file:
COMMENU	EXE	Program module — menu module
REPMAIN	EXE	Program module — main routine
REPSCRN	EXE	Program module — view selection module
RELATE	EXE	Program module — build relationships
REPUTIL	EXE	Utility module — export data
REPSORT	EXE	Program module — sort related databases
REPQRY	EXE	Program module — query
REPFORM	EXE	Program molule — display/print report
SELREP	EXE	Program module — user selections

624
PC-File III jr
Version 3
v1

This is Jim Buttons' very popular database filing program. Users comment on its ease of use and excellent documentation. It is a must for anyone desiring an inexpensive, useful filing system. This version is recommended for the PCjr. The version for all other systems can be found on Disk No 5.

Usage: Database management

System Requirements: 128K, one double-sided drive (two are advised) and a monochrome display

How to Start: Use the DOC file to print out the documentation and read it thoroughly! To load PC-FILE, place the program disk in your A drive and enter at the DOS prompt "PC-FILE" and press ENTER.

Suggested Donation: $49.00 which includes full Users Manual

File Descriptions:

GO	BAT	Explains how to start program and print documention
DOC	BAT	Batch file to print documentation file
PC-FILE	BAT	Batch file to start PC-File program
PC-DEF	EXE	Utility program to select system configuration
PC-FILE	DOC	Documentation file
PC-EXPOR	EXE	Part of PC-File
PC-FILE	EXE	Main program for PC-File
PC-FILE	PRO	Part of PC-File
PCFILE	XXX	Part of PC-File
PC-FIX	EXE	Part of PC-File
PC-IMPOR	EXE	Part of PC-File
PC-LABEL	EXE	Part of PC-File
PC-OVL	EXE	Part of PC-File
PC-PRINT	EXE	Part of PC-File
PC-SETUP	EXE	Part of PC-File
PC-SORT	EXE	Part of PC-File
PC-UTIL	EXE	Part of PC-File

662
DATABOSS
Version 3.00.01
(Disk 1 of 2)
v1

This is the first of a two-disk set comprising the DataBoss data management system. DataBoss is a database with flexible report generation and the ability to import and export data to Wordstar, PC-File III, DW III and many other programs. It sports user-defined color screens, up to eight different disk drives or subdirectories, pre-computed (equivalence) fields, wide standard reports, user-defined printer characteristics, a full alphabet keyboard enhancer, simple mathematical and statistical functions, sorting for up to eight levels, and enhanced search capabilities. This first disk holds the documentation for version 3.00.01 of the DataBoss system — 70 + pages of how-to information with some special tips on maximizing the use of your hard disk(s). NOTE: DataBoss runs in BASIC and needs MS/PC/DOS 3.xx and a hard disk for full functioning.

Usage: Database Applications

System Requirements: 128K and one disk drive floppy drives as well as hard drives (recommended).

How to Start: To print the documentation, enter COPY BOSS3.DOC LPT1: and press ENTER.

● To run, enter DB and press ENTER.

Suggested Donation: $50.00

File Descriptions:

BOSS3	DOC	The 70 + page user's manual.
CHANGES	DOC	Note about recent changes to the program.
README	DOC	The author's introduction to DataBoss.
AUTOEXEC	BAT	A sample of a program to auto boot DataBoss.

663
DATABOSS
Version 3.00.01
(Disk 2 of 2)
v1

This is the second of a two disk set comprising the DataBoss data management system. DataBoss is a database with flexible report generation and the ability to import and export data to Wordstar, PC-File III, DW III and many other programs. It sports user-defined color screens, up to eight different disk drives or subdirectories, pre-computed (equivalence) fields, wide standard reports, user-defined printer characteristics, a full alphabet keyboard enhancer, simple mathematical and statistical functions, sorting for up to eight levels, and enhanced search capabilities. The first disk holds the documentation for version 3.00.01 of the DataBoss system — 70+ pages of how-to information with some special tips on maximizing the use of your hard disk(s). NOTE: DataBoss runs in BASIC and needs MS/PC/DOS 3.xx and a hard disk for full functioning.

Usage: Database Applications

System Requirements: 128K and one disk drive but will support two floppy drives as well as hard drives (recommended).

How to Start: To print the documentation, enter COPY BOSS3.DOC LPT1: and press ENTER.

● To run, enter DB and press ENTER.

Suggested Donation: $50.00

File Descriptions:

DB	BAS	The DataBoss menu and control program.
*	01	A Database functional module (14 files)
FIXED	BAT	To load DataBoss onto a hard disk.
FLOPPY	BAT	To load the system onto a floppy.
COLOR	BAT	To start the color set up program.
DATABOSS	BAT	To load basic and start the program.

668
WORLD
Version 1.0
V1

WORLD is a simple, menu-driven database of statistical and demographic information about the nations. The information was extracted from "The Encyclopedia Britanica Year Book for 1986" and "Countries of the World and Their Leaders Yearbook 1986."

Through the main menu you can select information about the names, capitals, geography, population, per capita income, sovereignity of more than 100 countries. Probably the most interesting menu is the Vital Statistics which also gives the death and birth rates, infant mortality and life expectancy rates for male and female citizens.

Usage: Demographic and statistical information

System Requirements: 64K, one disk drive and monochrome display

How to Start: Enter WORLD and press ENTER.

File Descriptions:

WORLD	EXE	The program
DATABASE		The Data for the 1986 statistics

DESKTOP MANAGERS:

Desktop managers are the jack-of-all-trades for personal computer users. These combine many different accessories and utilities to use the storage and retrieval power inherent in computers.

Beginning as electronic calendars and appointment books, desktop managers have expanded to include address managers (often with sorting and printing abilities). Later, the ability to define macros (specific, reuseable, series of keyed-in tasks) and have a "notepad" structure available (for tagging notes to files) became popular and were integrated into most desktops.

Recently, new design applications have emerged which allow users to custom design a menu system for either floppy or hard disk systems. These are appealing for their style and ease of file management. You can see "at-a-glance" the major applications immediately available, and create a design to suit you! Many of our desktops are also appreciated for their ability to maintain file security through password protection.

87 Programmer's Calculator
v1.2

The Programmers Calculator offers a powerful Reverse Polish Notation format calculator to all those in the professions or students who have need of such a tool. With its on-screen stack display, complex calculations become much easier to follow; it also functions as good instructional tool for those who are just learning stack operations. With good documentation and informative displays, this is an excellent value.

Usage: Engineers, Scientists, and students.

System Requirements: 128K, one disk drive, color/monochrome display

Features:

- Auto configure for color or monochrome systems
- Up to 16-place precision
- Convert between octal, hex, decimal, and binary
- Toggle between Convert and Calculate modes
- Displays all functions and registers

How to Start: Read the MANUAL.DOC file or print it out with the MANUAL.BAT file

- To run, enter PC and press ENTER.

User Comments: "This is a great calculator. It replaces the need of a hand held calculator at your computer. It uses a visable stack structure which is very handy." "Excellent choice for any programmer working with hex numbers. Fun and easy to use. Should be recommended to anyone getting serious about computers but is weak on computer math"

File Descriptions:

PC	EXE	Programmer's calculator — main program
GC	EXE	Number base conversion program for use with PC.EXE
MANUAL	DOC	Documentation file (41K)
MANUAL	BAT	Batch file to print documentation
DUP	BAT	Batch file to copy program files to another disk

113
Three User-Supported Programs
v1.1

Here are three programs for system enhancement: 1) the Datamorphics Screen package for greater display control, 2) PC-COMPARE for comparing data files and; 3) DEFKEY, a keyboard reassignment program simular to Prokey. All of these programs can be quite helpful in streamlining and simplifying your daily operations.

Usage: System tools for Intermediate-Advanced level users

System Requirements: 128k, one disk drive, mono monitor

How to Start: Consult the .DOC and README files for directions and documentation

- To run the BASIC programs, consult the directions in GETTING STARTED for your configuration
- To run any of the programs with the suffix .COM or .EXE, just type its name, i.e., for COMPARE.COM, type COMPARE and press ENTER.

User Comments: ".. Can be of great help in reading documentation, tutorials, and other text files, one screen at a time." "All the tools on disk are quite good!"

Suggested Donation: PC-PAGE $20.00

File Descriptions:

— — — —	— —	Datamorphics Screen programs
READ	ME	Brief description of Datamorphics Screen programs
INVOICE		Form for generating invoice for screen package
PC-BW	DOC	Documentation for PC-BW (3 pages)
PC-PAGE	DOC	Documentation for PC-PAGE (3 pages)
PC-TTY	DOC	Documentation for PC-TTY (4 pages)
PC-TTY	COM	Program modifies TTY emulation of BIOS
WRAP	COM	Sets line wrapping on or off
PC-BW	COM	Program to make monochrome screen calls work on color board
PAGE	COM	Modifies page length setting of PC-PAGE
PC-PAGE	COM	Prevents text from scrolling off screen
*	D11	DOS 1.1 optimized versions of screen programs (3 files)

— — — —	— —	PC-COMPARE 1.30
RUN	BAT	Invokes the PC-COMPARE 4-part screen tutorial and program
COMPARE?	DOC	Part of PC-COMPARE documentation (6 files)
COMPLETE	DOC	Documentation for COMPARE.COM (3 pages)
PRINTDOC	BAT	Used to send COMPLETE.DOC to the printer
SAMP1	TXT	Sample file to be used with RUN.BAT
SAMP2	TXT	Sample file to be used with RUN.BAT
COPYCOMP	BAT	Makes a backup PC-COMPARE files from Drive A to Drive B
COMPARE	COM	The COMPARE program itself
CLS	COM	Utility to clear the screen, for running under DOS 1.10
BEEP	COM	Used by PC-COMPARE
FILES	LST	Listing of the PC-COMPARE files
— — — —	— —	DEFKEY
PROGRAM	DOC	Instructions for running DEFKEY program
DEFKEY	BAS	Program to reassign keyboard keys (Requires DOS 2.0)
DEFKEY	BAT	Batch file to automatically run DEFKEY program
DEFKEY	DOC	Instructions for running DEFKEY program (3 pages)
KEYS	BAS	Program to redefine BASIC program keys
BASICAK	BAT	Loads BASIC and runs KEYS.BAS from DOS
— — — —	— —	
MOD100IN	BAS	Program to load files from Radio Shack Model 100
MOD100IN	DOC	Documentation for MOD100IN.BAS (5 pages)

118
QSYS DOS Menu Version 3.0 (Disk 1 of 2)
v2

If you feel a need for some help in getting organized, then QSYS may be just the thing for you. QSYS is an operating environment, a menu system, an appointment calendar, and a message system. Major features of the program include password access for up to 24 users, and an extensive menu system. Documentation for QSYS is on Disk No 278.

Usage: Computer Organizing

System Requirements: 192K, color graphics, two disk drives, (hard disk recommended)

How to Start: Consult the .DOC and README files on Disk 278 for directions and documentation

- To run QSYS.EXE, just type its name, i.e., QSYS and press ENTER.

User Comments: "A well thought out program. Very useful in multi-user environments. "Good program, somewhat complicated." "Quite a good menu system for a low price."

Suggested Donation: QSYS $50.00 covers full documentation and update

File Descriptions:

QSYS	EXE	Main QSYS program
AUTOEXEC	BAT	Installation startup procedure batch file
QINST	EXE	Part of QSYS
QMSG	EXE	Message handler
QCNFG	EXE	Part of QSYS
QINT	EXE	Part of QSYS
QLDR	COM	Part of QSYS
CONFIG	SYS	Initial bootup file
MEMBRAIN	EXE	RAMdisk
MEMBRAIN	SYS	RAMdisk initial bootup file

278
QSYS DOS (3.0) Documentation (Disk 2 of 2)
v1

This disk contains the documentation for QSYS, a user-supported program. QSYS is a powerful operating environment, a menu system, an appointment calendar and message system, with many pluses. The programs are on Disk No 118.

Usage: Computer Organizing

System Requirements: 192K, color/graphics, two disk drives (hard disk recommended)

How to Start: Consult the README! files for directions and instructions on printing the documentation.

Suggested Donation: QSYS $50.00

File Descriptions:

MAKEDOC	BAT	Batch file to print documentation
MAKEDOC	TXT	Instructions for printing documentation
Q-*	DOC	Documentation files (17 files)
READ	ME!	Read this first

356
Fansi-Console Disk 1 of 2
v2.1

Fansi-Console is a sophisticated memory-resident program which replaces the standard IBM PC console drivers, extends the ROM BIOS, processes ANSI X3.64 control sequences, provides keyboard macro capabilities, and much more. You have two versions of Fansi-Console here: FCONSOLE.DEV is the commercial version and is usually the more stable more bugfree version of FansiConsole. It is the version which most closely matches the current printed user manual and is the version which you have purchased. The version of Fansi-Console in the file called FCONBETA.DEV is the beta test version. HAVE FUN COMPARING THEM!

NOTE: This is a two disk set, the second part being Disk No 650.

Usage: Some Fansi programming of and from your keyboard!

System Requirements: 128K, two disk drives and a monochrome display

How to Start: There is an on-disk abbreviated user manual for FANSI-CONSOLE in the file FCONSOLE.DQC. To unsqueeze it, use the UNSQZ program and this command: UNSQZ A:FCONSOLE.DQC B:FCONSOLE.DOC Once unsqueezed, it is much bigger so put it on a separate disk!

User Comments: "At last, a full ANSI device driver for the IBM-PC." "I have a lot of utility programs which do each function of this program. The virtue of this program is integration of all of them" "EXCELLENT, AGAIN! "I think this a great program. The best of its type that I've seen, but half the documentation is missing..." "Great program, but runs into other memory resident programs rather frequently. The screen writing speed is especially helpful." "This program is very interesting as it has shown me how differ drivers effect the operation of the computer."

Suggested Donation: Use license $25; $75 will get you the manual and the latest update.

File Descriptions:

-README-	NOW	Short instructions for printing the abbreviated user manual
123V2	PCH	Patch for Lotus 1-2-3 Version 2
ANSI80	TXT	Test data for 80 column screen displays
AT	LAY	AT keyboard layout file
CHARSETS	TXT	Demonstrates how to generate the entire IBM-PC character set
DEJAVU	EXE	Writes the lines from the scroll recall buffer to a file
DIZZY	C	Source for C program which generated part of ANSI80.TXT
DVORAK	TXT	Test data to set up a quasi-Dvorak keyboard layout
DVORAK2	TXT	Test data to set up a quasi-Dvorak keyboard layout (part 2)
EGALGCHR	COM	Decreases the number of lines of characters on the EGA
EGASMCHR	COM	Increases the number of lines of characters on the EGA
EXPAND	COM	Expands tab characters into spaces
FANSICAP	TXT	Termcap file for FANSI-CONSOLE when FANSI-VT100 is reset
FANSISET	EXE	Menu driven program for changing options at run-time
FANSISET	TXT	Example set-up file
FCONBBS	LST	List of Bulliten Board Systems
FCONBETA	DEV	"Beta Test" version of FANSI-CONSOLE
FCONSOLE	DEV	FANSI-CONSOLE itself
FCONSOLE	HST	Revision history
FLAYOUT	EXE	Program to rearrange your keyboard keys to your liking
LOGO	PCH	Patch for Logo
RAWMODE	MAC	Source for sub-routines useful to programmer's
SEND	EXE	Sends control sequences to the console or printer
SK111	PCH	Patch for Sidekick Version 1.11A
SNOW	COM	Test program for setting hardware options
SPIT	EXE	Program to slowly try test data
STANDARD	LAY	Standard keyboard layout file
STKSTRAW	COM	FANSI-CONSOLE utility program
TRAP	COM	Traps INT calls for problem reporting purposes
UNSQZ	COM	Unsqueeze utility
WATZITBE	COM	Displays the scan codes for each key pressed
WATZITDO	COM	Displays the effects of pressing keys
WORDSTAR	PCH	Patch for Wordstar 3.3
Z200	LAY	Sample keyboard layout file

387
Keep In Touch
3v1

Keep in Touch is a networking tool for all kinds of people and organizations. As networking is maintaining contact with people and organizations thereby sharing and distributing information, products, services, etc., tying them all together is key to success. Keep in Touch may be that key for you! Two other interesting observations about this program: while it is written in BASIC, Keep in Touch uses a menu structure similar to Lotus 1-2-3!

Usage: Desktop Manager

System Requirements: 64K, one disk drive and monochrome display

Features:

- Call using your automatic dialer
- Display the elapsed time of a call
- Show the Things-To-Do list
- Hang up the telephone and show elapsed time
- Check the time or use the alarm clock
- Games, visual relaxation and amusement
- Use the built-in calculator
- Examine information on your contacts and clients
- Create reports about your contacts and clients
- Print a phonelist report
- Print a report of dates
- Print mailing labels using Avery Tabulabel 4146 4" format
- Check the amount of memory available

How to Start: Consult the KIT.DOC file for directions and documentation

- To run this BASIC programs, consult the directions in GETTING STARTED for your configuration.

File Descriptions:

AUTOEXEC	BAT	Starts Keep In Touch when the system is booted.
CONFIG	BAS	Configures hardware, monitor, printer, telecommunications
CONFIG	KIT	Configuration data file
DEMO	BAS	Keep In Touch demonstration program
DEMO	BAT	Batch file to start the Keep In Touch demonstration

DEMO	KIT	Demo data file
DEMOSET	BAS	Part of the demonstration program
FILES	KIT	Directory data file
JAPAN	DAT	Sample file
KEYSET	BAS	Author's comments and copyright notice
KIT	BAS	The Keep In Touch program
KIT	BAT	Same as AUTOEXEC.BAT
KIT	DOC	Information about Keep In Touch
MENU	KIT	Menu data file
NEW	DAT	Sample file
TODO	DAT	Sample file

405 PC-DESKTEAM
Version 1.04
V2

PC-Deskteam is an all-in-one utility/accessory program that can be called from any program or DOS. It includes the following utilities: alarm clock, calculator, calendar, selected DOS commands, notepad, phone dialer, printer control, typewriter mode, and a handy ASCII chart. It is menu driven, has help facilities, can be used as a stand-alone program or in memory resident mode (with the ability to change the start key). This is a super alternative to commercial desktop managers, having many more features and good documentation, too.

Usage: Desktop Manager

System Requirements: 128K, one disk drive

Features:

- Menu driven operation
- On line help facilities
- Memory resident or stand alone operation
- Integrated printer control utility

How to Start: Consult the DESKTEAM.DOC and README files for directions and documentation

- To run, enter DESKTEAM and press ENTER.

User Comments: "This disk contains 8 personal utilities, any one of which would make its purchase worthwhile." "MANUAL long but well written" "Written for PC but I own a Zenith compatable. The documentation was unclear how to modify, but with perserverence I managed. Otherwise this is a most excellent 'SIDEKICK' program. I would RECOMMEND it to anyone." "In many ways this program is better than Sidekick. It is more usable

for me at home, but it does take a bit more RAM to keep."

Suggested Donation: Registration $25.00 gets extra documentation

File Descriptions:

ASCII	PAD	A file with ASCII/IBM character set chart
AUTOEXEC	BAT	Batch file for starting DESKTEAM in memory mode
CALENDAR	PAD	Sample calendar data
CLKFIX	COM	Program to fix clock display on LEADING EDGE and AT&T
CLKFIX	DOC	Documentation for CLKFIX.COM
DESKTEAM	CFG	Configuration file for DESKTEAM created by INSTALL.COM
DESKTEAM	COM	Main program
DESKTEAM	DOC	Documentation for DESKTEAM.COM (120k)
DISKETTE	BAT	Batch file for installing DESKTEAM on a floppy(ies)
EPSON	CFG	Printer configuration file for DESKTEAM and an EPSON
HARDISK	BAT	Batch file for installing DESKTEAM on a hardisk
HISTORY	DOC	List of changes from version to version
HOLIDAYS	PAD	File containing holiday dates
INSTALL	COM	Program to configure Deskmate to your system
MANUAL	BAT	Prints the manual (documentation) on using DESKTEAM
METRICS	PAD	Metric conversion Pad (displayed by Deskmate)
OKIDATA	CFG	Printer configuration file for DESKTEAM and an OKIDATA
PHONE	PAD	File containing sample telephone directory (displayed by Deskmate)
PLUGPLAY	CFG	Printer configuration file for DESKTEAM and an PLUG N PLAY roms
PRINTER	CFG	Configuration file with current printer selection
PROBLEM	DOC	Machines that have a problem run DESKTEAM
README		Introduction letter
README	BAT	Displays README file
STATES	PAD	File containing states and capitals

412 Personal Utilities
1.1

This disk contains an assortment of utility programs to aid you in organizational duties. PC-RECIPE will help you to keep track of your favorite recipes; DDCAL and PCYEARBK are both appointment book/calendar utilities; TELEFONE is a telephone book and dialer (requires a modem); and the Rolodex program is a simple filing system. All in all, a very well-rounded collection of handy helpers.

Usage: Personal organizational tools

System Requirements: 128K, monochrome display, one disk drive; Rolodex requires dBASE III

How to Start: Consult the .DOC and README files for directions and documentation

- To run the BASIC programs, consult the directions in GETTING STARTED for your configuration
- To run a program with the suffix .COM or .EXE, just type its name and press ENTER.

User Comments: "DDCAL colorful and very user friendly, EASY to use" (DIARY) This diary only goes from 7:00 to 8:30. Should be 24 hour diary. (DESK)" A little slow, but the price is right and it does all you need to have done. "(PC)Very useful. Needs updating to include variable envelope size;PC Yearbook is very useful to me everyday." (PC-DESK)" Good program — very useful" (PCRECIPE)"This is too complicated for average housewife."

Suggested Donation: PC RECIPE $25.00; DAILY DIARY $10.00; PC YEARBOOK $15.00; TELEPHONE $5.00

File Descriptions:

DDCAL	COM	Appointment book utility (like SideKick's)
PCRECIPE	DOC	Documentation for PCRECIPE.EXE program
PCRECIPE	EXE	A recipe filing system
PCYEARBK	DOC	Documentation for PCYEARBK.EXE program
PCYEARBK	EXE	An appointment book system
ROL????	COM	A name and address system — Rolodex simulator (for dBase II)
TELEFONE	COM	A telephone book and dialer (must have modem)

500 Soft-touch
v1

Soft-touch is a program that allows keys to be programmed with keystrokes. It operates as a sort of computer shorthand, allowing you to speed through often-repeated commands or entries. It has an excellent built-in tutorial. Soft-touch is a memory-resident program that may be activated any time through it's escape sequence. For the adventurous, the source code in assembly language is included.

Usage: Intermediate-Advanced user or programmer.

System Requirements: 64K, one disk drive, monochrome display

How to Start: Check the READ.ME and then the SOFTCH.DOC files for documentation and instructions

- To run, enter SOFTCH and press ENTER.

Suggested Donation: $25.00

File Descriptions:

SOFTCH	COM	Main Program.
MANUAL	BAT	A batch file to print out the operations manual.
README		An introductory text file.
MCRO	KEY	Tutorial and example micros.
SOFTCH	DOC	The operations manual text file.
TUTOR	BAT	A batch file to execute the tutorial.
TUTOR	DOC	Text information for the tutorial.
LIST	COM	Program to list the tutorial screens.

576 PC TICKLE
v1

PC-TICKLE is an appointments calendar/checkbook manager/record keeper program that can help users organize their schedules by tracking important appointments and dates, with reminders at the appropriate time. It also keeps track of checkbook expenditures, and can even be used as a calorie counter. It even includes its own "mini-editor" program to allow you to edit files.

Usage: A personal organizer, suitable for all user levels

System Requirements: 64K, one disk drive, monochrome display

How to Start: Check the README. Type TICKLE and press ENTER.

Suggested Donation: $29.95 plus $5.00 S & H

File Descriptions:

CAL	BAT	Batch file to print Calendar file
CALENDAR		Textfile of Calendar Appointments
CALORIES		Textfile with Calorie Consumption records
CHECKS		Textfile with Checking Account records
EXPENSES		Textfile with Expense records

HOLIDAYS		Textfile with Dates of Holidays
PCBOOK	COM	Program to read Documentation on screen interactively
PCBOOK	HLP	Help Screens for reading documentation on screen interactively
PCBOOK	MNU	Menus to select portions of documentation to read
PCLTRO	EXE	Auxiliary program to TICKLED
PRINTCAL	BAT	Batch file to print Calendar
PRINTDOC	BAT	Batch file to print Documentation
READDOC	BAT	Batch file to display Documentation on Screen
README		Introduction — How to print documentation or read it on screen
README	BAT	Batch file to display README file on Screen
TICKLE	COM	Main Program — Appointment Calendar/Checkbook Manager
TICKLE	DOC	Encrypted documentation file for PC TICKLE
TICKLED	COM	Mini-editor program to edit TICKLE Files

608 AUTOMENU Version 3.01
v1

AUTOMENU lets you access all your programs, batch files, even DOS commands in one easy menu system. Set it up once and let AUTOMENU take care of the rest! With or without a mouse, you can design your own access menus and then just "point and pick " what you want from plain English menus.

Usage: Personal Menu Design

System Requirements: 128K recommended as AUTOMENU needs minimum of 30K, monochrome/color monitors; can fit on floppy or hard disks.

Features:

* AUTOMENU can be memory resident (directions included)
* Execute any DOS command, program, or batch file directly without creating a batch file to be executed outside AUTOMENU.
* Password protection on any or all menu options
* Works on the PC, XT, PC Jr., Portable, AT, and 3270-PC
* Memory is allocated dynamically, using only what it needs
* Ability to define eight individual menus per Menu Definition File

* Eight menu options per menu
* Individually titled menus, automatically centered
* Help messages and optional helps
* Mouse support to choose menu options
* Supports all monitors including the Enhanced Graphics Adapter
* Automatic Screen Blackout to save monitor
* Current time displayed in 12-hour or 24-hour format while in menu

How to Start: Consult the excellent documentation in the AUTOMENU.DOC file for instructions. Run it by typing "AUTO" and pressing ENTER.

Suggested Donation: $30.00 for registration, update notification; $20.00 more for source code.

File Descriptions:

AUTO	BAT	Batch file to start a menu
AUTOMENU	COM	Main program for gemerating your own menus
AUTOMENU	DOC	Documentation for AUTOMENU.COM
AUTOINST	COM	Automenu installation program
*	MDF	Part of AUTOMENU (2 files)

618 MakeMyDay Version 2.0
v1

MakeMyDay! is a complete, computerized time management system for the PC family of computers. It contains an appointment calendar, a job scheduler, a time log and an expense account manager. It can be used to keep track of all of these things for one person or for several people. It makes use of your line printer to produce all the worksheets and printed reports you need to organize your business and personal schedule.

Usage: Personal Time Management

System Requirements: 128K, one disk drive (can be installed for floppy or hard disks) and a monochrome display

How to Start: Consult the documentation on MMD.DOC for directions. To run, first select the drive and (optional) path on which the MMD files reside, then type "MMD" and press ENTER.

Suggested Donation: $50 covers latest program disk and printed documentation. Commercial/governmental fee of $35.

File Descriptions:

MMD	COM	Time management program
MMD	000	Data file for MMD.COM
MMD	DOC	Documentation for MMD.COM

631 HARD DISK MENU
v1

HARD DISK MENU SYSTEM is a DOS shell which allows the user to create a 10-page menu (with up to 100 entries) of macros (Batch-like command sequences) for loading and running your favorite software or performing common DOS functions. The program is easy to set up and includes extensive help screens within the program. HDM-II allows the use of user-defined variables and parameters to create complex command sequences. Passwords can be set up to prevent unauthorized access to any (or all) menu selections or functions.

Usage: Hard Disk Management

System Requirements: Any hard/fixed disk with a floppy drive, 128K and a monochrome display

How to Start: Consult the HDM.DOC file for documentation and instructions. Then to install and use HDM: Copy all the files from the HDM II disk to the root directory or a subdirectory of your hard disk. Make that directory the default and enter HDM. Once in the system enter /H and read the HELP screens.

Suggested Donation: $15.00

File Descriptions:

README		Documentation for INSTALL.BAT AND UPDATE.BAT
HDM	BAT	Starts the Hard Disk Menu System
HDMX	BAT	Work file used by HDMENU
INSTALL	BAT	First time install of HDM-II
README	BAT	Displays the README file on screen
UPDATE	BAT	Update an existing HDM
HDMHELP	CHN	Help screens used by HDMENU
EPSON	COM	Sends control codes to EPSON printer
HDMENU	COM	Main program

IBMPRO	COM	Sends control codes to IBM ProPrinter
HDM	DOC	Hard Disk Menu documentation
HDMENU	TXT	Used by HDMENU

642 MENU-MASTER Version 2.1
v1

MENU-MASTER is a general-purpose menu utility designed to allow easy access to up to 12 applications and DOS functions on a fixed disk. Commonly used applications may be defined in terms that are meaningful to the user. Date changes and directory viewing are supported from within the menu system, which is designed to be loaded automatically through an Autoexec file.

MENU-MASTER is configured through a menu selection which defines an English language application name and a corresponding DOS path and program name combination. The configuration program features a context sensitive HELP Function, and the configuration page may be password protected to avoid unauthorized changes. The menu name itself is user-defined, as is the sub-function menu.

Usage: Hard Disk Management

System Requirements: 256K, any hard/fixed disk and a color or monochrome display

How to Start: After consulting the manual in file MENUMAST.DOC, start the program by entering MENU at the DOS prompt.

Suggested Donation: $29.00

File Descriptions:

MENU	BAT	The batch file to load MENU1.EXE
MENUSEG	HLP	Help file for the configuration process
MENUSET	EXE	Part of menu program
MENUSEG	USR	User's menu info file
MENUDIR	COM	A directory display program for use with MENU-MASTER
MENU1	EXE	The main MENU-MASTER program
README		Updates to the user's manual
MENUMAST	DOC	The MENU-MASTER Manual

650 Fansi-Console Version 2.00 (Disk 2 of 2)

V3.0

This is the second of the two disk set for Fansi-Console, a highly sophisticated memory-resident program which replaces the standard IBM PC console drivers, extends the ROM BIOS, processes ANSI X3.64 control sequences, provides keyboard macro capabilities, and much more.

NOTE: This is a two disk set, the FIRST part being Disk No 356.

Usage: Some Fansi programming of and from your keyboard!

System Requirements: 128K, two disk drives and a monochrome display

How to Start: There is an on-disk abbreviated user manual for FANSI-CONSOLE in the file FCONSOLE.DQC.

User Comments: "At last, a full ANSI device driver for the IBM-PC." "I have a lot of utility programs which do each function of this program. The virtue of this program is integration of all of them" "EXCELLENT, AGAIN! "I think this a great program. The best of its type that I've seen, but half the documentation is missing..." "Great program, but runs into other memory resident programs rather frequently. The screen writing speed is especially helpful." "This program is very interesting as it has shown me how differ drivers effect the operation of the computer."

Suggested Donation: Use license $25; $75 will get you the manual and the latest update.

File Descriptions:

-README-	NOW	Introductory text file
FCONSOLE	BQO	Squeezed advertisement for FANSI-CONSOLE
FCONSOLE	DQC	Squeezed documentation file for FANSI-CONSOLE

661 RESICALC Version 1.0

v1

RESICALC v.1.0 is a memory-resident calculator which can be "popped-up" whenever needed. The matrix functions supported in RESICALC are called by an "expressionfunc(x)" where x is a matrix expression. They include :

DIM returns the total number of components. ROWS returns the number of rows. COLS returns the number of columns. CSUM returns a row vector whose components are the sum of columns. RSUM returns a column vector whose components are the sum of rows. CAVG returns a row vector whose components are the averages of columns. RAVG returns a column vector whose components are the averages of rows. CSUM2 returns a row vector whose components are the sum of squares of columns. RSUM2 returns a column vector whose components are the sum of squares of rows.

Usage: Memory-resident higher math calculations

System Requirements: 128K, one disk drive and a monchrome display

How to Start: Check the README.DOC and MANUAL.DOC files for directions. To bring up RESICALC, press the ALT and F9 keys.

File Descriptions:

RESICALC	COM	Pop up calculator program
NAMELIST		Names of built-in functions of RESICALC.
ERRMSG		Run time error messages of RESICALC.
MANUAL	DOC	Short manual of RESICALC.
READ	ME	Quick start-up procedure for RESICALC.
FILES	DOC	Short description of files

687
IN-CONTROL
(Disk 1 of 3)
v1

The IN-CONTROL three-disk system (of which this is the first) is a very large and comprehensive business contacts tracking device. Using the power of compiled dBASE III code, five major business data sources (People Files — "Rolodex" — and Mailing Labels, Activities Files, Management Reports, Expense Reports and Appointments) are immensely enhanced. The primary example of this is the "layer-in" feature which allows you to "layer-in" lists of names from other sources, and still keep all reports and labels separate! This means that if you have 1,000 names in the electronic Rolodex and you purchase a list of prospects which has 10,000 names, you can enter them into the program and yet keep them separate from the original 1,000 when generating labels or reports.

Other major benefits include: 1) Complete on-line documentation: at every main level or menu, there is a HELP screen; 2) High speed data search capacity allows you retrieve names, activities, or messages by any word or words (including first or last name, phone number, city, or zip code) that you entered into the comments section Other search options; 3) Electronic Rolodex gives you detailed information on people: name, address, zip, city, comments, and 'referred by', including the ability to generate sorted lists from it; 4) Appointments: Ability to annotate appointments, expenses and keep a daily reminder — "tickler" — of all your appointments and commitments, as well as an on-line graphics display of appointments for any fourteen-day period.

This is Disk 1 which is the Help Disk containing the on-line documentation and data base and report form files; Disk 2 is the Program Disk; and Disk 3 contains the tutorial SALESDOC.

NOTE: ALL THREE DISKS ARE NECESSARY TO MAKE THE SYSTEM FUNCTION.

Usage: Comprehensive business tracking

System Requirements: 384K, two floppy drives, monochrome display DOES NOT REQUIRE DBASE III SOFTWARE TO RUN.

Features: System Specifications:

- Written in compiled DBASE III
- 1,000,000,000 records per file (person or activities)
- 99,999,999 categories or "layers" of data permitted

How to Start: The documentation and tutorial in file SALESDOC on Disk No 689 gives complete directions.

Suggested Donation: $49.00 registration; $50.00 for an additional service contract

File Descriptions:

*	DBF	Data base files (12 files)
*	DOC	On line help documentation (14 files)
LABEL1	I.BL	Label generation file
*	FRM	Report format generation files (9 files)

688
IN-CONTROL
(Disk 2 of 3)
v1

This is the second disk of the three-disk, comprehensive business contact tracking program called the IN-CONTROL system. It contains the main program files. Disk 1 is the the Help disk and contains the on-line documentation and Data base and report form files; and Disk 3 contains the tutorial SALESDOC.

NOTE: ALL THREE DISKS ARE NECESSARY TO MAKE THE SYSTEM FUNCTION.

Usage: Comprehensive business tracking

System Requirements: 384K, two floppy drives, monochrome display; DOES NOT REQUIRE DBASE III SOFTWARE TO RUN.

How to Start: The documentation and tutorial in file SALESDOC on Disk No 689 gives complete directions.

Suggested Donation: $49.00 registration; $50.00 for an additional service contract

File Descriptions:

ACS-PERS	EXE	Main executable file
ACS1OV	OVL	Overlay file
EPSON	MEM	Printer file
EPSON16A	MEM	"
LIST	COM	Help examination file
FLIP	COM	Key pad control file
MEMORY	COM	Memory varification file

689
IN-CONTROL
(Disk 3 of 3)
v1

This is the third disk of the three-disk, comprehensive business contact tracking program called the IN-CONTROL system. This disk contains the installation guide and tutorial/reference manual in the files INSTALL.DOC and SALESDOC, respectively.

NOTE: ALL THREE DISKS ARE NECESSARY TO MAKE THE SYSTEM FUNCTION.

Usage: Comprehensive business tracking

System Requirements: 384K, two floppy drives, monochrome display; DOES NOT REQUIRE DBASE III SOFTWARE TO RUN.

How to Start: The documentation and tutorial in file SALESDOC on Disk No 689 gives complete directions.

Suggested Donation: $49.00 registration; $50.00 for an additional service contract

File Descriptions:

INSTALL	DOC	Installation documentation

EDUCATION:

Like most good educational experiences, this category is a wide and wild collection of elemental to esoteric programs. Beginning with the basics (for BASIC see Computer Education) of letter recognition and vocabulary building (kindergarten through junior and senior high), our collection of educational software includes many levels of programs for learning:

- Spelling and vocabulary
- Mathematics (simple addition to complex equations!)
- Science (biology to chemistry)
- Typing for typewriter and computer keyboards
- Foreign languages (French, Italian, Spanish, Hebrew, German...even English!)
- American history
- Morse code
- Synonyms and antonyms
- And more!

To support the educational process and educators, we have a number of programs for tracking students' grades and attendance, determining grade distribution and preparing printouts for those parent-teacher meetings.

18 IQBUILD
v1

IQBUILDER is a program that will give you a solid mental workout. It features drills on synonyms, antonyms, and analogies. The games included range from simple (FRANKenstein, a variant of Hangman, and TRUCKER) to difficult (NIM, an ancient African strategy game, and MASTERMIND, a tough code-breaking series).

Usage: Educational for all!

System Requirements: Monochrome or graphics display, 64K of memory and two disk drives.

How to Start: To run BASIC programs consult the directions in GETTING STARTED for your configuration.

User Comments: "My son highly recommends this one. Fun and challenging." "Generally good. Program could benefit from more precise age and ability classifications."

File Descriptions:

MENU	BAS	Menu to select programs for execution
READING	BAS	Improve your reading speed
MASTER	BAS	Mastermind — guess the code
MATH	BAS	Drill of simple math problems
FRANK	BAS	HANGMAN by another name
WORDS	BAS	Data for FRANK
NIM	BAS	Ancient game of skill and strategy
BACKGAM	BAS	BACKGAMMON
BLACK	BAS	BLACKJACK — 1 or 2 players
TRUCKER	BAS	Make your fortune in the trucking business
— — — —	— —	IQBUILD
IQBUILD	BAS	Sub-menu to run the IQ-Builder Series
NUMBERS	BAS	Data 1 for numbers section of IQ-Builder Series
NUM2	BAS	Data 2 for numbers section of IQ-Builder Series
NUM3	BAS	Data 3 for numbers section of IQ-Builder Series
ANALOG	BAS	Data 1 for analogy section of IQ-Builder Series
ANALOG2	BAS	Data 2 for analogy section of IQ-Builder Series
ANALOG3	BAS	Data 3 for analogy section of IQ-Builder Series
ANALOG4	BAS	Data 4 for analogy section of IQ-Builder Series
ANALOG5	BAS	Data 5 for analogy section of IQ-Builder Series
ANALOG6	BAS	Data 6 for analogy section of IQ-Builder Series
SYNONYM	BAS	Data 1 for synonym section of IQ-Builder Series
SYNONYM2	BAS	Data 2 for synonym section of IQ-Builder Series
ANTONYM	BAS	Data 1 for antonym section of IQ-Builder Series
ANTONYM2	BAS	Data 2 for antonym section of IQ-Builder Series

76
History Education
v1

This is MYPRO's computer-based American History course taught as a game format that uses a time travel format. It covers seven periods from precolonization to World War II. It is well-designed with documentation for adding periods and varying question difficulty.

Usage: Junior to senior high students.

System Requirements: Monochrome/graphics display, 64K of memory and two disk drives.

How to Start: To run BASIC programs consult the directions in GETTING STARTED for your configturation.

User Comments: "Great format! The grid used as a game board is a neat idea. The questions are challenging enough for adult interest." "A great idea for a program. With more development and a few more bells and whistles it could be very interesting."

File Descriptions:

AUTOEXEC	BAT	Batch file to automatically invoke program
CATALOG	ASC	Additional programs from Mypro
HISTORY	BAS	Educational history program
QUEST	BAS	Program to create new lessons
*	DAT	Lesson data files for use HISTORY.BAS

95
Math Tutor
v1

This elementary grade level tutorial supplies age-graded exercises and tests for a variable student body. MATH TUTOR also supplies the opportunity to re-design for special problems. If you are involved with young children, this is a fun and easy way to teach them math. Suitable for parent-child use.

Usage: Home mathematics tutoring for grades 1-6.

System Requirements: Monochrome or graphics display and 64K of memory; a color display and adaptor is optional.

How to Start: To run BASIC program consult the directions in GETTING STARTED for your configuration. Consult README for program information.

User Comments: "It is fine, enjoyed some by my 11 year old but I modified it for my kindergartner (to add numbers ranging 1-5) and she enjoys it more!" "A good math tutorial for grades 1-6. Reviews should indicate that grade 6 is the highest level supported." "Good math training aide for my 6th grader."

File Descriptions:

ANSI	SYS	Enhanced version of program offered with DOS 2.0 (larger key buffer)
TUTOR	BAS	Math tutor program
INSTR	BAS	Part of Math Tutor package
SETUP	BAS	Part of Math Tutor package
MATH	BAS	Part of Math Tutor package
GRD?		Data files for grade levels 1 through 6 (6 files)
SAV?		Data files for grade levels 1 through 6 (6 files)
TDATA		Data files for grade levels 1 through 6
MIS		Data files for grade levels 1 through 6
READ	ME	Instructions for using Math Tutor

153
Norland
Software Hangman
Version 4.1
v1.1

Computerized version of the age-old game of Hangman. The program picks the problems for you to solve from a collection of data files. The words and phrases that this program can draw upon will probably serve to keep you on the edge of your seat. And, since this program has a surprisingly large vocabulary, it's one game that you won't tire of soon. Highly recommended!

Usage: Entertainment.

System Requirements: 128K, one disk drive, monochome monitor, color graphics needed if file marked by a plus symbol (+).

How to Start: To read DOCUMENT or README files simply enter TYPE filename and press ENTER.

• To run program, type HANGMAN and press ENTER.

User Comments: "Nice variations, literate and more challenging versions are particularly good, good for slow times at the office." "Excellent Hangman. It is fascinating and educational. Can't say enough good things about this disk." "One of the better educational games; easy to run; outstanding graphics and amusing musical programs."

Suggested Donation: $20.00

File Descriptions:

HANGMAN	EXE	Nifty Hangman game — larger vocabulary than most versions
AUTOEXEC	BAT	Automatic start-up file if set up on bootable disk
README		Start-up instructions
DOCUMENT		Documentation file
HANGADV1	WRD	Part of HANGMAN.EXE — Quotations
HANGBAS1	WRD	Part of HANGMAN.EXE — Riddles
HANGCMT	REF	Part of HANGMAN.EXE
HANGED1	WRD	Part of HANGMAN.EXE — Vocabulary words
HANGMAN	REF	Part of HANGMAN.EXE
HANGMUSE	MSC	Part of HANGMAN.EXE — Music

168

Music and Educational Programs

v1

MUSIC/ED is a far-ranging collection of items. The miscellaneous music includes the chance to write your own! The educational pieces range widely, from ALGEBRA (a graphic function demo), to both SPELL and SPELLING BEE (to teach spelling skills), to BABYMATH (a visual display of a selected number of objects. Other fun and educational programs are here too. Have fun, and teach your children well.

Usage: General (elementary through junior high) education.

System Requirements: Color graphics and display, 128K of memory and two disk drives.

How to Start: To run BASIC program consult the directions in GETTING STARTED for your configuration. Consult CLASROOM.DOC for program documentation.

User Comments: "The songs are entertaining, especially "Coffee", but my favorite is "BACH2" because you can play around with it and make tunes." "Euchre and the Funnels game had lots of documentation, but rest did not." "I wish most of the songs were compiled into a menu for easy loading." "My daughter is a music student and loves to use this diskette." "I especially like BABYMATH and TELLTIME. Great for my little girl and yet simple enough to teach her something."

File Descriptions:

ALGEBRA	BAS	Displays several algebra functions in 3-d (Color required)
BABYMATH	EXE	Select a number, displays same number of dots (Color required)
BACH	BAS	J. S. Bach Prelude 1 in C Major
BACH2	BAS	Compose your own music (Bach to BASIC Version 1.2)
BIBLE	BAS	The Bible Song
CHEMQUES	BAS	Chemistry test aid
CHEMTEST	BAS	Chemistry test aid
CLASROLL	BAS	Update, print class roll, attendance, labels
CLASROLL	DOC	Documentation
COFFEE	BAS	Percolating coffee (Color required)
GODFATHR	BAS	Theme from "The Godfather"
JESUSLOV	BAS	Jesus Loves Me
MINUET	BAS	Bach Minuet in D Minor
MINUET2	BAS	Bach Minuet
PIANO1	BAS	Play the piano from your keyboard (Color required)
PIANO2	BAS	Same as above, except it guides you through sample songs
SPELL	BAS	Spelling bee
SPELL?	DAT	Data files for SPELLBEE.BAS (4 files)
SPELLBEE	BAS	Another spelling bee program
SPELLDAT	BAS	Part of SPELLBEE.BAS
STORY	BAS	Supply the words to complete the story
TELLTIME	BAS	Good way to teach youngster to tell time (Color required)

ATC1	BLD	Part of ACT
ATC2	BLD	Part of ACT
AUTOEXEC	BAT	Part of ACT
ATC	DAT	Part of ACT
EUCHRE	BAS	"Squished" version of EUCHRE
EUCHRE	DOC	Rules for the card game EUCHRE
EUCHRE	SRC	Source code for EUCHRE including comments
EUCHRE	INS	Instructions for computer EUCHRE

229
Funnels & Buckets
v1

The major program on this disk is FUNNELS, an educational game which teaches math in a fun way. It's a fun way to get young ones interested in math and can be a very effective tool. They'll be too busy having fun to notice that they are learning something. The other programs are an air-traffic control game, which is challenging almost beyond human comprehension, and a good version of the old Euchre card game.

Usage: Entertainment.

System Requirements: 128K, one disk drive, monochome monitor, color graphics needed if file marked by a plus symbol (+).

How to Start: Type FUNNELS or ATC and press ENTER to start either game. To read DOC files, enter TYPE filename.ext and press ENTER. For instructions on running BASIC programs, please refer to the GETTING STARTED section in this catalog.

User Comments: "ATC: Try to handle an airport by being an air traffic controller. You must monitor planes taking off & planes landing. You can handle as many as 20 or so planes. You win if you can handle all of them without crashing. Quite challenging." "Very sophisticated and difficult to learn." "(EUCHRE) A thinking game which does not become boring and is very entertaining; have had problems running on my compatible computer, though" "If you enjoy playing bridge, you'll enjoy playing Euchre, although this is somewhat easier. Personally, I found it a ball, and you can even play it with 3 other players." "(FUNNELS) "good teaching program, and it is fun too; My 11 year old loves his math now!" " Good math game. Electronic flashcards in a game."

Suggested Donation: $10.00

File Descriptions:

FUNNELS	EXE	A user-supported Funnels & Buckets game
FUNNELS	DOC	Funnels documentation (15K)
FUNNELS	INV	Invoice for author contribution
ATC	EXE	Air Traffic Control game (US)

241
PCjr Educational Games
v1

This is an excellent collection of games for kids of ages 6 through 60. There are things to tease and tantalize the intellect and some that are just plain fun. For those wiith a PCjr, this disk really works to exploit the strengths of the computer, sound and graphics.

Usage: Education and fun.

System Requirements: PCJr with monochrome graphics display, 64K and two disk drives.

How to Start: To run BASIC programs consult the directions in GETTING STARTED for your configuration. Consult README.DOC for program information.

User Comments: "This disk is superior. The students in my class enjoyed working with it." "Some of the games, notably word match, hangman, mazes, and bowling, are good for kids. Maxit is fun for all ages. Main menu is too slow. Unfortunately, some of the programs had bugs or were incompatible with my system." "Excellent disk for grade schoolers! It is the family's favorite."

File Descriptions:

0	BAS	End program and goodbye screen
1	BAS	Spelling bee
2	BAS	Alphabetize a word list
3	BAS	Fun arcade type bowling game
4	BAS	A graphics display program
5	BAS	Maxit, a strategy numbers game
6	BAS	Othello, an old standby
7	BAS	Word problems game
8	BAS	Find-a-word puzzle (Requires printer)
9	BAS	Creates a unique maze each time (Requires printer)
10	BAS	Finds your age in days

11	BAS	Word matching game, similar to concentration
12	BAS	Black and white version of word matching game
13	BAS	Hangman, an old favorite
14	BAS	Word scramble number 1
15	BAS	Word scramble (1)
16	BAS	Screen machine, a draw program (Requires color graphics)
17	BAS	Mazes number 2
20	BAS	Program descriptions — called from menu
ACS	PIC	Picture file — used by ?
AUTOEXEC	BAT	A batch file that helps create a working disk
BRIEFLY	BAS	Part of titles used by TITLE.BAS
GRADE-?	LST	Wordlist for grade 1 through 5 (5 files)
MENU	BAS	Menu that allows selection and calls up the games
README	DOC	Documentation by authors
TITLE	BAS	Title page and pointer to other documentation
TITLE2	BAS	Additional titles

249
Equator/ PC-TOUCH Educational Programs
v1.2

Among the excellent educational programs on this disk, the star is EQUATOR, a user-supported educational system for teaching math, science, and finance. that uses a novel non-drill exploratory approach. It consists of 35 equations divided equally among the three subjects. Each equation appears on its own screen or worksheet. EQUATOR is designed to allow you to experiment with each equation as much as you like. The more you work with an equation, the easier it will be for you to understand it, remember it, and use it at home or at school.

The following equations are in the Math Menu of the EQUATOR:

1. Area of a square of rectangle. 2. Area of a circle. 3. Area of a triangle. 4. Hypotenuse of a right triangle. 5. Circumference of a circle. 6. Volume of a cylinder. 7. Surface area of a cylinder. 8. Volume of a cone. 9. Surface area of a cone. 10. Surface area of a sphere. 11. Volume of a sphere. 12. Distance between two points.

The following equations are in the Finance Menu of the EQUATOR:

1. Simple interest. 2. Compound interest. 3. Years to double investment. 4. Return needed to keep up with inflation. 5. Equivalent taxable return of a non-taxed investment. 6. Monthly mortgage payments. 7. Annual simple interest rate on loans. 8. Payoff balance on a loan. 9. Gross profit margin. 10. Net profit margin. 11. Earnings per share. 12. Price / Earnings ratio.

The following equations are in the Science Menu of the EQUATOR:

1. Celsius to Farhrenheit. 2. Farhrenheit to Celsius. 3. Density Ratio. 4. Average velocity. 5. Metric to English. 6. English to Metric. 7. Acceleration. 8. Force. 9. Work. 10. Power. 11. Pressure.

PC-TOUCH is a typing tutor which lets you go at your own pace and keeps track of how well you are doing. UTMP is a math drill program.

Usage: Education and skills development

System Requirements: 64K, one disk drive and a monochrome display.

How to Start: Load DOS and type PC-TOUCH or EQUATOR to enter the main programs. Consult the .DOC and .TXT files for program documentation.

User Comments: "EQUATOR should be a good tool for 7th to 12th grade students. Math drill is more a game of chance than a learning program." "The math lesson are suitable for middle and high school students. Area to Improve: the latter provides only the formula and answer to questions but does not accept student answer and then compare with the correct answer." "PC-TOUCH is very helpful in increasing anybody's typing speed and accuracy. Even if you are a pro at typing, you can still get something out of this program (things like words per minute, accuracy, & the ability to copy letter perfect."

Suggested Donation: EQUATOR $20.00

File Descriptions:

— — —	— —	EQUATOR 1.2 (u-s)
EQ	EXE	Main program — start by typing "EQ"
SCIENCE	EXE	Science lessons
MATH	EXE	Math lessons
PRT	BAT	To print documentation type: "PRT"
EQUATOR	TXT	Documentation (20K)
FINANCE	EXE	Finance lessons
— — —	— —	PC-TOUCH Touch typing tutor
PC-TOUCH	BAS	Source code for PC-TOUCH.EXE
PC-TOUCH	FIL	Part of PC-TOUCH
PC-TOUCH	EXE	Compiled version — type "PC-TOUCH" to start
PC-TOUCH	DOC	Documentation (4K)
— — —	— —	
UTMP	BAS	Math drill program

266 NAEPIRS
v1

This disk contains data from the National Assessment of Educational Progress Information Retrieval System (NAEPIRS) and programs to access the data. It is produced by the National Institute of Education. It has been designed so that users can ask for findings according to subject or age group; look for trends or attitudes; or compare findings between groups such as rural and urban students, males and females, students of different races, etc. Example of findings: About 10 percent of the surveyed students at each age do not read in their spare time.

Usage: Educators and students of education

System Requirements: 128K, two disk drives and monochrome display

How to Start: Load DOS and type NAEPIRS and press ENTER.

User Comments: "I got this for my wife, a soon to be school teacher. We were both very impressed with the program's operation." "Very interesting and useful to have if you're a teacher or an education student, otherwise not worth too much." "great database information source."

File Descriptions:

SETUP	BAT	Batch file to set up working disk
AUTOEXEC	BAT	Auto start file
SPOOL	EXE	Spooler, so you don't have to wait for your printer
NAEPIRS	EXE	Main program, type "NAEPIRS" to start
JSUM	BIN	Part of NAEPIRS system
JINT	BIN	Part of NAEPIRS system
REFYR	BIN	Part of NAEPIRS system
DBFIND	DAT	NAEPIRS data file
@??	OVL	Overlay files

320 Touchtype
v1

Here are two programs designed for gaining skill and getting skillful on the keyboard. The first is FASTYPE, a typing tutorial system to learn the IBM PC keyboard, and TYPERITE a program that turns your PC and it's printer into an electric typewriter. These programs can serve to improve the usefulness of your computer by increasing your capabilities with it. Both programs are simple to use.

Usage: Keyboarding skills.

System Requirements: Color graphics card and display, 128K of memory and two disk drives. NOTE: This program is not Hercules-compatible.

How to Start: Consult READ.ME and FASTYPE.DOC to read the program documentation. Type FASTYPE or TYPERITE and press ENTER to start either program.

User Comments: "(FASTYPE) Good beginning typing tutor. Colorful screens, clear menus, large variety of typing drills. Slow access to online help — it's easier to print these screens out and a program is included to make this easy. Only complaint; program is slow to load." "TYPERITE does the job that I had hoped it would. For something short and quick I think it is better than the word processor I have."

Suggested Donation: $20.00

File Descriptions:

————	——	FASTTYPE
README		Introduction for FASTYPE
PRTHELP	BAS	Prints all help screens for FASTYPE
AUTOEXEC	BAT	Self-booting batch file for FASTYPE
FASTYPE	BAT	Batch file to begin FASTYPE
PRINTDOC	BAT	Prints documentation file for FASTYPE
FASTYPE	DOC	Complete documentation for FASTYPE
FASTYPE	EXE	Main tutorial program
????		A large number of drill files for FASTYPE
————	——	TYPERITE
READ	ME	Intoduction to TYPERITE
TYPERITE	EXE	Turns your computer into an electric typewriter

359 Moonbeam
v1

For the would be astronomer or romantic this program may be for you. This program determines the phase, position, and illumination of the moon. To plot the star data graphics is required. It is not only educational, but can be just plain fun to play around with!

Usage: Astronomy education and enjoyment.

System Requirements: 128K, a color graphics card and display and one disk drive. The plotting routines will not work if STAR.REC is not present in the default drive.

How to Start: Load DOS and type MOONBEAM to enter the main program.

User Comments: "I love this program! Its fascinating to see the night sky on July 4, 1776...great for showing off the computer!" "Interesting prgram with best star database I have seen."

Suggested Donation: $5.00

File Descriptions:
READ	ME	Documentation on moonbeam program
MOONBEAM	COM	Main program for moonbeam system
STAR	REC	Star data file used by moonbeam to plot stars
MOONBEAM	V1	Source code for MOONBEAM

367 Flash Cards: Vocabulary & Spelling (Disk 1 of 4)
v1

This is the first of the 4-disk set of the Educational Package: Flash Cards with 7,500-Word Vocabulary Builder and Spelling Teacher. This disk contains the compiled form of the main program, the vocabulary file for the first part of the alphabet (a-de), and two files of flags to indicate words missed. An excellent tool to improve vocabulary and/or spelling at the high school, college, or higher level, it does not include the 4,000 most basic words but, rather, the 7,500 next most commonly-used words.

THIS FOUR DISK SET REQUIRES ALL FOUR DISKS TO FUNCTION PROPERLY.

Usage: Vocabulary and spelling improvement (Junior High and up)

System Requirements: 128K, one floppy drive and monochrome display.

How to Start: Load DOS and type FLASH to enter the main program. To use BASIC programs consult the directions in GETTING STARTED for your configuration. Consult MASTER.TXT on Disk 369 for program documentation.

User Comments: "Words:good for the kids." "This program was excellent for adult use, however, when I ordered it the write up suggested that this whole series (367-370) was a childrens education program, when in fact it was for teens or adults."

File Descriptions:
CARDS		Vocabulary words and definitions (a-de)
FLASH	EXE	Main Flash Cards program, compiled
FLAG		Flags for missed vocabulary words
SFLAG		Flags for missed spelling words

368 Flash Cards: Vocabulary & Spelling (Disk 2 of 4)
v1

This is the second of the 4-disk set of the Educational Package: Flash Cards with 7,500-Word Vocabulary Builder and Spelling Teacher. This disk contains the vocabulary file for the second part of the alphabet (de-in), the source code, in BASIC, for the main Flash Card program, the same source code as documentation giving excellent overall and line-by-line comments, and the two files of flags to indicate words missed.

THIS FOUR DISK SET REQUIRES ALL FOUR DISKS TO FUNCTION PROPERLY.

Usage: Vocabulary and spelling improvement
(Junior High and up)

File Descriptions:

CARDS		Vocabulary words and definitions (de-in)
FLASH	BAS	Main Flash Cards program, in BASIC
REMARKS	BAS	FLASH.BAS comments for documentation
SFLAG		Flags for missed spelling words
FLAG		Flags for missed vocabulary words

369 Flash Cards: Vocabulary & Spelling (Disk 3 of 4)
v1

This is the third of the 4-disk set of the Educational Package: Flash Cards with 7,500-Word Vocabulary Builder and Spelling Teacher. This disk contains the vocabulary file for the third part of the alphabet (in-pr), the two files of flags to indicate words missed, the documentation for the FLASH CARDS program, and the routine to print this documentation. In addition, this disk contains 27 files used by the database program should you desire to change the vocabulary file entries or create new ones.

THIS FOUR DISK SET REQUIRES ALL FOUR DISKS TO FUNCTION PROPERLY.

Usage: Vocabulary and spelling improvement
(Junior High and up)

System Requirements: See Disk 367

How to Start: Print the documentation by typing COPY MASTER.TXT PRN and press ENTER.

• To start the program type EQ and press ENTER; the program will prompt you to put the disk you want to work on — this is a four disk set — in the default drive.

File Descriptions:

CARDS		Vocabulary words and definitions (in-pr)
FLAG		Flags for missed vocabulary words
SFLAG		Flags for missed spelling words
MASTER	TXT	Documentation (manual) for Flash Cards (12 pp)
PRINTMAN	BAS	Program to print manual, in BASIC
????????		A bunch of data files used while changing vocabulary

370 Flash Cards: Vocabulary & Spelling (Disk 4 of 4)
v1

This is the fourth of the 4-disk set of the Educational Package: Flash Cards with 7,500-Word Vocabulary Builder and Spelling Teacher. This disk contains the vocabulary file for the last part of the alphabet (pr-z), the two files of flags to indicate words missed, and the database program, in BASIC, to enable you to make changes to the vocabulary words and/or definitions.

NOTE that the MAIN.BAS program does NOT work if you try to use the cursor control keys during data entry. To avoid problems, if you make an error, simply enter this incorrect entry into the file, then specify that you wish to make a change to this same entry and enter the correct data.

THIS FOUR DISK SET REQUIRES ALL FOUR DISKS TO FUNCTION PROPERLY.

Usage: Vocabulary and spelling improvement
(Junior High and up)

File Descriptions:

CARDS		Vocabulary words and definitions (pr-z)
FLAG		Flags for missed vocabulary words
SFLAG		Flags for missed spelling words
MAIN	BAS	Database program to change vocabulary files

394 Math Pak
v1

MATH PAK is a series of BASICA programs that teaches and helps to accelerate some math operations and helps the user to understand the importance of mathematics. It serves as a tutorial that covers basics to advanced math.

Usage: Basic to advanced mathematics practice

System Requirements: 128K, one disk drive and monochrome display

Features: MATHPAK covers basics to advanced math:

- Addition
- Subtraction
- Multiplication
- Division
- Hexidecimal and octal from decimal conversions
- Binary to decimal conversions
- Quadratic formula root solving(given $ax^2 + bx + c = 0$)
- Area of a circle calculations
- Area of a triangle calculations
- Metric to U.S. conversions
- U.S. to metric conversions
- Polar to rectangular and rectangular to polar conversions
- Finding points on an x-y coordinate system given $ay + b = mx + d$
- Finding the equation and slope of a line given two points
- Logarithmic functions(base 10 or base a)
- Second order determinant solving(x,y)
- Third order determinant solving(x,y,z)
- Trig functions and tables
- Plus other functions including an on-disk tutorial section

How to Start: To run BASIC programs consult the directions in GETTING STARTED for your configuration. Check the READ.ME and TEXT.DOC files for documentation.

User Comments: "Good as an educational backup tool for math, but not much else." "Thought the program was OK for myself but a little hard for my kids..if it had some colorful programs and or graphics it would be better." "I wanted something for high school level."

File Descriptions:

A	BAS	Main tutorial section
A1	BAS	Addition tutorial
B1	BAS	Hex/Octal conversion tutorial
C1	BAS	Trig. functions tutorial
COMPLEX	BAS	Complex functions section
D	BAS	Division tutorial
DETER	BAS	Determinant/line equations section
E	BAS	Area calculation tutorial
FLOW	BAS	Flow section of MATH PAK
FORM	BAS	Formula/conversion sheet/section
GAME	BAS	Game section
L	BAS	Binary to decimal conversion tutorial
M	BAS	Multiplication tutorial
MP	BAS	Graphics(box) display

MPK	BAS	MATH PAK main program
P	BAS	Printer use tutorial
Q	BAS	Quadratic formula tutorial
READ	ME	Instructions for the use of MATH PAK
S	BAS	Subtraction tutorial
START	BAS	Starting screen (use with letter; e.g., LOAD "START",R)
TEXT	DOC	Explanation of purpose of programs
Z	BAS	Metric conversions tutorial

407
VideoChem
EDUCATIONAL GAME
v1

VideoChem is an educational game designed to teach secondary school students about chemical valences, atomic bonding and structure. While limited in depth, VideoChem offers a fun introduction to an otherwise complex and difficult subject. Teachers may like to use this program for independent instruction. The game needs no special instructions to be played.

Usage: Chemistry instruction

System Requirements: 128K, one disk drive and monochrome display.

How to Start: Load DOS and type VCHEM to enter the main program. Consult VCHEM.DOC for program documentation.

User Comments: "A student printout would be nice. This would give the teacher an idea as to how the student did in 'hardcopy'. Otherwise, a good program dealing with the specific topic of a atomic structure and bonding. I will use it in my eigth grade physical science class." "This program gives a reasonable though limited overview of the chemical valence process. The graphics are great but I would like to see more elements and more exercises."

File Descriptions:

B1	DAT	Data file used by program
B2	DAT	Data file used by program
B3	DAT	Data file used by program
B4	DAT	Data file used by program
B5	DAT	Data file used by program
B6	DAT	Data file used by program
B7	DAT	Data file used by program
B8	DAT	Data file used by program
CART	DAT	Data file used by program

CEREAL	B	Picture file used by program
DATA		Data file used by program
DATA2		Data file used by program
DRUGS	B	Picture file used by program
LAB	EXE	A program file
LF-100%	DAT	Data file used by program
LOGO	EXE	Start with this program
RT-100%	DAT	Data file used by program
SLAB	EXE	A program file
SPACE	DAT	Data file used by program
TABLE	B	Picture file used by program
THIM2	B	Picture file used by program
VCHEM	DOC	Text file of instructions
VCHEM	EXE	A program file
VIDEO1	DAT	Data file used by program
WIZ	B	Picture file used by program

436 Ham Radio #1
v1

There are three different Morse code programs on this diskette to help the user learn and practice and review data. Other routines help the amateur radio operator compute various electronic formulas, design antennas, find satellites, and calculate satellite orbits. RTTY and TTY are two different communication programs using BAUDOT or ASCII or Morse code at varying speeds. RDSSTV2 is a fascinating program that takes audio (speaker output) and converts tones to a picture format; the user with a shortwave receiver can receive, view and print pictures from the ham operators (4 are here on the diskette for you to see).

Usage: Education in electronic and electric communications

System Requirements: 128K, two disk drives and monochrome display; RDSSTV2 requires a color graphics display

How to Start: To run BASIC program consult the directions for GETTING STARTED for your configuration.

User Comments: "(MORSE1)Helpful and easy to run. Once the code speed is set , changing can be done in only one word per minute increments." "The SSTV part is very intriguing. So is the RTTY program." "A nice collection for the Ham. Thank you for a fine disk." "I liked the computer interface for ham radio. Should work out OK for RTTY, etc. Other calc. programs may be simplified too much."

Suggested Donation: RTTY $5.00

File Descriptions:

ASCTTY	BAS	Transmits & receives 110 baud ASCII for TTY22.BAS
BAUDOTC	EXE	Demo of communication program
CQ	BDT	CQ message for TTY22.BAS
CWID	BDT	CW identification for TTY22.BAS
CWRCV	BAS	Copy EIA RS232C Morse code to screen
CWRCV	HLP	Description of CWRCV.BAS
FINDSAT	BAS	Azimuth & elevation to a synchronous satellite
HAMCALC	BAS	Computes miscellaneous electronic formulas
HAMHELP	BAS	Computations to aid in ham radio operations
HAMMODEM	BAS	Modem demonstration (ham radio or phone line)
LISTCOUN	TXT	Alphabetical list of counties in each state
SATFIND2	BAS	Locates TV satellites for given cities or locations
MORSE1	BAS	Morse code practice program, variable speed
MORSE2	BAS	Morse code generator, variable speed
OSCAR	BAS	Calculates satellite orbits
PARABOLA	BAS	Design of parabolic antenna reflector
EZCODE1	BAS	Learn & practice Morse code for amateur radio license
RTTY	DOC	Description of RS-232C interface
RTTYSUBS	BDT	RTTY unit
RTTYTALK	BAS	Transmit/receive, AEA CP-1 interface (like PC TALK-III)
RYT	BDT	RY message for TTY22.BAS
TTY	BAT	Gets date and time
TTY	DOC	Description of TTY22.BAS & updates
TTY22	BAS	TTY transmit and receive program
VHF-YAGI	BAS	Calculates dimensions of VHF Yagi antenna
OPTICS	PAS	Pascal; compute parameters of a reflecting telescope
RDSSTV2	EXE	Display Ham SSTV pictures on color monitor or print on graphics printer
RDSSTV2	DOC	Documentation for RDSSTV2.EXE
JUDY	PIC	Data for RDSSTV2.EXE
EYE	PIC	Data for RDSSTV2.EXE
OLDMAN	PIC	Data for RDSSTV2.EXE

437 Ham Radio #2
v1

The USAT program provides real time tracking of the OSCAR 9, 10, & 11 and the RS 5, 7, & 8 satellites; the user specifies the date, time, length of time, and tracking interval. Several programs calculate coil inductance, coil properties, signals for varying frequencies, resistance and reactance. NETWORK provides analysis of user-specified circuits, to aid the amateur radio or electronic user. The great circle distance between any two points is computed by GRCIRDIS when the latitudes and longitudes are entered. An alphabetized list of all of the counties in each state can be found in the COUNTIES files.

Usage: Ham radio operators and enthusiasts

System Requirements: 64K, one disk drive and monochrome display.

How to Start: To run BASIC programs consult the directions in GETTING STARTED for your configuration. Check the .DOC files for program documentation.

User Comments: "(NETWORK)A decent program for what it does. Quick analysis of fairly simple circuits is useful. Good for checking homebrew circuits." "Again needs documentation to run, no help files!!" "A very good collection of programs for the radio amateur. Would also like to have seen a program that graphically shows various lengths for different antenna types." "Another must for ham radio operators."

File Descriptions:

ELEMENTS	DAT	Data for USAT.BAS
GROUND	DAT	"
MAP	DAT	"
USAT	EXE	Real time tracking of OSCAR and RS satellites (XEQ form)
COILINDU	BAS	Coil length & no. of turns for user-specified inductance
DIPOLE	BAS	Loading coil inductance for loaded dipole antenna
INTERMOD	BAS	Signal, 3rd and 5th order product for >= 3 frequencies
SMITH	BAS	Resistance & reactance along transmission line,rho,vswr
SMITH	DOC	Description of SMITH.BAS
NETWORK1	LBR	NETWORK, below, in library form
NETWORK	DOC	Description of NETWORK
NETWORK	BAS	AC Electronic circuit analysis
NETWORK	EXE	" (XEQ form)
SAMPLE1	NET	Sample data for NETWORK.BAS
SAMPLE2	NET	"
SAMPLE3	NET	"
EDNTEST	NET	"
GRCIRDIS	BAS	Great circle distance between any two locations
COUNTIES	AK	Alphabetical list of counties in Alaska
COUNTIES	AL	" Alabama
COUNTIES	AR	" Arkansas
COUNTIES	AZ	" Arizona
COUNTIES	CA	" California
COUNTIES	CO	" Colorado
COUNTIES	CT	" Connecticut
COUNTIES	DE	" Delaware
COUNTIES	FL	" Florida
COUNTIES	GA	" Georgia
COUNTIES	HI	" Hawaii
COUNTIES	IA	" Iowa
COUNTIES	ID	" Idaho
COUNTIES	IL	" Illinois
COUNTIES	IN	" Indiana
COUNTIES	KS	" Kansas
COUNTIES	KY	" Kentucky
COUNTIES	LA	" Louisiana
COUNTIES	MA	" Massachusetts
COUNTIES	MD	" Maryland
COUNTIES	ME	" Maine
COUNTIES	MI	" Michigan
COUNTIES	MN	" Minnesota
COUNTIES	MO	" Missouri
COUNTIES	MS	" Mississippi
COUNTIES	MT	" Montana
COUNTIES	NC	" North Carolina
COUNTIES	ND	" North Dakota
COUNTIES	NE	" Nebraska
COUNTIES	NH	" New Hampshire
COUNTIES	NJ	" New Jersey
COUNTIES	NM	" New Mexico
COUNTIES	NV	" Nevada
COUNTIES	NY	" New York
COUNTIES	OH	" Ohio
COUNTIES	OK	" Oklahoma
COUNTIES	OR	" Oregon
COUNTIES	PA	" Pennsylvania
COUNTIES	RI	" Rhode Island
COUNTIES	SC	" South Carolina
COUNTIES	SD	" South Dakota
COUNTIES	TN	" Tennessee
COUNTIES	TX	" Texas
COUNTIES	UT	" Utah
COUNTIES	VA	" Virginia
COUNTIES	VT	" Vermont
COUNTIES	WA	" Washington
COUNTIES	WI	" Wisconsin
COUNTIES	WV	" West Virginia
COUNTIES	WY	" Wyoming

443

T-Score/ Education

v1.1

These are programs designed to grade your scores and score your grades! T-SCORE contains programs for asigning equitable grades to up to 60 students, based on 16 scores. PC GRADEBOOK is a program to maintain and display sorted lists of up to 12 classes with 35 students per class and 45 grades per student. Printouts and grades may be displayed by student or class as well as by assignment, grade to date or cumulative. PC Gradebook runs under the MicroSoft BASIC interpreter; the source code is GRADES.BAS and generates a report card which REPORTS.BAS prints. A FLASHcard spelling, MATH facts and TYPE(ing) tutor fill out this very educational disk.

Usage: Home education and teacher aids.

System Requirements: 128K, one disk drive and monochrome display. T-SCORE requires an 8087 math co-processor (source code is provided)

How to Start: To run BASIC programs consult the directions in GETTING STARTED for your configuration. Consult the .DOC files for program documentation.

User Comments: "Statistical package should accompany student and test prinout...for each test or paper." "Every teacher should have this disk." "Some real good stuff."

Suggested Donation: PC-GRADEBOOK $25.00

File Descriptions:

————	——	T-Scores Grading System (REQUIRES AN 8087 MATH COPROCESSOR!!)
TSCORE	DOC	Brief description file for T-Score (4K)
TSCORE	EXE	Calculate T-scores, to assign equitable grades.
TSCORE	S3I	SFtran source text for TSCORE.
TSCORE	S3L	Pretty 4 page listing, from SFtran processor.
TSCORE	FOR	Fortran source text, output from SFtran processor.
TSCORE	DAT	Sample data for input to TSCORE.
TSCORE	LIS	Output corresponding to TSCORE.DAT.
————	——	PC Gradebook
GRADES	BAS	ASCII BASICA program for main routine
NOTICE	BAS	ASCII BASICA plea for money
REPORTS	BAS	ASCII BASICA routine to produce printed reports
README	TXT	Introductory message and notes on operation (3K)
————	——	Flashcards
FLASH	BAS	A spelling program
FLASH	BAT	Batch file to load FLASH.BAS in DOS
FLASH	DOC	Documentation for FLASH.BAS (short)
————	——	HSO — High Score Organizer
HSO	BAS	High Score Organizer — a database for game scores
HSO	BAT	Batch file to start program from DOS
HSO-HELP	DOC	Documentation for HSO.BAS
————	——	ore Education Programs
MATH	BAS	A math program that will help you learn your math facts
MATH	DOC	Documentation for math.bas
MENU	BAS	Menu for this set of programs
TYPE	BAS	Program to improve your typing skills
TYPE	DOC	Documentation for TYPE.BAS
KILL	BAS	Utility to save you time in BASIC
KILL2	BAS	Updated version of KILL.BAS
KILL	DOC	Documentation for KILL.BAS and KILL2.BAS

506 BIBLIOGRAPHY OF BUSINESS ETHICS AND MORAL VALUES

V1

This BIBLIOGRAPHY OF BUSINESS ETHICS AND BUSINESS MORAL VALUES (third edition) contains a list of periodical references, texts, books, syllabi collections, and audiovisual materials compiled by Dr. Kenneth Bond of Creighton University. To give you an idea of how comprehensive it is, if a complete copy of this bibliography is loaded into WORDSTAR and printed, the document would be 142 pages in length. Some subjects: energy, environmental issues (strip mining, toxic chemicals and water pollution), worker issues (discrimination, sexual harassment, whistleblowing, etc.), privacy, distribution of wealth, third world issues. AN INCREDIBLE RESOUCE!

Usage: Researchers and students

System Requirements: 128K, one disk drive and monochrome display.

How to Start: Access directly with your wordprocessor or print/display using DOS commands COPY or TYPE.

File Descriptions:

README		Documentation for diskette (6K)
INTRO	ASC	Introduction to the Bibliography (12K)
JOURNAL	A-E	Text file containing journal articles (66K)
JOURNAL	F-M	Text file containing journal articles (78K)
JOURNAL	N-Z	Text file containing journal articles (67K)
BOOKS	ASC	List of books used (34K)
AV	ASC	AudioVisual Materials & Concordance (68K)

542
Polyglot & Letterfall
v1

POLYGLOT is a program that matches between two sets of data such as words and sentences, terms and definitions, questions and anwers. It takes the user's answers and displays the percentage of correct answers up to and including the most recent answer. It is an incredible educational tool for drill type studying. LETTERFALL is a tutorial game to teach you how to type using the touch method. It is set-up in a game enviroment and is very easy to use. There are seventeen different parts to this program, but the author has supplied only one part for you to look at. We don't normally include demos such as this but the program is outstanding.

Usage: Self instruction and drills

System Requirements: 128K, two disk drives and a monochrome display

How to Start: Type POLYGLOT or LETTERFA and press ENTER to start these programs.

Suggested Donation: $15.00

File Descriptions:

————	——	Polyglot
FACTS	DIC	A Polyglot dictionary file concerning Polyglot
FILLIN	DIC	A Polyglot dictionary file containing fill-in-theblanks.
INVST01	DIC	A Polyglot dictionary file for investment terms.
NETWORK	DIC	A Polyglot dictionary for computer networking
POLY001	DIC	A Polyglot dictionary for vocabulary set one.
POLY002	DIC	A Polyglot dictionary for vocabulary set two.
POLY003	DIC	A Polyglot dictionary for vocabulary set three.
POLY004	DIC	A Polyglot dictionary for vocabulary set four.
POLY005	DIC	A Polyglot dictionary for vocabulary set five.
POLYGLOT	DIR	Definiation file for Polyglot
POLYGLOT	EXE	Main program
————	——	Letterfall (V1.1)
LETTERFA	EXE	Executable program
SCORE	DTA	Data file to retain scores

612
Languages
v1

LANGUAGE TEACHER is a series of menu-driven language tutorial programs for vocabulary, verb conjugations and standard phrases in French, Spanish, German, Italian, and Hebrew. Most of the files on this disk are archived. The unarchiving file is included on this disk. The HEBREW is a separate program for language skills development.

SPANISH I: 750 Spanish/English word combinations, 1488 verb conjugations and 150 Spanish/English phrase combinations. SPANISH II: 800 Spanish/English word combinations and 2108 verb conjugation forms. FRENCH I: 784 French/English word combinations, 1600 verb conjugations and 196 French/English phrase combinations. FRENCH II: 864 French/English word combinations and 1600 verb conjugation forms. GERMAN I: 800 German/English word combinations, 1860 verb conjugations and 160 German/English phrase combinations. GERMAN II: 800 German/English word combinations and 2015 verb conjugation forms. ITALIAN: 816 Italian/English word combinations, 1500 verb conjugations and 114 Italian/English phrase combinations.

Usage: Self-paced language tutorials

System Requirements: 64K, one disk drive, color or monochrome display.

How to Start: Load DOS and check LANGUAGE.TXT and the GO.BAT for directions on using these programs; most must be un-archived using the ARC.EXE utility.

Suggested Donation: $5-10.00

File Descriptions:

ARC	EXE	Unarchiving program
FRENCH?	ARC	Archived files with French lessons (2 files)
GERMAN?	ARC	Archived files with German lessons (2 files)
HEBREW	EXE	Hewbrew lessons
ITALIAN	ARC	Archived file with Italian lessons
LANGUAGE	TXT	Documentation file
SPANISH?	ARC	Archived files with Spanish lessons (2 files)

MENU1	PIC	Picture screen for MENU program
ABC1	PIC	Picture screen for ABC program
BEARABC1	PIC	Picture screen for BEARABC program
BUNNY1	PIC	Picture screen for BUNNY program
BEAR1231	PIC	Picture screen for BEAR123 program
FROG1	PIC	Picture screen for FROG program
TRUCK1	PIC	Picture screen for TRUCK program

646
AMY'S FIRST PRIMER
PC,XT,AT Version
v1

Amy's First Primer is a collection of six games designed to teach basic skills to a pre-reading child. The collection includes a sing-along alphabet, a letter matching game, an alphabet tutorial, a numbers/counting game, a maze game, and a pattern matching game. The games stress positive reinforcement of these basic skills to promote a 'learning is fun' attitude.

The documentation, all 13 pages of it, is well written and explains everything necessary. Repeated suggestions that the parent use the games with their child adds a nice reinforcement towards family learning.

Usage: 4 to 8 year old children

System Requirements: 128K, a color graphics adapter (Hercules won't work) with an IBM Color display or color TV; at least one disk drive.

How to Start: To run BASIC programs consult the directions in GETTING STARTED for your configuration. Consult AMY.DOC for program documentation.

Suggested Donation: $15.00

File Descriptions:

README		Quick instructions for a fast start.
AMY	DOC	15 page User's Guide to print out.
GO	BAT	Batch file to start the programs.
AUTOEXEC	BAT	Batch file for auto-startup.
COPYRITE	BAS+	COPYRIGHT program to display initial information screen.
MENU	BAS+	MENU program to provide access to the other programs.
ABC	BAS+	ABC SONG Musical program for picture/word/letter association.
BEARABC	BAS+	BEARY FUN ABC'S program to learn keyboard and printed letters.
BUNNY	BAS+	BUNNY LETTERS program to learn alphabet.
BEAR123	BAS+	BEARY FUN COUNTING program to learn counting and numbers.
FROG	BAS+	HELP THE FROGGY Maze program for problem solving.
TRUCK	BAS+	LOAD THE TRUCK program for shapes, colors, patterns and order.

647
AMY'S FIRST PRIMER
PC-jr Version
v1

Amy's First Primer is a collection of six games designed to teach basic skills to a pre-reading child. The collection includes a sing-along alphabet, a letter matching game, an alphabet tutorial, a numbers/counting game, a maze game, and a pattern matching game. The games stress positive reinforcement of these basic skills to promote a 'learning is fun' attitude. PLEASE NOTE: This version is specially designed for the PC-jr.

The documentation, all 13 pages of it, is well written and explains everything necessary. Repeated suggestions that the parent use the games with their child adds a nice reinforcement towards family learning.

Usage: 4 to 8 year old children

System Requirements: 128K, a color graphics adapter (Hercules won't work) with an IBM Color display or color TV; at least one disk drive.

How to Start: To run BASIC programs consult the directions in GETTING STARTED for your configuration. Consult AMY.DOC for program documentation.

Suggested Donation: $15.00

File Descriptions:

README		Quick instructions for a fast start.
AMY	DOC	15 page User's Guide to print out.
GO	BAT	Batch file to start the programs.
AUTOEXEC	BAT	Batch file for auto-startup.
COPYRITE	BAS+	COPYRIGHT program to display initial information screen
MENU	BAS+	MENU program to provide access to the other programs.
ABC	BAS+	ABC SONG Musical program for picture/word/letter association.

BEARABC	BAS+	BEARY FUN ABC'S program to learn keyboard and printed letters.
BUNNY	BAS+	BUNNY LETTERS program to learn alphabet.
BEAR123	BAS+	BEARY FUN COUNTING program to learn counting and numbers.
FROG	BAS+	HELP THE FROGGY Maze program for problem solving.
TRUCK	BAS+	LOAD THE TRUCK program for shapes, colors, patterns and order.
MENU1	PIC	Picture screen for MENU program
ABC1	PIC	Picture screen for ABC program
BEARABC1	PIC	Picture screen for BEARABC program
BUNNY1	PIC	Picture screen for BUNNY program
BEAR1231	PIC	Picture screen for BEAR123 program
FROG1	PIC	Picture screen for FROG program
TRUCK1	PIC	Picture screen for TRUCK program

664 TEACHER'S SPECIAL
v1.0

This diskette contains a mix of educational programs designed to help both the teacher and the student. The Register, "written by a teacher for teachers and tested in the classroom," is a grade database that will keep track of students' marks by course. This is a fully featured demo version of the larger Register package.

It is limited to 13 students, up to 6 grades, no personalized information and default print (pica). The README.DOC file has a partial manual on disk.

The Atlas Software group as developed three color graphics and sound programs to drill students on history, our solor system and mathematical factors. The STAR program will generate star charts. Each program has well developed on-line documentation and Register comes with over 40k of documentation.

Usage: Educational Paperwork Management

System Requirements: 128K, one disk drive (two floppies recommended) and a monochrome display.

How to Start: To run BASIC programs consult the directions in GETTING STARTED for your configuration. Consult READSTAR.ME and MANUAL.DOC for program documentation.

Suggested Donation: $45.00 for REGISTER.

File Descriptions:

————	——	Atlas Package
ATLAS	BAS	Screen Image for Atlas package
ATLASARM	BAS	Screen Image
ERROR	BAS	Atlas program routine
HQ	BAS	Program: Historomaina
NTP	BAS	Program: Name That Planet
MENU	BAS	Main Menu program, run this first
MENU2	BAS	Atlas program routine
MULTID	BAS	Program: Multitime
REGISTER		Atlas registration information
————	——	Register Program (v1.0)
GRADE	000	Demonstration data
GRADE	COM	Main register program
GRADES	111	Demonstration data
INSTALL	COM	Installation program, read manual
MANUAL	DOC	Documentation for Register, about 40k
NAMES	11	Demonstration data
READ	ME	Startup information
RESET	COM	Program module
SETUP	BAT	Setup batch file, read documentation
————	——	Star Program
STAR	BAS	BASIC program, Star, will run from BASIC only
STAR	DAT	Program information
READSTAR	ME	Startup information
GO	BAT	Startup information for entire disk

ENTERTAINMENT:

Let us entertain you with our collection of adult and arts oriented programming that is both challenging and fun! In this category we include:

- Music software (Ragtime to Bach) to play, listen and write!
- Text adventure games
- Novelty programs (ESP, Origami, Tarot, etc.)

You'll have hours of fun with our selection of music software. Several allow you to compose and edit your own pieces! One program even turns your PC keyboard into a piano keyboard! Write music, store songs, or simply play a song from our growing library of music programs.

Our collection of text adventure games is great fun. This is a special category of imaginative play where you interact with the program through dialogue. Focus your wits and grit on unraveling the mystery/fantasy that the author has devised for you. Without graphics, you rely on joining your willing imagination and strong logical powers to the devilish and delightful quests our authors have devised for your entertainment.

You may find yourself in a great, dark dangerous cave full of treasures. You may find yourself seeking an ancient talisman of great magical powers with sorcerers and gnomes all around you. You may find yourself struggling to break out of a New York City ghetto. You may find yourself in a shotgun shack. You may find yourself behind the wheel of a large automobile...

92 MUSIC
v1

MUSIC provides some easy keyboard access to the built-in IBM PC's PLAY command. MUSIC allows you to enter one note at a time and lets you select the note on a regular music-sheet type display. The rest of the disk contains two excellent BASIC games, SQUARE (a version of Rubic's cube) and SW-PEG, a strategy board game, and miscellaneous files worth checking out.

Usage: Elementary music composition and home entertainment.

System Requirements: 64K, one disk drive and monochrome display. Files marked with " + " need a color/graphics card.

How to Start: To read DOC or TXT files, enter TYPE filename.ext and press ENTER. For instructions on running BASIC programs, please refer to the GETTING STARTED section in this catalog.

User Comments: "Good idea, but faces of cube are in monochrome letters (graphics mode 2 — high resolution). This makes it very difficult to work the puzzle. The Rubic's Cube really does need color." "A good bit of fun for such a small program. Good user interface." "Could not get the program to run on my machine; even when I loaded BASICA." "Not bad for an early program, but there's just no comparison to Pianoman. This is a jumble of various programs and should be reshuffled so that the music programs are on one disk and the game programs on another."

File Descriptions:

PATTERNS	BAS+	Creates patterns on graphics display
SOUNDEMO	BAS	Generates several sounds selected from menu
TWINKLE	BAS	Generates twinkling stars on screen (Use BASICA)
MUSIC	BAS	Music scoring system
MUSIC	DAT	Data file for MUSIC.BAS
NAMCNV	TXT	Naming convention suggestions for public domain software
QDCOPY	DOC	Diskcopy modification — eliminates prompts
RACE	BAS	Game
SCHROE	DER	Image of Schroeder in characters — may be printed
SQUARE	BAS	Rubic cube type game
SQUARE	DOC	Documentation for SQUARE.BAS
SQUARE	SUM	Part of SQUARE.BAS

STLOUIS	BBS	Information on using St. Louis bulletin board and others
SW-PEG	BAS+	Game — move the pegs to the other side of the board
UPVC	DOC	Instructions on how to make backups of VISICALC disks
VCCOM	DOC	How to make VISICALC load as a .COM file
GLOBE	REF+	Draws picture of earth on graphics adapter

ALIEN	DOC	Files for ALIEN.BAS
A2	SPC	Files for ALIEN.BAS
A5	SPC	Files for ALIEN.BAS
3DTT	BAS+	Play 3-D tic-tac-toe on a 4x4x4 board
ANIMATE	BAS+	Animation demo
EGGS	BAS+	Draws patterns of eggs on graphics screen
EGGS	DOC	Brief description of EGGS.BAS
MANOR	BAS	Adventure type game
TRADER	BAS	Interstellar trading game
CIA	BAS	Adventure type game

100 Jukebox
v1

From "Sunrise, Sunset" to "I Can't Get No Satisfaction," JUKEBOX plays your selection from 10 choices. If you want some more fun, there is a great variety of games here, too. The main three are ALIEN, 3DTT and EGGS. ALIEN is an adventure game in which you are the only survivor of a space crash on a very hostile planet. 3DTT is three dimensional Tic-Tac-Toe while EGGS is a short graphics display program that generates eggs of random colors, using paint and draw commands.

Usage: Entertainment.

System Requirements: 64K, one disk drive and monochrome display. Files marked with "+" need a color/graphics card and monitor.

How to Start: To read DOC or TXT files, enter TYPE filename.ext and press ENTER. For instructions on running BASIC programs, please refer to the GETTING STARTED section in this catalog.

User Comments: "Excellent! Challenging and solvable. Balloon graphics are a neat bonus. Puzzles are logical. I like this one (MANOR) for friends who love adventure game, but don't have access to a computer for long periods of time. It is a very well done game." "Very challenging! Possible to win. I was tic tac toe champ in grade school (No one would play with me), so I was intrigued by the computer version. The game keeps me coming back for more."

File Descriptions:

MENU	PGM	Menu program for running programs on this disk
BAGPIPES	BAS	Plays the bagpipes
JUKEBOX	BAS	Jukebox music player
*	MUS	Music for JUKEBOX.BAS (10 files)
ALIEN	BAS	Adventure type game
ALIEN	SPC	Files for ALIEN.BAS

127 PC-MUSICIAN
v1.2

With PC-MUSICIAN you can create and play songs on your PC. It enables you to enter music using musical notation, either from sheet music or your own original compositions. You may then hear the music played by the PC, change things around as needed, and finally save the song on disk. It can then be played anytime.

Usage: PC-MUSICIAN is a valuable tool for people who wish to write music regardless of their level of ability.

System Requirements: 64K, one disk drive and monochrome display.

How to Start: Be sure to read the documentation files READ.ME and MUSICIAN.DOC for program directions. Type MUSICIAN and press ENTER to start the program. You are then given the list of options, select your options as directed.

User Comments: "I have a Tandy 2000. This has been a particularly entertaining disk for our family — ages 8 to 35. There are certainly some aspects of design that could be improved upon. It would be nice, for example, if one could display more than just 4 or 5 measures at a time." "Some of the songs played very slooow! The documentation was good, but the disk needs some work." "I was expecting something more complex in the ability to reproduce music."

Suggested Donation: $20.00

File Descriptions:

READ	ME	How to list documentation
AUTOEXEC	BAT	Batch file for automatic execution
PRINTDOC	BAT	Batch file to print documentation

MAKECOPY	BAT	Batch file to files to disk b:
MUSICIAN	EXE	PC-MUSICIAN main program
TXTMUSIC	EXE	PC-MUSICIAN main program to use with monochrome display
EXNOTES	FNT	Part of PC-MUSICIAN
MUSICIAN	DOC	Documentation for PC-MUSICIAN (13 pages)
*	SNG	Song files (11 files)
MAKEMONO	BAT	Setup routine for monochrome display & >=128K memory
MAKEG64	BAT	Setup routine for graphics display & 64K memory
MAKEM64	BAT	Setup routine for monochrome display & 64K memory
GMUS64	EXE	Main program — see MAKEG64.BAT
TMUS64	EXE	Main program — see MAKEM64.BAT

173
Extra Sensory Perception
v1

The main program on this disk is a program which tests your ESP quotient. It makes for an interesting time as you test yourself and your friends. The disk also contains a couple of versions of the game PAC-MAN, for both monochrome and color systems. See if your ESP will tell you which way the ghosts will go!

Usage: Entertainment.

System Requirements: 128K, One disk drive, Monochome monitor, Color graphics needed if file marked by a plus symbol (+).

How to Start: To read DOC files, enter TYPE filename.ext and press ENTER.

- To run an EXE program, just type its name and press ENTER. For instructions on running BASIC programs, please refer to the GETTING STARTED section in this catalog.

User Comments: "The PACKMAN is not as good as disk #274. ESP is mildly interesting." "A novel disk! The pacman games are very good and the ESP portion make it a worthwhile disk to have." "Liked ESP. It was fun to test myself and my friends. I thought the explanation of mathematical calculation for odds was interesting." "Not the kind of program that should be distributed."

File Descriptions:

CPOKEMAN	EXE	Good monochrome Pacman-type game
ESP	DOC	Documentation
ESP	EXE	Extra Sensory Perception testing
PCMAN	BAS	Fair monochrome Pacman-type game
PACMANGL	EXE+	Slow Pacman-type game — good color (color graphics)
SELLERS		Part of ESP

259
C Adventure
v1

This is a fine D&D type adventure game that is written in 'C'. Not only can the game players have fun, but the hackers can get into this one and change things to suit their interests. It features a fairly good english parser, and can save or restore a game in progress. A very sophisticated piece of work. Try it out and see if you agree.

Usage: Entertainment.

System Requirements: 128K, One disk drive, Monochome monitor, Color graphics needed if file marked by a plus symbol (+).

How to Start: Type ADVENT and press ENTER to start. To read DOC or TXT files, enter TYPE filename.ext and press ENTER.

User Comments: "A fairly good interactive game, which suffers from the later development of similar such games, particularly in the area of two word commands." "A classic. Still fun, but easy to 'figure out'." "Excellent Adventure: well-written, clever, bug-free. Except for the parser that only handles two words, professional quality" " A classic. Frustrating, but so are all text adventure games. If you like this form of entertainment, this disk is a must."

File Descriptions:

— — — —	— —	ADVENTURE in "c" implementation by Jerry D. Pohl
ADVENT	EXE	Compiled adventure game ready to run
ADVENT0	EXE	Program utility to create ADVTEXT.H
CCADV	BAT	Batch file to compile ADVENT.C
CC	BAT	Batch file to compile an inserted variable program
CLADV	BAT	Batch file to link program after compiling
ADVENT	C	Initialization, save game, restore game
ENGLISH	C	Interpret game player's commands

DATABASE	C	Text file management & output
ITVERB	C	Intransitive verbs execution
VERB	C	Transitive verbs execution
TURN	C	Analysis & execution of player's command
ADVENT0	C	Utility to create "ADVTEXT.H" file
ADVENT1	TXT	Long cave description
ADVENT2	TXT	Short cave description
ADVENT3	TXT	Long & short object description
ADVENT4	TXT	Conversational descriptions & responses
ADVENT	DOC	ADVENTURE documentation file (3K)
STDIO	H	Standard I/O header
ADVENT	H	define & structure statements
ADVWORD	H	Words & codes array
ADVCAVE	H	Cave & travel arrays
ADVTEXT	H	TXT file message indexes
ADVDEF	H	Data constants & variables definitions
ADVDEC	H	Data constants & variables declarations
*	OBJ	Object files

279
PIANOMAN
Version 3.0
v2

PIANOMAN is Neil Rubenking's exceptional music composition tool. This well-designed group of programs allows you to play, record and edit your own music, with options for importing other music files, too. This disk contains four archived groups of music ready for you to play, edit, whatever, as well as the archiving tools and excellent documentation.

Usage: Suitable for both children and adults interested in music; it is appropriate for fun as well as serious music composition.

System Requirements: 128K RAM, color or monochrome monitor, and requires PC-DOS, not MS-DOS.

Features:

- Tune Playing:
- Tune Editing: both what you've saved and others', too!
- Help Windows: four small and eight large screens
- Note Changes in Length and Pitch:
- Block and Global Changes:
- Player Piano: a conversion utility to expand the horizons of your PIANOMAN tunes. It performs five types of conversion:

1) Tune into self-running program 2) Tune into external procedure for TURBO Pascal programs 3) Tune into BLOADable file for BASIC programs 4) Tune into SuperKey macro (really!) 5) 2 to 4 tunes into one "polyphonic" tune (fugues, etc.)

How to Start: To run an EXE or COM program, just type it's name and press ENTER. To read DOC files, enter TYPE filename.ext and press ENTER.

User Comments: "The program is very ingenious and shows a lot of musicality. One bug: the piano display freezes a lot when used with my Leading Edge Model D" "Although being a novice I had trouble getting some of the files to work. I did play around with it and enjoyed the sounds generated." "Look at this more as a game than a product for the serious musician. Since I am not a musician serious or otherwise, its great!" "Considering what the software has to work with, this program does an excellent job in creating and playing music."

Suggested Donation: $25.00

File Descriptions:

		PIANOMAN
READTHIS	1ST	Important information — do read it.
PIANOMAN	COM	Music playing, recording, and editing program
PIANOMAN	DOC	Documentation — to be screened, not printed
PLAYRPNO	COM	Utility for PIANOMAN files — turns them into programs
PIANOALT	COM	An alternative main program for PC Compatibles.
ARCX	COM	Program to unarchive Pianoman files.
COMTUNES	ARC	Music compiled from Pianoman (Archived)
COMTUNES	DIR	Listing of programs in COMTUNES.ARC
MACROS	ARC	Music in macro form (Archived)
MACROS	DIR	Listing of macro files in MACROS.ARC
TUNES	ARC	Music for Pianoman (Archived)
TUNES	DIR	Listing of files for TUNES.ARC
TUNES2	ARC	Music for Pianoman (Archived)
TUNES2	DIR	Listing of files for TUNES2.ARC

296 EAMON Master (Disk 1 of 2)
v1

EAMON is a computerized version of what are called "fantasy role-playing games." When you enter the universe of one of these games, you are no longer Jon (or Jane) Smith, mild-mannered computer hobbyist. Instead, you become a character in a land of adventure, doing almost anything you want to. EAMON was created by Donald Brown and converted to the PC by Jon Walker.

Usage: Entertainment.

System Requirements: 128K, One disk drive, Monochome monitor, Color graphics needed if file marked by a plus symbol (+).

How to Start: To read DOC files simply enter TYPE filename.ext and press ENTER. For instructions on running BASIC programs, please refer to the GETTING STARTED section in this catalog.

User Comments: "Please get some of the adventures themselves for the library; I like playing it." "The documentation was too long, but interesting reading." "We need more of these games or a source for them." "A classic example of interactive fiction. Major problem is its lack of graphics. Still, the program is interesting and challenging." "Mediocre documentation; all sorts of typos in the program itself — annoying in an interactive text game."

File Descriptions:

EAMON	BAS	Main program, type: RUN "EAMON" from BASICA
NEWGUY	BAS	Part of EAMON
MAINHALL	BAS	Main hall
CAVE	BAS	Cave
*	*	Other files used by system
PRINTMAN	BAS	Allows you to read manual on screen
README	EAM	Brief notes
EAMON	DOC	Documentation (30K)

297 EAMON Designer & Utilities (Disk 2 of 2)
v1

This disk is designed to be used with the EAMON master Disk No 293. It allows you to create new EAMON adventures. Perhaps one of your creations could become the next great adventure epic. We are always interested in receiving user-written EAMON games for inclusion in our library.

Usage: Entertainment.

System Requirements: 128K, one disk drive, monochome monitor.

How to Start: To read DOC files simply enter TYPE filename.ext and press ENTER. From BASIC, type LOAD"MENU", then RUN to start program.

User Comments: "Very nice program. really fun, & the documentation is a real help." "The description in the catalogue makes it appear as if anyone (with hard work, perhaps) can program new games. Hard work shouldn't need a PhD." "Tried to make a new EAMON game — failed. Documentation somewhat confusing." "Tough to understand use..have to experiment with it.."

File Descriptions:

----	--	Designer
MENU	BAS	Main program, run this program first
DUNINIT	BAS	Part of EAMON Designer
WORK	BAS	Part of EAMON Designer
MLIST	BAS	Part of EAMON Designer
LISTER	BAS	Part of EAMON Designer
DUNGEON	BAS	Part of EAMON Designer
CONFIG	BAS	Part of EAMON Designer
WEAPONS	DAT	Part of EAMON Designer
DESCRIPT	DAT	Part of EAMON Designer
AUTOEXEC	BAT	Part of EAMON Designer
DUNGEON	DOC	For those planning to create their own dungeons (6K text file)
DESIGN	DOC	Documentation (14K text file)
PRINTDOC	BAS	Prints documentation
----	--	Utilities
UTILITY	DOC	Notes about "utility" files
WEAPINIT	BAS	Program for initializing the weapon/artifact file
NEWCAVE	BAS	Basic program with SAVE and PLAY old game commands
STARTUP	BAS	Start into a dungeon with sword, gold
FILL	BAS	Makes it easier to make a dungeon full of artifacts and monsters
DAMON	ART	Artifact file for FILL.BAS program

DAMON	MON	Monster file for FILL.BAS program
DAMON	EFF	Description file for FILL.BAS program
README	UTL	Startup notes: use BASICA /S:256

322
Music Collection
v1

An amazingly diverse collection of music! The two main menus are Jukebox and Classics, which allow you to select one of more than dozen choices. Then there is a music composition program that plays scales, one that turns your PC keyboard into a piano and to top it off, the IBM Fight Song! All in all, a really fine collection of songs that will bring hours of fun.

Usage: Musical entertainment for all tastes and talents.

System Requirements: 64K, one disk drive, monochrome display.

How to Start: To read DOC or TXT files, enter TYPE filename.ext and press ENTER.

- To run an EXE or COM program, just type it's name and press ENTER. For instructions on running BASIC programs, please refer to the GETTING STARTED section in this catalog.

User Comments: "Very cute diskette. Very good music programming." "Some of the best IBM-PC music I have heard." "Cute. Recommended for music beginners like myself." "It is educational to be able to list the programs and analyze the program structure."

File Descriptions:

ANT2	BAS	Anteater Music II demo
ANVIL	BAS	A song
ARKTRAV	BAS	Arkansas Traveler
BACH	BAS	Classic: A song by Bach
BLUESBOX	BAS	Part of MUSICBOX.BAS
BOUREE	BAS	A song
CHOPIN1	BAS	Classic: A song by Chopin
CLASSICS	BAS	Menu for the selection of CLASSIC songs
DANCE	BAS	Dance of the Watchacallit
ELEPHANT	TUN	Baby Elephant Walk song that is part of TUNE.BAS
HAPPYB	BAS	Happy Birthday song
HEARING	BAS	Hearing test
HUNGRHAP	BAS	Hungarian Rapsody
IBMSONG	BAS	IBM fight song

JSB	BAS	Sonata VI in E Major, 1st Movement. by J.S. Bach
JSB	MUS	Same as JSB.BAS
JUKEBOX	BAS	Music menu program with a colection of songs
LIEBESTR	BAS	Franz Liszt
LUDWIG	BAS	Classic: Song by Bach [Ludwig]
MAGDALEN	BAS	Classic: From The Little Notebook For Anna Magdalena Bach
MESSIAH	BAS	Messiah
MINUET	BAS	Classic: Minuet by J.S. Bach
MINWALTZ	EXE	Minute Waltz
MTN-KING	BAS	A song
MUSICBOX	BAS	Compose your song and save to disk [requires graphics]
NUTCRAKR	BAS	Nutcracker Suite
NYLOGO	BAS	New York PC Users Group song and graphics demo [graphics]
PIANO	COM	Turns keyboard into piano keys to play music on
PRAELUD1	BAS	A song
PRAELUD2	BAS	A song
RAIL	BAS	Classic: I've Been Working On The Railroad
SCALES	BAS	Plays different music scales
SFG-BACH	BAS	Classic: Solfeggietto by Bach
SIREN	BAS	Alarm Siren
SOUNDS	BAS	Different sounds
SYMPH-5	BAS	A symphony
SYNTH	BAS	Demo
TRAUMERI	BAS	Traumerei
TUNE	BAS	Plays music files [ELEPHANT.TUN]
WILLTELL	BAS	Classic: William Tell Overture
XMAS	BAS	Collection of Xmas songs

327
Trivia
(Disk 1 of 2)
v1

This disk contains a very good trivia game program that is to be used with the category files on Disk No 328. The categories include Science and Nature, Entertainment, Sports and Recreation, and Mixed Bag. For your next party, try matching your knowledge against this one.

Usage: Entertainment.

System Requirements: 128K, one disk drive, monochome monitor.

How to Start: Enter TRIVMACH to start, or TYPE TRIVMACH.DOC to read documentation file.

User Comments: "Excellent disk. Easy to use and captivating. Can spend many entertaining hours here. The trivia questions are hard enough to be challenging but not so hard as to cause one to lose interest." "Would like to have the question displayed before the multiple choice answers are given and the timing starts. I'm a slow reader and get poor scores even when I know the correct answer." "This is a fair game at best. The questions are good but the way the game is played could be much better." "I thought the documentation on this one could have been improved since it did little to explain the game before you started. Also, by offering 4 chances to answer correctly between 4 multiple choice questions, its very easy to get points you don't deserve."

File Descriptions:

TRIVMACH	EXE	Trivia game program
TRIVMACH	DOC	Trivia game documentation

328 Trivia (Disk 2 of 2)
v1

This disk contains the category files for the trivia game program on Disk No 327. These files comprise several different categories of questions for the Trivia game, and should provide many hours of interest for all you Trivia buffs.

Usage: Entertainment.

System Requirements: 128K, one disk drive, monochome monitor.

File Descriptions:

CATEGORY	C	Science and Nature trivia questions
CATEGORY	A	Entertainment trivia questions
CATEGORY	B	Sports and Recreation trivia questions
CATEGORY	D	Mixed Bag trivia questions
TM	FNT	Support file for trivia game

329 Trivia & Others
v1.2

This disk contains a very challenging trivia game, and an equally excellent version of an Othello-type game titled ENTRAPP, which is a most entertaining strategy game. Also included, a couple of small BASIC programs concerning gambling entertainments. Enjoy, and try not to lose your next paycheck to your computer!

Usage: Entertainment.

System Requirements: 128K, one disk drive, monochome monitor.

How to Start: To read DOC files, enter TYPE filename.ext and press ENTER.

- To run an EXE or COM program, just type its name and press ENTER. For instructions on running BASIC programs, please refer to the GETTING STARTED section in this catalog.

User Comments: "Liked the trivia. ACEY has bug, can't win." " Craps: never heard of dice with 0s on them." "This is a good version of trivia, but why trivia? Trivia is a fun game because it sparks conversation with people. It makes little sense on a computer. But that's probably a minority opinion." "(ENTRAP)..Good, quick and clever version of this game, with the emphasis on clever. The machine plays very well. I wish the rest of the disk were as interesting." "The trivia program is not very good. The variety of questions is limited."

Suggested Donation: $10.00

File Descriptions:

ACEY	BAS+	Get insurance if this dealer gets an ACE
CRAPS	BAS+	Shoot craps in this casino
*	DAT	Data files used by TRIVIA.EXE (8 files)
ENTRAP	COM+	Great version of the popular OTHELLO game
ENT-BW	COM	Monochrome version of the OTHELLO game
ENTRAP	DOC	Documentation for both OTHELLO games
TRIVIA	EXE	Boggle your mind with this Triva program
TRIVIA	DOC	Documentation for TRIVIA.EXE

116

385
Phrase Craze Version 1.05
v1

For those of you who like to outguess those people on the TV quiz shows, here is a challenging phrase guessing game where you have to fill in a series of phrases that are outlined on the screen. This game is somewhat like the television show 'Wheel of Fortune', but without the commercials — Hurrah! — or Vanna White — Boo!

Usage: Entertainment.

System Requirements: 128K, One disk drive, Monochome monitor, color graphics needed if file marked by a plus symbol (+).

How to Start: To read DOC files, enter TYPE filename.ext and press ENTER.

• To run an EXE program, just type its name and press ENTER.

User Comments: "Anyone with a liking for word games will definitely want this one. My friends and I play it all the time. I only wish there were more phrases on the disk. But I am going to send the author the contribution and get the version with the extra phrases." "This is very fun and easy game to learn ... very enjoyable." "I find this game excellent, however please take this with a grain of salt, as I am not a games person." " A very entertaining program just like the wheel of fortune on TV." "Great Fun! Whole family had fun with this one."

Suggested Donation: $25.00 for enhanced version.

File Descriptions:

PHRASE	EXE	Program for in-game explanation of PHRASE CRAZE
EXPLAIN	EXE	Program to provide choice of game options
CRAZE	EXE	Program for actual play of PHRASE CRAZE
RANGE		File to store player scores and other data
DATA		File containing the game phrases
CMNT		File containing the explanations of phrases
PHRASE	DOC	Brief documentation file

408
ORIGAMI
v1

This disk will introduce you to Origami, the ancient art of paper folding. It starts you at the basics (the main starting folds), and proceeds to show you how to create many paper sculptures with step-by-step graphic instructions. Young and old alike will find many hours of enjoyment with these artistic creations.

Usage: Useful for school as well as home recreation.

System Requirements: 64K, one disk drive, monochrome display.

How to Start: For instructions on running BASIC programs, please refer to the GETTING STARTED section in this catalog.

User Comments: "If Origami is what you want, this is a delightful teacher." "This is a well written and fun program. It has colorful graphics and is one of the few programs my 11 year old non-computer type likes." "Very good demonstration, easy to follow, would like to see more of this author's work. Being used by my 7 year olds and they love it!" "If the subject matter is of interest, this disk is excellent — - my 10-yr-old son was fascinated with it — an excellent example of an instance where computer-aided-instruction is greatly superior to other forms."

Suggested Donation: $19.95 for individuals and from institutions an additional $5.00 for each disk made.

File Descriptions:

CHICK	BAS	Basic program that shows you how to fold a paper chicken
SHARE	BAS	Program and suggested donation info
MAIN	BAS	Main menu Program
INTRO	BAS	An introduction to origami
RABBIT	BAS	How to fold yourself a rabbit
JET	BAS	" " " " " jet plane
WATERFOW	BAS	" " " " " duck
CANDY	BAS	" " " " " candy box
PENGUIN	BAS	" " " " " penguin
BOXES	BAS	" " " " " two kind of boxes
HELMET	BAS	A two part exercise (1st — a samurai helmut, 2nd — a grouper)
BALLOON	BAS	How to fold yourself a balloon
PIG	BAS	" " " " " pig

CICADA	BAS	" " " " " cicada (?)
END	BAS	End message to main program
PUPPY	BAS	How to fold yourself a puppy
TITLEPG	BAS	Run this to start the program (Main Program Starter)
STATS	BAS	File that lists the stats for origami program files

ZORK2	DOC	Solution for Zork II.
ZORK3	DOC	Solution for Zork III.
ZT16	EXE	Zork Tools!! Great utility for any Infocom game.
ZT16	DOC	Documentation for ZT16.EXE. (11K)
CRISIS	EXE +	Space Game (c/g required)
GODCREAT	BAS	Advanced Dungeons & Dragons God Creation Program

446 Zork Utilities
v1

This disk is dedicated to the adventurers out there. Half of the disk is dedicated to the Zork trilogy of adventures by Infocom. Files include solutions to these programs and utilities to use with these programs. The other half is full of adventure and arcade game programs, and a utility to help Dungeons & Dragons players.

Usage: Entertainment.

System Requirements: 128K, One disk drive, Monochome monitor, Color graphics needed if file marked by a plus symbol (+).

How to Start: To read DOC files, enter TYPE filename.ext and press ENTER.

- To run an EXE or COM program, just type its name and press ENTER. For instructions on running BASIC programs, please refer to the GETTING STARTED section in this catalog.

User Comments: "(Q-BERT) Good graphics but way too slow." "Great. I go back to this one over and over again." "ZORKI.DOC is a lifesaver. The disk is pleasantly surprising with Q-BERT, ASTRO & X-WING as well as PIRATE and TEMPLE." "ZT16 is a useful ZORK tool. In addition to solutions and finding vocabularies, you can store two ZORK back-ups on one disk as DOS files." "The answers to Zork worked great! The games are very good as well!"

File Descriptions:

PIRATE	BAS	Adventure game. Find island, explore, and get treasure
PIRATE	DOC	Documentation for PIRATE.BAS
ASTRO	COM +	Asteroids game.
Q-BERT	EXE +	Like arcade game. Turn squares to different colors
TEMPLE	BAS	Temple of Loth! Like Dungeons and Dragons.
XWING	BAS +	Relive Star Wars.
ZORK1	DOC	Solution for Zork I.

451 Cavequest
v1

This is an user-supported adventure game, much in the vein as Epyx's Temple of Aphsai. You start as an Immortal, are allowed to chose your new mortal attributes, and are sent to Earth to seek out fame, fortune and adventure. This is a rich and complex adventure, and it is recommended that you read the documentation first before playing.

Usage: Entertainment.

System Requirements: 128K, one disk drive, monochome monitor.

How to Start: Enter TYPE READ.ME and press ENTER. Also recommended to copy SCROLL files to printer for reference. Then follow program instructions.

User Comments: "The graphics are well gone but the game is slow" "Entertaining. Works very well. However, immediate return to a level causes the program to abort." "It needs a switch for faster computers – real time games at 8 MHz are frenetic." "A good game, enough known that you can play it, enough unknowns that you will have problems. Probably my most frequently used game." "...the basic idea is a great one, but the instructions are poor, and some of the features, such as the shooting, do not appear to work as displayed. Despite this, my son has spent hours with it, and it is about as good as several similar commercial programs."

Suggested Donation: $35.00

File Descriptions:

CHECK	COM	Program checker
CHECK	TXT	Program checker text file
LEVEL1	DEF	Data file for level 1 of the adventure
LEVEL2	DEF	Data file for level 2 of the adventure
LEVEL3	DEF	Data file for level 3 of the adventure
LEVEL4	DEF	Data file for level 4 of the adventure

LEVEL5	DEF	Data file for level 5 of the adventure
MONSTER	DEF	Data file for adventure game
PLAYER	DEF	Data file for adventure game
QUEST	000	Part of game program
QUEST	001	Part of game program
QUEST	002	Part of game program
QUEST	003	Part of game program
QUEST	004	Part of game program
QUEST	005	Part of game program
QUEST	006	Part of game program
QUEST	COM	Main program
READ	ME	Text file
SCROLL	HNT	Hint file
SCROLL	OLD	Descriptions
SCROLL	USE	User Manual
SUPPORT		User support response form

452 THE AMULET OF YENDOR

v1

This Dungeons & Dragons type adventure comes from the Stichting Mathematisch Centrum in Amsterdam. Originally running on a Unix machine it was converted to MS-DOS by Don Kneller. This adventure game is played on 20 levels against many monsters and very powerful magic. You can be an explorer, warrior, magician, tourist, knight or a caveman with all their associated powers.

Usage: Entertainment.

System Requirements: 256k, Two disk drive, Monochome monitor, DOS 2.x or higher.

How to Start: Type HACK and press ENTER.

User Comments: "This is one of the best games I have ever played." "The kids and I can't stop playing this game." "It is one of the most addictive computer games that I have ever played. It is such a complex game that after six months of frequent play I am still discovering new things about the game." "This is a PC version of a superb unix game, but the documentation supplied leaves out some very important things, such as the command 'Z' (for zapping a wand) and an explanation of buying and selling in the various shops; the command 'S' to save the game."

Suggested Donation: $10.00

File Descriptions:

HACK	EXE	D & D adventure the 'Amulet of Yendor'
HACK	DOC	History and documentation for HACK.EXE
HACK	MSG	Hints on how to get through this adventure
DATA		List of objects and denizens of this empire
HELP		More documentation for the game
RECORD		Support file
RUMORS		Support file
README		Intro. file for ROGEHINT.TXT
ROGEHINT	TXT	More hints on how to get through this adventure

453 Adventureware

v1

Here is a collection of 5 text adventure games, ranging from a mystery adventure to an out and out horror film adventure. Many of the puzzles here will keep you intrigued for quite a while. If you like the challenge that these types of adventures offer, then you should find quite enough here to keep you happily occupied for days.

Usage: Entertainment.

System Requirements: 128K, one disk drive, monochome monitor.

How to start: To run an EXE or COM program, type its name and press ENTER.

User Comments: "Excellent game! Absorbing, with logical puzzles. The time element provided by the lamp keeps you on your toes. Same game feature is super." "Hints File necessary for novice gamers (like myself). I just didn't have the patience to keep dying to figure this out." "All the adventure games on this disk are challenging and highly entertaining. A must for adventure game fans!" "Just as maddening as Infocom games"

File Descriptions:

CRIME	EXE	Adventure Game
HAUNT	EXE	Adventure Game
ISLAND	EXE	Adventure Game
SUB	EXE	Adventure Game
TERROR	COM	Adventure Game
TERROR	DAT	Data file for Terror.com

473 *Trivial Towers (Disk 1 of 2)*

v1

Trivial Towers is a trivia game that tests the users knowledge on a variety of different subjects. It is a game that 2 to 4 people can play at a time. By answering questions correctly, you build "towers." When you complete all 4 towers, that are 6 blocks high, you win the game. There are special blocks on the gameboard, that when landed on, enable the user to choose any topic of his/her choice. Disk No 474 is the required second disk of this set.

Usage: Entertainment.

System Requirements: 128K, one disk drive, monochome monitor.

How to Start: To read DOC files, enter TYPE filename.ext and press ENTER. For instructions on running BASIC programs, please refer to the GETTING STARTED section in this catalog.

User Comments: "Very good education. Difficult questions. Would like to see a lot more disks with other subjects." "This is great!!! I'm a big fan of trivial pursuit and this is just about as good a program as the game." "Delightful game and especially liked the fact that I would be able to write my own questions."

Suggested Donation: $20.00

File Descriptions:

		Trivial Towers (v1.0)
TTENTER	BAS	Program that enables the user to write customized questions.
TTOWERS	BAS	Main program
TTRULES	BAS	Rules for TTOWERS.BAS and directions on how to customize.
TTNOTE	BAS	A letter from the authors of the program.
TTSHARE	DOC	A welcome letter from the authors giving definitions.

474 *Trivial Towers (Disk 2 of 2)*

v1

This disk holds all the questions and answers for the Trivial Towers program. The program files are on our disk No 473. Both disks are needed to play the game.

Usage: Entertainment.

File Descriptions:

		Trivial Towers (v1.0)
INCOMMON		Question and answer file
CAPITALS		Question and answer file
VANITY		Question and answer file
COMPUTER	S	Question and answer file
TVFILM		Question and answer file
WRITERS		Question and answer file

475 *Monopoly P.C. / Tune Trivia*

v1

Monopoly P.C. is a game developed to resemble the famous board game by Parker Brothers. This program follows the rules of the board game closely and allows one player to play against the computer, which rolls the dice moves the pieces on the board and updates the screen so that the player can follow along. There is also a graphics screen which displays the game board. Trivia Tune and its associated data files comprise a software package that allows players to hear music from the IBM's speaker and then attempt to guess the song's title. Trivia Tune then allows the players to answer trivia questions about musical history once a correct song has been guessed. The graphics card for the Monopoly P.C. game is optional.

Usage: Entertainment.

System Requirements: 128K, One disk drive, Monochome monitor, Color graphics needed if file marked by a plus symbol (+).

How to Start: To read DOC or README files, enter TYPE filename.ext and press ENTER. Type MONOPOLY or TUNETRIV and press ENTER to start either game.

User Comments: "Could be a 10 because I won my first EVER game of Monopoly. Such fun! Tune Trivia is great. Updates please." "Both games extremely good. Monopoly usable for single player only, but is well thought out and provides good entertainment. Tune Trivia is outstanding.... Best of it's kind that I've seen." "My son can seldom get anyone to play monopoly with him. Now he can play this!" "Two enjoyable programs — -very good "party games"."

Suggested Donation: $20.00 for Monopoly P.C., $30.00 for Tune Trivia.

File Descriptions:

————	——	Monopoly P.C.
MONOPOLY	EXE	Main program
MONOP	SCR	Data file to create graphic screen image
MONOPM	SCR	Data file to create graphic screen image
MONOPOLY	LCL	Modified "local rule" option text file
MONOPOLY	HLP	Brief help file displayed when requested during game
————	——	Tune Trivia (v1.0)
README		Brief information about authors and program
MANUAL		Program instruction manual (22k) set for 8.5" x 11" paper
TUNETRIV	EXE	Main Program for Tune Trivia
SET0??		Data files holding musical notes for TUNETRIV.EXE (22 FILES)
TRIV0??		Data files holding trivia questions for TUNETRIV.EXE (21 FILES)
SIGSOFT		Signature data file (Company name only)

477
Name Gram / Break Down / Fone Word
v2.1

Namegram is a wierd program that takes an input word, usually a name, and compares it to a set of compressed word files. In doing this, it can generate a set of anagrams of the word or name. Break Down is a strange, but interesting program. It has almost no practical uses, except perhaps for entertainment, but this does not limit its value. This algorithymn takes an input text file (I tried about two

paragraphs of an old English paper) and transforms the source text into a bunch of sentences that make little to no sense, but somehow they do!?

Usage: Entertainment.

System Requirements: 128K, one disk drive, monochome monitor, color graphics needed if file marked by a plus symbol (+).

How to Start: To read DOC or TXT files, enter TYPE filename.ext and ENTER.

● To run a COM program, just type its name and press ENTER.

User Comments: "Circus and Wild West are the best parts of this disk. I was extremely disappointed in Foneword. I expected more...more precise. I thought REAGAN.OUT was a political message, Could I be wrong?" "Mr. Rubenking's BREKDOWN, FONEWORD, and NAMEGRAM programs have amused me no end." "Fascinating and fun — and surely there ought to be some usefulness amid all these permutational games" "I'll never pay big $$ for copyprotected games again. This disk is dangerous; I've lost sleep running it."

Suggested Donation: $20.00

File Descriptions:

————	——	Name Gram
NAMESMAL	COM	Main program
MASHED	02	Compressed word files used by Namegram
MASHED	03	Compressed word files used by Namegram
MASHED	04	Compressed word files used by Namegram
MASHED	05	Compressed word files used by Namegram
MASHED	06	Compressed word files used by Namegram
READNAME	COM	Screen driven DOCumentation program for Namegram (33k)
————	——	Break Down
BREKDOWN	COM	Main Program
BREKDOWN	PAS	Pascal source code for Brekdown program
BREKDOWN	DOC	Short documentation for Brekdown (3 pages)
BREKDOWN	XMP	Some examples of text generated by Brekdown (3 pages)
BREK2	TXT	Associated text file used by Brekdown
ROMEO	O5T	Order-5 Breakdown of the "window scene" from Romeo & Juliet
ROMEO	O8T	Order-8 Breakdown of same, cleaned up and puntuated.
REAGAN	OUT	Order-8 Breakdown of the '85 State Of The Union address
————	——	Phone Word
FONEWORD	COM	Main Program
FONEWORD	DOC	Documentation of Foneword program
WORDFONE	COM	Reverses Foneword program
————	——	BONUS files: Created using my PIANOMAN program
WILDWEST	COM	"The Wild West Is Where I Wanna Be" by Tom Lehrer

WILLTELL	COM	"The William Tell Overture" by G.A. Rossini
INVENTN4	COM	Two-part Invention #4 in D-Minor, by J.S. Bach
MNTPYTHN	COM	Theme from Monty Python's Flying Circus, by J.P. Sousa

539
Adventure Solutions
v1

HINTS gives hints for solving some games: Zork I, II, & III, Starcross, Deadline, Witness, Mask of the Sun, Serpent's Star, Dark Crystal, Planetfall, The Enchanter, Death in the Caribbean, Infidel, Sorcerer, Seastalker, Hitchhiker. ZorkTools is a collection of utility programs which provide capabilities not normally available for INFOCOM games: copies, converts to DOS file, protects from DOS, makes unprotected copies, lists all words in the game. Requires any IBM PC or compatible, DOS 2.0 or higher, 22 to 128K of free space above DOS depending on the menu option selected. The other programs on this disk provided the actual solutions to some of the hardest aventure games, including adams, another large maker of adventure games, and solutions to others from companies like IBM.

Usage: Entertainment.

System Requirements: 128K, one disk drive, monochome monitor, color graphics needed if file marked by a plus symbol (+).

How to Start: Type ZORKTOOL and press ENTER to start program. Enter TYPE UNARC.TXT for instructions on making archived files usable.

File Descriptions:

— — — —	— —	HINTS
HINTS	DOC	Hints, 17152 bytes long.
— — — —	— —	ZORKTOOL 1.6
ZORKTOOL	COM	Main Program
ZORKTOOL	DOC	Documentation
— — — —	— —	GAME SOLUTIONS
ARC	EXE	Program to unarchive the soulutins.
UNARC	TXT	Text on how to unarchive the files, so that they can be used
INFOCOM	ARC	An archived file containing soulutions for INFOCOM games
ADAMS	ARC	An archive file containing soulutions for ADAMS games
OTHER	ARC	This file contains the solutions to games by other companys

567
DND Version 1.2
v1

DND is a computer fantasy role game inspired by Dungeons And Dragons, the "grandaddy" of all the computer games that was developed and played on mainframe computers back in the 60's. Different than most games, it uses text characters in the upper right corner of the screen instead of graphics.

Usage: Entertainment.

System Requirements: 256K, one disk drive, monochome monitor, PC-DOS 2.1 or MS-DOS 2.1.

How to Start: To read DOC files simply enter TYPE filename.ext and press ENTER. To start the game, type DND and press ENTER.

Suggested Donation: $25.00

File Descriptions:

DND	EXE	Main program
????????	BIN	Various binary files for the different dungeons you can play
????????	DOC	Several files containing the documentationf for DND
NOTICE	DAT	Datafile containing the author's notice
README		Note from the author

591
GENESIS Version 1.0
v1

GENESIS is a program designed to work with TRAVELLER (a science fiction role playing game) from Game Designers Workshop. It helps to speed up the process of setting up planets by the referee and handles aspects such as planetary size, atmosphere and population.

Usage: Entertainment.

System Requirements: 128K, one disk drive, monochome monitor, Traveller software.

How to Start: To read DOC files, enter TYPE filename.ext and press ENTER.

- To run a BAT file, just type its name and press ENTER.

File Descriptions:

README	NEW	File with list of revisions
SETUP	BAT	Batch file for setup
SECTOR	CHN	Planet sctor detail file
SUBSEC	CHN	Planet subsector detail file
PLANET	CHN	Planet detail file
GENESIS	COM	Main GENESIS program
SYSTEM1	DAT	System data file to set up planet
GENESIS	DOC	System documentation with users guide
AUTOEXEC	BAT	Auto-execute file
README	NOW	Introduction to GENESIS with feature list
PLANET	000	Sample planet detail file
— GNSS10	DID	Genesis system work file

604 Landing Party

v1

Landing Party is a different type of adventure game in that your favorite movie stars, historical figures, friends and relatives can become characters in this adventure. That's because before you become the Captain of this starship, you get to pick your crew!! You must then overcome the intricacies of dealing, blasting or running through the planet's zones before you can get the energy crystals you need desperately — without which your life supports fail! Landing Party is menu driven and easy to play. Individual games are short and different each time. This adventure is text based and has no graphics.

Usage: Entertainment.

System Requirements: 64K, one disk drive and monochrome display.

How to Start: To begin playing, type in LPARTY and press ENTER, and select "PLAY THE GAME" from the menu. Or type in LP to skip the initial menu.

Suggested Donation: $10.00 covers latest version and BASIC source code.

File Descriptions:

— — —	— —	Landing Party (v1.0)
LP	EXE	Add your favorite movie stars or heros to this adventure
LPARTY	EXE	Menus and utilities for Landing Party
LPARTY	DAT	File of characters for Landing Party
LPARTY	DOC	Documentation for LP.EXE (6k)

614 New York Version 1.0

v1

New York is a cleverly designed adventure program written in BASIC. The goal is to escape from a New York City ghetto. There are many obstacles to overcome, and many hardships to endure. After you escape the dangerous ghetto areas, you must find adequate food and shelter, or you will soon die from the rough exposure of the city. Unlike other interactive text games in which only one solution exists, New York can be solved different ways with different endings depending upon how you play the game! For example, you can overcome your opponents using violent/ evil tactics, or you can try using less violent methods. The choice is entirely up to you!

Usage: Entertainment.

System Requirements: 128K, monochrome monitor, one disk drive.

How to Start: Read the NEWYORK.DOC and .TXT files for instructions. To display the help information about New York, load BASICA and enter: RUN "NEWYORK" and press ENTER and follow menu options for instructions.

File Descriptions:

— — —	— —	New York (v1.0)
NEWYORK	BAS	Escape from New York city
NEWYORK	DOC	Documentation for NEWYORK.BAS

628 BibleQ
v1

BIBLEQ is a trivia-type game with 1000 multiple-choice questions drawn from the Bible. It tests you on a wide range of topics including geography of the biblical lands, personalities, and incidents and teachings of the Gospels. Bible students and teachers of the Church School variety will certainly want this in their collections. Combined with WordWorker (#581-2) you have the foundations of an excellent on-line scripture study system.

Usage: Entertainment

System Requirements: 128K, one disk drive, monochrome display

How to Start: To start, type BIBLEQ and press ENTER. Since "BIBLEQ" program uses files cat1.dat through cat4.dat for data, the program and these files must be on the default drive.

Suggested Donation: $7.00. Also, if you would like the source code, written in BASIC, and a couple programs for making your own multiple-choice trivia-type game, please include $2 for postage and handling with your registration fee of $7 (total $9).

File Descriptions:

BIBLEQ	EXE	Main program
BIBLEQ	DOC	Documentation for program and file
CAT1	DAT	Questions on Old Testament
CAT2	DAT	Questions on Bible geography
CAT3	DAT	Questions on the Four Gospels
CAT4	DAT	Questions on the New Testament
GO	BAT	Startup instructions

641 MAHJONG
v1

MAHJONG is one of the most fascinating games from the Orient. It is similar to western card gambling games in that it has stakes options, different suits (Characters, Circles, and Bamboos) and special tiles resembling wild cards: there are special tiles called The Four Winds (East, South, West and North) and The Three Dragons. Combining these gives you 136 tiles to play with. In play it is similar to the card game Rummy in that each player picks up a tile until four complete sets are gotten.

What sets this game apart is the extraordinary quality of the graphics employed to display the tiles. Also, beginners need not be daunted: the documentation is excellent. And this version allows the player to practice against three simulated opponents. with levels of play from beginner to expert.

Usage: Entertainment

System Requirements: 128K, one disk drive and a color/graphics monitor and card

How to Start: After consulting MAREAD.DOC for instructions, begin the game by entering MAHJONG at the DOS prompt.

Suggested Donation: $20.00

File Descriptions:

MA	INS	File needed by MAHJONG
MA	C	File needed by MAHJONG
MA	S	File needed by MAHJONG
MA	P	File needed by MAHJONG
MA	A	File needed by MAHJONG
MA	B	File needed by MAHJONG
AUTOEXEC	BAT	This file makes the disk self booting if MS/PC/DOS is added
MAHJONG	EXE+	The main game playing program
MAREAD	DOC	A short explanation of the program and the game of MAHJONG

678 The Golden Wombat of Destiny

v1

Four Very Noteworthy Things About This Program:

First, it is one of the better all-text adventure games we have seen. The program is able to handle full sentence commands, much in the same way as the major commercial programs. Also it accepts a good-sized vocabulary, viz., here is a list of some of the verbs which it currently understands: break, drink, drop, eat, examine, get, hit, kick, kill, listen, look, open, pick up, press, pull, push, put, read, shout, shut, smash, feel, give, feed, go, drink, smell, take, taste, throw, touch, wake.

Second, even though the program is a text adventure, it does require a color-graphics adapter. This is due to the ability it has to change the color of the screens and the text to fit the wishes of the user.

Third, Your quest is to discover the Forbidden City of the Great Lost Empire and unearth the mysteries it contains.

Fourth, this is the first text adventure entered into the library from our growing pool of authors in England and Europe. And it shows it in the humour and styling, delightfully so! To quote the author of The Golden Wombat:

SCORE: Much as in life, there is no scoring in The Golden Wombat.

THE POINT: The point of The Golden Wombat is Destiny itself. Obviously. You'll know when you've found it. Possibly.

Usage: Entertainment

System Requirements: 64K, one disk drive, color adaptor and display

How to Start: READ the WOMBAT.DOC, type WOMBAT and press ENTER, and then you're on your own...

File Descriptions:

COLOURS?	ALT	Alternate color data files (3 files)
NEW–ADV	???	Overlay files which the game calls when running (7 files)
???	DAT	Data files (4 files)

READ	COM	Program to read READ.TXT file
READ	TXT	Introductory text file from the author (accessed by READ.COM)
SETUP	COM	Program to change colors in display
WOMBAT	COM	Main game file
WOMBAT	MAN	Users manual

683 Buttonware Adventures

v1

This diskette contains two of Jim Button's latest in his expanding text-adventure series. In the first game, Castaway, you find yourself the sole survivor of a shipwreck who has now drifted onto a small island. Not only are you without supplies, you find plenty of treasures and clues, but your main problem is to survive and get home. The other text-adventure is more educational as you are to travel throughout South America collecting information for the United States. Players learn basic geography playing this adventure. Each is well documented during program execution.

Usage: Entertainment

System Requirements: 128K, one disk drive, monochrome display

How to Start: Read the INFO.DOC for directions; both run from DOS.

Suggested Donation: $29.95 + $5 s/h

File Descriptions:

– – – –	– –	Buttonware Adventures (v1.0)
CASTAWAY	EXE	Castaway adventure, will run directly from DOS
SAMERICA	EXE	South America Trek adventure, runs from DOS
INFO	DOC	Program startup documentation
GO	BAT	Initial program information, type: go (enter)

694

Sleuth
Version 4.1

v1

As you begin a game of SLEUTH a murder has just been committed. Your job is to mingle with the houseguests and to search the contents of the house until you feel you have solved the crime. Every game of SLEUTH is different so you must fully explore the house each time that you play.

The objective is to determine among six suspects which one has committed a murder, discover his or her murder weapon, find the location that the murder took place, and accuse the murderer in everyone's presence. Unfortunately, the guilty one quickly tires of the investigation and plots to end the game for you prematurely.

One Hint: The murder weapon will be obvious as soon as you EXAMINE the correct object. (Though you will need to find the magnifying glass before you can really conduct an adequate search of the various objects.) You probably should not GET the weapon at first since the murderer is likely to become nervous if you are carrying the evidence around with you...

Usage: Entertainment

System Requirements: 64K, one disk drive and monochrome display

How to Start: To see the documentation for SLEUTH, select the 'Review Instructions' option from the main menu of the SLEUTH program.

• To run, enter SLEUTH and press ENTER.

Suggested Donation: $10.00

File Descriptions:

– – – –	– –	Sleuth (V4.1)
SLEUTH0	EXE	Main program.
SLEUTH	DOC	Documentation for SLEUTH0.EXE.
AUTOEXEC	BAT	Runs SLEUTH.BAT.
SUNDRIES		Contains data used to understand commands.
ALIBI1		Contains ways in which suspects may respond to questions.
ALIBI2		Contains the pleas of suspects.
DESCR	V1	Contains descriptions of portions of the house.
SUSPICT	V1	Random file containing binary data.
RMDEF	V1	Sequential file containing lots of numbers.
ACT	V1	Contains the actions of people in the house.

WEAPN	V1	Contains descriptions of potential murder weapons.
DESCR	V2	Contains descriptions of portions of the house.
SUSPICT	V2	Random file containing binary data.
RMDEF	V2	Sequential file containing lots of numbers.
ACT	V2	Contains the actions of people in the house.
WEAPN	V2	Contains descriptions of potential murder weapons.
README		Tells how to run SLEUTH.
BW	BAT	Removes all color from the houses shown on the screen.
SUSPICT	V3	Random file containing binary data.
SUSPICT	V5	Random file containing binary data.
SUSPICT	V0	Random file containing binary data.
SUSPICT	V7	Random file containing binary data.
SUSPICT	V9	Random file containing binary data.
SUSPICT	V4	Random file containing binary data.
SUSPICT	V6	Random file containing binary data.
SUSPICT	V8	Random file containing binary data.
PLUG		A list of games by Norland Software.
SLEUTH	BAT	Runs SLEUTH0.EXE, then types PLUG.

705

KIDGAMES

v1

KIDGAMES is a BLAST! This collection of games specifically geared toward the ages of 2-10 years has excellent graphics and a straight-forward approach to making fun educational. Your children will not only have fun with these games but will also learn from them.

For education, easily the top on this disk is HANGMAN which both teaches basic spelling and allows for growing a vocabulary by expanding the dictionary of the game. For pure fun, MOSAIC which teaches pattern matching and allows for pattern building gets my vote! Also here are:

ALPHABET teaches the alphabet and alphabetic sequence ANIMALS teaches simple preschool math CLOCKGAME teaches how to read an analog clock MOSAIC teaches pattern matching

If you really like the sprites that accompany the games, there is a sprite designer package included (MAKEICON.COM). You may also use the more fully featured sprite designer form this author's Sprites and Animation package : DESIGNER.COM on Disk No 511.

Usage: Educational Fun!

System Requirements: 64K, one disk drive and monochrome display

How to Start: Consult the .DOC files, especially the HANGMAN.DOC.

Suggested Donation: $10.00

File Descriptions:

ALPHABET	—2	Part of ALPHABET.COM
ALPHABET	—1	Part of ALPHABET.COM
ALPHABET	COM	Main ALPHABET program
ANIMALS	—2	Part of ANIMALS.COM
ANIMALS	—1	Part of ANIMALS.COM
ANIMALS	COM	Main ANIMALS program
ANIMALS	TAB	Part of ANIMALS.COM
CLOCKGAM	COM	Main CLOCKGAM program
CLOCKGAM	PIC	Part of CLOCKGAM program
DICTNARY		Auxiliary dictionary for hangman
GO	BAT	ypes out kidgames.doc
HANGMAN	COM	Teaches letter sounds and spelling
HANGMAN	DIC	Dictonary for hangman
HANGMAN	DOC	Documentation for hangman
KIDGAMES	DOC	Brief description about the games on this disk
MAKEICON	COM	Icon maker program
MAKELIST	COM	Program which allows you to add word to HANGMAN dictionary
MOSAIC	COM	Mosaic main program
MOSAIC	PIC	Part of MOSAIC program
MOSAIC	TAB	Part of MOSAIC program

FINANCIAL APPLICATIONS:

The Library focuses here on the analysis and management of your financial affairs. The selected programs are of different dimensions and complexity. Topics covered include :

- Stocks and bonds portfolio management
- Stocks and bonds performance
- Business graphs and trend analysis
- Loan analysis
- Asset management
- Tax management
- Accounting programs (also see BUSINESS)
- Depreciation
- Interest
- Present and future valuation
- Amortization tables
- Personal finances (also see HOME)
- Leasing versus purchasing

The more complex programs are designed for portfolio tracking and analysis, as well as graphing stocks and bonds performance. Other programs calculate depreciation, interest, yields and, of course, taxes on assets.

There are many small programs for analyzing loans, creating amortization tables and different payment schemes, compare leasing vs buying, and figure present versus future values. Several disks of BASIC and LOTUS 1-2-3 templates pertain to financial and real estate analysis as well as tracking personal finances.

Finally, several accounting packages for small to medium sized businesses have been included. They are mainly encumbrance or double entry accounting systems that require a high level of financial knowledge. For less sophisticated packages, see the BUSINESS section.

14 BARGRAPH

v1

Bargraph is a graphic display program that accepts your input data and creates custom bar graphs. These graphs that can be used to track financial data, grades or profits. Bargraph includes an option to graph against the mean average. You can specify whether the graph is to be presented in percentages or in decimal figures.

Usage: Educational and financial graphing program, Intermediate level users

System Requirements: 64K, one disk drive and monochrome display

How to Start: To run BASIC programs consult the directions for GETTING STARTED for your configuration. To use the VISICALC files consult your VISICALC manual. Consult PDSOFTWR.DOC for addition information.

User Comments: "The best bargraph program for anyone." "It is tremendous in that it gives actual examples and then lets you go to work." "Does what it says; works best when used with a PrtSc than with program Print command."

File Descriptions:

BASMENU	BAS	Automatic menu for BASIC programs
METEOR	BAS	Fast-moving game using cursor movement keys
YAHTZEE	BAS	Yahtzee game rolls the dice & keeps score
COREFIX	BAS	BASIC program to inspect & patch storage
BIRDS	BAS	Sound effects
BLKLETER	BAS	Generate block letters on the printer
SPSHIPS	BAS	Sound effects
TICKTOCK	BAS	Sound effects
FINANCE	BAS	Large package of financial programs
SHELLSRT	BAS	Shell-metzger sort written in BASIC
SORT	BAS	Another sort written in BASIC
PDSOFTWR	DOC	Package of public domain software
ASYN-PGM	BAS	Asynchronous communication program
BKSPACE	BAS	Patch for DOS-disk COMM.BAS to handle backspaces
DWNLOAD	BAS	Patch for DOS-disk COMM.BAS to download files
PRINTER	BAS	Patch for DOS-disk COMM.BAS to toggle printer
BRKEVEN	VC	VISICALC program — break-even points
COSINES	VC	VISICALC program — calculate table of cosines
FEDTAX	VC	VISICALC program — federal income tax
GRAPHS	VC	VISICALC program — plotting points
HOMEBDGT	VC	VISICALC program — home budget program

PRTSETUP	VC	VISICALC printer setup hints
— — — —	— —	BARGRAPH
BARGRAPH	BAS	Program to produce bargraphs on the mono display — well liked
BACKLOG	BAR	Sample BARGRAPH input
FCST	BAR	Part of BARGRAPH
PLANACT	BAR	Part of BARGRAPH
QTR2G	BAR	Part of BARGRAPH
S	BAR	Part of BARGRAPH
SS	BAR	Part of BARGRAPH
SSS	BAR	Part of BARGRAPH
SSSSS	BAR	Part of BARGRAPH
SSSSSS	BAR	Part of BARGRAPH
YR17	BAR	Part of BARGRAPH
YR20	BAR	Part of BARGRAPH

25 FINANCE
v1.1

Finance is a collection of standard financial programs, designed so that anyone can use them. The programs prompt for input and are easy to run. Some of the routines included are; Depreciation, Interest and Bond yield calculators. A perfect item for all of you budding financial geniuses.

Usage: Educational and financial tools for investors, accountants, and college students

System Requirements: 64K, one disk drive and monochrome display

How to Start: To run BASIC programs consult the directions in GETTING STARTED for your configuration.

User Comments: "The finance program is menu driven, fast, and very helpful. Amortization tables are breeze with this!" "A good selection of financial programs. Covers just about all needs." "Program needs a little more documentation"

File Descriptions:

FINANCE	BAS	20 Miscellaneous financial programs
FINANCE1	BAS	5 more financial programs
GROWTH	BAS	Growth rate and projections
GROWTH1	BAS	Calculates compound growth
REPORTS	BAS	Budget management report
PRLIST	BAS	Miscellaneous printer routines
KALCOL	BAS	Kaleidescope — mono/color (Subroutine form)

40 Stock Market Analyser
v1

This is a stock market analysis program for creating, analyzing and plotting security data files. Stock Market Analyser is a stock tracking program that enables the user to update the history files of a particular stock, either with current activity or a past record. It then displays the data in graphic form so the user may analyze the stock trend. Stock Market Analyser comes complete with routines to plot the compiled stock data.

Useage: Analysis tools for stock traders

System Requirements: 64K, one disk drive and monochrome display

How to Start: To run BASIC programs consult the directions in GETTING STARTED for your configuration. Consult MAKSTKFL.DOC for program documentation.

User Comments: "Great for technical stock analysis. It's one of the few disks I actually use every week! It has sparse documentation, but the program is fairly intuitive" "Needs a utility to download data into the proper format via modem fron Compuserve, The Source, or Dow Jones info service. Manual data entry is tedious."

File Descriptions:

MAKSTKFL	BAS	Main program to create stock data file
MAKSTKFL	DOC	Documentation for MAKSTKFL.BAS
PLTSTKFL	BAS	Main program to print stock data
PLTSTKFL	DOC	Documentation for PLTSTKFL.BAS
SCHWABCM	BAS	Part of stock market program
TRANSFER	BAT	Backup batch file
*	NYS	Stock data file (14 files)
PUTNAMHL	MUT	Stock data file
INDUST	DJA	Stock data file
COMSHARE	OTC	Stock data file
KELLYSER	OTC	Stock data file
GEMAR70	OPT	Stock data file
MONEYMKT	INT	Stock data file
UPDSTKFL	ALL	Lists all securities files
PLTSEQFL	ALL	Lists all plot files
UPDSTKFL	DAT	Lists all active files

101
The Portworth Package
v1

The Portworth Package is a user-supported set of applications programs that you can use for monitoring and evaluating your stock portfolios. Portfolios of up to 25 stocks can be processed. It has graphing capabilities, and includes documentation and sample files to illustrate usage.

Usage: Stock portfolio tracking and evaluation

System Requirements: 64K, one disk drive and monochrome display

How to Start: To run BASIC programs consult the directions in GETTING STARTED for your configuration. Consult the .DOC files for program documentation.

User Comments: "I did not like having to use an editor to generate the data files. Once you have the data files created, the program works fine." "It is best used by someone who holds onto their stocks for a long time so their portfolio isn't changing a lot."

Suggested Donation: $15.00

File Descriptions:

DLTAFILE	DTA	Sample input file
DLTAPLOT	BAS+	Portfolio valuation change line graph program
DLTAPRNT	BAS	Portfolio valuation change bar chart program
DRIVE	DTA	System configuration parameter file
HOLDLIST	DTA	Sample input file
PORTCHNG	DOC	Documents changes to this version of package
PORTCOST	BAS	Portfolio cost valuation program
PORTMRKT	BAS	Portfolio current valuation program
PORTPACK	BAT	Prints PORTPACK.DOC
PORTPACK	DOC	32-page user guide
SETDRIVE	BAS	System configuration program
README	TXT	Description of files on disk
PORTCNGZ	DOC	Documents changes to this program

151
Finance Manager by Hooper International Version 3.1
v1.1

The Finance Manager is a very powerful double-entry bookkeeping system. It allows multiple accounts, many report capabilities, sorting, and more. A very nice tool for either small businesses or sophisticated personal finances. This is an evaluation version of the program. It is fully functional and has only certain ommissions from the on-disk manual. Registration gets an update and full, printed documentation.

Usage: Bookkeeping system suitable for small business or personal use.

System Requirements: 64K, one disk drive and monochrome display

Features:

- Powerful reporting and summary capabilities.
- Customising capabilities for screen and printer.
- Multiple sets of books.
- Automated closings.

How to Start: Load DOS and type FM to enter the main program. Consult FM.DOC for program documentation.

User Comments: "Recommend that a user have pre-existing knowledge of double-entry bookkeeping before using this program." "For the first-time user the program is very difficult to use without sufficient documentation"

Suggested Donation: $40.00.

File Descriptions:

README		Description of files listed below
FM	DOC	Documentation file (55K)
FM	EXE	Main program
FMUTIL	EXE	Configuration program
FM	DEF	FM system file
FM	CNF	System active configuration data file
IBM	CNF	Configuration file for IBM/Epson printer (copy to fm.cnf)

JUKI	CNF	Configuration file for Juki 6100 printer (copy to fm.cnf)
AUTOEXEC	BAT	Autoboot batch file
INSTALL	BAT	Batch procedure to install/configure program for first use
WORK	???	Small Business example
HOME	???	Home use example

164
TeleWare
CASHTRAC Version 5.15
v3.1

CASHTRAC-5 is is a commercial quality software package for managing home, club, and small business checking, savings, and investment accounts. Data entry and reporting are simple and speedy in operation. The continuous checking account balance display and adjustable low balance warnings help prevent overdrafts. The Unpaid Bill feature warns of upcoming due dates and has one-time-only or automatic monthly and yearly reminders.

CASHTRAC-5 offers multiple checking account capabilities, each with up to 99 user-selected budget catagories. The account balance is always displayed, and a low-balance warning helps prevent overdrafts. Here is a listing of the reporting facilities also available to help you track your activities:

- Overall account statement
- Tax deductions
- Summary of all expenditures, with grand total
- Detail of expenditures in one budget area
- List of deposits
- Unpaid bills
- Summary of transactions within time frame and entire
- account.
- Budget Summary
- Budget Details

Usage: Financial management package for personal/business use.

System Requirements: 192K, 1 disk drive, monochrome monitor

How to Start: Load DOS and type CT510 to enter the main program. Consult READ.ME and CT510.DOC files for program documentation.

User Comments: "(CASHTRAC)..Best checkbook balancing program I've found yet, at any price." "Excellent home finance manager; user supported software well worth the money " "CashTrac does take a little getting use to, but works very well once you understand the system."

Suggested Donation: Registration of $35.00 entitles user to receive an associated graphics and utility program, bulletin board access, and update notices.

File Descriptions:

CT510	EXE	Main program
CT510	DOC	Documentation (90K)
PRINTDOC	BAT	Batch file to print-out documentation
READ	ME	Text file

171
Finance and Inventory
v1

The financial portion of this disk contains 20 useful, easy-to-use progams, including such handy routines as loan amortization, asset depreciation, and bond yield. The inventory portion of this disk is well documented and includes routines to take cash register input data, generate pick lists and report inventory.

Usage: Point-of-sale and accounting tools. Intermediate-advanced usage.

System Requirements: 64K, one disk drive and monochrome display

How to Start: To run BASIC programs consult the directions in GETTING STARTED for your configuration. Consult INVENTORY.DOC for additional program documentation.

User Comments: "I needed a program to do loan and future value analysis quickly as I was doing financial planning for investments. This collection of programs has all the calculations in one place." "Many useful routines for the business user." "I highly recommend this disk for financial calculations."

File Descriptions:

B1	BAS	Future value of an investment
B2	BAS	Future value of regular deposits
B3	BAS	Regular deposits
B4	BAS	Regular withdrawals from an investment
B5	BAS	Initial investment
B6	BAS	Minimum investment for withdrawals
B7	BAS	Nominal interest rate
B8	BAS	Effective interest rate on investment
B9	BAS	Earned interest table
B10	BAS	Depreciation table
B11	BAS	Depreciation amount
B12	BAS	Salvage value
B13	BAS	Discount commercial paper
B14	BAS	Principal on a loan
B15	BAS	Regular payment on a loan
B16	BAS	Last payment on a loan
B17	BAS	Remaining balance on a loan
B18	BAS	Term of a loan
B19	BAS	Annual interest rate on loan
B20	BAS	Mortgage amortization table
BUSIN	BAS	Menu for above B??.BAS programs
FINANCE	BAS	Amortization, present values, future values, interest rate
INTEREST	BAS	Prints compound interest factors
————	——	POS Inventory
CASHREG	BAS	POS Inventory — Cash register transaction processing
INVENPRC	BAS	POS Inventory — Inventory transaction processing
INVENRPT	BAS	POS Inventory — Inventory reporting
INVENTRY	DOC	POS Inventory — Documentation
PICKER	BAS	POS Inventory — Picking list generation
PICKTRAN	BAS	POS Inventory — Picking list transaction processing
START	BAS	POS Inventory — Main menu

227
Financial Programs
v2.0

A user-supported finance program to determine present and compound values. FINANCE is a well written, well documented, user-friendly series of menu driven software from Computer Handholders. It runs well and even includes such useful programs as a personal loan tracker and a home mortgage routine. This is a fine collection for the homeowner or student who doesn't want, or have, time to calculate these formulas for themselves.

Usage: Financial tools for budget management and control.

System Requirements: 64K, one disk drive and monochrome display

How to Start: To run, type "FINANCE" and press ENTER. Consult FINANCE.DOC for program documentation.

User Comments: "Good program to start learning about finance" "Easy, quick — great for the non-finance person" "..people who get the most out of it are taking a college Finance course."

Suggested Donation: $30.00, or $10.00 for students.

File Descriptions:

FINANCE	EXE	Main program
FINANCE	DOC	Documentation (20K)

242
Sage Trader
v1

Sage Trader was written to provide the commodity trader with an analysis and graphics program that would run on the IBM monochrome display. This program features an autosave feature that saves your data to disk whenever you change files or end the program. 'Typewriter' graphics are used, so a graphics card is not required, and graphs can be printed with a dot-matrix or daisywheel printer.

Usage: Stock market analysis package.

System Requirements: 64K, one disk drive and monochrome display

How to Start: To run, type "ST" and press ENTER. Consult TRADER.PRN for program documentation (NOTE: this program prints documentation directly to your printer).

Suggested Donation: $50.00

File Descriptions:

ST	EXE	Main program
ST	HLP	On line help for ST.EXE
ST	SPC	Points to data files
ST	ARF	Same as above
*	CCC	Example data files (4 files)
INSTALL	BAT	Makes a working copy of original disk
TRADER	PRN	Documentation for Sage Trader

246
Stock Charting System V1.7
v2.2

This disk contains a surprisingly sophisticated system to draw and print volume-high-low-close charts for any stock, bond, commodity, or security that has high-low-close prices. Short and longterm moving average can optionally be included on the chart. A color graphics adapter is required to display the graphs.

Usage: Graphic display of stock trends for analysis.

System Requirements: 128k, 1 disk drive, color graphics, and a graphics compatible printer.

How to Start: To run BASIC programs consult the directions in GETTING STARTED for your configuration. Consult SMSYSM2.DOC for program documentation.

User Comments: "A great buy for the money for charting." "The program works well (I tested all functions), and produces professional results." "Overall, a very good program."

Suggested Donation: $25.00 contribution for registration, documentation update and a newletter.

File Descriptions:

INDEXFIL	SMX	Index to data files
READ	ME	Instructions for printing documentation file
REL2–2		Release marker
SMADDEL2	BAS	Maintains index file directory
SMENTRY2	BAS	Sets up data entry to data files
*	HS?	Help screen that displays on line documentation (7 files)
SMSETUP2	CTL	System control file
SMSYSTM2	DOC	12 page user guide
*	SMP	Sample data files (5 files)

323
TRANSTOCK
v1.40

This program package allows those interested in the stock market to easily download information from two databases on the Source (a communication utility). It acts as a translator, enabling any data-management software, (spreadsheets, graphics programs, etc), to use this data to analyse and spot trends. It also provides tools for manipulating files of selected stocks, simplifying these otherwise time-consuming tasks.

Usage: Stock analysis assistance package.

System Requirements: Requires a modem & access to the Source communication service.

Features:

- Very complete documentation.
- Easily settable program default parameters.
- Multiple translation formats
- Menu-driven for ease of use

How to Start: Load DOS and type TRANSTOK to enter the main program (NOTE: first set default configuration through DEFAULTS.EXE). Consult TRANSTOK.DOC for program documentation.

Suggested Donation: $25.00, includes update to latest version.

File Descriptions:

READ	ME	How to use Printdoc.bat
PRINTDOC	BAT	Batch file to print documentation
PRINTDOC	MSG	Documentation message
TRANSTOK	DOC	Full Documentation for TRANSTOK
TRANSTOK	EXE	Main program
TRANSTOK	DFL	Default information file
TRANSTOK	DF2	Copy of TRANSTOK.DFL
DEFAULTS	EXE	Customizes TRANSTOK for you — do first.
AMEX	STB	Stock name abbreviations
NYSE	STB	Stock name abbreviations
STOKCHEK	DJI	Sample data file
UNISTOX	DJI	Sample data file
UNISTOX	DJC	Sample data file

360
PFROI
Version 2.15
v2.15

PFROI is used to maintain a securities (stocks, bonds, CDs, etc.) portfolio and to measure periodically the return on investment. A demonstration data file is included. This package can help you handle many functions of managing an extensive portfolio and can aid the user in tax planning and preparation.

Usage: Analysis and portfolio management for investors.

System Requirements: 64K, one disk drive and monochrome display

How to Start: Load DOS and type PFROI to enter the main program. Consult PFROI.DOC for program documentation.

User Comments: "Well thought out program. This is a good way to organize investments."

Suggested Donation: $15.00 covers update disk with additional features, or $22.00 includes printed documentation.

File Descriptions:

READ	ME	Documentation for the PFROI program
PFROI	COM	PFROI program
PFROI	DOC	PFROI documentation.
DEMOPF		A demo portfolio file
SETFA	EXE	Program that sets the file attribute byte (hidden, etc)
SETFA	DOC	Documentation for SETFA.EXE
GRFX	COM	Plots math functions of the form: $Y = F(x)$
GRFX	DOC	Documentation for GRFX
READ-ME	A	Description of other Techserv, Inc. software
BONDPRO	COM	Bondpro demo
BONDPRO	000	Bondpro overlay file
BONDPRO	HLP	Bondpro help file
BONDS		Bondpro demo data file

406
FINANCIAL PROGRAMS & LOTUS WORKSHEETS
v1

A variety of BASIC programs and LOTUS 1-2-3 worksheet templates suitable for personal and business use, including such tasks as; financial and real estate analysis, portfolio and personal property worksheets, and others to help analyze and control your finances. Also included is a spreadsheet program written in BASIC and an address book program.

Usage: Financial management tools, Intermediate level.

System Requirements: 64K, one disk drive and monochrome display

How to Start: To run the BASIC programs consult the directions in GETTING STARTED for you configuration

- To run the LOTUS 1-2-3 files consult your LOTUS 1-2-3 manual.

User Comments: "The templates were easily adaptable to specific needs which I liked. Another good value, saving hours it would take to build these models from scratch." "The AUTO2-1.BAT and MENU2-1.BAT are the greatest things that I have seen to help a person to run BASIC and BASICA programs."

File Descriptions:

AUTO1-1	BAT	Autoexecute batch file DOS 1.X
AUTO2-1	BAT	Autoexecute batch file DOS 2.X
MENU1-1	BAT	Main program for use with BASICA 1.0
MENU2-1	BAT	Main program for use with BASICA 2.0
BUSPGM	BAS	Business financial program
CHECK	BAS	Home check book program
DATAPGM	BAS	Statistical analysis program
FINANCE	BAS	Home finance program
FINPGM	BAS	Financial analysis program
KALK	BAS	Compound interest computation program
LOANS	BAS	Loan analyzer
MORTGAGE	BAS	Amortization program
PC-PAD	BAS	Editor/spreadsheet/viewer program
PERPCAL	BAS	Calendar for any year
PERS	BAS	Data file for personal address book
PERSONAL	BAS	Personal address book
PRINTCON	BAS	Printer setup

REALPGM	BAS	Real estate analysis program
STOCK	BAS	Stock market analysis
BUDGET	WKS	LOTUS 123 — budget worksheet
DIVIDEND	WKS	LOTUS 123 — dividend and interest report
EDFNDWKS	WKS	LOTUS 123 — plan for educational expenses
GROWTH	WKS	LOTUS 123 — accumulation planning worksheet
INSURE	WKS	LOTUS 123 — insurance calculator
INVEST	WKS	LOTUS 123 — portfolio summary worksheet
PAYMENTS	WKS	LOTUS 123 — expenditures and cash flow worksheet
PROPERTY	WKS	LOTUS 123 — personal property tracking worksheet
RETIRE	WKS	LOTUS 123 — retirement analysis
SECURITY	WKS	LOTUS 123 — social security analysis worksheet
TX5J	WKS	LOTUS 123 — 5 year income tax averaging worksheet
WEALTH	WKS	LOTUS 123 — compute your networth worksheet

519
BUDGETRAK
Version 1.2 (Disk 1 of 2)
V1

BUDGETRAK is an excellent accounting package for those who have a desire or a need to track their budget and expenses more closely than possible using an ordinary accounting system. Encumbrance accounting (the method used here) tracks obligations and planned expenses rather than actual expenses. When the actual expense is known, it is entered and the encumbrance amount and budget are updated. This gives a more accurate picture, for budgeting purposes, than waiting to record an actual expense. This is the first of a two disk set.

Usage: Accounting system for asset management, Intermediate-Advanced users.

System Requirements: 128k, 2 disk drives, (hard disk recommended)

Features:

- Handles single & double entry systems
- Built-in password system
- Five running balances are maintained

How to Start: Load DOS and type BINT to initialize and setup your personal budget. Review the various text files for program documentation and setup information (i.e.: BUDGDOC, READ.ME, and the .DOC files).

Suggested Donation: $49.00

File Descriptions:

BUDGDOC		Documentation for BUDG.EXE
BUDPASWD	EXE	Password Program
BINT	EXE	Initialization program
BUDG	EXE	Budget set up program
BMST	EXE	Master file set up program
BTRN	EXE	Transaction creation program
READ	ME	Introduction to BUDG.EXE
BRIEFDOC		Short documentation to get you up and running quickly
CONVERT	DOC	Conversion documentation

520
BUDGETRAK
Version 1.2 (Disk 2 of 2)
V1

This is the essential second disk of the BUDGETRAK accounting system. It is essential to have both disks in order to run the programs successfully. Please see description of disk No 519.

File Descriptions:

README		Brief notes on using BUDGETRAK
BPRN	EXE	Print transaction file with summaries
BSPR	EXE	12 month spreadsheet program
B3MO	EXE	3 month spreadsheet program
GIND86DD		Data file — 1
BSRT	EXE	Sorts transaction file and master file
SOFFSET		Data file — 2
BUDPASS		Data file — 3
???DD1		Data files (Created by month)
BBAL	EXE	Audit transaction file balances
GNAM86DD		Data file — 4
GLMS86DD		Data file — 5
GCTL86DD		Data file — 6
BCON	EXE	Conversion program
CONVERT	DOC	Documentation for BCON.EXE

532 PC-MONEY Version 1.1

V1

PC-MONEY is a personal and family financial and tax recording system with sections for portfolio management and federal tax estimating. You can use this in conjuntion with disk #458 to print out your income tax return. It is menu-driven for ease of use, and includes a checkbook program that creates tax records.

Usage: Financial tracking aids for all users

System Requirements: 64K, one disk drive and monochrome display

Features:

- Includes two sample data files for familiarization purposes.
- Menu driven
- Support for multiple checking accounts

How to Start: Load DOS and type PC-MONEY to enter the main program. Consult PC-MONEY.DOC for program documentation.

Suggested Donation: $25.00

File Descriptions:

PC-MONEY	COM	Main PC Money program
PC-MONEY	DOC	PC-Money documentation
README	DOC	Quick introduction to PC-MONEY
INITDATA		Initialization data used by PC-MONEY
CONTENTS		In-depth description of the files on this diskette
TAXES85	DTA	Sample datafile — 1
BANK185	DTA	Sample datafile — 2

575 PC-STOCK

v2.4

PC-STOCK Finance Program is a stock evaluation and tracking system. It is meant as a tool to enable the user to analyze stock trends, and tries to meet this objective with an easy to use, menu-driven system and informative graphics. Support is also included for graphics printers, enabling you to save your analysis to hard copy.

Usage: Graphics oriented stock analysis tool for all levels.

System Requirements: 128K, one disk drive, color graphics

How to Start: Load DOS and type PC-STOCK to enter the main program. Consult PC-STOCK.DOC for program documentation.

File Descriptions:

PC-STOCK	EXE	Stock trend analysis program (128K + colorgraphicard)
PC-STOCK	DOC	Documentation
PC-STOCK	INF	Over lay program for PC-Stock
README		Documentation (brief) for printing manual
DAYTON	STK	Stock Trend Files
DJ20BND	STK	Stock Trend Files
DJIND	STK	Stock Trend Files
INTHARV	STK	Stock Trend Files
MESABI	STK	Stock Trend Files
MIDSUT	STK	Stock Trend Files
AMFESCO	STK	Stock Trend Files
FRANKUS	STK	Stock Trend Files
PANAM	STK	Stock Trend Files
S&P20T	STK	Stock Trend Files
S&P400I	STK	Stock Trend Files
S&P40FIN	STK	Stock Trend Files
S&P40UT	STK	Stock Trend Files
S&P500	STK	Stock Trend Files
TESORO	STK	Stock Trend Files
AUTOEXEC	BAT	Batch file to automatically start PC-STOCK.EXE
SILVER	STK	Silver Trend Files
GOLD	STK	Gold Trend Files

644
The Stock Trader
v1

The Stock Trader is a menu driven program requiring a graphics monitor for tracking selected stock performance and generating buy-and-sell signals according to trends over user-selected periods of time. There are 8 stocks at the start for demo purposes. Stocks may be added and deleted, and the DOW performance, or other accepted market average, is also displayed. Stock performance is graphed in x-y mode, and graphs may be printed.

Usage: Stock tracking and analysis

System Requirements: 128K, two disk drives and monochome/graphics or color display system

How to Start: Load DOS and type STOCK to enter the main program. Consult READ.ME for program information.

Suggested Donation: $35.00

File Descriptions:

README		Text file instructions for starting The Stock Trader
CONFIG	DAT	Configuration data file used to format screens and graphs.
CONTROL	DAT	Screen data for help screen to set printer codes and color.
MONEY	DAT	Call-up screen for info on donations, copyrights, etc.
SCREENA	DAT	Stock update help screen #1.
SCREENA2	DAT	Stock update help screen #2.
SCREENA3	DAT	Stock update help screen #3.
SCREENB	DAT	Help screen #1 for adding a stock to the list.
SCREENB2	DAT	Help screen #2 for adding a stock to the list.
SCREENC	DAT	Help screen for deleting a stock.
SCREEND	DAT	Graphing help screen #1.
SCREEND2	DAT	Graphing help screen #2.
SCREEND3	DAT	Graphing help screen #3.
SCREENE	DAT	Screen for posting the data entry date.
SCREENF	DAT	Help screen for printout of stock performance.
SCREENG	DAT	Help screen for writing updated data to disk.
SCREENH	DAT	Handling a stock split help screen.
SCREENI	DAT	Help screen for color display and printer codes.
SCREENJ	DAT	Help screen for entering modifications to trading indicators.
SCREENJ2	DAT	Trading indicators help screen #2.
SCREENJ3	DAT	Trading indicators help screen #3.
SCREENM	DAT	A first menu help screen.
SCREENM2	DAT	A second menu help screen.
SCREENM3	DAT	A third menu help screen.

STOCK	COM	Command file for The Stock Trader
STOCKS	DAT	Data file for stocks for demonstration and additions.

656
Real Estate Systems
v1

RES is a menu-driven program developed to assist the "typical" real estate office to store and retrieve information concerning: properties for sale, pending sales, and closed sales as well as details about your agents. RES keeps detailed records for each sale and one can search for pending/closed sales at any time. It keeps track of the agents' records for current and the previous year's commissions and enables the user to add an agent or search records of an agent.

RES generates valuable reports, such as an office or agent commissions reports, projected income reports, pending/closed sales reports, unsold property listing reports. RES also has the added special feature of year-end processing which purges all closed sales from the system.

Usage: Real Estate Office Management

System Requirements: 256K, two floppy drives (a hard disk is strongly recommended) and a monochrome display

How to Start: Consult and print out the Documentation in file RES.DOC — beware it is 80+ pages

- To run, enter RES at the DOS prompt; it will bring you to a Master Menu Screen from which you can choose the module you need.

Suggested Donation: $15.00 covers a complete, bound manual and makes you a member of the RES USERS GROUP.

File Descriptions:

RES	EXE	Main Program
SALE	DBF	Record of sale-search for pending/closed sale
AGENT	DBF	File on agents-add/search
SELLER	NTX	Record of details of sale just made
AGNTNAME	NTX	Keeps agents record-current/previous years. Updates commissions
READ-ME	TXT	Information on program
RES	DOC	77 pg. documentation file

GAMES:

From chess to ping pong, from anagrams to Hangman, from the ancient African strategy game of Nim to Ms Packgal, you can find every level and variety of games in here! Games that run on monochrome monitors, games that run on color monitors, arcade games, word games, adventure games, educational games, games for the young, and games for the not-so-young.

And if someone starts to get on your case about "wasting your time playing those silly games", just explain that to effectively strategize the parameters of emerging Expert Systems development, it is crucial to our national security that you can outthink PANGO, escape from The Castle and make it to the 10th level of Ms Packgal.

1 Game Series No 1
v1.1

This disk is one of the original game disks for the IBM PC. Many of these games are primitive compared to ones on later disks, but they may be of interest to those who'd like to see where we've been. And, as an added bonus, all can be addressed from a single menu.

Usage: Entertainment.

System Requirements: 64K, One disk drive, Monochome monitor, Color graphics needed if file marked by a plus symbol (+).

How to Start: From BASIC, type LOAD MENU, and press ENTER.

User Comments: "Most games somewhat simple but generally easy to run." "A very interesting disk because of the age of the programs." "One can not appreciate how good the current game programs are until one has has seen original games such as these."

File Descriptions:

PATTERNS	BAS+	Generates random patterns on color monitor
BLACKJCK	BAS	Blackjack game on the monochrome display
YAHTZEE	BAS	Yahtzee game on the monochrome display
MENU	BAS	Menu for selecting programs on this disk
DOTS	BAS	Displays dot patterns for display characters
HATDANCE	BAS	Plays the Mexican Hat Dance song
KALEID	BAS+	Generates random patterns on the color display
MAXIT	BAS+	Number game
STRINGS	BAS+	Generates random patterns on the color display
WOMBAT	BAS	Generates word problems
CIRCLES	BAS+	Draws random patterns on the color display
PONGPONG	BAS	Pong type game
COPYOVER	BAT	Copies games from DOS 1.0 or 1.1 disk
COPYOVER	DOC	Description of how to use COPYOVER.BAT

16 Game Series No 2
v1

This disk covers a wide spectrum of entertainment. For the cerebral, we have a version of Chess. For the adventurous, we have a Star Trek simulation. And for the arcade player, we have Breakout. For the gamblers, we have included a version of the game Craps. And if you feel like working with your modem instead, we have one of the earliest versions of PC-Talk III.

Usage: Entertainment.

System Requirements: 128K, one disk drive, monochome monitor, color graphics needed if file marked by a plus symbol (+).

How to Start: For instructions on running BASIC programs, please refer to the GETTING STARTED section in this catalog.

User Comments: "These are still the best games I've found for myself and also for my 10-year-old. He can play for hours on these -only one commercial game program measures up to these in keeping his interest."

File Descriptions:

BREAKOUT	BAS	Uses cursor keys to move paddle
CHESS1	BAS	Multi-level skills (Slow)
CRAPS	BAS	Casino type game for a single player
MASTMIND	BAS	Guess numbers instead of colored pegs
SUPRTREK	BAS	Another version for the "Trekies"
STARTREK	BAS	Minor updated version of STARTREK on Disk No 13
STARTREK	HOW	Documentation used by STARTREK.BAS
STARTREK	DUM	Data used by STARTREK.BAS
PC-TALK	BAS	Original version of popular communications program
PC-TALK	DOC	Extensive documentation for PC-TALK 2
LPCTALK	BAS	Used with PC-TALK.OR SCREEN
REMOVE	BAS	Used with communications (PC-TALK)

17 Game Series No 3
v1

A nice collection of different kinds of entertaining games. The text adventure will keep you busy for quite a while. And the arcade games will keep you entertained for hours. To make things easy, all programs on this disk may be accessed from a single menu.

Usage: Entertainment.

System Requirements: 128K, one disk drive, monochome monitor, color graphics needed if file marked by a plus symbol (+).

How to start: From BASIC, type LOAD MENU, and press ENTER.

User Comments: "Seeing older programs such as these and being able to see different treatments of the same game is interesting." "This has a good set of games some are a bit simple." "PCMAN slow, FENCE interesting and challenging."

File Descriptions:

MENU	BAS	Menu to execute programs on this diskette
PCMAN	BAS	Pac-Man look alike for 80 column display
SURVIVAL	BAS	Can you survive a trip to the moon?
MOON	BAS	Enhanced version of SURVIVAL
STARTREK	BAS	Another STARTREK version with minor changes
STARTRK2	BAS	Documentation for STARTRK game
STARTREK	DUM	Overlay module for STARTREK
JBREAK	BAS	Bounce the ball off of the wall (BREAKOUT)
BREAKOUT	BAS	A more sophisticated version of BREAKOUT
METEOR	BAS	Enhanced version of game on Disk No 14
FENCE	BAS	Enhanced version of game on Disk No 12
PCINIT	BAS	Initialize a high score file for PCMAN

21 PCMAN
v1

This disk contains a splendid example of what can be done graphically without the need of a graphics card, either monochrome or color. PCMAN and PCGIRLA are two different versions of the age-old run-and-eat maze game that revolutionized the computer and arcade industries. PCGIRLA uses ASCII characters to draw out the maze, while PCMAN uses the same character but in a 40-column color mode, to represent the player and the monsters that live in the maze.

Usage: Entertainment

System Requirements: 128K, one disk drive and monochrome or color graphics adaptor and display; files marked "+" require color setup

How to Start: While PCCHEERS requires BASIC, all the other can be run from DOS by typing their filename and pressing ENTER.

User Comments: "Great fun for those of us unwilling to go broke at the shopping centers." "I like having PCMAN and PCGIRL on the same disk; makes you appreciate the programming tricks." "Can't get this one away from the kids!"

File Descriptions:

JOYSTICK	DOC	Documentation file for JOYSTICK.EXE
JOYSTICK	EXE	Program to test your joystick's positions
PACGIRLA	EXE	Monochrome version of PAC-MAN
PCHEERS	BAS	THE TWELVE DAYS OF CHRISTMAS for the computer age
PCMAN	EXE+	Color version of PAC-MAN
PCMANHI	FIL	High score data file for PCMAN

24 Game Series No 4
v1.1

A fine collection of games from the earlier years of PC-SIG. All these games have been in the library since the early 1980's, but many are still quite popular, as well as having almost historic interest at this point. These programs are not only entertaining, but will show you the origins of some of later programs in the library.

Usage: Entertainment

System Requirements: 128K, one disk drive, monochome monitor, color graphics needed if file marked by a plus symbol (+).

How to Start: For instructions on running BASIC programs, please refer to the GETTING STARTED section in this catalog.

User Comments: "(NEWTREK) Same as all the rest." "(PACKMAN) is interesting." "PACKMAN is quite good and the best game on the disk!"

File Descriptions:

WUMPUS	BAS	Hunt the Wumpus in its cave
JAMMER	BAS	"Head On" Variation
RACJAM	SCO	Data for JAMMER game, scoring categories
GOBBLE	BAS	PAC MAN variation
TICTACTO	BAS	Tic-Tac-Toe
MOON	BAS	Survival on the MOON
NEWTREK	BAS	Another version of StarTrek
NEWTREK	HOW	Documentation for NEWTREK.BAS
OPERATOR	BAS	Simulates S/370 VM Operator Console
PACKMAN	EXE+	Excellent graphics version of PacMan
PACKMAN	DOC	Documentation for PACKMAN.EXE
————	——	SONGS
SONGS	BAS	Choose from several on "menu"
YESTER	BAS	Yesterday
EVRONWRD	BAS	Ever Onward
RANGERD	BAS	The William Tell Overture (Lone Ranger Theme)
PUFF	BAS	Puff the Magic Dragon
LITUPLIF	BAS	You Light Up My Life

35
Game Series No 5
v1

Another collection of games from the earlier years of PC-SIG. All these games have been in the library since the early 1980's. These programs are not only entertaining, but will show you the origins of some of later programs in the library. Some programs here have some practical uses as well. Simple phone lists, checkbook programs, and others provide useful functions for you to enjoy.

Usage: Entertainment.

System Requirements: 128K, one disk drive, monochome monitor, color graphics needed if file marked by a plus symbol (+).

How to start: For instructions on running BASIC programs, please refer to the GETTING STARTED section in this catalog.

User Comments: "I'm disappointed that the computer takes so much time making a decision about which move it wants to make in the chess program. The instructions are not what I would call detailed. For instance, it never indicates how to quit the game." " ..nice group of basic games." "GOLF, STRIKE9, DESERT, BULLSEYE are good. LEM seems rather meaningless. ZAP-EM, and MISSLE have glitches. I'll try CHESS when I have more time." "The disk seems to offer some diversions, good for my kids."

File Descriptions:

23MATCH	BAS	The match game
ADDRESS	BAS	Addresses and phone numbers
BANKER	BAS	Checking account maintenance, expense categories
BARGRAPH	BAS	Creates bargraphs
BULLSEYE	BAS	Simulated dart game
CAPTURE	BAS	Logic game, try to capture the enemy space ship
CHESS	BAS	Play chess with the computer
CHIEF	BAS	Math game
DECIDE	BAS	Helps decide between alternatives
DESERT	BAS	Try to cross the desert without getting killed
GOLF	BAS	Play golf, pick your club and stroke
ICICLE	BAS	A race to the top of the screen
KENO	BAS	Nevada style bingo
KINGDOM	BAS	Can you survive your term as king?
LANDER	BAS	Another moon lander program
LEM	BAS	A moon lander program
LOAN	BAS	Loan amortization program

MISSLE	BAS	Earth under attack from another planet
SECRETNO	BAS	You try to guess the number
STARS	BAS	Challenging permutation puzzle to solve
STORY	BAS	Creates four stories from user-supplied words
STRIKE9	BAS	Dice roll numbers game
TRAP	BAS	Number guessing game
ZAP-EM	BAS	Space shoot'em on the monochrome

37
Game Series No 6
v1

Yet another collection of games from the earlier years of PC-SIG. All these games have been in the library since the early 1980's. These programs are not only entertaining, but will show you the origins of some of later programs in the library. For the BASIC programmers among you, these can be very informative if you yearn to write your own games someday.

Usage: Entertainment.

System Requirements: 128K, one disk drive, monochome monitor, color graphics needed if file marked by a plus symbol (+).

How to start: For instructions on running BASIC programs, please refer to the GETTING STARTED section in this catalog.

User Comments: "A list of the top ten highest scores would be a great addition to many of the games on this disk." "Games are entertaining and a lot of fun for the beginner and as they are in BASIC, they can be used as a learning tool for the novice. My daughter loves SCRAMBLE." "INVEN program was superb. I have used it on lots of different occasions."

File Descriptions:

ATTACK	BAS+	Destroy the Apple computer manufacturing plant
BLACKBOX	BAS	A game of strategy
CHR	BAS	Displays complete character set on screen
CIAGAME	BAS	An adventure to recover the stolen ruby
EQNSOLVE	BAS	Solves n linear equations in n unknowns
GALLERY	BAS	Arcade game
INVEN	BAS	48K inventory program
MATH	BAS	Addition, subtraction, multiplication & division problems
PERMUTE	BAS	Displays all possible permutations of a set of characters
ROMCHAR	BAS	Displays dot matrix characters from ROM patterns

SCRAMBLE	BAS	Guess scrambled words in shortest time
SERPENT	BAS	Guide a serpent through obstacles
SLOTMACH	BAS	Play the slot machines
SPINOUT	BAS+	High resolution version of breakout
SURROUND	BAS	Guide expanding character through a maze
WILLTELL	BAS	Music — An amazing musical selection
WILLTELL	DAT	Data for WILLTELL.BAS
ZAP'EM	BAS	Shoot the bugs
MENU	BAS	Menu program — run it to assess other programs

45 Games Series No 8

v1

Yet another collection of vastly different programs. There are number of educational games on this disk, plus a couple of games which will keep you guessing. For the general in you, we have a simulation of the Civil War. The artists can connect the dots, or have Snoopy come to life on their printer. For anyone interested in seeing a bit of history, or enjoying some vintage good times, this disk warrants investigation.

Usage: Entertainment.

System Requirements: 128K, one disk drive, monochome monitor, color graphics needed if file marked by a plus symbol (+).

How to Start: For instructions on running BASIC programs, please refer to the GETTING STARTED section in this catalog.

User Comments: "Some programs are fun but most are simplistic and after use, very little point in running again. SYNONYMS was the most fun." "Most programs lack any explanation of rules. What does exist is poorly written or says so little as to be useless. The exception is TRADE.BAS. That one is worthwhile and is very interesting." "Some of the games are pretty mediocre, but LIFE2 is a lot of fun."

File Descriptions:

ANTONYMS	BAS	Learn your antonyms
AWARI	BAS	Classic African sticks and stones
BACCRRT	BAS	Card game
BASEBALL	BAS	Baseball game
BIO	BAS	Biorythms for printer
BIRTHDAY	BAS	Find the day of the week you were born
BOMB	BAS	Find the bomb

CIVILWAR	BAS	The blue against grey
CLIMATES	BAS	Educational game
CLOUD-9	BAS	Educational game
DOTS	BAS	Connect the dots and make a picture
DRAGRACE	BAS	Race the circuit
FOOTBALL	BAS	Football simulation
GALAXY	BAS	Behold the stars
GALAXY2	BAS	Behold the stars and be inspired
GREEKRTS	BAS	Match Greek words with their meaning
HIDESEEK	BAS	Search for hidden objects
IQUEEN	BAS	Problem solving with chess pieces
MEMBRAIN	BAS	Keep cells alive
MINIMATH	BAS	Math
REVERSE	BAS	Arrange the numbers correctly
SHOP	BAS	Go shopping
SNOOPY	BAS	Print Snoopy on printer
SQUARE	BAS	Competitive square building
SWARMS	BAS	You are attacked by bees
SYNONYMS	BAS	Learn your synonyms
TAXMAN	BAS	Beat the taxman
TRADE	BAS	Intergalactic trading game
WEATHER	BAS	Predict the weather

47 PC-SIG Sampler No 1

v1

A virtual potpourri of programs, which range from games and musical programs to utilities that calculate electic usage and dump pictures to your printer. The CASTLE program, an adventure in a wizard's castle, is an old favorite. And the FINPAK package is a collection of useful financial aids.

Usage: Entertainment.

System Requirements: 128K, one disk drive, monochome monitor, color graphics needed if file marked by a plus symbol (+).

How to Start: To read DOC files, enter TYPE filename.ext and press ENTER.

● To run an EXE program, just type its name and press ENTER. For instructions on running BASIC programs, please refer to the GETTING STARTED section in this catalog.

User Comments: "CASTLE.BAS is a good program but it is included on disk 274. XMAS.BAS is good as is FINPAK. I would not reccomend this disk because the rest of the programs are phony." "FINPAK and maillist used, both simple but useable." "I loved the adventure games. Good challenge" "Again, I really enjoyed the Christmas music program."

File Descriptions:

CASTLE	BAS	Wizards castle game from July/Aug, Recreational Computing
CASTLE	DOC	Documentation for CASTLE game
CHRONSET	BAS	Sets Hayes stack chronograph
COMCHRON	BAS	Program to read Hayes stack chronograph
DISRTN	EXE	Disk file utility — undeletes and recovers lost sectors
ELECTRIC	BAS	Computes electric usage
FINPAK	BAS	Package of 20 financial programs
GDUMP1	BAS	Graphics dump program
GDUMP2	BAS	Graphics dump program
KILLNULL	BAS	Removes nulls from sequential files
MAILLIST	BAS	Mailing list program
PLOT	BAS+	Creates plots on color display
SORT-BLK	BAS	Sorts fixed length record files
XMAS	BAS	Plays Christmas song

49 PC-SIG Sampler No 2
v1

Another virtual potpourri of programs, which includes programs which will allow you to print 3x5 cards, display dot matrix characters, on-screen digital clock, play with a Rubic cube simulation, use a calendar program, calculate great circle crossings, try a hearing test, run a loan amortization statistics program, or hit the bouncing ball.

Usage: Entertainment.

System Requirements: 128K, one disk drive, monochome monitor, color graphics needed if file marked by a plus symbol (+).

How to Start: To read DOC files, enter TYPE filename.ext and press ENTER. For instructions on running BASIC programs, please refer to the GETTING STARTED section in this catalog.

User Comments: "(3BY5).. This program is only limited by your imagination as to what data you what to catalog. I particularly like the search capabilities." "(HEARING)Only checks top audio pitch you can hear, but I hooked up a stereo earphone set to my PC and am able to check each ear separately. Very good!" "Cube and hearing are very good. In a quiet room, the hearing test is surprisingly reproducible.

File Descriptions:

ADDRFLCD	BAS	Prints 3x5 cards
BIGTYPE1	BAS	Displays dot matrix characters in ROM pattern
CALEPSON	BAS	Modification to CALENDAR.BAS (1.0 & 1.1) for Epson printer
CALEPSON	DOC	Documentation for CALEPSON
CHARDISP	BAS	Displays screen character set
CLOCK	BAS	On screen digital clock
CUBE	BAS	Rubic cube simulation
DAYLOG	BAS	Calender program
EMBEDDED	BAS	Demonstrates embedded printer commands
FINISH	BAS	Text formatter written in BASIC
FINISHTX	BAS	Documentation for FINISH.BAS (Use FINISH.BAS to list)
GREATCIR	BAS	Calculate great circle crossings
GREATRHM	BAS	Great circle calculations
HEARING	BAS	Hearing test
JOYSTEST	BAS	Test joystick
JOYSTICK	BAS	Display joystick values
LOAN3	BAS	Loan amortization
NCCLSPRE	BAS	Statistics program — precision based on collected data
PCHALLEN	BAS	Game — hit the bouncing ball
PRINTER2	BAS	Sets up printer and lists files
PRINTSET		Sets up Epson printer to 1/8 inch line spacing
PRINTSET	DOC	Description of how to use PRINTSET
RHMLINE	BAS	World navigation
SEC&BYTE	BAS	Prints a table listing number of bytes as a function of sectors
SPINOUT	BAS+	Game using color graphics
XREFMOD	BAS	Produces cross-reference of variables used in a BASIC program

55 Game Series No 9
v1

Your Basic Games Package: Games for all ages, IQs, biorhythms and genders. Games of chance, games of skill, games for just about everyone. Do for yourself and your friends, play poker against your computer, race across a desert, or race around the horse track. And when you're finished, let your computer serenade you with one of several tunes.

Usage: Entertainment.

System Requirements: 128K, one disk drive, monochome monitor, color graphics needed if file marked by a plus symbol (+).

How to Start: To read DOC files, enter TYPE filename.ext and press ENTER. For instructions on running BASIC programs, please refer to the GETTING STARTED section in this catalog.

User Comments: "(LANDER) Great game for those of us that were not brought up on arcade games. At least I have a chance to win this one!" "CRAZY8 is nicely done, but I could make no sense out of JETPILOT or LANDER. Loved the tunes, though." "Biorythm program makes nice copy to send with birthday card."

File Descriptions:

BIO	BAS	Biorythms — from today's date
CRAZY8	BAS	Uses character graphics for cards
DESERT	BAS	Try to cross the desert in this adventure game
HRSERACE	BAS	Horserace
IPCOGOLF	BAS	Golf
IPPOKER	BAS+	Buck Mann's poker for one — uses graphics
IPPOKER	DOC	Documentation for IPPOKER.BAS
JETPILOT	BAS	Fly from pilots control panel
JETPILOT	DOC	Documentation for JETPILOT.BAS
LANDER	BAS+	Land space vehicle — graphics and sound
LANDER	BIN	Used by LANDER.BAS
LANDER	SCR	Used by LANDER.BAS
NADIA	BAS	Song
PHOENIX	BAS	Song
ROULETTE	BAS	Roulette
SESAME	BAS	Song
STARWARS	BAS	Song

71
Game Series No 10
v1

This is truly a game collection for the adventurous. Can you fly a starship into a hostile galaxy? How about finding the minerals you need? Can you survive a journey into a dangerous castle, hunt the elusive, (and sometimes dangerous), Wumpus? Challenge the unknown, accompanied by your trusty computer, and live to tell about it!

Usage: Entertainment.

System Requirements: 128K, one disk drive, monochome monitor, color graphics needed if file marked by a plus symbol (+).

How to Start: To read DOC files, enter TYPE filename.ext and press ENTER. For instructions on running BASIC programs, please refer to the GETTING STARTED section in this catalog.

User Comments: "(WIZARD)The game captures ones interest for about 6 to 10 sessions, where I was able to solve the game completely. Once the game was solved, there was no challenge...The humor used by the author in some of the situations was

amusing." "Same re games for kids and new users good!" "Best adventure games I have seen."

File Descriptions:

ZAP'EM	BAS	IPCO shoot'em type game
STARTREK	BAS	Another Startrek
STARTREK	DOC	Documentation for STARTREK.BAS
CYCLE	BAS	IPCO motorcycle race, Q&A type game
DROIDS	BAS	IPCO Hunt for minerals (board game)
LOSTGOLD	BAS	IPCO Adventure type game
WIZARD	BAS	IPCO The Wizards Castle
MEMORY	BAS	IPCO game to test your memory
SPELLER	BAS	IPCO spelling word drill (input your own words)

72
Game Series No 11
v1

A mind-boggling collection of programs. If you're confused, you can discuss your problems with Eliza or the Doctor. If you like puzzles, enter the world of the atom and try the Black Box. And, if games of chance are your field, how about a game of Blackjack? It's guaranteed to be safer for your wallet than a trip to Reno.

Usage: Entertainment.

System Requirements: 128K, one disk drive, monochome monitor, color graphics needed if file marked by a plus symbol (+).

How to start: For instructions on running BASIC programs, please refer to the GETTING STARTED section in this catalog.

User Comments: "The instructions on how to play the games are not clear. I never knew how to get out of any of the programs when they were dull. tictacto too simple. doctor stupid." "I enjoy playing with Eliza and my boys like the Blackjack game." "One of the best reasons I give people to contact PC-SIG" "ELIZA & DOCTOR fantastic!" "A very fun disk. At college, this disk is one I am always asked to swap!" "Blackbox, Doctor, and Eliza were all most entertaining. Othello did not allow enough time to examine the computer's moves."

File Descriptions:

TICTACTO	BAS	IPCO Tic-tac-toe
DOCTOR	BAS	IPCO Talk your problems out with the doctor
ROADRALY	BAS	IPCO Roadrally — Q&A type game
BLCKJACK	BAS	IPCO Blackjack — no color

BLACKBOX	BAS	IPCO Discover position of atoms by projecting rays
FIFTEEN	BAS	IPCO Puzzle game
ELIZA	BAS	The psychoanalyst

83 Wormcity
v1

For all of you who can't afford the ticket to the planet Arrakis of Dune fame, here is Wormcity, home of another voracious creature. Among the other BASIC fun'n'games here are the Towers of Hanoi, the 15Puzzle and TARGET, a really decent arcade shoot-em-up (which requires a monochrome graphics system). Filling out the disk are several utilities, the best of which are a program for taking a compiled file back to Assembly (COM2ASM) and Keyflags, which lets you track your use of NumLock and ScrollLock in the upper right hand corner of your screen.

Usage: Entertainment.

System Requirements: 64K, one disk drive, monochome monitor, color graphics needed if file marked by a plus symbol (+).

How to start: For instructions on running BASIC programs, please refer to the GETTING STARTED section in this catalog.

File Descriptions:

15PUZZLE	BAS	Fit the 15 numbers into their right places
COM2ASM	BAS	Program for taking .COM files back to assembly
COM2ASM	DOC	Documentation for COM2ASM.BAS
DISKMDF2	BAS	Allows you to modify disk tracks and sectors
GRPH64K	BAS	Guide to upgrading graphics boards
GRPH64K	DOC	Documentaiton for GRPH64K.BAS
HANOI	BAS	Towers of Hanoi, famous programming exercise
KEYFLAGS+	COM	Displays status of CapsLock and NumLock on the screen
KEYFLAGS	ASM	Assembly source code for KEYFLAGS.COM
LANDER	BAS	Try for a soft landing — Just Try!
MENU2	BAS	Main menu for the whole system
NWCLOCK	BAS	On screen digital clock
PCGLOBE	BAS	Display perspective views of a 3-d Earth
STARMAP	BAS	Look up!
TARGET	BAS	Arcade shoot-em-up
TARGET	DOC	Documentation for TARGET.BAS
TARGET	PIC	Picture file for TARGET.BAS
WORMCITY	BAS	Attack Saturn and it's cities

91 PC-SIG Sampler No 4
v1.1

Another fine collection of different kinds of entertaining games. The text adventure will keep you busy for quite a while, and the arcade games will probably keep you entertained for a few hours as well. And, for the more cerebral types among you, how about a nice game of chess??

Usage: Entertainment.

System Requirements: 128K, one disk drive, monochome monitor, color graphics needed if file marked by a plus symbol (+).

How to Start: To read DOC or TXT files, enter TYPE filename.ext and press ENTER. For instructions on running BASIC programs, please refer to the GETTING STARTED section in this catalog.

User Comments: "(Adventure)I could not make the program work as per documentation Adventure." "Additional files found on diskette; useful "readme" file helpful; would like to see better hard copy documentation; like the map." "The rotating globe is nice as is the golf game but the adventure compiler would not work." " A good mix of compiler options."

File Descriptions:

ADVENT	DOC	Documentation for Adventure game compiler
BASCOM	PAT	Patches for IBM BASIC compiler
BOGGLE	BAS	Find as many words as you can
CHESS	BAS	New version of the old game
COMPIL	BAS	Adventure system database compiler
DKSPAT	TXT	DISKCOPY and DISKCOMP patches for large memory (320K+) machines
DRIVER	BAS	Driver for Adventure system
GLOBE	BAS+	Creates rotating globe on graphics screen
GLOBE	DAT	Data file for GLOBE.BAS
GOLF2	BAS	Golf game
HIQUE2	BAS	Puzzle game (uses lightpen if you have one)
MUGGER	DAT	Sample adventure definition

120 PC-CHESS
v1

PC-Chess is a user-supported program that allows you to play chess against the computer or a human opponent. This game requires a color graphics adapter. These are large files, and are provided in a squeezed format, copy the files onto blank floppies before unsqueezing to insure sufficient room.

Usage: Entertainment

System Requirements: 128K, one disk drive, color graphics monitor

How to Start: For program instructions, type COPY PCCHESS.PRT PRN and press ENTER to print the manual.

User Comments: "Plays a good game of chess. Works as a good learning tool for the game of chess." "Best chess program I have ever seen, and I'm not much of a chess player." "It's amazing the things that can be done while playing. Even level one is a challenge for me." "Good but no match for Sargon. Shouldn't complain about something this sophisticated for this price." "Plays bad chess, at any speed that I can tolerate, fun to pit it against other chess programs." "Good buy. Documentation hard to follow. Should make provision for printing on non-graphics type printer. Print too small for good reading."

Suggested Donation: $15.00

File Descriptions:

PCCHESS	EXE	Initialization/setup program
PCCH1M	EXE	Player vs computer (monochrome display)
PCCH2M	EXE	2 Player version (monochrome display)
PCCH1G	EXE	Player vs computer (graphics display)
PCCH2G	EXE	2 Player version (graphics display)
PCCHESS	PRF	Save file for game setup parameters
PCCHESS	PRT	Documentation

174 Game Series No 12
v1.1

This disk in our entertainment series contains several different and challenging adventure games, a football simulation or two, several good arcade-type games, including SEAWOLF, an excellent game that DOES NOT require graphics capabilities. Also included, a VERY challenging, and very honest, game of Solitaire. (It won't let you cheat!)

Usage: Entertainment.

System Requirements: 128K, one disk drive, monochome monitor, color graphics needed if file marked by a plus symbol (+).

How to Start: To read DOC or TXT files, enter TYPE filename.ext and ENTER.

- To run a BAT file, just type its name and press ENTER. For instructions on running BASIC programs, please refer to the GETTING STARTED section in this catalog.

User Comments: "(GRINCH) Uses colors for the bushes and the grinch instead of the standard white on black on the color monitor . The children really like it." "(MARS-ESC) This is a cute text adventure game. There aren't that many rooms to explore; however it will take you awhile figuring out what to do with all the objects you find." "(SEAWOLF) This is an excellent action game for those of you who don't have color or graphics. You must try to shoot ships. Bonus times are given for certain scores. The hardest boats — PT boats, move very fast — a real challenge." "(SOLITARE) If you enjoy playing solitaire, this is an excellent version. I tried to cheat, but it wouldn't let me. If you win, there is a cute little surprise afterwards." "(CIA) This game is impossible to start without documentation."

File Descriptions:

?	BAT	Letter A-L for MENU.BAT
CIA	BAS	CIA adventure simulation
CIVILWAR	BAS	Civil war simulation
COMBOT	BAS	Program two robots to fight each other with lasers
COMBOT	DOC	Documentation for COMBOT.BAS
FOOTBAL	BAS	Big-8 football simulation — K.U. versus your choice

FOOTBALL	BAS	Another football simulation
FROG	EXE	Good Frogger type game — graphics required
GRINCH	BAS	El Grinch game — cute, neat game
MARS-ESC	BAS	Escape from Mars adventure
MENU	BAT	Menu for the files on this disk
MENU	SCR	Part of MENU.BAT
RACECAR	BAS	Good race car game
SEAWOLF	BAS	Excellent game — sink subs, PT's, tankers
SOLITARE	BAS	Solitare card game — you can't cheat with this one
XWING	BAS	Re-live Star Wars — outstanding game — graphics req'd

BLKFRDY	BAS	Stock market simulation
BLOCK	EXE	Pong — requires graphics and BASRUN.EXE
CHECKERS	BAS	Checkers — slow but okay
HUSTLE	BAS	Like Hoser — good game
HUSTLE	DAT	Part of HUSTLE.BAS
HUSTLE	DOC	Documentation
KNOCK	ASC	Documentation
KNOCK	BAS	Knock-knock joke teller
MUSICFIL	BAS	Music class management program
JHORCH	MUS	Sample data created by MUSICFIL.BAS
JHBAND	MUS	Sample data created by MUSICFIL.BAS
SHORCH	MUS	Sample data created by MUSICFIL.BAS
MEDLEY	BAS	Name that tune-plays favorite songs (Requires DOS 2.0)

175
Simulation & Board Games
v1

Have you ever wanted to play baseball when it is raining? Or explore a distant planet? Or try to keep your money on the stock market, while everyone else is jumping out of windows? This disk will let you do all those things, plus much more.

Usage: Entertainment.

System Requirements: 128K, one disk drive, monochome monitor, color graphics needed if file marked by a plus symbol (+).

How to Start: To read DOC files, enter TYPE filename.ext and press ENTER.

- To run an EXE program, just type its name and press ENTER. For instructions on running BASIC programs, please refer to the GETTING STARTED section in this catalog.

User Comments: "(VERSION) We mainly use HUSTLE which is a fine game. BASIC BASEBALL is OK too. The others are hard to understand and use." "Not much fun — too time consuming." "ALIEN is worth the price of the disk although I get a lot of error messages as I progress through the game. BASEBALL is fun. good selection." "Good board games, especially Acey-duecy and Black Friday."

File Descriptions:

ACEY-DUE	BAS	Acey-duecy card game
ALIEN	BAS	Adventure version
BASEBALL	BAS	Baseball simulation
BLACKBOX	BAS	Find the balls in an 8x8 grid using rays

177
Arcade Series No 1
v1

The first in a series of disks which display some of the best, in our opinion, of the games we have to offer in the library. For a good test of your heart rate, try to find the BOMB before it explodes. Or battle the vicious BUGS! JUMPJOE is a real test of your reflexes, and BREAKOUT is always a popular offering. After all that, grab your PENCIL and sketch your cares away.

Usage: Entertainment.

System Requirements: 128K, one disk drive, monochome monitor, color graphics needed if file marked by a plus symbol (+).

How to Start: To run an EXE or COM program, just type its name and press ENTER. For instructions on running BASIC programs, please refer to the GETTING STARTED section in this catalog.

User Comments: "Excellent assortment. For the price, can't beat it. some of the games did not operate on my PCjr. JUMPJOE is great. Rest are OK. How many versions of BREAKOUT are in your library?" "JumpJoe and Bugs good. Other basic programs are not much fun, More music- color & sounds needed." "Breakout didn't work and most had poor graphics. JumpJoe was good." "Archaic games !!!" "BUGS and JumpJoe: Two great games! Both me and the Missus have gotten more enjoyment out of these two games than any three of our store bought games!"

File Descriptions:

BOMB	BAS	Find the bomb in 1 of 1,000,000 rooms before BLAM!
BREAKOUT	BAS+	Hard Pong game (Requires color graphics)
BUGS	EXE	Centipede-like game — good version
BUGS!	SCR	Part of BUGS.EXE
CUBE	BAS+	Cube game (Color required)
DRIVER	BAS	Drive racecar around track — tough on eyes!
HS	DAT	High scores for JUMPJOE.EXE
JUMPJOE	EXE+	Version of Miner 2049'er or Donkey Kong (Color required)
JUMPJOE	SOL	Part of JUMPJOE.EXE
PENCIL	BAS+	Sketch on color monitor with joystick

178
Game Series No 13
v1

Are you ready for a challenge? Then grab your hat and let's go! First stop, your very own Kingdom, where you are responsible for the well-being and prosperity of yourself and your subjects. Next, stop the mad bomber in COLLIDE, it'll really blow you away! Then off to deep space with STARTREK, destroy Klingons and save your command. Afterward, sit back and let the stars of STAR3D relax you.

Usage: Entertainment.

System Requirements: 128K, one disk drive, monochome monitor, color graphics needed if file marked by a plus symbol (+).

How to Start: To read DOC files, enter TYPE filename.ext and press ENTER.

• To run an EXE program, just type its name and press ENTER. For instructions on running BASIC programs, please refer to the GETTING STARTED section in this catalog.

User Comments: "(CHESS) This game offers 6 different levels. it has the different aspects of chess such as castling. The game has some amazing moves." "(STARTREK) An outstanding game, great documentation." "STARTREK needs more documentation."

File Descriptions:

AWARI	BAS	Old African game played with 7 sticks & 36 stones
CHESS	EXE	Color Graphics — plays well at first, not tough later
CHESS88	EXE	Same as above game, either later or earlier version
COLLIDE	BAS	Simple minded but not easy — shoot falling bombs
HAMURABI	BAS	Play King and find out its not such a good life
STAR3D	DOC	Documentation for STAR3D.EXE
STAR3D	EXE	Sensation of traveling through space on color monitor
STARTREK	BAS	Super version of Startrek
STARTREK	EXE	Outstanding version of Startrek

197
Two Treks
v2.1

There are two version of Treks on this disk. MS-TREK is a user-supported version from MapleLeaf Software. Galaxy Trek is a fast moving, interactive version of the game. To read/print instructions and run the game type: TREKPIK. It is amazing how many different versions of Star Trek exist, but it is also worthy of note that each different version has something different to offer. These are two of the best, in our opinion. See if you agree.

Usage: Entertainment.

System Requirements: 128K, one disk drive, monochome monitor, color graphics needed if file marked by a plus symbol (+).

How to Start: To read DOC files, enter TYPE filename.ext and press ENTER. Type MS-TREK or TREKPIK and press ENTER to start either game.

User Comments: "This is a well designed, varied and yet simple game that all our family (with the exception of my wife who isn't into "sci fi") enjoys. There is a sufficient number of different possible game scenarios under a common theme to keep us playing for hours." "The documentation failed to provide some critical information, such as how to affix a tracking device to an enemy vessel. The program also had bugs in it: instructions too numerous, and complex." "There are two Star-Treks here, the first is very simple, too simple in fact, the second is very fun, a real challenge."

Suggested Donation: $10.00

File Descriptions:

————	——	MS-TREK
MS-TREK	EXE	Excellent Trek with many advanced features
MSTREK	DAT	Data file for MS-TREK
MS-TREK	DOC	Documentation file for MS-TREK.EXE (32K)
————	——	Galaxy Trek
TREKPIK	EXE	Galaxy Trek real time TREK game — start by typing TREKPIK
TREKRUN	EXE	File used by Galaxy Trek
TREK	DOC	Note that documentation is in TREKPIK
DATA	DAT	File used by Galaxy Trek

203 Game Series No 14
v1

This entry in our Game series offers you ADVEN1, a version of the classic Adventure, and a related game, SURVIVAL. Both should present you with a challenge. The classic Lunar Lander is here also, accompanied by an ASTEROID game to keep you space-jockeys happy. Many other challenges await you here, try it and see!

Usage: Entertainment.

System Requirements: 128K, one disk drive, monochome monitor, color graphics needed if file marked by a plus symbol (+).

How to Start: For instructions on running BASIC programs, please refer to the GETTING STARTED section in this catalog.

User Comments: "(FLY) Funniest PC game ever!!! Never failed to make friends laugh with this game. Good to test your hand-and-eye coordination also. LOVE the graphics!" "(NEWCHESS) I got this to play with (my own chess program), it plays pretty poorly but it's in BASIC and gives me a start" "(Games & Music) One of the better game disks, music worth little." "Excellent disk, should receive best games award." "ADVEN1 (Adventure), MOON, FLY, are big hits and are also, like the games on disk 72, always requested at school." "ASTEROID is a challenge and NEWCHESS is enjoyable, albeit slow game. The music isn't bad either." "FUN! Adventure was a GREAT deal of fun. The other programs were mildly amusing, but not great."

File Descriptions:

ADVEN1	BAS	Adventure by Scott Adams
ASTEROID	BAS	Asteroid Pilot by Dorn Stickle & R A Bower (Color graphics)
BLESS	BAS	God Bless America (With flag display)
FLY	BAS	Simple fly swatting game (Color graphics)
HINT1	DOC	Part of ADVENT1.BAS
HINT2	DOC	Part of ADVENT1.BAS
HINT3	DOC	Part of ADVENT1.BAS
MOON	BAS	Lunar lander (Color graphics) (Allan & Andrew Lee)
NEWCHESS	BAS	Chess game by M. C. Rakaska (Modified by S. W. Huggins)
SLOTCOLR	BAS	Good color graphics slotmachine (Modified by Arnold Thomson)
SOLITAIR	BAS	Klondyke solitaire (Jeff Littlefield, modified by Ken Handzik)
SURVIVAL	BAS	Space adventure-like game (Allan and Andrew Lee)
TRAILER	BAS	Trailer for rent
TRUMPET	BAS	Trumpeters Lullaby (Leroy Anderson)
WELLTEMP	BAS	Praeludium I from The Well-Tempered Clavier by J S Bach
WHEEL	BAS	Wheel of Fortune (David Lien)
WORDPLAY	BAS	Generates sentences from lists of nouns,adjectives and verbs

208 PC-SIG Sampler No 7
v1

A fine graphically oriented collection of programs, whether through your monitor screen or your printer. DESIGN is an intriguing graphics demo, and MASTER2 is a good version of the classic Mastermind board game. Also included are two cute music pieces, and several nice examples of printer art.

Usage: Entertainment.

System Requirements: 128K, one disk drive, monochome monitor, color graphics needed if file marked by a plus symbol (+).

How to Start: To run an EXE program, just type its name and press ENTER. For instructions on running BASIC programs, please refer to the GETTING STARTED section in this catalog.

User Comments: "Fun for a change!" "Graphics are excellent for demonstrations. Master2.bas and JSB.bas are they only two worthwhile programs on this disk for me since my system doesn't have the capabilties to run the design program."

File Descriptions:

DESIGN	EXE	Neat graphics demo
FLASHDAN	BAS	Flashdance (Music — Judith Penner)
JSB	BAS	J.S. Bach Violin Sonata No 6, in E Major, 1st Movement
MASTER2	BAS	Mastermind (Les Penner)
NUDE	BAS	Graphics nude (G. Wesley)
NUDE84	TXT	Text nude with 84 calendar
PRF	PRF	Part of MASTER2.BAS
SMURF	BAS	Smurf printer art (James Card, Phil Gill)

209 Arcade Series No 2
v1

Three of our better graphic programs. DATNOIDS is a very good robot-type arcade game, very challenging. JUMPJOE2 demands a lot of hand-eye coordination, and is interesting enough to keep your attention for quite a while. NUKE-NY isnt a game, it's a graphic demo of the effect of a nuclear bomb on the N.Y. area.

Usage: Entertainment.

System Requirements: 128K, one disk drive, monochome monitor, color graphics needed if file marked by a plus symbol (+).

How to Start: To read DOC files simply enter TYPE filename.ext and press ENTER. Type JUMPJOE2 and press ENTER to start that game. For instructions on running BASIC programs, please refer to the GETTING STARTED section in this catalog.

User Comments: "Arcade games: The JUMPMAN game has gotten much use." "The nuke-ny program is super. The other programs are fine. This is a good disk for anyone wanting graphic games."

File Descriptions:

JUMPJOE2	DOC	Documentation & hints (Tim McClarren)
JUMPJOE2	EXE+	Improved version of Miner 2049'er-like game (Kevin Bales)

DATNOIDS	BAS+	Similar to robot arcade game (Casey Roche)
NUKE-NY	BAS+	Simulation of nuclear attack on NYC area (J. R. Dukat)

210 Game Series No 15
v.1

This disk contains three of our most popular games. CASTLE is an adventure-quest game, find treasure and slay the monsters. PACKGAL is a good translation of the arcade favorite. And SPACEVAD is one of the best versions of the classic Space Invaders.

Usage: Entertainment.

System Requirements: 128K, one disk drive, monochome monitor, color graphics needed if file marked by a plus symbol (+).

How to Start: To read DOC files, enter TYPE filename.ext and press ENTER.

• To run an EXE or COM program, type its name and press ENTER.

User Comments: (CASTLE)"My most played game, provided much entertainment. One MAJOR frustration is that even when armed with sword and helmet, it is virtually impossible to slay monsters. They just will not die as the instructions claim they will." "I gave it a 7 because it could be better." (SPACEVAD) "Good game. Challenging, but solvable. Graphics are imaginative. This is an excellent choice for computer neophytes, even adult neophytes."

Suggested Donation: $10.00

File Descriptions:

CASTLE	DOC	Documentation for CASTLE.EXE adventure game
CASTLE	EXE	Main program
CASTLE	RAN	Required data file for CASTLE.EXE
SLOWDOWN	COM	Slows down fast PC's for CASTLE play.
PACKGAL	COM	Travel trough a maze eating dots and avoiding ghosts
SPACEVAD	EXE+	Save the world from the extra-terrestrial invaders.

228
Game Series No 16
v1

Ever have the urge to blow up something? Try NUKE-SF, it is a graphic demo of nuclear destruction. Then relax with a game of CRIBBAGE or SLOT, or try two adventure games, VAMPIRE and T-ROAD. Then try your reflexes against FIREFIRE. And when you're sure that you are the fastest thing on two fingers, try PAC-GAL and see.

Usage: Entertainment.

System Requirements: 128K, one disk drive, monochome monitor, color graphics needed if file marked by a plus symbol (+).

How to Start: To run an EXE program, just type its name and press ENTER. For instructions on running BASIC programs, please refer to the GETTING STARTED section in this catalog.

User Comments: "(PAC-GAL) I'm addicted to this game. My record is 26 wins in a row running at speed 0 with a NEC V-20 and Fansi-Console." "Cribbage game is incomplete and won't play at all." "NUKE-SF is very informative and interesting, very well done. "A lot of really nice games. NUKE-SF is a good visual display of what-if?" "CRIBBAGE game is wonderful! It caught me cheating. The slot machine was cute."

File Descriptions:

CRIBBAGE	BAS	Game — same rules as board game one player vs PC
CRIBBAGE	BLD	Subroutines for CRIBBAGE.BAS
PAC-GAL	EXE	Game — eatem up dots
COLSLOT	BAS	One arm bandit in color — its a winner (Requires color)
FIREFIRE	BAS	Game — reflexes on keyboard
MAZE	BAS	Produces mazes of any size for screen or printer
T-ROAD	BAS	A neat and interesting adventure game
SLOT	BAS	Same as you have, but graphics are much better and in color
VAMPIRE	BAS	Adventure game
NEWFONT	BAS	The program in PC — bugs?
NUKE-SF	BAS	A well done nuclear war demo

229
Funnels & Buckets
v1

The major program on this disk is FUNNELS, an educational game which teaches math in a fun way. It's a fun way to get young ones interested in math and can be a very effective tool. They'll be too busy having fun to notice that they are learning something. The other programs are an air-traffic control game, which is challenging almost beyond human comprehension, and a good version of the old Euchre card game.

Usage: Entertainment.

System Requirements: 128K, one disk drive, monochome monitor, color graphics needed if file marked by a plus symbol (+).

How to Start: Type FUNNELS or ATC and press ENTER to start either game. To read DOC files, enter TYPE filename.ext and press ENTER. For instructions on running BASIC programs, please refer to the GETTING STARTED section in this catalog.

User Comments: "ATC: Try to handle an airport by being an air traffic controller. You must monitor planes taking off & planes landing. You can handle as many as 20 or so planes. You win if you can handle all of them without crashing. Quite challenging." "Very sophisticated and difficult to learn." "(EUCHRE) A thinking game which does not become boring and is very entertaining; have had problems running on my compatible computer, though" "If you enjoy playing bridge, you'll enjoy playing Euchre, although this is somewhat easier. Personally, I found it a ball, and you can even play it with 3 other players." "(FUNNELS) "good teaching program, and it is fun too; My 11 year old loves his math now!" " Good math game. Electronic flashcards in a game."

Suggested Donation: $10.00

File Descriptions:

FUNNELS	EXE	A user-supported Funnels & Buckets game
FUNNELS	DOC	Funnels documentation (15K)
FUNNELS	INV	Invoice for author contribution
ATC	EXE	Air Traffic Control game (US)
ATC1	BLD	Part of ACT

ATC2	BLD	Part of ACT
AUTOEXEC	BAT	Part of ACT
ATC	DAT	Part of ACT
EUCHRE	BAS	"Squished" version of EUCHRE
EUCHRE	DOC	Rules for the card game EUCHRE
EUCHRE	SRC	Source code for EUCHRE including comments
EUCHRE	INS	Instructions for computer EUCHRE

JETSET	DOC	Documentation for JETSET.DOC
CRIBBAGE	BAS	Game of cribbage
SCROLL1	ML	Data file for CRIBBAGE.BAS
SIMONSEZ	BAS +	Remember the sequence game for young children
SIMONSEZ	DOC	Documentation for SIMONSEZ.BAS
SLOTMACH	BAS	Nevada style — putting a coin box on your CPU is illegal!
MORSE	BAS	Morse code learning program
TRONLC	BAS +	Game of TRON
TRONLC	EXE	Compiled version of TRON

260 Game Series No 17

v1

This is a good game disk with some neat stuff like JETSET, a flight simulator program, and a couple of cribbage games. SIMONSEZ is a fun way for the youngest of kids to get hooked on computers, while training their memories at the same time. Dueling Starships and the Tron game are made for two people and are both highly recommended.

Usage: Entertainment.

System Requirements: 128K, one disk drive, monochome monitor, color graphics needed if file marked by a plus symbol (+).

How to Start: To read DOC files, enter TYPE filename.ext and press ENTER.

- To run an EXE program, just type its name and press ENTER. For instructions on running BASIC programs, please refer to the GETTING STARTED section in this catalog.

User Comments: "Jetset is too slow, all have poor graphics, and TRON is only one of the many levels. I thought JETSET was very well doc. and also a challenge." "DSS and TRON were great. Used Jetset with some interest until I bought Microsoft Flight Simulator. There was no comparison. Jetset needs graphics of a better kind to be worth even looking at with FS available at low costs." "Tronlc is a real action game and the cribbage is nice." "JETSET cleared up some hazy areas in Microsoft 'Flight Simulator'. DSS is mindboggling and CRIBBAGE is great. You can dump CRIB2."

File Descriptions:

DSS	EXE	Dueling Starships
DSS	DOC	Documentation for Dueling Starships
CRIB2	BAS	Game of Cribbage, enjoy
JETSET	BAS	Real Time Simulation of B747 jet flight

274 Best Games

v1

This disk is a collection of some of the better games in the PC-SIG library. With a good selection of Adventure games, Arcade games, and the amusing game of 'LIFE', there should be something here for everyone. All games run on a 128k PCjr (though you may have to type "MODE CO80" first).

Usage: Entertainment.

System Requirements: 128K, one disk drive, monochome monitor, color graphics needed if file marked by a plus symbol (+).

How to Start: To read DOC or TXT files, enter TYPE filename.ext and press ENTER.

- To run an EXE program, just type its name and press ENTER. For instructions on running BASIC programs, please refer to the GETTING STARTED section in this catalog.

User Comments: (BREAKOUT)"A good copy of the original game but too slow!" (CASTLE)"Good combo of adventure/graphics, but once you figure it out, it doesn't change, you can only "solve" it once. Monsters too tough!" "The classic wizard's castle game: endlessly fascinating." "(PACKMAN) A good copy of my favorite. Good for beginners." "A good simulation of arcade version, except that it's slow!" "(SPACEVAD)It was just like the arcade! Very realistic." "PLEASE put in the directions that you should use the cursors to bring the ships down to the bottom of the screen before pressing space to start firing."

THE DISK AS A WHOLE: "Great disk! Lots of fun games for you to use. The graphics on most of them are very good. Castle and Wizard are about the best." "I like some of the games very well. The best are Space Wars, Lander, and Pacman. There are, however, some bugs which need to be worked out." "The games were very boring — some were purposeless, others were too slow, yet others incomprehensible. I was enjoying playing with life2 until I realized the program was giving invalid results." "Without color/graphics, it is hard to review the rest of this disk, but the games we were able to use are superior and BUGS! is outrageous."

File Descriptions:

GAMES	TXT	Comments from the person who selected these programs
CASTLE	EXE	Find your way out of the castle and get treasures, kill monsters
CASTLE	RAN	Part of CASTLE game
SPACEVAD	EXE +	Shoot invaders before they invade earth
PACKMAN	EXE +	Gobble power pellets and eat monsters
PACKMAN	DOC	Documentation for PACKMAN.EXE
BREAKOUT	BAS +	Try to break out of a brick wall, like tennis
LANDER	BAS +	Land a space ship on a pad without crashing
LANDER	BIN	Part of LANDER
LANDER	SCR	Part of LANDER
BUGS	EXE	Shoot crawling creatures before they get you
BUGS!	SCR	Part of BUGS
LIFE2	EXE	Try to make your bacteria live
LIFE2	BAS	Source code for LIFE2
WIZARD	BAS	A role game to find the ORB of ZOT
XWING	BAS +	Try to destroy the deathstar

292
SPACEWAR
Version 1.71

v1

The primary program on this disk, SPACEWAR, is an excellent asteroid type arcade game. The three versions, SWC for color graphics, SWATT for the ATT 6300 using 640x400 graphics mode, and SWH for the Hercules graphics card, provide good detail in a fast paced game. Other games include some Turbo Pascal offerings and a large number of BASIC games and demos. The large number of small simple BASIC demos with a few Turbo programs to add spice make this an excellent package for the novice programmer.

Usage: Entertainment.

System Requirements: 128K, one disk drive, monochome monitor, color graphics needed if file marked by a plus symbol (+).

How to Start: To read DOC or TXT files, enter TYPE filename.ext and press ENTER.

- To run an EXE or COM program, just type its name and press ENTER. For instructions on running BASIC programs, please refer to the GETTING STARTED section in this catalog.

User Comments: "The Spacewars program itself is nicely put together and seems to run well but the rest of the programs on the disk seem of little or no value." "Your catalogue was correct — a fine arcade type game. My children really enjoy this disk." "Spacewars itself is not bad....but not good. The rest of the disk (80%) is incredibly useless." "This is a fun game. I like its sounds and graphics. I had heard that this was a fun disk." "These small Basic programs (some of which are pretty bad!) are great for teaching kids beginning programming. I had my 6-year-old grandsons listing and rewriting the smallest ones very quickly."

Suggested Donation: $20.00

File Descriptions:

SONGS	BAS	Menu driven tune player
MAZEMAKE	BAS	Creates mazes up to 25 x 25 on screen and printer
LMAZE	BAS	Makes larger mazes direct to printer
GUESSNUM	BAS	Out guess the computer
LIFE	BAS	The game of LIFE in basic
LLIFE	BAS	More LIFE
ROCKET	BAS	Don't blink or you will miss this mini demo
MARINE'S	BAS	A musical bit of artillary
PRODUCT	BAS	Product of two numbers
NAME	BAS	Mini demo prints your name
BAD	BAS	Bad version of above
DIVIDE	BAS	Simple division
ADD	BAS	It all adds up
SUBTRACT	BAS	And subtracts
STARS	BAS	Graphics demo that works well on Hercules
SORCERER	BAS	A nice little adventure game
MACDONAL	BAS	As in Old
STATION	BAS	Mini motion demo
DOODLE	BAS	As in Yankee
VACATION	BAS	Mini vacation demo
ANTHEM	BAS	As in Natonal
CREATURE	BAS	Tell it which way to nibble
AMERICA	BAS	The beautiful
FLOWER	BAS	With its own bee
MOVINGAL	BAS	More music
JINGLEBE	BAS	More music
OATSPEAS	BAS	More music
OLDFOLKS	BAS	More music
SWELLING	BAS	More music
TRACK	BAS	More music
SAINTS	BAS	More music
HOTCROSS	BAS	More music
LIGHTLYR	BAS	More music
MORNING	BAS	More music

SAILBOAT	BAS	A mini demo
SWIMMER	BAS	A mini demo
AVERAGE2	BAS	Averages numbers
AVERAGE#	BAS	Averages numbers
COUNTING	BAS	Sums up
PRINT	BAS	Prints a line
BIRTHDAY	BAS	Mini cake
BALL	BAS	Toss a ball
CSTLDFNS	BAS	An adventure game to defend your castle
AVERAGE	BAS	Averages numbers
GRAPHICS	BAS	Simple graphic display
CIVILWAR	BAS	Second guess the Civil War generals
EQUAT?	BAS	Simple algebra equations (4 files)
TYPE	BAS	Mini typing test (may have bugs)
————	——	Spacewars (user-supported)
SWC	EXE	For use with color graphics card
SWH	EXE	Hercules graphics version
SWATT	EXE	AT&T 640X400 mode
SPACEWAR	DOC	Three pages of documentation for Spacewar
————	——	Life game in Turbo Pascal
LIFEC	COM	Compiled for non graphics monitor
LIFECG	COM	Compiled for graphics with 99 x 99 grid
LIFEC	PAS	Source code for above
LIFECG	PAS	Source code for above
————	——	Turbo Pascal demo
NEWSPIRO	PAS	Random character display in a curvy pattern
NEWSPIRO	COM	Compiled version of above

293 Arcade Series No 3
v1

A really fine collection of colorful arcade games. If you can't find a game to suit you here, perhaps you're just not a game player. This collection of games for the color tube will catch and hold your attention for hours. They work well on the 128k PCjr also.

Usage: Entertainment.

System Requirements: 128K, one disk drive, monochome monitor; most require color graphics.

How to Start: To read DOC files, enter TYPE filename.ext and press ENTER.

- To run an EXE program, just type its name and press ENTER. For instructions on running BASIC programs, please refer to the GETTING STARTED section in this catalog.

User Comments: "(PANGO)... Response is slow, but otherwise game is excellent. A fun and, on an 8mHz machine, furious game even at the easiest level." "I strongly recommend it be played with a joystick as control is quicker and easier. Arcade quality, no question about it." "(3-DEMON)...Fantastic graphics! The map showing where you are is confusing to follow. I love the scoring and all the Scott Joplin music." "The music is great! Fun,challenging, but not too fast or difficult." "Fascinating, fresh concept. Fast action. Easy to get started, but still interesting after numerous sessions."

OVERALL: "Some of the games (i.e., PANGO) are really awesome, but others could stand some improvement, such as PC-GOLF. Many such as PYRAMID should be rewritten to take into account an IBM AT's blazing speed." "The golf game was enjoyable but I was disapointed in the fact the ball did not show location on the fairways." "A very good disk, especially Pango (if only one could get rid of the repetitious opening introduction)." "PC-Golf was fun, but could be more sophisticted. Bricks and 3-Demon were both good."

File Descriptions:

3-DEMON	EXE +	A fascinating 3-d Packman type game
BRICKS	EXE +	Another colorful breakout type game
FORTUNE	EXE	Word game like Wheel of Fortune on TV (mono)
KONG	EXE +	Jump the barrels and watch out for the gorilla
PANGO	EXE +	Use blocks to squish the bees before they get YOU
PC-GOLF	EXE +	Plays golf on your color tube
PITFALL	EXE	Diving down a long pit but don't touch the walls (mono)
PYRAMID	EXE +	Climb the pyramid and the blocks change color
BRICKS	DOC	Documentaion for BRICKS
3-DEMON	HI1	Score keeper for 3-DEMON
PANGO	HGH	Score keeper for PANGO

354 PCjr Games
v1

For those of you PCjr owners out there who may feel forgotten sometimes, fear not! The games on this disk will work ONLY on the PCjr. They include a combat simulation game to try out your skills as a tactician, an entertaining Dungeons & Dragons type game, and, if that's not enough mayhem to suit you, how about a nice Global Thermonuclear War?

Usage: Entertainment.

System Requirements: IBM PCjr, 128K, one disk drive, monochome monitor, color graphics needed if file marked by a plus symbol (+).

How to Start: To read DOC files, enter TYPE filename.ext and press ENTER. For instructions on running BASIC programs, please refer to the GETTING STARTED section in this catalog.

User Comments: "The programs on the disk were good, but there should have been more." "Challenging and interesting games. I enjoyed the playing and experimenting that I could do with them." "Dungeon Master's assistant can be very helpful. War is made to be very entertaining." "These games rate poorly against commercial games, however commercial games don't utilize the PCjr's special capabilities. The dungeon game is very good."

File Descriptions:

————	——	Tactical Combat
COMBAT	BAS	Tactical combat simulation
COMBAT	DOC	Documentation for combat game
———	——	Dungeons and Dragons
DUN	DOC	Documentation for dungeon quest
DUNCHAR		Data file of players for dungeon quest
DUNCHAR	BAS	Update program for player file
DUNEND	BAS	File update program for dungeon quest
DUNMAP	BAS	Map creation utility
DUNMAP	1-9	Maps of dungeons used by dungeon quest
DUNPLAY	BAS	Main play program of dungeon quest
DUNQUEST	BAS	Initilization program to load arrays for play
DUNSHOP		Data file of supplies, etc
DUNSHOP	BAS	File update program for supply file
MAP		Data file of world map for war program
MENU	BAS	Main menu program for dungeon quest
————	——	Global Thermonuclear War
WAR	BAS	Global thermonuclear war game
WAR	DOC	Documentation for war game

390 Game Series No 18

v1

This disk contains one of the finest collections of color graphic games in the library. They cover a wide range of interests. ABC is a fun way to teach your children the alphabet. ACQB is armchair fun for you football fans. BRICK and BABY are fast-paced challengers, and the list goes on. For a good time, try this disk.

Usage: Entertainment.

System Requirements: 128K, one disk drive, monochome monitor, color graphics needed if file marked by a plus symbol (+).

How to Start: To read DOC files, enter TYPE filename.ext and press ENTER.

- To run an EXE program, just type its name and press ENTER. For instructions on running BASIC programs, please refer to the GETTING STARTED section in this catalog.

User Comments: "The Flightmare game itself has the best graphics I have seen on a shareware program." "My family likes Flightmare and Brick the best." "Flightmare makes hours seem like minutes." "It is excellent! A very good program, apart from an occasional bug that will drop the user back to the original engagement screen. A choice of difficulty levels would make it even better." "(ACQB)..Super game! Brian, 11 years old, loves this one !"

File Descriptions:

ABC	BAS	Kids use the computer and learn the alphabet.
ABC	DOC	Documentation for ABC.DOC.
ACQB	EXE	Armchair quarterback strategy football game.
BABY	EXE+	Try to catch the bouncing babies in time.
BRICK	EXE+	Knock down the brick wall game.
FLIGHTM	EXE+	Protect the Omegan's from the Desert Warriors.
QUIMBEE	BAS+	Dice game requires BASICA and color monitor.
SOVIET	BAS	Escape From Soviet Science And Detention Base.
SOVIET	DOC	Documentation for SOVIET

WILLY	COM	Willy the Worm — executable main program
WILLY	SCR	Data: Top ten high scores and names
WILLY	DAT	Data: Eight game screens
WILLY	CHR	Data: Modified character set for WILLY.COM
WILLY	DOC	Complete documentation for WILLY.COM (5K)
EDWILLY	COM	Allows user to edit game screens
EDWILLY	DOC	Complete documentation for EDWILLY.COM (4K)
VIS	COM	"Hides" files on directory
INVIS	COM	"Un-hides" files on directory
READ	ME	Brief description on Willy the Worm

445
Willy the Worm & more
v1

Willy the Worm is a high quality game, in the same mode as Donkey Kong or Lode Runner, that allows you to build your screens. In this way, the program never grows old. And there are other points of interest here as well. Several other games, some artwork routines, and a handy file hiding utility round out this collection.

Usage: Entertainment.

System Requirements: 128K, one disk drive, monochome monitor, color graphics needed if file marked by a plus symbol (+).

How to Start: To read DOC files, enter TYPE filename.ext and press ENTER. For instructions on running BASIC programs, please refer to the GETTING STARTED section in this catalog

- To run an EXE or COM program, just type its name and press ENTER.

User Comments: "FLIGHTMARE used to be my favorite. Willy the worm is twice as good though and I highly recomend it. I love the sound effects, color and being able to edit it with Edwilly." " Challenging and fun. Good choice to develop timing and coordination. Kids like it. Excellent game, but it would be nice to control the speed of movement since it is quite fast." "My stepson (13 yrs old) likes the game but does not play it often. When questioned, he said it's OK, but lacking enthusiasm." "(GRIME) The main problem is the complete lack of documentation. Another main drawback is the need to turn off the PC after you are done playing."

Suggested Donation: WILLY $10.00

File Descriptions:

CHASE	PAS	Can you evade the robots chasing you? — in Pascal
CHASE	COM	Can you evade the robots chasing you?
GRIME	COM+	game similar to centipede but things come at you from 4
KIRK	PIC	Printer art. Subject: James T. Kirk
DSK	EXE	Disk Crash (yes, it is a game)
SHUTTLE	BAS	will draw the space shuttle from any angle in 3D
———	——	Willy the Worm

448
Assorted games
v1

A fine collection of arcade type games, most of which require color graphics. Pinball is an absorbing video version of the old pool hall favorite, and MAZE, KANGAROO, and RIBIT will all keep you hopping! The rest of these are all equally entertaining, but BABY may not appeal to all tastes.

Usage: Entertainment.

System Requirements: 128K, one disk drive, monochome monitor, color graphics needed if file marked by a plus symbol (+).

How to Start: To read DOC files, enter TYPE filename.ext and press ENTER.

- To run an EXE program, just type its name and press ENTER. For instructions on running BASIC programs, please refer to the GETTING STARTED section in this catalog.

User Comments: "(PINBALL) Very fine program — option of keyboard input would be nice." "This program tries to emulate as much a real pinball game except for the fact that there are no bonus balls or bonus games!" "PINBALL is the one game that appeals to everybody who uses the computer. It is a flawless simulation." "(BABY) "Absolutely the most disgusting game I have ever seen!!" "Challenging game with an unusual concept." "SICK, SICK, SICK! (but fun)" "(BOOGERS!) Incredibly slow. Obnoxious noise that is not controllable. The game also totally screws up the computer clock!" "Boogers! is challenging and fun. The game was much easier to use after I tinkered with it and changed the right direction key from ` to]."

File Descriptions:

KANGAROO	BAS+	Donkey Kong-like game
AF	DOC	Documentation file for AF.EXE
AF	EXE+	War game based in Afghanistan
BABY	EXE+	Catch the falling babies as they jump from a building
PINBALL	EXE+	Pinball game made using Electronic Arts pinball program
RIBIT	EXE+	Frogger clone
MAZE1-2A	EXE+	Hi-Res maze game (tough!)
BOOGERS!	BAS	Shoot your way out of a maze
ZYLGIS	BAS	Another PAC-MAN clone
ZYLGIS	SCR	High scores for ZYLGIS.BAS

450 Assorted BASIC Games

v1

A good collection of games. Some shoot-em-ups, two different stock market simulations for you financial wizards, and other assorted entertainments. All are written in BASIC, so you can play with and change 'em around if you have the desire to experiment. All will run on a monochrome system, too!

Usage: Entertainment.

System Requirements: 128k, one disk drive, monochrome monitor

How to start: For instructions on running BASIC programs, please refer to the GETTING STARTED section in this catalog.

File Descriptions:

DICE	BAS	A simple dice game
ELECTION	BAS	You get to run for President
FUN	BAS	A fun with numbers game
MONEYMKT	BAS	Can you succeed in the stock market?
PRESCH	BAS	A word game for pre-schoolers
RIEMAN	BAS	Can you survive in the intergalactic trading circle
ROBOTNKA	BAS	Shoot the tank before it gets to you
STAR2001	BAS	Another space game
WALLST	BAS	Another Stock Market simulation

456 Assorted games

v1

Here is another fine collection of games that will keep you busy for years to come. FIRE.EXE is a good strategy game in which you must use fire breaks and water drops to keep your section of the forest from burning up. AIRTRAX.EXE is a very good game in which you, as a air traffic controller, try to land a number of planes. PTROOPER.EXE is a good arcade shoot-em-up that will keep you guessing. And for you gamblers out there, we've got a version of the old favorite, POKER.EXE.

Usage: Entertainment.

System Requirements: 128K, one disk drive, monochome monitor, color graphics needed if file marked by a plus symbol (+).

How to start: To run a COM or EXE program, type its name and press ENTER.

User Comments: "I may never fly again...very good game!" "These are the best games I've ever seen for such a price! Some of these games could be sold individually for 3 times as much as you charge for a library of games! Please keep it up!" (POKER)..A great game, but maybe a little too easy to beat. I played for about three hours the first time I turned it on." "Good general game package. Some very good, some poor, but good selection provided"

File Descriptions:

AIRTRAX	EXE	A very good air controller game
FIRE	COM	Can you keep a forest from going up in smoke?
HEART	EXE+	good graphic version of Pac-man
HOSTAGES	EXE+	Shoot your way through walls to let prisoners free
LANDMINE	EXE+	Can you make it across a mine field without going boom!
PACKGAL	COM	Version of Ms. Pac-man, doesn't need graphics card
POKER	EXE	The old card game favorite
PTROOPER	EXE+	Keep the invading paratroopers from landing in your country
QUBERT	EXE+	Good version of Q-bert

457 Greatest Arcade Games

v1

This disk contains an assortment of our finest "arcade-type" games. You can play anything from Scramble to Donkey Kong in programs that are similar to the arcade versions. Also on this disk are games that aren't in the arcades but should be!

Usage: Entertainment.

System Requirements: 128K, one disk drive, monochome monitor, color graphics needed if file marked (+).

How to Start: To read DOC files, enter TYPE filename.ext and press ENTER.

● To run an EXE program, just type its name and press ENTER.

User Comments: "This disk is a SUPER collection of games. The games are fast paced and exciting. Please continue to put out games of this nature in your library for all of us who like a little recreation." "I enjoyed it very much, in fact I accidently destroyed the disk and I am going to ask for it again." "Games are good but some need more instructions" "Flightmare alone makes this disk worth the money. It is an excellent game."

Suggested Donation: $20.00

File Descriptions:

FLIGHTM	EXE+	Protect the Omegan's from the Desert Warriors
JUMPJOE	EXE+	Donkey Kong like game using Mario as a Janitor
MISFAC	DAT	Stores an image of the missile factory in Striker
SOLITARE	EXE	Play solitare against the computer
SPACEWAR	DOC	Documentation for SWH.EXE and SWC.EXE
STRIKER	DOC	Documentation for STRIKER.EXE
STRIKER	EXE+	Public Domain version of Scramble
STRKHINS	BAT	This file will install striker on a hard disk drive.
STRKLOGO	DAT	Stores the image of inital helicopter logo.
STRKPARM	DAT	Stores screen position parameters and the key assignments.
SWC	EXE+	Spacewar program for use with a color graphics card
SWH	EXE	Hercules graphics version of Spaceware
SWATT	EXE	AT&T 640X400 mode
SPACEWAR	DOC	Three pages of documentation for Spaceware
TUNNELS	DAT	Stores the tunnel terrain data.

476 Patrick's Best Games

v1

These games were gathered from previous PC-SIG disks to provide a good representation of high quality games for the new user. In answer to complaints that most of the best games require color screens, only 3-DEMON and SPACEVAD out of the seven included games need a color graphics card.

Usage: Entertainment.

System Requirements: 128K, One disk drive, Monochome monitor, Color graphics needed if file marked by a plus symbol (+).

How to Start: To run an EXE or COM program, just type its name and press ENTER. For instructions on running BASIC programs, please refer to the GETTING STARTED section in this catalog.

User Comments: "Because we do not have a color card, it was great to get a disk with games we could play on a monochrome monitor that were not just adventure games." "PACKGAL, CASTLE and 3-DEMON are good but most others mediocre. Would be better to have only monochrome games on one disk." "(BUGS)..It's an excellent imitation of the arcade game. It can be improved by giving more than one "life" to each player, and keeping track of a number of high scores. Still it is excellent and quite addictive." "CASTLE and SPACEVAD are well done and easy to play. 3-DEMON is slick but could use some documentation. BOOGERS! without documentation is unplayable and impossible."

File Descriptions:

GO	BAT	File that prints help messages
README1	*	Four help files
PACKGAL	COM	Multiscreen version of MS. PACMAN with a few twists.
POKER	EXE	The school of implemented Casino probability theory.
BOOGERS!	BAS	A maze game that requires destruction of blockades.
CASTLE	EXE	An adventure game with clever animation and graphics,
CASTLE	RAN	it has elements of role-playing and strategy games.
BUGS	EXE	A good version of the classic arcade game Centipede

3-DEMON	EXE	Three-D view of PACMAN-like game from inside the maze.
SPACEVAD	EXE	Excellent version of Space Invaders, great graphics
3-DEMON	HI1	Records the High score of 3-Demon Game for posterity.

487 REFLEX POINT
v1

This is a BASIC program in which you, a Freedom Fighter, combat the evil Invid Alien Invaders. Through the course of the game your cyclone changes into battle armor. Then when you reach the alpha fighter you can can change into battloid form. Reach the Reflex Point and kill the Evil Alien Prince. This game will run on a 128k PCjr.

Usage: Entertainment.

System Requirements: 128K, one disk drive, color monitor, color graphics needed, IBM BASIC or IBM PCjr BASIC.

How to Start: From BASIC, type LOAD REFLEX and press ENTER; then RUN and press ENTER.

User Comments: "The graphics are impressive, but this does not play well on my PCjr. I suspect that the Jrs slow speed is the problem." "Reflex Point was made with good intentions, but it is ridden with bugs. Also, the key buffer gets filled up too quickly and action is slow." "...excellent graphics; program's response to input is slow" "Very difficult game. I still have not experienced most of it."

File Descriptions:

ALPHA	PIC	Image file of Alpha Fighter
CYCLONE	KEY	Subprogram for REFLEX.BAS
CYCLONE	PIC	Image of Cyclone
CYCLONE2	PIC	Image of jumping Cyclone
POWER	PIC	Graphic image
REFLEX	BAS	Reflex Point game
REFLEX	KEY	Subprogram for REFLEX.BAS
REFLEX	PIC	Image of Reflex Point
RP-HELP	BAS	Tips on how to play
TITLE	PIC	Image of title screen

514 FOLLIES
v1

This games disk has 8 programs which will give you hours of fun and relaxation. Roulette and Keno might be used to develop your own system of beating the casinos. I found the 3D tic-tac-toe and the Othello games to be just great fun, for they match your wits against the computer. The PC-Othello game is meant to be played by two computer users over the telephone. If you are a serious internals person with experience in Assembly you may find Corewars to be both fun and a learning experience. The biorythms charting program is very good. All in all, a nice collection of computer games.

Usage: Entertainment.

System Requirements: 128K, one disk drive, monochome monitor, color graphics needed if file marked by a plus symbol (+).

How to Start: To read DOC or TXT files, enter TYPE filename.ext and press ENTER.

● To run an EXE or COM program, just type its name and press ENTER.

Suggested Donation: $10.00 each for OTHELLO, PCOTHELL, and ROULETTE

File Descriptions:

3DTICTAC	EXE	3-Dimensional Tic-Tac-Toe game against the computer
BIORHY	TXT	Short Intoduction to biorythm and its use
BIORHY	COM	Program to calculate your biorythm on any date
BRIDGE	EXE	Program which randomly deals bridge hands for practice
BRIDGE	DOC	Notes about the use of BRIDGE.EXE
COREWAR	EXE	Executable corewar game program
COREWAR	DOC	Complete instructions on COREWAR.EXE
KENO	EXE	The program file for the keno game
OTH-BW	COM	The Program for monochrome or b/w computers
PCOTHELL	DOC	Documentation for PCOTHELL.EXE
PCOTHELL	EXE	Executable program for othello
PCOTHELL	PN1	Communication file for com1
PCOTHELL	PN2	Communication file for com2
ROULETTE	EXE	The program file for roulette

557 PINBALL RALLY
v1

Here is a disk for the pinball addict. It has three games which have been created using the program "Pinball Construction Set" by Bill Budge. The games vary in the level of difficulty but they are all interesting. The three games include PINBALL which is the standard pinball game; RAIN is more complicated as it uses 5 pinballs at the same time and TWILZON2 is perhaps the most difficult, something for the Rod Serling fans.

Usage: Entertainment.

System Requirements: 128K, one disk drive, monochome monitor, color graphics needed if file marked by a plus symbol (+).

How to start: Type PINBALL, RAIN, or TWILZON2 and press ENTER to start.

File Descriptions:

PINBALL	EXE+	Program to execute a standard pinball game
RAIN	EXE+	Pinball program with 5 balls!
TWILZON2	COM+	Twilight Zone pinball, a must for the pinball player

705 KIDGAMES
v1

KIDGAMES is a BLAST! This collection of games specifically geared toward the ages of 2-10 years has excellent graphics and a straight-forward approach to making fun educational. Your children will not only have fun with these games but will also learn from them.

For education, easily the top on this disk is HANGMAN which both teaches basic spelling and allows for growing a vocabulary by expanding the dictionary of the game. For pure fun, MOSAIC, which teaches pattern matching and allows for pattern building, gets my vote! Also here are:

ALPHABET teaches the alphabet and alphabetic sequence
ANIMALS teaches simple preschool math
CLOCKGAME teaches how to read an analog clock
MOSAIC teaches pattern matching

If you really like the sprites that accompany the games, there is a sprite designer package included (MAKEICON.COM). You may also use the more fully featured sprite designer form this author's Sprites and Animation package: DESIGNER.COM on Disk No 511.

Usage: Educational Fun!

System Requirements: 64K, one disk drive and monochrome display

How to Start: Consult the .DOC files, especially the HANGMAN.DOC.

Suggested Donation: $10.00

File Descriptions:

ALPHABET	—2	Part of ALPHABET.COM
ALPHABET	—1	Part of ALPHABET.COM
ALPHABET	COM	Main ALPHABET program
ANIMALS	—2	Part of ANIMALS.COM
ANIMALS	—1	Part of ANIMALS.COM
ANIMALS	COM	Main ANIMALS program
ANIMALS	TAB	Part of ANIMALS.COM
CLOCKGAM	COM	Main CLOCKGAM program
CLOCKGAM	PIC	Part of CLOCKGAM program
DICTNARY		Auxiliary dictionary for hangman
GO	BAT	Ypes out kidgames.doc
HANGMAN	COM	Teaches letter sounds and spelling
HANGMAN	DIC	Dictonary for hangman
HANGMAN	DOC	Documentation for hangman
KIDGAMES	DOC	Brief discription about the games on this disk
MAKEICON	COM	Icon maker program
MAKELIST	COM	Program which allows you to add word to HANGMAN dictionary
MOSAIC	COM	Mosaic main program
MOSAIC	PIC	Part of MOSAIC program
MOSAIC	TAB	Part of MOSAIC program

GRAPHICS:

Create computer graphics with our selection of simple to sophisticated graphics programs. Whatever the level of your interest and your equipment, you will surely find something here to catch your eye.

PC-based graphics programs have significantly advanced from programs for designing clever screen logos or printing naughty pictures to BASIC-structured joystick/keyboard input paint programs to high-quality, full resolution paint and animation design programs.

Admittedly, the higher-end programs require excellent equipment (Color Graphics Adaptors with RGB/color monitors and perhaps color printers, too) but many of the more recent packages rival the more expensive commercial programs in features and versatility. Even on the lower end, such programs as The Designer can be a terrific programming tool for BASIC users working with animated graphics on a PC. Such tools can be of significant value to people writing graphics-based games, interactive learning programs and for computer-oriented artists interested in experimenting with animation.

13 PDRAW
v1

This disk contains two sections. STARTREK is a fine implementation of the game that has been around since time sharing has been popular on college campuses. The game runs uder BASIC and has sound effects. PDRAW is a simple line, circle, square, etc. drawing program. It doesn't require a mouse, and has color fill for the enclosed areas of your drawing, not real powerful but a good starting program. Last and least, IBMSONG is something that everyone should see at least once.

Usage: Game buffs and computer artists.

System Requirements: 128k, 1 disk drive, color graphics, printer recommended.

How to Start: To run BASIC programs consult the directions in GETTING STARTED for your configuration. Consult PDRAW.DOC for program documentation.

User Comments: "This is the perfect PC artist. It even gives competition to the big-name PC artists." "The documentation is clear and concise...help screens are also very useful." "This is my first experience with color drawing on a color monitor. The help screen are very useful."

File Descriptions:

STARTREK	BAS	Starship Enterprise — space war with sound effects
STARTREK	HOW	Screens of instructions — invoked by BASIC program
STARTREK	DUM	Data file used by program
PDRAW	DOC	Comprehensive documentation of PDRAW package (15K)
PDRAW	BAS+	Drawing program
COLOR	BAS+	Color sub-program
MONO	BAS+	Monochrome sub-program
*	BAT+	Batch files used by PDRAW (4 files)
*	PIC+	Pictures used by PDRAW (6 files)
IBMSONG	BAS	IBM rally song — lyrics & bouncing ball — 80 screen

20
Draw
v1.1

Besides the four games on this disk, most of the programs on this disk have something to do with either drawing or displaying a picture on your screen. Some are games which are visually displayed, while the DRAW program allows you to, as the name implies, draw pictures with your computer. Two other programs are for the BASIC programmer. CROSSREF is a cross-referencing utility, and B-SIMPLE is an aid for structured BASIC programming.

Usage: Entertainment

System Requirements: 128K, one disk drive, monochome monitor, color graphics needed if file marked by a plus symbol (+).

How to Start: From BASIC, type RUN "BASMENU", and press ENTER.

User Comments: "(SPOOLER) Good as any commercial spooler." "A good disk!" "HDRAW is pretty interesting. Do have slight problems with saving & restoring on my Tandy 1000."

File Descriptions:

CHSONG	BAS	Music — Christmas songs ('Tis the Season!)
WORM1	BAS	Watch him tunnel through the ground
SCOPE	BAS+	Display symmetric random patterns
DRAW	BAS+	Program to draw pictures on color screen
HANGMAN	BAS+	Color version of HANGMAN
BLACKJCK	BAS	Upgraded to use color monitor if on
YAHTZEE	BAS	Upgraded to use color monitor if on
B-SIMPLE	BAS	Utility aid to create & structure BASIC programs
CROSSREF	EXE	Utility cross-reference program for BASIC programs
CROSSREF	SCR	Documentation for CROSSREF (SCRIPT source)
EDIT	BAT	Utility to invoke RV-EDIT from DOS (See Disk No 19)
BASMENU	BAS	AUTOMATIC MENU FOR BASIC PROGRAMS (See Disk No 14)
CONTROL	BAS	Lets this diskette run under PCS

38
BASIC DRAWING
v1

With DRAW, you can draw, and then some! Easy to understand and use graphics program, plus DOS utilities you've been wishing for. Set your display to color/monochrome from DOS, examine and modify disk directory, list files to screen, a page at a time, or even remove control characters from down-loaded files!

Usage: Intermediate, advanced.

System Requirements: 64K, 1 disk drive, color graphics

How to Start: Load DOS and type any .EXE file

- To run BASIC programs consult the directions in GETTING STARTED for your configuration. Consult the .DOC files for additional program information.

User Comments: "(SPOOLER)Good as any commercial spooler." "A good disk!" "HDRAW is pretty interesting. Do have slight problems with saving & restoring on my Tandy 1000."

Suggested Donation:

File Descriptions:

COLOR	EXE	Sets display to color from DOS
MONO	EXE	Sets display to monochrome from DOS
SCROLLK	BAS	Allows scrollock key to enable/disable scrolling
SCROLLK	COM	Compiled version of SCROLLK.BAS
WS-DOS	BAS	Converts WordStar files to DOS files
SPOOLBAS	BAS	Allows scrolling to continue from BASIC to DOS
SPOOLER1	COM	Printer spooler for monochrome display card
SPOOLER2	COM	Printer spooler for color display card
SPOOLER	DOC	Documentation file for spooler programs
DISKRTN	EXE	Examine and modify disk directory
DISKRTN	DOC	Documentation for DISKRTN
FILTER	BAS	Removes control characters from downloaded files
FILTER	DOC	Documentation for FILTER program
DM	BAS	Sets up Dot Matrix printer under WORDSTAR
DMLQ	DOC	Documentation for DM and LQ
LQ	BAS	Sets up Letter Quality printer for use under WORDSTAR
LIST	EXE	Lists files to screen, one page at a time
— — — —	— —	DRAW Programs
DRAW	DOC	Documentation file for MDRAW and HDRAW
DRAW	CMT	Comment lines for HDRAW and MDRAW programs
MODROW	TXT	Additional information on graphics programs

MDRAW	BAS	Medium resolution DRAW program
HDRAW	BAS	High resolution DRAW program
HELP1	PIK	Help picture for DRAW programs
HELP1	PIC	Help picture for DRAW programs

69 DESIGNER
v1.1

THE DESIGNER is a programming tool for IBM PC BASIC users working with animated graphics. Source code in BASICA is included for study or modification for those who want to write graphics games or experiment with animation. A beginning knowledge of programming and BASIC are recommended to use this package.

Usage: Graphic design for programmers.

System Requirements: 128k, 1 disk drive, color graphics

Features:

- Full PC function key use to control programming functions
- On-line help
- Printable reference card.

How to Start: To run BASIC programs consult the directions in GETTING STARTED for your configuration. Consult DESIGNER.DOC for program documentation.

User Comments: "Good animation. Should have been done for Turbo Pascal." "A very good program. I have been impressed with its possibilities and continue to investigate all it has." "I found that designer is very hard to use...entirely too complicated for the novice."

Suggested Donation: $20.00.

File Descriptions:

DESIGNER	BAS	DESIGNER main program (Requires BASICA)
DESIGNER	DOC	Documentation for DESIGNER.BAS (45K)
DEMO	BAS	Animation demo
MAZE	BAS	Part of DEMO
MAZE	RES	Part of DEMO
MOUSE	SPR	Part of DEMO
TEXTCHAR		Text character images
VERBIAGE		Used by DESIGNER.BAS — messages, menus, etc.

73 3D
v1

3D is a collection of freeware or public domain programs which perform useful or interesting functions...catalog your books or records, figure growth rates and projects or calculate miles per gallon, percentages, or windchill factors. Also included are graphic figures which can be rotated and displayed, plus a program to create your own 3Dimensional figures.

Usage: Beginner or the curious.

System Requirements: Color graphics for 3D programs.

How to Start: To run BASIC programs consult the directions in GETTING STARTED for your configuration.

User Comments: "Interesting." "Not much here. It seems to be a demo only." "Not enough documentation to know just what it could do." "The test picture is handsome, but beyond that I don't see much use for this."

File Descriptions:

TEMPCONV	BAS	IPCO Temperature conversion
MPG-CAL	BAS	IPCO Miles per gallon calculator
%-DIFF	BAS	IPCO Calculates percentages — educational value
MOLY-PAY	BAS	IPCO Catalog books in your library
SERIALNO	BAS	IPCO serial number generator
GROWTH	BAS	IPCO Growth rates and projections
WINDCHIL	BAS	IPCO Calculates windchill factors
SHIP		Data file for 3-D-ROT.BAS
JET		Data file for 3-D-ROT.BAS
CUBE		Data file for 3-D-ROT.BAS
PYRAMID		Data file for 3-D-ROT.BAS
3-D-ROT	BAS +	IPCO Rotate and display objects
3D	GRF	BASIC source for 3D.EXE
3D	DOC	Documentation for 3D
3D	EXE +	Creates 3D images on graphics board
3DTEST1	PLT	Part of 3D — image file
3DTEST2	PLT	Part of 3D — image file
PCFILECH	BAS	Recreates PC-FILE data base in different format
CLERK	BAS	IPCO Record keeping program
SHIFTS	BAS	Subroutines to set/test shift keys

136
PC-Picture
Graphics by E. Ying
v1

PC-Picture allows you to create graphics images on your color monitor. A number of readymade images are included. You can digitize to a plotter, create your own graph files and even your own slide show. If you wish to create a nice-looking visual presentation without spending thousands, give this disk a try.

Usage: Graphics design tool

System Requirements: Graphics board, color monitor.

How to Start: Load DOS and type PCPG to enter the main program.

User Comments: "Extremely well done graphics program! It rivals the stuff I've paid lots of good money for." "Takes a little tinkering to understand it but results are terrific." "The basic documentation was somewhat difficult to understand." "Fine graphics program; two fonts don't work; excellent library of graphics."

Suggested Donation: $20.00.

File Descriptions:

PCPG	EXE	Great graphics drawing package (Requires graphics board)
PCPG	FT?	Part of PC-Picture
PCPG	HLP	PC-Picture help file
PCPG	PIC	Part of PC-Picture
PCPG	SYM	Part of PC-Picture
DEMO*	GFL	Demo files for PC-Picture containing graphic immages

154
Printer Art
v1

PRINTER ART is a disk full of exactly what its name implies...art for you to screen display or print. From the Pink Panther to Schroeder and Snoopy and a lot of unclothed ladies in between. You can even get Darth Vader and the Enterprise from Startrek in BASIC-run programs. Visual fun.

Usage: Artistic endeavors for the dot-matrix set.

System Requirements: 64K, one disk drive and monochrome display.

How to Start: To run BASIC programs consult the directions in GETTING STARTED for your configuration.

User Comments: "Some of these pictures were excellent, especially the McDonnel-Douglas fighter plane." "Some humorous art work." "Disk would be better if it had a tutorial on how to make these types of pictures."

File Descriptions:

CLOWN	ART	Clown
ENTEP	BAS	Enterprise (From Startrek)
SNOOPY	BAS	Snoopy
DARTH	BAS	Darth Vader
SANTA	BAS	Santa and his raindeer
SNOOPY3	BAS	Snoopy
SCHROE	DER	Schroeder (From Peanuts)
*	NUD	Nude female printer pictures (9 files)
PANTHR	PIC	Pink Panther
PHANT	PIC	McDonnell Douglas F-4E Phantom II
SHUTTL	PIC	Challenger space shuttle

191 BASIC PAINT: Easel and Easygraf

v1

Here are three very interesting, very basic BASIC "Paint" programs.

The EASEL program is a set of standalone programs used for preparation of artistic graphics done in medium resolution mode. Color, line size and dimensions are controlled by function key usage.

It has a companion system here in EASYGRAF, a menu-driven facility for producing medium or high-resolution graphics images. With it, it is possible to store up to 10 images per diskette. Once recorded, these images may be used with other programs since they are recorded in standard BSAVE format. Optionally they may also be displayed and printed by using the print feature of EASYGRAF.

The Digidraw is a general purpose drawing tool designed to run in the high resolution mode (640 x 200). With Digidraw you can create, store, change any picture or image which can be drawn in the IBM high resolution graphics mode. Routine shapes such as boxes, circles, ellispses, arcs, etc. can be easily drawn with two or three keystrokes any place on the screen.

For documenting all your work, here is DVED, a compact, screen-oriented text editor. As its documentation is part of the program, loading DVED with no parameters will enter the help facility which interactively provides the documentation of all DVED features. This help facility can be printed out as a complete, formatted reference manual.

Usage: Screen editing and programming

System Requirements: 128K, the color or monochrome display card and one disk drive; files marked with "+" require color/graphics system. EASEL uses a Light Pen.

How to Start: Consult the .DOC and README files for directions and documentation

● To run the BASIC programs, consult the directions in GETTING STARTED for your configuration.

User Comments: "EASYGRAF and EASEL have been fun but are limited. My brother says he can do better." "I have used DVED for casual editing for over a year now. It is one of the most secure editors I have ever worked with. It's error recovery facilities can't be beat." "Wish it could handle more than 80 columns. Am using PC-Write instead."

Suggested Donation: DIGIDRAW $25.00

File Descriptions:

COLOR	BAS+	Part of PIECHART.BAS
DIGIDRAW	BAS+	Nifty drawing program (Requires graphics & BASICA)
DIGIDRAW	DOC	Documentation for DIGIDRAW.BAS
DVED	COM	Good screen-oriented text editor (Version 6.02) — Can use with mouse
READ	ME	Part of DVED.COM
GRAPH	BAS+	Graphs data (x, y coordinates and function)
GRAPH2	BAS+	Graphs data (x, y coordinates and function)
HISTGRAM	BAS+	Displays and prints simple histogram
INFO	BIN	Binary file for DIGIDRAW.BAS
LOGO	BIN	Binary file for DIGIDRAW.BAS
PIECHART	BAS	Draws pie charts — Version 1.0
PLOT	BAS	Creates plots from your coordinates
SKETCH	BAS	Etch-a-sketch with cursor keys
————	——	EASEL
EASEL	BAS+	Easel drawing package (Requires light pen, color graphics)
EASEL	ASC+	Part of EASEL.BAS — documentation
PENCIRC	BAS+	Part of EASEL.BAS — draw circles
PENCLEAR	BAS+	Part of EASEL.BAS — clear screen
PENDRAW	BAS+	Part of EASEL.BAS — draw dots
PENLINE	BAS+	Part of EASEL.BAS — draw lines
PENPAINT	BAS+	Part of EASEL.BAS — demo — color train with light pen
PENSAVE	BAS+	Part of EASEL.BAS — save drawing
————	—— +	EASYGRAF
EASYGRAF	BAS+	EasyGraf drawing package (Requires color graphics)
BUILGRAF	BAS+	Part of EASYGRAF.BAS — build graph file
COLRGRAF	BAS+	Part of EASYGRAF.BAS
DISPGRAF	BAS+	Part of EASYGRAF.BAS — display graph
DISPGRDR	BAS+	Part of EASYGRAF.BAS — display graph directory
DRAWGRAF	BAS+	Part of EASYGRAF.BAS — draw a graph
EASYGRAF	ASC+	Part of EASYGRAF.BAS — documentation
EZGDOCM	BAS+	Part of EASYGRAF.BAS — use BASIC LIST to view
GRAPHIT	BAS+	Part of EASYGRAF.BAS — draws with cursor & function keys
MONOGRAF	BAS+	Part of EASYGRAF.BAS — monochrome graph
PRINGRAF	BAS+	Part of EASYGRAF.BAS
PRN2GRAF	BAS+	Part of EASYGRAF.BAS
PRNTGRAF	BAS+	Part of EASYGRAF.BAS
PRNTSAVE	BAS+	Part of EASYGRAF.BAS
SAMPDRAW	BAS+	Part of EASYGRAF.BAS — sample drawing — part of house
SAVEGRAF	BAS+	Part of EASYGRAF.BAS
TEMPGRAF	BAS+	Part of EASYGRAF.BAS — temporary graph storage
TESTPRNT	BAS+	Part of EASYGRAF.BAS

195 PC-GRAF
v1

A BASIC program to plot line drawing graphs of data sets. Three different versions of the program are provided (PC-GRAF2, 3, 4,) to allow the user to choose the number of features and degree of IBM PC compatablilty required. Data entry is from the keyboard or read in from data files. Additional programs include computer use log, screen color control, and keyboard redefinition.

Usage: Intermediate level users, computer graph makers

System Requirements: 128k, 1 disk drive, color graphics.

How to Start: To run BASIC programs consult the directions in GETTING STARTED for your configuration. Consult the .DOC files for additional program information.

Suggested Donation: $20.00

File Descriptions:

INSTALL	BAT	Batch file to install DOS system and BASICA on PC-GRAF disk
PC-GRAF	DOC	PC-GRAF documentation — to view use "Type pc-graf.doc"
PC-GRAF4	BAS	PC-GRAF with color and B&W plots and plotter output
LOGPRINT	BAS	Program to print the computer use log.
PC-GRAF2	BAS	Fastest version of PC-GRAF with the least features
DEMOSUB	BAS	Demo BASIC program...How to call SUBGRAF from your own program
SUBGRAF3	BAS	Plotting subroutine from PC-GRAF3
SUBGRAF2	BAS	Plotting subroutine from PC-GRAF2
SUBGRAF4	BAS	Plotting subroutine from PC-GRAF4
PC-GRAF3	BAS	PC-GRAF with color and B&W plots... no plotter support
SIMPLEX	BAS	Simplex function fitting algorithm
CONVERT	BAS	Convert old graph files for GRAPH2 program to PC-GRAF format
SORT	EXE	Program to sort graph data
LOGON	BAS	Program to log start of computer session in log file
README	DOC	Disk description — to view use "type readme.doc"
README	BAK	Backup of disk description

LOGON	BAT	Batch file to run LOGON program
LOGOFF	BAT	Batch file to run LOGOFF program
LOGOFF	BAS	Program to log end of session in log file. Gives total time
LOGPRINT	BAT	Batch file to run LOGPRINT
AUTOEXEC	BAT	Batch file for PC-GRAF disk
CONFIG	SYS	System file required to install ANSI.SYS screen driver
COLOR	BAS	Program to set screen foreground and background colors
COLOR	SCR	File that contains screen color commands. Type to activate
COLOR	BAT	Batch program to run COLOR program and activate color change
KEYDEF		File containing key redefinition commands. Type to activate
KEYDEF	BAS	Program to allow redefinition of keyboard keys in DOS
KEYDEF	BAT	Batch file to run KEYDEF
TESTPLOT	DTA	Demonstration plot for use with PC-GRAF

219 MapMaker
v1

This disk contains some powerful programs designed for making computer plotted maps. MM1 is the simplest requiring only a color graphics card and single monitor. MM2 is more complex and requires both a color and a monochrome monitor, for enhanced graphics. The major benefit from this program is that it allows the user to easily turn statistical data based on area into a form representing the data displayed as a map.

Usage: Intermediate to advanced level cartographers.

System Requirements: 128k, 1 disk drive, color graphics.

How to Start: Load DOS and type MAPMAKER to enter the main program. Consult MANUAL.DOC for program documentation.

User Comments: "This is a very good program, however, the authors need to simplify the documentation for people without a cartographic or geography background." "Makes nice maps from pre-existing data sets but is difficult to make new sets for new maps."

Suggested Donation: $55.00 MapMaker

File Descriptions:

MANUAL		Documentation (Approximately 20 pages)
MAPMAKER	EXE	Main program
FLAPAN		Data set — NW Florida
GNV		Data set — Gainsville, Florida
OFFICES		Data set — sample floorplan
USA		Data set — contigous USA
FLA-POP		Statistical data — number of residents by county (FLAPAN)
FLA-INC		Statistical data — per capita income (FLAPAN)
OFF-YRS		Statistical data — number of years of occupancy by present occupa
GNV-65		Statistical data — percent of residents 65 years and older in 197
GNV-POP		Statistical data — number of residents in 1970
USA-SUN		Statistical data — percent sunny days during an average year
USA-FUND		Statistical data — Federal funding of universities in 1979
FLA-CENT		Centroid data set (FLAPAN)
USA-CENT		Centroid data set (USA)
SCREEN1	BAS	Screen image files — Choropleth — Office Residency
SCREEN2	BAS	Screen image files — Circle — Gainesville Population
SCREEN3	BAS	Screen image files — Circle — N.W. Florida Population
SCREEN4	BAS	Screen image files — Choropleth — Gainesville Elderly
SCREEN5	BAS	Screen image files — Choropleth — U.S. Sunny Days

238 SPRITE Graphics
v1

There are several unrelated programs on this disk. SPRITE is a user supported program which lets you conveniently create Sprite charaters. A Sprite character is a graphics figure made from a set of colored pixels. Instead of displaying this figure pixel by pixel, BASIC lets you display the figure in one step with the graphics form of the PUT statement. This is similar to the Sprite graphics available on other microcomputers. Other files included are various files to explain how to unprotect some popular software. A benchmark is here as well as a program to print foreign language characters on an EPSON printer.

Usage: BASIC users with graphics interest

System Requirements: 128K, one disk drive, color graphics.

How to Start: Load DOS and type SPRITE to enter the main program. To run BASIC programs consult the directions in GETTING STARTED for your configuration. Consult the .DOC files for additional information.

User Comments: "SPRITE makes creating graphic sprites in BASIC much easier." "All in all, SPRITE makes programming much easier." "Fantastic. Simple and easy to use." "Great results. This program takes all the drudgery out of creating sprites."

Suggested Donation: $20.00

File Descriptions:

SPRITE	COM	This is the SPRITE Program
SPRITE	SAV	This is a sample SPRITE save file.
SPRITE	BAS	A sample BASIC program created with the SPRITE program
SPRITE	DOC	Documentation message — SPRITE is self documenting
BASTOD	BAS	BASIC program shows how to call DOS functions (50K)
SEIV	DOC	Benchmark test for several computers including c test program
CVTBIN	BAS	Converts CIS (Intel hex format) .BIN files to true Binary files
TIMER		Explains how to get around PRINT/SIDEKICK incompatibility
QUIET	DOC	How to quiet Tandon drives (DOS 2.0+)
HARDBO	DOC	How to reboot off hard disk
NKYPKY	TXT	Comparison of NEWKEY and PROKEY
TKSOLVER	UNP	How to unprotect TKSOLVER
PROKEY	UNP	How to unprotect PROKEY
LAYOUT	UNP	How to unprotect LAYOUT
RBASE	UNP	How to unprotect RBASE
SK	UNP	How to unprotect Sidekick
PC-PRINT	EXE	German, Spanish, Banner, EPSON printer utilities
PC-PRINT	DOC	Documentation file (11k)

244 *Slide Generation*
v1

The purpose of this program is the production of medium quality slides and overhead transparencies. Images may be created, edited, saved, displayed and printed using this program. Overhead transparancies are produced by copying the printed output onto transparent material. Photographic slides are produced by photographing the printed output.

Usage: All users requiring slides or transparancies for education or business presentations.

System Requirements: 128K RAM, 1 disk drive, a mono display, a graphic printer and photographic equipment to turn the printed output into either a slide or an overhead transparency.

How to Start: Load DOS and type SLIDE to enter the main program. Type -README- for additional instructions.

User Comments: "This is great for creating overhead transparencies. For slides it requires extra work." "It does a very good job in printing text and text graphics. I will use it alot!" "Couldn't get to work on Kaypro 2000 — program doesn't specify need for graphics card." "A great disc."

Suggested Donation: $25.00

File Descriptions:

SLIDE	EXE	Slide master program
SLIDE	SDE	Character definition file
SLIDE	CTR	Printer control code file
-README—	BAT	Initiates the display of instructions
INSTRUCT	ION	Instructions for printing the slide manual and running the slide
SLIDEDOC	EXE	Expand and print slide manual
SLIDE	MAN	Squeezed manual

336 *ABC Design (Disk 1 of 2)*
v1

The ABC Design character-graphics, color-image editor program allows one to create and use many sets of fonts for the Epson printer, create drawings and dump them with graphics mode. If you've ever felt frustrated by the difficulty of getting the most out of your printer's capabilities, check this one out! See accompanying documentation Disk 337 for complete operating instructions for this program.

Usage: Intermediate, advanced.

System Requirements: 128K, graphics printer, color graphics, and BASIC. Mouse Systems optical mouse is optional.

How to Start: Load DOS and consult ME.TXT for program information. Consult MANUAL.EXE on disk 337 for program documentation.

User Comments: "All graphics are in COLOR." "Has more limited use than I had imagined from the catalog." "Too techie for me." "Something else that I am playing around with, COLOR."

Suggested Donation: $5.00/Year.

File Descriptions:

ALPHA?	PIC	Block symbol images (3 files)
ASCREF?		Documentation file (2 files)
ASKDICK	PIC	Documentation file
BW	PIC	Symbol Dictionary Image
CHARDOC?		Documentation file (5 Files)
D??????	PIC	Symbol Dictionary Image (3 files)
*	SET	Character Set (19 files)
EDDIE	BAS	Character graphics color image program
EDDIE	BAT	Batch file to run Eddie
EP	BAT	Batch file to create script files
FEED	TXT	Text for Form Feed
FIXPIC	BAS	Blanks the 25th Line of an Eddie Image
GET	BAT	Batch File to copy Eddie Program
GETEDDIE	BAT	Batch File to copy Eddie Program
GETPETE	BAT	Batch File to copy Pete Program
*	BIN	Binary output (3 files)
INSERT	TXT	Instructions for printing documentation
LICENSE	TXT	License information
ME	TXT	Instructions for this Disk
MEDDIE	COM	Monochrome version of EDDIE
MOUSE	BAT	Batch file to run mouse version of Eddie
*	QUE	Script file (3 files)
PART?	TXT	Instructions for printing documentation (4 files)

PETE	EXE	Uses screen images to create symbols
PETE	SET	Character Set
PETEDOC1		Documentation file
PETEDOC2		Documentation file
PRINT	SET	Character Set
PUSH	BAS	Character Set Conversion Utility
PUSHOVER	BAT	Batch file to run Push Program
READ	BAT	Batch file to print documentation
REGFORM	TXT	Registration form
SCUT	PIC	Symbol Dictionary Image
SEE	BAT	Batch file to list documentation to screen
SETREF		Documentation file
WARRENTY	TXT	Warranty form

337
ABC Design
(Disk 2 of 2)
v1

This is the accompanying documentation disk for the ABC Design character-graphics color-image editor which allows one to create and use many sets of fonts for the Epson printer, create drawings and dump them with graphics mode.

Usage: Intermediate, advanced.

System Requirements: 128K, graphics printer, color/mono display and adapter, and BASIC. Mouse Systems optical mouse is optional.

File Descriptions:

MANUAL	EXE	Program to print ABC Design documentation
MAN	SET	which takes about 1 1/2 hours
MAN	QUE	to print
MAN	DOC	Documentation for ABC Design

344
PC-Key Draw
No 1 (Disk 1 of 2)
v3.22

PC-KEY DRAW is a very powerful combination of programs providing keyboard to screen drawing, graphics printing, and slide show capability. Recently improved, PC-KEY DRAW is now more powerful than ever and easier to use. Documentation has been expanded from 20 to 65 pages. The drawing program allows a full range of computer art and computer graphics creation. Built in technical functions allow use as a CAD system. A big advantage is that this program is easy to use with or without a mouse. Demonstration files are on Disk No 345.

Usage: Intermediate to advanced.

System Requirements: 256K, color-graphics, two disk drives

How to Start: Load DOS and type DRAW to enter the main program. Consult DRAW.DOC for program documentation.

User Comments: "Offers an outstanding CAD program for the experienced computer user. The program is not easy to use, but I haven't seen a CAD system that is." "The program offers many features such as demonstration shows." "Very nice!" "Wow! This is quite sophisticated!"

Suggested Donation: $100.00 for full user registration

File Descriptions:

AUTOEXEC	BAT	Batch file to run KD.BAT
KD	BAT	Batch file to run PC-KEY DRAW
KD-INTRO		Introduction screen
KD-COPY	BAT	Batch file to copy the disk
KD-DRAW	EXE	PC-KEY DRAW drawing, paint, slide show and printing
KD-DRAW	TXT	Menu text for KD-DRAW.EXE
KD-DRAW	HLP	Help file used by KD-DRAW
KD-DRAW	80C	Status screen overlay
KD-PAINT	PIC	Picture of 16 basic colors used to paint with
KD-PTRN	PIC	64 Patterns used with pattern fill
KD-FONT1	FNT	Font definition (Large filled text)
KD-FONT2	FNT	Font definition (Large outlined text)
KD-MOUSE	MSC	Mouse Systems mouse source driver
KD-MOUSE	COM	Mouse Systems mouse driver for PC-KEY DRAW

KD-MSMOS	DEF	Microsoft mouse source driver
KD-MSMOS	MNU	Microsoft mouse source driver for PC-KEY DRAW
KD-PRNT1	TBL	Printer table for Okidata 92
KD-PRNT2	TBL	Printer table for Okidata 93
KD-PRNT3	TBL	Printer table for Citizen MSP-15
KD-PRNT4	TBL	Printer table for Epson and IBM graphics
SAMPLE	MCR	Sample macro showing many program features
EGA	MCR	Macro to set hi-res mode of EGA
KD-READ	ME	Basic information on program and registration
DATEIT	EXE	Replacement for DOS DATE
DATEIT	DAT	Date file used by DATEIT.EXE
BASRUN	EXE	Runtime overlay used by KD-DRAW.EXE
KD-DOC	BAT	Batch file to send print manual
KD-USER	MNL	65 page manual for versio 3.0
KD-DEMO	BAT	Batch file to load KD-DRAW and run SAMPLE.MCR
COMPARE	TXT	Compares PC-KEY DRAW to several commercial programs
KD-UPDAT	TXT	Provides update information for version 3.22
MOUSER	TXT	Provides mouse use information

345
PC-Key Draw
No 2 (Disk 2 of 2)
v3.22

Demonstration files to be used with PC-KEY-DRAW To run slide show demo (DEMO.SHW) disk must be in drive B:. All .PIC files can be retrieved using F7. All .SCN files are retrieved using F10. The main program is located on Disk No 344.

Usage: Intermediate to advanced.

System Requirements: 256K, two disk drives, color-graphics .

File Descriptions:

HOUSE	SCN	Simple floor plan of a house
PANDM	PIC	Planet and moon
OED	PIC	OEDWARE logoe
SOFTNOW	PIC	Text sample
PCKEYDRW	PIC	Text sample of PC-KEY DRAW
GIRL	SCN	Girl with sheep on hill
SUDSFISH	SCN	Submersible Dye System for towing
SINE	PIC	Sine curve used in SCNSHOW.MCR
SADDLE	SCN	Submersible recovery saddle
ESCHER	PIC	Escher style outline
GRAPH1	PIC	Sample edited Bar Graph
GRAPH2	PIC	Sample edited Line Graph
GRAPHT	PIC	Graphic text screen
COMET	PIC	Comet (shades of Halley's)
SPACE2	SCN	Outer space scene
SPACE4	SCN	Outer space scene

JOES	SCN	Eat at Joes — humerous space screen
GPLANE	PIC	Geometric plane
GPLANE	PIC	Geometric vertical plane
SAUCERS	PIC	Small saucer picture
RECOVERY	SCN	Recovery of small submersible
SAUCERL	PIC	Large saucer picture
HANDLING	SCN	Motion compensated Launch Recovery Crane
DESIGN2	PIC	Oriental rug design
SAUCERM	PIC	Medium saucer picture
COUCH	VCT	Vector image of couch
PATTERNS	PIC	Samples of patterns
SAUC	PIC	Another saucer created by SCNSHOW.MCR
PUMP	PIC	3-D picture of IV pump design
INVEST	PIC	Letterhead logo of world
PLAN	PIC	Simple planetoid created by SCNSHOW.MCR
PLANE	MCR	Macro to create 3-D plane
ESCHER1	MCR	Recursive macro to create 3-D image
XMAS	SCN	Christmas scene
GLASHOUS	PIC	Letterhead logo of building
SUBURB	SCN	Suburb made from HOUSE.SCN
PART3D	PIC	Simple wire frame model
README		Text file of information
SCNSHOW	MCR	Macro to cerate slide shows
HEAD	PIC	SHeep's head in animation of GIRL.SCN
KEYDRAW2	PIC	Text of PC-KEY DRAW
BIRDS	PIC	Flying birds used in animation of GIRL.SCN
HAT	PIC	Hat used in animation of GIRL.SCN
LRTITLE	SCN	Title screen for presentation on Launch Recovery
MOUNTBAS	SCN	Mounting base for an LRMC-18

380
GLUDRAW
v1

GLUDRAW offers good graphics generation software with extensive on-line help and sample drawings. It is a simple easy to use program for both children and adults. This software requires BASRUN.EXE which is part of the BASIC compiler, a commercial program. If you need to generate graphics images with any regularity, this is a program worth your consideration.

Usage: Graphics tools for all users

System Requirements: 128k, 1 disk drive, color/graphics monitor

How to Start: Load DOS and type GLUDRAW. (BASRUN.EXE must be in the path.) To run BASIC programs consult the directions in GETTING STARTED for your configuration.

User Comments: "On my PCjr it was difficult to use the function keys. "Overall, it seemed as useful and easy as a drawing program could be, but it needed an introduction on how to get started."
"Recommended for everybody who has a child using the PC !!"

File Descriptions:

GLUDRAW	EXE	Main executable program
DRAW2	EXE	Part of GLUDRAW.EXE
DRAW3	EXE	Part of GLUDRAW.EXE
DRAW4	EXE	Part of GLUDRAW.EXE
DRAW5	EXE	Part of GLUDRAW.EXE
*	PIC	Sample picture file (30 Files)
DRAWHELP	DIR	On-line help system
DRAW????	HLP	Part of on-line help system (32 Files)

418
PC-GRAPH
v1

PC-Graph is a program that allows you to create plots from database and report files which have been created by PC-File. It can produce line graphs of report & database files of up to 1000 records; define the area on the screen to use for your graphs; view all or part of your data; put labels and comments on your graphs; save graphs to disk; or print your graphs. This is an evaluation copy, the full supported software is available elsewhere.

Usage: PC-File users wanting to graph their data.

System Requirements: 192K RAM, one disk drive, a color-graphics card and monitor; PC-FILE software needed, too.

How to Start: Load DOS and type PC-GRAPH to enter the main program. Consult PC-GRAPH.DOC for program documentation.

User Comments: "Good for plotting x-y graphs of any data you have in a PC-FILE III data file." "Very easy to use. Scaling feature is great."

Suggested Donation: Registration of $49.00 brings full manual and limited technical support.

File Descriptions:

DOC	BAT	Batch file to print the manual contained in PCGRAPH.DOC
PC-GRAPH	DOC	The User manual (28 pages)
PC-GRAPH	EXE	The PC-GRAPH program (menu driven)

PCTEXT	BIN	Text screens used by PC-GRAPH program
PLOT1	PLT	Sample Graph files
PLOT2	PLT	Sample Graph files
PLOT3	PLT	Sample Graph files
PMCONFIG	PCG	Configuration file used by PC-GRAPH program
SCREEN	BAS	Picture screens used by PC-GRAPH
TUTOR1	LST	Sample data files used in the tutorial
TUTOR2	LST	Sample data files used in the tutorial

471
Present (5.1)
v1

This diskette contains the complete set of PRESENT programs (version 5.1), and associated utilities. It also has a set of pictures (.PIC) that can be used to provide a demonstration. The PRESENT program provides the ability to have your computer act as an automatic or manual slide projector. But this slide projector is special, it has fades, color changes, picture "piecing", and other things that a computer can do to video.

Usage: Users wishing a "Slide Projector" type of presentation on a color monitor.

System Requirements: 128K RAM, color graphics, and joysticks.

How to Start: Load DOS and type PRESENT to enter the main program. Consult PRESENT.DOC for program documentation.

User Comments: "Similar to IBM's PC STORYBOARD, even the HELP menu is the same. There is no provision for drawing pictures, but you can steal pictures from other graphics programs with CAMERA." "Professional. Program is easy to use. Results are first rate. This is as good as (if not the same as) IBM STORYBOARD software." "Programs of this caliber are usually very expensive, graphics were great."

Suggested Donation: $40.00

File Descriptions:

*	PIC	Present slide picture file (51 files)
CAMERA	COM	Memory resident utility takes pictures of screen images
COMPRESS	COM	Converts Basic Bsave files to Present's internal format
DEMO		This program is a demonstration of the features of PRESENT

EXPAND	COM	Converts PRESENT files to Basic Bsave format
PIC2RAS	COM	Picture to raster utility program
PREPARE	COM	Use this program to "prepare" slides for presentation
PREPARE	HLP	This is PREPARE'S help file
PRESENT	COM	The main executable file
PRESENT	DOC	Author supplied documentation file
PRESENT	HLP	Help file for PRESENT program
RAS2PIC	COM	Raster to picture utility program
README	1ST	User supplied documentation file

484
Graphics Font Design Utility Version 2.0

v1

Graphics Font Design Utility is a program that allows the user to design alternate sets of fonts for the ASCII characters in the high set (numbers 128 to 255). The new set of fonts may then be loaded into any Turbo Pascal program and used in place of 128 to 255. Graphics Font Design Utility then presents two ways which may be used to save the font sets created.

This utility was born to alleviate the pain of hand-coding each of the characters. This can be done on graph paper, but the final result does not always look the way that is expected. With Newfonts.com the design of these character sets can be done interactively and without the headaches of bit manipulation. Plus, the program is well documented!

Usage: Screen and font designers

System Requirements: 256K, one disk drive and monochrome/graphics display and a CGA card. A Pascal compiler is advisable.

How to Start: Type TYPE NEWFONT.DOC from the DOS prompt and follow the instructions.

User Comments: "Just wish I had some instructions on like how to use this program." "Takes the tedious job of creating fonts and simplifies it Very useful and efficient. Shareware price is reasonable." "Could not find any help to get program started." "Nice and very useful program for designing one's own characters."

Suggested Donation: $10.00; Source code $20.00

File Descriptions:

NEWFONTS	COM	Main program
NEWFONT	DOC	Complete documentation and insructions (20k)
USEFONTS	LIB	Small library file with procedures to use the files
FNTDEMO?	PAS	Pascal source code for FNTDEMO?.COM (4 Files)
FNTDEMO?	COM	Executable file for main program (4 Files)
HI–ASCII	FNT	Standard Ascii fonts in disk file form
LO–ASCII	FNT	Standard Ascii fonts in disk file form
CHEMFONT	FNT	Subscipts, superscripts, and some special symbols
CHEMMATH	FNT	Combination file with file merging option for
SAMPLE??	FNT	Sample fonts that can be used or modified (12 Files)
HIASCII	INC	Included file of standard ascii fonts
LOASCII	INC	Included file of standard ascii fonts
CHEMFONT	INC	Included file of numbers for ascii fonts
CHEMMATH	INC	Included file for merge of HI–ASCII.FNT and CHEMFONT.INC
NEWLORES	PAS	Pascal source code
LORES	PIC	Graphics of NEWLORES.PAS
JUNIOR16	PAS	Pascal source code

511
Turbo Sprites and Animation

v2.5

Turbo Sprites and Animation is a series of utilities, library files and demo programs to create, maintain and animate sprites (user defined graphics images) in the Turbo Pascal environment. It is an excellent program for exploring the world of animation using Turbo Pascal.

Usage: Turbo Pascal users

System Requirements: 256K, one disk drive, a CGA color card, RGB display and PASCAL compiler.

How to Start: Consult DESIGNER.DOC for program documentation.

Suggested Donation: $10.00; $20.00 for source code

File Descriptions:

DESIGNER	COM	Sprite design utility (version 2.5, Jan 1987)
DESIGNER	—0	Screen file for DESIGNER.COM
DESIGNER	—1	Screen file for DESIGNER.COM
DESIGNER	—2	Screen file for DESIGNER.COM
DESIGNER	DOC	Documentation for DESIGNER.COM (formatted for printer)

ADDENDA	DOC	Additions to documentation for new version 2.5
COMPOSER	COM	Pogramming utility to load screen file and sprite tables
COMPOSER	DOC	Documentation for COMPOSER.COM (formatted for printer)
SPRITES	LIB	Sprite definitions and driver routines
DEMO?	PAS	Turbo Pascal source code of demo program (8 Files)
DEMO?	COM	Compiled versions of some of demos (4 files)
DEMO?	TAB	Sprite table for DEMO.PAS programs (5 Files)
ANIMALS	TAB	Example Sprite table
??????	SPR	Individual sprite for demo programs
SANTA	INC	Individual sprite converted to typed constant array
DRAGON	INC	Individual sprite converted to typed constant array
SAVESCRN	COM	Utility to import PC Paint screens to Turbo Pascal programs
SAVESCRN	LIB	Library routines to save and load Turbo Pascal screens
READTHIS	NOW	Program overview

515
THE DRAFTSMAN
Version 1.1
v1

The Draftsman is a sophisticated package for producing presentation-quality charts, graphs, simple illustrations, or slide shows. You can input and edit you data with ease; also, data can be drawn from such programs as Lotus 1-2-3, Symphony, and Visicalc files that are in DIF (Data Interchange Format), or user-created data files.

Many graph types are available with The Draftsman; it can generate pies and exploded pies, stacked or cluster bar charts, scatter plots, and line graphs. Each graph may be sized and moved, and several may be placed on the same screen. This disk contains the full documenation for The Draftsman in archived form.

Usage: Intermediate or advanced graphics/spreadsheet users.

System Requirements: 192K, one disk drive, graphics adapter and monitor, Epson MX Printer or HP 7470 Plotter.

Features:

- Context-sensitive help screens
- Comprehensive User's Manual
- Freehand edit mode with ample options
- Support for Mouse Systems mouse
- 24 hour BB support.

How to Start: Load DOS and type DRAWMAN to enter the main program. Consult DRAWMAN.DOC (on Disk 516) for program documentation.

Suggested Donation: $25.00

File Descriptions:

INSTALL	BAT	Batch file to unarchive the program and manual
PRINTMAN	BAT	Batch to print the manual
README		Introduction letter from author
README	BAT	Batch file to read README file
ARC	EXE	Un-archiving program
BROWSE	COM	Text-file display utility
DRAWDOC	ARC	Contains the following files:
DRAWMAN	DOC	Documentation for DRAWMAN.EXE
DRAWMAN	ARC	Contains the following files: MOUSE BAT Batch file to attach a mouse to the system DRAWMAN EXE Main program to edit business graphs ERROR DAT Contains error messages used by DRAWMAN.EXE FILE DAT Contains file pointer information used by DRAWMAN.EXE HELP DAT Contains help messages used by DRAWMAN.EXE MENU DAT Contains the menus used by DRAWMAN.EXE VIO DAT Additonal programs segments, this is part of DRAWMAN.EXE WORK DAT Data work file used for slide shows and plotting and printing

620
Danal (1.0)
V1

DANAL is a graphically oriented data analysis tool that provides a quick means of manipulating and processing data files as if they were continuous functions. This program would be especially useful to: scientists and engineers when coupled to a data acquisition system; mathematically oriented businessmen; those tracking the stock market; students and teachers; and to anyone with data to be plotted.

Two different versions of DANAL are included on the distribution disk; one for an IBM PC or compatible with a color graphics adapter (CGA) and one for a PC equipped with a Hercules monographics card. The IBM color graphics adapter version is called DANALI and the Hercules version is called DANALH.

Usage: Graphic manipulation of data

System Requirements: 256K; IBM CGA compatible graphics interface capable of supporting the 640x200 high resolution mode or a Hercules monographics card; one floppy disk or hard disk; an 8087 math coprocessor and a text editor (e.g., EDLIN) or a word processor (e.g., Wordperfect) capable of outputting ASCII text files.

How to Start: Consult the thorough documentation in DANAL.DOC for directions on installing and running

● To run, select appropriate version and enter its program name at the DOS prompt.

Suggested Donation: $35 is full registration for individuals and first copy for schools, universities, government agencies, companies; for more, a fee of $60 for every 3 copies made by the organization. EGA versions and versions not requiring an 8087 available for $35.00.

File Descriptions:

DANALI	EXE+	Function plotting program for use with 8087 coprocessor
DANALH	EXE	Function plotting program for use with 8087 and Hercules card
DANFIG	EXE	Sets default configuration parameters
DANAL	DOC	Documentation for DANALI.EXE and DANALH.EXE
DEFAULT	FIG	Default values and configuration data for DANAL?.EXE
IBMJET		Graphics interface and printer configuration file
IBMOKI		Graphics interface and printer configuration file
IBM		Graphics interface and printer configuration file
HERCLJET		Graphics interface and printer configuration file
HERCOKI		Graphics interface and printer configuration file
LISAJOU		DANAL source file examples
MAKEDATA		DANAL source file examples
PLOTSTOK		DANAL source file examples
VIBRATIO		DANAL source file examples
PLOTSPOT		DANAL source file examples
FUTURE	VAL	DANAL source file examples
BIORHYTH		DANAL source file examples
SINE-5X		Predefined data files used with the LISAJOU example
COS-3X		Predefined data files used with the LISAJOU example
EG&G		Corporation stock quotes and portfolio activity for PLOTSTOK
NUMEG&G		Corporation stock quotes and portfolio activity for PLOTSTOK
SUNSPOT	DAT	ASCII data file used by PLOTSPOT example

629 PC-ART

v1

PC-ART is an excellent multi-function graphics drawing program that allows you to create color pictures and designs utilizing the standard color graphics adaptor on the PC.

What makes it especially worthwhile is the extreme care the author employed to make this not dependant upon having a mouse, light pen, koala pad, etc. He has produced a solid graphics package with maximum functionality from the keyboard. Another big plus is the high ease-of-use level with a fairly uncluttered screen which allows almost the entire screen for drawing.

Usage: Graphics design

System Requirements: 128K, one disk drive (two are recommended) color monitor and color graphics card

Features:

● Crayon function for freehand drawing in any color with varying line boldness;
● Paint brush function that paints in any color using any one of 15 different patterns;
● Line and Box functions with 4 different line patterns;
● Circle function with concentric repeat feature;
● Text function in one of two different fonts in any color and
● in 10 different character sizes;
● Retrieve or save entire screen for later processing;
● Snapshot function to take a picture of a portion of the screen and store it;
● Image library to store and later retrieve drawn figures;
● Easy-to-use window panels to select functions, colors, etc.

How to Start: Consult the users manual in file PC-ART.DOC can be printed out

● To run the program, enter PC-ART and press ENTER.

Suggested Donation: $15.00

File Descriptions:

DEMO	SCN	Data file for SCNDSIGN.COM
GENERAL	INC	
HELP	SCN	Data file for SCNDSIGN.COM
PC-ART	DOC	Documentation file for PC-ART.DOC
PC-ART	EXE	Graphic drawing program
PC-ART	IMG	PC-ART image libary file
PRTDOC	BAT	Batch file print PC-ART.DOC
READ	ME	File listing programs for PC-ART.DOC
READ1ST		Letter to PC-SIG from author of SCNDSIGN
README		Documentation for the ScnDsign program
SCNDSIGN	COM	Screen design utility
VAR	SCN	Data file for SCNDSIGN.COM

633 DRAWPLUS & SECRET QUEST
v1

DRAWPLUS is a Graphics/Drawing program written in BASICA for the PC/PCjr. It uses pull-down menus and a joystick to control the various functions. It operates in Medium Resolution Graphics Mode.

SECRET QUEST 2010 is a graphic/text adventure that takes place aboard a star ship in orbit around the earth. Uses standard commands and graphics created with the DRAWPLUS program.

Usage: Graphics design and fun!

System Requirements: 128K, two disk drives, a color monitor and a color/graphics card. NOTE: the DRAWPLUS program requires a joystick.

How to Start: To run BASIC programs consult the directions in GETTING STARTED for your configuration.

File Descriptions:

DRAWPLUS	BAS	Drawing program
HELPPLUS	BAS	Help screen and instruction printout menu
FILES	TXT	Author's list of files descriptions
QUEST	BAS	SECRET QUEST 2010 game
*	PIC	33 Picture files for Secret Quest

652 HI-RES RAINBOW Version 1.00
v1

HI-RES RAINBOW is a full featured paint package which includes pull-down windows, icons, multiple device inputs (joysticks, mouse, keyboard, tablet). A partial list of the features include Connecting lines, Ray, Zoom, Erase, Draw (two modes), Spray, Lines, Brush, Box, Fill, Circle, Arc lines, Connecting arcs, Undo, Reflexing, and each has its own icon.

Usage: Full featured graphics "painting"

System Requirements: 256K, two disk drives and a color/graphics monitor display with appropriate card

How to Start: After consulting the documenation file README.1ST, start the program by entering HIRES at the DOS prompt.

Suggested Donation: $25.00 for a a full implementation of 'HI-RES RAINBOW' plus full documentation; $50.00 for two full copies (both the 256k and 320k) with more screens, documentation with a hint section, plus a second disk with additional utilities and art parts for your own use.

File Descriptions:

*	WIN	Files which are needed to run 'HI-RES' (11 files)
*	BIN	Files which are 'HI-RES' format picture files (11 files)
HIRES	EXE+	The HI-RES drawing program
QUICKEYS	COM	Program to speed up program use while in keyboard mode
README	1ST	Documentation file

GTPR	COM	Printer driver
GTPRS	EXE	Printer driver
PORT	COM	Program to assign ports; like MODE.COM
MAC1	GTM	Macro to run demo
ADMIN	GTD	Data file for Business Graphics demo
DPBUDGET	GTD	Data file for Business Graphics demo
PARTS	GTD	Data file for Business Graphics demo
SALES	GTD	Data file for Business Graphics demo
WAGES	GTD	Data file for Business Graphics demo
RAND	GTD	Data file for Business Graphics demo
TEXT	GTT	Sample text screen, user can insert screens in "slide shows"
GTSTART	EXE	Main menu program for Graphtime;
BRUN10	EXE	Runtime module
GTLINE	EXE	Line chart module
GTFILE	EXE	File Input/Edit Module
GTPIEBL	EXE	Pie chart module
T1	GTB	A sample block file
LPIE	GTP	A sample "PAINT" file to view or print.
LCAR	GTP	A sample "PAINT" file
HCOLUMN	GTP	A sample "PAINT" file
GTPATERN	GTX	Paint Pattern Library
HDRAGON	GTP	A sample "PAINT" file
NEWSREVU	TXT	A review published in an Australian newspaper

669
GRAPHTIME II (2.5A) (Disk 1 of 2)
V1

This is the first of a two disk Demo Set contains a business presentation graphics program of considerable power. GRAPHTIME II does various line, column and pie charts. The charts can be printed or plotted, viewed individually, or set up to run as an unattended "slide show" on the monitor. Extensive on-line help information is available with the Help key.

Graphtime accepts data from dBase II/III, Multiplan, and LOTUS, or you can enter data directly into Graphtime. There is a Font editor and macro editor. There are math functions including moving averages. There is even an "undo" function. A Microsoft mouse (or compatible) is recommended.

NOTE: This Demo version does not have the pen plot driver and supports only color graphics adapters. This version will plot only 24 data points. The commercial version can handle 365 data points. This Demo version will not save "Paint" files, but it will print them.

Usage: Business graphics

System Requirements: 256K, two floppies or a floppy/hard disk, the color/graphics adaptor, the monitor can be colour or composite monochrome.

How to Start: If the online help isn't enough, you can print it out by inserting the RUNTIME disk in drive A: enter CTRL/PrSc then: PRINTHLP. The README file contains complete instructions and installation guides.

Suggested Donation: $35.00 for the full version

File Descriptions:

README		Publisher's remarks about the Graphtime II v.2.5A
GT	BAT	Start up batch file, parallel print driver for A size prints
GTS	BAT	Start up batch file, parallel driver for 1/2 size prints
GTC1	BAT	Start up batch file, serial print driver for A size prints

670
GRAPHTIME II (2.5A) (Disk 2 of 2)
V1

This is the second of a two disk Demo Set contains a business presentation graphics program of considerable power. GRAPHTIME II does various line, column and pie charts. The charts can be printed or plotted, viewed individually, or set up to run as an unattended "slide show" on the monitor. Extensive on-line help information is available with the Help key.

This disk contains the Text/Font Generator, the Text/Font Editor, three fonts, and the Drawing and Graphing Modules. It also contains the HELP screens with a file for printing them out as a reference manual.

Usage: Business graphics

System Requirements: 256K, two floppies or a floppy/hard disk, the color/graphics adaptor, the monitor can be colour or composite monochrome.

How to Start: See the README file for full directions on setup and running.

Suggested Donation: $35.00 for the full version

File Descriptions:

PRINTHLP	BAT	A batch file to print out the Help screens from GRAPHTIME II
GT	BAT	A batch file to load the program
TFR	GTZ	Part of Graphtime II
GTPATERN	GTX	Pattern file for GTDRAW
GTDRAW	EXE	The Drawing Module of GRAPHTIME
GTGRAPH	EXE	The Graphing Module
GTFONTPR	EXE	The Text Generator and Font Editor Module
GTFILE	EXE	The File input/edit Module
GTTEXTED	EXE	Text and Macro Editor
GTPIEBL	EXE	Part of Graphtime II
FONT1	GTF	Font number 1
FONT2	GTF	Font number 2
FONT3	GTF	Font number 3
*	GTH	Help files (19 files)
README		The publisher's introduction to GRAPHTIME II.

701 DANCAD3D Version 1.30 (Disk 1 of 4)

v1

This is the first of the four disk set DANCAD 3D. It contains the powerful DANCAD 3D program and its documentation. The next three disks — 702, 703, 704 — contain the DANMOVIE program with working demos of that program. While DANCAD 3D can function by itself, DANMOVIE must have DANCAD3D.COM to work properly.

DANCAD 3D will let you do complex tasks like stereoscopic 3D wire frame animation or just draw simple things like a letter head. DANCAD3D is a program that lets you draw with lines, be they lines in a plane (2D drawing) or in space (3D drawing). These lines can be formed into both simple and complex "elements". These can be: saved, loaded, magnified, rotated, flipped, offset (moved), and used over and over again, by keeping them as a file on a disk (give them names like cube, sphere, and cylinder).

You can also work with complex forms, such as lettering, blocks of text, and dimensioning can be automatically generated as elements made of lines. Since the elements are separate they can be moved and displayed repeatedly to simulate the effects of motion on the objects you have drawn. You can put a list of elements, their position, and the view point from which they are to be displayed in a macro

(ASCII text file), so DANCAD3D can run itself without you having to enter the commands manually through the menus and keyboard.

DANCAD3D prints out very sharp lines and is useful for: line drawings, mechanical drawing, technical illustration, wire-frame animation, engineering simulation to verify the fit of three dimensional shapes, business forms, page layout combining text and drawings, and automatic computer "slide" shows.

Usage: CAD applications

System Requirements: 640K, one floppy/one hard disk, color graphics.

How to Start: Consult the README and the MANUAL.DOC for installation and operations guidance.

Suggested Donation: $10.00

File Descriptions:

DANCAD3D	COM	Main program and code editor with help screens
DANCAD3D	00?	overlay file loaded by DANCAD3D.COM (8 files)
DANCAD3D	MSG	Message file
DANCAD3D	COL	.COL for color or .B&W for CGA black and white
SHOW-20X	MAC	DANCAD3D Macro file
DEMO	1	Demo program written with DANCAD3D's commands
README	BAT	Help for first time user
INSTALL	BAT	Installs DANCAD3D
MANUAL	DOC	Documentation and Tutorial for DANCAD3D

702 DANCAD3D — Demo Examples (Disk 2 of 4)

v1

This is the second of the four disk set DANCAD 3D. It contains the DANMOVIE program, a full demo and its documentation. The next two disks-703 & 704 — also contain the DANMOVIE program with working demos of that program. NOTE: While DANCAD 3D can function by itself, DANMOVIE must have DANCAD3D.COM to work properly.

DANMOVIE works with DANCAD 3D to animate screens saved as pixel bit maps. DANCAD 3D can print out or plot the drawings at very high resolution (greater than 4 million pixels) if you like the way the animation looks using DANMOVIE.

DANMOVIE is a useful engineering tool since you can program DANCAD 3D to make an animated close-up of parts in a layout drawing. In that way you can confirm the fit of moving parts. You can also program DANCAD 3D to produce a animated perspective view of the whole assembly with all its parts in motion!

Usage: CAD applications

System Requirements: 640K, one floppy/one hard disk, color graphics

How to Start: Consult the DANMOVIE.DOC and the MANUAL.DOC on Disk 701 for installation and operations guidance.

Suggested Donation: $10.00

File Descriptions:

FRAME	??	DANCAD 3D pixel frame files (20 files)
DANMOVIE	COM	Program that shows the frame files
DANMOVIE	DOC	Documentation for DANMOVIE.COM
README	BAT	Types documentation
GO	BAT	Runs demo

703 DANCAD3D — Demo Examples (Disk 3 of 4)
v1

This is the second of the four disk set DANCAD 3D. It contains the DANMOVIE program, a full demo and its documentation. The next two disks-703 & 704 — also contain the DANMOVIE program with working demos of that program. NOTE: While DANCAD 3D can function by itself, DANMOVIE must have DANCAD3D.COM to work properly.

Usage: CAD applications

System Requirements: 640K, one floppy/one hard disk, color graphics

How to Start: Consult the DANMOVIE.DOC and the MANUAL.DOC on Disk 701 for installation and operations guidance.

Suggested Donation: $10.00

File Descriptions:

FRAME	??	DANCAD 3D pixel frame files (20 files)
DANMOVIE	COM	Program that shows the frame files
DANMOVIE	DOC	Documentation for DANMOVIE.COM
README	BAT	Types documentation
GO	BAT	Runs demo

704 DANCAD3D — Demo Examples (Disk 4 of 4)
v1

This is the fourth of the four disk set DANCAD 3D. It contains the DANMOVIE program, a full demo and its documentation. NOTE: While DANCAD 3D can function by itself, DANMOVIE must have DANCAD3D.COM to work properly.

Usage: CAD applications

System Requirements: 640K, one floppy/one hard disk, color graphics

How to Start: Consult the DANMOVIE.DOC and the MANUAL.DOC on Disk 701 for installation and operations guidance.

Suggested Donation: $10.00

File Descriptions:

FRAME	??	DANCAD 3D pixel frame files (20 files)
DANMOVIE	COM	Program that shows the frame files
DANMOVIE	DOC	Documentation for DANMOVIE.COM
README	BAT	Types documentation
GO	BAT	Runs demo

HOME:

Organize your home and safeguard your valuables with our home applications software. In this category are programs that:

- Identify and catalog your household valuables
- Manage your household finances (checkbooks to home budgets)
- Research your family genealogy

Have you ever been burglarized? Do you know someone who has? You can protect your valuables by identifying and cataloging your property using any of our excellent home inventory programs. Many of these programs are highly recommended for insurance purposes.

Tracking household finances and maintaining the family budget are the next most popular home applications programs. Personal finance managers come in a variety of shapes and sizes. Many are designed to keep track of items of special interest when April 15th rolls around. In fact, we have several programs solely for that purpose!

For many families, extending their family roots by genealogy has become a means of bridging miles and years, and it's fun, too! Our selection goes from simple to complex, the latter having programs for printing out questionnaires and family tree structures suitable for framing.

90 Genealogy ON DISPLAY Version 5.0

v5.0

Genealogy ON DISPLAY, Version 5.0, is an integrated, menu-driven group of thirty-one BASIC programs for PCs (including the PCjr), which assist users in organizing, entering, and reporting their own genealogical data. It provides for 500 persons and 200 marriages within its data base, with no specific generation limit.

Information can be displayed and printed. Output available for printing or displaying includes:

1. Pedigree (Family Tree) Charts. 2. Family Group Charts. 3. Descendents Charts (30 generation default) 4. Detailed Personal Information. 5. Detailed Marriage Information.

Additional output available for printing includes:

1. Lists of Persons (by number or alphabetized). 2. Lists of Marriages (by number or alphabetized). 3. A list of Parent/Child Relationships.

NOTE: A companion disk with more functions is available on Disk 594 Notes On Display.

Usage: Genealogical research and family fun.

System Requirements: 96K, at least one floppy drive, color or monochrome display and a printer (manual is 80+ pages)

How to Start: To run BASIC programs consult the directions in GETTING STARTED for your configuration.

User Comments: "A great program. I love it." "...very easy to work with" "An excellent program for the PC-JR. A very colorful and interesting program." "One problem: I can't motivate my relatives enough to provide me with enough information..."

Suggested Donation: $35.00 for registration and updates

File Descriptions:

RUNFIRST	BAS	Copy of cover letter — how to start
MENU	BAS	Program to run first
DISPLAY	BAS	Displays file information
CREATMAR	BAS	Creates marriage file
INDEXMAR	BAS	Creates marriage index
CREATORD	BAS	Creates ordinances file
CREATPER	BAS	Creates persons file
INDEXPC	BAS	Creates persons index
UPDATMAR	BAS	Updates marriage file
UPDATORD	BAS	Updates ordinance file
UPDATPER	BAS	Updates persons file
LISTMAR	BAS	Lists marriages
LISTPCI	BAS	Lists parent/child index
LISTPER	BAS	Lists persons file
ALPHAMAR	BAS	Prints alphanumeric marriage list
ALPHAPER	BAS	Prints alphanumeric persons list
DESCEND	BAS	Prints descendents
FAMILY	BAS	Prints family group sheets
PRINTMAR	BAS	Prints marriage file
PEDIGREE	BAS	Prints pedigree charts
PRINTPER	BAS	Prints persons and ordinance file
DIRECTOR	BAS	Prints program directory
TESTFILE		Test file to verify BASIC /S:256
— —	— —	Programs to run to print documentation
TABLEOFC	BAS	Program to print table of contents (1)
INTRODUC	BAS	Program to print manual introduction (2)
GENERAL	BAS	Program to print general information (3)
USINGTHE	BAS	Program to print "Using the programs" (4)
REFERENC	BAS	Program to print reference material (5)
APPENDIX	BAS	Program to print Appendices (6)
PRINTERS	BAS	Program to print documentation on other printers

107 *Home Finance*
v1

Among several financial applications, the standout program is FOS, the Financial Operating System. This program will maintain all your financial records whether they are checking accounts, savings accounts, CD's, stocks, bank notes, cash expenditures or just about any other transaction. Many reports are available to inform you of your current 'net worth' and to aid you in controlling your liquid assets.

Usage: Personal financial management

System Requirements: 64K, at least one disk drive and a 80 column display, BASICA. A printer is optional.

How to Start: To run BASIC programs consult the directions in GETTING STARTED for your configuration.

User Comments: "FINANCE is good. I just wish it would print all the nice material that it gives." "FOS is nice but requires time to keep records up to date." "On our PC Jr program disables and changes certain keys,(i.e. the cursor keys). This can be eliminated by pressing ALT-Fn-N after loading." "Pretty good check register."

Suggested Donation: $10.00 — includes registration and updates.

File Descriptions:

SCRNSAVE	COM	Program to turn off screen if no keys depressed after 3 minutes
SCRNSAVE	DOC	Short description for SCRNSAVE.COM
MUSIC	BAS	Plays notes
SETUP	BAT	Initialization routine for this diskette
FOS	BAS	Home financial management system
FOS2	BAS	Second part of FOS
FOS	DOC	FOS documentation
FINANCE	BAS	A collection of financial analysis routines
TAX1982	VC	A VISICALC template for 1982 Federal Income Taxes
HAL-PC	TXT	Description of how one PC users group formed

116 *microGOURMET (Disk 1 of 2)*
v1

microGOURMET is a two-disk software package, which functions through dBASE II. It was designed to help those of you who spend lots of time looking through cookbooks and rummaging through scraps of paper to find recipes. It will help reduce the time spent choosing recipes to prepare for both family and guest meals. It is also an aid to menu planning. You can select recipes for whatever time period you wish, print the recipes, and prepare and print a shopping list to take to the store. You can also add and change recipes.

Usage: Developing your culinary skills!

System Requirements: 180K of disk storage (with at least 90k bytes per disk), monochrome display and at least two disk drives, dBASEII software. Can be configured for hard disks.

How to Start: Access microGOURMET through DBASEII. At the dot prompt, type DO MENU. Consult MANUAL.DOC for program documentation.

User Comments: "More than worth the cost. Saved me seemingly endless programing time." "SLOW! 116 and 117 should be combined." "Fun program." "When I got it working it turned out to be just about what I wanted. I'm really enjoying this one."

File Descriptions:

READ	ME	Notes about MicroGOURMET programs and listing documentation
GOURMET	HI	Version of MicroGOURMET for 360K or HDU drives (rename .PRG)
GOURMET	LOW	Version of MicroGOURMET for single-sided drives (rename .PRG)
ITEM	DBF	MicroGOURMET dBASE II database file
SHOP	DBF	MicroGOURMET dBASE II database file
TYPE	NDX	MicroGOURMET dBASE II index file
NUMBER	NDX	MicroGOURMET dBASE II index file
ITEM	NDX	MicroGOURMET dBASE II index file
MANUAL	DOC	MicroGOURMET manual in listable DOS file format

117 microGOURMET (Disk 2 of 2)
v1

This is the companion disk to Disk No 116.

File Descriptions:

GOURMET	DBF	MicroGOURMET dBASE II database file
MANUAL	TXT	MicroGOURMET manual (WORDSTAR format)
UNWS	BAS	Program for converting WORDSTAR files to DOS files

193 FREEWILL
v1

The California Legistlature approved, effective Jan. 1, 1983 the use of a "Fill-in-the-blanks" approach for executing a valid will in California. They apparently felt this was better than having people die without a will or with an invalid holographic will. Two standard will forms have been approved. This diskette contains both forms (printable) and a copy of the California civil code that covers the forms. The documentation should provide some background for deciding whether you should have a will, whether either of the two California statutory will forms can serve your needs, or whether you should obtain the services of a lawyer to draft your will.

Usage: Preparing a personal will in California

System Requirements: 64K, one disk drive and monochrome display

How to Start: Load DOS and type WILL or TRUST to enter the California wills program.

User Comments: "Useless outside of California; requires too much modification." "Freewill is a good introduction BUT it may not be valid in states other than California and it deals with only the very simplest of estate situations. Mainly good to get you thinking about a will and what is involved." "Found it easy to understand and use. Although I do not live in California, my attorney said most parts apply generally and only slight modifications had to be made to the will I wrote with it."

File Descriptions:

FREEWILL	DOC	Introduction
PRINTING	DOC	Information on printing FREEWILL GROUP
C2	BAT	Execute "C2" in default drive for explanation
BANNER	ASC	FREEWILL LOGO
PAGE????	ASC	Explanation text (8 files)
WILL		First of two FORMS for your "Do-It-Yourself" will
TRUST		Second choice of FORMS

240 Family-Tree, Etc Genealogy
v3.01

'Family-Tree, Etc' (Version 3.01) is a general purpose genealogy system designed for charting and maintaining family tree information and relationships between individuals. The system is menu driven with single keystroke commands, scrolling, mini-windows and screen/printer/disk file report output capability. Default options may be changed by user to select disk drive. screen colors and printer control codes.

The MAINTENANCE function allow the entry of Names, Sex, Dates/Places of Birth/Death/Marriage and freeform text remarks. Spouse and Parent/Child are established after data is entered.

The REORG function automatically ensures data is correctly sequenced through an internal numbering scheme.

CHARTS uses the database created through MAINTENANCE to generate reports by pedigree, ancestors, family groups, decendants and relationships.

Usage: Serious genealogical work.

System Requirements: 128K, at least one diskette drive and a monochrome display. Access to a printer is strongly suggested!

How to Start: Load DOS and type FT-ETC to enter the main program. Consult FT-ETC.TXT for program documentation.

User Comments: "Easier to use than Genealogy on Display (DISK #90), but not as thorough." "Both my wife and I use it at least twice a week. It has also encouraged us to get in touch with our families to add more folks to our Family Tree."

File Descriptions:

FT-ETC	EXE	This is the main genealogy program
FT-ETC-C	EXE	One of the branches
FT-ETC-M	EXE	Another branch
FT-ETC-R	EXE	Still another branch
FT-ETC	PCS	Documentation
FT-ETC	TXT	Documentation and directions

275 PC-CHECK Version 3.0
v3.0

Here is an excellent user-supported personal finance program. PC-Check Manager is an easy to use, menu-driven checkbook and personal general ledger with printout and check writing capabilities. This enhanced version will sort data files, find payees, print checks, track income tax deductions, list data by month, quarter, payee, or ledger account. It can handle multiple checkbooks by assigning different names to each file. The drive on which the data is located can be selected from the Maintenance Menu. The last active data file is saved and automatically called up the next time the program is used. The user can assign up to 78 payees to which checks are regularly written and 100 ledger accounts, to speed data entry. The program will automatically assign the ledger account number when an assigned payee is selected. Version 3.0 is new and expanded.

NOTE: IT IS NOT COMPATIBLE WITH PREVIOUS VERSIONS!

Usage: Personal Checkbook and Tax Management

System Requirements: 192K, two disk drives, mono display

How to Start: Load DOS and type PCC to enter the main program. Consult PCC.DOC for program documentation.

User Comments: "This is a very good program for people who are selfemployed. However, some of the documentation is unclear." "Except for one bug this checkbook manager has made a pleasure out of daily management, as well as being a big assistance at tax time." "I use PC-Check writer for my personal checking accounts."

Suggested Donation: $35.00 for PC-CHECK MANAGER

File Descriptions:

----	--	PC-CHECK Manager
PCC	EXE	Compiled version PC-Check Manager
PCC		User data file (sample)
PCC	DOC	Documentation for PC-Check Manager
PCCL	DAT	List of ledger catagories used by PCC.EXE
PCCP	DAT	Data file for PCC.EXE

295

TAX-FILE

v2.1

TAX-FILE is a complete tax record keeping system written for Ashton-Tate's dBASE II. It enables a person to collect financial records throughout the year and then print several reports making the yearend tax job quick and easy. The system keeps complete personal records for all types of deductions and income. Recording of business related expenses is also included.The TAX-FILE makes use of the menu approach for entering and editing data and has several built-in reports.

Usage: Complete personal tax recordkeeping.

System Requirements: 192K, two disk drives, a monochrome display and dBASEII software.

How to Start: Access through dBASEII.

Suggested Donation: $10.00 for registration and updated manual.

File Descriptions:

MENU	PRG	The main TAX-FILE menu
TAXFILE	DBF	Database for income tax record transactions
CHKORDER	FRM	Report form for check list in check number order
SALESTAX	MEM	Memory variables for sales tax computation
INTRCOST	PRG	Program to report on the interest paid during the year
SALETAX	PRG	Program to compute sales tax
ADDCHEK	PRG	Program to record a check
CHECKS	DBF	Database for checks
MISCLIST	FRM	Report form for printer list of miscellaneous deductions
INCOME	FRM	Report form for list of sources of income during the tax year
INCOME	DBF	Database for income earned
TAXLIST	FRM	Report form for list of tax deductible payments
SECURITY	FRM	Report form for list of securities purchased during the year
READ	TXT	Text file describing TAX-FILE
INTRPAID	FRM	Report form for interest paid
READ	BAT	Batch file to read program description text files
DONACOST	FRM	Report form for charitable donations
AUTOCOST	FRM	Report form for business related automobile expenses
COMPCOST	FRM	Report form for computer related expenses
MISC	FRM	Report form for screen list of miscellaneous deductions
EDITCHEK	PRG	Program to edit a check entry
MEDICOST	FRM	Report form for medical costs
TAXPAID	FRM	Report form for state taxes paid

MEDIPAY	FRM	Report form for list of mileage incurred with medical cost
TAINCOST	FRM	Report form for business related entertainment costs
STOKLIST	FRM	Report form for stock and bond list
INTRLIST	PRG	Program to list interest earned
MEDICAL	PRG	Program to run report on medical deductions
MEDICAL	DBF	Database of medical deductions
DONATION	PRG	Program to run report on charitable donations
TAXES	PRG	Program to run report on taxes that are deductible
AUTOCOST	PRG	Program to run report on business automobile expenses
COMPCOST	PRG	Program to run report on computer related expenses
MISCCOST	PRG	Program to run report on miscellaneous deductions
INTEREST	PRG	Program to run report of interest expense incurred
TAXCOST	PRG	Program to run report on state taxes paid
READ1	TXT	Second text file continuing program description
OTHRCOST	PRG	Program to run report on miscellaneous deductions
SALECOST	PRG	Program to run report on sales tax paid
SETUP	PRG	Menu lists as sales tax setting, actually program setup
INTRLIST	FRM	Report form for list of interest payments made to lenders
GEMINI	DBF	Database for printer control for Gemini 10X or 15X
TAXDATA	MEM	Memory variable for tax year
SETPRINT	PRG	Program to set up printer
DATABASE	BAT	Batch file to setup data files on drive B for dual floppy
TAXES	DBF	Database for taxes paid
MISC	DBF	Database for miscellaneous deductions
DONATION	DBF	Database for charitable donations
INTEREST	DBF	Database for interest paid
AUTO	DBF	Database for business related automobile expenses
COMPUTER	DBF	Database for computer related expenses
MENUREPT	PRG	Report menu
CHKPAYEE	FRM	Report form for check list in payee order
ADDSTOK	PRG	Report form to add a stock transaction to the database
BUSICOST	FRM	Report form for list of business expenses incurred
INTRCOST	FRM	Report form for list of interest expenses incurred
MISCCOST	FRM	Report form for list of miscellaneous deductible expenses
WORKCOST	FRM	Report form for non-entertainment business expenses
EDITRECD	PRG	Program to edit a payment
TRANFILE	MEM	Memory variable for next transaction number
WORKCOST	PRG	Program to run report of non-entertainment business expenses
BONDSTOK	PRG	Program to report securities bought and sold during the year
POLICOST	FRM	Report form for political compaign contributions
CHKINX	NDX	Index file for check database by check number
INTRPAID	PRG	Program to run report on interest paid

STOCKS	DBF	Database for stocks and bonds
ADDRECD	PRG	Program to add a payment
PAYINX	NDX	Index file for check database by payee
PRNTIT	PRG	Program to setup printer
MENUMILE	PRG	Travel menu
TRAVEL	DBF	Database to record travel mileage and expenses
CHEKVIEW	PRG	Program to list checks in the system
MENUCHEK	PRG	Checkbook menu
ADDINCO	PRG	Program to enter income earned
TESTRUN	PRG	Program to set the default data drive
INCOFILE	MEM	Memory variable for next income identification number
MANUAL	PRG	Program to print order form for TAX-FILE manual on diskette
MANUAL	TXT	Text file for MANUAL.PRG
FILEDRIV	MEM	Memory variable to store data drive letter
INVOICE	TXT	Invoice form for TAX-FILE and manual order
TAINCOST	PRG	Program to run report of business entertainment expenses
STOKINDX	NDX	Index file for stocks database
FILELIST	TXT	Text file describing the types of files used by TAXFILE
DIVDLIST	FRM	Report form for list of dividend income received
OKIDATA	DBF	Database for printer control for Okidata 92 or 93
MENUINCO	PRG	Income menu
ORGANIZE	PRG	Program to organize files
MILEGONE	FRM	Report form for mileage traveled
PLACGONE	FRM	Report form for overnight expense
INCOINDX	NDX	Index file for income database by income code
EPSON	DBF	Database for printer control for Epson family of printers
POLICOST	PRG	Program to run report of political campaign contributions
EDITINCO	PRG	Program to edit income earned
DIVILIST	PRG	Program to list dividends earned
DIVIDEND	DBF	Database for dividends earned
INTRINDX	NDX	Index file for income database by type and source

321
Home Applications
v1

A wide and wild collection of programs! Programs range for guitar tuning to analysis of IRAs to picking against the NFL point spreads to data encryption. Easily the most appreciated is the Home Inventory program which is excellent for insurance purposes.

Usage: Something for everybody at your house!

System Requirements: 64K, one disk drive and monochrome display; files marked with " + " need a color/graphics card and monitor

How to Start: To run BASIC programs consult the directions in GETTING STARTED for your configuration. Consult the .DOC and .TXT files for program documentation.

Users Comments: "Anxious for football season to try NFL-PIX. CRYPT1 is very heavy. Love calendar. CALENDAR.BAS is the best I have seen for flexibility of use." "Several programs were good (e.g. home inventory, lifetime, calendar); several would probably be good IF I knew what they meant or how to use them (e.g. alarm, biorythm, — documentation of any kind would be welcome." "This seems to be mostly a "fun" program disk."

File Descriptions:

$-EXCHNG	BAS	International Currency Exchange Program
ALARM	BAS	Program to set Alarm Clock on PC
AREACODE	EXE	Area Code Finder Program
AVEGRATE	BAS	Stock Growth, Rate and Projections Program
BIORYTHM	BAS	Program to determine Biorythms
BUZZWORD	TXT	Data Processing Definitions
CALENDAR	BAS	Prints Monthly Calendars from 1583 to 4046
CALL	BAS	Program to Evaluate Stock calls
CAS-REEL	BAS	Provides timing information for reel to casette
CHEKBOOK	COM	Checking account statement/reconciliation program
PC-CRYP2	EXE	Data Encryption and De-Cryption Program
PC-CRYP2	DOC	Documentation for PC-CRYP2.EXE
DECIDE	BAS	Decision Making Program
DECISION	BAS	Another Decision Making Program
FUNDANAL	BAS	Fundamental Analysis Program
GUITAR	BAS	Guitar Tuning Program
HAIKU	BAS	Generates Random Haiku's
HEATCALC	BAS	Performs SENES Building Energy Load Modeling
HOME-INV	BAS	Program for Home Inventory Tracking
HOME-INV	DAT	Data for HOME-INV
HOME-INV	DOC	Documentation for HOME-INV
HURRICAN	BAS	Hurricane Tracking Program
DEBBIE		Data for Hurricane Tracking Program
INSAT	BAS	Calculates Aiming Angles for Satellites
IRA-CALC	BAS	Individual Retirement Account Calculation Program
JOBJAR	BAS	Job Tasking Program
LAYAWAY	BAS	Lawaway Account Management Program
LIFETIME	BAS	Life Expectancy Determination Program
LOTTERY2	BAS	Lottery Number Choosing Program
NFL-PIX	BAS	NFL Point Spread Calculation Program
OPTION	BAS	Option Analysis Program
SOUNDEFF	BAS	Sound Effects Generation Program
STAR	BAS	Astronomical Calendar Program
STAR	DAT	Data for STAR
STARFIND	BAS	Astrologic and Astronomical Calculator
TEMPER	BAS	Temperature Conversion Program
TIMECALC	BAS	Time Calculation Program
TIMECALC	DOC	Documentation for TIMECALC

TOLLFREE	TXT	Toll Free numbers for Computer Products
WEA1986	DAT	Sample database for WEATHER.EXE
WEATHER	DOC	Documentation for WEATHER
WEATHER	EXE	Weather record and statistics program
WNDCHIL	BAS	Wind Chill Calculation Program
ZELLER	BAS	Determines Day of Week from Zeller's Congruence
WEA0000	DAT	Database template for WEATHER.EXE

361
FAMILY HISTORY
(Disk 1 of 2)
v1.1

This 'Family History System' — of which this is the first of a two disk set — is noteworthy among computerized genealogy programs for its modular design, use of Fixed Formatted screen displays, and thorough use of function keys. The system uses a set of 'linked random access' datasets for storing information about individuals, including all family relationships. No limits are placed upon the number of relationships that may exist for each individual or for the number of generations of ancestors or descendants that may be recorded. Information for up to 3200 individuals may be stored on a single DS/DD diskette (up to 9999 on a hard disk). The system produces Ancestor, Descendant, and Family Group reports and Ancestor (tree) Charts. Blank worksheets and charts may be produced for recording information for entry into the system.

This, the first of a two disk set (disk 2 on DISK 632), contains the 38 page manual, the interpreted BASIC versions of the programs, and installation utilities. DISK 632 contains the compiled versions of the programs and a set of sample files built using the descendents of Adam as recorded in the Book of Genesis in the Bible.

Usage: Serious family tracking!

System Requirements: 128K, one disk drive, monochrome display; printer recommended.

How to Start: To run BASIC programs consult the directions in GETTING STARTED for your configuration. Consult README and CONTENTS.DOC for program information.

User Comments: "Well handled screen presentation enhances this software. Moreover, it represents a comprehensive genealogical system. Speed is its primary problem, inability to print all data is another." "Excellent buy for the genealogist. Very glad I bought it. Will use it a lot." "This is a great little program.

Suggested Donation: $35.00 for registration and extended options

File Descriptions:

READ	ME	'Bootstrap' document
CONTENTS	DOC	Documentation
PCINSTAL	BAT	Batch file for installation using BASICA
JRINSTAL	BAT	Batch file for installation on PCJR
GWINSTAL	BAT	Batch file for installation using GWBASIC
SSINSTAL	BAT	Batch file for installation for single side drives
XTINSTAL	BAT	Batch file for installation on PC XT (hard disk)
AUTOEXEC	BAT	Batch file for 'autostarting' Family system
AFAMILY	DAT	System defaults for 1 drive systems
BFAMILY	DAT	System defaults for 2 drive systems
CFAMILY	DAT	System defaults for hard disk system
PCFAMILY	BAT	Batch file for starting system using BASICA
GWFAMILY	BAT	Batch file for starting system using GWBASIC
XTFAMILY	BAT	Batch file for starting system on PC XT (hard disk)
FAMINIT	BAS	Entry program for Family History System
FAMMENU	BAS	Main Menu program
FAMILY	BAS	Display/Update/Create Family files
FAMANCST	BAS	Produce Ancestor report
FAMDSCND	BAS	Produce Descendant report
FAMGROUP	BAS	Produce Family Group report
FAMCHART	BAS	Produce Ancestor Charts
FAMLIST	BAS	Undocumented function F2-E
FAMFILES	BAS	Change default file names
FAMSCRNA	BAS	Change default screen attributes
FAMPRNTC	BAS	Define (up to 9) printer 'setups'
FAMILY	BAT	Batch file for starting sample session
FAMILY	DAT	System Defaults for sample session
GENESIS	NAM	Sample Name file
GENESIS	ADR	Sample Address file
GENESIS	OTH	Sample 'Miscellaneous information' file
VIEWDOC	BAT	Batch file for viewing the documentation on screen
PRINTDOC	BAT	Batch file for printing documentation
*	DOC	Documentation for Family History (8 files)
BASIC	BAT	Startup file for FAMILY HISTORY using IBM BASIC
GWBASIC	BAT	Batch file to start FAMILY HISTORY with GWBASIC
RSFAMILY	BAT	Starts and initializes FAMILY HISTORY
RSINSTAL	BAT	Startup file to make working copy of FAMILY HISTORY
VERSIONS	DOC	Documents changes in FAMILY HISTORY

PRINTERS	BAS	How to customize to utilize other printers.
RECDELET		Record Deletion
REDISPLA		Redisplay the Menu
RUNFIRST	BAS	The 'cover letter', showing how to start.
STOPPING		How to Stop
SUBARRAY		Initial Content of the Specific Categories
TABLEOFC		Title, Copyright, and Table of Contents
TERMCOND		Terms and Conditions
TEXTPROC	BAS	Text Processor, to produce the documentation.
VECTOR1		Initial Content of the Rooms
VECTOR2		Initial Content of the Owners
VECTOR3		Initial Content of the Colors
YOURVOWN	BAS	To enter, inquire, personalize and report data.

395

Home Inventory System
v2

YOURVOWN — Your Very Own — keeps track of everything you own (furniture, collections, etc.). What is unique is that it uses your own words to describe all the data you store; also, your data can be stored and retrieved by several categories, rooms, etc. The documentation for the system is very complete; in fact it occupies approximately 80% of the diskette. A must for every homeowner!

Usage: Complete home inventory system

System Requirements: 128K, two disk drives, a monochrome monitor and a printer.

How to Start: To run BASIC programs consult the directions in GETTING STARTED for your configuration. Consult DOCHANGE and TEXTPROC.BAS for program documentation.

User Comments: "Documentation was too long (107 pages) but thorough. Program speed was good and no bugs were found." "I had to call your tech to help me get into the program." "The best home inventory program that I have seen. It is easy to install and simple to use."

Suggested Donation: $35.00

File Descriptions:

ARRAY		Initial Content of the General Categories
CLEANDOC	BAT	To remove the documentation programs and files from the
CREATFIL		Creating and Extending Data Files
DATAENTR		Data Entry
DIRECTOR		Program Directory (this document)
DOCHANGE		Documentation which is unique to YOUR VERY OWN HOME INVENTORY
FIRSTIME		First Time Usage, Startup and Backup
GENINFOR		General Information
HIGH		Initial Setting of Highest Records Used.
INQUIRYS		Formation of Inquiries
INTRODUC		Introduction and Care of Diskettes
INTROPER		Introduction to Personalization
MESSAGES		Program Messages
PERARRAY		Personalizing the General Categories
PERSUBAR		Personalizing the Specific Categories
PERVECT1		Personalizing the Rooms
PERVECT2		Personalizing the Owners
PERVECT3		Personalizing the Colors

397

Checkbook System (3.31)
v1.3

CHEKLIST is a PC, XT, or AT program dedicated to the maintenance of bank account records. It is designed to be simple and convenient to use and to provide all functions that one might need with such records. The CHEKLIST disk actually has two programs. The CHEKLINE program presents all entries in the form of a list. The CHEKLIST program works the same way, but offers a choice of having the entries shown on a list or showing them one at a time on a form that looks like a bank check.

Usage: Comprehensive bank account record keeping

System Requirements: 256k, two disk drives, color graphics capability.

Features:

- Up to 1700 check or other entries
- Up to 10 bank accounts
- Up to 22 special tags (ledger accounts)
- Many data-entry conveniences
- Search on any item, like check number, amount, payee, tag, date, etc.
- Easy bank statement reconciliation
- Instant balances
- Move, delete, store on disk, and print-out modes.
- No disk reading or writing except at start and end.

How to Start: Load DOS and type CHEKLINE or CHEKLIST to enter the demo programs. Consult the .DOC files for program documentation.

File Descriptions:

CHEKDEMO	DOC	Documentation for CHEKLINE.EXE
CHEKLINE	EXE	Presents all entries in the form of a list
CHEKLIST	EXE	Offers choice of showing entries as a list or singly in
CHEKLIST	DOC	Documentation for CHEKLIST.EXE
CHEKDATA	???	Demo Data files (3 files)

458 INCTAX (1.1)

v1.1

INCTAX.COM is a program which accepts data either from a file or the keyboard or both, and calculates your federal income tax for calendar 1985. Recalculations can be made to see how such changes affect income tax liabilities. A summary and details for form 1040 and schedules A, B, and D may be displayed or printed. Tax data can be entered from a tax file developed by the PC-MONEY program (available from Keith Consulting), or it can be entered from the keyboard. Data can be entered from the tax file and modified, item by item as necessary.

Usage: 1985 Federal Tax Returns

System Requirements: 64K, one disk drive, monochrome display

How to Start: Load DOS and type CK to start the main program. Consult CK.DOC for program documentation.

Suggested Donation: $25.00

File Descriptions:

CONTENTS		Text file giving a small description of the program
INCTAX	CHN	Inctax program that may use in conjuction with PC-MONEY
INCTAX	COM	Inctax program that stands alone
INCTAX	DOC	Documentation file
INITINC		Initialzation data file for Inctax.com
README	DOC	Introdutory text file
TAXES79	DTA	Sample data file

462 CK SYSTEM (Disk 1 of 2)

v1

The CK SYSTEM is a two disk set of programs that tracks your income and expenses in checkbook form and prints many types of reports. With CK SYSTEM you can generate bar charts on income/expenses and keep an orderly check register/deposit record. It also prepares a month by month yearend summary of all your income and expenses for up to 9 separate accounts. The program comes with extensive, detailed documentation for the inexperienced user. The programs on Disk #1 are used to enter check data, examine files, correct mistakes, add files together, set-up income/expense categories and list of checking accounts. The User Manual is contained on this disk also.

Usage: Comprehensive personal and household financial management

System Requirements: 128K RAM, two disk drives and a monochrome/graphics display.

How to Start: Load DOS and type CK to start the main program. Consult CK.DOC for program documentation.

User Comments: "OK program with limited capabilities for a small user." "Needs clearer prompts, wider code # fields. Pretty serious program but well written."

Suggested Donation: $25.00

File Descriptions:

CK	EXE	Main program
CKACCTS	EXE	Sub-program : set-up your list of accounts
CKADD	EXE	Sub-program : adds data files together
CKEXSET	EXE	Sub-program : set-up income and expense categories
CKEXTOT	EXE	Sub-program : totals expenses
CKINPUT	EXE	Sub-program : enter/change at check information
CKLOOK	EXE	Sub-program : look at check information
CKMSG		Text file containing messages used by program files
CK	DOC	Documentation/User manual (ASCII — 28 pgs)

463
CK SYSTEM
(Disk 2 of 2)
v1

This is the companion disk to 462 and while it can be used by itself, the documentation is there so don't buy one without the other!! The programs found here on Disk #2 are used to do year-to-date reports and bar charts. They rely for their data upon the programs on disk 462 which track your income and expenses, prints many types of reports regarding what you've earned and where you've spent, cross-referenced many ways, draws bar charts on income/expenses, keeps an orderly check register/deposit record, etc.

Usage: Comprehensive personal and household financial management

System Requirements: 128K RAM, two disk drives and a monochrome/graphics display.

How to Start: Load DOS and type enter CK to enter the main program.

Suggested Donation: $25.00

File Descriptions:

CK	EXE	Main program
CKAMTD	EXE	Sub-program : prepare report sorted by amount spent
CKCAT	EXE	Sub-program : prepare report sorted by expense category
CKCHRT	EXE	Sub-program : prepare a chart
CKDATE	EXE	Sub-program : prepare report sorted by date of expense
CKINST	EXE	Sub-program : used by system to create memory map
CKNAME	EXE	Sub-program : prepare report sorted by account name
CKNUMBR	EXE	Sub-program : prepare report sorted by check number
CKSORT	EXE	Sub-program : sortmenu program
SORT	EXE	Sub-program : used by CKSORT.EXE program

465
Family Ties
v1.17

The Family Ties Genealogy program is designed for the organized compilation of personal genealogical information. All of the names entered in this program are automatically linked to each other. Starting with one individual (usually yourself) use the edit mode to enter your information. Then add a person linked to this first individual eg. parents, spouse, other spouse or child and enter their information. You may start with any **MALE** person and then ancestors or decendants may be added in any order. You may jump around and add as you please. **NOTE:** This program has a regular mode and an LDS (MORMON) option mode.

Usage: Tracking personal genealogical information

System Requirements: 128K, one disk drive and a monochrome display, preferably a 132 column display

How to Start: Load DOS and type FT to enter the main program. Consult MANUAL and DEMO for program documentation and demonstration.

User Comments: "It was fairly easy to use. Would recommend it." "This is by far the best genealogy program that I have ever run. It is very complete and ... one can move through the program with ease and with speed." "Excellent. Well organized. Very quick to learn and to use." "An excellent, strong program for genealogy — undoubtly the best I have ever seen."

Suggested Donation: $50.00

File Descriptions:

COPYPROG	BAT	Batch program to copy the program files
FGRSH	INS	Messages file
FT	EXE	The main FAMILY TIES program
FTCOLOR	DAT	Data file containing color settings
FTDEMO	EXE	Demo/tutorial program
FTINSTAL	DAT	Printer data used by the installation program
FTINSTAL	EXE	Installation program for FAMILY TIES
LICENCE	DOC	Information on the licence for the program
MANUAL		The user manual/documentation text file (20 pages)
NAMES	DA1	Database constants
NAMES	NTS	Blank notes file
PRINT	CTR	Printer control file
README		Information regarding the files on this diskette

README	BAT	Batch file to display the README file
REGISTRN	FRM	Text file of the Registration form
UPDATE	DOC	Information on how to uppdate early versions
UPDATE	BAT	Batch program to update early versions of Family Ties
USER-NO	EXE	Program to change the USER number encoded in a FAMILY TIES
QUERY	COM	

479
AM-TAX 1986
v1

AM-Tax (formerly ACCU-TAX 1985) is a software product designed to assist you in the preparation of your 1986 federal tax return. It will do most calculations for you and, where possible, check to see that information entered by you is consistent and valid. Because of the power of the software, you can try out any "what if" situation. Change an income or deduction figure and instantly see the result on your tax balance or refund.Besides the 1040 form, many other commonly used forms and schedules are supported. Information entered or calculated for a supporting form is automatically transferred to the appropriate line that it supports. All of the forms can be printed and filed directly with the IRS.

Usage: Personal federal income tax

System Requirements: 256k, one disk drive, monochrome monitor. Printer recommended.

Features:

• Tax forms supported:
  Federal Form 1040 — Individual Tax Return
  Schedule A: Itemized Deductions
  Schedule B: Interest/Dividend Income
  Schedule C: Business Income or Loss
  Schedule D: Capital Gain or Loss
  Schedule E: Supplemental Income
  Schedule F: Farm Income
  Schedule G: Income Averaging
  Schedule R: Credit for Elderly
  Schedule SE: Self-Employment Tax
  Schedule W: Marriage Deduction
  Form 2106: Employee Business Expense
  Form 2119: Sale of Residence
  Form 2441: Child Care Credit
  Form 3903: Moving Expenses
  Form 4136: Special Fuels credit
  Form 4562: Depreciation

Form 5695: Energy Conservation Credit
Form 6251: Alternative Minimum Tax
• AccuTax uses special 'worksheets' to handle specific situations on the federal tax form. The worksheets are:
  #1:   W-2 Wages (5 employers)
  #2:   Other Dependents (5 copies)
  #3,4: Capital Gain (10 copies)
  #5:   Car Expenses (5 cars)
  #6:   Sec. 179 Expenses (5 copies)
  #7:   ACRS Non-Listed Property (30 copies)
  #8:   Amortization Worksheet (5 copies)
  #9:   Rent/Royalty Income (5 properties)
  #10:   Partnership/S Corp Income (15 copies)
  #11:   Estate/Trust Income (3 copies)
  #12:   ACRS Listed Property (10 copies)
  #13:   Non-ACRS Depreciation (15 copies)

How to Start: Load DOS and type TAX86 to enter the main program. Consult AMTAX.DOC for program documentation.

User Comments: "This program seems to be an extremely well thought out, well planned, and well documented income tax preparation program. It looks to me like something that would cost $100-200." "It helped me enjoy doing a job that I normally dislike."

Suggested Donation: $35.00

File Descriptions:

????????	86	59 Separate files containing forms and parts for ACCUTAX
TAX86	EXE	ACCU-TAX program
ACCUTAX	DOC	Documentation on ACCU-TAX
REGISTER		How to become a registered user of ACCU-TAX
FEEDBACK		Form for errors and other feedback for ACCU-TAX
STARTUP		Information on how to start ACCU-TAX

INITVAL	SOL	A sample installation file generated with SOLSTALL.
HOUSE	DAT	A sample definition of a house.
READ	ME	A brief description of how to use the program.

486
TELISOLAR
v1

The Teli/Solar package is a program which provides the user with an easy, quick method of evaluating energy-saving alternatives in the areas of hot water usage, building heating/cooling load, and solar collector design. Teli/Solar enables the average homeowner to make intelligent decisions about energy-related home improvements and/or investments.

Usage: Designed for direct use by architects, contractors, and homeowners.

System Requirements: 64K, one disk drive and monochrome display

Features:

- 1 Disk storage of building design for later use
- 2 Menu driven (with ability to bypass menus)
- 3 Accepts American or metric units
- 4 Provides interactive response
- 5 Runs on IBM-PCs and compatibles

How to Start: Consult TELISOL,DOC and READ.ME files to review program documentation (strongly urged). Type TELISOL to enter the main program. To run the BASIC program consult the directions in GETTING STARTED for your configuration.

User Comments: "Very thorough — the documentation even has a primer on disk formats and handling for novices. Only problem is that you must have lots of information on your house in order to fill in the blanks and have he program run well." "This is the first program of its kind that I have seen that allows the user to design a solar energy system for a building based on the integrated solar design tutorial."

Suggested Donation: $50.00 registration provides technical support, one version upgrade and a letter-quality printed manual.

File Descriptions:

TELISOL	EXE	The actual energy analysis program.
TELISOL	DOC	An 80 page document for TELISOL.
SINSTALL	BAS	A BASICA version of the installation program.
SOLSTALL	EXE	A compiled version of the above.

497
HOMEWARE (3.2)
(Disk 1 of 2)
v3.2

HOMEWARE Version 3.2 contains a great series of miscellaneous household routines. The program tracks information the following areas: Household Inventory, Automobile Expenses, Meal Schedules, and Shopping List, Mixed Drinks, Name & Address Book, and Hobbies Record Keeping. The HOMEWARE series is written in C programming language and is very easy to use. The documentation is comprehensive and the system comes with data files for mixed drinks and recipes.

NOTE: The companion disk to HOMEWARE, which contains program documentation, is on Disk 630.

Usage: Comprehensive home environment tracking

System Requirements: 256k, 2 disk drives, monochrome monitor, printer

How to Start: Load DOS and type HWS00 to enter the main program. Consult HW.DOC (see disk 630) for program documentation.

Suggested Donation: $25.00

File Descriptions:

HAS00	EXE	Automobile expense program
HWS00	EXE	Main control program
HIS00	EXE	Household inventory program
HMS00	EXE	Meal / Recipe / Shopping list program
HNA00	EXE	Name and Address Record Book program
HHS00	EXE	Hobbies Record Keeping
HW	BAT	Main menu loader batch program

594 NOTES ON DISPLAY
v1

NOTES ON DISPLAY is an extension of the Genealogy ON DISPLAY program disk #90 in the library. This program enhances and organizes the search for your ancestral past by allowing you to save notes upon each new find.

Usage: Genealogical research.

System Requirements: 96k, one disk drive, monochrome display

How to Start: To run BASIC programs, consult the directions in GETTING STARTED for your configuration.

File Descriptions:

		NOTES ON DISPLAY
RUNFIRST	BAS	A short note on the use of the programs provided
PRINTERS	BAS	A note enabling you to modify print control characters
DIRECTOR	BAS	Main documentation output controlling program
TABLEOFC	BAS	Documentation file to be printed
INTRODUC	BAS	Documentation file to be printed
GENERAL	BAS	Documentation file to be printed
USINGTHE	BAS	Documentation file to be printed
REFERENC	BAS	Documentation file to be printed
APPENDIX	BAS	Documentation file to be printed
NOTESAND	BAS	Dcoumentation file to be printed
VERIFILE		Data file verifying source and type codes
SOURFILE		Data file containing all source codes
TYPEFILE		Data file containing all type codes
HIGH		Record number controlling data file
CLEANDOC	BAT	Batch file to erase all documentation files from data disk
OVERVIEW	BAS	A screen oriented program presenting Program operation

613 Managing Money with IBM PC Version 1.0
v1

Written by A. Glazer, an economics professor at the University of California, this disk contains all the BASIC programs contained in his book Managing Money With Your IBM PC (Prentice-Hall, 1985). Among other things, the programs can determine the after-tax cost of a loan, demonstrate the advantages of an Individual Retirement Account, compare loans which have different interest rates and different origination fees, and calculate the amount of monthly savings necessary to finance a college education. Anyone interested in short, useful investment calculation programs will find this package very valuable. Many different types of loans are also well demonstrated and make more easy using this package.

NOTE: Each program is independent and must be run directly from BASIC.

Usage: Personal Money Management

System Requirements: 64K, one disk drive and monochrome or color/graphics (needed for the text graphics)

How to Start: To run BASIC programs consult the directions in GETTING STARTED for your configuration. Consult README for additional information.

Suggested Donation: $10.00

File Descriptions:

		Managing Money (v1.0)
AMORTIZE	BAS	Amortization schedule for a mortgage and monthly loan payment
BALREM	BAS	Balance remaining on a mortgage
CHARGEHI	BAS	Monthly status of a revolving charge account
CREDITCA	BAS	The gains from using a credit card instead of paying in cash
CREDITPU	BAS	Minimum payment schedule for a credit purchase
DAILYODO	BAS	Date that is a specified number of days away from starting date
DATEDIST	BAS	Number of years, months, and days between two dates
DATESINM	BAS	Dates in a month on which a specified day of the week falls

DAYOFWEE	BAS	Day of week on which a specified date falls
DEPGROWS	BAS	Balance in a savings program with deposits that grow with time
INTRATE	BAS	Interest rate on a loan
INVHISTO	BAS	Annual description of an investment; value, rate of return,
INVINCOM	BAS	Annual or monthly income that yields a specified rate of return
INVPRICE	BAS	Sales price of an asset that yields a specified rate of return
INVVALUE	BAS	Present value of an investment
INVYIELD	BAS	Annual rate of return on an investment
IRA	BAS	The benefits of saving in an Individual Retirement Account
LOANCOST	BAS	After tax cost of a loan
LOANQUAL	BAS	Size of loan available at interest rate and monthly payment
LOANTERM	BAS	How many payments you must make on a loan
MNTHINCM	BAS	Monthly income you can obtain from a specified amount of money
MONTHLYO	BAS	Date that is a specified number of months away from starting date
NUMDAYS	BAS	Number of days between two dates
PAYBACK	BAS	How long it takes to recover an investment
PERBALAN	BAS	Balance in savings account after any number of deposits
PERDEPOS	BAS	How much to deposit each month or year to reach a savings goal
PERRATE	BAS	The interest rate you must earn on your savings to reach
PERTERM	BAS	How many monthly or annual deposits to make to reach a goal
POINTS	BAS	Effective interest rate on a loan that charges points
README		General information and file information
RULEOF78	BAS	Amortization schedule for consumer and automobile loans
SAVHISTO	BAS	Annual balance in a savings program with deposits that grow
SIMPINV	BAS	Analysis of an investment that produces no annual income
TERMDEPO	BAS	Balance in a savings plan

630 HOMEWARE (3.2) (Disk 2 of 2)
v1.1

This diskette contains the second disk of the HOMEWARE package and contains documentation and supplemental data files. The documentation, approximately 50 pages, includes separate sections for each application. The data files consist of recipes and mixed drinks and can be changed or printed as desired. HW.FLE describes all HOMEWARE file descriptions.

NOTE: Disk 1 is on Disk 497

Usage: Comprehensive home inventory

System Requirements: 256K, two floppy disk drives, color or monochrome display, and an Epson dot matrix printer

How to Start: Consult HW.DOC for program documentation. Executable files are found on Disk 497.

Suggested Donation: $25.00

File Descriptions:

HW	DOC	Homeware documentation for household inventory,
HW	FLE	Homeware file descriptions
HMU00	DAT	Homeware recipe data file
HMU00	IDX	Homeware recipe data file index
HDU00	DAT	Homeware mixed drink data file
HDU00	IDX	Homeware mixed drink file index

632 FAMILY HISTORY (Disk 2 of 2)
v1.1

This disk contains the second diskette of The FAMILY HISTORY, a family history tracking system. The first disk of this set (Disk 361) has a 38 page manual and program versions written in interpreted BASIC. This disk contains the compiled versions of the programs, and run 3-10 times faster than the interpreted version, but require at least 256K RAM. Refer to Disk 361 for more information.

Usage: Family History Tracking

System Requirements: 256K, 1 disk drive, monochrome monitor (a printer is recommended — but not required — for full use of the system).

How to Start: Enter TYPE README and press ENTER for program information.

Suggested Donation: $35.00

File Descriptions:

BRUN20	EXE	QuickBasic 2.0 runtime support module
FAM?????	EXE	System subprograms (8 files)
FAMILY	DAT	Data file
FAMILY	EXE	Main system program
INSTALL	BAT	Installation batch file
README		Documentation file
ZERO	COM	Initialing program

700 MEALMATE and others

v1

MEALMATE is a planning aid for people preparing meals for someone on a carefully controlled diet. MEALMATE is an easily operated program that can present nutritional information on many common foods. It can also combine the information from meal plans or menus to check the total nutritional content of a planned diet. It can make it easier to plan more varied meals and to help in choosing substitutes for hard to find diet items. MEALMATE should be a big help to anyone preparing meals that have to meet strict requirements for calories, proteins, carbohydrates, and fats.

This program is targeted for the 10 percent of our population who are diabetic as it is a readily available source of complete nutritional information concerning glucose level control. However, it is of value to anyone who must or wishes to precisely control intake. It is consistent with the guidelines established by the American Diabetes Association, the American Medical Association, WeightWatchers International, and the Grace L. Furgenson Aluminum Storm Door and Fat Control Monday Night Fellowship Society.

The utilities include a screen blanker, a disk error reporter, a system equipment reporter, a screen dump for compiled BASIC programs, and a simple game with a bug in it. Consider it a personal challenge to fix it!

Usage: Nutritional planning

System Requirements: 64K, one disk drive and monochrome display

How to Start: Consult the .DOC and README files for directions and documentation

- To run the BASIC programs, verify your procedures according to the GETTING STARTED section
- To run any program suffixed .EXE or .COM, just enter its programname, e.g., type MEAL and press ENTER.

Suggested Donation: $25.00

File Descriptions:

————	——	Mealmate
FORM	TXT	Registration form
MEAL	EXE	MEALMATE main program
*	BLD	Data file for MEALMATE (5 files)
README		Information about the program
DATA		Data base 9/86 U.S.
DATA	BUP	Read only data backup
————	—	Miscellaneous Programs
CARDS	BAS	Graphics Demonstration
5INLINE	EXE	A game; THIS COPY HAS A BUG
5INLINE	BAS	Source for above
GAME	PIC	Save file for above
BLANK	COM	Dim screen at 3 min. Run from autoexec
EQMENT	EXE	Tells about your system
DISKPRAM	BAS	Displays the floppy disk driver settings. Reboot after use!
BOOT	BAS	Warm start from basic
DUMP	BAS	Yet another screen dumper but for compiled basic
DSKWATCH	ASM	Source
DSKWATCH	COM	Reports ALL disk errors. DOS only reports 5 in a row
EQUIP	BAS	Tells about your system
NODUP	BAT	Deletes duplicate files

LANGUAGES:

Beyond BASIC, FORTRAN, COBOL or Assembler, computer programmers now are fluent in a multitude of tongues and dialects. The appearance of Pascal, Turbo Pascal, FORTH and C in the PC world has led to an amazing cross-fertilization of programming features and syntax.

Among the current selections are programs to structure, re-structure and analyze most forms of BASIC, compiled or otherwise. Similarly, this section contains entire libraries of Pascal and C routines and subroutines for finding special tools and alternate means of attacking special problems. For more intricate and arcane usages, check out the Language and Programmer Utilities sections.

3 RATBAS

v1

RATBAS stands for RATionalized BASic. RATBAS allows BASIC programs to be written in a more structured way without line numbers. Programs written in Rationalized BASIC are converted by the RATBAS translator into standard BASIC. RATBAS is a translation program that takes your RATional BASic programs and converts them to standard BASIC. RATBAS forms the bridge between Pascal-like Rational Basic and Standard BASIC by making conversion easier.

Usage: For advanced BASIC programmers.

System Requirements: 64K, 1 disk drive and monochrome display.

How to Start: To start program, type RT and press ENTER.

User Comments: "This is a great program for building up structured BASIC code using the same techniques as are commonly used in Pascal and C." "It is the perfect step between interpretive BASIC and learning other languages where routines can be labeled." "The thing I like most about this program is the ability to program BASIC in a more structured manner."

File Descriptions:

RT	EXE	The RatBAS translator
RT	UM	User's Manual for RT.EXE
RATBAS	UM	User's Manual for the RatBAS language
RATBAS	TXT	Paper on RatBAS by the authors. The RatBAS article in
TEST	RAT	A sample program written in RatBAS
SORT	INC	An 'include' routine which will be used by TEST.RAT
TEST	BAS	TEST.RAT after being processed by RT.EXE. This is an

10
CHASM
Version 4.09
V4.2

CHASM stands for CHeap ASseMbler. It is a user-supported assembler useful for those wishing to learn about assembly language. Programs are converted directly into .COM files. CHASM comes with extensive documentation and an excellent introduction file called PRIMER.DOC for those inexperienced with assembly language.

Usage: For beginner through advanced assembly programmers.

System Requirements: 64K, 1 disk drive and monochrome display.

How to Start: To read DOC files, enter TYPE filename.DOC and press ENTER.

• To start program, type CHASM and press ENTER. For instructions on ASM listings, refer to your Assembler manual.

User Comments: "A good, inexpensive assembler for those of us who can't afford the MASM." "Very interesting for a beginner like me. I could follow the instructions and what was required to make the program work." "Good program, excellent price/performance, excellent documentation, good tutoring documentation."

File Descriptions:

CHASM	CFG	Configuration file for CHASM
CHASM	COM	CHeap ASseMbler version 4.00
CHASM	DOC	Documentation for CHASM
CHMOD	ASM	Changes file status: hidden, read-only, normal, system
CHMOD	DOC	Documentation for CHMOD.ASM
COM2DATA	ASM	Converts machine language into BASIC DATA statements
DUP	ASM	Reads data, removes adjacent, duplicated lines.
DUP	DOC	Documentation for DUP.ASM
EXAMPLE	ASM	Example file for CHASM
FREEWARE	DOC	The freeware concept and other freeware programs and authors
LABEL	ASM	Adds volume label to an already formatted disk
LABEL	DOC	Documentation for LABEL.ASM
LC	ASM	Program to convert text files to lower case letters
LC	DOC	Documentation for LC.ASM
PRIMER	DOC	Primer to introduce assembly language to the novice.

WC	ASM	Filter that counts words, lines, and characters
WC	DOC	Documentation for WC.ASM

30
Pascal I/O
v1

The Pascal programs on this disk show how to do disk I/O with Pascal. PASCAL I/O is logical well written and documented code. At the heart of PASCAL I/O is INTRPT.OBJ which in conjunction with IOSTUFF.OBJ and IOSTUFF.INC demonstrate IBM I/O routines in Pascal. Also included is DISKREAD which displays the disk contents using IBM BIOS.

Usage: For intermediate and advanced IBM PASCAL progammers.

System Requirements: 64K, 1 disk drive, monochrome display and the IBM PASCAL compiler.

How to Start: To read DOC files, enter TYPE filename.DOC and press ENTER.

• To start program, type CHASM and press ENTER. For instructions on ASM listings, refer to your Assembler manual.

File Descriptions:

IOSTUFF	DOC	Describes files below
DISKREAD	EXE	Displays disk contents by sector
DISKREAD	OBJ	Object for DISKREAD.EXE
DISKREAD	PAS	Source for DISKREAD.OBJ
INTRPT	OBJ	Object to be linked to your Pascal program object
INTRPT	ASM	Source for INTRPT.OBJ
IOSTUFF	OBJ	Object to be linked to your Pascal program object
IOSTUFF	PAS	Source for IOSTUFF object
IOSTUFF	INC	Source to be INCLUDED with your Pascal program source
PRIME	PAS	Source for DEMO
SAMPLE	PAS	Source for DEMO

31 MVP-FORTH
v1.1

This disk contains the Mountain View Press Public Domain FORTH language. For documentation refer to the book "Starting Forth" by Leo Brodie. MVPFORTH is a fully executable FORTH compiler that can be either started from DOS or booted from scratch. This system requires familiarity with the FORTH language.

Usage: For Advanced FORTH programmers, college or graduate level.

System Requirements: 64K, 1 disk drive and monochrome display.

How to Start: To read the documentation enter TYPE MVPFORTH.DOC and press ENTER. The documentation refers to the book "Starting Forth", and it is a good idea to have a copy on hand.

User Comments: "An excellent implementation of a fine language." "This is a good implementation of Forth." "Great!"

File Descriptions:

COMMAND	COM	Boots FORTH on initial startup
MVPFORTH	ASM	Assembly language source for MVPFORTH
MVPFORTH	EXE	Executable FORTH — type MVPFORTH to start from DOS
MVPFORTH	DOC	Where to look for documentation — "Starting Forth"

36 PASCAL Collection No 1
v2

These programs are intended as illustrations that will help you to get started with IBM Pascal. The language is left unclear by the reference manual so having these sample programs will be helpful. This disk is a collection of useful IBM Pascal software that includes routines like GETDIR.PAS, a Pascal directory program. TOOLS.PAS is full of BASIC keyword subroutines, ie:, INKEY, LOCATE and ESCAPE. This collection even includes SIDEWAYS for custom printing on an Epson MX-80 printer.

Usage: For intermediate and advanced IBM Pascal applications programmers at the high school, college, or graduate level.

System Requirements: 64K, 1 disk drive and monochrome display.

How to Start: The pertinent documentation can be read by entering TYPE CONTENTS.TXT or TYPE MATH.DOC for information on the math subroutine. Refer to your Pascal manual for details on running .PAS program files.

User Comments: "Analyzing these programs helped me understand the usage of some Pascal terms." "Helpful, but very few comments in the source code."

File Descriptions:

CONTENTS	TXT	Description of files on this disk
TABSET1	PAS	Sets tabs on Epson mx-100 printer
TABSET2	PAS	Similar to tabset1 but treats printer as binary file
TIMM	PAS	Illustrates concept of Pascal unit (main program)
TIMI	PAS	Illustrates concept of Pascal unit (interface)
TIMU	PAS	Illustrates concept of Pascal unit (unit)
SCREEN	PAS	Short program to assess specific memory addresses
SCREENC	PAS	Color/graphics version of SCREEN.PAS
PRINTER	PAS	Utility to print multiple files
*	P	Part of PRINTER.PAS (3 files)
XREF	PAS	Cross-reference utility
COPYFILE	PAS	Program to show how files are defined, read and copied
DUMPFILE	PAS	Produces hexadecimal and ascii dump of a disk file
UNSQ	PAS	Unsqueezes files compressed by huffman encoding
PRETTY	PAS	Utility for listing pascal programs in pretty format
PART?	PAS	Part of PRETTY.PAS (3 files)
GETDIR	PAS	Program to read disk directory
GETDIR	OBJ	Object module of getdir
GETSEC	ASM	Assembly language utility used by getdir
GETSEC	OBJ	Object module of getsec
GETDIR	EXE	Executable program to read disk directory
VIDEO	ASM	Pascal callable routine to perform bios video interrupts
VIDEO	OBJ	Object module of video
PASCLG	BAT	Batch file to compile, link and go
PASCL	BAT	Batch file to compile and link
PASC	BAT	Batch file to compile only
C	BAT	Batch file to compile only (no prompts)
C-LST	BAT	Batch file to compile/list (no prompts)
CL	BAT	Batch file to compile/link (no prompts)
CL-LST	BAT	Batch file to compile/list/link (no prompts)
FLUSH	BAT	Batch file to clean up Pascal compilation and test residue
BUILD	PAS	Index building program by Peter Norton Corp 1983
BUILD	EXE	Executable file of build.pas

MATH	DOC	Documentation file for the math subroutine library
MATH	INT	Pascal interface for the math subroutine library
MATH	OBJ	Pascal v2.0 object module of the math subroutine library
MATHV1	OBJ	Pascal v1.0 object module of the math subroutine library
MATHTEST	EXE	Pascal v2.0 executeable version of the combined math subroutine
MATHTEST	PAS	Pascal driver program demonstrates how to use the subroutine
OKIDATA	PAS	Sets mode of operation on the Okidata Microline 92 printer
MERGE	PAS	Index merging program
MERGE	EXE	Executable version of MERGE.PAS
CLEAN	BAT	Cleans up residue from compile
IBMPAS	DOC	Notes/info/patchs for IBM PASCAL
SIDEWAYS	PAS	Prints a file sideways on the epson mx-80 printer
TOOLS	PAS	MS and IBM PASCAL screen and I/O tools

108
Programmer's Utilities No 1
v1

This disk contains a collection of utilites for the APL or DOS programmer. All APL programs on this disk require the IBM APL compiler or similar APL interpreter/compiler. BATMENU is a simple batch file enhancement which allows the user to inquire choices within a specified range of options. Provided documentation should be adequate for even the non-programmer to make sucessful use of this utility. Programmer's Utilities is a toolbox like group of software. Contained within a well documented menu program are four handy APL programs including a depreciation routine, a forecasting model and a determinant function.

Usage: For intermediate and advanced APL programmers at college or graduate level.

System Requirements: 64K, 1 disk drive and monochrome display.

How to Start: To read DOC files, enter TYPE filename.ext and press ENTER.

• To run an EXE or COM program, just type its name and press ENTER. For instructions on running BASIC programs, please refer to the GETTING STARTED section in this catalog. For instructions on ASM listings, refer to your Assembler manual.

User Comments: "..useful utilities accompanied by good documentation."

File Descriptions:

BASTODOS	BAS	Subroutines for BASIC to access DOS 1.1 and 2.0 functions
BATMENU	COM	Flexible menu prompting for batch files
BATMENU	DOC	Documentation for above
DEPRE—	APL	Depreciation functions in APL
DISKTYPE	EXE	Tells you a diskette's format (Sides, sectors/track)
DISKTYPE	DOC	Documentation for above
FORECAST	APL	Forecasting model in APL
MATH—	APL	Determinant, integrate by Simpson's rule, in APL
MUSIC	BAS	Color graphics music editor/player
MUSIC	DOC	Documentation for above
NOECHO	DOC	Tells how to make DOS 2.0 batch default to no echo
PEPATCHS	DOC	Add color to Personal Editor and other improvements
PMODE	COM	Command to set EPSON printer modes and fonts
PMODE	ASM	Source and documentation for above
PRTSCFX	COM	Allows PrtSc to print the FULL monochrome character set
PRTSCFX	DOC	Documentation for above
PRTSCFX	ASM	Source for above
UNDOC	DOC	Lots of undocumented DOS 2.0 bugs and gotchas
UTILITY—	APL	String, time/date, and other utility functions in APL

114
Assembly Language Tutorial
v1

The file ASM. is a tutorial on the assembly language for the IBM-PC's 8088 processor and was distributed by IBM itself. It is a concise description of the essentials of IBM-PC assembly language programming. NEWCLOCK is a fixit device driver addressing the 24 hour rollover problem as well as mis-stamped file times. UASMLS is a utility that will enable the creation of an almost-assembler-ready listing from the output of a DEBUG dis-assembly. The PCTALK files are overlays to the original PCTALK III release and support VT100 or VT52 terminal protocols. TERM is overlay for the IBM ASYNC.BAS program.

Usage: For beginner and intermediate assembly programmers at the high school, college, or graduate level.

System Requirements: 64K, 1 disk drive and monochrome display.

How to Start: To read DOC files, enter TYPE filename.ext and press ENTER.

• To run an EXE program, just type its name and press ENTER. For instructions on running BASIC programs, please refer to the GETTING STARTED section in this catalog.

User Comments: "The problem with this disk is the ASM tutorial, it is mostly a waste of time and is certainly not an Assembler primer." "Since the disk is billed as an Assembler Tutorial, it is all documentation-which is poor." "I had hoped for more from the ASM tutorial."

File Descriptions:

ASM		Tutorial on Assembly Language programming
BASCOM	DOC	Four patches for the BASIC Compiler
FPLOT	BAS	Plots math functions in polar and Cartesian coordinates
FPLOT	DOC	Documentation file for FPLOT.BAS
KBDFIX	BAS	Fix for keyboard buffer program in September Softalk
NEWCLOCK	SYS	Fix for DOS 2.0 clock update function
NEWCLOCK	DOC	Documentation file for NEWCLOCK.SYS
PCT3VT	BAS	Adds Vidtex, VT52, VT100 & ANSI cursor control to PCTalk III
PROFEEL	DOC	Review of Sony KX 1211 HG monitor/TV
CABLE	DOC	Procedure for making a cable for the Sony Profeel
TERM	BAS	Adds auto-dial and auto log-on to IBM ASYSC. Comm. 2.0
TERM	DOC	Documentation file for TERM.BAS
TREND123	MAC	LOTUS 123 macro for straight line/exponential curves
TREND123	DOC	Documentation file for TREND123.MAC
UASMLS	EXE	Formats DEBUG unassemble output file
UASMLS	DOC	Documentation file for UASMLS.EXE

263 Laxon & Perry FORTH (Disk 1 of 2) v1

This is a FORTH language system put together by Henry Laxen and Mike Perry. This FORTH uses the files of the host operating system. Although this reduces performance, it is much more portable and more convenient for novices. Many FORTH extensions such as an assembler, editor, and decompiler are included in this version of FORTH. L & P FORTH is a well stuctured introduction to the FORTH language. The recommended reading for this FORTH is "Starting FORTH" by Leo Brodie. If a user is not familiar with FORTH then definitely README.PC is an advantage to have.

Usage: For intermediate and advanced FORTH Programmers.

System Requirements: 64K, 1 disk drive and monochrome display.

How to Start: To read documentation — A MUST FOR BEGINNERS IN FORTH-enter TYPE README.PC and press ENTER. Type "F83" to start program, and "BYE" to quit.

User Comments: "Excellent implementation of FORTH for PC's." "Could use more doc for beginners — doc is fine for reference but poor to learn from." "This is a good implementation of the Forth language but the documentation is very brief."

File Descriptions:

F83	COM	Main program — type: F83 to start
F83-FIXS	TXT	Fixes made for this version (5K)
README	PC	Notes about using L&P FORTH (16K)
*	BLK	Source code for L&P FORTH extensions (5 files)
KERNEL	COM	Source code for L&P FORTH extensions

264
Laxon & Perry
FORTH (Disk 2 of 2)
v1

This disk has additional extensions to the Laxon & Perry FORTH on Disk No 263.

File Descriptions:

*	BLK	Source code for L&P FORTH extensions (2 files)

341
C Utilities No 5
v1

This disk contains a collection of programs and subroutines in 'C', which can serve as time savers for those who don't wish to have to write everything themselves. Ii is also useful as a learning tool for the novice, since you can inspect the source code and see how others do it. Many of the routines/programs perform elemental functions similar to those found on many "seasoned" UNIX or XENIX systems.

Usage: Language programming.

System Requirements: 64K, 1 disk drive and monochrome display, 'C' compiler.

How to Start: To read TXT files simply enter TYPE filename.ext and press ENTER. For instructions on ASM or 'C' listings, refer to your Assembler or 'C' language manuals.

User Comments: "Amortization program helped with a school project but no documentation to tie programs together." "A useful set of C programs." "Good to use, but not good to try to learn C from."

File Descriptions:

ADDLF	C	Program to add linefeeds to text if found absent
CC	ASM	C shell for Lattice C and DOS 2.00
CONIO	C	Source for console I/O routines
CRC	C	Cyclic Redundancy Check functions
DOS–ERR	TXT	Documentation on DOS 2.00 redirection of I/O bug
DUMP2	C	Program to print parts of large files in dump format

FRAME	C	Function to draw a frame on the screen
FUNKEY	C	Program to build function key reassignment files
GETSEG–C	ASM	Function returning current register values
INKEY	C	Input from keyboard function
IOS1–20	ASM	Level 1 I/O routines for DOS 2.00 and Lattice C
ISCHECK	C	Program to verify Microsoft's "isxxxxxx" routines
LEJ–LIB	C	Example functions from Kernighan & Ritchie book on C
LIFE	C	"Game of Life" written in C
M8087	MAC	Assembler macros for 8087 coprocessor support
MEMCLEAN	C	Program to "clean" memory above 640K
MEMCLEAN	DOC	Documentation for the above
PRINT	C	Program to print ASCII file with heading on each page
RENAME	C	Functional equivalent of a DOS "rename" in C
SNAP	C	Dump memory area in hex/character format
SNAP	OBJ	Object code for the above
STRING	C	Source for standard string functions (a la K&R book)
SYSINT	ASM	General interrupt call function
TIMEMARK	TXT	Timestamping functions and benchmarks tests
TINKEY	C	Program to test "inkey" function
TOWERS	C	"Towers of Hanoi" game written in C
TYPECONV	C	Demo of type conversions in C
XC	C	C concordance utility
–MAIN	C	New version of "–main" for DOS 2.00 and Lattice C

352
Two FORTHS
v1

Here are two FORTHS that are ready for the beginner to use. They also include the documentation and source code for experienced programers who want to extensively expand or modify their FORTH. Good examples for those who want to write their own FORTH engine are provided in the assembly language source files. MVPFORTH and FORTH-H can be assembled using IBM's assembler.

Usage: For beginner — advanced FORTH programmers.

System Requirements: 64K, one disk drive and monochrome display. MVPFORTH and FORTH-H source files can be assembled IBM's assembler, but FORTH requies the Seattle Computer products assembler.

How to Start: Read the accompanying .DOC file. To start MVPFORTH: type MVPFORTH to load the MVPFORTH operating system from DOS. Then typing VLIST will list the available FORTH words (FORTH-79 compatible).

User Comments: "Need additional information on FORTH language to take full advantage of these programs." "FORTH is a lot of fun."

File Descriptions:

MVPFORTH	WDS	List of code level words for MVPFORTH
MVPFORTH	DOC	Documentation for MVPFORTH
MVPFORTH	ASM	Source code for MVPFORTH IBM assembler format
MVPFORTH	COM	FORTH-79 compatible forth interpiter
FORTH-H	ASM	Source for Glen Haydon's version of MVPFORTH
FORTH-H	COM	Glen Haydon's FORTH interpreter
FORTH-H	DOC	Documentation for Glen Haydon's FORTH

381 BASIC Aids No 4
v1

The BASICAID program will compress a BASIC program (by removing extra spaces, etc.), expand a program, and generate a cross reference of BASIC reserved words. The TBASIC program allows the creation and execution of TINY BASIC programs. TINY BASIC is a limited version of the BASIC language. Included is an internal TINY BASIC editor.

Usage: For beginner — advanced BASIC programmers.

System Requirements: 64K, one disk drive and monochrome display.

How to Start: Type BASICAID or TBASIC and press ENTER to start either program. To read DOC files, enter TYPE filename.ext and press ENTER.

User Comments: "TBASIC was quick and simple to learn. Now I'm ready for regular BASIC." "I didn't have much use for BASICAID."

Suggested Donation: $10.00

File Descriptions:

BASICAID	BAS	BASIC source file for BASICAID.EXE
BASICAID	DOC	Documentation for BASICAID.EXE
BASICAID	EXE	Multi-fuction BASIC programmers utility
BRENTBAS	EXE	A translator from a structured BASIC to Microsoft BASIC
BRENTBAS	UM	BRENTBAS.EXE Users Manual
TBASIC	ASM	Source code for TBASIC.COM
TBASIC	COM	TINY BASIC language. A very limited subset of BASIC
TBASIC	DOC	Documentation for TBASIC.COM

392 Compiled Pascal Routines Library
v1

A library of useful Turbo Pascal procedures to be used when linking Pascal object files. It includes CIRCLE which is a circle drawing procedure, and REBOOT which is a system reboot without clearing RAM. If you wish to speed up your programming, consider including some of these routines.

This library of routines for use with Pascal compiler includes:

ALLFILES, EXISTFIL, GETINTGR, KAVAIL, MOVEFILE, REBOOT, SUCCESS CIRCLE, EXTENDIO, GETKEYS, KEYBOARD, NEWINT9, RECTANGL, TITLES CURSOR, FANCYKEY, GETSECTR, KEYCHART, NOSOUND, REGPACK, WINDOWS DISKMOD, FILEATTR, GETSETDD, LABEL, NUMDISKS, SAFEWRIT DISKTYP, FILENAME, GRFXTABL, LESSRAM, PARAMETR, SCANCODE EQUIPMNT, GETFILE, GTSETDIR, MKRMDIR, POPSCREN, SCREEN ERRMESSG, GETFREE, HEXFUNCT, MONITOR, QUEUE, SCREENS

Usage: For intermediate and advanced Turbo Pascal programmers.

System Requirements: 64K, one disk drive and monochrome display, Turbo Pascal.

How to Start: Access this library through your Pascal software.

User Comments: "Excellent subroutines which I already have put to work in a number of programs." "Good and useful programs." "Too complicated for a beginner to use."

Suggested Donation: $10.00

402 Cross Assembler for the IBM 370 Version R1.1

v1.1

PC/370 Virtual Machine is a cross assembler that runs on the IBM PC, AT, or XT and lets you compile and run IBM 370 assembly language programs. These programs are well documented with an excellent example demo set up to be run by a batch file. This is as complete an emulation of the VM370 assembler as can be found in the public domain. A generous debugging and trace facility is also provided to facilitate complete development cycles without the big blue box.

Usage: For beginning through advanced S/370 assembly language programmers.

System Requirements: 64K, one disk drive and monochrome display.

How to Start: Type GO and press ENTER.

User Comments: "Very good implementation of a mainframe emulator." "This program is very good for the programer who does not have an IBM 370 accessible to him since it tries to almost duplicate the functions needed on the PC." "Very well done!"

File Descriptions:

A370	COM	PC/370 Assembler Program (Convert ALC file to OBJ file)
A370	TRC	A370 trace id's
DAT	ALC	Date and Time subroutine
DEMO8Q	ALC	Solve 8 Queens problem with recursive routine
DEMOAST1	ALC	Assist demo program with output to log file
DEMOAST1	DAT	Data input to DEMOAST1 demo program
DEMOAST2	ALC	Assist demo program with input and ouput files
DEMOAST2	DAT	Data input to DEMOAST2 demo program
DEMOIO	ALC	Demo I/O Source program
DEMOPNUM	ALC	Prime number assembler source program
DEMOSRC	ALC	Analize all source programs on diskette
DEMOSVC	ALC	Demo SVC interface program
E370	EXE	PC/370 Emulator Program
E370	TRC	E370 trace id's
GO	BAT	Program to explain how to print documentation
HATCHECK	ALC	Hatcheck algorithm to calculate value of e
L370	COM	PC/370 Linkage Editor Program (convert OBJ files to COM file)
L370	LIB	Library of object code subroutines for L370 (PET,TIMER)
L370	TRC	L370 trace id's
MMS	TRC	Common subroutine trace id's
PC370	DOC	PC/370 user documentation
PET	ALC	Date, Time, Elapsed Time, Instructions per second subroutine
RUNDEMO	BAT	Run demo programs (batch commands)
TIMER	ALC	Time of day subroutine
Z86SUB	ASM	8086 subroutine demo source program
Z86SUB	EXE	8086 subroutine linked loadable object code for DEMOSVC

409 SNOCREST BASIC #1

v1

This is a BASIC interpreter that is made for multiusers. It includes SNOTERM which allows the IBM PC to act as an asynchronus terminal at 19,200 baud. SNOBACK backs up and SNOREST restores all files from a number of floppy disks to a hard disk. The companion disk No 410 contains much additional documentation. Please note that programs written under SNOBASIC will be incompatable with IBM BASICA.

Usage: For beginning through advanced BASIC programmers.

System Requirements: 256K, one disk drive and monochrome display.

How to Start: To read DOC files, enter TYPE filename.ext and press ENTER.

● To run an EXE or COM program, just type its name and press ENTER.

User Comments: "I used this program over DOS's BACKUP and was impressed by the speed of backup." "Needs easier method of accessing user files." "The restricted variable names and one statement per line constraints make it hard to use existing programs with SNOBASIC."

File Descriptions:

README	DOC	Updates for SNOBASIC
INSTALL	DOC	Installation instructions for SNOBASIC
CONFIG	DOC	Configuration instructions for SNOBASIC
STARTUP	BAT	Startup batch file for SNOBASIC (1 user)
STARTUP2	BAT	" " " " " (2 users)

STARTUP3	BAT	" " " " (3 users)
DK0	<DIR>	Contains files needed to run SNOBASIC
SNOBASIC	EXE	SNOBASIC for machines without 8087
SNOBAS87	EXE	" " " with 8087
SNOTERM	EXE	Terminal emulator (fast — up to 9600 baud)
SNOBACK	DOC	Documentation for SNOBACK.COM
SNOTERM	DOC	Documentation for SNOTERM.EXE
SNOBACK	COM	Fast backup routine
SNOBACK	ASM	source for SNOBACK.COM
SNOREST	DOC	Documentation for SNOREST.COM
SNOREST	COM	Fast restore routine
SNOREST	ASM	Source for SNOREST.COM
DIREC	DOC	Disk directory

410
SNOCREST BASIC #2
v1

This is the companion disk to the SNOCREST BASIC package. Please note that both disks are needed to sucessfully use this program series.

File Descriptions:

DIREC	DOC	Disk directory
DK1	<DIR>	Contains a number of files,for use with SNOBASIC
USERMAN	DOC	Users manual for SNOBASIC

424
Pascal Compiler
v1

This is a p-code compiler for an extended subset of Pascal. It is written in Turbo Pascal for the IBM PC. The compiler adheres closely to the standard Pascal of Jensen and Wirth, but does not implement file I/O. For those who are interested in inspecting or using an alternate Pascal compiler, this disk is a good educational tool.

Usage: Students and Pascal programmers.

System Requirements: 192K memory, IBM-PC/XT/AT or true compatible.

How to Start: To read the documentation for getting started, enter TYPE FACILIS.UM and press ENTER.

User Comments: "This program shows mainly how a Pascal compiler operates." "Sparse comments and the use of inline assembly code make the compiler HARD to follow what its doing." "Good compiler."

File Descriptions:

FACILIS	COM	Pascal compiler
FACILIS	000	A required overlay file
FACILIS	UM	Users manual for this pascal compiler
FACILIS	DOC	A 1-page description of the diskette contents
ZELLER	PAS	Short demo program
FACILIS	IM	Implementation manual for this pascal compiler
TEST	PAS	Overall confidence test for the compiler
STEST	PAS	Exercises the string facility of the compiler
FACILIS	PAS	Main program in Turbo to compute day of the week
BLOCK	PAS	A required include file. Contains most of compiler
INTERPRT	PAS	A required include file. Contains run-time interpreter

425
Engineering Pascal
v1

Most of these programs come from the book entitled "Pascal Programs for Scientists and Engineers", published by Sybex. They include commonly-used routines for engineering and statistics. The MATHPACK.PAS is a collection of mathematical and geometrical functions. For example, MEANS.PAS will compute the mean and standard deviation of a set of numbers. RANDOM.LIB is a random number generator.

Usage: For any Turbo Pascal programmer or student interested in solving engineering type problems.

System Requirements: 64K, one disk drive, monochrome display, and Turbo Pascal.

How to Start: To read the documentation enter TYPE PAS-ENG.DOC

User Comments: "An excellent set of functions, especially for occasional use." "Excellent for anyone doing mathematical modelling in TURBO PASCAL." "Great stuff!"

File Descriptions:

BESY	PAS	Evaluation of the Bessel function of the 2nd kind
CFIT1	PAS	Linear least-squares curve fit
CFIT1A	PAS	" (with a random number generator)
CFIT2	PAS	Plotting program using PLOT.LIB
CFIT4	PAS	Linear least-squares fit
DETERM	PAS	Calculate the determinant of a 3x3 matrix
DIFFUS	PAS	An example of FITPOL: diffusion of Zn in Cu
ERF4	PAS	An improved Gaussian error function
ERFD	PAS	Infinite series expansion for Gaussian error function
ERFD3	PAS	Gaussian error function and its complement
ERFSIMP	PAS	Gaussian error function by Simpson's rule
FITPOL	PAS	Linear least-squares fit to the ratio of two polynomials
GAUSID	PAS	Simultaneous solution by Gauss-Seidel
GAUSS	PAS	Simultaneous solution by Gaussian elimination
GAUSSJ	LIB	Gauss-Jordan matrix inversion and solution
GD-LINF1	LIB	Linear least-squares fit with Gauss-Jordan routine
GD-LINF2	LIB	"
JULIAN	LIB	Converts date to Julian
LEAST1	PAS	Linear least-squares fit using a parabolic curve
LEAST2	PAS	Linear least-squares fit with Gauss-Jordan routine
LEAST3	PAS	Linear least-squares fit with Gauss-Jordan routine
LEAST6	PAS	Linear least-squares fit with Gauss-Jordan routine
LINFIT1	LIB	Fits a straight line through n sets of x,y points
LINFIT2	LIB	Fits a straight line through n sets of x,y points
MATRI1	PAS	Matrix multiplication
MEANS	PAS	Computes mean and standard deviation
NEWDR	PAS	Solves equations by Newton's method
NEWDR2	PAS	Solves equations by Newton's method
NEWTON	LIB	Solves equations by Newton's method
NEWTON-L	LIB	Newton program with an iteration counter
NLIN3	PAS	Linear least-squares fit with nonlinearized e-function
PAS-ENG	DOC	Description of files on this diskette
PLOT	LIB	A plotter (printer) subroutine
RANDG	LIB	Random number generator with gaussian distribution
RANDOM	LIB	Random number generator (0..1)
RANDOM	PAS	Source code for random number generator
ROMB1	PAS	Integration by the Romberg method
ROMB3	PAS	" (with adjustable panels)
SIMP1	PAS	Integration by Simpson's rule
SIMPS	LIB	" (with end-correction)
SIMQ1	PAS	Solves three simultaneous equations by Cramer's rule
SOLVEC	PAS	Performs simultaneous solution for complex coefficients
SOLVGJ	PAS	Simul. equations, Gaussian elimination, Gauss-Jordan
SOLVGJ2	PAS	" (using more equations than unknowns)
SOLVGV	PAS	" (with multiple constant vectors)
SORT-B	LIB	Bubble sort
SORT-Q-N	LIB	Nonrecursive Quick-sort
SORT-Q-R	LIB	Recursive Quick-sort
SORT-S	LIB	Shell-Metzner sort
SQUARE	LIB	Matrix multiplication
TRAP1	PAS	Integrations by the trapezoidal rule
TRAP2	PAS	"
TRAPEZ	LIB	" (with end-correction)
TSTBES	PAS	Tests the Bessel function
TSTGAM	PAS	Tests the Gamma function
TSTSORT	PAS	Test speed of sorting routine
MATHPACK	PAS	Mathematical & geometrical function package

429 Elementary C

v1

A collection of C language routines that will help a programmer learn the language and will also provide a shortcut library for more experienced users. Included are some basic data movement routines, a help facility, amortization programs, and matrix manipulation. A short but succinct example shows how to initialize a Hayes Smartmodem out of Lattice C. An entire set of functions is provided for string processing of a list of arguments, with an example showing how to use these functions for Command Tail Processing.

Usage: For any beginning or intermediate C programmer.

System Requirements: 64K, one disk drive and monochrome display.

How to Start: To read DOC files, enter TYPE filename.ext and press ENTER.

● To run an EXE program, just type its name and press ENTER. For instructions on 'C' program listings, refer to your 'C' language manual.

User Comments: "It is elementary as stated. It covers numerical and matrix applications." "Good for learning C. The examples are very helpful when trying to understand how the language works." "Nice help in learning C."

File Descriptions:

ABOUT	C	Elementary help facility for C functions
ABOUT	DAT	Descriptions for ABOUT.C help facility
ABOUT	EXE	Object code for help facility
AMORTIZ1	C	Link of AMORTIZE.EXE
AMORTIZ2	C	"
AMORTIZ3	C	"
AMORTIZE	EXE	Amortization, where user or PC specifies payment
AMORTPRN	EXE	Same as AMORTIZE.EXE with data also sent to disk

BACKUP	C	Create backup copy of a file with the extension .BAK
BACKUP	EXE	''
C	DOC	Description of some of files on diskette
CLS	C	Clear screen
DOSDATE	C	Return system date in characters
DOSTIME	C	Return system time in characters
GETPOS	C	First part of comments on Lynn's routines
INTEREST	C	Link of AMORTPRN.EXE
LOCATE	C	Position cursor
LYNN	DOC	Middle part of comments on Lynn's routines
LYNN	LIB	Object code only
MAT	H	Matrix source and object code
MATRIX	3L	Matrix manipulation subroutine descriptions
MATRIX	S	Matrix manipulation subroutine descriptions
MENU	C	Link of AMORTPRN.EXE
M–COFACT	C	Cofactor of element of matrix
M–COPY	C	Duplicate copy of matrix
M–DETERM	C	Determinant of matrix
M–DUMP	C	Print matrix
M–INVERT	C	Inverse of matrix
M–MULTIP	C	Multiply matrix 1 x matrix 2
M–READ	C	Read into matrix
M–SOLVE	C	Matrix linear equations
M–TRANSP	C	Transpose matrix
OUTSTNG	C	Short section of LYNN.DOC
PRINT	C	Print from ASCII file, with tabs
PRINT	EXE	''
PRINTAB	C	Print from ASCII file, with spaces
PRINTAB	EXE	''
PRTSCN	C	Print screen to printer
PYMT	C	Link of AMORTPRN.EXE
SETHAYES	C	Hayes Smartmodem initialization routine
STRINGS	C	String processing of list of arguments

442
SPA:WN Structured Programming/ Warnier Diagram
v1

SPA:WN is an acronym for 'Structured Programming Automated: Warnier Notation'. This disk serve provides both a tutorial on the concepts of structured programming, and a working tool for design and documentation of the programs. Any target language is accomodated, but structured languages (Pascal, dBASE, True BASIC) work best. Design, automated code generation, and long range documentation for maintenance are all provided for. This package is targeted at serious programmers, and may be daunting to the casual user, but the potential benefits are great.

Usage: Structured language programmers

System Requirements: 192K of memory, two disk drives

How to Start: To read LST or READ.ME files, enter TYPE filename.ext and press ENTER.

- To run a COM program, just type its name and press ENTER.

User Comments: "Very good tutorial for structured programming." "A must for every civilized programmer who wants structure and not 'wildlife' in his programs." "Very useful but somewhat cumbersome in practice."

Suggested Donation: $50.00

File Descriptions:

DIR	DIR	Short description of the files contained on this disk
PWARN	COM	Executable object code for Pascal Warnier program
PWARN	PAS	Turbo Pascal source for Warnier program
PWARN	WAR	SPA:WN source for Pascal Warnier program
READ	ME	Miscellaneous matters; expl'n of files
RODGERS	WAR	Example SPA:WN source for a FORTRAN program
SPAWN	BAT	Batch file for doing SPA:WN runs: 'SPAWN fn'
SUMMARY	USE	Brief, cryptic reminder of input requirements
WARNCMS	LST	Detailed use instructions for CMS mainframe users
WARNIEEE	LST	Academically oriented paper about SPA:WN
WARNINTR	LST	Introduction for Structured Programming beginners

---

454
UNIFORTH
v1

The UNIFORTH Sampler from Unified Software Systems is a subset of the full Professional UNIFORTH. It provides a full assembler, video editor and software for floating-point arithmetic. It supports the FORTH-83 Standard with few exceptions. You will find the Sampler to be the equivalent of several commercial systems.

Usage: For beginning through advanced Forth programmers.

System Requirements: 64K, one disk drive and monochrome display.

How to Start: For complete information on how to start enter TYPE UNIFORTH.DOC and press ENTER. This file also gives documentation on the FORTH language.

● To start program type UNIFORTH and press ENTER.

User Comments: "This is a good subset of FORTH and, even though limited in comparison with the full bore program, is powerful and useful." "A good starter set of FORTH words and procedures." "Great for learning FORTH."

Suggested Donation: $25.00

File Descriptions:

UNIFORTH	COM	UNIFORTH main program
UNIFORTH	DOC	Documentation for UNIFORTH (87K)
FORTH	FTH	The default file that is opened when UNIFORTH is executed.
VEDITOR	FTH	The configuration file for the video editor
WORDS	DOC	The vocabulary word list

510 VISIBLE-PASCAL
v1

VISIBLE-PASCAL, a Pascal compiler, is particularly useful aid for teaching and learning the Pascal language. With this package, users can watch the operation of a program as it runs. There are 19 different sample programs which can be edited to run. An excellent tool for anyone interested in finding out how Pascal works.

Usage: For beginning Pascal programmers.

System Requirements: 128K, one disk drive and monochrome display.

How to Start: Type PRINTMAN and press ENTER to print users manual.

● To start program type RUN and press ENTER.

User Comments: "An interesting program, it really helped me understand program flow." "Useful for beginning to learn PASCAL, otherwise it's very tedious."

Suggested Donation: $35.00

AUTOEXEC	BAT	Starts program from boot after system has been put on the disk
EDIT	BAT	Batch file to start the editor
ERR	TXT	Text file containing error messages
G	BAT	Batch file that explains how to start the program
MANUAL	1	User manual part 1 of 2 (27K)
MANUAL	2	User manual part 2 of 2 (52K)
PRINTMAN	BAT	Batch file that prints the manual
RUN	BAT	Batch file to run a program
VISBUG	EXE	Part of Compiler
VISED	EXE	Part of Compiler
VISPAS	EXE	Part of Compiler

512 Programs From "The Complete Turbo Pascal"
v1

This disk contains the example programs, subprograms, and data files from Jeff Duntemann's book, The Complete Turbo Pascal, ISBN: 0-673-18111-1. The disk is meant to augment Duntemann's book by illustrating Pascal programming. Source and compiled versions of most routines are included, so you can run the routines, and review the code to see how they work.

Usage: For Turbo Pascal programmers.

System Requirements: 64K, one disk drive and monochrome display, Turbo Pascal.

How to Start: Enter TYPE READ.ME and press ENTER for a note from the author. For instructions on PAS listings, refer to your Pascal manual.

User Comments: "Some nice programs, but very little documentation." "I recommend getting Mr. Duntemann's book, then looking at these programs."

File Descriptions:

BEEP	SRC	Turbo Pascal source function/procedure
BOXSTUFF	SRC	Turbo Pascal source function/procedure
BOXTEST	PAS	Turbo Pascal source program
CASE	COM	Compiled, executable Turbo Pascal program
CASE	PAS	Turbo Pascal source program
CLRAREA	SRC	Turbo Pascal source function/procedure
CURSOFF	SRC	Turbo Pascal source function/procedure
CURSON	SRC	Turbo Pascal source function/procedure
DISKFREE	SRC	Turbo Pascal source function/procedure
FACTRIAL	SRC	Turbo Pascal source function/procedure

FATPAD	COM	Compiled, executable Turbo Pascal program
FATPAD	PAS	Turbo Pascal source program
FLIPFLD	SRC	Turbo Pascal source function/procedure
FRCECASE	SRC	Turbo Pascal source function/procedure
FRIENDS	KEY	Support routine or data file for example program
FRIENDS	NAP	Support routine or data file for example program
GENESIS	PAS	Turbo Pascal source program
GETSTRIN	SRC	Turbo Pascal source function/procedure
HEXDUMP	COM	Compiled, executable Turbo Pascal program
HEXDUMP	PAS	Turbo Pascal source program
INTSWAP	SRC	Turbo Pascal source function/procedure
ITERM	PAS	Turbo Pascal source program
KEYSTAT	C86	Support routine or data file for example program
KEYSTAT	CPM	Support routine or data file for example program
KEYSTAT	PC	Support routine or data file for example program
KSEARCH	SRC	Turbo Pascal source function/procedure
MAKE	BAT	Batch file for SCRNBLT.ASM program
MONOTEST	SRC	Turbo Pascal source function/procedure
MOUSE	SRC	Turbo Pascal source function/procedure
OVLTEST	000	Overlay file for example program
OVLTEST	001	Overlay file for example program
OVLTEST	PAS	Turbo Pascal source program
PARSTAIL	SRC	Turbo Pascal source function/procedure
POINTERS	PAS	Turbo Pascal source program
POWER	SRC	Turbo Pascal source function/procedure
PULL	SRC	Turbo Pascal source function/procedure
PUSHPOP	PAS	Turbo Pascal source program
QUIKSORT	SRC	Turbo Pascal source function/procedure
RANDOMS	KEY	Support routine or data file for example program
READ	ME	A note from the author
ROLLEM	PAS	Turbo Pascal source program
RVRSNAME	SRC	Turbo Pascal source function/procedure
SCREEN	PAS	Turbo Pascal source program
SCRNBLT	ASM	Assembler source code program
SCRNBLT	COM	Compiled, executable Turbo Pascal program
SHELSORT	SRC	Turbo Pascal source function/procedure
SHOWNAME	COM	Compiled, executable Turbo Pascal program
SHOWNAME	PAS	Turbo Pascal source program
SNAPSHOT	PIC	Support routine or data file for example program
SORTTEST	PAS	Turbo Pascal source program
STRIPWHT	SRC	Turbo Pascal source function/procedure
VARDUMP	SRC	Turbo Pascal source function/procedure
WHICH	PAS	Turbo Pascal source program
WRITEAT	SRC	Turbo Pascal source function/procedure
WRITEHEX	SRC	Turbo Pascal source function/procedure
YES	SRC	Turbo Pascal source function/procedure

527 B-WINDOW TOOLBOX Ver 2.0, C-WINDOW VER 1.2

V1

BASIC WINDOWING TOOLBOX (B-WINDOW) is a collection of functions that give windowing capability to a BASIC programmer using an IBM PC or compatible. Windows can be opened over sections of the screen and, when closed, the overwritten section of screen is restored. With B-WINDOW, BASIC programs look much more visually exciting and professional. B-WINDOW works with both compiled and interpreted BASIC. Special windowing cursor control, and string, character display and border drawing are included. Everything happens at top speed because B-WINDOW was written in C, converted to assembler, and hand-optimized. The C WINDOWING TOOLBOX (C–WINDOW) programs on this disk perform the same function for the programming language C. (Lattice C or Microsoft C version 3 or 4).

Usage: For BASIC and C programmers who want windowing capabilities in their programs.

System Requirements: 64K, one disk drive and monochrome display, 'C' compiler FOR C–WINDOW.

How to Start: Type GO and press ENTER for directions on how to display or print the documentation of both software packages

● To run an EXE program, just type its name and press ENTER.

User Comments: "I was impressed by the different kinds of capabilities available." "A nice accessory to have."

Suggested Donation: $20.00 for BASIC WINDOWING TOOLBOX, $15.00 for C–WINDOW C source code

File Descriptions:

— — —	— —	BASIC WINDOWING TOOLBOX Version 2.0
B-WREAD	ME	B-WINDOW updates & notes
B-WINDOW	DOC	System documentation for B-WINDOW
B-WIN5I	BIN	Interpreted BASIC windowing support file, 5K buffer

B-WIN10I	BIN	Interpreted BASIC windowing support file, 10K buffer
B-WIN20I	BIN	Interpreted BASIC windowing support file, 20K buffer
B-WINI	MRG	Program to be merged with your BASIC program
BWDEMO1	BAS	Interpreted BASIC demo program — 1
BWDEMO2	BAS	Interpreted BASIC demo program — 2
BWDEMOC	EXE	Compiled BASIC demo program
————	——	C WINDOWING TOOLBOX Version 1.2
C-WREAD	ME	C-WINDOW updates & notes
C-WINDOW	DOC	Documentation for C-WINDOW
C-WINLAT	OBJ	Windowing for C. Link to your Lattice C programs
C-WINMSC	OBJ	Windowing for C. Link to your Microsoft C programs
C-WDEF	H	Include file. Defines C-WINDOW functions, variables
C-WDEMO	C	Windowing demo source code
C-WDEMO	EXE	Windowing demo program

TU	DOC	Tutorial on creating a Tiny Pascal compiler
TU	GRM	Tiny Turbo Pascal grammar
TU	TBL	Table file created by QPARSER table generator
TUDBUG	PAS	Skeleton source file
TUDECLS	PAS	Skeleton source file
TUFILES	PAS	Skeleton source file
TUPROG	COM	Executable compiler
TUPROG	PAS	Tiny Pascal compiler program
TURPT	TXT	QPARSER report file (from compiler creation)
TURUN	ASM	Compiler output (8086 assembly code)
TURUN	COM	Assembled (executable) sample program
TURUN	LST	Chasm assembler list file
TURUN	TXT	Sample program for compiler
TUSEMS	PAS	Skeleton source file
TUSKEL	PAS	Main "skeleton" file used by QPARSER to create TUPROG.PAS
TUSYMS	PAS	Skeleton source file
TUUTILS	PAS	Skeleton source file

540
Tiny Pascal Compiler Builder
v1

This disk will let you design and implement a small subset Pascal compiler, using the Turbo Pascal compiler. It will let you translate the program into 8086 symbolic assembly language which you can compile. Not only can you build a small compiler, you learn how to create your own language translators and compilers.

Usage: For intermediate or advanced PASCAL programmers.

System Requirements: 64K, one disk drive and monochrome display, and a TURBO PASCAL compiler.

How to Start: To read TXT files, enter TYPE filename.ext and press ENTER.

- To run a COM program, just type its name and press ENTER. For instructions on PAS listings, refer to your Pascal manual.

File Descriptions:

CHASM	CFG	Configuration file for use with CHASM assembler
PMACS	TXT	Macro forms file for use with QPARSER program generator
STDIO	HDR	Standard assembly IO routines needed for Tiny Pascal

553
LLSQ (FORTRAN Programs)
v1

This disk contains LLSQ, a package of 14 basic, high-quality mathematical FORTRAN subprograms that can be utilized in your applications programs. These first appeared in the "IMSL Numerical Computations Newsletter", "User News", and "Directions".

Usage: Intermediate-advanced FORTRAN programmers.

System Requirements: 64K, one disk drive and monochrome display.

How to Start: For instructions on FOR listings, refer to your FORTRAN language manual.

User Comments: "These routines are exceptionally well documented in the Prentice-Hall book, "Solving Least Squares Problems", by Charles L. Lawson and Richard J. Hanson. This book is, in fact, almost a prerequisite to properly use these routines."

File Descriptions:

LINK?	BAT	Batch files to properly link the various modules
PROG?	FOR	Test drivers for the various modules
????????	FOR	LLSQ FORTRAN source code modules

556
FORTRAN & A Little Assembly

v1

This is a mixed collection of games, usable programs, and utilities that can be called from FORTRAN programs. Included is PLTSPEC which is useful in analyzing spectra with broad asymmetric peaks on a sloping background. DIR–ASM.ASM is a routine which lists to the console the names of the files in the current directory. There are also some .PIC files which are ASCII files to copy to a printer. They contain drawings of various figures.

Usage: For intermediate to advanced FORTRAN programmers.

System Requirements: 64K, one disk drive and monochrome display.

How to Start: To read DOC files, enter TYPE filename.ext and press ENTER.

- To run an EXE program, just type its name and press ENTER. For instructions on ASM or FOR listings, refer to your Assembler or FORTRAN language manual.

User Comments: "Some interesting programs, but I didn't have much use for them." "I'm not a nuclear engineer, so I wasn't much interested in PLTSPEC."

File Descriptions:

README		Description and documentation for the files on this disk
DOSFN	ASM	Gives access to DOS functions from an MS-FORTRAN program
DOSFN	OBJ	Assembled version of DOSFN
DOSFUNC	FOR	FORTRAN routines for use with DOSFN
KYBD–EX	FOR	Example program using DOSFUNC and DOSFN
DIR–ASM	ASM	A disk directory from FORTRAN
DIR–ASM	OBJ	Assembled version of DIR–ASM
DIR–FOR	FOR	Example FORTRAN program using DIR–ASM
DIR–FOR	EXE	Compiled and linked version of above
DAT–TIME	ASM	Routines for getting the date and time in FORTRAN
DAT–TIME	OBJ	Assembled version of DAT–TIME
TIME2	FOR	Example FORTRAN routines using DAT–TIME
TIME2	EXE	Compiled and linked version of above
PLTSPEC	FOR	Interactive processing of gamma-ray pulse height spectra
MANSPT	FOR	Part of PLTSPEC; requires MS-FORTRAN
EDITS	FOR	Part of PLTSPEC; MULTI-HALO graphics library

PLOT1	FOR	IDS Micro Prism printer
PLOT2	FOR	Dump routines for PLTSPEC
EFFIXSP	FOR	Detector efficiency correction of gamma-ray spectra
EXAMPLE	DAT	Example data set for PLTSPEC
CALENDAR	CPM	Calendar source code — CP/M
CALENDAR	FOR	Calendar source code
CHESS	DOC	Chess documentation
CHESS	FOR	Chess source code
EDITM	FOR	Edit program source code
LINUS	PIC	Linus portrait
MAZE	CPM	Maze generator source code — CP/M
MAZE	FOR	Maze generator source code
OTHELLO	FOR	Othello program source code
OTHELLO	DOC	Othello program documentation
PINUP?	PIC	Pinup portraits
RND	FOR	Random numbers generator source code
SSPLIB	FOR	Linear least squares program source code

573
XASM Cross assembler

v1

XASM is a cross-assembler that allows the use of a PC as a development station for several target CPUs. Among those supported are the Zilog Z8 family, the Intel 8048 and 8041 series, and many more. The assembler uses a text macro to specify the target machine, making the assembler user-configurable for a specific target machine. Also on this disk are demo versions of four APL language workspaces.

Usage: For assembly language programmers or those interested in APL.

System Requirements: 64K, one disk drive and monochrome display and NOTE: The APL workspaces require STSC's APL*PLUS(tm), version 3.0+, and at least 192K.

How to Start: With the disk in the driver, type GO. Information on starting XASM is given in XASM.DOC.

Suggested Donation: $50.00

File Descriptions:

XASM	EXE	Macro configured Cross-assembler for single-chip computers.
XASM	DOC	XASM cross-assembler documentation.

6805MACS	ASM	Sample XASM macro file
ALL6805	ASM	Sample source file for XASM
QSCAN	AWS	APL workspace file — Scan/clean/edit functions and variables.
QDOC	AWS	APL workspace file — Make neatly paged workspace documentation.
ZPLEX	AWS	APL workspace file — Complex number mathematical functions.
APLDEMO	AWS	APL workspace file — 115 public domain utility functions.
README	1ST	Information on APL workspace files.

606
Polymath
v1

This disk contains the Polymath language. Developed much in the light of Forth, Polymath is highly modulated and structured upon a set of defined words that themselves define other words and so build a powerful programming dictionary based on simple functions. Polymath is specially designed to be user friendly with on-line documentation and user guides. The most powerful feature of Polymath, however, lies in its number processing abilities. With syntax much like Hewlett Packard programmable calculators, Polymath bridges the gap between hand held programmable calculators and computer languages. Although this program is only a sampler version, it was found to be very powerful, easy to use, useful and just fun to play with. Included are sample application programs written in Polymath.

Usage: Mathematicians, programmers, general PC users

System Requirements: 192K of memory, one disk drive

How to Start: Type GO and press ENTER to obtain starting instructions.

Suggested Donation: $40.00

File Descriptions:

POLYMATH	COM	The executable file for the Polymath program
POLYMATH	HLP	Random access word glossary called by Polymath (76k)
POLYMATH	PKG	Dictionary file for the word glossary
GUIDE	HLP	Random access text for the tutorial
GUIDE	PKG	Dictionary file for the guide
CONVERT	PM	Text source file for the convert application
CONVERT	HLP	Random access help file (80k)

CONVERT	PKG	Dictionary for the convert application
COMPLEX	PM	Text source file for the application
COMPLEX	HLP	Random access help file
COMPLEX	PKG	Dictionary for the application
PRINTER	PM	Text source file for the printer application
PRINTER	HLP	Random access help file
PRINTER	PKG	Dictionary for the printer application
REGRESS	PM	Text source file for the polynomial regression application
REGRESS	HLP	Random access help file
REGRESS	PKG	Dictionary for the application
TOWERS	PM	Text source file for the Towers of Babble demo application
TOWERS	HLP	Random access help file
TOWERS	PKG	Dictionary for the application
GO	BAT	Quick help batch file for documentation presentation

643
TASM
Version 2.2
v1

TASM is an assembler which runs on the IBM PC/XT/AT or compatibles and creates code for any of three 8 bit processors: 8048, 8051, or 6502. The user can customize TASM to produce code for other processors by creating a proper Instruction Definition Table for the target chip.

Usage: Assembly language programming

System Requirements: 128K, one disk drive and a monochrome display

How to Start: After consulting carefully the manual found in file TASM.DOC, execute it from DOS by typing TASM at the prompt.

Suggested Donation: $30.00 which includes: the latest version of TASM, the source code (in C), and a bound manual.

File Descriptions:

TASM	EXE	TASM Assembler, executable
TASM48	TAB	8048 Instruction definition table
TASM51	TAB	8051 Instruction definition table
TASM65	TAB	6502 Instruction definition table
TASM	DOC	TASM Documentation
README		Brief Explanation of Disk contents
COPYRIGH	T	Copyright notice

666 Structured Programming Language

v1

This disk contains a very powerful and easy to use structured programming langauage (SPL). This program, SPL, is a hybrid mix of structured BASIC with Pascal-style programming architecture. For example, the language revolves around procedures, functions and programming blocks defined by BEGIN and END statements.

The SPL compiler takes an input source code and produces an ASCII file in BASIC that can be executed in BASICA or compiled using the BASIC compiler. SPL supports many IF THEN style programming codes as well as REPEAT WHILE commands. SPL also comes with graphics ability with excellent mathematical operators and strong string manipulation commands. In short, almost every command available in BASIC is also available in SPL, with a few additions. A reference manual is also included. This package is intended for the experienced user of the IBM-PC.

Usage: Advanced BASIC programming

System Requirements: 64K, one disk drive and monochrome display; Requires the SORT.EXE utility.

How to Start: Both program and documentation are archived in SPLLIB.ARC. Use the enclosed ARC to get them.

Suggested Donation: $50.00-$100.00 is encouraged

File Descriptions:

————	——	Structured Programming Language
ARC	EXE	Un-archiving program
READ		Introductory text file from author
SPLLIB	ARC	Archived file which contains the following files:
SP	EXE	Source compiler for SPL
SPA	EXE	Support program for the compiler
SPLLIB	ARC	Library for SPL in archived format
README	DOC	Short author documentation and general information
ARC	EXE	The archive utility
ARC	TXT	Documentation for the archive utility
BLACKJAC	SP	A program written in SPL
IPLOT	SP	Another program written in SPL
MANUAL		The SPL reference manual, error codes with index (96k)

685 New FIG FORTH

v1

For fans of FORTH, here is the latest version of this unusual programming language. This version of FIG-FORTH incorporates a number of significant changes to the FIG version. The following is a partial list:

- Written for Microsoft's MACRO-86 assembler
- Full MS-DOS file interaction, as well as usual FORTH disk access
- All I/O is vectored and may be re-directed within FORTH
- Command line interpretation

The accompanying documentation includes a user's guide, a technical reference manual, and a FORTH glossary (a list and explanation of each FORTH word which has been changed or added to this version).

Usage: FORTH programming

System Requirements: 128K, one disk drive, monochrome display system CPU must be 8086 or 8088

How to Start: Use the UNPACK file to de-archive the enclosed files.

File Descriptions:

CONTENTS	A list of the contents of the FORTH.ARC file
GLOSSARY	List of FORTH words for use with FIND (see User Guide)
README	List of all files and instructions on how to unarchive

MATH/SCIENCE/ STATISTICS:

Perhaps no one has appreciated the advent of personal computing power more than those in the "hard sciences" (referring to the complexity of computations needed for their work). Chemists, mathematicians, physicists, statisticians and the students of such sciences will find this category extremely useful.

Actually, there is no one discipline that gets the lions share of this category. Rather, most programs are for the statistically minded user. The capabilities for data analyses (i.e., market/demographic analysis, multiple regressions, linear equations, etc.) are quite staggering. Still, two noteworthy newcomers to this field should be cited. The first is a pair of NMR — Nuclear Magnetic Resonance — programs that assist chemists in preparing advanced analyses of spectroscopic samples. The second is a graphics-oriented statistical analysis package that imports from many different sources, including dBASE II and III and ASCII, and can produce histograms as well as 3D bar charts and graphs.

88 EPISTAT Statistics Package (3.0)

v2

This package contains a set of routines for use in analysis of small data sets, and is meant to be used by a person well-versed in math and computer operations. This is a fairly complex disk and is not recommended for the casual user. But for those with an interest, it can be of great help.

Usage: Chemistry students

System Requirements: 256K memory, one disk drive, color graphics card and high-res display, graphics printer.

How to Start: To run BASIC programs consult the directions in GETTING STARTED for your configuration. Consult PRINTDOC for documentation.

User Comments: "Not a program for a novice in statistics, yet a comprehensive and broad approach to the subject is covered in the programs." "An excellent program, especially for the person who is less than expert in this field." "Plenty of helpful hints to assist you."

Suggested Donation: $15.00

File Descriptions:

ANOVA	BAS	One and two way analysis of variance
AUTOEXEC	BAT	Batch file to auto boot program
BAYES	BAS	Uses Bayes theorem to calculate rates of false positive and negative tests
BINOMIAL	BAS	Binomial distribution
CHISQR	BAS	Chi-square test
CORRELAT	BAS	Calculates Pearson's correlation coefficient
DATA-ONE	BAS	Main data entry program
EPIMRG	BAS	Used by every EPISTAT program
EPISETUP	BAK	Backup for EPISETUP.DAT
EPISETUP	DAT	Used by every EPISTAT program
EPISTAT	BAS	Lists available programs and guides user to proper program to use
FILETRAN	BAS	Transfers data from one data file to another
FISHERS	BAS	Fisher's exact test to evaluate 2 by 2 tables of discrete values
FORTRANS	BAS	Transfers FORTRAN to EPISTAT files
HISTOGRM	BAS	Graphs data sample on high resolution graphics screen
LNREGRES	BAS	Linear regression
MCNEMAR	BAS	McNemar's test or paired Chi-square test

MHCHIMLT	BAS	Mantel-Haenszel Chi-square test for multiple controls
MHCHISQR	BAS	Mantel-Haenszel Chi-square test
NORMAL	BAS	Calculates normal distribution
POISSON	BAS	Calculates Poisson distribution
PRINTDOC		Documentation file (25K)
RANDOMIZ	BAS	Random sample generator
RANKTEST	BAS	Three tests — signed rank, rank correlation and rank sum
RATEADJ	BAS	Rate adjustment program
SAMPLSIZ	BAS	Calculates sample sizes for statistical significance
SCATRGRM	BAS	Graph scatergrams
SELECT	BAS	Select from other programs
T-TEST	BAS	T-test compares mean of 2 samples
XTAB	BAS	Print crosstab reports
EXAMPLE		Sample data set

180
Math and Statistics Routines
v1

This collection of math and financial analyst programs are intended for the either the professional or student. This package has a menu shell for each of the two main functions, which allow you to easily access the related routines. Many handy analysis tools.

Usage: For advanced math students and financial analysts.

System Requirements: 128K memory, one floppy drive, color or mono display.

How to Start: To run BASIC programs consult the directions in GETTING STARTED for your configuration.

User Comments: "This is a good program for the college student like me." "Math/Stat is going to save me a lot of wasted time that I would normally do figuring out the prime numbers, etc." "A few of the programs are very primitive but have potential."

File Descriptions:

TRADENET		TRADENET network sampler
DATANET		DATANET network sampler
M1	BAS	Greatest common demonator
M2	BAS	Prime factors of integers
M3	BAS	Area of polygon
M4	BAS	Analysis of two vectors
M5	BAS	Parts of a triangle

M6	BAS	Operations on two vectors
M7	BAS	Coordinate conversion
M8	BAS	Coordinate plot
M9	BAS	Angle conversion
M10	BAS	Plot of polar equation
M11	BAS	Plot of function
M12	BAS	Linear interpolation
M13	BAS	Curvilinear interpolation
M14	BAS	Integration: Simpson's rule
M15	BAS	Integration: Gaussian quadrature
M16	BAS	Integration: Trapesoidal rule
M17	BAS	Derivative
M18	BAS	Roots of quadratic equation
M19	BAS	Real roots of polynomials: Newton
M20	BAS	Roots of polynomials: half interval sear
M21	BAS	Trig polynomial
M22	BAS	Simultaneous equations
M23	BAS	Linear programming
M24	BAS	Matrix add, subtract & scalar multiplication
M25	BAS	Matrix multiplication
M26	BAS	Matrix inversion
MATH	BAS	Menu for above math programs
MATRIX	BAS	Solves simultaneous equations
NCCLSPRE	BAS	Calculates a sample's precision
NORMAL-Z	BAS	Normal distribution routines
REGRESS	BAS	Regression analysis
S1	BAS	Permutations & combinations
S2	BAS	Mann-Whitney U test
S3	BAS	Geometric mean and deviation
S4	BAS	Binomial distribution
S5	BAS	Poisson distribution
S6	BAS	Normal distribution
S7	BAS	Chi-square distribution
S8	BAS	Chi-square test
S9	BAS	Student's T distribution
S10	BAS	Student's T test
S11	BAS	F-distribution
S12	BAS	Linear correlation coefficient
S13	BAS	Multiple linear regression
S14	BAS	Linear regression
S15	BAS	Nth order regression
S16	BAS	Geometric regression
S17	BAS	Exponential regression
S18	BAS	Mean, variance, standard deviation
STAT	BAS	Menu for above S??.BAS statistics programs

232
SPPC System Demo (3.0) (Disk 1 of 2)
v3

This is a demo of SPPC, a fully interactive statistical package that enables you to enter, manage and analyze simple and complex sets of data. In order to use the SPPC, you must enter your data and store it on a diskette or hard disk file. You can then conduct any statistical analysis that is available. NOTE: This is a two disk program and must be used together. Disk 2 is on DISK 623.

Usage: Statistical analysis

System Requirements: 128K, two disk drives, and a monochrome/graphics display

How to Start: Unarchive the programs following the instructions on disk in files named README.* .

File Descriptions:

ARCE	COM	Archiving program
README	*	Instructions files
SPPC0	ARC	Archived sections of SPPC demonstration
SPPC1	ARC	"
SPPC2	ARC	"
SPPC3	ARC	"

234
TPNCALC
v1

This is a user-supported program, intended for use by Pharmacists to calculate intravenous electrolyte additives needed to compound a Hyperalimentation order according to the medical doctors specifications. A rather specialized field, it's true, but for those with a need, it's a real timesaver.

Usage: Pharmacists

System Requirements: 128K memory, one drive, printer, and either a color or mono display.

How to Start: Load DOS and type TPNCALC to invoke the program. Consult TPNDOC for program documentation.

User Comments: "Great program!" "The author has done an excellent job." "A useful program for pharmacists involved in the preparation of TPN if they are using the manufacturers products included on the disk."

File Descriptions:

TPNCALC	EXE	Main program
TPNDOC		Documentaion (14K)

391
NMR Spectroscopy and Statistics
v1

This series of programs are simulations and problems for the serious chemistry enthusiast of NMR — Nuclear Magnetic Resonance Spectroscopy. A set of statistical analysis programs are also included. The programs are useful for students and professionals.

Usage: Chemist or student of Nuclear Magnetic Resonance Spectroscopy.

System Requirements: 128K memory, one drive, printer, graphic card and a hi-res color monitor.

How to Start: To run BASIC programs consult the directions in GETTING STARTED for your configuration.

User Comments: "Good for chemical scientist or college students. Good if you are learning NMR. It could be better documented." "An interesting teaching program and the statistical routines are fantastic. They alone are worth far more than the price of the disk."

File Descriptions:

ADIABAT	BAS	NMR — Adiabatic slow passage experiment
AUTOEXEC	BAT	Starting batch file — lists directory, starts MENU.BAS
BASHADAM	BAS	NMR — Calculates surface tension by use of the BASFORTH
BASTAT2V	BAS	Basic statistics — two variables

BESSELJN	BAS	Calculates Bessel functions Jn(x)
BESSELYN	BAS	Calculates Bessel functions Yn(x)
BR2DIFFN	BAS	Diffusion of Bromine in a tube
BUBLSORT	BAS	A bubble sort
CHISQDIS	BAS	Chi-square distribution
CUBICFIT	BAS	Least squares cubic fit
CUBICSPL	BAS	Cubic spline function interpolation
CURVEFIT	BAS	Curve fitter
DEBYESOL	BAS	Heat capacity of Debye solid
DIFFCAP	BAS	Differential capacitance of the electric double layer
ERFERFC	BAS	Calculates erf(x) and erfc(x)
ERRANAL	BAS	Error analysis — root mean square
EXPFIT	BAS	Exponential curve fit
FOURIER	BAS	Fourier coefficients
GAMMA(X)	BAS	Gamma functions by Stirling's approximation
GATDECUP	BAS	Homonuclear gated decoupling for solvent peak suppression
HARMOSC	BAS	Harmonic oscillator function Hn(x) by recursion
INTERP3	BAS	4-point polynomial interpolation
INTERP4	BAS	Quartic interpolation
INVRECOV	BAS	NMR measurement of T1 by inversion recovery
L2FILMS	BAS	Equation of state of L2 films in surface chemistry
LARMOR	BAS	NMR Spectroscopy Larmor precession and other effects
LEGENDRE	BAS	Calculation of Legendre polynomials by recursion
LINEQNS	BAS	Simultaneous linear equations
LINLSQR	BAS	Linear least squares
LINREGR	BAS	Linear regression
LOGCURVE	BAS	Logarithmic curve fit
LSQPARAB	BAS	Least squares parabola
LSQREXP	BAS	Non-linear least squares exponential curve fit
MATERBAL	BAS	Material balance equations
MATRDIAG	BAS	Matrix diagonalization by partial pivot method
MATRINV	BAS	Matrix inversion
MENU	BAS	Main menu program to gain access to all NMR programs
MOMSKKUR	BAS	Moments, skewness, kurtosis
MORSECRV	BAS	Morse curves for diatomic molecules
MULTPULS	BAS	Multiple pulses in NMR
NEWTONRT	BAS	Newton's method for real roots of polynomials
NMR-ABC	BAS	ABC proton spectrum
NMR-ABCD	BAS	ABCD proton spectrum
NMR-WEFT	BAS	Water peak supression by WEFT — Water Elimination by
NMRAPP	PIC	Diagram of NMR apparatus
NMRAPP2	PIC	Diagram of NMR apparatus
NMREXCH	BAS	NMR lineshapes in chemical exchange
NMREXEC	BAS	Older version of MENU.BAS — interesting graphics
NMRFOURT	BAS	Free induction decay in spectra with several signals
NMRPHASE	BAS	NMR line phasing simulation
NMRRELAX	BAS	Effect of correlation time on the longitudinal NMR
NMRROT	BAS	NMR — behavior of the magnetization vector
NUMDIFF	BAS	Numerical differentiation — symmetrical 4-point formula
OFFRES	BAS	Procession on and off resonance
POWRCURV	BAS	Power curve fit

ROOTFHLF	BAS	Roots of functions / Half-interval search
RUTHEXPT	BAS	Rutherford scattering apparatus & trajectories experiment
RUTHSCAT	BAS	Rutherford scattering — calculates & plots trajectories
SHELSORT	BAS	A shell sort routine (300 entries max.)
SIMPINT	BAS	Integration by Simpson's rule
SPECPROB	BAS	NMR Spectroscopy spin echo measurements problem
SPINECHO	BAS	Spin echo simulation in NMR
TRIDIAG	BAS	Tridiagonal systems of linear equations
TWOMEANS	BAS	Compares the means of two populations
XRAYDIF1	BAS	X-ray diffraction simulations

394 Math Pak
v1

Math Pak is a collection of BASICA programs designed to solve various math problems while improving problem-solving skills. The programs are easy to understand. Programmers, engineers and computer science students should find the binary to decimal octal to hexidecimal conversions especially useful. Other routines handle polar to rectangular to polar conversion, second and third order determinants and logarithmic functions.

Usage: Basic to advanced mathematics practice.

System Requirements: 128K, one disk drive and monochrome display.

Features: MATHPAK covers basic to advanced math:

- Hexidecimal and octal from decimal conversions
- Binary to decimal conversions.
- Quadratic root formula root solving given ay^2 + bx + c = 0)
- Polar to rectangular to polar conversions
- Finding points on an x-y coordinate system given (ay + b = mx + d
- Logarithmic functions (base 10 or base a)
- Second order determinant solving (x,y)
- Third order determinant solving (x,y,z)

How to Start: To run BASIC programs consult the directions in GETTING STARTED for your configuration. Consult TEXT.DOC for program documentation.

User Comments: "Good as an educational backup tool for math, but not much else." "Interesting, but calculators do the same things only faster." "This is a teaching program."

File Descriptions:

A	BAS	Main tutorial section
A1	BAS	Addition tutorial
B1	BAS	Hex/Octal conversion tutorial
C1	BAS	Trig functions tutorial
COMPLEX	BAS	Complex functions section
D	BAS	Division tutorial
DETER	BAS	Determinant/line equation section
E	BAS	Area calculation tutorial
FLOW	BAS	Flow section of MATH PAK
FORM	BAS	Formula/Conversion sheet/section
GAME	BAS	Game section
L	BAS	Binary to decimal conversion tutorial
M	BAS	Mutiplication tutorial
MP	BAS	Graphics (box) display
MPK	BAS	MATH PAK main program
P	BAS	Printer use tutorial
Q	BAS	Quadratic formula tutorial
READ	ME	Instructions for the use of MATH PAK
S	BAS	Subtraction tutorial
START	BAS	Starting screen (use with letter: e.g., LOAD "START",R
TEXT	DOC	Explanation of purpose of programs
Z	BAS	Metric conversions tutorial

Usage: Math and Science students who need to do complex calculations in manuscript form.

System Requirements: 256K memory, graphics card and printer, FORTRAN complier, one drive and color display.

How to Start: Load DOS and type PC-SIZE to enter the main program. Consult PC-SIZE.DOC for program documentation.

Suggested Donation: $10.00

File Descriptions:

————	——	PC-SIZE
PC-SIZE	EXE	Main program for PC-SIZE
PC-SIZE	DOC	Documentation for PC-SIZE (31K)
PC-SIZE	FOR	FORTRAN source code for PC-SIZE
————	——	PC-MULTI
PC-MULTI	EXE	Main program for PC-MULTI
PC-MULTI	DOC	Documentation for PC-MULTI (9K)
PC-MULTI	FOR	FORTRAN Source Code for PC-MULTI
————	——	FORGET-IT
FORGET	EXE	Main program for FORGET
FORGET	DOC	Documentation for FORGET (12K)
FORGET	FOR	FORTRAN source code for FORGET

508 Stat Tools (Disk 1 of 2) v1

PC-SIZE determines the sample size requirements for single factor experiments, two factor experiments, randomized blocks designs, paired T tests, and other experiments. PC-SIZE can calculate the power of specific sample sizes as well as determine the sample size needed to achieve specific power. Double precision calculations are used throughout. PCMULTI constructs simultaneous confidence intervals for pairwise mean differences using Tukey's honest significant differences (Studentized range statistic). FORGET-IT produces Forget-it plots, also called two-way plots. These were introduced by Tukey (1970, chapter 16) as a graphical technique for representing the interaction structure in a two-way table.

509 Stat Tools (Disk 2 of 2) v1

STAT-SAK, the statistician's Swiss Army Knife, is meant as a supplemental tool for anyone who analyzes data regularly and has access to a large statistical package. STAT-SAK will not do calculations that require the entry of the original observations. STAT-SAK calculates distributions (Normal, T, Chi-square, F), tests of independence/homogeneity of proportions in two dimensional contingency tables, Mantel-Haenszel test, McNemar's test, correlation coefficients, Bartholomew's test. Double precision calculations are used throughout. PC-PITMAN performs exact randomization tests. It also performs Wilcoxon signed-rank tests and Wilcoxon-Mann-Whitney U tests in the presence of an arbitrary number of ties in the data. PC-EMS uses the algorithm of Cornfield and Tukey(1956) to calculate tables of Expected Mean Squares for balanced experiments. PCPLAN generates randomization plans. The resulting file can be used as input to a word processing program for touch up and entry into a report.

Usage: Math and science students.

System Requirements: 256K, color display, graphics printer, graphics card, one drive unit.

How to Start: Load DOS and type STAT-SAK to invoke the main program. Consult STAT-SAK.DOC for program documentation.

Suggested Donation: $10.00

File Descriptions:

— — — —	— —	STAT-SAK
STAT-SAK	EXE	Main program for STAT-SAK
STAT-SAK	DOC	Documenatation for STAT-SAK
STAT-SAK	FOR	FORTRAN source code for STAT-SAK
— — — —	— —	PC-PITMAN
PITMAN	DOC	Main program for PITMAN
PITMAN	EXE	Documenatation for PITMAN
PITMAN	FOR	FORTRAN source code for PITMAN
— — — —	— —	PC-EMS
PC-EMS	EXE	Main program for PC-EMS
PC-EMS	DOC	Documenatation for PC-EMS
PC-EMS	FOR	FORTRAN source code for PC-EMS
— — — —	— —	PC-PLAN
PC-PLAN	FOR	Main program for PC-PLAN
PC-PLAN	EXE	Documenatation for PC-PLAN
PC-PLAN	DOC	FORTRAN source code for PC-PLAN

---

554 LINPACK Library (FORTRAN Programs)
v1

The Linear Equation Package (LINPACK) is a set of routines which solves systems of linear equations and related problems. This package was developed by the Applied Mathematics Division of Argonne National Laboratory; this source code was taken from a distribution disk provided by International Mathematics and Statistical Libraries, Inc. (IMSL).

Usage: Math and science students.

System Requirements: FORTRAN compiler, 256K memory, color monitor, one drive, graphics card and printer.

How to Start: For instructions on FORTRAN listings, refer to your FORTRAN language manual. Consult the INDEX file to review the routines included on this disk.

User Comments: "For the experienced user and/or FORTRAN programmer." "Fortran programs are very well written." "No documentation or help files."

Suggested Donation: $10.00

File Descriptions:

INDEX		An index of all the routines on the library and driver disks
SCH	FOR	Main routine/driver for testing the SCH routines.
SCHDC	FOR	Real Cholesky decomposition decompose
SCHDD	FOR	Real Cholesky decomposition downdate
SCHEX	FOR	Real Cholesky decomposition exchange
SCHUD	FOR	Real Cholesky decomposition update
SEX	FOR	Main routine/driver for testing the exchange routines.
SG	FOR	Main routine/driver for testing the SG routines.
SGBCO	FOR	Real general band condition estimate
SGBDI	FOR	Real general band determinant, inverse, inertia
SGBFA	FOR	Real general band factor
SGBSL	FOR	Real general band solver
SGECO	FOR	Real general condition estimate
SGEDI	FOR	Real general determinant, inverse, inertia
SGEFA	FOR	Real general factor
SGESL	FOR	Real general solver
SGT	FOR	Main routine/driver for testing the SGT routines.
SGTSL	FOR	Real general tridiagonal solver
SP	FOR	Main routine/driver for testing the SP routines.
SPBCO	FOR	Real positive definite banded condition estimate
SPBDI	FOR	Real positive definite banded determinant, inverse, inertia
SPBFA	FOR	Real positive definite banded factor
SPBSL	FOR	Real positive definite banded solver
SPOCO	FOR	Real positive definite condition estimate
SPODI	FOR	Real positive definite determinant, inverse, inertia
SPOFA	FOR	Real positive definite factor
SPOSL	FOR	Real positive definite solver
SPPCO	FOR	Real positive definite packed condition estimate
SPPDI	FOR	Real positive definite packed determinant, inverse, inertia
SPPFA	FOR	Real positive definite packed factor
SPPSL	FOR	Real positive definite packed solver
SPTSL	FOR	Real positive definite tridiagonal solver
SQR	FOR	Main routine/driver for testing the SQR routines.
SQRDC	FOR	Real orthogonal triangular decompose
SQRSL	FOR	Real orthogonal triangular solver
SQRTS	FOR	Real orthogonal triangular
SS	FOR	Main routine/driver for testing the SS routines.
SSICO	FOR	Real symmetric indefinite condition estimate
SSIDI	FOR	Real symmetric indefinite determinant, inverse,inertia
SSIFA	FOR	Real symmetric indefinite factor
SSISL	FOR	Real symmetric indefinite solver
SSPCO	FOR	Real symmetric indefinite packed condition estimate
SSPDI	FOR	Real symmetric indefinite packed determinant, inverse, inertia
SSPFA	FOR	Real symmetric indefinite packed factor
SSPSL	FOR	Real symmetric indefinite packed solver

SSV	FOR	Main routine/driver for testing the SSV routines.
SSVDC	FOR	Real singular value decomposition
ST	FOR	Main routine/driver for testing the ST routines.
STRCO	FOR	Real triangular condition estimate
STRDI	FOR	Real triangular determinant, inverse, inertia
STRSL	FOR	Real triangular solver
SUD	FOR	This is the test driver for matrix update subs.
SMACH	FOR	Computes machine dependent parameters of floating
ISAMAX	FOR	This and the following are the support
SASUM	FOR	routines from the "Basic Linear Algebraic
SAXPY	FOR	Subroutine" library. These handle vector
SCOPY	FOR	movement and arithmetic calculations.
SDOT	FOR	
SNRM2	FOR	
SROT	FOR	
SROTG	FOR	
SSCAL	FOR	
SSWAP	FOR	
NOTES554	TXT	A comprehensive writeup on use of these routines

SEX	FOR	Main routine/driver for testing the exchange routines.
SG	FOR	Main routine/driver for testing the SG routines.
SGT	FOR	Main routine/driver for testing the SGT routines.
SP	FOR	Main routine/driver for testing the SP routines.
SQR	FOR	Main routine/driver for testing the SQR routines.
SS	FOR	Main routine/driver for testing the SS routines.
SSV	FOR	Main routine/driver for testing the SSV routines.
ST	FOR	Main routine/driver for testing the ST routines.
SUD	FOR	This is the test driver for matrix update subs.
SCH	LNK	The link list of binaries for the single precision
SEX	LNK	The link list of binaries for the SEX test set.
SGT	LNK	The link list of binaries for the single precision
SP	LNK	The link list of binaries for the single precision
SQR	LNK	The link list of binaries for the single precision
SS	LNK	The link list of binaries for the single precision
SSV	LNK	The link list of binaries for the single precision
ST	LNK	The link list of binaries for the single precision
SUD	LNK	An undocumented link list.

555 LINPACK Drivers
v1

The Linear Equation Package (LINPACK) is a set of routines which solves systems of linear equations and related problems. This package was developed by the Applied Mathematics Division of Argonne National Laboratory; this source code was taken from a distribution disk provided by International Mathematics and Statistical Libraries, Inc. (IMSL).

Usage: Math and science students.

System Requirements: Fortran complier, 256K memory, color display, graphics card and printer and one drive unit.

How to Start: Consult README and INDEX for program information.

Suggested Donation: $10.00

File Descriptions:

INDEX		An index of all the routines on the library and driver disks
README		A comprehensive writeup on use of these routines
SEX	CAL	Undocumented file
SUD	CAL	Undocumented file
SCH	FOR	Main routine/driver for testing the SCH routines.

590 Nuclear Magnetic Resonance (NMR)
v1.0

This disk contains a highly technical and useful NMR analysis program. Nuclear Magnetic Resonance is used in many advanced chemistry applications and this program allows the analysis of this technique. Written by a professor of chemistry at the University of South Florida, this package is unique in the fact that it displays the calculated spectrum including adjustable peak broadening. Simulated plotting of very complex molecules, such as strong coupled proton spectra are also allowed. Parameters for up to seven spins (nucleii) can be calculated.

Usage: For the advanced chemistry/physics student.

System Requirements: 256K memory, graphics printer and card, mono or color display, and one disk drive.

How to Start: Type NMR to enter the main program. Consult NMR.DOC for program information.

Suggested Donation: $10.00

File Descriptions:

————	——	NMR submissions
NMR	BAT	Batch file to start program
NMR	DOC	Short documentation about the program
NMR?	BAS	Basic code for program modules 0 — 7
NMR?	EXE	Compiled version of module 0 — 7
SCRATCH	MNR	Misc data file for program

623
SPPC System Demo (3.0) (Disk 2 of 2)
v3

This is a demo of SPPC, a fully interactive statistical package that enables you to enter, manage and analyze simple and complex sets of data. In order to use the SPPC, you must enter your data and store it on a diskette or hard disk file. You can then conduct any statistical analysis that is available. NOTE: This is the second of a two disk program. The first disk is on DISK 232.

Usage: Statistical analysis

System Requirements: 128K, two disk drives, monochrome/graphics display

How to Start: Unarchive the programs following the instructions on disk in files named README.* .

File Descriptions:

ARCE	COM	Archiving program
README	*	Instruction files
SPPC0	ARC	Archived sections of SPPC demonstration
SPPC3	ARC	"
SPPC4	ARC	"

638
SST Version 1.00 (Disk 1 of 2)
v1

SuperSTat Share is a shareware statistical package for analyzing the results of market surveys and poles. The statistical analysis is very complete. The program is operated by choosing items from menus and filling in forms on the screen. This version allows 25 variables and 50 data columns with up to nine values to the variable.

THIS IS A TWO DISK SET THAT REQUIRES BOTH TO FUNCTION.

Usage: Statistical analysis of market surveys

System Requirements: 128K, two disk drives, Hercules graphics display, Epson-compatible printer.

How to Start: After consulting the NOTES638.TXT and SST.DOC for information, initiate the program by entering SSTMENU at the DOS prompt.

Suggested Donation: $35.00; $20.00 for students

File Descriptions:

SCATTER	EXE	Scatter plot program
CROSS	EXE	Cross tabulate program
FREQ	EXE	Frequency distribution analysis program
SSTMENU	EXE	Main menu and system management program
SST	DEF	System configuration file
TEST	VRN	Analysis Module
TEST	APD	Analysis Module
TEST	DTA	Analysis Module
TEST	TTL	Analysis Module
INT	DTA	Analysis Module
INT	APD	Analysis Module
INT	TTL	Analysis Module
INT	VRN	Analysis Module

639
SST Version 1.00
(Disk 2 of 2)
v1

SuperSTat Share is a two disk, shareware statistical package for analyzing the results of market surveys and polls. The statistical analysis is very complete. The program is operated by choosing items from menus and filling in forms on the screen. This version allows 25 variables and 50 data columns with up to nine values to the variable.

THIS IS A TWO DISK SET THAT REQUIRES BOTH TO FUNCTION.

Usage: Statistical analysis of market surveys.

File Descriptions:

SSTMENU	EXE	The menu and system management program
SST	DEF	Configuration file
DATAMAN	EXE	The data management module
CODEMAN	EXE	The code entry module
FILEMAN	EXE	The file management module
SST	DOC	The short form of the SST Manual

654
KWIKSTAT
(Disk 1 of 2)
v1

KWIKSTAT is a graphics-oriented program for scientific statistical analysis. It can import ASCII files and DBF (dBase III) files, as well as building it's own databases. It is entirely menu-controlled. There is a brief tutorial with the program, but this program assumes knowledge of statistics. The major modules on this disk include:

1. DATA Create a database, enter and edit data

2. STAT1 Descriptive statistics, graphical presentations including:

HISTOGRAM : examine the distribution of a continuous variable SCATTERPLOT : examine the relationship between two variables BOX PLOT : method of looking at the distribution of the data (0, 25th, 50th, 75, and 100 percentile) 3-D BAR CHART: examine three dimensions of a table of counts

3. STAT2 Comparative statistics, T-tests and One Way Analysis of Variance (ANOVA) on independent or repeated observations.

NOTE: FULL DOCUMENTATION IS ON THE SECOND DISK, Number 655!

Usage: Statistical Analysis

System Requirements: At least 196K, a graphics, EGA or PGA monitor (Monochrome or Hercules won't work for the graphics) and two disk drives, though a hard disk is recommended.

How to Start: To read program information, consult the READ.ME and print the manual in KS.DOC

● To run, enter: KWIKLOAD and press ENTER.

Suggested Donation: $35.00 plus $4.00 S&H covers full documentation in bound manual and upgrade information

File Descriptions:

GO	BAT	Tells you preliminary information
READ	ME	File containing current information — READ IT!
DATA	EXE	KWIKSTAT program to create, enter and edit data
STAT1	EXE	KWIKSTAT descriptive statistics & graphics
STAT2	EXE	KWIKSTAT T-tests and ANOVA
KS	BAT	Batch file to begin KWIKSTAT
KWIKLOAD	BAT	Used to load KWIKSTAT to hard disk
KWIKSTAT	HLP	KWIKSTAT help file
ORDER		How to become a registered user, order manuals

655
KWIKSTAT
(Disk 2 of 2)
v1

KWIKSTAT is a graphics-oriented program for scientific statistical analysis.

The major modules on Disk 2 are:

1. REPORT Outputs reports about the data, output ASCII text files, and examine the contents of the database or other files.

2. STAT3 Regression:Simple and Multiple Linear Regression

3. STAT4 Survival Analysis, Life Tables, Plots

4. KS.DOC Documentation

Usage: Statistical Analysis

File Descriptions:

READ	ME	File containing current information — READ IT!
REPORT	EXE	Report module
STAT3	EXE	Simple linear and multiple linear regression
STAT4	EXE	Survival Analysis
KS	DOC	This document, condensed manual
*	DBF	Some sample databases
*	DAT	Some sample ASCII data files
KWIKLOAD	BAT	Used to load KWIKSTAT to hard disk
KSROOT	BAT	Batch file for root directory
KWIKSTAT	HLP	KWIKSTAT help file.

REFERENCE MATERIALS:

Here like nowhere else does the PC-SIG Library resemble your local branch of the public library. This section is composed almost entirely of compiled databases prepared for your investigation through the use of a specific database manager. Interestingly, the overwhelming choice for these databases has been PC-FILE III (Disk No 5) as it provides for a solid retrieval structure which is well-designed for multiple keyword searches.

It is no surprise that a majority of our databases are designed to assist in identifying information about the early years of The Computer Age. The LETUS series, PC Firing Line and even our Magazine Bibliographies grouping are all such documentation; however, please note that they are indexes, not abstracts or compilations. The minority contains recipes and recipe indexes as well as a small business database.

121 Letus A-B-C Volume 1
v1

Letus A-B-C is a database in PC-FILE III format containing references to articles in the major PC-oriented magazines, beginning with 1982. This release of Letus A-B-C — the first! — covers for the following five magazines devoted to the IBM PC: Softalk (SOFT), Personal Computer Age (PCAGE), PC Magazine (PCMAG), PC World (PCW), and PC Tech Journal (PCTEC). This database provides the PC user with a tool for easily performing literature searches at a very nominal cost in one's office or home.

The search is done by keyword fields as well as identification fields (i.e., author, title, magazine issue, and page); also, the authors have included three lines that give a general description of the article.

PLEASE NOTE: THIS DISK CONTAINS THE DOCUMENTATION FOR DISKS 122, 123, 348, AND 349.

Usage: Anyone interested in broadening their knowledge of personal computers or doing a survey of how the industry grew.

System Requirements: 128K, 2 disk drives, PC-FILE III (Disk No 5)

How to Start: It is very important to read the Documentation file (Letus.doc) either by screening it (entering TYPE LETUS.DOC at the A> and using CTRL-S to pause it) or accessing it with your word processor.

- To run it, "boot-up" the DOS system and put PC-FILE system disk in drive A; enter PC-FILE and press ENTER. PC-FILE will ask where the database is; you will have put Letus A-B-C Disk No 1 in drive "B", so you will enter B:LETUS and press ENTER. The various files on this disk, corresponding to magazine and year, will be displayed on the screen for your selection.

User Comments: "A very thorough indexing that is extremely useful." "A great concept. Wish I'd thought of it myself. Too bad updating costs so much, but that's not PC-SIG's problem." "As a consultant, this saves me a lot of time."

Suggested Donation: $10.00 per disk

File Descriptions:

SOFT82	???	Softalk 1982 magazine reference files (4 files)
PCMAG82	???	PC Magazine 1982 magazine reference files (4 files)
PCAGE82	???	PC Age 1982 magazine reference files (4 files)
BYTE82	???	Byte 1982 magazine reference files (4 files)
LETUS	BAT	Batch file for starting Letus
LOGO82	COM	Generates Letus logo
LETUS	DOC	Documentation for using Letus (11 pages)

122 Letus A-B-C Volume 2
v1

Letus A-B-C is a database in PC-FILE III format containing references to articles in major PC-oriented magazines, beginning with 1982. This disk of Letus A-B-C covers the following three magazines devoted to the IBM PC: Softalk (SOFT), Personal Computer Age (PCAGE), and PC Magazine (PCMAG). This database provides the PC user with a tool for easily performing literature searches at a very nominal cost in one's office or home.

The search is done by keyword fields as well as identification fields (i.e., author, title, magazine issue, and page); also, the authors have included three lines that give a general description of the article.

Usage: Anyone interested in broadening their knowledge of personal computers or doing a survey of how the industry grew.

System Requirements: 128K, 2 disk drives, PC-FILE III (Disk No 5)

How to Start: Refer to the Documentation file (Letus.doc) located on Disk No 121

● To run, load PC-FILE drive A: with your Letus A-B-C disk in B:.

User Comments: "A very thorough indexing that is extremely useful." " Great indexing device; lots of fun to cruise around looking for helpful hints." "Almost a time capsule feeling reading this stuff..."

Suggested Donation: $10.00 per disk.

File Descriptions:

SOFT83	???	Softalk 1983 magazine reference files (4 files)
PCMAG83A	???	PC Mag. first 6 months 1983 magazine ref. files (4 files)
PCAGE83	???	PC Age 1983 magazine reference files (4 files)
LETUS	BAT	Batch file for starting Letus
LOGO83A	COM	Generates Letus logo

123 Letus A-B-C Volume 3
v1

Letus A-B-C is a database in PC-FILE III format containing references to articles in major PC-oriented magazines, beginning with 1982. This disk of Letus A-B-C covers the following four magazines devoted to the IBM PC: PC Magazine (PCMAG), PC World (PCW), and PC Tech Journal (PCTEC), Byte Magazine (BYTE). This volume covers the first half of 1983.

Usage: Anyone interested in broadening their knowledge of personal computers or doing a survey of how the industry grew.

System Requirements: 128K, 2 disk drives, PC-FILE III (Disk No 5)

How to Start: Refer to the Documentation file (Letus.doc) located on Disk No 121

● To run, load PC-FILE drive A: with your Letus A-B-C disk in B:.

User Comments: "Excellent for finding early design problems and watching how people outthunk them." "If you don't have access to old copies — which is hard even in libraries — this is the next best thing." "Once I got PC-File figured out, this proved a real treasure trove."

Suggested Donation: $10.00 per disk.

File Descriptions:

PCW83	???	PC World 1983 magazine reference files (4 files)
PCMAG83B	???	PC Magazine 2nd 6 months 1983 magazine ref. files (4 files)
PCTEC83	???	PC Tech Journal 1983 magazine reference files (4 files)
BYTE83	???	Byte 1983 magazine reference files (4 files)

| LETUS | BAT | Batch file for starting Letus |
| LOGO83B | COM | Generates Letus logo |

159
PC Firing Line/PC Underground Issue #1
v1

This is the first issue of the PC Firing Line Newsletter. It has been positioned as the underground newspaper for the IBM user. You will be presented with the untold tales and in-depth programming aids. Some of the articles are about ADA, Assembly routines, and items not written about by IBM. It also contains many sample program listings with accompanying documentation.

Usage: PC users who want programming information.

System Requirements: 64K, one disk drive, monochrome display

How to Start: To read, enter PCFL and press ENTER.

Users Comments: "Only of marginal use. newsy but not meaty." " I have all three 159, 160, 161. very good articles." "... I enjoyed reading PCFL, and hope you publish more." "I had problems running this on a PCjr, but with the "ST" utility you can get along."

Suggested Donation: $12.00

File Descriptions:

DOS1	TXT	PC-DOS and Firmware
DOS2	TXT	A bug in DOS 2.0
DOS3	TXT	The interrupt phone book
INTRO	TXT	Introduction to PC-Firing Line
LIST1	???	Test the ADS compiler in ADA, Pascal, Assembly, and C
MEMORY	TXT	Memory Management
METABAS	TXT	Bigger Basic
PRETTY1	COM	Program embellisher
SPONSORS	TXT	Sponsers/Adviters list
TXT	ADS	Advertisments
WRITEUS	TXT	Write to the company

160
PC Firing Line Issue #2 (Disk 1 of 2)
v1

This is the second issue of PC Firing Line, with the magazines official title. It has been positioned as the underground newspaper for the IBM user. You will be presented with the untold tales and in-depth programming aids. Some of the articles are ADA, Assembly routines, LISP, Fortran, and items not written about by IBM. It also contains many sample program listings with accompanying documentation.

Usage: Users who want programming information.

System Requirements: 64K, one disk drive, monochrome display

How to Start: To read, enter PCFL and press ENTER.

Users Comments: "Only of marginal use. newsy but not meaty." "I have all three 159, 160, 161. very good articles." "... I enjoyed reading PCFL, and hope you publish more." "I had problems running this on a PCjr, but with the "ST" utility you can get along. This & #161 weren't as informative as the catalog would lead you to believe."

Suggested Donation: $12.00

File Descriptions:

ADA1	TXT	A tutorial on using ADA (Part 1)
ADABOOK	REV	Book reviews on 6 different ADA books
ASM1	TXT	Introduction to Assembly language
ASM2	TXT	Using routines in DOS 1.1 and DOS 2.0
BASIC1	TXT	Simple Maze program written in BASIC
C1	TXT	Introduction to C programming
CHANGES	TXT	What is new with PC-Firing Line
DOS1	TXT	DOS — Past, Present and Future
DOS2	TXT	Is it IBM-Compatible?
EDITOR	TXT	Letter from the Editor
FORT1	TXT	Roots of 3rd and 4th Order Polynomials
FORTH1	TXT	Articles on FORTH (3 files)

161
PC Firing Line
Issue #2 (Disk 2 of 2)
v1

This is part two of the second issue from PC Firing Line. It has been positioned as the underground newspaper for the IBM user. You will be presented with the untold tales and in-depth programming aids. Some of the articles are ADA, Assembly routines, LISP, Fortran, and items not written about by IBM. It also contains many sample program listings with accompanying documentation.

Usage: For IBM users who want some more programming information.

System Requirements: 128K, one disk drive, monochrome display

How to Start: To read, enter TYPE (filename).TXT and press ENTER.

Users Comments: "Only of marginal use. newsy but not meaty." "I have all three 159, 160, 161. very good articles." "...I enjoyed reading PCFL, and hope you publish more." "I had problems running this on a PCjr, but with the "ST" utility you can get along. this & # 161 weren't as informative as the catalog would lead you to believe."

Suggested Donation: $12.00

FORTH	BAT	Will display the FORTH.MSG file
FORTH	MSG	Tells you how to create a self-booting FORTH disk
FORTH	OBJ	Ojbect code to create a self-booting FORTH disk
MANUAL	BAT	File to print the Manual for Programmer's Calculator
MANUAL	DOC	Documentation for PC.EXE
PC	EXE	Programmer's Calculator
POLYMAZE	EXE	Maze Program
SQ	C	C source code for SQ.EXE
SQ	EXE	Program to compress files

247
BOBCAT —
Business Database
v1.1

BOBCAT is a database of small business computer information. Reviews, tutorials, general articles, buying guides, even ads on special products that apply to small businesses are listed. The database may be searched by any combination of category, subject, form, product or company name. BOBCAT is distributed as user-supported software in Jim Button's PC-File III format. BOBCAT needs PC-File III, or other similar program to sort and print information and indexes in a usable format.

Usage: Small business database tool

System Requirements: 128K, 2 disk drives, PC-FILE III (Disk No 5)

How to Start: It is very important to read the Documentation file BOBCAT.TXT

● To run it, bring up PC-FILE and enter BOBCAT as you would any database/data file.

Suggested Donation: $10.00

File Descriptions:

BOBCAT01	DTA	Data base
BOBCAT01	INX	Index
BOBCAT01	HDR	Header information
BOBCAT	TXT	Help program
ORDERFRM	TXT	Order form and information to communicate with author
MAG	HDR	Header information
MAG	INX	Index
MAG	DTA	Data base
MAG	RPT	Formats a report for data from BOBCAT01.DTA
CATEGORY	RPT	Part of BOBCAT

280
Magazine Bibliographies
v1.1

This disk contains references to articles in two areas: Amateur Radios and Computers. The computer magazine bibliography begins approximately August, 1983. The Amateur Radio and Shortwave bibliographies begin January, 1982. Most technical articles are listed. Also, many letters or other comments that refer to technical topics are listed. Articles of a short "news" nature and other general articles are not listed. Software announcements are not listed but many true software reviews are listed.

Usage: For those interested in amateur radio or technical information.

System Requirements: 64K, one disk drive, monochrome display

How to Start: Consult the .DOC and .TXT files for each program.

● To run a program suffixed .COM or .EXE, enter its name and press ENTER.

User Comments: "These files have been extremely helpful in researching the ham radio literature. The RTTY program that was buried on the disk has performed well."

File Descriptions:

HAMINDEX	1	Index of codes and settings for a ham radio operator
HAMINDEX	2	Index of codes and settings for a ham radio operator
HAMINDEX	3	Index of codes and settings for a ham radio operator
HAMINDEX	DOC	Documentation for hamindex 1,2,3
CONFIG	TTY	Configuration file for PCRTTY.EXE
CWP	DOC	Documentation for CWP.EXE
CWP	EXE	Easy to use code practice tutor(char & word rates)
PCFILTER	EXE	Many feature file cleanup up program
PCFILTER	DOC	Documentation for PCFILTER.EXE
PCRTTY	EXE	Full featured ham radio RTTY baudot program
PCRTTY	DOC	Documentation for PCRTTY.EXE

281
Recipe Index
v1.1

iRecipe83(tm) is a database index to 1800 recipes that appeared in the 1983 issues of Women's Day and Family Circle magazines. If these magazines are saved in your home, this database will provide the advantages of computer indexing. Note: it is necessary that you have saved the magazines, or have them readily available from a library. iRecipe83 is an INDEX ONLY, not a repeat of the recipes.

Usage: For those interested in finding new recipes.

System Requirements: 128K, 1 disk drive, monochrome display

How to Start: Read documentation in IR83PCF.DOC. To print documentation, place disk in A: drive and enter DOC and press ENTER.

User Comments: "Not very useful unless you have access to GOOD HOUSEKEEPING MAGAZINE back issues." "Wish it gave the recipies, too. It only tells where to find them." "Requires a database that I do not have." "Wife loves it!!!"

Suggested Donation: $20.00

File Descriptions:

DOC	BAT	Prints documentation (IR83PCF.DOC)
IR83PCF	DOC	Documentation (55K)
*	DTA	Data base files
*	RPT	Report formats
NESTMENU	DOC	List of menus
NESTMENU	BAT	Prints NESTMENU.DOC

348
Letus A-B-C
Volume 4
v1

Letus A-B-C is a database in PC-FILE III format containing references to articles in major PC-oriented magazines, beginning with 1982. This disk of Letus A-B-C covers the following eight magazines devoted to the IBM PC: Softalk (SOFT), Personal Computer Age (PCAGE), PC Magazine (PCMAG), PC World (PCW), PC Tech Journal (PCTEC), Byte Magazine (BYTE), PCjr Magazine (PCJR), PCjr WORLD Magazine (PCJRW). This volume covers the first quarter of 1984.

Usage: Anyone interested in broadening their knowledge of personal computers or doing a survey of how the industry grew.

System Requirements: 128K, 2 disk drives, PC-FILE III (Disk No 5)

How to Start: Refer to the Documentation file (Letus.doc) located on Disk No 121

- To run, load PC-FILE drive A: with your Letus A-B-C disk in B:.

User Comments: "Great indexing." "I thought it had the magazine's articles too." "Great for backtracking computer developments."

Suggested Donation: $10.00 per disk.

File Descriptions:

LETUS	BAT	Batch file for starting LETUS A-B-C
LOGO84A	COM	generates LETUS logo part 1
PLOGO84	COM	generates LETUS logo part 2
BYTE84A	???	BYTE Magazine Jan-Mar 1984 reference files (4 files)
PCAGE84A	???	PC AGE Magazine Jan-Mar 1984 reference files (4 files)
PCJR84A	???	PCjr Magazine Jan-Mar 1984 reference files (4 files)
PCJRW84A	???	PCjr WORLD Magazine Jan-Mar 1984 reference files (4 files)
PCMAG84A	???	PC Magazine Jan-Mar 1984 reference files (4 files)
PCTEC84A	???	PC TECH JOURNAL Jan-Mar 1984 reference files (4 files)
PCW84A	???	PC WORLD Magazine Jan-Mar 1984 reference files (4 files)
SOFT84A	???	SOFTALK Magazine Jan-Mar 1984 reference files (4 files)

349
Letus A-B-C
Volume 5
v1

For descriptions, see Disk No 348.

Suggested Donation: $10.00 per disk.

File Descriptions:

FILES	TXT	Description of LETUS A-B-C
LETUS	BAT	Batch file for starting LETUS A-B-C
LETUS	DOC	Information about LETUS
LOGO84N5	COM	Generates LETUS logo part 1
PLOGO82	COM	Generates LETUS logo part 2
BYTE84B	???	BYTE Magazine Apr-Jun 1984 reference files (4 files)
PCMAG84B	???	PC Magazine Apr-Jun 1984 reference files (4 files)
PCTEC84B	???	PC TECH JOURNAL Apr-Jun 1984 reference files (4 files)
PCW84B	???	PC WORLD Magazine Apr-Jun 1984 reference files (4 files)

350
Letus A-B-C
Volume 6
v1

For descriptions, see Disk No 348.

PLEASE NOTE: THIS DISK CONTAINS THE DOCUMENTATION FOR DISKS 544, 545, 546, 547, 548, 549, 550, AND 551.

Suggested Donation: $10.00 per disk.

File Descriptions:

FILES	TXT	Description of LETUS A-B-C
LETUS	BAT	Batch file for starting LETUS A-B-C
LETUS	DOC	Information about LETUS
LOGO84N6	COM	Generates LETUS logo part 1
PLOGO82	COM	Generates LETUS logo part 2
PCAGE84B	???	PC AGE Magazine Apr-Jun 1984 reference files (4 files)
PCJR84B	???	PCjr Magazine Apr-Jun 1984 reference files (4 files)
PCJRW84B	???	PCjr WORLD Magazine Apr-Jun 1984 reference files (4 files)
PCPRO84B	???	PC PRODUCT REVIEW Apr-Jun 1984 reference files (4 files)

| PNUT84B | ??? | PEANUT Magazine Apr-Jun 1984 reference files (4 files) |
| SOFT84B | ??? | SOFTALK Magazine Apr-Jun 1984 reference files (4 files) |

544
LETUS A-B-C
Volume 7
v1

For descriptions, see Disk No 348.

Suggested Donation: $10.00 per disk.

File Descriptions:

BYTE84C	???	Byte Magazine Third Quarter 1984 reference files (4 files)
PCMAG84C	???	PC Magazine Third Quarter 1984 reference files (4 files)
PCTEC84C	???	PC Tech Journal Third Qtr 1984 reference files (4 files)
PCW84C	???	PC World Third Quarter 1984 reference files (4 files)
LETUS	BAT	Batch file to generate Letus logo
LOGO84N7	COM	Executable program that generates Letus logo

545
LETUS A-B-C
Volume 8
v1

For descriptions, see Disk No 348.

Suggested Donation: $10.00 per disk.

File Descriptions:

BCOMP84C	???	Business Computing 3rd Qtr 1984 reference files (4 files)
PCJR84C	???	PCjr Magazine 3rd Quarter 1984 reference files (4 files)
PCJRW84C	???	PCjr WORLD Magazine 3rd Qtr 1984 reference files (4 files)
PCPRO84C	???	PC PRODUCT REVIEW 3rd Qtr 1984 reference files (4 files)
PCWK84C	???	PC WEEK Third Quarter 1984 reference files (4 files)
PNUT84C	???	PEANUT Magazine 3rd Quarter 1984 reference files (4 files)
SOFT84C	???	SOFTALK Magazine 3rd Quarter 1984 reference files (4 files)

| LOGO84N8 | COM | Executable file to generate Letus logo |
| LETUS | BAT | Batch file to generate logo |

546
LETUS A-B-C
Volume 9
v1

For desccriptions, see Disk No 348.

Suggested Donation: $10.00 per disk.

File Descriptions:

PCMAG84D	???	PC Magazine 1984 4th Quarter reference files (4 files)
PCWK84D	???	PC Week 1984 4th Quarter reference files (4 files)
BCOMP84D	???	Business Computing 1984 4th Qtr reference files (4 files)
PCJRW84D	???	PCjr WORLD Magazine 1984 4th Qtr reference files (4 files)

547
LETUS A-B-C
Volume 10
v1

For descriptions, see Disk No 348.

Suggested Donation: $10.00 per disk.

File Descriptions:

PCW84D	???	PC WORLD Magazine 1984 4th Qtr reference files (4 files)
CPUT84	???	COMPUTING Magazine 1984 4th Qtr reference files (4 files)
JR84	???	jr Magazine 1984 4th Qtr reference files (4 files)
PJ84	???	Programmers Journal 1984 reference files (4 files)
PCJR84D	???	PCjr Magazine 1984 Fourth Quarter reference files (4 files)
PCTEC84D	???	PC TECH JOURNAL 1984 4th Qtr reference files (4 files)
BYTE84D	???	BYTE Magazine 1984 4th Qtr reference files (4 files)
PCPRO84D	???	PC PRODUCT REVIEW 1984 4th Qtr reference files (4 files)

548 LETUS A-B-C
Volume 11
v1

For description, see Disk No 348.

Suggested Donation: $10.00 per disk.

File Descriptions:

BCOMP85A	???	Business Computing 1985 1st Qtr reference files (4 files)
BYTE85A	???	BYTE Magazine 1985 1st Quarter reference files (4 files)
PCMAG85A	???	PC Magazine 1985 First Quarter reference files (4 files)
PCPRO85A	???	PC Professional 1985 1st Quarter reference files (4 files)
PCTEC85A	???	PC Tech Journal 1985 1st Quarter reference files (4 files)

549 LETUS A-B-C
Volume 12
v1

For descriptions, see Disk No 348.

Suggested Donation: $10.00 per disk.

File Descriptions:

PCWK85A	???	PC Week 1985 First Quarter reference files (4 files)
PJ85A	???	Programmers Journal 1985 1st Qtr reference files (4 files)
PCW85A	???	PC Week 1985 First Quarter reference files (4 files)
PCJRW85A	???	PCjr WORLD 1985 First Quarter reference files (4 files)

550 LETUS A-B-C
Volume 13
v1

For descriptions, see Disk No 348.

Suggested Donation: $10.00 per disk.

File Descriptions:

BYTE85B	???	BYTE Magazine Second Quarter 1985 reference files (4 files)
PCWK85B	???	PC Week Second Quarter 1985 reference files (4 files)

551 LETUS A-B-C
Volume 14
v1

For descriptions, see Disk No 348.

Suggested Donation: $10.00 per disk.

File Descriptions:

PCMAG85B	???	PC Magazine Second Quarter 1985 reference files
PCPRO85B	???	PC Professional 2nd Quarter 1985 reference files (4 files)
PCW85B	???	PC WORLD Second Quarter 1985 reference files (4 files)
PCJRW85B	???	PCjr WORLD Second Quarter 1985 reference files (4 files)
PCTEC85B	???	PC Tech Journal Second Quarter 1985 reference files (4 files)
PCOMP85B	???	Personal Computing 2nd Qtr 1985 reference files (4 files)
PJ85B	???	Programmers Journal 2nd Qtr 1985 reference files (4 files)

572
Federal Building
Life Cost Comparison
V1

The Federal Building Life-Cycle Cost (FBLCC)
program diskette contains the FBLCC programs and
data files referred in the National Bureau of
Standards Technical Note 1222, "A User's Guide to
the Federal Building Life-Cycle Cost Computer
program," April, 1976. This program should not be
used without the Reference Users Guide.
Information on how to obtain this doccumentation
can be obtained from:

U.S. Department of Energy
Office of the Assistant Secretary for Conservation
and Renewable Energy
Federal Energy Management Program CE 10.1
Washington, D.C. 20585

SPECIAL APPLICATIONS:

These are the most unique programs in the Library. They are specialized in format, content and application. They deal with unusual subjects not covered in our other categories. Topics include:

- Astronomy
- Farming and agricultural
- Personal health
- Nutrition
- Bible reference
- Manuscript management
- Word processing aids
- And more!

Yes, this selection encompasses the heavens and the earth. For example, there are four disks of programs for astronomical computations (including a two disk set for ephemeris calculations) as well as a three disk series on computerized applications for farming situations.

Some programs deal with specialized personal health problems, like our two different databases for nutrition analysis or the health risk appraisal program from the Center for Disease Control. Some, like the three-disk set The World Digitized, have unique data. There are also some with special formats for special data, like The Wordworker (a two disk reference tool for word study in the New Testament). If you anticipate going to Europe soon, you might need the foreign language tutorials covering French, German, Spanish and Italian vocabularies.

Due to the impact of word processing on publishing, we have two special programs worth noting: one prepares a database of references and modifies them according to the bibliographic dicta of any particular scholarly or technical journal. Another tracks your manuscripts as they seek publication. For the royalties, consider the BUSINESS section.

23 Bowling League Secretary
v3

The Bowling League Secretary is comprised of twelve programs that cover everything needed to run a league. This highly generalized system handles: League Name, Team, Configuration, Handicap basis, and Schedule. As distributed, the system can handle 24 teams, up to 9 bowlers per team, and up to a 50 week season. Programs are provided to initialize all master files, enter scores and print standings (weekly), as well as prepare Bookaverage listings, final team/bowler standings, and display or print individual team/bowler record sheets.

Usage: TOTAL documentation for your Bowling League!

System Requirements: 64K, two disk drives, monochrome display; a color/graphics adaptor and color monitor are required for files marked "+".

How to Start: To run BASIC programs consult the directions in GETTING STARTED for your configuration. Consult BOWLING.DOC for program documentation.

User Comments: "Inexpensive method of maintaining bowling records. The bowlers of America salute you and the writer." "One of the most useful I have received from you yet, despite the documentation."

File Descriptions:

— — — —	— —	BOWLING
BOWLING	DOC	Documentation for Bowling League Secretary Programs
BOWLFILE	FD	Part of League Secretary Bowling application
BOWLING	BAT	Batch programs to run Bowling League Secretary programs
MENU	BAS	Bowling League Secretary application — run this program first
SCORES	BAS	Program used to enter bowling scores
RECAP	BAS	
CREATE	BAS	
SCHEDULE	BAS	Program used to create and use bowling schedules
CHANGE	BAS	Program used with SCHEDULE.BAS
PRINT	BAS	Program used with SCHEDULE.BAS
DETAIL	BAS	Program used with SCHEDULE.BAS
SORTFILE	BAS	Program used with SCHEDULE.BAS

RECORDD	BAS	Program used with SCHEDULE.BAS
RECORDP	BAS	Program used with SCHEDULE.BAS
FINAL	BAS	Program used with SCHEDULE.BAS
RESET	BAS	Program used with SCHEDULE.BAS
BOWLPRT1	EWF	EASYWRITER format documentation for Bowling programPart 1
BOWLPRT2	EWF	EASYWRITER format documentation for Bowling programPart 1
*	BAS	League Secretary Bowling application program files (11 files)
DRAW2	BAS+	Update to PDRAW (graphics)
MOUNTAIN	BAS	Enhanced version of Artillery
STARWARS	BAS	PC adaptation of popular space game
TAXRETRN	VC	VISICALC template to use for your income taxes

192 Health Risk

v1

A PC conversion of the Center For Disease Control health risk appraisal program will help MANY medical professionals — doctors, nurses, public health administrators, etc. — in delivering quality care. Dr. Arden Aston, M.D., the author/converter, placed it here, and says: ".. I have found it very useful in my patient education program. I feel my patients are more likely to change their health habits if I can show them how this will benefit their long term health." He recommends that the program only be use by qualified health professionals who have the experience and training to adequately interpret individual results. Further information on the program can be obtained directly from the Center for Disease Control in Atlanta, Georgia.

Usage: Risk analysis and patient education

System Requirements: 128K, one or two disk drives, printer urged.

How to Start: Load DOS and type HRA1 to enter the main program. Consult HRA.DOC for program documentation.

User Comments: "Interesting way to demonstrate health risks to the lay person. "The program is well put together, easy to run and very informative." "The health risk appraisal is valuable to those health practitioners who can sit a patient (or friend) down to answer these questions. They can also be used by non-health professionals to help establish some goals to improving the health of the individual."

File Descriptions:

HRAINP1	EXE	Interactive input module
HRA1	EXE	Main health/risk program
HRAPRINT	EXE	Program to set up printer
*		Data tables (17 files)
HRADOC	TXT	Documentation

231 REFLIST

v2.1

REFLIST is a user-supported program that makes lists of references, bibliographies and footnotes. It was written to be easy to use and menu- driven. REFLIST consists of two programs and several files. One program reads through your own text file and formats references. The second program enters the refences into a master catalog, maintained in the support files. Other files serve as reference formats from various journals for the formatting program to copy.

Usage: For authors of scientific and technical manuscripts.

System Requirements: 64K, one disk drive, monochrome display

Features:

- REFLIST reads the manuscript and compiles a list of the citations to other publications.
- It draws the full reference out of a Master File.
- Formats the reference list according to the style requirements of almost any journal.
- It can return to the text file and replace the citations with the appropriate numbers.
- Change the example formats to add new ones to the collection.

How to Start: After reading the REFLIST.DOC manual, run it by entering REFLIST and pressing ENTER at the DOS prompt.

User Comments: "A very useful program for those who do a lot of scholarly or technical writing. It make compiling bibliographies and checking references much less tedious." "A good idea, but a poor program- apparently written to satisfy the author's needs...The formats are not flexible enough to adapt to bibliographic styles and needs that differ from the author's." "An absolute godsend for those who write scientific manuscripts or any scientific publications. Use of this program with WordStar makes manuscript writing easier by a factor of 100." "Very handy program for science and technical writers. Does a nice job of sorting and reformatting literature references, a very dull and disagreeable task."

Suggested Donation: $25.00

File Descriptions:

FILEREFS	EXE	Program to file your reprints
REFLIST	EXE	Program to formats references
REFLIST	DOC	Instruction manual (32K)
MASTFILE		Reprint master file
PROTOTYP	???	Prototype formats
EXAMPLE	MSS	Text to practice on
FILECATA	LOG	List of files on disk

262
PC-GOLF
Version 1.5
v1.2

PC-GOLF measures and analyses your golf performance. The professional golf instructor can also use the convenience and clarity of PC-GOLF to the student's benefit. It keeps track of your scores and your putts for each hole on your home course. Use it with confidence that it will help raise your level of achievement and enjoyment on the course. By inputing your golf score and the courses you play, this program will find the problem areas in your game. The program does the work so you can sit back and enjoy your game!

Usage: Enjoying and improving your golf game!

System Requirements: Monochrome or graphics display, 64K of memory and two disk drives.

How to Start: To run BASIC programs consult the directions in GETTING STARTED for your configuration. Consult USER.DOC for program documentation.

User Comments: "This is a good program for the serious golfer." "I enjoy this program because of the ease of looking back at my previous scores and seeing the pretty good graphics chart on screen." "It analyzes several areas of golf scores and presents them in a useful format. It is quite slow, however."

File Descriptions:

————	——	PC-GOLF Package
AMAIN	ZRO	Main program
AUTOEXEC	BAT	Used to autostart program (BASICA required)
USER	DOC	Used to print documentation — type: BASICA USER.DOC to start
*	*	Additional PC-GOLF files

298
Planets/Wator/
Leygref's Castle
v1.3

PLANETS computes information relating to the position, distance, magnitude, etc. for the major planets on a specified date and time. It also computes the position of four of the major asteroids and HALLEY'S COMET and allows you to move the charts forward and backward in time to see the positions on certain dates! WATOR — in forms WATERMON for monochrome and WATORCOL for color — is a battle-for-survival game where you are in charge of developing a harmonious ecology between them. A real figure-juggling act and good fun to watch! LEYGREF'S CASTLE is a fantasy adventure game. The castle is randomly stocked for each game, thereby ensuring a different adventure each time you play.

Usage: Astronomical charting and fun!

System Requirements: 64k, two disk drives, some programs on this disk require color graphics.

How to Start: Load DOS and type PLANETS to enter the PLANETS program, LEYGREF1 to play LEYGREF'S CASTLE, WATORMON (for monochrome) or WATORCOL+ (for color monitor) to play WATOR. Consult the .DOC files for program documentation.

User Comments: "PLANETS is a good informative program for those interested in space and astronomy." "Good ephemeris. I intend to use this together with disk 489 to cast true natal horoscopes." "Leygref's castle is pretty good (similar to Wizard on #274)."

Suggested Donation: $10.00 for PLANETS

File Descriptions:

——	——	Planets
PLANETS	DOC	Documentation
PLANETS	COM	Is for use without an 8087
PLANETSA	COM	Is for use with an 8087 Arithmetic coprocessor
——	——	WATOR — Fish & sharks engage in battle for survival
WATORMON	PAS	Source code, Turbo Pascal, for monochrome card
WATORCOL	PAS	Source for color card
WATORMON	COM	Compiled code for mono card
WATORCOL+	COM	Compiled code for color card
WATOR	DOC	List of files
READ	ME	Notes from author
——	——	LEYGREF'S CASTLE
LEYGREF1	BAS	Main program
LEYGREF	INS	Instructions (7K text file)
LEYGREF	PIC	Part of LEYGREF
LEYGREF	DAT	Part of LEYGREF
LEYGREF	CMD	Part of LEYGREF

342
Golf Scorecard
v1

A menu-driven system that keeps track of golf scores. Keeps track of a number of golfers, courses, and golf rounds. Good way to track the improvement of your golf game. It is written in BASIC, and includes a compiled, as well as the source files. For the computer-oriented golfer, or the golf oriented computist, a handy analysis tool.

Usage: Golf game improvement

System Requirements: Monochrome or graphics display, 64K of memory and two disk drives;

How to Start: Load DOS and type GOLFCARD to enter the main program. Consult README.DOC for additional program information.

File Descriptions:

COURSE	DAT	Golf course data
COURSPTR	DAT	Pointer for number of courses in COURSE.DAT
GOLFCARD	BAS	Basic source for GOLFCARD program
GOLFCARD	EXE	Main program [type in to run GOLFCARD program]
GOLFERS	DAT	Contains data on golfers
GOLFPTR	DAT	Pointer for the number of golfers in GOLFERS.DAT
README	DOC	Introduction
ROUND	DAT	Golfers round data
ROUNDPTR	DAT	Pointer for the number of rounds in ROUND.DAT

347
PC-FOIL
v1

PC-FOIL and its companion program FOIL-EDIT combine to provide a multipurpose tool creation of overhead transparencies and attractive documents. When you combine the large print, bold print, and boxes with your own creativity, the effect can be dramatic. You develop the presentation or document using FOIL-EDIT and print it using PC-FOIL. FOIL-EDIT is an excellent general purpose full-screen editor. You can use it for creating programs, as a word processor, or for just modifying any standard DOS file that you have, such as BAT files or data base files. It is fast and easy to use and offers both menus and commands, depending upon your skill level. PC-FOIL is complete with on-line help.

Usage: Presentation graphics and transparencies

System Requirements: 128k, two disk drives, 80-column display, graphics printer. This program has been tested on a 128k PCjr and an IBM 3270 PC.

How to Start: Load DOS and type E to enter the FOILEDIT program or F to enter the PC-FOIL program. Consult PC-FOIL.DOC for program documentation.

User Comments: "Great program; Good wordprocessor with graphics capabilities if you are using an IBM compatible printer." "Looks to be a great product! Getting the documentation was very straight forward and the material is very easy to follow. A little more variety in type fonts might be useful."

File Descriptions:

FOIL	LET	Font to let printer print large letters
FOILEDIT	EXE	Main full screen editor program
FOILEDIT	HLP	Help screens for editor
PC-FOIL	DOC	Instructions on how to print manual
PC-FOIL	EXE	Main presentation program
PC-FOIL	FOI	PC-FOIL program to display or print manual
PC-FOIL	HLP	Help screens for PC-FOIL and FOILEDIT
PC-FOIL?	FOI	Manual for FOILEDIT and PC-FOIL programs (5 Files)
PROFILE	DEF	Easy to set up default parameters for output,line widths, ect.

CENTRAL	DAT	Data file for AIRNAV.BAS covering the central area of USA
EASTCST	DAT	Data file for AIRNAV.BAS covering the east coast of USA
USA	DAT	Data file for AIRNAV.BAS
AIRNAV	BAS	Program to prepare a flight log
——	——	Starfinder
RUNFIRST	BAS	Introduction
PRINTERS	BAS	
DIRECTOR	BAS	Prints out a directory for the program
USERMANU	BAS	User's Manual
STARFIND	BAS	Star and constellation finder program (in basic)
STARFIND	EXE	Star and constellation finder program (executed)

447
The Sky
v1.1

Two astral programs: AIRNAV helps prepare a flight log for flight over a predetermined route of up to twenty points (for most light aircraft this provides waypoints close enough together, and enough waypoints for one leg without refueling). The log gives the geographic coordinates of the point, the distance between points, the true course and the estimated time between points. It prints space on the log for entering actual time between points. All flight planning is done on the basis of one estimated speed for the entire series of legs. The second program, STARFINDER, allows you to locate the various stars and constellations.

Usage: Plotting flight plans, scanning the skies!

System Requirements: 64k, two disk drives, color-graphics.

How to Start: Load DOS and type STARFIND to enter the STARFIND program

- To run the BASIC programs consult the directions for GETTING STARTED for your configuration. Consult AIRNAV.DOC for program information on AIRNAV.BAS.

User Comments: AIRNAV: "This program has helped me a great deal in planning my flying trips." "This program is another great find in the public domain jungle." STARFIND: "Terrible documentation; Interesting programs — not that useful but educational." "The documentation itself is good, however I dislike manuals on designed for any size less than 8-1/2 x 11 — it wastes too much paper." "I had hoped the STARFINDER program would be more comprehensive; good, though, for very basic information."

Suggested Donation: $35.00 for STARFINDER

File Descriptions:

——	——	Air Navigation
READ	ME	Text file
REVIEW	BAS	
AIRNAV	DOC	Documentation file
WESTCST	DAT	Data file for AIRNAV.BAS covering the west coast of USA
NORCOAST	DAT	Data file for AIRNAV.BAS covering the north coast of USA

459
Assorted Agricultural Programs
v1

From the Department of Agriculture and Applied Economics at the University of Minnesota comes this wide-ranging collection of BASICA decision aids for Farm Management. MINN-AIDS covers a set of topical papers for small to large sized farms and makes you appreciate the intricacies of efficient farming!

Usage: Analysis of farm management problems and opportunities

System Requirements: 64k, two disk drives, color-graphics.

How to Start: To run BASIC programs consult the directions in GETTING STARTED for your configuration. Consult README.DOC for additional program information.

File Descriptions:

ACRSCALC	BAS	Analysis of Federal Depreciation Computations
AUTOEXEC	BAT	Automatic instructions to read this file
BESTCROP	BAS	Price & Yield Analysis of Crop Choices (Equal-margin)
DATECALC	BAS	Computes Future (Gestation) Dates & Calendars
DRYSTORE	BAS	Analysis of Harvest and Storage Cost & Alternatives
FARMBID	BAS	Determines the Maximum Bid Price for Land or a Farm.
FEEDPIGS	BAS	Should I Feed Out a Batch of Feeder Pigs ?
FEEDSILO	BAS	Calculates Likely Dairy Feed in a Silo Given Feed Rate
FEEDVALU	BAS	Given Corn & SBM Values, What's a Feed Worth ?
MENU	BAS	Menu program for BASIC pgms on this disk

PEARSON	BAS	Balances 1 Ration Nutrient from 2 Feed Sources
READ	BAT	Batch file to provide instructions for SCROLLCK.COM
README	DOC	Documentation file
RUN	BAT	Batch file requests date, loads BASICA & starts MINNAIDS
SCROLLCK	COM	Scroll lock — control with shift keys
SDIR	COM	2 column directory +
SOWINDEX	BAS	Determines a Sow Index, Relative to the Group
STEERBID	BAS	Calculates Equivalent FOB prices for Fat Steers at Farm
TIMEC	COM	Help program
ULOGO	BAS	University of Minnesota Logo — START HERE
USERDOCS	BAS	Explains How to Make Hardcopy Documentation of MINNAIDS

DIET	BAS	Diet Detective Jr. — March 1983
DOLLAR	BAS	Dollar Detective — personal budgeting — March 1983
HAYCRAB	BAS	Hay cost returns and analysis — March 1982
HELLO	BAS	Alberta Agriculture menu program — August 1984
INSTALL	BAT	Batch file to add system and BASICA to disk
LANDPUR	BAS	Land purchase decisions — February 1983
LOAN	BAS	Loan calculator — August 1984
RATION	BAS	Ration balancing — May 1984
README	DOC	Author supplied documentation file

460
Alberta Agricultural Programs
v1

Another useful collection of decision aids for Farm Management. This one is from Alberta College's Department of Agriculture, and each one analyzes a specific farming related situation. If you are involved in any aspect of farming, or are a student of analysis methods, this disk holds a lot of information.

Usage: Farm management

System Requirements: Monochrome display, 64K and one disk drive.

How to Start: To run BASIC programs consult the directions in GETTING STARTED for your configuration. Consult README.DOC for additional program information.

User Comments: "Good collection of AG software suitable for fairs, farm shows, etc." "Talking old conservative ranchers into computers is hard enough; this helps." "Our the local school district AG department likes it."

File Descriptions:

AUTOEXEC	BAT	Batch file BASICA HELLO
BESTCROP	BAS	Breakeven prices & yields — March 1982
BFP	BAS	Breakeven feeder prices — July 1984
CARCOST	BAS	Car or truck costing program — January 1984
CFP	BAS	Comparative feed pricing — June 1984
COWCRAB	BAS	Cow calf risk analysis budget — July 1983
CRCROP	BAS	Concensus research crops model — July 1984

461
Ridgetown College Programs
v1

From Ridgetown College of Ontario comes this fine collection of Farm Management tools. Besides a handy Metric Conversion program, disk highlights include: LUMBER brings you into the world of computer carpentry: fed your basic design and constraints, it produces reliable estimates of all the construction materials you will need for your project, and it keeps a running total of the costs. USLE does the same for the problem of Soil Loss Evaluation on Irregular Slopes: this program gives a fast, accurate estimate of such soil loss. The documentation also includes the code for Hewlett Packard (HP-41c) calculators. As many if not most fields have irregular slopes, the farmer or the conservation specialist can benefit from this computerized aid.

Usage: On-line farming

System Requirements: 64K, one disk drive, monochrome monitor.

How to Start: To read DOC or TXT files, enter TYPE filename.ext and press ENTER.

- To run an EXE or COM program, just type its name and press ENTER. For instructions on running BASIC programs, please refer to the GETTING STARTED section in this catalog.

User Comments: "Some good software for fairs, farm shows, etc." "Used CONV.BASon some other files; worked great."

File Descriptions:

AVERAGE	DAT	Unkown ??? data file for this disk
CONV	BAS	Converts programs from EXE or COM to BAS
LUMBER	BAS	Lumber requirements for building
LUMBER	DOC	Documentation for LUMBER.BAS
METRICON	BAS	Metric conversion program — source
METRICON	EXE	Metric Conversion program — compiled
QUIZ	BAS	Do you need a farm computer quiz — source
QUIZ	EXE	Do you need a farm computer quiz — compiled
README	DOC	Author supplied user documentation file
SHRINK	EXE	Shrinks BASIC files prior to compilation
SILENCE	COM	Silences your computer speaker
TREEFIX	BAS	Fixes output from TREE.COM
TREEFIX	BAT	Batch file to produce useful form of TREE.COM
USLE	BAS	Universal Soil Loss Equation
USLE	DOC	Documentation for USLE.BAS
WOODHEAT	BAS	Economics of wood heating
WOODHEAT	TXT	Documentation for WOODHEAT.BAS

492
NUTRIENT
v1.21

NUTRIENT analyzes an individual's (infant to old age) food intake over 3 days for nutrient adequacy. After inputting your diet (chosen from a 700 food database which can be expanded) the program lists the average daily nutrient intake of 27 nutrients (including alcohol and cholesterol) and compares them to the 1980 Recommended Daily Allowance. It also generates personal graphs of the results.

Usage: Personal nutritional evaluation

Features:

- Individualized Analysis of Food Intake: NUTRIENT will analyze the diet of healthy individual's in all stages of the life cycle, from infancy through old age (I sometimes feel I'm at both extremes).
- Multiple Day Analysis: 3 days of 45 foods each day are permitted to be entered.
- 700 Food Database: The main database is a database of food names and their nutrient content. This is called FOODFILE. It can be customized by entering your own food preferences by using the routine called ADD A FOOD. FOODFILE is expandable to a size only limited by the disk capacity and speed of your machine.
- 27 Nutrients: There are 27 nutrient values for most foods, including some not often evaluated by other programs, such as cholesterol and alcohol. Of course alcohol is not considered a

nutrient or dietary substance essential for humans. However, it is included with the nutrient listings for the sake of continuity.
- Food Groups: NUTRIENT categorizes foods by food groups to enable one to select foods that are close to the one actually eaten, in its nutrient content and/or general characteristics.
- Daily Averages: Receive a display and/or printout of the average daily nutrient intake for up to three days. This average is then compared to the 1980 RDA (expressed as Percent of RDA).
- Printouts: Produced for an individual's Food Intake Analysis, including a simple graph, and comments on low and high nutrient intakes. You can print out individual food values; or all foods in the database by food group; also printout the entire Foodfile which will be a necessary reference for each person's food intake data entry.
- Display: Besides printouts, you will be able to display a simple graph of an individual's Food Intake Analysis; individual food values; foods by food group; and the entire Foodfile.
- Bibliography: A list of references used in the writing of NUTRIENT are provided for your referral.

System Requirements: 64K, one disk drive, monochrome monitor.

How to Start: To run BASIC programs consult the directions in GETTING STARTED for your configuration. Consult READNUT1.DOC and READNUT2.DOC for program documentation.

User Comments: "I needed to read the docs 2 or 3 more times before I fully understood the power of this excellent program." "Doesn't give all the output that would be useful; help & print routines are not included until you send in payment." "OK for elementary diet control."

Suggested Donation: $35.00

File Descriptions:

FOODFILE		Food and nutrient database
METRO	DAT	Adult height and weight database
ENERGY	DAT	Energy allowance database
RDA	DAT	Recommended Dietary Allowances
CHILD	DAT	Height and weight %iles, to 18 yrs
NUTRIENT	BAS	Main program in BASIC
DSPLYNUT	BAS	Displays food, food groups, etc.
SORTNUT	BAS	Sort used with DISPLYNUT & PRINTNUT
READNUT1	DOC	Documentation, first 40 pages
READNUT2	DOC	Documentation, last 12 pages

494
The World Digitized (1 of 3)
V1.1

The World Digitized is a collection of more than 100,000 points of latitude and longitude, all grouped under specific continents: Australia, Africa, Antarctica, Europe, Asia, North America and South America. When connected together, these co-ordinates form outlines of the entire world's coastlands, islands, lakes, and national boundaries in surprising detail. This first disk contains the documentation, the batch files for hard disk installation and the program to expand the condensed shipping format to ASCII. The philosophy adopted in making The World Digitized available to the public is the exercise of ones own creativity and imagination is much more interesting and profitable than the acquisition of a fixed program. The World Digitized is, therefore, simply a raw data base sprinkled with a few suggestions to be used as jumping off points in your personal quest to create significant and dazzling programs. NOTE: THIS IS A THREE DISK SET — BUY IT AND USE IT TOGETHER!!

Usage: Cartographers, geography students and graphics freaks

System Requirements: 128K, two disk drives, and monochrome-graphics display; hard disk seriously recommended (1.3 Mb required).

How to Start: Consult the comprehensive READ.ME file on disk 494 for complete directions and documentation on installing The World Digitized on your hard disk.

User Comments: "This is probably a very good program for geographers and cartographers." "It only works on my hard drive." "The detail is surprising. The documentation is highly technical."

Suggested Donation: $60.00 personal registration (for all three disks); $65.00 for special educational registration

File Descriptions:

AFRICA	DIR	Data directory containing Africa information
ANTARCTI	DIR	Data directory containing Antartica information
AUSTRALI	DIR	Data directory containing Austrailia information
COPYING		Text file containing copying information

DEMO	DIR	Demo system directory
EXPAND	BAT	Database convertor
INSTALL	BAT	Installation program 1
INSTALL1	BAT	Installation program 2
MPSTOMP1	C	Source of convertor
MPSTOMP1	EXE	Ship ASCII file to Convertor
READ	ME	Instructions file
SOUTHAME	DIR	Data directory containing Southern Hemisphere information

495
The World Digitized (2 of 3)
V1.1

This disk contains the databases for Asia and Europe in The World Digitized Series (disks 494, 495, 496).

Usage: Cartographers, geography students and graphics freaks

System Requirements: 128K, two disk drives and monochrome/graphics display; hard disk seriously recommeded

File Descriptions:

ASIA	Data directory containing ASIA information
COPYING	Introductory and copying program
EUROPE	Data directory containing EUROPE information

496
The World Digitized (3 of 3)
V1.1

This disk contains the databases for North America in The World Digitized Series (disks 494, 495, 496).

Usage: Cartographers, geography students and graphics freaks

System Requirements: 128K, two disk drives and monochrome/graphics display; hard disk seriously recommended

File Descriptions:

COPYING		Copying & introductory program
NORTHAME	DIR	Northern Hemisphere Data Directory

507 PC-SPRINT
v1

PC-SPRINT contains step-by-step directions on how to accomplish a low cost ($25 — $50) speed up for the IBM PC/AT/XT. It can achieve processor performance increases of up to 2 times normal, does not use an expansion slot, doesn't make any permanent changes to the computer and maintains software compatibility without restrictions. Also, it adds a true hardware reset — no more "keyboard lockup". NOTE: This package makes extensive use of printer graphics. It is intended to be printed on EPSON compatible printers only since most files contain embedded EPSON control codes. The DOS "PRINT" command cannot be used because of this — all printable files must use COPY filenmae PRN" instead. The batch file PCSPRINT.BAT will copy all relevant files for you.

Usage: Increase your processor speed

System Requirements: 128K, one disk drive and monochome/graphics display, Epson-compatible printer recommended.

How to Start: Enter TYPE 1STREAD.ME or TYPE PCSPRINT.DOC and press ENTER for program documentation and printing instructions.

File Descriptions:

1STREAD	ME	List of files on diskette (this list)
ARTWRK1X	BOT	Bottom layer printed circuit artwork 1x size
ARTWRK1X	TOP	Top layer printed circuit artwork 1x size
ARTWRK2X	BOT	Bottom layer printed circuit artwork 2x size
ARTWRK2X	TOP	Top layer printed circuit artwork 2x size
FEEDTHRU		Top — bottom "feed through" connection diagram
NOPRTYCK	COM	Program to disable parity checks
PARTLIST		Parts list & placement drawing
PCSPRINT	BAT	Batch file to print PC-SPRINT info & drawings
PCSPRINT	DOC	Description & construction info
SCHEMATC		Electronic circuit diagram
WARMBOOT	COM	Program to set "warm boot" flag

538 Astronomy Collection #1
v1

MOONBEAM is a program that takes the date and time, as well as your time zone, and gives you a lot of general information regarding the position of the moon and its relationship to Earth. SUNSET accepts the date, time and location of position and displays general information about the sun in relation to Earth. SOLAR is a duplicate of the SUNSET program mentioned above, with some slight variations. OPTICS gets optical parameters from the sophisticated lens user and returns a myriad of technical information about reflecting lenses or telescopes. STORM is an amusing program which accepts detailed storm information incrementally by time and plots the movement of that storm in the area.

Usage: Astronomical and atmospheric calculations

System Requirements: 64K, one disk drive and monochrome display

How to Start: Load DOS and type MOONBEAM to enter the MOONBEAM program, OPTICS to run the OPTICS.COM program

- To run BASIC programs consult the directions in GETTING STARTED for your configuration. Consult the .DOC files for program documentation.

File Descriptions:

— — —	— —	Moonbeam (V1.0)
MOONBEAM	COM	Executable program for Moonbeam
MOONBEAM	DOC	Documentation for the use of the program
STAR	REC	Yale Observatory Bright Star database
— — —	— —	Sunset
SUNSET	BAS	Basic program in source code
— — —	— —	Solar
SOLAR	BAS	Basic program in source code
— — —	— —	Optics
OPTICS	COM	Executable code to run Optics
OPTICS	PAS	Source code in Pascal for Optics
— — —	— —	Storm
STORM	BAS	Storm program
STORM	DOC	Documentation for Storm.BAS
????????		Files with no extensions are data files for storm program

562
PC-HAM
Version 1.5
V1

PC-HAM is a set of amateur radio database programs for the use of a microcomputer in amateur radio based, in part, on programs described in the book, Software For Amateur Radio, written by Joe Kasser. There are seven files covering aspects of computer aided design, fifteen contests and logging awards — including a WAS Package and a DXCC Pack — eight antenna position and pointing programs and six files making up a DBASE II Data Base Logbook package.

Usage: Hams who want to get on-line.

System Requirements: 64K, one disk drive and monochrome display; 128K and DBASEII for the Logbook Package.

How to Start: Enter TYPE PC-HAM.DOC and press ENTER for program documentation

• To run BASIC programs consult the directions for GETTING STARTED for your configuration. To read the DBF files, consult the directions in your DBASE II manual.

Suggested Donation: $36.50

File Descriptions:

*	PRG	Part of DBASE2 logbook package (11 Files)
2MFUND	BAS	Part of computer aided design package
BLANKLOG	DBF	Part of DBASE2 logbook package
CKLSTGEN	2	Part of BASIC contest package
CKLSTRD	2	Part of BASIC contest package
CONTEST	BAS	CONTEST OPERATING PROGRAM
CONTST16	2	Part of BASIC contest package CONTEST PROGRAM
CQSS	BAS	Sweepstakes contest game (simulation)
DXCC	DBF	Part of DBASE2 logbook package
DXCC????	BAS	Part of DXCC record keeping package (5 Files)
FIELD85	CHK	Part of contest package
FIELD85	DBF	Part of DBASE2 package (SAMPLE DATABASE LOG)
FIELD85	LOG	Part of contest package (SAMPLE BASIC LOG)
FIELD85	NDX	Part of DBASE2 package (SAMPLE INDEXED LOG)
FIELD85	RUN	Part of contest package (SAMPLE AS RUN LOG)
FILES	2	Part of BASIC logging package
FREQPLOT	BAS	Part of computer aided design package
HELP	2	Part of BASIC logging package

LOG?????	2	Part of BASIC logging package
LOGCONV	BAS	Reformats BASIC contest logs after contest
MBCKLSTG	2	Part of BASIC contest package
NEWLOG	2	Part of BASIC logging package
OSCFREQ	BAS	Part of computer aided design package
OSCPLOT	BAS	Part of computer aided design package
OSCUPLK	BAS	Part of computer aided design package
PC-HAM	DOC	Documentation for package
PHASE1	2	OSCAR Orbit calculator
PHASE2	2	OSCAR antenna AZ-EL calculator
QSLPRINT	2	Part of BASIC logging package
QTH?????	2	Part of antenna direction pointing package (7 Files)
RESISTOR	BAS	Part of computer aided design package
STNINFO	2	Part of BASIC logging package
SWPSTAKS	2	Part of BASIC contest package SWEEPSTAKES CONTEST
SYSTEM	2	Part of BASIC logging package
UPLINK	BAS	Part of computer aided design package
W3	DX	Part of DXCC package (Sample DXCC record file)
WASENTER	BAS	Part of WAS record keeping package
WASGEN	BAS	Part of WAS record keeping package
WASPRINT	BAS	Part of WAS record keeping package

581
WORDWORKER
(Disk 1 of 2)
v1

Wordworker is a cross-reference program for the New Testament with over 14,800 cross references to 7956 verses. It can also provide the number of occurences for over 6063 words. This disk also contains a complete editor to genterate letters, sermons or other text with the information contained in the set. After starting the program you should examine each help screen to learn about program operation. A complete Wordworker system with a manual and disks is available from The Way International.

Usage: New Testament word study

System Requirements: 128K, two disk drives and monochrome display

How to Start: Load DOS. With WORDWORKER disk 1 in drive A, and WORDWORKER disk 2 in drive B, type WW to enter the WORDWORKER program.

Suggested Donation: $45.00

File Descriptions:

ALPHSHEL		Alpha-shell file
EXT	DCT	List of words — 2
INT	DCT	List of words — 1
ORDERFRM		Order form
PROFILE	WWP	Batch file
PUNFILE		Punctuation file
README		Introduction to system files & installation
REFFILE		External cross reference
RESPONSE		Response form
WW	COM	Main WORDWORKER program
WW	DEF	File with different term definitions
WW	HLP	Explanation of function keys & operations
WWSETUP	COM	WordWorker setup program
XPOINT		Cross point program for system
XREF		Cross reference program

582 WORDWORKER
(Disk 2 of 2)
v1

Wordworker is a cross-reference program for the New Testament with over 14,800 cross references to 7956 verses. It can also provide the number of occurences for over 6063 words. This disk contains the data disk for disk number 581.

615 Oracle
Version 1.0
v1

The ORACLE package is useful for people learning to use the I Ching or Tarot cards, or for those who use them frequently and would like to spend less time shuffling oversized cards, counting sticks, etc. Two programs make up the ORACLE package. TAROT automatically goes through the procedure for TAROT card fortune telling. ICHING very similarly goes through the I Ching fortune telling procedures by coin-toss and yarrow stick techniques. Both programs allow for an "interactive" or an "automated" procedure.

Usage: Fortune Telling/Entertainment

System Requirements: 64K, one disk drive.

How to Start: READ ORACLE.DOC for instructions.

- To run, enter "TAROT" or "ICHING"and press ENTER. Menus will lead you from there.

Suggested Donation: $15.00 includes upgrade notification

File Descriptions:

——	——	Oracle (v1.0)
ICHING	EXE	Makes hexagrams by coin-toss and yarrow-stick techniques
TAROT	EXE	Performs deal and layout of Tarot cards with interpretations
ORACLE	DOC	User's manual for the ICHING and TAROT (12k)
GO	BAT	Startup batch information

616 Corbin Handbook
(Disk 1 of 2) Version 1.0
v1

This disk is the first of a two disk set containing the Corbin Handbook of Bullet Swaging, No. 7 written by Dr. Corbin. This one has the table of contents and the first 11 chapters. It is saved in ASCII text format.

The subject of bullet swaging is the manufacture of projectiles using high pressure to flow ductile metals at room temperature into the precise dimensions of a strong, highly-finished steel die. The process is discussed both as a hobby for the firearms enthusiast and as a highly profitable part-time business venture, supplying handloaders with high quality, special purpose bullets. Utility programs on this diskette facilitate the retrieval of the Corbin Handbook information.

Usage: Specialty Firearms

System Requirements: 64K, one disk drive, a monochrome display and an ASCII text editor or word processor.

How to Start: Consult the READ.ME and INTRO.TXT for directions. To run, prepare two formatted disk with the DOS system command and add files FIND.EXE and ANSI.SYS; copy 616 to one and 617 to another using the COPY *.* command. Either can now be run by placing in A: and hitting CRTL-ALT-DEL and following the access menus that then appear.

Suggested Donation: The handbook is available in a bound, printed book format for $4.00 by ordering directly from Corbin Manufacturing & Supply.

File Descriptions:

— — — —	— —	Corbin Handbook
ANSI	SYS	System information
AUTOEXEC	BAT	Start up batch file
*	TXT	Documentation for the Corbin Handbook (11 files) (245k)
CONFIG	SYS	System information
FIND	EXE	Find utility
HB7	BAT	Introduction Batch file
HB7	BAK	Backup of HB7.BAT
INTRO	TXT	Short introduction text of Corbin
READ	ME	Documentation about Corbin and Bullet Swaging
SCRNSAVE	COM	Screen save utility
SDIR	COM	Show directory utility batch file
SHOW	BAT	Display text file utility
SHOW	DOC	Documentation for SHOW.BAT
ST	COM	Display text file program
ST	DOC	Documentation for ST.COM

617
Corbin Handbook
(Disk 2 of 2) Version 1.0
v1

This is the second disk of the two disk set containing the Corbin Handbook of Bullet Swaging, No. 7 written by Dr. Corbin. This one has has the table of contents and chapters 12 through 22 of saved in ASCII text format.

The subject of bullet swaging is the manufacture of projectiles using high pressure to flow ductile metals at room temperature into the precise dimensions of a strong, highly-finished steel die. The process is discussed both as a hobby for the firearms enthusiast and as a highly profitable part-time business venture, supplying handloaders with high quality, special purpose bullets. Utility programs on this diskette facilitate the retrieval of the Corbin Handbook information.

Usage: Specialty Firearms

System Requirements: 64K, one disk drive, a monchrome display and an ASCII text editor or word processor.

How to Start: Consult the READ.ME and INTRO.TXT for directions.

● To run, prepare two formatted disk with the DOS system command and add files FIND.EXE and ANSI.SYS; copy 616 to one and 617 to another using the COPY *.* command. Either can now be run by placing in A: and hitting CRTL-ALTDEL and following the access menus that then appear.

Suggested Donation: The handbook is available in a bound, printed book format for $4.00 by ordering directly from Corbin Manufacturing & Supply.

File Descriptions:

— — — —	— —	Corbin Handbook (Chptr 12-22)
ANSI	SYS	System information
AUTOEXEC	BAT	Startup Batch file
AUTOEXEC	BAK	Startup Batch file backup
*	TXT	Documentation for the Corbin Handbook (10 Files) (168k)
CONFIG	SYS	System information
FIND	EXE	Text search utility
FKEY	BAT	Batch file
HB7	BAK	Backup batch file
HB7	BAT	Setup Corbin chapters
READ	ME	Information from the author
SCRNSAVE	COM	Screen save utility
SDIR	COM	Show directory utility
SHOW	BAT	Batch file for text display
SHOW	DOC	Documentation for SHOW.BAT
ST	COM	Text display utility
ST	DOC	Documentation for ST.COM

619
Hotboot/Insults
V1

This disk contains a couple of practical joke files that are fun for the PC user and PC victim. Hotboot is by far the most "fun" PC practical joke disk around. This hotboot file is a public domain version, if you think this is great get the "real" program from Left-handed Software, you won't be disappointed. Insults can randomly generate 22 million insults on the unsuspecting PC user, not for the weak of stomach.

Usage: Practical Joking

System Requirements: Both will run on 64K, one disk drive and monochrome though some HOTBOOT tricks require color or graphics adaptor.

How to Start: Consult HOTBOOT.DOC for directions; INSULTS has on-line helps. Both can be run directly from DOS by typing their program names.

Suggested Donation: $35.00 for HOTBOOT gets full version and documentation.

File Descriptions:

HOTBOOT	COM	Hotboot program file
HOTBOOT	DOC	Documentation for HOTBOOT.COM
INSULTS	EXE	Lists various insults

635
MUSE
(Disk 1 of 2)
Version 5.12
v1

MUSE is a program for authors and their agents to organize the circulation of manuscripts to publishers. It is a very specialized data base which helps keep track of publishers' responses as well as current mailings. It also mail merges the address in the files with appropriate form letters. Disk 1 contains the main MUSE program and the archive/unarchive program used to unarchive the data files on disk 2.

Usage: Manuscript tracking

System Requirements: 256K, two floppies or one floppy and a hard disk and a monochrome display

How to Start: Enter TYPE MUSEARC.DOC and press ENTER for documentation on unarchiving the .EXE files. Once unarchived, type MUSE to enter the main program. Consult MUSES.DOC (disk 636) for program documentation.

Suggested Donation: $15.00

File Descriptions:

AUTOEXEC	BAT	A sample file for an auto boot disk.
CONFIG	SYS	A file to set the number of files for DOS to open.
MUSE	EXE	The MUSE menu program.
MUSE1	EXE	Data Base module
MUSE2	EXE	Data Base module
MUSEARC	DOC	How to unARC these disks

636
MUSE
(Disk 2 of 2)
Version 5.12
v1

This is the second disk of the MUSE manuscript tracking program. Disk 2 of 2 contains the documentation for MUSE and the data files (archived) used by MUSE.

Usage: Manuscript tracking

File Descriptions:

Contents of file MUSE2.ARC

ACCEPT	LET	A form letter
COVER	LET	A form letter
MERGEP		Explains merging with Wordstar documents
MUSE3	EXE	The print program
MUSE4	EXE	The set up program
MUSES	DOC	The 30 + page manual
PUBCY	LET	A form letter
QUERY1	LET	A form letter
QUERY3	LET	A form letter
QUICK	MUS	How to start MUSES without reading the manual
README		Basic info from the author
SNIDE	LET	A form letter

Contents of file MUSE3.ARC

C		Data Files
COUNT	BAT	Lists how many publishers have accepted, rejected, etc.
D3		Data Files
D6		Data Files
D7		Data Files
D8		Data Files
D9		Data Files
E		Data Files
G		Data Files
I		Data Files
P		Data Files
PARA	MUS	Set up information file
R		Data Files
TALLIES		Publication/Circulation statistics
UPREPORT	!BAT	Adds a new daily report to the monthly report.

648
WALMYR PROGRAMS
(Disk 1 of 2)
v1

This is the first of a two disk set of programs from WALMYR Publishing. Their orientation is in the field of interactive, computer-assisted learning and assessment programming for the helping professions. All these programs are stored in compressed form on the original disks. The decompression program is included and should be run first. Most are intended as demonstration versions so their capabilities are intentionally curtailed. The two major programs on this disk are:

CAS — The CLINICAL ASSESSMENT SYSTEM is a computer based clinical environment designed for use by social workers, psychologists, and other helping professionals to help solve or reduce personal and social problems of clients when used interactively by both professional and client.

ITA — The INDEX OF TEACHING ABILITY program is used to evaluate teacher performance in the classroom.

Please note that the Documentation is on the second disk!

Usage: Computer Assisted Instruction and Evaluation

System Requirements: 256K, two floppy drives and a monochrome display

How to Start: Enter TYPE README. and press ENTER to read the files giving installation and unarchiving instructions. After running the ARC program to un-archive the programs, follow the enclosed documentation files to install and run them. Consult WALMYR.DOC (on disk 649) for program documentation.

Suggested Donation: $10.00

File Descriptions:

ARC	EXE	Archive Utility
CAS1	ARC	First half of the CAS program
CAS2	ARC	Second half of the CAS program
ITA	ARC	Index of Teaching Ability program
README	BAT	Batch file for system implementation procedures
README	1ST	Installing on a hard disk system
README	2ND	Installing on a two floppy system
README	3RD	Archiving and Authors notes
WALMYR	ARC	Archived files from WALMYR

649
WALMYR PROGRAMS
(Disk 2 of 2)
v1

This is the second of a two disk set of programs from WALMYR Publishing. Their orientation is in the field of interactive, computer-assisted learning and assessment programming for the helping professions. All these programs are stored in compressed form on the original disks. The decompression program is included and should be run first. Most are intended as demonstrations version only so their capabilities are intentionally curtailed. The two major programs on this disk are:

ICES — The INTERACTIVE COMPUTER EXAMINATION SUPERVISOR is a general CAI program aid for university instructors of graduate and undergraduate courses in preparing, administering, grading and reporting on tests, quizzes and homework assignments to their students.

WPC — The WALMYR PRINTER CONFIGURATOR a printer configuration program.

Usage: Computer Assisted Instruction

Suggested Donation: $10.00

File Descriptions:

README	?	System implementation procedure
ARC	EXE	Archive utility
ICES?	ARC	Interactive Computer Examination Supervisor
PRNCON	ARC	Walmyr Printer Configurator
WALMYR	DOC	System documentation

MEMBER	XNM	"
CONTR	DAT	"
CONTR	XEV	"
MANUAL	DOC	Manual for church contribution system
INVOICE	DOC	Invoice to order church contribution system
README		Notes on how to begin
README	BAT	Batch file to type out readme

659
VIANSOFT® CHURCH CONTRIBUTIONS
v1

This is a user supported program to allow you to record pledged and unpledged contributions in twenty different categories, for each member of your church. It prints out a variety of reports based on this information. Notable features include:

- Easy entry of contributions
- Two formats for Member Summary
- Contribution List by date (Ledger Sheet)
- Contribution totals for period of time by category
- Mailing Labels
- Member Directories with any combination of the following:
  Name
  Family Members
  Address
  Phone
  Envelope Number
  Pledge Amount
  Contributions to Date

Usage: Church Finance Management

System Requirements: 128K, two disk drives, or one floppy and a hard disk, a monochrome monitor and an IBM compatible printer.

How to Start: Type README and press ENTER for program instructions.

- To print the documentation file, type COPY TUTOR.DOC PRN or COPY MANUAL.DOC PRN and press ENTER. Load DOS and type CHURCH to enter the main program.

Suggested Donation: Sending in $60.00 will secure the password to turn your DEMO into a working version and receive a complete, bound manual.

File Descriptions:

CHURCH	COM	Viansoft(r) church contribution main program
CHURCH	000	Overlay for CHURCH.COM
TUTOR	DOC	Tutorial for church contribution system
CHINFO	DAT	Sample data for tutorial
MEMBER	DAT	"
MEMBER	XEV	"

660
MAROONED AGAIN & EMS
v1

The EMPLOYEE MANAGEMENT SYSTEM (EMS) is a system for describing a set of personality characteristics that would fit a certain job and then using them as a benchmark to test prospective employees with. EMS uses responses to a series of descriptive statements to determine an employers requirements for a position. It then tests employees/applicants for their suitability in that job. Based on the responses, EMS prints out a 5 page report on the personality outlined by the responses.

MAROONED AGAIN is not your standard text adventure game. In the first place, it's logical. It tells you this every time you try to do something illogical. The basic plot is you are marooned on an alien planet with a broken spaceship and a bunch of retarded clones who can only respond to two word commands. There is hope however! Also on this planet is an alien spaceship that can be made to work with some minor repairs. All you have to do is fix the ship with your clones and take off.

Usage: Management analysis and Fun!

System Requirements: 128K, one disk drive and monochrome display

How to Start: To read DOC files, enter TYPE filename.DOC and press ENTER.

- To run an EXE program, just type its name and press ENTER.

Suggested Donation: $85.00 for EMS gets you: 1. Hard bound instruction manual. 2. Call-in telephone support. 3. Places you on our mailing list for notification of future updates. 4. For every one of your friends that registers, we will pay you $20. "Whatevers fair" for MAROONED AGAIN

File Descriptions:

		EMPLOYEE MANAGEMENT SYSTEM v1
INSTALL	EXE	Installation program for Color or Monochrome
READ-ME	DOC	"GO.BAT" for EMPLOYEE MANAGEMENT SYSTEM
EMS	EXE	Main Program
EMSHIST	EXE	Subprogram
EMSSHEET		Employee response sheet for use with program
JOBSHEET		Form for describing characteristics to be tested for
INSTRUC	DOC	Brief instructions, registration pitch and registration form
EMSINST		Directs data storage for EMS
EMS??		Data files for EMPLOYEE MANAGEMENT SYSTEM (21 files)
		MAROONED AGAIN v1
MAROONED	EXE	MAROONED AGAIN game
MAROONED	DOC	Instructions for MAROONED AGAIN game

665
PC Demonstration System
v1

The PC Demonstration system is an excellent program for putting together a presentation on the system or laying out the specifications of a package. There are three programs in the PC Demonstration System:

Screen Formatter — which is used to create the screens for your presentation.

Demo Maker — which is used to create a "sequence file" that describes the order in which your screens will be displayed, along with the valid keys that can be used to branch within your presentation.

Demo Run — which takes your screens and your sequence file and "runs" your presentation.

This shareware/evaluation version of PC Demonstration System limits sequence file size to 10 records. It also has a reminder-to-register screen in place of a blank edit screen in Screen Formatter. The registered/enhanced version allows sequence files of 450 records and does not have the reminder-to-register screen.

Usage: PC-based presentations

System Requirements: 256K, one disk drive and color/monochrome display MUST BE RUN in 80 column mode

How to Start: Documentation in READ.ME and MANUAL.DOC

- To run, enter "DR" for DEMO RUN or "SF" for SCREEN FORMATTER.

Suggested Donation: $35.00 registrations covers the latest enhanced version, update notification ($10.00), technical support, SHOW.COM (will allow the use of screens created by Screen Formatter in batch files and even dBase III programs), and a supplement to the User's Guide that gives tips on how Screen Formatter screens can be used within their own programs.

File Descriptions:

DM	COM	Demo Maker program
DM	SCN	Demo Maker screens
DMHLP	SCN	Demo Maker help
DR	COM	Demo run program
MANUAL	DOC	Actual text of system documentation
PCDEMO	???	Segments of introductory demonstration (41 files)
PRINTDOC	BAT	Batch file to print documentation
READ	ME	System introduction on how to run Demo
SF	COM	Screen formatter program
SF	SCN	Screen formatter screen file
SFHLP	SCN	Screen formatter help

674
Enable Reader Speech System (3.0) (Disk 1 of 4)
V1.0

The Enable Reader 4.0 Professional Speech System is a four disk set. This is disk one — The Program Disk. It contains all the programs for the seven speech synthesizers currently supported. The addresses for the companies producing the speech synthesizers are located in the APPENDIX of the manual under RESOURCES.

The Enable Reader 3.0 Speech System is actually two programs in one. The Full Screen Speech Review System is designed for visually impaired and blind people. With Full Screen Speech Review, a visually impaired person has access to the wide selection of commercial software available for MSDOS compatible machines, such as the IBM PC and dozens of other machines. Whether it is WordStar, dBASE, or Lotus 1-2-3 , a visually impaired person can now use these programs efficiently.

The second program built into the Enable Reader 3.0 Speech System is the Talking Tutorial Programmer's Aid. Professional programmers now have access to many of the speech functions of the Enable Reader 3.0 Speech System for writing talking tutorials for their software. This gives blind and visually impaired people the best of both worlds. One, they have access to the Review Mode of the Enable Reader 3.0 Speech System for running commercial software. And two, any program that is written with the Talking Tutorial Programmer's Aid will run for them.

This system consists of 4 disks. They are as follows:

Disk No. 674 is the main program disk.
Disk No. 675 contains the manual.
Disk No. 676 contains the Votrax word processing programs.
Disk No. 677 contains the Dectalk word processing programs.

Contents of Disk 674:

There are seven sub-directories containing the Enable Reader 4.0 programs. The names of the sub-directories and the synthesizers they support are:

SUB-DIRECTORY	SYNTHESIZER TYPE
ARTIC	ARTIC TECHNOLOGIES — SPEECH BOARD
CALLTEXT	SPEECH PLUS — CALLTEXT 5050
DECTALK	DIGITAL EQUIPMENT CORP. — DECTALK.
ECHO	STREET ELECTRONICS — ECHO GP
VOTALKER	VOTRAX, INC. — VOTALKER IB
VOTRAX	VOTRAX, INC. — VOTRAX PSS
VOTRAX–B	VOTRAX, INC. — VOTRAX PSS/B

Each sub-directory contains a version of Enable Reader for the that unit. Any table for any synthesizer can be loaded into the the program and the Enable Reader will run for that synthesizer.

Usage: Computer accessibility for visually impaired/blind

System Requirements: 256K, two floppy drives but HARD DISK IS STRONGLY RECOMMENDED, monochrome display and speech synthesizer hardware

How to Start: Refer to documentation on disk 675.

675
Enable Reader Speech System (3.0) (Disk 2 of 4)
V1.0

The Enable Reader 4.0 Professional Speech System is a four disk set. This is disk two — The Manual Disk. It contains all the files for the Enable Reader 4.0 Speech System Operations Manual.

CHAPTER 1 gives a general overview of the logic behind the development of the Enable Reader program, and some of the design concepts.

CHAPTER 2 details the contents of the Enable Reader package. It also explains how to set up your speech synthesizer and your disks in preparation for using the Enable Reader program.

CHAPTER 3 introduces you to the actual use of Enable Reader. It covers the general organization of the commands, and relates them to the structure of the Enable Reader program.

CHAPTER 4 gives a detailed description of each function key. You should read through the commands once to become familiar with the capabilities of Enable Reader.

CHAPTER 5 is the Talking Tutorial Programmer's Aid and is used as a reference section only. If you are not a programmer you can skip over this chapter.

CHAPTER 6 is the reference chapter for the Integration Keys, a special category of functions which was not described in Chapter 4 .

CHAPTER 7 takes you through the use of Matchup Integration with the Wordstar wordprocessor program and the use of Macro Screen Review keys and automatic configuration.

CHAPTER 8 is similar to chapter 7 only it describes the Matchup setup for Word Perfect and the use of all three modes of screen review available.

CHAPTER 9 provides an augmented tutorial for using Superkey. The short tutorial is designed to help with the instructions in the Superkey Manual. This chapter should be read before attempting to create your own macro keys.

The APPENDIX contains reference tables and charts. The most useful will probably be the Enable Reader Command Summary listed in Appendix E. Complete charts of the Enable Reader Punctuation Word Table and the Letter-to-Word Translation Table are included.

THE MANUAL IS ALSO AVAILABLE ON FIVE NINETY MINUTE CASSETTE TAPES.

Usage: Computer accessibility for visually impaired/blind

System Requirements: 256K, two floppy drives but HARD DISK IS STRONGLY RECOMMENDED, monochrome display and speech synthesizer hardware

How to Start: Refer to the STARTING section.

676 The Votrax Word Processing Program

3

The Enable Reader 4.0 Professional Speech System is a four disk set. This is disk three — The Votrax Word Processing System. AS IT IS DESIGNED TO WORK WITH THE ENABLE SYSTEM, REFER TO THE MANUAL ON DISK 675 FOR ALL TECHNICAL INFORMATION.

The VOTRAX and DECTALK disks have two sections. The root directory and the sub-directory called WORDSTAR. Both disks contain the same structure. They have programs, tables, and macro files for SUPERKEY for the respective synthesiser the disk is named for. The root directory contains the Automation Package for WordPerfect. The WordStar sub-directory contains the Automation Package for WordStar.

677 DECtalk Word Processing Programs.

The Enable Reader 4.0 Professional Speech System is a four disk set. This is disk four — The DECtalk Word Processing System. AS IT IS DESIGNED TO WORK WITH THE ENABLE SYSTEM, REFER TO THE MANUAL ON DISK 675 FOR ALL TECHNICAL INFORMATION.

The VOTRAX and DECTalk disks have two sections. The root directory and the sub-directory called WORDSTAR. Both disks contain the same structure. They have programs, tables, and macro files for SUPERKEY for the respective synthesiser the disk is named for. The root directory contains the Automation Package for WordPerfect. The WordStar sub-directory contains the Automation Package for WordStar.

690 Best-Plan Planning System (Disk 1 of 2)

v1

BEST-PLAN is a mathematical modeling package which simplifies analysis by having a build-in modeling language, a report writer and multiple analyses "what-if" capability thru a built-in database management system. Such a system is projected for large-scale material allocations and factory-level production planning. The supplied system for PC-SIG will allow you to tryout the system which is large, twelve programs usually supplied on four disks but here on two.

The general goal of designing a linear programming planning system like BEST-PLAN was to put the maximum amount of analytical power into the hands of the people directly concerned with the problem, to require only a minimum of specialized knowledge or experience on the part of the user, and at the same time giving him the advantages of mathematical modeling for planning.

LIMITATIONS in this DEMO PACKAGE: Systems operations are intended for demonstrations ONLY!

The user is allowed only to execute the supplied samples. In summary:

- The user CANNOT create a NEW problem/model.
- The user CANNOT Optimize a master PLAN.
- The user CANNOT modify the BEST-PLAN environment file (BP-ENV.CON) other than change screen color and disk assignments.
- The problem size has been limited to 6,000 elements elements = (no. of rows) * (2 * no. of rows + no. of columns)

Usage: Mathematical modeling for large-scale planning

System Requirements: 64K, one disk drive and monochrome display

Features:

- Flexible, user-oriented interface to the planner. English-like input data language that the planner can relate to. The data input concept is through a materiel-flow dialogue and not mathematical equations.
- Automatic generation of models from this materiel-flow data entry concept. Specialized knowledge of linear programming is not required, and conveniently made transparent to the user.
- Efficient and dependable optimization of the models using well accepted algorithms.
- Report writing of the optimization results in concise, easy-to-use terms, requiring no programming expertise.
- Integration with the PC/XT, completely self-contained, menu-driven; giving the planner the convenience and accessibility and of the PC.
- Interfaces or links to other decision-support systems or the like, such as VISICALC, LOTUS 1-2-3, etc., thus extending any current planning activity to include profit maximization and/or cost minimization.

How to Start: Enter TYPE LISTME and press ENTER for program information.

Suggested Donation: $199.00 gets you: SAMPLES MANUAL (103 pages) discussing the four test cases plus eleven more sample problems; A USERS GUIDE and PLANNING GUIDE (100 pages) discussing the modeling language, report writer, screen editor, etc; Upgrade disksto increase problem size to 20,000 elements, plus: 8087 math-coprocessor support; and three poster-size flow charts and a

keyboard overlay for the system.

File Descriptions:

INSTALL	EXE	Install file
BP-EDT	EXE	Program modules (13 files)
BP-ENV	CON	"
BP-ENV	COM	"
CONFIG	SYS	Configuration file
CONTINUE	BAT	Program batch files
BP	BAT	"
MODIFY0	BAT	"
TEST	BAT	"
LISTME		Documentation file

691
Best-Plan Planning System (Disk 2 of 2)
v1

BEST-PLAN is a mathematical modeling package which simplifies analysis by having a build-in modeling language, a report writer and multiple analyses "what-if" capability thru a built-in database management system. Such a system is projected for large-scale material allocations and factory-level production planning. The supplied system for PC-SIG will allow you to tryout the system which is large, twelve programs usually supplied on four disks but here on two.

Usage: Mathematical modeling for large-scale planning

System Requirements: 64K, one disk drive and monochrome display

Suggested Donation: $199.00 (see description of Disk 690)

File Descriptions:

DATA	<DIR>	Data directory
HELP	<DIR>	Help directory containing on-line help files
README		File containing overview of BEST-PLAN

692

Astrosoft Ephemeris(ACE) (Disk 1 of 2

v1

The AstroSoft Computerized Ephemeris, or ACE for short, is a general purpose astronomy software package consisting of three separate parts, AceCalc and AceSolar being on this disk and AceCat being on the second of the two disk set.

AceCalc is a menu-driven Astronomical Ephemeris. It can perform the most needed astronomical calculations involving the sun, moon and planets. The menu displays the local time, date and time zone name, universal time, local mean sidereal time, Julian day, and the name of the location designated in the installation. This program will also calculate astrophotography exposures, precession of coordinates, phases of the Moon, Equinoxes and Solstices, Galilean satellites of Jupiter, print a perpetual calendar, and execute DOS commands without exiting.

AceSolar provides information on objects in the solar system. The first two menu selections provide numeric data on the sun, the planets and their satellites. The next function displays narrative descriptions of the sun and planets. The observational data provides information on observing the planets.

Usage: Astronomical computations

System Requirements: 128K, one disk drive, monochrome display, DOS 2.10 or above; FX-80 printer is supported

How to Start: To read DOC or TXT files, enter TYPE filename.ext and press ENTER.

• To run an EXE or COM program, just type its name ENTER.

Suggested Donation: $25.00

File Descriptions:

		Volume ACE1
ACE	DOC	Users manual
ACECALC	000	Overlay file for ACECALC
ACECALC	COM	The Astronomical Ephemeris Program
ACESOLAR	EXE	The Solar System Data Program
ASPECT	DAT	Planetary Observational Data

DESCRIP	DAT	Planetary descriptive data
HELP	TXT	Help file (Acecalc)
INSTALL	COM	The Installation Program
SATINF	DAT	Planetary data
SATINF	DAT	Satellite data
SITE	DAT	Site information
SUBMOD	CHN	Overlay file

693

AstroSoft Ephemeris(ACE) (Disk 2 of 2)

v1

The AstroSoft Computerized Ephemeris, or ACE for short, is a general purpose astronomy software package consisting of three separate parts, AceCalc and AceSolar being on the first disk and AceCat being here on the second of the two disk set.

AceCat is a menu-driven sky catalog program that will alow the user to search the sky catalog for objects by name, catalog number, position in terms of R.A./Declination, object type, and constellation. This Sky Catalog provides data on over 2000 deep-sky objects, the entire Messier Catalog, 100 "named objects", all bright stars to magnitude 2.00, and 100 prominent double stars, with detailed commentary on nearly 400 of these objects. Objects may be searched for on the basis of one criterion or by a combination of criteria.

Usage: Astronomical computations

System Requirements: 128K, one disk drive, monochrome display, DOS 2.10 or above; FX-80 printer is supported

How to Start: Full documentation is on Disk No 692 in ACE.DOC.

Suggested Donation: $25.00

File Descriptions:

		Volume ACE2
ACECAT	COM	The Sky Catalog Program
DBLCAT	DAT	Double star catalog
DBLCOM	DAT	Double star commentary
DBLCOM	NDX	Double star commentary index
DEEPCAT	DAT	Deep sky catalog
DEEPCOM	DAT	Deep sky commentary
DEEPCOM	NDX	Deep sky commentary index
DEEPMES	DAT	Messier catalog

DEEPNAM	DAT	Named objects catalog
HELP2	TXT	Help file
README		Information about ACE
SITE	DAT	Site information
STARCAT	DAT	Bright star catalog
STARCOM	DAT	Bright star commentary
STARCOM	NDX	Bright star commentary index

700
MEALMATE and others
v1

MEALMATE is a planning aid for people preparing meals for someone on a carefully controlled diet. MEALMATE is an easily operated program that can present nutritional information on many common foods. It can also combine the information from meal plans or menus to check the total nutritional content of a planned diet. MEALMATE should make it easier to plan more varied meals or to help in choosing substitutes for hard to find diet items. MEALMATE should be a big help to anyone preparing meals that have to meet strict requirements for calories, protiens, cabohydrates, and fats.

This program is targeted to the 10 percent of our population who are diabetic as the only source of complete nutritional information readily available for glucose level control but is of value to anyone who must or wishes to precisely control intake. It is consistent with the guidelines established by the American Diabetes Association, the American Medical Association, WeightWatchers International, and the Grace L. Furgenson Aluminum Storm Door and Fat Control Monday Night Fellowship Society.

The utilities include a screen blanker, a disk error reporter, a system equipment reporter, a screen dump for compiled BASIC programs, and a simple game with a bug in it. Consider it a personal challenge to fix it!

Usage: Nutritional planning

System Requirements: 64K, one disk drive and monochrome display

How to Start: Consult the .DOC and README files for directions and documentation

- To run the BASIC programs, verify your procedures according to the GETTING STARTED section
- To run any program suffixed .EXE or .COM, just enter its programname, e.g., type MEAL and press ENTER.

Suggested Donation: $25.00

File Descriptions:

		Mealmate
————	——	
FORM	TXT	Registration form
MEAL	EXE	MEALMATE main program
*	BLD	Data file for MEALMATE (5 files)
README		Information about the program
DATA		Data base 9/86 U.S.
DATA	BUP	Read only data backup
————	—	Miscellaneous Programs
CARDS	BAS	Graphics Demonstration
5INLINE	EXE	A game; THIS COPY HAS A BUG
5INLINE	BAS	Source for above
GAME	PIC	Save file for above
BLANK	COM	Dim screen at 3 min. Run from autoexec
EQMENT	EXE	Tells about your system
DISKPRAM	BAS	Displays the floppy disk driver settings. Reboot after use!
BOOT	BAS	Warm start from basic
DUMP	BAS	Yet another screen dumper but for compiled basic
DSKWATCH	ASM	Source
DSKWATCH	COM	Reports ALL disk errors. DOS only reports 5 in a row
EQUIP	BAS	Tells about your system
NODUP	BAT	Deletes duplicate files

SPREADSHEETS AND TEMPLATES:

Everyone who has ever worked in accounting or with any large scale inventory knows how valuable spreadsheets are for tracking purposes. They have proved their usefulness for columnar calculations, planning departmental forecasts or performing any other numbers-based analyses. Spreadsheets are GREAT for "what if" type questions because an entire forecast can be quickly generated from changes in a few numbers.

The spreadsheets here do not have the "power user" capacities of the mammoth and expensive spreadsheets. However, what they lack in total power they make up for in ease of use and many are equivalent in overall features. (Who really needs 6450 rows by 9000 columns, anyway?) For small to medium-sized applications (12 X 20 to 30 x 45) the selection here can offer you excellent alternatives to "the higher priced spread."

However, if you are stuck with one of the large commercial packages, we can still make your life happier. Two thirds of this section are templates for Lotus 1-2-3, Symphony, and VisiCalc. Some are specialized collections of worksheets designed to make that big package responsive and some will even analyze your worksheets. Some perform special functions, for example, there is a desktop manager based on the Lotus 1-2-3 environment, and some offer special macro-driven templates to enhance your productivity in diverse areas as inventory tracking and project management.

64 DESKTOP (Disk 1 of 2)
v1

DESKTOP is a LOTUS 1-2-3 worksheet featuring a menu-driven manager's appointment calendar, phone directory, and more. It is particularly useful for consultants and people who need to track time and expenses. DESKTOP is sophisticated and relatively easy to use. The companion tutorial and documentation disk is available on Disk #65.

Usage: Desktop organization, time management

System Requirements: 265K RAM, two disk drives, monochrome display and LOTUS 1-2-3 version 1-A

How to Start: Access through LOTUS 1-2-3

User Comments: "Directory and scratch pad very handy. Latter would be better if could save to disk. Clock helpful. Printer functions also handy." "There are better and easier to use desk-top programs which are also inexpensive."

Suggested Donation: $25 (for 2 disks)

File Descriptions:

SAMPLE	WKS	DESKTOP sample worksheet
DESKTOP	WKS	DESKTOP main worksheet
COPYIT	BAT	Batch file to copy DESKTOP
DTCOPY	BAT	Batch file

65 DESKTOP (Disk 2 of 2)
v1

This is the companion disk to #64 DESKTOP. DESKTOP is a LOTUS 1-2-3 worksheet featuring a menu-driven manager's appointment calendar, phone directory, and more. It is particularly useful for consultants and people who need to track time and expenses. This disk contains program documentation and instructions.

Usage: Desktop organization, time management

System Requirements: 265K RAM, two disk drives, monochrome display and LOTUS 1-2-3 version 1A

How to Start: Access through LOTUS 1-2-3.

Suggested Donation: $25 (for two disks)

File Descriptions:

DESK	DOC	Documentation for DESKTOP
INSTRUCT	WKS	DESKTOP instruction worksheet

170 Spreadsheets
v1.2

Spreadsheets is actually FreeCalc version 1.01, which is a reasonably good Lotus clone. However, many of the bugs and limitations present in this program are removed in version 2.0, which is available on Disk #574. The Pad (PC-PAD) is an interesting calculator and spreadsheet that can be used with FreeCalc worksheets. Both FreeCalc and The Pad are menu driven and fairly easy to use, but the documentation (provided) is important to read. The spreadsheet itself is 100 rows by 25 columns wide. Another odd utility program is Minicalc, which is a small compiled spreadsheet. Minicalc is interesting to look at, but not very useful.

Usage: Financial, simple accounting

System Requirements: 192K, two disk drives, monochrome display

How to Start: To read DOC or TXT files, enter TYPE filename.ext and press ENTER.

- To run an EXE or COM program, just type its name and press ENTER. For instructions on running BASIC programs, please refer to the GETTING STARTED section in this catalog.

User Comments: "The templates are simple, but they do work." "Width of cells limited to 10 characters." "It is a simple program to use and the documentation is very clear."

Suggested Donation: $25

File Descriptions:

————	——	FreeCalc
FC	EXE	FreeCalc Version 1.01 — main FREECALC spreadsheet program
FC	HLP	FreeCalc Version 1.01 — help files used by FC.EXE
FC	DOC	FreeCalc Version 1.01 — documentation for FC.EXE
READ	ME	FreeCalc Version 1.01 — how to print FC.DOC
DEMO?	FC	FreeCalc Version 1.01 — sample spreadsheet (3 files)
————	——	PC-PAD
AUTOEXEC	BAT	Part of PC-PAD — boot start up file
PC-PAD	ABS	Part of PC-PAD — abstract of PC-PAD
PC-PAD	BAS	PC-PAD Version 1.3 text oriented spreadsheet main program
PC-PAD	BAT	Part of PC-PAD — start PC-PAD spreadsheet
PC-PAD	DOC	Part of PC-PAD — documentation
PC-PAD	LST	Part of PC-PAD — commented source & 20 add-on functions
ROWCOL	BAS	Part of PC-PAD — instruction for row/column totaling
TEMPLE	KEY	Part of PC-PAD
VOLKSWTR	KEY	Part of PC-PAD
BASIC	KEY	Part of PC-PAD
COPYPAD	BAT	Part of PC-PAD
DEMOPAD		Part of PC-PAD
EW	KEY	Part of PC-PAD
————	——	MINICALC
MINICALC	DOC	Documentation for MINICALC.EXE
MINICALC	EXE	Small compiled spreadsheet

199 PC-CALC
v3

PC-CALC is a nice simple spreadsheet that is easy to use and well documented. Although somewhat limited, PC-CALC is able to handle most spreadsheet functions. This spreadsheet can even be used as a simple database, limited only by memory size. PC-CALC comes with its own tutorial and sample spreadsheets to be used with the extensive documentation.

Usage: Simple accounting, financial analysis

System Requirements: 128K, two disk drives and monochrome display

How to Start: Load DOS and type PC-CALC to enter the main program. Consult PCCALC.DOC for program documentation.

User Comments: "Simple and limited, but works well." "PC-CALC is an excellent little spreadsheet. Good learning disk." "I love it!" "Adequate for home or small business; not for heavy duty work."

Suggested Donation: $59.95

File Descriptions:

PC-CALC	EXE	Spreadsheet program from author of PC-FILE
PCCALC	DOC	Documentation for PC-CALC (86K)
DOC	BAT	Batch file to print documentation
PCCALC	EXE	Part of PC-CALC
PCCALC2	EXE	Part of PC-CALC
PCCALC3	EXE	Part of PC-CALC
PCCALC	MSG	Part of PC-CALC
PCOVL	EXE	Part of PC-CALC
EXAMPLE		Part of PC-CALC
RESPONSE		Part of PC-CALC

207
LOTUS
Worksheets No 1
v1

This disk contains a collection of some really nice worksheets. AUTO.WKS records every auto expense and tracks repair history. JOGLOG.WKS, a memory hog (needs 340k), is designed for the serious runner who must track performance at every level. FEDTAX83.WKS is complete. PAD.WKS is a sophisticated demo of Desktop-like templates. Additional spreadsheets are available from the author. AUTO and JOGLOG are especially well designed for professional performance management.

Usage: Expense management, physical training, performance management

System Requirements: 340k, two disk drives, monochrome display, LOTUS 1-2-3 version 1A

How to Start: Access through LOTUS 1-2-3

User Comments: "I liked AUTO best." "Definately worth it if you're a serious runner!" "Interesting collection of spreadsheets."

File Descriptions:

123KEY	BAT	Batch start up file
123KEY	DOC	Documentation
123KEY	PRO	Prokey template — permits using numeric key pad with LOTUS
AUTO	WKS	Calculates your gas usage and mileage (Vince Heiker)

FEDTAX83	WKS	1983 Tax Schedules 1040, 1040A, B, C, W (Les Wheeler)
JOGLOG	WKS	Simple jogging log (Vince Heiker)
PAD	WKS	Version 1.2 (Frank Girard) — Desktop-like template
TREND123	DOC	Documentation
TREND123	MAC	Version 1.0 (John Dannenfeldt) — Curve fitting macro for LOTUS

224
Gordon's
PC-Calc
v1

Gordon's PC-Calc is a small spreadsheet written by John Vandegrift and Guy Gordon. Although limited, PC-Calc even comes with some of its own utilites, such as keyboard buffer expander, advanced screen save and enhanced directory. PC-Calc is distributed free and should not be confused with a later program of the same name by Jim Button (of PC-FILE fame).

page 266

File Descriptions:

123DOC	BAS	BASICA Program to document the formulas in 1-2-3 worksheets
123DOC	DOC	Documentation file for 123DOC
123DOC	EXE	Compiled version of 123DOC.BAS
123MAIL	TXT	Tech notes on mail labels & SYMPHONY Q & A
123PREP	DOC	Documentation file for 123PREP.EXE
123PREP	EXE	Prepares data for file import to 1-2-3
123Q&A	TXT	Questions and answers from Lotus
123RANGE	BAS	Creates a table of range names/location in 1-2-3 worksheets
123XIMAC	TXT	Tech notes of using the /XI macros
ADDLABEL	DOC	Documentation file for ADDLABL3.WKS
ADDLABL3	WKS	Address label macros on WKS
DATAFILL	TXT	Tech notes on using the /Data Fill
FOR–NEXT	WKS	123 macros to demonstrate equivalent of a FOR-NEXT loop
LOOPMAC	TXT	Tech notes on using loops in macros
LOT101	TXT	Tech notes from Lotus
LOT102	TXT	Tech notes on memory use in 123
LOT103	TXT	Tech notes on using @IF in 123
LOT105	TXT	Lotus tech notes
MACROLIB	TXT	Notes on making a library of macros
MENU	WKS	123 template to make menu macros
PICFIL	TXT	Analysis of the .PIC files (graphs)
PHOTOEST	DOC	Documentation file for PHOTOEST.WKS
PHOTOEST	WKS	Photography fee estimation worksheet (standard ASMP form)
RATIO	WKS	123 template to do financial analysis
TEXTDEMO	WKS	Example of using text in @IF functions

257 Utility 1-2-3
v1

Utility 1-2-3 (not affiliated with LOTUS) is a useful tutorial and utiltity package that contains helpful hints and aids for LOTUS. The program is menu driven and features excellent screen graphics. ASCIITUT.WKS and ASCII.WKS illustrate how graphics are generated through LOTUS. Also included are various macros and Prokey templates. Utility 1-2-3 is a must for any serious LOTUS user.

Usage: Utilities and ASCII generator for LOTUS 1-2-3 worksheets

System Requirements: 256K, two disk drives, monochrome display and LOTUS 1-2-3 version 1A

How to Start: Access through LOTUS 1-2-3

User Comments: "This disk is really a good buy!" "The ASCII generator is nice for dressing up worksheets, but it takes some getting used to." "Some great 123 utilities, especially the graphics macros." "A great learning tool."

Suggested Donation: $25

File Descriptions:

ASCII	WKS	Reference file for extended ASCII character set
ASCIIDOC	BAT	Displays ASCII character table on screen
ASCIIDOC	PRN	Prints ASCII character table
ASCIITUT	WKS	Tutorial for ASCII character generator
AUTO123	WKS	Part of printed documentation files
END	PRN	Part of printer documentation files
HINTSTUT	WKS	Hints and techniques tutorial
INTROTUT	WKS	Introduction to tutorials
LOTUS	PRO	UTILITY 1-2-3 Prokey macros
MACROTUT	WKS	Macro samples
PRINTER	WKS	Reference file for generation of printer control characters
PRINTTUT	WKS	Tutorial for printer control generator
PROKYTUT	WKS	ProKey templates
README	BAT	Starts printout of documentation
SCREEN?	PRN	Part of printed documentation files (4 files)
SETUP	BAT	Installs UTILITY 1-2-3 on your LOTUS 1-2-3 system disk

289 Power-Worksheets
v1

Power-Worksheets is a user-supported program which relieves you of the need to set up (or program) and test 1-2-3 worksheets. A collection of financial calculators, the worksheets are easy to use, sophisticated and well graphed. Also included is a phone databes and Desktop-like appointment calendar. Over 70 pages of documentation is included with this disk, which is actually one of two disks available. Disk #2, which contains additional graph-supported worksheets, is available for $49 from the author.

Usage: LOTUS 1-2-3 templates, financial, desktop

System Requirements: 265K, two disk drives, monochrome display and LOTUS 1-2-3 v2.0

How to Start: Access through LOTUS 1-2-3

User Comments: "Very useful disk." "Very nice for sophisticated financial analysis." "Even though a little complicated, the spreadsheets are very useful."

Suggested Donation: $49 (includes printed manual and second disk) or $5 per worksheet.

File Descriptions:

README	1ST	Descriptions of worksheets on this disk
AUTO123	WKS	Lotus autostart file
AGENDA	WKS	Allows you to go from one worksheet to another.
BSTAT	WKS	Accepts data and performs two major analytical tasks.
DEPREC	WKS	A comprehensive worksheet.
NPV	WKS	Calculation program.
PROFIT	WKS	Analysis worksheet.
ROR	WKS	Another calculation program.
SREGR	WKS	Linear Regression program
TEST	WKS	Test worksheet
TV	WKS	Part of Power Worksheet
PRINTDOC	BAT	Prints 72 pages of documentation
INTRO	DOC	Introduction (6K)
BSTAT	DOC	Part of documentation (18K)
DEPREC	DOC	Part of documentation (24K)
NPV	DOC	Part of documentation (20K)
PROFIT	DOC	Part of documentation (44K)
ROR	DOC	Part of documentation (27K)
SREGR	DOC	Part of documentation (33K)

290 FITT Lotus 1-2-3 Tax Worksheets
v2

FITT, a user supported program, is a Lotus 1-2-3 worksheet (or template) for calculating your 1985 Federal Income Tax. Complete, with more than 20 pages of documentation included, this worksheet produces forms 1040, 2106, 2119, 2210, 2441, 3903, 4684 and Schedules A, B, C, D, E, F, R, SE and W. The worksheets are simple to use and well detailed. This disk is one of the best 1985 Federal Tax spreadsheets available. Even though the template is outdated now by the new tax laws, it can provide much needed references and help if you wish to write worksheets for the current times.

Usage: 1985 Federal Tax worksheet

System Requirements: 265K RAM, two disk drives, monochrome display and LOTUS 1-2-3 v2.0

How to Start: Access through LOTUS 1-2-3

User Comments: "Useful if being audited." "It's a good tax program." "Well documented, easy to use."

Suggested Donation: $35.00

File Descriptions:

————	——	FITT
README	1ST	Introduction
FITT85	DQC	Documentation — 20 pages
FITT85	WQS	Main worksheet file
STATES85	WQS	Optional state sales tax tables
USQ	COM	Unsqueeze program

301 Lotus Worksheets No 2
v1

Lotus Worksheets No 2 is a collection of technical notes, utility programs, operation hints and miscellaneous templates. FOR–NEXT.WKS, for example, illustrates how macros can be used to create FOR NEXT loops. MENU.WKS is a template used for designing menu macros. Tech notes include tips on printing mailing labels, the use of text in @IF fubctions, memory management and more. Power users will find this disk very useful. Beginners should have this disk just for the Q & A discussion on what Lotus can and cannot do.

Usage: Utilities, macros, tech notes

System Requirements: 265K RAM, two disk drives, monochrome display and LOTUS 1-2-3 v2.0

How to Start: Access through LOTUS 1-2-3

User Comments: "Recommended for serious LOTUS users." "A good collection of files and worksheets." "The Q&A section is great."

File Descriptions:

123DOC	BAS	BASICA Program to document the formulas in 1-2-3 worksheets
123DOC	DOC	Documentation file for 123DOC
123DOC	EXE	Compiled version of 123DOC.BAS
123MAIL	TXT	Tech notes on mail labels & SYMPHONY Q & A
123PREP	DOC	Documentation file for 123PREP.EXE
123PREP	EXE	Prepares data for file import to 1-2-3
123Q&A	TXT	Questions and answers from Lotus
123RANGE	BAS	Creates a table of range names/location in 1-2-3 worksheets
123XIMAC	TXT	Tech notes of using the /XI macros
ADDLABEL	DOC	Documentation file for ADDLABL3.WKS
ADDLABL3	WKS	Address label macros on WKS
DATAFILL	TXT	Tech notes on using the /Data Fill
FOR–NEXT	WKS	123 macros to demonstrate equivalent of a FOR-NEXT loop
LOOPMAC	TXT	Tech notes on using loops in macros
LOT101	TXT	Tech notes from Lotus
LOT102	TXT	Tech notes on memory use in 123
LOT103	TXT	Tech notes on using @IF in 123
LOT105	TXT	Lotus tech notes
MACROLIB	TXT	Notes on making a library of macros
MENU	WKS	123 template to make menu macros
PICFIL	TXT	Analysis of the .PIC files (graphs)
PHOTOEST	DOC	Documentation file for PHOTOEST.WKS

PHOTOEST	WKS	Photography fee estimation worksheet (standard ASMP form)
RATIO	WKS	123 template to do financial analysis
TEXTDEMO	WKS	Example of using text in @IF functions

302

Lotus
Worksheets No 3

v1

Lotus Worksheets No 3 is a collection of miscellaneous but useful worksheets. Investors, in particular, may find the stock analysis worksheets very helpful for what-if analysis and portfolio management. The cash and checkbook management worksheets are designed well, too. Business professionals are sure to find most of these worksheets useful, which are easy to use and nicely detailed.

Usage: Financial, simple accounting, investment management

System Requirements: 256K, two disk drives, monochrome display and LOTUS 1-2-3 v2.0

How to Start: Access through LOTUS 1-2-3

User Comments: "Very nice for beginner and sophisticated users." "Some very useful programs...we used parts of this disk in our business." "Scattered in interest, but generally good in quality."

File Descriptions:

2X2DISC	WKS	2 x 2 Linear Discriminant Function (Fisher's Method)
ACRS	WKS	ACRS depreciation
AMORT1X	WKS	Loan amortization self study
BIORYTHM	WKS	Biorythm calculator and graph
CARCOST	WKS	Auto operating expense
CASH	WKS	Checkbook/cash management system & journal
CASHMAN	WKS	Manual for CASH.WKS
CASHREAD	WKS	Instructions for CASH.WKS
DATEWR	WKS	Date value to string form
EXPENSRP	WKS	Travel business expense report
FLCHART	WKS	Draw & place flowchart symbols
GOLF	WKS	Golf handicapper
HANGROBO	WKS	Game of hangman — very slow
ICR–CALC	WKS	IRS interest calculator for tax underpayment
INDUST	WKS	Industry Analysis — Transportation sector stocks
IRR	WKS	Internal rate of return calculator

LEDGER	WKS	Checkbook ledger
MISTOX	WKS	Stock portfolio analysis-what-ifs
NLBE	WKS	Non-linear breakeven analysis
OPTIONZ	WKS	Options manager/stock current price
PAD	WKS	123 template-notepad/calendar/phone directory — menu driven
PRNTMENU	WKS	Menu for enhanced printer control — for EPSON
RENTAL	WKS	Rental property analysis
TAXPLAN	WKS	Five-year tax planner
TREND123	DOC	Documentation file for TREND123.WKS
TREND123	WKS	Macros-trend analysis-curve fitting

303

Lotus
Worksheets No 4

v1

Lotus Worksheets No 4 contains the OptionWare demo for solving mathematical problems. Reports and graphs can be printed from the demo. This disk also contains tips on converting Lotus 1-2-3 worksheeks to Symphony worksheets, a 1984 Federal Income Tax template and a template to create letters and labels. Documentation is included for all worksheets.

Usage: Simple accounting, math analysis, financial analysis

System Requirements: 256K, two disk drives, monochrome display and LOTUS 1-2-3 v2.0

How to Start: Access through LOTUS 1-2-3

User Comments: "Interesting, fun, but not very useful." "Too much advertising."

Suggested Donation: $25

File Descriptions:

AUTO123	WKS	Demo of OptionWare 1-2-3 models — self start with 1-2-3
MAGEE	DOC	Documentation file for MAGEE.WKS
MAGEE	WKS	Ledger/database date math + reports — menu driven
MAIL	WKS	123 template to form letters/labels
PREVIEW	WKS	Part of demo for OptionWare — used with AUTO123.WKS
TAX1984	DOC	Documentation file for TAX1984.WKS
TAX1984	WKS	Individual tax planning model
WSFF1	TXT	Worksheet File Format 1-2-3/Symphony:Intro & quick ref.

WSFF2	TXT	Worksheet File Format 1-2-3/Symphony:Summary of record types
WSFF3	TXT	Worksheet File Format 1-2-3/Symphony:Appendix A>
WSFF4	TXT	Worksheet File Format 1-2-3/Symphony:Appendix B

MACRO–1	DOC	Documentation for MACLIB.WKS (5K)
MACS	PRN	Macro set in PRN format
NVB	WKS	New Venture Budget
OLDBULL	DOC	Documentation file of all bulletins from the Capitol PC BBS
PVA	WKS	Price Volume Analysis
QA1	WKS	Queue Analysis (single-station service facility)
QAM	WKS	Queue Analysis (multi-station service facility)
QGN	WKS	Quote Generator — Form and Tracker
RAR	WKS	Ratio Analyzer
STC	WKS	Statistics Calculator

304
Lotus Worksheets No 5
v1

Lotus Worksheets No 5 is a great collection of Lotus 1-2-3 worksheets from the Capital PC Users Group BBS and Astrix Computer System. This disk includes worksheets for small business, fiancial and accounting use, a and macro library. The Check Book Balancer and cash flow managers are easy to use, even for beginners. The macro library is sophisticated and requires reading of the documentation (included).

Usage: Small business, accounting and financial analysis

System Requirements: 256K, two disk drives, monochrome display and LOTUS 1-2-3 v2.0

How to Start: Access through LOTUS 1-2-3

User Comments: "Excellent collection of useful worksheets." "I have used this disk in my business classes and have found it very helpful, a few flaws, but I recommend overall." "The macro library is extremely useful for us." "Good collection of financial macros." "Good overall models."

File Descriptions:

ADC	WKS	ACRS Depreciation Calc.
ARC	WKS	Accounts Receivable collections tracker
CBB	WKS	Check Book Balancer
CDB	WKS	Cash Disbursements
CFM	WKS	Cash Flow Manager
CFP	WKS	Cash Flow Projection
EIO	WKS	EOQ Inventory Ordering
FFS	WKS	5-in-1 Financial Statement
GCC	WKS	Growth Capacity Calc.
IIB	WKS	Interactive Income Statement
IRR	WKS	Internal Rate-of-Return
LCT	WKS	Line-of-Credit Tracker
LNA	WKS	Loan Amortization
LNP	WKS	Loan Payoff Calculator
MACLIB	WKS	Lotus 1-2-3 Macros Library — combined into most worksheets

305
Symphony Worksheets No 1
v1

Symphony Worksheets No 1 is good assortment of miscellaneous worksheets, macro aids, setting sheets, application add-in programs and tech notes. One useful application included is a Wordstar to Symphony conversion utility. Technical tips explain differences between 123 and Symphony macros, database conversion from 123 and wordprocessing in 2 columns. For fun, there is a biorythm worksheet and a roulette game. For the serious, there is a Desktop-like appointment calendar and phone directory (nice graphics).

Usage: Utilities, entertainment, tech tips, desktop

System Requirements: 512K, two disk drives, monochrome display and Lotus SYMPHONY

How to Start: Access through Lotus SYMPHONY

User Comments: "Great collection, something for everyone." "Gave me some good examples and ideas for a class I'm in." "Helpful in learning macros."

File Descriptions:

ADDRS	WRK	Name & Address notebook and mailing list label printer
APPT	WRK	Appointment Calendar
BIORYM	WRK	Plots Biorythm graph
CHCKWR	WRK	Converts numbers to spelled-out words
CLFORM	WRK	Macro to allow use of a FORM window without leaving window
COMDOC	WRK	Documentation for COMMA.APP
COMMA	APP	Application add-in for file import (comma-delimited)
COMPSV	CCF	Setting sheet for Compuserve
COMPSV	CTF	Translation table for Compuserve
COMTST	PRN	Test file to use with COMMA.APP

DBSEQ	WRK	Example of FORMs with record #'s
DECODE	EXE	Analyzer of 123 and Symphony worksheets
DECODE	WRK	Can be used with DECODE.EXE
FROMTO	TXT	Tech notes on 123 vs Symphony macros
FTMAC	WRK	File transfer utilities (macros) — XMODEM
HAMMER	WRK	Demo of graphics macros with trig. functions
LOTUSM	WRK	Automatic message retrieval from 'World of Lotus'
MENUBR	WRK	Examples of {menubranch} uses
NYNEW	TXT	New York Lotus SIG Newletter 10/84 (78K file)
REDIAL	WRK	Redial phone-and-login branch macro
ROULET	WRK	Roulette wheel game
SPACER	TXT	Data dependent line spacing/database
SYM102	TXT	Tech notes-database conversion from 123
SYMQ&A	TXT	Questions and answers from Lotus
SYNC	WRK	Synchronized windows macros
TWOCOL	WRK	Hints re: wordprocessing in two columns
WIDE	APP	Application add-in for file import: allows for long lines,etc.
WIDEDOC	WRK	Documentation for WIDE.APP
WIDTST	PRN	Test file for WIDE.APP
WNDWSY	WRK	Macro for synchronizing windows like 1-2-3
WRDST	CTF	Translation for Wordstar files to Symphony

File Descriptions:

1LETTER	WRK	Used with DIRECTRY.WRK
10_KEY	7WRK	A 10-key calculator
1MACROS	WRK	Used with DIRECTRY.WRK
1SHEET	WRK	Used with DIRECTRY.WRK
ADDR	WRK	Address Book
CHKBK	WRK	Macro-driven Checkbook
CHKBOO	DOC	Documentation file for CHKBOO.WRK
CHKBOO	WRK	Checkbook manager for home or small business
CTLBRK	APP	Break menu handling add-in
DIRECTRY	WRK	Create a library for file names and descriptions
DISKLABL	WRK	Prints out list of disk contents
INPUT	APP	1-2-3 'Range Input' feature add-in
LABELS	WRK	Name and address labels for printer
MCA	APP	1-2-3 Macro conversion aid add-in from Lotus
MCA	HLP	On disk help for MCA.APP
MCARI	WRK	Documentation for MCA.APP
PHNBRS	WRK	Database using find functions
PHONE	WRK	Phone dialer sample
SYSERR	APP	DOS error retry disable
UN1	CCF	Unattended operation .CCF file
UN1	WRK	Unattended operation see UN1.CCF

306
Symphony Worksheets No 2
v1

Symphony Worksheets No 2 is a mixed-bag selection of small business oriented worksheets and modem utilities. The macro-driven Checkbook program is quite sophisticated and can be used for any home or small business. Additional macro aids help manage disk contents, addresses and phone nubers (using find functions), 1-2-3 macro conversion, and more. DIRECTORY.WRK is an excellent program for creating a library for file names and descriptions, printing labels, letters, etc.

Usage: Home & small business accounting, file management, misc. utilitiies.

System Requirements: 512K, two disk drives, monochrome display and Lotus SYMPHONY

How to Start: Access through Lotus SYMPHONY

User Comments: "Good checkbook program, utilities may be useful."

389
Home Budget Template for LOTUS 1-2-3
v1.1

Pam's Home Budget Template for LOTUS 123 is well designed for managing personal and household finances. This disk contains 12 monthly files, complete with expense management for tax purposes. Because the files are standalone files, only 256k RAM is necessary. Each file is macro-drive and easy to use. Because of the size of the files, the disk is quite full. Therefore, it is recommended that you copy half the files to a work disk for more efficient disk management. The worksheets are well documented, but assumes a limited understanding of simple single entry accounting.

Usage: Home accounting

System Requirements: 256K, two disk drives, monochrome display and LOTUS 1-2-3 v1A

How to Start: Access through LOTUS 1-2-3

User Comments: "Very flexible, adaptable for most home users." "Easy to use and understand." "Could use some power macros to simplify handling."

File Descriptions:

????EXP	WKS	Expense template for each month (12 files)
AUTOEXP	WKS	Keep track of auto expenses, gas milage, etc.
DOCUMENT	WKS	Documentation template.

524
ExpressCalc
Version 3.09
(Disk 1 of 2)
v1

ExpressCalc is an excellent Lotus 1-2-3 clone with the capability of handling spreadsheets up to 64 columns by 256 lines. Each column may be up to 75 characters long, requires 256k RAM, and DOS 2.x or higher. It even works on 40 and 80 column displays. Like LOTUS 1-2-3, ExpressCalc can be used in a wide variety of application ranging from business forecasts to financial analysis to simple database management. No programming background is necessary to create a spreadsheet. ExpressCalc is definately one of the better LOTUS 1-2-3 clones. It performs almost as well and is limited only by memory. The tutorial is extensive and is highly recommended (see Disk #525). The program can be easily configured

Usage: Simple accounting, financial analysis, simple database

System Requirements: 256K, two disk drives, monochrome monitor, DOS 2.x or higher

How to Start: Load DOS and type CALC to enter the main program. Consult CALC.DOC (on disk 525) for program documentation.

Suggested Donation: $10 per disk, $49 for disks & printed manual

File Descriptions:

CALC?	EXE	ExpressCalc programs (5 Files)
CALC	MSG	Error messages displayed when using ExpressCalc
EXAMPLE		Sample spreadsheet
BW	PRO	Parameter file for setting black and white display
40	PRO	Parameter file for setting 40 column display
BW40	PRO	Parameter file for setting black & white, 40 column display
SL	PRO	Parameter file for slowing down the screen display

525
ExpressCalc
Version 3.09
(Disk 2 of 2)
V1

This is the companion disk to #524 and contains the tutorial and the documentation necessary to use ExpressCalc. See Disk #524.

Usage: Tutorial for ExpressCalc

System Requirements: Same as disk 524

How to Start: Same as disk 524

Suggested Donation: $10 per disk, $49 for disks and manuals

File Descriptions:

CALC?	DOC	Different sets of user documentation total about 190 pages
PRINTDOC	BAT	Batch file to print out documentation
RESPONSE		Response text file

531
Alan's Text
Editor & Spreadsheet
V1

Alan's Text Editor & Spreadsheet is a full screen ASCII text processor program with simple wordprocessing functions, including multi-file capabilities. The program is well supported with documentation and help menus, but does require an understanding of ASCII text editing. The spreadsheet is functional, but clumsy. Sample spreadsheet files include balloon payments, loan mortgages and other simple accounting uses.

Usage: Programming, simple financial uses

System Requirements: 128K, two disk drives and monochrome display

How to Start: Load DOS and type AE to enter the ASCII editor program. Type AC to enter the spreadsheet program. Consult README and the .DOC files for program documentation.

Suggested Donation: $35

File Descriptions:

————	——	Alan's Editor
AE	EXE	Alan's Editor ASCII Text Processor Program
AE	DOC	Documentation for Alan's Editor — printer formatted manual
AE	HLP	Help Screens for Alan's Editor
————	——	Alan's Spreadsheet
AC	EXE	Alan's Calc Spreadsheet Program
AC	DOC	Documentation for Alan's Calc — printer formatted manual
BALLOON	AC	Sample Spreadsheet File — Balloon Payments for car purchase
MORT	AC	Sample Spreadsheet File — Amortgage on a loan
BALANCE	AC	Sample Spreadsheet File — Checkbook Balancing exercize
SUMMARY	AC	Sample Spreadsheet File — Business Budget Summary
BUDGET	AC	Sample Spreadsheet File — Household Budget Calculations
SHEET1	AC	Sample Spreadsheet File — Linked Work Sheet #1 for Summary
SHEET2	AC	Sample Spreadsheet File — Work Sheet #2 for Summary
XYZCO	AC	Sample Spreadsheet File — Financial Data, XYZCO
README		Author's Introduction to files on disk.

568
LOTUS UTILITIES
v1

Lotus Utilities (not affiliated with LOTUS Corp.) is a mixed-bag selection of worksheets and utilities. OPTIONZ.WKS is a useful stock option program, with tables for calculating profit by option, buying/selling long or short, and more. NEWCOLOR.IN is a utility to enhance the color performance of LOTUS 1-2-3. Also included are utilities for archiving and unarchiving 12-3 worksheets, a program that sets up a 640k RAM disk, and a program for adding text to numeric cells. Another utility (123DOC.WKS) prints out worksheets with readable formulas. Finally, there is a 1985 Federal Tax template, complete with documentation.

Usage: 1985 Federal Tax, misc. utilities, stock option analysis

System Requirements: 256K, two disk drives, monochrome display, LOTUS 1-2-3 v2.0

How to Start: Access through LOTUS 1-2-3

File Descriptions:

123DOC	ARC	Archived file — Documentation Utility
123EGA	ARC	Archived file — Extended Graphics Adapter Utility
123PREP	ARC	Archived file — Text file to Lotus Prep Utility
123RANGE	EXE	Spreadssheet file print Utility Program
ARC	EXE	Archive Utility Program
CLRJET	ARC	Archived file — IBM Color Jet Printer Drivers
FEDTAX85	DOC	Text file — Documentation for FEDTAX85.WKS
FEDTAX85	WKS	LOTUS worksheet — Federal Income Tax for 1985
NEWCOLOR	DOC	Text file — Documentation for NEWCOLOR.IN
NEWCOLOR	IN	Program to change display colors for LOTUS 1-2-3
OPTIONZ	WKS	LOTUS worksheet — Stock Options
UNARC	TXT	Directions on expanding archived files on disk
TRYVM123	COM	Virtual memory system for 1-2-3 Release 2.0
TRYVM123	DOC	Documentation for TRYVM123
WKS-FRMT	TXT	Worksheet files format

571
1-2-3 Worksheets No 7
V1

1-2-3 Worksheets #7 contains various useful worksheets for financial analysis and accounting applications. PAYROLL.WKS is a standalone payroll system that can be used in many small businesses. It even includes graphs. LOAN.WKS requires 340k RAM and calculates amortization on loans up to 50 years. PAD.WKS is a Desktop-like electronic notepad. RENTAL.WKS is a detailed management system for income property owners. This disk requires that you have LOTUS 1-2-3 version 1.1a, or you can convert to version 2 of LOTUS. It will work with any system that runs LOTUS.

Usage: Simple finance, accounting, stock management, payroll

System Requirements: 256K, two disk drives, monochrome display, LOTUS 1-2-3 v1.1

How to Start: Access through LOTUS 1-2-3

File Descriptions:

BAR	WKS	LOTUS worksheet — Data Entry for Curve Smoothing
CHR256	WKS	LOTUS worksheet — Display all IBM characters in worksheet
LOAN	WKS	LOTUS worksheet — Amortization on 50 year loan
PAD	WKS	LOTUS worksheet — Menu driven Notepad
PAYROLL	WKS	LOTUS worksheet — Menu driven Payroll
PRNCINT	WKS	LOTUS worksheet — Principal, Interest and Insurance
PRTFOL	WKS	LOTUS worksheet — Portfolio Manager
RENTAL	WKS	LOTUS worksheet — Rental Units financial Manager
SCHEDULE	WKS	LOTUS worksheet — Project Scheduler
TREND123	DOC	Documentation for TREND123.MAC
TREND123	MAC	LOTUS 1-2-3 Trend line curve fitting macro
CHR256	DOC	Documentation for using IBM characters in a Lotus Worksheet
PAYROLL	PIC	Payroll grafix

574
FreeCalc
V2.0

FreeCalc is a spreadsheet program with numerous features. It has been expanded from Version 1.0 and is a mature product. While it lacks some of the features and power of a product like Lotus 1-2-3, it also lacks Lotus' high price. As a better than average spreadsheet, it is quite adequate for most applications. Like Lotus, FreeCalc uses all available memory (up to 640k) and is command bar driven. FreeCalc also allows for a color monitor. The disk manual is very complete and is 106 pages long.

Usage: Simple accounting, financial analysis, simple database

System Requirements: 256K, two disk drives, monochrome display,

Features:

- 250 rows by 25 columns
- Column width of 0 to 70 characters
- Text can be entered
- Left or right justified
- Display 0 to 6 decimal places
- Macros
- Print spreadsheet by disk
- Export spreadsheet to other programs
- Load ASCII text files

- Support for 8087 and 80287 coprocessors
- Up to 15 significant digits
- Wordprocessing mode
- Move, copy, delete and insert columns/rows

How to Start: Load DOS and type FC to enter the FREECALC program. Consult FC.DOC for program documentation.

Suggested Donation: $35

File Descriptions:

READ	ME	Instructions on how to print the manual
FC	EXE	Main FreeCalc program
FC	HLP	FreeCalc help file
FC	DOC	106 page FreeCalc manual
DEMO?	FC	Sample spreadsheets
COLOR	EXE	Program to set colors for color monitor
NO-COLOR	FIL	Parameter file to set colors to black/white
ONE2TWO	EXE	Program to convert from FreeCalc V1 to FreeCalc V2

583
LOTUS 1-2-3 — THE WHITEROCK ALTERNATIVE
v1

The Whiterock Alternative is a very user-friendly macro-driven worksheet shell (AUTO123.WKS) with several applications. AUTO123.WKS is a worksheet manager that allows access to other worksheets. Supported by clever screen graphics, the Whiterock Alternative is a pleasure to use. Checkbook, Maillist and loan amortizer worksheets are very complete and easy to use. A library of 1-2-3 macros is also included. This disk is highly recommended for serious Lotus users.

Usage: Checkbook management, mail listing, macro library

System Requirements: 256K, two disk drives, monochrome display, LOTUS 1-2-3 v2.0

How to Start: Access through LOTUS 1-2-3, use AUTO123.WKS

User Comments: "AUTO123 is very nice. CHECK.WKS is excellent." "The macros shell is worth the price of the disk."

Suggested Donation: $15 for shell, $15 per application

File Descriptions:

AUTO123	WKS	Auto-run file — Whiterock Alternative Menu & File Driver.
LIBRARY	WKS	Library of LOTUS 123 Macros
CHEKBOOK	WKS	Checkbook ledger worksheet
LOANTABL	WKS	Installment loan amortizer worksheet
MAILLIST	WKS	Mailing list maintenance worksheet
WEEKRPT	WKS	Jobcosting time management worksheet

LOANTABL	WKS	Installment loan analyzer.
MAILLIST	WKS	Mailing list database.
NEWCOLOR	IN	Redirect output for DEBUG program to change LOTUS 123 colors.
NEWCOLOR	WKS	Instructions for NEWCOLOR.IN.
POLREG	WKS	Calculate polynomial regressions.
PRTGRAPH	WKS	Instructions for using PRTGRAPH.COM for special fonts.
TITLES	WKS	Prepare chronological dates as titles for columns.
TRIANGLE	WKS	Solve for triangles given sides.
VENDOC	WKS	Documentation for VENDORS.WKS
VENDORS	WKS	Macro driven data base of suppliers for business.
WEEKRPT	WKS	Time management/Job logging utility.

584
COLLECTED LOTUS 1-2-3 WORKSHEETS
v1

This disk contains a variety of spreadsheets, ranging from printing utilities to common financial applications (loan amortization, checkbook manager, etc.). Included is the demo version of Toolkit and ACII driver, with mathematical calculators for solving triangles, creating ASCII tables and more. Another math spreadsheet performs polynomial regressions. Miscellaneous utilities allow default colors to be changed, the preparation of using chronological dates as column titles, intructions for using PRTGRAPH.COM to generate special fonts, etc. There are also worksheets for time management, mail list database and vendor database.

Usage: Small business, checkbook management, math, utilities

System Requirements: 256K, two disk drives, monochrome monitor, LOTUS 1-2-3 v2.0

Features: LOTUS 1-2-3 spreadsheets, utilities and databases

How to Start: Access through LOTUS 1-2-3

File Descriptions:

ASCIIUSE	WKS	How to use CHARS2 worksheet.
CHARS2	WKS	File of ASCII characters not directly accessible by LOTUS 123.
CHEKBOOK	WKS	Personal checkbook ledger.
CODESAMP	WKS	Printer driver for specialized fonts.
CONTENTS	WKS	Toolkit Shell and ASCII driver.
LOAN	WKS	Loan analysis worksheet.

587
SYMPHONY WORD PROCESSING TIPS & MACROS
v1

This disk contains a variety of prize-winning tips and Macros for SYMPHONY, including tips on importing wordprocessor files, Multiplan files, using SIDEKICK with SYMPHONY, and much more. In addition to great tips, there are also worksheets for creating a phone and address directory, creating and printing mailing labels, creating macros, and setting up multi-column documents. Utilities perform hexadecimal to decimal conversions (and vice versa), simulation of 123 window sychronization capability, calculation of metric values of resistance and tolerance of resistors. Also included is a macro demonstration and macro tips using the {get} function. These utilities seem to solve many of the conversion problems for major programs (WordStar, etc.).

Usage: Utilities, wordprocessing conversion, desktop

System Requirements: 512K, two disk drives, monochrome display and Lotus SYMPHONY

How to Start: Access through Lotus Symphony

File Descriptions:

TWOCOL	WRK	Sets up a multi-column document.
WORDST	CTF	Converts a WordStar document for Symphony.
WRDPRF	WRK	Use Word Proof in conjunction with Symphony.
SEARCH	APP	Searches spreadsheet for specific character.
HEX2DE	WRK	Converts hexadecimal to decimal numbers and vice versa.

CALC2	WRK	Calculates elapsed calendar and business days between two dates.
WNDWSY	WRK	Simulates 123 window synchronization capability.
RESICO	WRK	Returns metric values of resistance and tolerance of resistors.
MPLAN	APP	Imports Multiplan data into Symphony.
SEARCH	WRK	Worksheet using search capability.
SEARCH	PRN	Printable documentation on search capability.
SEARDOC	WRK	Worksheet format Search documentation.
SKPROB	WRK	How to use SideKick with Symphony.
ADDRMAC	WRK	Create an address book.
APPTMENT	WRK	An appointment and time management system.
DUALDS	WRK	Install Symphony with two monitors
DEMO	WRK	Demonstration file.
FLIPPER	APP	Data mover extension.
LABELS	WRK	Produces labels based upon a mailing list.
LEEVFORM	WRK	Offers an important macro concept using {get}.
MACRO1	WRK	Demonstration macro.
MOVIE	WRK	Use Symphony to display moving graphics.
ORD–ENT	WRK	Uses almost all Symphony commands for order-entry program.
USERTIPS	DOC	Protocols for use of some of these capabilities.

588 SYMPHONY BANK/INSURANCE/ MEDICAL APPLICATIONS
v1

This disk contains Symphony sample files that illustrate how Symphony can be used in banking, medical and insurance applications. Business professionals can use some of the sample files directly in their applications with simple modification. Financial analysis worksheets are quite sophisticated and can be used for developing ratios, creating forecasts, tracking performance. BUDGET.WRK is useful in calculating the financial prospects of medical practice. Medical practitioners can track and graph patient data and generate reports from the findings. Homeowners can calculate the appropriate amount of home owner's insurance. Small businesses can manage and track their inventory throurgh INVENTORY.WRK.

Usage: Small business, insurance, banking, medical, simple accounting

System Requirements: 512K, two disk drives, monochrome display and Lotus SYMPHONY

How to Start: Access through Lotus SYMPHONY

File Descriptions:

ASSET	WRK	Assists in asset-liability management.
2–APPLIC	WRK	Example file for APPLIC worksheet
2–ASSET	WRK	Example file for ASSET worksheet
2–BOND	WRK	Example file for BOND worksheet
2–CASH	WRK	Example file for CASH worksheet
2–EXCHAN	WRK	Example file for EXCHANGE worksheet
2–HUMANR	WRK	Example file for HUMANRES worksheet
2–MORTGA	WRK	Example file for MORTGAGE worksheet
AUTODEMO	WRK	Autorun Demo
BOND	WRK	Calculates a bond market price.
CASH	WRK	Forecasts cash flow.
DEMO	PIC	Graphics file for demo.
EXCHANGE	WRK	Effects of exchange rates on loan payments.
HUMANRES	WRK	Organizes employee information.
MORTGAGE	WRK	Determines if customer qualifies for mortgage loan
1–APPLIC	WRK	Example file for APPLIC worksheet
1–AUDIT	WRK	Example file for AUDIT worksheet
1–CLIENT	WRK	Example file for CLIENT worksheet
1–FORECA	WRK	Example file for FORECAST worksheet
1–IVENTO	WRK	Example file for IVENTORY worksheet
1–LIFE	WRK	Example file for LIFE worksheet
AUDIT	WRK	Calculate the appropriate amount of home owner insurance.
CLIENT	WRK	Manage client information. Make follow-up sales call schedule.
FORECAST	WRK	Calculates historical growth figures for insurance products.
IVENTORY	WRK	Maintain, stock and order inventory items.
LIFE	WRK	Estimate appropriate life insurance coverage for client.
1–BUDGET	WRK	Example file for BUDGET worksheet
1–CAPEQP	WRK	Example file for CAPEQPT worksheet
1–RESEAR	WRK	Example file for RESEARCH worksheet
1–SCHEDL	WRK	Example file for SCHEDULE worksheet
BUDGET	WRK	Forecast the financial prospects of a medical practice.
CAPEQPT	WRK	Determine investment quality of potential purchases.
DEMI	PIC	Graphics file for demo
RESEARCH	WRK	Track and graph patient data. Generate reports from findings.
SCHEDULE	WRK	Schedule patient appointments.

596
Symphony Worksheets No 3
v1

Business planners and investors will find this disk especially valuable to Symphony users. 5YEAR.WRK allows the financial planning of any business over a five year period, including the appropriate pro forma calculations. PROJECT.WRK enables planners to determine production and performance timetables for implementing and executing project oriented businesses. Both spreadsheets are macro-driven but do require reading the documentation and assumes basic knowledge of buiness plan development.

Usage: Business plan development

System Requirements: 512K, two disk drives, monochrome display and Lotus SYMPHONY

How to Start: Access through Lotus SYMPHONY

File Descriptions:

5YEAR	WRK	Five year business plan macro
PROJECT	WRK	Project oriented company planner macro
0–DESCR	WRK	Description of macros on this disk
0–HIGHLT	WRK	Expalanation on where to locate files
0–README	WRK	Library disk highlights

597
Symphony Worksheet No 4
v1

Symphony Worksheet #4 contains three macros for managing a checkbook (complete with a built in budget and IRS codes), developing loan tables and creating mailing lists. The spreadsheets are quite extensive and are easy to use. Another worksheet included is a discussion on creating and using Symphony macros. MAILLIST.WRK produces mailing labels and up to 3 different form letters.

Usage: Checkbook, loan analysis, mailling labels.

System Requirements: 512K, two disk drives, monochrome display and Lotus SYMPHONY

How to Start: Access through Lotus SYMPHONY

File Descriptions:

AUTOLOAD	WRK	Macro to display systems on disk
0–HIGHLT	WRK	Instructions on where to find details
0–HIGHLT	WRK	Instructions on where to find details
0–README	WRK	Details about new revisions and location of files
0–README	WRK	Details about new revisions and location of files
CHEKBOOK	WRK	Check Book Macro
LOANTABL	WRK	Loan Table Macro
MAILLIST	WRK	Mailing List Macro
PRODUCTS	WRK	Brief description of some macros
0–DESCR	WRK	Instructions on executing demo

625
PC-Calc jr
v2

This is Mr. Jim Button's famous spreadsheet program PC-Calc. This version of the program was included to fill a void for PCjr users. It is recommend that PCjr users and owners purchase this version of the program, and all others purchase the version on disk no 199.

Usage: Small to medium size spreadsheet applications

System Requirements: 128K, one double-sided drive (two are advised) and a monochrome display

How to Start: Type GO and press ENTER to print out the on disk documentation. When ready, enter PC-CALC at the DOS prompt to start.

Suggested Donation: $48.00 includes full Users Manual

File Descriptions:

PC-CALC	EXE	Spreadsheet program
PCCALC	DOC	Documentation for PC-Calc (86k)
DOC	BAT	Batch file to print documentation
PCCALC	EXE	Part of PC-Calc
PCCALC2	EXE	Part of PC-Calc
PCCALC3	EXE	Part of PC-Calc
PCCALC	MSG	Part of PC-Calc
PCOVL	EXE	Part of PC-Calc
EXAMPLE		Part of PC-Calc
RESPONSE		Part of PC-Calc

651

Turbo Calc /
AsEasyAs
Spreadsheets

v1

Turbo Calc is a spreadsheet program of about medium size; 512 rows by 64 columns. It is relatively easy to use and supports the usual range of functions, as well as text entries. Commands are by letter entry and there is onscreen display of command choices.

AsEasyAs is a refined spreadsheet program supporting 52 columns and 200 rows. Worksheet extension is .wks and files are compatible with another popular spreadsheet program. Function keys are utilized, and operation is by use of complete on-screen menus. AsEasyAs creates x-y graphs and bar charts as well.

Usage: Small to medium spreadsheet applications

System Requirements: 256K, two floppy drives and a monochrome display; AsEasyAs requires a graphics option for its x-y graphs and bar charts.

How to Start: Consult all documentation files before starting either program (they are marked with filename.DOC). While the TurboCalc program can be run immediately, you must use the ARC utility to un-archive the AsEasyAs program. Once done, either may be started from the DOS prompt.

Suggested Donation: TurboCalc $20.00; AsEasyAs $25.00

File Descriptions:

————	——	Turbo Calc (V5.01)
ARC	EXE	Program for archival storage and retrieval.
UNARC		Notes: How to retrieve AsEasyAs files from archive.
TC511	TXT	Notes about Turbo Calc overlay file.
TC511-EX	SSF	Sample Turbo Calc worksheet (template). Family budget.
TC511	000	Turbo Calc overlay file.
TC511	COM	Turbo Calc command file.
TC511	DOC	User documentation file for Turbo Calc.
ASEASYAS	ARC	Archived AsEasyAs System files.
————	——	AsEasyAs (V1A)
ASEASY	COM	AsEasyAs system command file.
AUTOEXEC	BAT	Batch file for root directory, hard disk, color.
CMODE	COM	Command file, switches mono to color.
PRINTER	COM	Printer control routine.

PS-READ	DOC	Notes about S-DUMP.COM and PRINTER.COM.
README	DOC	User documentation — Instructions. 7 pages.
README	WKS	Complete function list available with AsEasyAs running.
S-DUMP	COM	A Hires graphic screen dump routine.
SPREAD	MSG	Data file for spreadsheet messages.

695

EZ-SPREADSHEET

v1

EZ-SpreadSheet is designed to be an easy to use but powerful spreadsheet for the first time user. Many experienced spreadsheet users will find the straight-forward implementation of commands easy to understand and logical. Its particular virtures are that it is fast, full-featured as well as compact, being just 512 columns by 64 rows which is enough for most folks anyway.

In most cases you can just use the worksheets supplied and enter your own data into the worksheet and EZ-Spread will do all the calculations for you (my 9-year old has been eyeing this capability). Applications worksheets supplied for the home include calculating budgets, loans, savings plans, etc. Business applications include everything from simple loan calculations to complete financial statements.

LIMITATIONS: Although none of the prime functions are limited, EZS does not allow you to print to a file (which would allow the use of one of the many "sideways" programs) nor allows a page length longer than 66 lines, or a page width wider than 80 characters. Registered users will have full control over these functions as well as the ability to modify or eliminate the timed "screen save" message.

Usage: Small business spreadsheet users

System Requirements: 256K, two disk drives and monochrome/graphics display

How to Start: Enter TYPE EZS.DOC and press ENTER to read program information. To start, type EZS and press ENTER.

Suggested Donation: $49.95 Full individual registration gets a unique registration number; latest version of EZ-Spread; Printed users manual; Free phone support for 30 days; and Membership in the Worksheet Exchange Service. Mail in several of your worksheets (on diskette), and they will return your diskette with a selection of other worksheets in your requested field of interest; Site licenses available for $250.00

File Descriptions:

EZS	000	Data for the Main program
EZS	COM	Main program
EZS	DOC	Documentation for EZ Spreadsheet
?????	EZS	Spreadsheets
REGISTER	FRM	Registration form

696

QubeCalc

v1

QubeCalc is a spreadsheet with many advanced features and some features which are so unique it would be hard to find them collected anywhere else at any price (SEE FEATURES below). However, the special power of QubeCalc is in its being a TRUE three dimensional spreadsheet. As opposed to some two dimensional spreadsheets which let you link cells of multiple spreadsheets together, it gives you the ability to look at your data in more ways than you ever imagined possible.

QubeCalc may be thought of as a large cube — the WorkQube — with 262,144 cells, arranged into 64 rows, 64 columns and 64 pages, named X,Y and Z. So configured there are six faces on the WorkQube named A through F. Face A is the opposite side of Face D; B is opoposite E and C is opposite Face F. Here is the Power of QubeCalc: You may view, enter or manipulate your data from ANY of the six faces, providing a different perspective of the data stored within the WorkQube. Thus you have the ability to turn columns into pages, pages into columns, etc, to allow you to look at your data in any perspective you desire.

Usage: Heavy spreadsheet users

System Requirements: 256K (640K recommended), two floppy or one floppy/one hard disk drive and color/graphics display;

Features:

- Interactive context help screens
- Ability to recalculate only specific block if needed

- Ability to recalculate, graph and DataFill in all 6 possible orders of rows, columns, and pages
- A DataFill command to generate sine curves, exponential curves and any othe sequences of data required
- Forty-four predefined functions (including math, trig, statistical)
- Create bar charts and line graphs from data
- A very powerful Macro facility
- The ability to turn rows into columns, columns into pages, etc.
- Selective Recalculation: only a specific block if you wish.

How to Start: QUBECALC.DOC has the documentation for installation and operation.

Suggested Donation: $49.95 + $5 s/h covers registration fee and full manual

File Descriptions:

EXAMPLE	QUB	Sample spreadsheet
IMPORT	COM	Part of setup
INSTALL	BAT	Installs QUBECALC to your hard drive
PRINTDOC	BAT	Batch file to print the documentation for you
QUBECALC	000	QUBECALC data
QUBECALC	COM	Main program
QUBECALC	DOC	Documentation for QUBECALC
QUBECALC	HLP	Help file for QUBECALC
SETUP	COM	Setup program for your system

WORD PROCESSORS:

This category includes the major tools of document processing:

- Text processors
- Text editors
- Word processors

Text processors, editors and word processors are all text processing tools of different strengths and applications. The primary differences are that text editors do not have the special printing powers of word processors (for cut & paste, boldfacing, italics, etc.) and are used primarily for technical documentation applications. Text formatters, on the other hand, are specialized tools for preparing text for printing and are relatively "weak" for word processing.

A major trend in this field is "power word processing" and we have several outstanding examples: full-featured word processors with integrated spelling checkers, mail merge capability, even automatic footnoting and indexing! These user-supported programs are highly popular and we encourage you to check others to see which word processor meets your needs.

For text editors, our selection ranges from several solidly programmer-oriented ones to a recent pair that have significant word processing features (macro capacity, print formatting and even windowing!). Text formatters vary in complexity from simple print batch jobbers to a number of advanced models that can do large scale print management.

For the special needs of writers and editors, there is special software for evaluating the quality and qualities of your writing. Got a hot idea to sketch out? Use one of our outlining devices. There's even a specially configured word processor for the dramatically inclined, whether it be the silver screen or the TV screen you're writing for.

78 PC-WRITE (2.7/4) (Disk 1 of 2)

v2.7

PC-WRITE is a powerful, easy to use, word processor that has been around, and has been recognized as one of the best for some time. Though a quite sophisticated package, the substantial on-line help facilities make it easy for the novice user to gain proficiency in a comfortable manner. The program possesses a wide array of powerful features, some not available on expensive, commercial packages. If you are in need of a package you won't soon outgrow, PC-WRITE is an excellent choice.

Please note this is the first of a two disk set; No 627 is the second.

Usage: Full-featured word processing

System Requirements: 128K, one disk drive, and monochrome display

Features:

- On-line help screens
- Table of Contents and Indexing support
- Split-screen editing
- Supports imbedded printer commands
- File and field merge
- Alternate language character support

How to Start: Consult the READ.ME for an introduction. To get the Tutorial and Quick Guide, insert the program disk in drive A, and enter one of the following at the A> prompt: PRINTMAN (prints copy of 17 page Tutorial) TYPEMAN (types Tutorial on screen, with pause to read); use FILEMAN MANUAL1.CRN B:PART1.DOC to un-compress manual; do for all THREE files marked MANUAL*.DOC. Files MANUAL2.DOC and MANUAL3.DOC are a 44 page instructions manual called QUICK GUIDE. When uncompressed, you can print or screen read them.

- To run, enter ED and press ENTER.

User Comments: "Superior word-processing program. A joy to use and easy to learn. This is a powerful and complete word-processing program. Superb!!!!" "ABSOLUTELY THE CLASS OF SHAREWARE. This is my word processor of choice!!"

Does any more need to be said?" "It will be super once I get the hang of it, I am encouraging my family to learn on this rather than get "polluted" by another word processer." "This word-processing program is loaded with features. You can do almost anything imaginable with it if you can decipher the documentation which is confusing at times. I would not recommend this one for beginners."

Suggested Donation: $79.95 plus $5.00 S & H for full version and printed manual and tech support number.

File Descriptions:

GO	BAT	Types READ.ME
READ	ME	Introductory note
QUICKS	ME	How to get started note
ED	EXE	Edit program
PR	EXE	Print program
WORKDISK	BAT	Creates a working diskette or directory
PRINTMAN	COM	Prints Tutorial and Quick Guide
TYPEMAN	COM	Types Tutorial and Quick Guide on screen
FILEMAN	COM	Uncompresses Tutorial and Quick Guide
MANUAL1	CRN	Tutorial (compressed)
MANUAL2	CRN	Quick Guide, part one (compressed)
MANUAL3	CRN	Quick Guide, part two (compressed)
STORY		Sample text file used in tutorial
ED	HLP	Edit program help file
ED	DEF	Edit control file — for normal use
ED	TRS	Edit control file — for Tandy 1000
ED	SPC	Edit control file — for special cases
PCWMOUSE	DOC	Information about Microsoft Mouse
PCWMOUSE	DEF	Microsoft Mouse menu control file
PCWMOUSE	MSC	Mouse Systems Mouse control file
UPDATE27	CRN	Update notes, 2.6 to 2.7 (compressed)
GETYN	COM	Used by Workdisk
ED	DIR	Directory of files

86 *SCREEN Text Editor*
v1.1

A straightforward and powerful text editor which provides all the essential functions that are really needed for most routine text development. Its commands are simple and easy to remember and where appropriate, needed responses are clearly prompted. If you need a basic text editor, you can't overlook this one!

Usage: Text and simple word processing

System Requirements: 128K, one disk drive, monochrome or color display

Features:

- Line lengths to 240 characters long
- Full insert and delete capabilities
- Block operations (move,copy,delete)
- Upper & lower case conversions of text
- Split a line in two
- Concatenate two lines
- Center screen around a line
- Exchange two lines of text
- Repeat a line of text
- Go to absolute or relative page numbers
- File length may exceed memory
- External files may be written or read
- Search, replace & global replace
- All function keys utilizied
- Supports the MICROSOFT MOUSE.
- Works with DOS 1.1, 2.X OR 3.X!
- Pop-up menus

How to Start: Check the HELPME.BAT to get started and SCREEN.TXT for documentation

- To run it, just type SCREEN and press ENTER.

User Comments: "Very good. The best editor I have used at the PC level. I am using Screen as an editor to write dBase II programs." "SCREEN seems to fit the bill. This is an excellent, easy to use screen editor and is certainly comparable to TEXTRA or other much more expensive text editors." "Can't make this run on DOS 3.1." "Very easy to use. Only a few limitations — doesn't use all memory — no programmability — auto backup — difficult to save file with different name."

Suggested Donation: $35.00 registration brings full manual, function key overlay and the latest update.

File Descriptions:

SCREEN	EXE	Main program
SCREEN	TXT	Documentation file (125K)
AUTOEXEC	BAT	Batch file to autoboot SCREEN
HELPME	BAT	Instructions on how to begin
INSTALL	BAT	Batch file to install program
MMOUSE	BAT	Batch file to copy Microsoft Mouse software onto disk
PRTCOM1	BAT	Batch file to copy documentation to com1:
PRTCOM2	BAT	Batch file to copy documentation to com2:
PRTLPT1	BAT	Batch file to copy documentation to lpt1:
PRTLPT2	BAT	Batch file to copy documentation to lpt2:
STRIPPER	EXE	Strips out Tabs and replaces with spaces

146
EasyRite/ LablFile from GINACO
v2

Two very basic and effective programs from GINACO. EasyRite is a elementary text editor/word processor that is styled to make the computer perform like a typewriter. With its onscreen documentation you can do most everything from the main menu. The four modes of EasyRite are (1) LOAD and then review a file; (2) CREATE a file; (3) EDIT a file; and (4) PRINT a hard copy. Several nice features that go beyond the simple stuff, for instance, a new or edited EasyRite file may be saved to any drive.

LablFile is a self-documented, highly flexible file-management and label-print program which compliments EasyRite. Both of the programs are provided in expanded ASCII, BASIC and compiled form; also, both can function on the PCjr.

Usage: Basic word processing and file management

System Requirements: 64K, one disk drive and monochrome display

How to Start: Read the TEXT.ONE, README and FACTS files for information about the programs. Both LablFile and EasyRite may be run from DOS by typing LF or ER ENTER.

User Comments: "Good for learning word processing." "Pales in light of other programming available. I really haven't used this program and that is probably due to the fact I have a word processor already and the documentation is so brief (1 Page for a word processor!) that I thought it would be more trouble than it was worth."

Suggested Donation: $10.00

File Descriptions:

		EasyRite
ER	EXE	Word processor program (compiled)
DEMOFILE		Sample Word Processor file
EASYRITE	BAS	Word processor source code
FACTS		EasyRite instructions
TEXT	ONE	Sample text file — information about EasyRite/LabelFile
TEXT	TWO	Sample text file — information about Blueberry from GINACO
		LabelFile

LF	EXE	Label/File program (compiled)
LABLFILE	BAS	Source for Label/File program
README		Notes about using programs (short!)

190
Text Editors and Misc
v1

Most of the programs on this disk are in BASIC and must be run under the Interpretive BASIC provided on PC's and most clones. The central program on the disc is FULLSCREEN which is a fullscreen editor for use with BASIC instead of the cranky line editor provided with PC BASIC. It is simple to use, driven by the function key menu at the bottom of the screen just as in standard BASIC. The function key menu has several levels which provide most all the functions offered by most text editors. The other programs provide a variety of functions, such as form building, memo building, string search, file converions, directory changes and the like.

Usage: All around BASIC full-screen editor

System Requirements: 64K, one disk drive and monochrome display

How to Start: Consult the RV-EDIT.DOC and INFO.DOC (FULLSCREEN) files for instructions; the others have onscreen help

- To run a BASIC program (suffix .BAS), type BASICA filename and press ENTER. Please note that you must either put a copy of BASICA on this disk, or have BASICA on your current DOS path.
- To run programs suffixed .EXE, just type its name, i.e., for X.EXE, type X and press ENTER.

File Descriptions:

CUSTOM	BAS	Custom characters by Gary Antrim
FIX-TEST	BAS	Inserts carriage returns & line feeds
MEMO	BAS	Quick memo writer (John Harrington)
PC-FORM	EXE	PC-FILE form generator Version 1.1 (William Bailey)
RV-EDIT	BAS	Full screen editor Version 1.2 (Bob Vollmer)
RV-EDIT	DOC	Documentation
TXTSCAN	BAS	Searches ASCII file for character string
VUE	BAS	Nifty look into text files Version 1.0 (Buzz Hamilton)
		FULLSCRN
FULLSCRN	BAS	Full screen data entry

PGMCVRT	BAS	Part of FULLSCRN.BAS
XXXX	DAT	Part of FULLSCRN.BAS
FULLSCRN	BSC	Part of FULLSCRN.BAS
FRM001	DAT	Part of FULLSCRN.BAS
FUL001	DAT	Part of FULLSCRN.BAS
FULLSCRN	BSN	Part of FULLSCRN.BAS
INFO	DOC	Part of FULLSCRN.BAS — Documentation

194
ROFF and PC-READ
v2

PC-READ is a compiled Pascal program that accepts a text file and grades it on a slightly modified Gunning Fog Index. The Gunning Fog Index measures the complexity of writing. It represents the complexity as an average grade level (elementary, high school, college) at which the text could be easily read. For instance, a Fog Index of 9 means 9th grade reading level. Most successful popular writing grades below a 13 on a Fog Index scale.

ROFF is a text formatter. Using ROFF, you can make nice printouts of a file with as little or as much help from the program as you want, depending on the commands. There are default values for all parameters, so if you don't put any commands in at all, your file will come out with filled, right-justified lines. The default line-length is 80 characters and the default page-length is 66 lines per page.

Usage: Text formatting and writing analysis

System Requirements: 64K, one disk drive and a monochrome display

How to Start: Consult the PC-READ.DOC and the ROFF.DOC files for directions. Both ROFF and PC-READ can be started directly from DOS.

User Comments: PC-READ: "There is not enough explanation of the readability concept; also, all that comes out is the final value. I need to know how it is calculated and what the wordcount, sentence number, etc. are." "PC-Read is a fun program, especially when trained on pompous writers!" ""I found it to be very helpful to me. It makes me take more time to think about how I am writing things. I would highly recommend it to anyone who does any type of writing." "Only used it twice but I believe that it is unnecessarily restricted in order to force

the user into paying the $35.00 charge without adequate evidence of the program's usability."

Suggested Donation: $35.00 for PC-READ

File Descriptions:

INTEGRAL	C	Source in C for integration routine
INTEGRAL	PAS	Source in Pascal for integration routine
INTEGRAL	DCL	Declaration of integral for calling Pascal program
TSTINTEG	C	Source in C for example of use of integral
TSTINTEG	PAS	Source in Pascal for example for use of integral
RKF45	C	Source in c for RKF45 integrator
RKF45	PAS	Source in Pascal for RKF45 integrator
RKF45	DCL	Declaration of RKF45 for calling Pascal program
TSTRKF45	C	Source in C for example of use of RKF45
TSTRKF45	PAS	Source in Pascal for example of use of RKF45
— — —	—	ROFF
ROFF	H0	Header common to all ROFF source
ROFF	H1	Header specific to ROFF1
ROFF	H2	Header specific to ROFF2
ROFF1	C	Part 1 of ROFF source (Modified from PC-SIG Disk No 50).
ROFF2	C	Part 2 of ROFF source
ROFF3	C	Part 3 of ROFF source
ROFF	DOC	Documentation of ROFF
ROFF	EXE	Version of ROFF produced from source code on this disk
— — —	— —	PC-READ by Joey Robichaux
PC-READ	COM	Program to determine the clarity of text
PC-READ	DOC	Documentation for PC-READ.COM
WRITENOW	COM	Writes to printer imediately using Diablo codes

294
EDIT (1.16)
v1.17

EDIT is a general purpose text editor and word processing program. It supports a wide array of editing operations, including powerful commands that are often not available even in very expensive word processors. For example, it supports not only "word wrapping", but fully automatic paragraph reformatting as well. Under versions 2.0 or later of DOS, EDIT even allows you to execute DOS commands, or start another program without leaving EDIT. Files are limited to about 50,000 characters (25 single-spaced pages).

Usage: Basic word processing

System Requirements: 96K (128K recommended), one disk drive and monochrome display; IBM matrix printer or compatible.

How to Start: Consult the README and .TXT files for documentation; use the PRINTDOC.BAT file to print it

- To run EDIT.EXE, just type EDIT and press ENTER.

User Comments: "I am just learning this editor and the more that I use it, the better that I like it. I would highly recommend it to everyone." "Excellent general purpose word processor and text editor. Far better than most $200 and up word processors." "Very straight forward Word Processor & Editor. Would recommend this program to anyone who desires a no frills WP."

Suggested Donation: $25.00

File Descriptions:

EDIT	EXE	Main program — type "edit" to start
EDIT	SET	Setup parameter file
EDIT	HLP	Help text
*	TXT	Documentation files (70K total)
*	SET	Print format files
PRINTDOC	BAT	Batch file to print documentation
*	PRN	Documentation files to print
READ	ME	Brief description

343 Word Processing
v1

This program provides a simple word processing environment for children. Using a high degree of graphics displays, it offers children a distinctively bright, friendly environment for young ones to learn in. It features easy-to-understand graphic menus, automatic word wrap, and extra large characters, perfect for small people.

Usage: Writing tool for the younger set.

System Requirements: 128K, 1 disk drive, color/graphics monitor and adaptor card

How to Start: Excellent documentation is in the WPK.DOC file

- To run the program, enter WPK and press ENTER.

User Comments: "This is a great program for Kids, 4 to 8 years old. It provides a complete wp system that is attractive to them and encourages them to write." "Tried it out on my two grandsons (both 6)

with good results." "Very nice program for the kids. Our 10 yr old loves it; very easy and powerful." "This is one of the finest writing programs that I have ever seen for children. The documentation is clearly written for the young user. The program is snag-proof for the younger set (who might be more prone to forgetfulness). EXCELLENT!"

Suggested Donation: $10.00

File Descriptions:

WPK	EXE	Executable children's word processing program
THE–CAT	WPK	Sample text file
THE–DOG	WPK	Sample text file
RHYMES	WPK	Sample text file
STORY	WPK	Sample text file
PRACTICE	WPK	Sample text file
WPK	DOC	Documentation for WPK.EXE

379 WordStar Aids
v1

An all-star collection of useful WordStar utilities to enhance your usage of this valuable word processor. The collection includes keyboard redefinitions, printer patches, color, and editing features. Among others: WS2000.DIR gives you a full description of that versions keyboard defintions. Also here is ST — the SuperTyper program — an improved version of the DOS "TYPE" command.

Usage: Any WordStar user looking for improved performance

System Requirements: 64K, one disk drive and monochrome display

How to Start: Consult the files suffixed .DOC, .KEY and .TXT for documentation

- To run a program with the suffix .COM or .EXE, just type its name, i.e., for ST.COM, type ST ENTER.

User Comments: "CAT is a very good program, the program to change colors in WordStar did not run on my Leading Edge model "D" without scrambling the WordStar comfile....still use CAT, and several of the WS files." "This is definitely a program for an experienced wordstar user. Judy Epstein's work is definitely not for the beginner." "Good for WordStar users who have not yet updated to WordStar 2000. Depending upon your version of WS, some of the programs are redundant (such as WSMOD and WSMX80G)." "I've only used the UNWS program, but this program alone is worth much more than the price of the disk to anyone who needs to convert WordStar text into a database program."

File Descriptions:

MODWS1	ASM	Strips underline from WS files
MODWS1	EXE	"
ST	COM	Supertyper for WordStar
ST	DOC	Documenatation for ST.COM
UNWS	EXE	Removes high-order bits from WS
WS — 3·24	PAT	WS printer patches
WS-PROKY	KEY	Function key redefinitions
WS2	KEY	Keyboard redefinition
WS2000	DIR	Keyboard redefinition
WS2KEY	DOC	Keyboard redefinition
WS3530	WS	Printer patches for NEC3530
WSFIX3	TXT	Function key redefinitions
WSFXNEC	TXT	Function key redefinitions
WSMOD	COM	Adds color to WS
WSMX80G	WS	Patches for MX-80G
WSNUM	EXE	Numbers paragraphs in ws files
WSPNEC35	BAS	Patches for various printers
WSUNNUM	EXE	Unnumbers paragraphs in WS files

415
W-ED, Word Processing Previewer
v1

Three very powerful text-oriented programs can be found on this disk.

1. W-ED is a small (14K) editor and word processor which is very simple to use. It's commands are easy to remember and it creates an ASCII file which can be printed or re-edited.

2. The Word Processing Previewing System (WPPS) gives you a picture of page layouts from any ASCII word processor file without your having to print a hard copy. WPPS draws up to 18 rectangle "pages" on your color display, then fills them with microscopic output to show exactly how your document will look. Repeating the operation, up to 18 pages at a time, it is invaluable in saving reams of paper, and your time, especially for documents with tens or hundreds of pages.

Usage: Special text/word processing applications

System Requirements: 128K, one disk drive and monochrome display WPPS requires color/graphics board for 640x200 resolution.

How to Start: Consult the WED.DEF, MANUAL and files suffixed .DOC for documentation. As all three programs may be run from DOS, just type its name, i.e., for W-ED, type WED ENTER.

User Comments: "Very useful in previewing multipage printouts" "Superb program, one of the real shareware gems. I've given copies of this disk to everyone I know and am giving a presentation on it to the user group. If I'd had this back when I started, I could have paid the shareware fee in paper saved by now!" "Difficult to setup." "I was disappointed that WordPerfect was not directly supported, but only if I save my files as ASCII text...at least according to the documentation."

Suggested Donation: W-ED $39.95 covers a printed manual, the newest W-ED version and notification of product enhancements; WPPS $40.00 includes a wire-bound, typeset, and illustrated manual.

File Descriptions:

WED	BGN	Screens describing each section of W-ED
WED	PGM	Describes the programmable version of W-ED
INSTALL	EXE	Changes the W-ED default options, such as margins
WED	SAL	Sales information to obtain W-ED
WED	TUT	Screens for W-ED tutorial
WED	DEF	Documentation for W-ED (10 pages)
ORDER	WED	WyndhamWare order form for W-ED
WED	EXE	The W-ED Word-processing EDitor (executable program)
TSTBRD	EXE	Demonstrates the programmer's version (for DEMO only)
DEMO	EXE	Demonstration of W-ED, including a tutorial
WEREAD	ME	Short description of W-ED (2 pages)
WED-DESC	1LN	One-line description of W-ED files
&	EXE +	Word Processing Previewing System (executable program)
&	CUE	Configuration file for W.P.P.S.
&	DOC	Documentation for W.P.P.S. (33 pages -or- 10 with "type")
&PCW	CUE	Configuration file for PC-Write users
&READ	ME	Short description of W.P.P.S. (1 page)

416
ROFF4
v1

A complete and well documented version of ROFF with test and sample files. This formatter contains features important for the preparation of technical manuscripts. Special symbols or fonts that can be defined by or for the user can be produced (if the hardware is capable!). Super and subscripts can be handled as well as backspace, even for printers without reverse scrolling or backspacing hardware capabilities.

Using ROFF4, you can make nice printouts of a file, with as little or as much help from the program as you want, depending on the commands. There are default values for all parameters; so if you don't put any commands in at all, your file will come out with filled, right-justified lines.

Usage: Text formatting

System Requirements: 128K, one disk drive and a monochrome display

How to Start: To read the manual on screen, enter: ROFF4 ROFF4.DOC To print the manual, type: ROFF4 ROFF4.DOC+

● To run, enter ROFF4 and press ENTER.

User Comments: "The readme.1st file gave an incorrect command for getting a printed copy of the manual. The command should have been: 'roff4 roff4.doc +)'. Once I got a copy of the manual I was able to format documents without much trouble." "Very complex! But powerful. Documentation needs a command summary, and SOME description of how to use the sample files." "Great formatter although I usually don't often need all its features" "Have used mainframe ROFF. This version compared well."

File Descriptions:

EQN		Demonstrates macro use for equation numbering
CATALOG	DSK	List of files on disk
FNOTES		Test for footnotes
SUPER5	ROF	
README	1ST	Describes how to print documentation
FOOT		Footnote demo
FORM		Demonstration creating form letters
LIST		Initialize to list
MATRIX		Demonstrates postional control for equations
MX80		Initialize for epson MX-80 with graftrax

ONE		Test used with sotest
PAGES		Test for pagination
READ	ME	Comments on ROFF4 formatter in public domain
ROFF4	C	Main source module
ROFF4	EXE	Executable form of formatter
ROFF4	DOC	19 pages of documentation
ROFF4	PRN	Formatted version of ROFF4.DOC
ROFF4	H	Source (common declarations)
COMPILE	BAT	Batch file to create roff4.exe from sources
ROFF4A	C	Source module (7 files)
SOTEST		Test and demo of nested .so(urce) commands
THREE		Used with sotest
TWO		"
HEADER	ROF	Header file for Epson printer
NRO	ROF	Another header file
TESTNRO	ROF	Sample file for NRO.ROF
DESCRIPT	ROF	Brief description of ROFF4 v1.61

422
ScreenWriter
v1

ScreenWright Professional is a complete word processing program specifically designed for screenplays and teleplays. Special care has been taken to keep ScreenWright Professional simple to use, so you can concentrate on your writing instead of on a stack of computer manuals. ScreenWright Professional is the first complete word processor for film and television writers — it includes both a complete text editor and formatter, so no other software is needed. If you have ever tried to use a regular W-P program to generate this very complex format, you'll really appreciate this one.

Other programs on this disk include Turbo Script a word processor designed specifically for the 128K PCjr along with a host of assorted text processing utilities that can count words, help create indexes, and one to convert Displaywrite files to ASCII text format.

Usage: Text processing for screenplays and teleplays

System Requirements: 128K, one disk drive and monochrome display

How to Start: The documentation for ScreenWright is in SWMANUAL.DOC; print it by entering "SWMANUAL.DOC LPT1". TSCRIPT has a small .DOC file and a big HELP.HLP

- To run a program with the suffix .COM or .EXE, just type its name, i.e., for ScreenWright, type SW and press ENTER.

User Comments: "Good special use program. Inclusion of macro program to insert printer commands would have been very useful. tcount program good." "Okay for beginners: simpler than using a macro-maker. But also more limited: it doesn't calculate page-breaks, which is crucial for formatting scripts."

Suggested Donation: $10.00 for every piece you get published using ScreenWright! Bravo!

File Descriptions:

— — — —	— —	ScreenWriter Text Preparer
SW	COM	Screenwriter — prints stageplays/teleplays from prepared text
SWINST	COM	ScreenWriter installation program
SWINST	MSG	File used for Screenwriter installation
SWINST	DTA	File used for Screenwriter installation
SWMANUAL	DOC	Documentation for ScreenWriter (47K)
SWTRY	ME	Sample ScreenWriter input
SWREAD	ME	How to get started with ScreenWritter — list this file first
— — — —	— —	Junior Word Processor
TSCRIPT	COM	Word processor for Jr only
TSCRIPT	DOC	Documentation file — brief
TSCRIPT	PAS	Pascal source code for TSCRIPT
HELP	HLP	More documentation for TSCRIPT (9K)
— — — —	— —	Counters and such
WORDFREQ	COM	Counts the usage of each individual word
WPINDEX	COM	Creates an index for a given set of words
DWASC	EXE	Converts DisplayWrite documents to ASCIII
TCOUNT	COM	Counts characters, words, lines and pages
TCOUNT	DOC	Documentation file (7K)

455
PC-TYPE+
by Jim Button
(Disk 1 of 3)
v1.1

This is the first of the three disk set of PC-TYPE+, Jim Button's supercharged new version of PC-TYPE. Instead of a simple, clean word processor, PC-Type+ now comes equipped with all of the standard word processing features plus many advanced features — Mail Merge that works hand-in-hand with PC-File databases, Wordstar files and straight ASCII files; 100,000 word Fault Finder that checks for misspellings; WHOOPS Key to recover up to 10 lost or deleted lines.

This disk contains the main program; the second (#681) contains an extensive on-line help system; and the third (#682) contains the spelling checker, mailmerge, and printer supports.

NOTE: THIS SYSTEM REQUIRES ALL THREE DISKS TO WORK.

Usage: Power word processing

System Requirements: 256K, two disk drives, monochrome display

How to Start: Refer to the READ.ME and INSTALL files for installation and directions.

User Comments: "Good documentation and a fairly versatile program." "I find that PC-TYPE does not seem to have as many features as their other word processing program PC-WRITE. I still find it useful for quick edits."

NOTE: all above comments were pertinent to PC-TYPE version.]

Suggested Donation: The full fledged working version is available from Mr. Button for $69.95 + $5 for shipping charges.

File Descriptions:

PCTYPE	EXE	PC-TYPE+ main program
PCTYPE	EVL	PC-TYPE+ main program
INSTALL	EXE	Installation program to configure PC-TYPE to your machine
READ	ME	Intoductory text file
PATHS	LOC	Help for fixed disk users
FINSTALL	BAT	PC-Type+ installation for fixed disk users
GETRSP	COM	Program to support FINSTALL.BAT

480
PC-OUTLINE
Version 3.21
v2

PC-OUTLINE is a program comparable to Thinktank. It gives you the capacity to outline and organize any item by helping you arrange and re-arrange them using different catagories of classificiations. Additional hot features: hot-key definition; auto-numbering and auto-indent; levels can be hidden; and it can easily interact with ProKey, SideKick and other such memory resident programs without RAMJAM occurring.

Usage: Outlining and creative thinking on the fly!

System Requirements: 64K, one disk drive and monochrome display

How to Start: Type BBO to run the program. Check out the README1 & 2 files first. PRINTDOC.BAT will print the documetation.

User Comments: "Very useful program. I plan to subscribe." "More doc please, otherwise it appears to be first class software..." "Almost as good as ThinkTank; better than Ready. It works very well as a memory resident program with the Leading Edge Word Processor (v. 1.3a) and the Word Finder thesaurus." "The memory resident feature makes it very useful for brainstorming while writing." "This superbly crafted gem is a prime example of what shareware can and should be. It is a great idea, well developed and coded and the documentation is excellent, given the limits of what the author intended."

Suggested Donation: $89.95 plus $5.00 S & H for registration brings you the full manual, the latest update and a tech line number.

File Descriptions:

BBO	EXE	Executable file for running Outline!
README	1	The latest notes about Outline! not included in the manual
README	2	Descriptions of the utility programs included on the disk
GLOBAL	COM	Utility program #1 (see README.2)
CPY	COM	Utility program #2 (see README.2)
DIRS	COM	Utility program #3 (see README.2)
MOVE	COM	Utility program #4 (see README.2)
MEM	COM	Utility program #5 (see README.2)
BEEP	COM	Utility program #6 (see README.2)
PUSHDIR	COM	Utility program #7 (see README.2)
POPDIR	COM	Utility program #8 (see README.2)
DOC	PRN	Brief documentation in printable form
DOC	BBO	Brief documentation in a Outline! file
EPSON	CFG	The EPSON printer driver
IBM	CFG	The IBM printer driver
BLANK	CFG	A dummy printer driver that will ignore all print codes
PRINTDOC	BAT	A batch file that will print DOC.PRN to LPT1
PCPRINT	COM	A program for changing printer drivers
KEYSET	COM	A program for customizing the Outline! invoke key
BBOPRN$	CFG	A printer substitution file for correctly printing graphics characters on non-IBM printers.
*	7BBO	Sample outlines covering many of Outline!'s features.

*	7BBO	Sample outlines covering many of Outline!'s features.
GOODCLK	COM	A program to make the time display in Outline! work correctly on some compatibles (AT&T, EPSON, and others). To use it, just run it in your autoexec.bat file (or any time before loading Outline!).

505 PC-STYLE

v1

PC-STYLE analyzes text files (ASCII or WordStar) for readability, personal tone, and action. It makes these decisions based on the number of words per sentence, the percentage of words of certain lengths, the percentage of personal words, the percentage of action words, and other tests. PC-Style in essence analyzes the "readability" of your writing and thereby determines readability level. This version is enhanced even further by a built-in lexicon and complete manual on disk.

Usage: Writing analysis

System Requirements: 64K, one disk drive and monochrome display

How to Start: From the DOS prompt you can get all the information in this manual by typing HELP, MENU, CONTENTS, or READHELP. The PC-Style manual has been designed to be online or printed out. Enter PCSTYLE at the DOS prompt.

Suggested Donation: $29.95 plus $5 S&H

File Descriptions:

PCBOOK	COM	Documentation menu program
PCBOOK	HLP	Utility for documentation menu program
PCBOOK	MNU	Menu for documentation
PCS	DOC	Documentation on disk
PCSTYLE	COM	PCSTYLE main program
PCSTYLE	PRO	Optional profile file for customizing program
PCSTYLX	COM	PCSTYLE main program for less compatible machines
PCSTYLX	PIF	Program Information File to run PC-Style in Topview or Windows
PRINT	BAT	Batch file to print documentation
READ	BAT	Types read me file to screen
READ	ME	Read Me text file

528
NEW YORK
WORD Version 2.1
V1

New York Word is a very powerful word processor that allows up to 12 windows on the screen, movement of text between windows, the creation of macros that perform functions with just a few keystrokes, footnoting, EGA support, automatic table of contents and index generator, automatic hyphenation, mail merge, and even an on-board programming language.

Even with all these fancy features, NYW at heart is an outstanding word processor with a full complement of text editing features. For instance, the cursor movement commands allow you to move up and down lines, paragraphs, and pages. Or you can go directly to any line number, or any number of lines relative from where the cursor currently is. You can place up to 26 bookmarks at various points in the document, and return to any point at any time. You can scroll continuously up or down the document with a user-selectable scrolling speed.

Usage: Sophisticated word processing

System Requirements: 256K, two disk drives, monochrome monitor

Features:

- Split screen editing
- Column operations
- Two calculators
- Automatic hyphenation
- Keyboard macros
- Reconfigurable keyboard
- Fully programmable mail merge
- Regular expression searching
- Integrated spelling checker
- Automatic table of contents and index generation

How to Start: As NYW is archived, you must first un-archive the files marked *.ARC using the ARC.COM program (see the GO.BAT file for more instructions). If you have a hard disk, then use the INSTALL file

- To run, enter WP and press ENTER.

Suggested Donation: $35.00 which covers: The NYWord manual which is 100 pages long, and utilities for NYWord, including the mail merge program, a multi-column utility, and other sundries.

File Descriptions:

NYWORD21	ARC	Archive file: contains the actual program files
NYWREMAP	ARC	Archive file: contains a keyboard remapping program
NYWSPELL	ARC	Archive file: contains the accompanying spelling checker
READ	ME	Introductory text file
UPDATE	DOC	List of changes from different versions of New York Word
ARC51	COM	Un-archiving program which "unfolds" into two working files

530
FreeWord
Version 1.0
V1

FreeWord is a powerful and easy to use, menu-driven word processor. It is capable of right and left justification of text; moving the cursor either by character, word, line, screen or page; searching a document for a word or phrase and also moving and copying blocks of text. FreeWord even permits printing in the background mode so that the user can proceed with other work!

Usage: Text processing for all users

System Requirements: 256K, two disk drives, color or monochrome monitor; printer is optional.

Features:

- Cursor movement by character, word, line, screen, page
- Move, copy, delet boxes
- Automatic formatting
- Supports forced page breaks
- Typewriter mode
- Search and replace
- Displays page breaks on screen

How to Start: Documentation in FW.DOC

- To run, enter FW and press ENTER.

Suggested Donation: $49.00 makes you a registered owner of FreeWord. You will receive a printed copy of the manual, be eligible for support from us, and you will also receive a spelling checker called SSP's SPELL.

File Descriptions:

FW	EXE	Actual FreeWord program
FW	HLP	Help text file
FW	DOC	Documentation on FreeWord
DEMO2		Demonstration file
COLOR	EXE	Configuration file for color monitors
NO-COLOR	FIL	Monochrome monitor configuration file

563
MAX — Freeware Editor
v1

MAX is a freeware text editor that is a downsized version of the popular EMACS editor. Down in size but not much in power! It is quite fast and has some very powerful text-editing features. If you have used the mainframe version, you'll feel right at home. The program is distributed in versions for both color and monochrome systems, and the source code is provided for the curious programmers among you. However, for those not it that league, there is included an optional menu-driven interface for novices.

Usage: Intermediate level users, especially DEC & UNIX users.

System Requirements: 128K, one disk drive and monochrome display

Features:

- Move by word, or globally
- Search for text
- Search and replace text by other text
- Switch buffers
- Multiple buffers and windows
- Incremental search
- Use windows or split screens (limited to 64K)
- Give arguments to functions
- Insert Control-Characters
- Kill and yank back lines, words or regions

- Format paragraphs
- Define and invoke macro commands
- And many more things...

How to Start: NOTE: the Documentation, Color version and the Source code are all in separate subdirectories with their appropriate documentation files

- To run it, type MAX and press ENTER.

Suggested Donation: $20.00 for individuals; $25.00 per copy for commercial and governmental sites.

File Descriptions:

— — ROOT	DIRE	TORY — —
MAX	BAT	Starts the Max Editor Program
MAXC	BAT	Starts the Max Editor Color Program
PRINTDOC	BAT	Prints the Max Documentaion
— — MAX	UB-D	RECTORY — —
WELCOME	MSG	Introductory message
MAX	COM	MAX Editor program
— — SOUR	E SU	-DIRECTORY (UNDER MAX) — —
MAKEFILE		Assembler/Linker Control file
ALLOCATE	ASM	Buffer Allocation
CTRLC	ASM	Command control handling
CTRLXC	ASM	Command control handling
DOSFILES	ASM	File Handling
ESCC	ASM	Command control handling
ESCXC	ASM	Command control handling
HELP	ASM	Help execution
LAST	ASM	Last Command filer
MAIN	ASM	MAX Mainline
MODELINE	ASM	Modeline display
MORESCRE	ASM	Screen control
PARSE	ASM	Command parser
SCREEN	ASM	Screen builder
SEARCH	ASM	Search command
WINDOWS	ASM	Window and buffer control
— — DOCU	ENTA	ION SUB-DIRECTORY (UNDER MAX) — —
CONTRACT		Software Agreement
MAX-REF	DOC	Reference file
MAX	HLP	Help text file
MAX-REF	MSS	Reference file — 2
TUTORIAL	TXT	Tutorial
— — COLO	SUB	DIRECTORY (UNDER MAX) — —
FDEF	DEF	Color definition globals
MAX	COM	MAX Editor for Color systems

627

PC-WRITE
Version 2.7/4
(Disk 2 of 2)
v2.8

PC-WRITE is a powerful, easy to use, word processor that has been around, and been recognized, as one of the best of its kind for some time. It has on-demand documentation, its own pagination and print utility and a whole lot more.

NOTE: This is the second disk of the two-disk set (first is disk no. 78) and the first is required to use this one!

Usage: Word Processing

System Requirements: 128K, two disk drives and monochrome display

How to Start: REFER TO DISK NO 78: To get the Tutorial and Quick Guide, insert the program disk in drive A, and enter one of the following at the A> prompt: PRINTMAN (prints copy; best at 12 chars/inch) TYPEMAN (types on screen, with pause to read) FILEMAN MANUAL1.CRN B:PART1.DOC (un-compresses AND prints manual).

File Descriptions:

GO	BAT	Types READ.ME
READ	ME	Introductory note
WORKDISK	BAT	Creates a working diskette or directory
GETYN	COM	Used by WORKDISK
MENUPRT	EXE	Printer picker, all but laser printers
MENULAZ	EXE	Printer picker, laser printers
HPDOWN	BAT	Downloads HP LaserJet Plus Softfonts
PSDOWN	TXT	PostScript prefix file to download
PRINT	TST	Printer font effects test
CHARS	TST	Printer extended character set test
JUSTIFY	TST	Printer microspacing test
MANYCOPY	BAT	Copies a file to the printer forever
MULTCOPY	BAT	Copies a file to the printer N times
WORDS	MAS	Master word list for spelling check
WORDS	EXE	Adds WORDS.USE file to WORDS.MAS file
ED	DIR	Directory of files

640

LIST
v1

LIST is a printer-related utility program designed to aid programmers and others with simple document printing requirements. The program controls printing of documents, providing automatic pagination, page numbering, titling, printing of headers and footers, and a number of other similar features. Most significantly, the program easily handles printing multiple documents, such as might occur when a programmer wishes to print out all program source code files used on a project.

Usage: Document printing

System Requirements: 256K, one floppy drive and a monochrome, black & white, or color monitor. To print hardcopy documents, a parallel (LPT) printer is required.

How to Start: After consulting the documentation in LIST.DOC, initiate the program by running INSTALL and then LIST.

Suggested Donation: $10.00

File Descriptions:

README	DOC	Contents, installation and execution of LIST
INSTALL	BAT	Batch file to install LIST for display type
LINSTALL	COM	Program run by the BAT file
LIST	COM	Main program
LIST	DOC	Documentation file

657

Zuri Editor
v1

This diskette contains the Zuri text editor, which is a very powerful program made up of many features. Primarily, it is very easy to use; Zuri is intended for someone who easily forgets the common commands. The program can edit as big a file as will fit into memory (maximum 480K in a 640K machine) and text lines can be up to 225 characters, also lines longer than 75 characters are wrapped to the next line. Zuri supports text macros with search and replace options and also block commands which are available. A great deal of documentation comes with Zuri as well as on-screen help menus.

IMPORTANT NOTE: The Zuri editor works ONLY on the MONOCHROME adapter card.

Usage: Text Editing

System Requirements: 190K, at least one disk drive and a moncohrome display. With this memory, the maximum editable file is 32K. Each additional 32K memory adds that much to the maximum editable file, up to the maximum 640K giving a possible file size of 480K!

How to Start: Read carefully the ZURI.DOC file and all other .DOC files for the different parts of the editor. To start the editor, enter ZURI and press ENTER, making sure that the file zuri.com is on the drive being used.

Suggested Donation: $15.00 includes update and Turbo Pascal source code if you request it.

File Descriptions:

— — — —	— —	ZURI EDITOR (V3.2)
DI	COM	This is a program to list a directory in sorted form
DI	DOC	Documentation for di.com (28k)
Z	COM	The control file for the .chn programs, must be on same disk
ZMAKEKEY	CHN	This program provides an easy way to make text macros on Zuri
ZMAKEKEY	DOC	Documentation for zmakekey.chn
ZURI	COM	The zuri editor. Start it by typing zuri
ZURI	DOC	Documentation for the zuri editor
ZURI	HLE	Help file for the editor. Can be omitted if desired
ZURICHS	CHN	A program to choose records by certain criteria
ZURICHS	DOC	Documentation for zurichs.chn
ZURICOMP	CHN	Compare two files, line by line
ZURICOMP	DOC	Documentation for zuricomp.chn
ZURICONV	CHN	Convert special characters; see also zurirein.chn
ZURICONV	DOC	Documentation for zuriconv.chn
ZURICOUN	CHN	Counts lines and words in a file
ZURICOUN	DOC	Documentation for zuricoun.chn
ZURIDELL	CHN	Eliminates duplicate lines in a file
ZURIDELL	DOC	Documentation for zuridell.chn
ZURIEXTR	CHN	Extracts specified lines from a file
ZURIEXTR	DOC	Documentation for zuriextr.chn
ZURIINST	COM	To install go-to-DOS feature on the editor; see zuri.doc
ZURIJUST	CHN	A program to word-wrap and justify a file
ZURIJUST	DOC	Documentation for zurijust.chn
ZURIMERG	CHN	To merge two sorted text files
ZURIMERG	DOC	Documentation for zurimerg.chn
ZURIPRNT	CHN	A program to print a specified file
ZURIPRNT	DOC	Documentation for zuriprnt.chn
ZURIREIN	CHN	Cleans up a file;
ZURIREIN	DOC	Documentation for zurirein.chn
ZURISEQ	CHN	Checks that a file is in a given order

ZURISEQ	DOC	Documentation for zuriseq.chn
ZURISORT	CHN	Sorts a text file, which can be quite big
ZURISORT	DOC	Documentation for zurisort.chn
ZURISPLT	CHN	To split a file into several parts
ZURISPLT	DOC	Documentation for zurisplt.chn
ZURITWO	CHN	Display two files simultaneously, in windows
ZURITWO	DOC	Documentation for zuritwo.chn
GO	BAT	Startup information, type: GO (enter)

667 The Writer's Toolkit

v1

The Writer's Toolkit is a collection of 20 executable utility programs inspired by Kernighan and Pike's Software Tools. Most of the utilities are filters that process text files. These utilities include: converting lower case to upper case and upper case to lower case, encrypting and decrypting files, etc. Each utility has a well written documentation file with examples for each utility.

The most interesting program is MEMO. This program will display memos that have the same date as the system date. Runnerup is the FREQ.EXE which determines frequency of use but only works on a sorted list of words. You will have to use the WORDS and SORT programs first; very handy for anyone doing a lot of wordprocessing and documentation.

Usage: Word processing chores

System Requirements: 64K, one disk drive and monochrome display

How to Start: To run, enter its filename, e.g., for WORDS.EXE enter WORDS and press ENTER.

Suggested Donation: $15.95

File Descriptions:

????????	DOC	Documentation files (20 files)
BOOP	EXE	Beeps the speaker.
CAL	EXE	Calendar for any month between 1901 and 1989.
CAPITALS	EXE	Capitalization filter. Converts lower case to upper case
CC-CLCL	EXE	Carriage return filter.
COLOR	EXE	Change the backgnd and foregnd colors.
DECRYPT	EXE	Decrypt files encrypted with encrypt.
DETAB	EXE	Converts tabs into spaces. From Software Tools.

DUP	EXE	Duplicate line filter.
ENCRYPT	EXE	Encryption program from Software Tools.
ENTAB	EXE	Converts 8 spaces into a tab char. From Software Tools.
FREQ	EXE	Word frequency counter. Must use words and sort first.
LL-CLCL	EXE	Carriage return filter.
LOWCASE	EXE	Lowercase filter. Converts upper case to lower case.
MEMO	EXE	Display memos that have the system date.
NL	EXE	Line numbering filter.
RS	EXE	Removes whitespace at ends of lines.
SLEEP	EXE	Pauses for given number of seconds.
TEE	EXE	UNIX tee filter.
WHITE	EXE	Whitespace counting filter.
WORDS	EXE	Unix words filter.
READ	ME	Writer's Toolkit information.
SAMPLE	MEM	Sample memo file for the memo utility.
WRITERS	TXT	Writer's Toolkit information.

681
PC-TYPE+
by Jim Button
(Disk 2 of 3)
v1.1

This is the second in the three disk set of PC-TYPE+, Jim Button's supercharged new version of PC-TYPE. Instead of a simple, clean word processor, PC-Type+ now comes equipped with all of the standard word processing features plus many advanced features — Mail Merge that works hand-in-hand with PC-File databases, Wordstar files and straight ASCII files; 100,000 word Fault Finder that checks for misspellings; WHOOPS Key to recover up to 10 lost or deleted lines.

This disk contains the 76 files for a comprehensive on-screen help system for quick reference or in-depth explanations. It also contains seven major printer drivers and test devices. NOTE: THIS SYSTEM REQUIRES ALL THREE DISKS TO WORK.

Usage: Power word processing

System Requirements: 128K, one disk drive and monochrome display

How to Start: Refer to Disk No 455 for installation and directions.

Suggested Donation: PC-Type+ registered version with manual for $69.95 + $5 for shipping and handling.

File Descriptions:
PCT-HELP   <DIR>   Subdirectory containing all help files

682
PC-TYPE+
by Jim Button
(Disk 3 of 3)
v1.1

This is the third in the three disk set of PC-TYPE+, Jim Button's supercharged new version of PC-TYPE. Instead of a simple, clean word processor, PC-Type+ now comes equipped with all of the standard word processing features plus many advanced features — Mail Merge that works hand-in-hand with PC-File databases, Wordstar files and straight ASCII files; 100,000 word Fault Finder that checks for misspellings; WHOOPS Key to recover up to 10 lost or deleted lines.

This disk contains the 240K dictionary and the program overlays for the MailMerge and Spelling Checker. NOTE: THIS SYSTEM REQUIRES ALL THREE DISKS TO WORK.

Usage: Power word processing

System Requirements: 256K, two disk drives, monochrome display

How to Start: Refer to Disk No 455 for installation and directions.

Suggested Donation: PC-Type+ registered version with manual for $69.95 + $5 for shipping and handling.

File Descriptions:
PCT-DIC   <DIR>   Subdirectory containing dictionary program files

684
PAGEONE
v1

The PAGEONE programs provide a powerful, flexible document processor for small to medium size files where the major emphasis is print formatting. PAGEONE is a hybrid type of word processor; it contains many features either not found on many large word processors (for instance, a chain-printing device) or so difficult on them that most people do not use them (line oriented formatting with embedded commands).

It is especially useful for making letters, flyers, documents and forms of all types; there is even a "typewriter" mode for dashing something off! It is easy to learn, and over 90% of its instructions are displayed on the screen at all times alongside the work processed. For greater efficiency of operation, formatting is line oriented and editing capabilities are fully screen oriented.

Usage: Processing small to medium size documents

System Requirements: 128K, one disk drive and monochrome display NOTE: If the DOS SHELL feature is invoked, 256K will be needed for

How to Start: Documentation in PAGEONE.DOC

● To run, enter PAGEONE and press ENTER.

Suggested Donation: $34.00 brings you the Advanced Version 4.01pc which supports a color monitor, embedded printer codes in text files, extended directory features, and updated documentation, telephone support, and product updates at reasonable cost.

File Descriptions:

CODES	EXE	Sub-program accessed by PAGEONE
DEMO	TXT	Demonstration file of PAGEONE features
????????	DAT	Data files for running various printers (3 files)
FILECONV	COM	File conversion utility that strips high bits from Wordstar
FILESOND	ISK	Text file listing the major files on this disk
PAGEONE	COM	Main program file
PAGEONE	DOC	The operators manual
PRINFILE	COM	Menu driven print queue utility
README	TXT	Instructions for starting program
STYLES	DOC	Documentation ad registration form for STYLES.EXE
STYLES	EXE	Sub-program accessed by PAGEONE

UTILITIES SOFTWARE :

An Introduction:

The Utilities category contains a huge assortment of special service and data modification programs which enhance and expand other Library programs. It was just because of this immense number of programs that they were placed in these special categories of utilities for:

- DOS Level
- General System Level
- Language
- Programmer
- Screen
- Printer
- Copy/Uncopy
- Encode/Decode

The DOS and General Systems utilities are used for understanding and enhancing the Disk Operating System (for MS/PC DOS).

The Languages and Programmers sections contain specialty items relating to the major languages listed in our regular Language section. Language Utilities include refinements within one language's structure, syntax and command operations. Programming utilities relate more to applications. There is some overlap between these groups; it is always worthwhile to check both groupings.

Related to these two is the Screen Utilities section which concerns the special aspects of designing data input and their accompanying documentation, in particular the help and on-line documentation. These programs deal with screen design, generation, and modification as well as the refining of data input devices. Programmers will find it worthwhile to look here!

Printer utilities are a necessity for anyone contemplating getting the best out of a bewildering variety of printers, fonts and documentation needs. While the Epson/compatible line is obviously the leader now, you have an enormous selection to consider here.

Finally, we have two sections for very special purposes, Copy/Uncopy and Encode/Decode. Copy/Uncopy is designed to remove the burdensome copy protection schemes. The Encode/Decode section contains encryption/decryption and data security devices. We selected them out (not being applications per se) by considering them as specialty data modifiers. We hope that you will find them useful and worthwhile.

COPY/UNCOPY UTILITIES:

This collection contains a huge number of procedures for removing those cranky, bothersome copy protection schemes from specific programs. These procedure require your careful, step-by-step use of the directions in them. Important here is your willingness to employ the little appreciated DEBUG program, which is one of the overlooked powerhouses of your DOS disk.

PLEASE NOTE: We urge you to TAKE CARE to search for your software version's EXACT counterpart. There is no MEGA-STRIPPER applicable to all programs in our collection.

And if someone does offer you one, check out the opportunities in beachfront property in downtown Denver while you're at it.

184 DOS Utilities No 9
v1.1

Among this disk's collection are programs that allow you to copy "protected" disks, generate a listing of directories, alter file attributes, clean your disk drives, purge files, fix DOS 1.1 bugs, and other miscellaneous utilities. The remainder is a group of early devices for removing copy protection schemes from your software.

NOTE: CAREFULLY EXAMINE THE UNPROTECT FILES TO BE SURE THAT YOUR VERSION IS HERE.

Usage: System enhancement tools, all user levels.

System Requirements: 64K, one disk drive and monochrome display; files marked with " + " need a color/graphics card and monitor

How to Start: There is a .DOC file for almost every file/program.

- To run a program with the suffix .COM, .EXE, or .BAT, just type its name, i.e. for COVERPRO.COM, type COVERPRO and press ENTER.

User Comments: (COVER) "This is the best directory print utility I've used." "I use the program COVER all the time. The other programs on this one are good too." "Various unprotect schemes, while well documented, cumbersome. Most did not work." "old, dated; with the exception of a few programs, I found the documentation to be inaccurate or unclear." "CHMOD alone worth 10 times the price."

File Descriptions:

COVER	COM	Generates a listing of a directory to put into disk envelope
(READ	ME)	Part of COVER.COM
COVER	DOC	Part of COVER.COM (13K)
COVER	ASM	Part of COVER.COM
COVERPRO	COM	C.Itoh Prowriter version of COVER.COM.
COVERPRO	ASM	Source for COVERPRO.COM.
CO*	ASM	Assembly language source code for COVER.COM modules
CO*	OBJ	Object modules for COVER.COM
ALTER	COM	Alter file attributes
ALTER	DOC	Documentation

CHMOD	BAS	Change file attributes
CHMOD	DOC	Documentation
CLEAN2	COM	Update to disk drive cleaning utility
CLEAN2	DOC	Documentation
COPY40	COM	Copy utility that breaks some protected items
COPY40	DOC	Documentation
COPYALL	COM	Copy utility that breaks some protected items
CV	COM	Changes disk labels (DOS 1.1, 2.0, 2.1)
CV	DOC	Documentation
DCOPY	COM	Copies some protected items
DFORMAT	COM	Format utility (Buggy)
DOSBUG	DOC	Fix DOS 1.1 bugs
MINIPRT	DOC	Prints directory in small shape for disk envelopes
PURGE	COM	Deletes selected files
PURGE	DOC	Documentation
RAMDSK16	COM	160KB RAM disk
RAMDSK18	COM	180KB RAM disk
RAMDSK32	COM	320KB RAM disk
RAMDSK36	COM	360KB RAM disk
RM18	ASM	Assembler source for RAM disks
SPEEDUP2	DOC	DOS 2.0 disk drive speed up utility
123STAR	UNP	How to unprotect LOTUS 123
BASIC	UNP	How to unprotect BASIC compiler
EASYWR11	UNP	How to unprotect EASYWRITER
FLTSIM	UNP	How to unprotect FLIGHT SIMULATOR
LOTUS1A	UNP	How to unprotect LOTUS 123 1A
MEMSHIFT	UNP	How to unprotect MEMORY SHIFT
MS2	UNP	How to unprotect MEMORY SHIFT
NEW123	UNP	How to unprotect LOTUS 123
PFSFILE	UNP	How to unprotect PFS File
VISICALC	UNP	How to unprotect VISICALC
WORD	UNP	How to unprotect WORD
WORDNEW	UNP	How to unprotect WORD
ZORK3	UNP	How to unprotect ZORK

204 — DOS Utilities No 12

v1

This disk holds many DOS system chore-handling programs: FCOPY copies and formats single-sided disks in 30 seconds; GCOPY copies files from one drive to another; GDEL can be used to delete files from current drive; MSPOOL2 allows up to 4 printer spoolers simultaneously; VDL is a file delete utility for DOS 2.0 only, VISIPROT converts VISICALC DISK to a disk that can be copied by DISKCOPY; WRTE sets and resets the read-only bit on a file to protect it from being deleted or updated; and FILECOPY paginates and prints test files.

Usage: File and copy utilities, Intermediate/Advanced users.

System Requirements: 256K RAM, two disk drives and a monochrome display

How to Start: Check the .DOC files for each program

- To run a program with the suffix .COM or .EXE, just type its name, i.e. for GDEL.COM, type GDEL and press ENTER.

User Comments: "Only a few programs on this one, but they are pretty good." "Not great, but useful."

File Descriptions:

FCOPY	EXE	Copies & formats SS disk in 30 sec (Peter Norton)
FCOPY	PAS	Pascal source code
FCOPY	OBJ	Object code
FCOPY	LNK	Part of FCOPY
READ	ME	FCOPY documentation
FCMAGIC	ASM	Assembler routines for FCOPY.EXE
FCMAGIC	OBJ	Object code
FILECOPY	BAS	Paginates & prints text files
FILEOUT	BAS	Epson printing utility (Don Withrow)
GCOPY	DOC	Documentation
GCOPY	EXE	Enhanced DOS copy utility (Gordon Waite)
GDEL	DOC	Documentation
GDEL	EXE	Enhanced DOS delete utility (Gordon Waite)
MSPOOL2	COM	Up to 4 simultaneous printer spoolers (Rich Winkel)
MSPOOL2	DOC	Documentation
VDL	COM	File delete utility for DOS 2.0 (Tom Roberts)
VDL	DOC	Documentation
VISIPROT	DOC	Unprotect VISICALC
WRT	DOC	Documentation — WRTE.COM & WRTP.COM (Kent Quirk)
WRTE	COM	Make a read-only file copyable
WRTP	COM	Make a file read-only

376 — Patches

v1

PATCHES is our mega-collection for unprotecting and patching specific programs. The programs on this disk allow you to place the indicated programs on your hard disk or to make backup copies, inspect file descriptions, and includes a multitude of information on such subjects as BASIC patches, CLOCKS, VisiCalc back-up, and a WordStar 3.3 patch for PC AT. There is even a demonstration of building and searching a tree structure, and how to run a non-serialized program with PRO Basic.

CHECK CAREFULLY TO BE SURE YOUR
PROGRAM'S UNPROTECT PROGRAM IS HERE
BY VERSION.

Usage: File copy patch files, Intermediate/Advanced
users.

System Requirements: 128K, one disk drive,
monochrome display

How to Start: Except for three litte BASICs, these
are all documentation files (suffix .UNP (for
unprotect), .DOC (for DOCument), or .TXT (for
TeXT) files. Screen read with TYPE, then PRINT
what you need.

User Comments: "Worked VERY well with Lotus
and dBase III." "PATCHES are for old versions of
the programs." "Documentation is for advanced
user. Many programs have been updated. It is
important to update this type of collection as often
as possible." "GREAT!!! Used the Symphony patches
so that we could use Symphony on hard disks at
work. Excellent utilities for making backups of my
most often used software."

File Descriptions:

123	UNP	How to make backup copy of 123 (& run without key disk)
123-LOGO	PAT	How to eliminate 123 logo page
123A	UNP	How to make backup copy of 123 Ver A (& run without key disk)
123STAR	UNP	How to make backup copy of 123 Ver A*
8088	TXT	How to identify defective 8088 chips which crash systems
NEWCOLOR	123	Changes colors displayed by original 123
BASCOM	FIX	Documentation for patching bugs in Basic Compiler Ver 1.0
BASCOM	PAT	Latest BASCOM patches
BASLIB	PAT	Latest BASLIB patches
BASRUN	PAT	Latest BASRUN patches
DB3ZAP	BAT	Batch file for unprotecting DBIII
DB3ZAP	UNP	Parameters needed by DB3ZAP.BAT
C86MOD	DOC	Enables C86 function MAIN to return an error code to DOS 2.0
FILECMD	PAT	Add color to IBM's FileCommand
XTALK	PAT	Bypass the sign-on screen on Crosstalk Rel 3.4
CLOCKFIX	DOC	Info on PC DOS 2.0 CLOCK$ that doesn't change date at midnight
CLOCKFIX	SYS	Installable driver to replace PC DOS2.0 CLOCK$
COMCOM20	PAT	DOS 2.0 patch parameters for COMMAND.MOD
COMMAND	MOD	Makes transient portion of COMMAND.COM become resident at IPL
VCBACKUP	DOC	How to backup VisiCalc disk (1982 version)
COMMOD	TXT	Adds resident commands to COMMAND.COM
DB3-NEW	DOC	Documentation for DB3ZAP.UNP and DB3ZAP.BAT
DOSBUG	MOD	Fixes DOS 1.1 bug relating to random access I/O

FRMWK1	DOC	How to make backup copy of Framework Ver 1.0
DOS–ERR	DOC	How to fix 'C' programs to get around DOS 2.0 redirection bug
DSKCPY20	MOD	Modifies DISCOPY to eliminate messages to user
EWBACKUP	UNP	How to make backup copy of EasyWriter 1.0
FIND	MOD	Patch to eliminate header inserted by DOS 2.X FIND filter
FLT-SIM	MOD	Allows an RGB monitor to show colors using Flight Simulator
FORMAT20	MOD	Patch to cause DOS 2.0 FORMAT to prompt for volume label
GENPATCH	BAS	Generates patches for PATCHER.BAS
JRAM123	MOD	How to use 123 V1.0 with JRAM memory board in IBM-XT
LAYOUT	UNP	How to make backup copy of PROKEY 3.0
MEMSHIFT	UNP	How to make backup copy of MEMORY/SHIFT
NORTONS	MOD	Patch to Norton Utilities V2.01 to access tracks beyond #39
FRMWK1	BAT	Batch file to backup Framework (see FRMWK1.DOC)
PATCHER	BAS	Program to patch other programs using a patch (.PAT) data file
PCM	UNP	How to make backup copy of IBM Personal Comm. Manager V 1.0
FRMWK1	UNP	Parameters needed by FRMWK1.BAT
PE-COLR	MOD	Patch to set colors in IBM Personal Editor
PE-LOGO	PAT	Patch to eliminate logo screen on IBM Personal Editor
POOLCOPY	DOC	Patch to fix POOLCOPY monitor bug and to make backup copy
PRINT20	DOC	Patch to have DOS 2.0 PRINT.COM skip prompt for list device
PROKEY	UNP	How to backup PROKEY V3.0
NEWCOLOR	IN	Unidentified color patches
RESCMD	BAS	Program to make COMMAND.COM totally memory resident
RESCMD	DOC	Documentation to RESCMD.BAS
SAMNA	UNP	How to backup SAMNA WORD II Ver 1.1
TIME-MGR	UNP	How to backup IBM Time Manager
XTFORMAT	DOC	Batch utility for a PC XT that allows user to format A: only
BASIC2	MOD	Patch to fix LOF bug in BASIC and BASICA 2.0
MSWORD	UNP	How to backup Microsoft Word
WS33-AT	PAT	Patch to allow Wordstar 3.3 to work properly on the PC AT
CLOUT256	UNP	How to backup Clout V1.0 256K Disk 1
CLOUT384	UNP	How to backup Clout V1.0 384K Disk 1
TKSOLVER	UNP	How to backup TK Solver Ver TK-1(2J)
RB4000	UNP	How to backup RB4000 Ver 1.11
COPYWRIT	UNP	How to backup Copywrit
EXECUVSN	UNP	How to backup ExecuVision for Dos 1.1
FLTSIM	UNP	How to backup Flight Simulator Ver 1.00
MLINK	UNP	How to backup Multilink 2.07
PCDRAW	UNP	How to backup PC-Draw V1.2
PCDRAW14	UNP	How to backup PC-Draw V1.4
PROBASIC	UNP	How to run non-serialized program with Pro Basic by Morgan
HARVARD	UNP	How to backup Harvard Project Manager V1.1
HPMV116	UNP	How to backup Harvard Project Manager V1.16
PFS-PROG	UNP	How to backup PFS File/Report/Write

TANK	UNP	How to backup ThinkTank Ver 1.00 and Ver 1.001
SK111C	UNP	How to backup Side Kick Ver 1.11C
TIMEMGR	UNP	How to backup Time Manager Ver 1.00
XENOCOPY	UNP	How to backup Xenocopy Plus Ver 1.09
SK	UNP	How to backup Side Kick Ver 1.00A
TKNEW	UNP	How to backup TK Solver TK-1(2J)/PC-DOS/IBM5150
MLINK206	UNP	Notes to accompany MULTILNK.UNP
MULTILNK	UNP	How to backup MultiLink Ver 2.06
SK111A	UNP	How to backup Side Kick Ver 1.11A
MLINK207	UNP	How to backup MultiLink Ver 2.07
FLGHTSIM	UNP	How to backup Microsoft Flight Simulator Ver 1.00
ZORK12	UNP	How to backup Zork I and Zork II
ZORK3	UNP	How to backup Zork III
SARGON3	UNP	How to backup Sargon 3
TREE	BAS	Demonstrates building and searching a tree structure
SYMPH	DOC	Explanation of the instructions for SYMPHONY.UNP
SYMPH	COM	Executable version of program given in SYMPHONY.UNP
SYMPHONY	UNP	Program to run Symphony Ver 1.0 without a key disk
— NOTICE	— —	Information on copyright law and file extensions
ML28-30	UNP	How to backup MultiLink Ver 2.08,2.08c, and 3.00c
SK110A	UNP	How to backup Side Kick 1.10A (another version)
SK100A	UNP	How to backup Side Kick 1.00A (another version)
DB3	UNP	Used in conjunction with DB3ZAP.UNP

414
Copy Protection/Unprotect Utilities
v1

Here's a gold mine of information about running copy-protected and "key-disk" programs from your hard disk, and how to save your original as backup. Generally, these are step-by-step detailed instructions to walk thru a DEBUG session that will allow easier use of over 30 of the most popular copy-protected software products.

CHECK CAREFULLY TO BE SURE YOUR SOFTWARE'S UNPROTECT PROGRAM IS HERE BY VERSION.

Also included are programs to make your disk files 'read-only' and back to 'read-write' (including BASIC programs saved with protection).

Usage: Program copy utilities, Intermediate/Advanced users.

System Requirements: 128K, two disk drives and a monochrome display

How to Start: Check the files with the suffix .DOC (for DOCument), or .TXT (for TeXT) files. Also look for files marked .UNP which are text files for unprotection procedures.

User Comments: "We give this disk the same high rating as the 376. The many programs make great backup utilities especially if you know the DOS debug program." "The program to unlock Symphony worked beautifully." "Documention unclear for those that are not familiar with assembly language programming. A better explanation of how to use DEBUG would help." "Many dated fixes. My Lotus 1A didn't succumb to the patch... Suppose that there's some gold in the that hills, but I couldn't find it!"

File Descriptions:

ALTER	COM	Program to allow user to change file attributes (hidden/
ALTER	DOC	Documentation for ALTER.COM program
CHARTMAS	UNP	Procedure on how to unprotect CHARTMASTER v6.04
COPYALL	COM	Disk-Saver program : copies most disks
COPYPC	COM	A more intelligent alternative to DOS DISKCOPY program
COPYPC	DOC	Documentation for COPYPC.COM program
DB3V21	BAT	Batch file to unprotect dBaseIII vers. 1.0, Edition 1
DB3V21	BIN	Overlay file needed by DB3V21.BAT
DB3V30	BAT	Batch file to unprotect dBaseIII vers. 1.0, Edition 2
DB3V30	BIN	Overlay file needed by DB3V30.BAT
DB3V30	DOC	Documentation for all DB3???.* unprotection methods
DB3ZAP	BAT	Batch file to provide an executable backup copy of dBaseIII
DB3ZAP	BIN	Overlay file needed by DB3ZAP.BAT
DB3ZAP	DOC	Documentation for DB3ZAP.BAT
DOUBLDOS	UNP	Instructions on how to unprotect the DoubleDOS SoftGuard
DSAVER	COM	Disk-Saver vers. R2.01 — copies disks
DUPE	EXE	Backup utility
ENABLE	UNP	Procedure to unprotect the ENABLE v1.0 integrated package
EXECUVSN	UNP	Procedure to unprotect the EXECUVISION graphics package
EZWRITR	UNP	Procedure to unprotect EZWRITER 1.1
FLTSIM	CPY	Procedure to make backup copies of Microsoft Flight
FLTSIM	UNP	Procedure to unprotect Microsoft Flight Simulator v1.00
FOCUSNEW	UNP	Procedure to eliminate need for 'activator' disk in A-drive

File	Type	Description
FRMWK1	BAT	Batch file to create executable backup copy of FRAMEWORK v1.0
FRMWK1	DOC	Documentation for backup of FRAMEWORK v1.0
FRMWK1	UNP	To create executable backup copy of FRAMEWORK v1.0
GRAFWRTR	UNP	Procedure to unprotect GRAPHWRITER v4.21
INFOCOM	COM	Utility programs to operate on INFOCOM games (ZORK) — copy/
INFOCOM	DOC	Documentation for use of INFOCOM.COM program
LAYOUT	UNP	Procedure to unprotect LAYOUT program
LOAD-US	COM	Utility program to allow running Lotus 1-2-3 & Symphony
LOAD-US	DOC	Documentation for use of LOAD-US.COM program
LOADCALC	UNP	Procedure to create a backup copy of LOADCALC v4.13
MANY	UNP	Procedure to unprotect dBaseIII v1.1 (bypass SoftGuard
MEMSHIFT	UNP	Procedure to unprotect MEMORY/SHIFT program
MLINK206	UNP	Procedure to unprotect MULTILINK v2.06 and allow direct
MOD123	COM	Procedure to unprotect LOTUS 1-2-3
MOD123	DOC	Directions for use of MOD123.COM program
MS2	UNP	How to unprotect MEMORY/SHIFT v2.1
123STAR	UNP	Procedure to unprotect LOTUS 1-2-3 Release 1A*
NEW123	UNP	Procedure to unprotect LOTUS 1-2-3 Release 1A
NEW123UN	V1A	Procedure to unprotect LOTUS 1-2-3 Release 1A
PCDRAW	UNP	Procedure to unprotect PC-DRAW
PCDRAW14	UNP	Procedure to unprotect PC-DRAW v1.4
PCM	UNP	Procedure to unprotect IBM Personal Communications Manager
PFS	UNP	Procedure to unprotect PFS-File, PFS-Report, PFS-Write
PFS-ZAP	UNP	Procedure to ZAP PFS-File & PFS-Report to allow running on
PFSFILE	UNP	Procedure to unprotect PFS-File & PFS-Report
PRODWN	TXT	Patches to allow PROKEY v3.0 to run with SIDEKICK
PROKEY	COM	Program referred to as part of procedure in PRODWN.TXT
PROKEY30	UNP	Procedure to unprotect PROKEY v3.0
RB4000	UNP	Procedure to unprotect RBase 4000 v1.11
READONLY	COM	Program to make a file read-only to protect from accidental
READONLY	DOC	Documentation for READONLY.COM
READWRIT	COM	Program to reset read-only files to read/write and allow
READWRIT	DOC	Documentation for READWRIT.COM
SDKIK	UNP	Procedure to unprotect SIDEKICK v1.10A
SIGNMAST	UNP	Procedure to unprotect SIGNMASTER v5.04
SK	UNP	Procedure to unprotect SIDEKICK v1.00A
SK11C	UNP	Procedure to unprotect SIDEKICK v1.11C
SYMPH	COM	Program to allow running SYMPHONY from hard disk without
SYMPH	DOC	Documentation for SYMPHONY.COM program
SYMPHONY	UNP	Procedure to patch SYMPHONY to allow it to run without
SYMPHONY	UP2	Same as SYMPHONY.UNP — simpler instructions
TIMER	SK	Patch to fix SIDEKICK/DOS PRINT.COM conflict
TM	UNP	Procedure to unprotect IBM TIME MANAGER (80 col, v1.00)
TRIVIA	UNP	Procedure to unprotect TRIVIA FEVER (game & demo disks)
ULTIMA	UNP	Procedure to unprotect ULTIMA II, PROKEY 3.0 & other .COM
UNP123	TXT	Procedure to unprotect LOTUS 1-2-3 Release 1 & 1A
UNPROT	B	BLOAD file from BASIC, designed to unprotect a BASIC
UNPROT	DOC	Documentation on how to use UNPROT.B
VISICALC	UNP	Procedure to convert VISICALC to a .COM file
WORD	UNP	Procedure to unprotect Microsoft WORD
WORD1–1	UNP	Procedure to unprotect MS WORD v1.1 using Ultra-Utilities
WS2000	UNP	Procedure to unprotect WordStar 2000 v1.00
ZORK12	UNP	Procedure to make backup copies of INFOCOM's ZORK I and

DOS LEVEL UTILITIES:

Utilities at this level deal primarily with modifications of DOS commands and functions as well as defining new means of accessing them. The majority of this category contains a multitude of such tiny re-programmed and often highly improved versions of the system's internal commands. These are the "system tweakers" that hackers so enjoy creating and using.

For the rest of us, the value of these utilities lies in their alternate mode: often they can provide a shell or overlay system that goes DOS one better by its improved "user-friendliness." In this collection we have several such shells that allow you to select and perform arcane operations with ease. Also worthy of note are a pair of programs that extend visibly the DOS commands by allowing you to query an on-line dictionary for syntax and examples of use. Both are extremely well-documented and will teach you more about DOS than you thought possible!

If you are frustrated by DOS, this is your section!

28 DISKMODF
v1.1

A variety of BASIC and DOS tools, directory listers, machine tutorials, graphics and games. Utilities are included to let you design your own graphics characters, generate a resident COMMAND.COM, or generate a large block font set from BASIC. Some amusing games are here as well. DOS utilities include directory handlers, diskette speed-up, one to confirm files when doing wildcard deletes, a function to give status info on all drives, and others.

Usage: Beginning/intermediate system tools.

System Requirements: Programs marked "+" require color graphics.

How to Start: To run an EXE or COM program type its name and press ENTER. For instructions on running BASIC programs, please refer to the GETTING STARTED section in this catalog. To read DOC files enter TYPE filename.ext and press ENTER.

User Comments: "This documentation for unprotecting protected BASIC programs is clear and complete. I have been looking for this technique for some time. Thanks!" "Corrects for shortcoming in DOS." "One of the best utility collections I've seen."

File Descriptions:

BIGTYPE	BAS	Displays character set in large block font
DDATE	COM	Allows quick updating of date and time on bootup
DISKMODF	BAS	Improved version of disk sector modifier program
JUMBLE	BAS	Permutes jumbled words
PALLETTE	BAS+	Displays colors available in low-res (160x200) graphics
SPEED411	COM	Sets disk step rate to 4 ms — test with format and copy
TIMING	BAS	Accurately times the execution of short BASIC programs
HALS	DOC	Doc on above files
LF	COM	Directory lister sorted by extension & filename
VDEL	COM	Provides for OK's when doing wildcard deletes
CD	COM	Sets default drive, file information, & sorts directory
WAIT	COM	Batch file PAUSE for three seconds
GUMUP1	DOC	Doc on LF, VDEL, CD, WAIT
SYSTAT	COM	Status report on all drives
SYSTAT	DOC	Documentation on SYSTAT.COM
FK	COM	Function key handler (with reset) for DOS 1.0 & 1.1

FK	COM	Function key handler (with reset) for DOS 1.0 & 1.1
FK	DOC	Documentation on FK.COM
SD	COM	Directory lister, 4 up
SDIR	EXE	Directory lister, 2 up — upgrade of SDIR.COM on Disk #2
UNPROT2	TXT	Ultra simple technique for unprotecting BASIC programs
ARTILL	BAS+	Artillary for 2, random terrain & winds — Quite good
GRAFGE	BAS+	Uses graphic screen to develop your own upper ASCII set
GRAFGE	DOC	Documentation for GRAFGE.BAS
MEMPEEK	BAS	Similiar to disk modify programs except for RAM memory
SQUISH	SRC	Upgrade of SQUISH on Disk No 9, modified for compiler
SQUISH	EXE	Compresses BASIC programs, removes REM's, etc
SQUISH	DOC	Documentation on SQUISH
GSDUMP	BAS+	Graphics Sideways memory DUMP (C.Itoh 8510 or NEC8023)
COLOUR	DOC	Tutorial + small routines re: Artifacting, high-res
CPCPRO	DOC	Tutorials -BASIC PrtSc, Printer bit graphics, Keyloc
RESCMD	BAS	Generates resident COMMAND.COM
RESCMDCK	BAS	Resident COMMAND.COM with BEEP, PAGE, CLS
RESCMD	DOC	Documentation on resident COMMAND.COM

33
DOS and Printer Utilities
v1.1

A host of useful system enhancements. Do a graphic dump to an Epson or C.Itoh printer (in two sizes), turn off printer bell, change print pitch, and others. This disk also contains some patches to existing DOS routines, and simplify or speedup some operations. In addition to the DOS and printer utilities, there are some simple (but useful) communication utilities.

Usage: Enhance printer functions and some DOS commands.

System Requirements: 128K, one disk drive, some programs require color graphics.

How to Start: To run an EXE or COM program type its name and press ENTER. For instructions on ASM listings, refer to your Assembler manual. For instructions on running BASIC programs, please refer to the GETTING STARTED section in this catalog. To read DOC files enter TYPE filename.ext and press ENTER.

User Comments: "Best diskette in the first 100 I bought." "All of the utilities are very good and usable." "Useful utilities!"

File Descriptions:

BATMAN	BAS	Sample menu/batch manager program; requires SHELL.BAT
BATMAN	DOC	Documentation file
BSR	BAS	Simple program to drive ABM/BSR controller
BSR	DAT	Data file for BSR.BAS
BUZOFF	COM	Turn off paper out buzzer on Epson (Can execute from WORDSTAR)
COMPRS	COM	Enables compressed print on Epson (Can execute from WORDSTAR)
CVTHEX	EXE	Binary/hex conversion for files larger than 32K
DCPATCH	DOC	Patch for DISKCOPY.COM 2.0
DIAL	COM	Dials Hayes Smartmodem
DIR	BAS+	Disk cataloging program — very colorful
DIR	DAT	Sample data file
DIR	DOC	Documentation file
FK203	ASM	Source code for FK203.EXE
FK203	EXE	Function key reassignment program for DOS 2.0
GRAFTRAX	ASM	Screen dump using PrtSc key for Epson/Nec/C.Itoh
GRAFTRAX	BAS	Sample BASIC program to call GRAFTRAX.COM as a subroutine
GRAFTRAX	COM	Executable program file
GRAFTRAX	DOC	Documentation file
HANG	COM	Hangs up Hayes Smartmodem
HOST	BAS	Communication program for remote access
HOST	DOC	Documentation file for HOST.BAS
PEPATCH	DOC	Patch to IBM's Personal Editor
POSTER	BAS	Prints large character posters
PRTFIX	COM	Corrects "DEVICE TIMEOUT" errors with printer
PRTFIX	DOC	Documentation file
QD	COM	Quadram RAMDRIVE program — FOR QUADRAM BOARD ONLY
QD	DOC	Documentation file
SCROLL	ASM	Scrolls specified area of display screen
SCROLL	BLD	Program file to "BLOAD" from BASIC
SCROLL	DOC	Documentation file
SCROLL1	BAS	Sample program
SCROLL2	BAS	Sample program
SHELL	BAT	Bat file used with BATMAN.BAS
SOUNDS	BAS	Generates different sounds — contains documentation

34
Sorted Directory Version 2.2
v1.1

This collection includes a program to redefine your keyboard, one to let you add volume labels to disks without reformatting, two RAM-disk programs, and a very nice directory display, SDIR.COM, that is a vast improvement over DOS's "DIR" command. Assembly source code is included for these last two. Also included are two routines meant to be merged with the PC-TALK III program. One adds split-screen capabilities to the program, and the other adds the X-modem protocol.

Usage: Communication and DOS enhancements.

System Requirements: 128K, 1 disk drive, monochrome monitor.

How to Start: To run an EXE or COM program type it's name and press ENTER. For instructions on ASM listings, refer to your Assembler manual. To read DOC files enter TYPE filename.ext and press ENTER.

User Comments: "For my particular problem — a compatable computer with no switch for additional disk drives, this RAMdisk program is a lifesaver." "VDISK as stated in the catalog description is from the IBM DOS 2.0 manual; however, it works quite well with DOS 2.11." "Very good collection of utilities. The SDIR22 program is very well documented...I'll be working with PC3SC soon."

File Descriptions:

PC3SC	MRG	Adds split screen capability to PC-Talk III
PC3SC	DOC	Documentation file
SDIR22	ASM	Sorted directory program for DOS 2.0
SDIR22	COM	Executable program file
VDISK	ASM	Sample RAM disk program from DOS 2.0 manual
VDISK	COM	Executable program file
VDISK2	ASM	Same as VDISK.COM modified for double-sided disk
VDISK2	COM	Executable program file
VOLSER	COM	Program to write 2.0 volume labels on diskettes
VOLSER	DOC	Documentation file
XOFF	MRG	Adds XMODEM protocol to PC-Talk 2.0
XOFF	DOC	Documentation file
DEFKEY	COM	Keyboard reassignment program; DOS 1.1 and 2.0
ORIGINAL	KEY	Original keyboard configuration file
BSLASH	KEY	Backslash keyboard configuration file
DEFMAIL	EXE	Mail/donation assistance
DEFCOPY	BAT	Copies distribution disk
DEFKEY	DOC	Documentation file

46
Screen Utilities No 1
v1.3

This disk contains two keyboard-definition programs (Dvorak and QWERTY styles), a full-screen editor, printer-control utilities, and more. Also included is a simple checkbook balancing program, a BASIC database program, and several other possibly useful utilities.

Usage: Word processing and system enhancements.

System Requirements: 128K, 1 disk drive, monochrome monitor.

How to Start: To run a COM or BAT program type it's name and press ENTER. For instructions on running BASIC programs, please refer to the GETTING STARTED section in this catalog. To read DOC files enter TYPE filename.ext ENTER.

User Comments: "Most programs would not run. ASDA, CHECKCON, FORMSDISP, DVORAK all ran fine but none other. You should also warn people that DVORAK changes the keyboard before warning that it will do so." "Some items lock-up machine. Those using BASIC are OK." "Some good utility programs here, as on disk # 80 (which I also have)."

Suggested Donation: $10.00

File Descriptions:

CLOCK	COM	Puts clock in upper right corner of display
CONFIG	SYS	Setup for alternate keyboard programs (DOS 2.0)
DVORAK		Alternate keyboard program (DOS 2.0 only)
DVORAK	DOC	Documentation for above
DVORAK	BAT	Batch file for above
QWERTY		Alternate keyboard program (DOS 2.0 only)
QWERTY	BAT	Batch file for above
MA	BAT	Batch file for above
FULLEDIT	BAS	Stopgap full screen editor
PRINTFIX	COM	Run once to be rid of early DOS 1.1 printer bug
WS-ASCII	BAS	WORDSTAR-to-ASCII conversion
EFS	BAS	Electronic (database) file system
ASDADEL	BAS	Part of screen format program
ASDA	BAS	Part of screen format program
ASDARUN	BAS	Part of screen format program
HELPCOM	BAS	Part of screen format program
EDIT	BAS	Part of screen format program
FORMDISP	BAS	Part of screen format program

RESTATTR	BAS	Part of screen format program
HIDEFILE	BAS	Remove/modify hidden files
CHECKCON	BAS	Simple checkbook balancing program
CPRINT	BAS	Setup parameters of C-Itoh 8510 (NEC 8023) printer
GPRINT	BAS	Setup parameters of IBM/Epson printer
MEMDUMP	BAS	Memory dump program
DVORAK	COM	Command file for DVORAK
CONTROL	COM	Part of alternate keyboard system
QWERTY	COM	Command file for QWERTY
KEYMOVE	BAS	Part of alternate keyboard system

51 HYPERDRIVE

v1

There are two different configurations of the Hyperdrive RAM-disk program on this disk, as well as the source code to let users generate their own configurations. Note, however, that the documentation states that you must reset DIP switches on your system board to use this program. Also included is an interesting BASIC program to figure future. And for all you heretics who still believe that computers can be fun, too, a version of the game GOMOKU is included. Translated into Pascal from HP Basic, this is guaranteed to keep you up late for a few nights.

Usage: System enhancement and entertainment.

System Requirements: 128K, 1 disk drive, monochrome monitor.

How to Start: To run an EXE program type its name and press ENTER. For instructions on running BASIC programs, please refer to the GETTING STARTED section in this catalog. For instructions on ASM listings, refer to your Assembler manual. To read DOC files enter TYPE filename.ext and press ENTER.

File Descriptions:

FOUR	EXE	Game — get four in a row
FUTRDATE	BAS	Determines date — x days, months, years from now
FUTRDATE	DOC	Documentation for FUTRDATE.BAS
GOMOKU	DOC	Documentation for GOMOKU.EXE
GOMOKU	EXE	Game — simular to tic-tac-toe but played on 20x20 board
GOMOKU	PAS	Source code for game of GOMOKU
HDD512	EXE	RAM disk program for 512K of memory
HDS320	EXE	RAM disk program for 320K of memory
HYPERDRV	DOC	Documentation for RAM disk program
INTERUPT	MAC	Macro assembly language interrupt routine

PCGLOBE	BAS	Draws globe
RAMDISK	ASM	Source code for RAM disk program
TMDAY	BAS	Digital clock

70 DISKCAT

v1

DISKCAT and DC-SORT: These two programs combine for a disk cataloging and sorting/pring system for keeping track of your disk files. It works with DOS 1.1 format disks only (not DOS 2.0).

PAGESKIP : This utility simply skips to the top of form from DOS 2.0, so that you do not have to push buttons on your printer. Just key "PAGE" and hit enter to run, if the utility is on a diskette in your default drive. NOTE: it requires an EPSON MX or FX compatible.

SMALLPRT and USMALLPRT: These install (and uninstall) a utility that skips you to the top of form then sets the printer to compressed double-strike mode. While slow, it saves paper and makes printouts more readable and xerox-able, when printing documentation like this.

Usage: Cataloging your Disks, Controlling your Printer!

System Requirements: 96K, one disk drive and a monochrome drive

How to Start: Consult the .TXT and .DOC files for directions. The BASIC programs require GWBASIC; the .EXE and .COM programs can be run directly from DOS.

File Descriptions:

PAGE	BAT	Sends formfeed to printer
PAGES	KIP	Formfeed character
PAGESKIP	DOC	Documentation for PAGESKIP.BAS
SMALLPR	INT	Commands to put Epson in condensed, double-strike mode
SMALLPRT	BAT	Batch file to put Epson in condensed, double-strike mode
SMALLPRT	DOC	Notes for using SMALLPRT.BAT
UNSMALLP	BAT	Batch file to reset Epson in normal print mode
UNSMALLP	DOC	Notes for using UNSMALLP.BAT
UNSMALLP	RNT	Commands to put Epson printer back to normal mode
DISKCAT	BAS	Disk cataloging program
*	EXE	Compiled version of DISKCAT BASIC files (2 files

DISKCAT	DOC	Documentation for DISKCAT.BAS
DC-SORT	BAS	Sort program for DISKCAT
VPRINT	COM	Redirects printer output to file
VPRINT	ASM	Assembly language source for VPRINT.COM
VPRINT	DOC	Documentation for VPRINT.COM
DIRMANIP	EXE	Directory manipulation program

80

DOS Utilities No 3

v1

Here's a little bit of everything for anyone looking to add some functionality to their system. DOS Utilities No 3 has some great routines, including two improved directory utilities, SD20 & XDIR, which let you alter file attributes EASILY! (Keep someone from erasing those important files!) Also of interest is MOVE, which can combine the functions of COPY and ERASE (much quicker, too). There are also color-setting routines, an expanded ANSI.SYS driver, modification to let you use the ALT, CTRL, and SHIFT keys as toggles (on/off). Toggle on/off functions can help people who have problems depressing multiple keys to more safely use their PC functions. There's much more, explore and enjoy!

Usage: System enhancement and customization.

System Requirements: 128K, 1 disk drive, monochrome monitor.

How to Start: To run an EXE or COM program type its name and press ENTER. For instructions on running BASIC programs, please refer to the GETTING STARTED section in this catalog. For instructions on ASM listings, refer to your Assembler manual. To read DOC files enter TYPE filename.ext and press ENTER.

User Comments: "I like the compact, but full information display it presents." "Odd mix of utilities and BASIC games/word processors." "Some utilities (Alter, Ask, Move) were useful; rest were either too specialized or outdated." "Super utilities."

File Descriptions:

ALTER	COM	Utility to change file attributes (DOS 2.0)
ALTER	DOC	Documentation file for ALTER.COM
ASK	COM	Allows interactive input to a batch file (DOS 2.0)
ASK	DOC	Documentation file for ASK.COM
BIGANSI	SYS	Enlarged ANSI.SYS (DOS 2.0) — allows for redefinition of 40 keys

CISEXE	COM	Communications program that supports CompuServe protocol
CISEXE	DOC	Documentation file for CISEXE.COM
CL	ASM	Source for CL.COM
CL	COM+	Sets blue bkgnd, yellow frgnd. and block cursor on C/G monitor
CL	DOC	Documentation file for CL.COM
COLOR	COM+	Machine language equivalent of BASIC's COLOR statement
COLOR	DOC	Documentation file for COLOR.COM
EDITNO	BAS	Formats numeric output in ways that PRINT USING cannot
EDITNO	DOC	Documentation file for EDITNO.BAS
ET4	BAS	BASIC text file line editor — an alternative to EDLIN
ET4	EXE	Compiled BASIC version
FCBCRT	BAS	Creates BLOADable program for reading directories from BASIC
FCBEXM	BAS	Demonstrates use of BLOADable file
FCBREAD	BSV	BLOADable file created by FCBCRT.BAS
FKREST	ASM	Source for FKREST.COM
FKREST	COM	Companion to FKSET.COM — resets keys to original functions
FKSET	ASM	Source for FKSET.COM
FKSET	COM	Upgrade of function key definition routine for DOS 2.0
FLIGHT	NEW	How to modify Flight Simulator for color on a RGB monitor
HIQUE	BAS+	Board game that supports light pen input
KEYLK	DOC	Documentation for KEYLK and KEYLK3
KEYLK3	ASM	Source code for KeyLock program for latest BIOS ROM
KEYLK3	EXE	KeyLock program for BIOS ROM.
MEM640	DOC	Documentation file for MEM640.ZAP
MEM640	ZAP	Modifies BIOS to handle memory greater than 544KB
MOVE	COM	Utility to move files across directories without copying
MOVE	DOC	Documentation file for MOVE.COM
OKIMOD	DOC	Documentation on how to modify MODE.COM for different printers
SD20	COM	Sorted directory for DOS 2.0. Includes several run options
SD20	DOC	Documentation file for SD20.COM
SOLFE	BAS	Plays "Solfeggietto" by Carl Phillip Emanual Bach
WMTELL	BAS	Plays William Tell Overture
XDIR	COM	Extended directory — shows file attributes
XDIR	DOC	Documentation file for XDIR.COM

89
PC-SIG Sampler No 3
v1

Some interesting programs reside on this disk. MINICALC is a small (11 x 22) spreadsheet, with graphing capabilities, and is useful for quick jobs. MSPOOL is a quite flexible print spooler which allows you to print on three printers simultaneously. There are also programs to blank your monitor to prevent phosphor burn, a text-tool package that lets you catalog disks, generate mail-list mailings, and generate multi-column lists from single-column data.

Usage: System enhancement.

System Requirements: 128K, 1 disk drive, monochrome monitor.

How to Start: To run an EXE or EXE program type its name and press ENTER. For instructions on running BASIC programs, please refer to the GETTING STARTED section in this catalog. To read DOC files enter TYPE filename.ext and press ENTER.

User Comments: "I use VOLSER constantly — an excellent utility! I am not entirely sure what the "PC-LIB" program does (better documentation perhaps?)." "I certainly enjoyed Texttools."

Suggested Donation: TEXTTOOL: $25

File Descriptions:

COLBLNK1	COM	Blanks color display after 5 minutes
MINICALC	DOC	Documentation for MINICALC.EXE
MINICALC	EXE	Single screen spreadsheet calculator — 11 columns, 22 rows
MONBLNK1	COM	Blanks monochrome display after 5 minutes
MONBLNK1	DOC	Documentation for MONBLNK1.COM and COLBLNK.COM
MSPOOL	COM	Flexible spooler program
MSPOOL	DOC	Documentation for SPOOL.COM
PC-LIB	BAS	Disk file library program
PC-LIB	DOC	Documentation for PC-LIB
VOLSER	COM	Create/alter volume labels
VOLSER	DOC	Documentation for use of VOLSER.COM
————	——	Text Tools programs
XUP	BAS	Prints textfiles in columnar tables
PRNT2	BAS	Wild card print program
MAIL	BAS	Mailmerge program
MAIL	TXT	Sample input file for MAIL.BAS with instructions for use
PR1	LET	Sample letter for MAIL.BAS

109
DOS Utilities No 5
v1.1

A grabbag of utilities aimed mostly at the needs of the more advanced programmer types among us. BREAKPT lets you do a breakpoint within any program, FILEDUMP will do a hex dump to your screen. There are routines to demonstrate structured macros and one on APL. One of the most interesting programs here is UTIL. This is a DOS utility that allows you to do things like: sort directories, do paged display of text files, redefine your keyboard, and others. This could be quite useful for anyone interested in a simple, effective way to enhance their system.

Usage: Intermediate/advanced programmer tools.

System Requirements: 128k, one disk drive, monochrome display.

How to Start: To run an EXE or COM program type its name and press ENTER. WKS files are for use with LOTUS 1-2-3. For instructions on ASM listings, refer to your Assembler manual. To read DOC and read-me files enter TYPE filename.ext and press ENTER.

User Comments: "Good items: util (very good) & filedump BREAKPT.COM and UTIL.EXE are worth the money !" "The UTIL program is the best I have used from PC-SIG we need more programs like this please someone tell the writer he has done a damn good job."

Suggested Donation: UTIL $10.00, $15.00 includes latest version and printed documentation.

File Descriptions:

BREAKPT	COM	Makes ctrl-esc do a breakpoint to trace any program
BREAKPT	DOC	Documentation for above
BREAKPT	ASM	Source for above
DATE	PRG	dBASE II program to validate dates
FEDTAX83	WKS	123 worksheet for 1040 form, schedules A, B, C, W
FILEDUMP	COM	Hex dump a file to screen
MACTEST	ASM	Illustrates structured assembler macros in STRUCT.MAC

PV——	APL	Present value functions in APL
REGDISP	ASM	Source for program to display 8088 regs in real time
STRUCT	MAC	Assembler macros for structured programming
UTIL	EXE	Fantastic set of screen/file/directory, etc. functions
UTIL	DOC	Documentation for UTIL.DOC
UTILREAD	ME	Introductory note about these utilities
DATABASE		Sample database
READ	ME	List of files on this diskette

111
File Utilities No 1
v1

Here's a big package of some handy file and text utilities. ST — for SuperTyper — is an improvement over the DOS "TYPE" command. It features a paged display, with page numbers if desired. Another program prints your disk directories onto labels. Use it to track of your software. Several other routines aid in file management. There are a few text utilities, a Wordstar utility (blanks to tabs, and tabs to blanks). DOS utilities include a file comparator (improved over the DOS "COMP") and The Shell. The SHELL program was written to fix a DOS 2.0 COMMAND.COM bug, nice if you need it. Finally, for those with special needs, BIGCALC is an 8100-digit precision calculator.

Usage: File management and text handling.

System Requirements: 128K, 1 disk drive, monochrome monitor.

How to Start: To run an EXE or COM program type its name and press ENTER. For instructions on ASM or 'C' listings, refer to your Assembler or 'C' language manuals. For instructions on running BASIC programs, please refer to the GETTING STARTED section in this catalog. To read DOC files enter TYPE filename.ext and press ENTER.

User Comments: "Unfortunately, this method (MEMDRIVE) of 'fooling' the boot-up procedure is not compatible with all commercial software. The first time this occurred, I spent considerable time in troubleshooting a non-existent software problem." "MYM and AUTOCAD are 2 good ones, nice package to have available." "Several very useful utility programs on this disk :COVER,CAL,LAR

and ST are good basic programs for the person just starting out with pd software."

File Descriptions:

BIGCALC	BAS	100 digit precision calculator!
BIGCALC	DOC	Documentation for above
CAL	COM	Prints calendar for any month/year after 1900
CAL	DOC	Documentation for above
COVER	COM	Prints file directory on Epson
DETAB	C	Convert tabs in file to blanks (Source program)
DETAB	EXE	Executable file for above
DIRECTRY	BAS	Creates machine program to read disk directory
ENTAB	C	Convert blanks in file to tabs (Source program)
ENTAB	EXE	Executable file for above
FIXTEXT	BAS	DOS-to-WORDSTAR converter, better than UNWS
GETMEM	ASM	Program to reserve memory areas (Source program)
GETMEM	COM	Executable file for above
LABELPRT	BAS	Print diskette directory as a diskette label
LAR	DOC	Program to manage file libraries (Documentation)
LAR	EXE	Executable file for above
MEMDRV	ASM	DOS 2.0 device driver to allow 640K RAM (Source program)
MEMDRV	SYS	Executable file for above
PI-COMP	COM	Replacement for DOS COMP command — better!
PI-COMP	DOC	Documentation for above
PRINT	C	Print text files on printer (Source program)
PRINT	EXE	Executable file for above
SHELL	COM	Fix for DOS SHELL command bug
SHELL	DOC	Documentation for above
ST	COM	Type files to full screen with PgUp/PgDn
ST	DOC	Documentation for above

138
Programmer Utilities No 4
v1

A hackers paradise! Utilities let you set printer modes from DOS, diagnose parity errors and display interrupt vectors, and give you a 100line virtual screen. There are instructions on accessing DOS enviornment variables from within batch files, and much, much, more!

Usage: System tools for more advanced users.

System Requirements: 128K, 1 Disk drive, monochrome monitor.

How to Start: To run an EXE or COM program type it's name and press ENTER. For instructions on ASM or 'C' listings, refer to your Assembler or 'C' language manuals. For instructions on running BASIC programs, please refer to the "Getting Started" section in this catalog. To read DOC files enter TYPE filename.ext and press ENTER.

Suggested Donation: RE-VIEW $15.00

File Descriptions:

BLYPROGS	DOC	General description of BLY programs
RE-VIEW	COM	BLY's color card support for 100-line virtual screen in DOS!
RE-VIEW	DOC	Documentation for above
ANSIPCH	EXE	Part of RE-VIEW
CLA	COM	Part of RE-VIEW
UP	COM	Part of RE-VIEW
BRICKS	EXE	BLY's version of BREAKOUT
SETPRN	COM	BLY's printer setup program
SETPRN	ASM	Source for above
SETPRN	DOC	Documentation for above
CASE	COM	BLY's resident utility for auto case switching during program entry
CASE	ASM	Source for above
VTYPE	EXE	BLY's replacement for DOS type command, many extensions
VTYPE	C	Source for above
VTYPE	DOC	Documentation for above
C	ASM	DOS 2.0 version of entry point routine for Lattice c
–MAIN	C	DOS 2.0 version of main routine for Lattice c
IOS1–20	ASM	DOS 2.0 version of level 1 I/O routines for Lattice c
ENVIRON	DOC	How to access DOS environment variables from batch files
LIBRIAN	MRG	Merge file to upgrade IBM diskette librarian to DOS 2.0
LIBRIAN	DOC	Documentation for above
NORTPAT2	DOC	Patch to Norton Utilities 2.0 to support Teac 42 track drives
RMSPC	COM	Interrupt handler for diagnosing parity errors
RMSPC	ASM	Source for above
VECTS	EXE	Program to display interrupt vectors

139 Screen Utilities No 2

v1

Some nice routines for handling screen output, as well as other utilities. The LORES program lets you design screens using the 160x100 16-color mode of the CGA card. Fun and colorful, there are both BASIC and compiled versions. The PRINTXT1 routines are for Dbase II programmers (allows you to display long (80 chars) text lines on screen. Also included, the BAT200D program, and associated .BAT files, allow you to explore the many possibilities of batch files.

Usage: Screen handlers, batch utilities, and programmers tools.

System Requirements: 128K, 1 Disk drive, monochrome monitor.

How to Start: To run an EXE program type its name and press ENTER. For instructions on ASM or 'C' listings, refer to your Assembler or 'C' language manuals. For instructions on running BASIC programs, please refer to the GETTING STARTED section in this catalog. CMD files are for use with dBASE II. To read DOC files enter TYPE filename.ext and press ENTER.

User Comments: "NUSQ is a great improvement in speed and size over other unsqueeze utilities." "Too much DOS 2.0 and IBM-specific for use with clones!"

Suggested Donation: LORES $10.00 or $5.00 and a formatted diskette. This gets you the latest version of the program and demos, as well as printed documentation.

File Descriptions:

DOSPATH	C	Lattice c functions for DOS 2.0 command line args and pathnames
CHAROP	ASM	Used by DOSPATH.C. Reads/sets switch char and device available
DIR201	BAS	Diskette cataloging program. Very friendly user interface
DIR201	EXE	Compiled version of above
LORES	BAS	Does 160x100 16-color graphics
LORES	DOC	Documentation for 160x100 graphics support package
LORES	ASM	Assembly language subroutines for 160x100 16-color graphics

LORES	OBJ	Assembled version of LORES.ASM
LODEMO	BAS	Demo of 160x100 16-color graphics on IBM PC
LORES	EXE	Another 160x100 demo program
LORES	USR	BASIC-callable 160x100 graphics functions
NUSQ	COM	Assembly-coded version of unsqueeze program, super fast!
PRINTXT1	CMD	dbase II command to print multiple text lines on screen
PRINTXT1	DOC	Documentation for above
PRINTXT1	INC	Include routines for PRINTXT1.CMD

124 Extended Batch Language Ver. 2.04a by Seaware

v2

The Extended Batch Language is a program which adds additional features to the batch processing supported by DOS. With the Extended Batch Language, you can write batch file programs that prompt for responses and keep track of values of variables.

Usage: Intermediate/advanced DOS enhancements.

System Requirements: 128K, 1 disk drive, monochrome monitor.

How to Start: To run a COM or BAT program type its name and press ENTER.

User Comments: "Real good examples. Will be useful in future, but really need hard disk." "A wonderful and most welcome upgrade of the batch file processor. Now the DOS programmer has the power and options that should always have been there, without having to resort to a series of "utility" batch routines." "This is a must for automated systems — documentation in the form of a text file would be much better."

File Descriptions:

BACKUP	BAT	Utility to backup BAT
BAT	COM	Extended Batch Language
BATDEMO	BAT	Demonstrations — number guessing, menu, directory, etc.
BATDOC	BAT	Documentation start
EDIT	BAT	General purpose "editor & file to be edited" caller
ERRATA		Items corrected from previous BAT versions
TELE	BAT	Telephone list sample program
VCOPY	BAT	Demo of READSCRN command to copy file with 80 col. display

COLORTST	BAT	Demo color test routine
DIAL	BAT	Demo Dialer
KEYTEST	BAT	Sample and test keyboard strobe

133 Ultra-Utilities 4.0

v2

The Ultra-Utilities are a collection of useful tools everyone with a PC should have. With these utilites you can recover a file that you may have accidently erased, modify and look into any file on a disk, or create a database program written in BASIC. Unsqueezed copies of files from this disk are on Disk No 245.

Usage: Intermediate/advanced DOS tools and enhancements.

System Requirements: 128K, 1 Disk drive, monochrome monitor.

How to Start: Enter TYPE README.NOW and press ENTER for instructions on running this package.

User Comments: "Documentation too sophisticated and too skeletal." "Too technical." "I ordered it specifically for Ultra-file's file recovery function, which worked very easily when I tested it." "In some instances this program was better than Norton's Utilities." "Documentation skips too much information."

Suggested Donation: Ultra-Utilities $30.00

File Descriptions:

README	NOW	Instructions for files on disk
U-ZAP	EXE	Program to look at disk sectors
U-FILE	EXE	Modify/recover disk files
U-OPT	EQE	Squeezed U-OPT (Optomize) program
U-OPT	DQC	Squeezed documentation for U-OPT
U-FORMAT	EXE	Disk format utility
U-MIND	BQS	Squeezed U-MIND BASIC program
U-MIND	DQC	Squeezed documentation for U-MIND
SKELETON	BQS	Squeezed BASIC program for U-MIND
TEST	ATR	Part of U-MIND
TEST	HDR	Part of U-MIND
USQ	COM	Unsqueeze program
DOC41	TQT	Squeezed documentation for Ultra-Utilities — Part 1
DOC42	TQT	Squeezed documentation for Ultra-Utilities — Part 1

144

Fabula 1
(Disk 1 of 2)

v1

A fine collection of tools for communications users and others. The SQIBM and USQIBM programs compress and expand files to save on costs when using modem transmission. TALK450 shows how to add 450 baud capacity to your Hayes 300 modem. There are other goodies like SCRNSAVE, which prevents phosphor burn on your monitor, and a series of batch files to give sorted directory listings.

Usage: Communications and system enhancement.

System Requirements: 128K, 1 disk drive, monochrome monitor.

How to Start: To run a COM or BAT program type its name and press ENTER. To read DOC files enter TYPE filename.ext and press ENTER.

User Comments: "SCRNSAV is great! I've got it on every bootable disk I use." "FABULA is fabulous! I lusted for SCREENSAVE & SQEEZER/ UNSQUEEZER!" "Most interested in screensave but that has the weakest documentation."

File Descriptions:

ASMGEN	COM	Converts EXE and COM to ASM files
ASMGEN	DOC	Documentation for ASMGEN.COM
BASICAID	BAS	Squeezes and unsqueezes files
BASICAID	DOC	Documentation for BASICAID.BAS
BINSIX	DOC	Documentation for BINSIX.DOC
BINSIX	EXE	New squeeze program, 20% less then hex
COMP	BAS	Compares two tokenized BASIC files
CROSSOPT		Data file for CROSSREF.EXE
DIP-MEM	COM	Bypasses power-up memory test
DIP-MEM	DOC	Documentation for DIP-MEM.COM
MAKEDATA	BAS	Checksumed data files for COM/EXE
RSVD	COM	Changes the size of VDISK
SQIBM	COM	Squeezes files for faster transfer
SQIBM	DOC	Documentation for SQIBM.DOC
TABS	BAS	Puts tab codes in or removes them
UPNUM	COM	Shows if NumLock or CapsLock in use
UPNUM	DOC	Documentation for UPNUM.DOC
USQIBM	COM	Unsqueezes files squeezed by SQIBM
USQIBM	DOC	Documentation for USQIBM.COM
VDISK	COM	160k RAM disk program (see RSVD.COM)
WRITECOM	BAS	Converts data to EXE/COM
WRT	DOC	DOC for WRTE.COM and WRTP.COM
WRTE	COM	Erases read-only attribute from a file
WRTP	COM	Sets read-only attribute of a file

145

Fabula 2
(Disk 2 of 2)

v1

Another fine collection of tools worth adding to almost anyones library. BINSIX is an improvement over HEX for you modem-types who can't transmit 8-bit code, VDISK and RSVD are ram-disk utilities, and WRTE and WRTP let you easily set or release write-protection on any file. For the hackers, ASMGEN converts .EXE and .COM files to assembly format.

Usage: Communications and system enhancement.

System Requirements: 128K, 1 disk drive, monochrome monitor.

How to Start: To run a COM or EXE program type its name and press ENTER. For instructions on running BASIC programs, please refer to the GETTING STARTED section in this catalog. To read DOC files enter TYPE filename.ext and press ENTER.

User Comments: "Excellent but the user needs to be warned some programs may not be useable on his/her machine."

File Descriptions:

ASMGEN	COM	Converts EXE and COM to ASM files
ASMGEN	DOC	Documentation for ASMGEN.COM
BASICAID	BAS	Squeezes and unsqueezes files
BASICAID	DOC	Documentation for BASICAID.BAS
BINSIX	DOC	Documentation for BINSIX.DOC
BINSIX	EXE	New squeeze program, 20% less then hex
COMP	BAS	Compares two tokenized BASIC files
CROSSOPT		Data file for CROSSREF.EXE
DIP-MEM	COM	Bypasses power-up memory test
DIP-MEM	DOC	Documentation for DIP-MEM.COM
MAKEDATA	BAS	Checksumed data files for COM/EXE
RSVD	COM	Changes the size of VDISK
SQIBM	COM	Squeezes files for faster transfer
SQIBM	DOC	Documentation for SQIBM.DOC
TABS	BAS	Puts tab codes in or removes them
UPNUM	COM	Shows if NumLock or CapsLock in use
UPNUM	DOC	Documentation for UPNUM.DOC
USQIBM	COM	Unsqueezes files squeezed by SQIBM
USQIBM	DOC	Documentation for USQIBM.COM
VDISK	COM	160k RAM disk program (see RSVD.COM)
WRITECOM	BAS	Converts data to EXE/COM
WRT	DOC	DOC for WRTE.COM and WRTP.COM
WRTE	COM	Erases read-only attribute from a file
WRTP	COM	Sets read-only attribute of a file

MSBEDIT	EXE	Compiled version of editor written in Pascal
PAS-BEEP	DOC	How to create a beep in Pascal
PORTS	DOC	Documentation for PORTS.EXE
PORTS	EXE	Program to examine I/O ports
PORTS	PAS	Source code for PORTS.EXE
PRNSTATS	BAS	Program to examine status of lineprinter port
PRNSTATS	DOC	Documentation for PRNSTATS.BAS
RAMDISK	COM	Virtual disk driver from DOS 2.0 manual
RAMDISK	DOC	Documentation for RAMDISK.COM
SETKEY	BAS	Keyboard reassignment program (Requires DOS 2.0 up)
SETKEY	DOC	Documentation for SETKEY.BAS

172
Steve's Utilities
v1

This is a very nice collection of utilities that would make a worthwhile addition to almost anyone's system. Included are routines to: let you change the beep tone of your PC to suit yourself, clear your display screen, several different programs to let you determine status of your machines ports, rework your keyboard arrangement, and much more. The source code is included along with most of these programs. Those of you so inclined may use this to make changes, or simply examine it to find out how other programmers do things. This is an excellent way to enhance your machines capabilities, as well as your own.

Usage: Intermediate to advanced users.

System Requirements: 128K, 1 Disk drive, monochrome monitor.

How to Start: To run an EXE or COM program type its name and press ENTER. For instructions on running BASIC programs, please refer to the GETTING STARTED section in this catalog. For instructions on ASM or PAS listings, refer to your Assembler or Pascal manual. To read DOC files enter TYPE filename.ext and press ENTER.

User Comments: "SETKEY is too primitive to be of any value."

File Descriptions:

BEEP	ASM	Source code for BEEP.EXE
BEEP	COM	Program to produce "tone" on speaker
BEEP	DOC	Documentation for BEEP program
BEEP	EXE	Program to produce "tone" on speaker
CLS	ASM	Source code for routine to clear screen
CLS	DOC	Documentation for CLS.ASM
DSKTEST	BAS	Examines the status byte from the floppy controller
DSKTEST	DOC	Documentation for DSKTEST.BAS
EDIT-MOD	PAS	Source code for part of editor
EDITOR	DOC	Documentation for editor written in Pascal
EDT-MAIN	PAS	Source code for main editor module
INPORT	ASM	Routine to interrogate requested port
INPORT	DOC	Documentation for INPORT.ASM
LOCATE	ASM	Routine to locate curser position
LOCATE	DOC	Documentation for LOCATE.ASM

182
AutoFile, EasyFile and Time, Date Utilities
v1

The AUTOFILE program is a free-form sort of database. Your data is stored as an 80-column by 20-line "page", indexed and searchable by up to 42 keywords. A very useful program for keeping track of information that might not work as well under a "conventional" database program. EASYFILE is another simple file manager with a host of support routines.

Usage: Simple database managers.

System Requirements: 128K, 1 Disk drive, monochrome monitor.

How to Start: For instructions on running BASIC programs, please refer to the GETTING STARTED section in this catalog. To read DOC files enter TYPE filename.ext and press ENTER.

User Comments: "Easyfile is a good program."

File Descriptions:

————	——	AUTOFILE
AUTOFILE	BAS	AUTOFILE small indexed file system
AUTOFILE	BAT	AUTOFILE batch start up file
AUTOFILE	DOC	AUTOFILE documentation
AUTOFILE	FIX	Part of AUTOFILE
————	——	EASYFILE
EASYFILE	BAS	EASYFILE main program — small simple file manager
ADDFILE	BAS	Part of EASYFILE — add to a file
BUILFILE	BAS	Part of EASYFILE — builds initial file
COLRFILE	BAS	Part of EASYFILE — switches to color monitor
COPFILE	BAS	Part of EASYFILE — copies file

DCATFILE	BAS	Part of EASYFILE — displays file categories
DISPFILE	BAS	Part of EASYFILE — displays files
DTEXFILE	BAS	Part of EASYFILE — displays text
EZFDOCM	BAS	Part of EASYFILE — documentation — use BASICA LIST to view
FILEFILE	BAS	Part of EASYFILE — file selection
FILEMENU	BAS	Part of EASYFILE — EASYFILE menu
LISTFILE	BAS	Part of EASYFILE — list file
MONOFILE	BAS	Part of EASYFILE — switch to monochrome
STATFILE	BAS	Part of EASYFILE — status report
————	——	Date and Time Utilities
AREACODE	BAS	Displays major cities within an area code
CALENDAR	BAS	Displays calendar for any month & year (Irvan Krantzler)
DDATE	COM	Last date used routine
MONOCLKF	COM	Monochrome clock time display
MONOCLKF	DOC	Documentation
SPEC-OCC	BAS	Keeps track of special occasions by month (Phil Michitsch)
SPEC-OCC	DOC	Documentation
TCLOCK	BAS	Displays large date & time, has alarm feature (William Vath)
TIME	BAS	Displays time

183 DOS Utilities No 8

v1

An assortment of the old and the new reside on this disk. For those with older PC's, MEM640 patches to allow you to get 640k in your machine, RESCMD lets you have a memory-resident command processor. Of more general appeal, MOVE combines the functionality of both COPY and DELETE into one easy package. VTYPE is an improved TYPE command. And COMSPEC4 lets you run COMMAND.COM from subdirectories. Many more programs of interest are also included.

Usage: Beginning/intermediate users.

System Requirements: 128K, 1 disk drive, monochrome monitor.

How to Start: To run an EXE or COM program type its name and press ENTER. For instructions on running BASIC programs, please refer to the GETTING STARTED section in this catalog. To read DOC files enter TYPE filename.ext and press ENTER.

User Comments: "SUNDRY is a hardware hacker's handful — a few outdated patches, but a couple of useful routines for ROM inspection." "Good for all DOS 2.xx and DOS 1.1 users only !"

File Descriptions:

BOARD	TST	Check for famous QUADRAM parity error design defect
CHECKOUT	BAS	Diagnostics on all ports
CMD99	COM	Command processor
COMPROM	EXE	Compares two ROM programs from diskettes
COMSPEC4	ASM	Assembler source
COMSPEC4	COM	DOS patch to activate COMMAND.COM in subdirectories
COMSPEC4	DOC	Documentation
CONFIG	EXE	Displays your PC's configuration
COPYROM	EXE	Copies ROM programs onto diskette for later use
CRL	BAS	Change cursor shape & size (John Herzfeld)
CRL	COM	Compiled version
CRS	BAS	Change cursor shape & size (John Herzfeld)
CRS	COM	Compiled version
INFO1	BAT	Documentation for COPYROM.EXE & COMPROM.EXE
MEM640	DOC	Documentation
MEM640	ZAP	DOS patch to permit older BIOS PC's to use 544KB-640KB memory
MY-DATE	BAT	Part of COPYROM.EXE utility
OLD-NEW	BAT	Part of COMPROM.EXE utility
RESCMD	BAS	DOS 1.1 patch to make COMMAND.COM memory resident
RESCMD	DOC	Documentation
ROMREAD	BAS	Reads & displays ROM BIOS dates, type IBM PC (Tom Allen)
ROMREAD	DOC	Documentation
VTYPE	DOC	Documentation
VTYPE	EXE	Improved TYPE command (Vincent Bly)
MOVE	COM	Utility — COPY command which prompts at each file
MOVE	DOC	Documentation for MOVE.COM

185 DOS Utilities No 10

v1

A variety of handy utilities to help manage your files. Two different squeeze/unsqueeze programs, SQIBM/USQIBM, and ZSQ/ZUSQ save time when transmitting files by modem, and save disk space when archiving files. Several directory managers let you view/save your file listings the way you want, including hidden files.

Usage: System enhancement tools.

System Requirements: 128K, 1 disk drive, monochrome monitor.

How to Start: To run an EXE,COM, or BAT program type its name and press ENTER. For instructions on running BASIC programs, please refer to the GETTING STARTED section in this catalog. To read DOC files enter TYPE filename.ext and press ENTER.

User Comments: "SDIR24C is great! this is now my standard directory program,set to F10. It is indispensible." "Only weaknesses are that it does not list subdirectories and is a little slow."

File Descriptions:

CATALOG	COM	Sorted directory
DD	BAT	Directory sorted by date (Part of DNXSD.BAT)
DIR2	BAS	Diskette sorted directory by Wes Meier, Version 2.0
DN	BAT	Directory sorted by filename (Part of DNXSD.BAT)
DNXSD	DOC	Series of batch sorted directory utilities
DS	BAT	Directory sorted by file size (Part of DNXSD.BAT)
DX	BAT	Directory sorted by file extension (Part of DNXSD.BAT)
DXSAVE	BAT	Sample change in BAT to save sorted directory on disk
SDIR	COM	Sorted directory by Ted Reuss
SDIR	DOC	Documentation
SDIR24C	ASM	Assembler source
SDIR24C	COM	Sorted directory Version 2.4 by John Ratti
SDIR24C	DOC	Documentation
SEC&BYTE	BAS	Prints table of diskette sectors & bytes
SQIBM	COM	Squishes a file
SQIBM	DOC	Documentation
USQIBM	COM	Unsquishes a squished file
USQIBM	DOC	Documentation
ZSQ	EXE	Squishes a file
ZSQ-ZUSQ	DOC	Documentation
ZUSQ	EXE	Unsquishes a squished file

205
DOS Utilities
No 13
v1.1

DOS Utilities No 13 is a collection of miscellaneous programs for serious computer users. NDOSEDIT is a fine DOS command editor. BROWSE lets you view files (better than TYPE). Other utilities allow you to change cursor shape, enhance your COMMAND.COM, and more.

Usage: Intermediate users.

System Requirements: 128K, 1 disk drive, monochrome monitor. Some programs require color graphics.

How to Start: To run an EXE or COM program type its name and press ENTER. For instructions on running BASIC programs, please refer to the GETTING STARTED section in this catalog. To read DOC files enter TYPE filename.ext and press ENTER.

User Comments: "NDOSEDIT is a dream — it gives me as much control over command line editing as I have on my mainframe." "Extremely useful DOS command stack editor. Saves me lots of time. "BROWSE is a useful program for examining a text file (or any file, for that matter)."

File Descriptions:

BROWSE	COM	View file contents — similar to CMS BROWSE command
BROWSE	DOC	Documentation
CGCLOCK2	COM	Color display clock, beeps every 15 minutes
CGCLOCK2	DOC	Documentation
CMD185	COM	Creates resident COMMAND.COM with good internal commands
CMD185	DOC	Documentation
CURSOR	COM	Changes cursor shape — enter "cursor8" for block shape
CV2	COM	Changes diskette labels under DOS 2.0
EDLIN	BAS	Better documentation for EDLIN (Mel Rothman)
FILELIST	BAS	Displays text files with pause for each full screen
KEY	BAS	Something like simple Prokey for DOS 2.0
NDOSEDIT	COM	VM style editor for DOS commands, with command stack
NDOSEDIT	DOC	Documentation

217
NELIST and Disk ALIGNment
v2

NELIST is a Pascal source lister, capable of automatically enhancing your printouts, and configurable to your own needs. WA-TOR is a fascinating predator-prey simulation, try changing it's parameters and watch what happens! SUPERDIR is a diskette file manager that allows you to give each file a descriptive comment line.

Usage: System enhancement tools.

System Requirements: 128k, 1 disk drive, monochrome monitor.

How to Start: To run a COM program type its name and press ENTER. For instructions on running BASIC programs, please refer to the GETTING STARTED section in this catalog. For information on PAS programs, consult your Pascal manual.

User Comments: "WA-TOR is a cute demonstration of Turbo Pascal's graphics capabilities. I use it when showing off my Tandy 1000. NELIST has been superceded by Turbo's LISTT (version 3)." "Align is not very useful to me — I don't know anything about oscilloscopes!" "NELIST/ALIGN's proceedures require more equipment than I have. Equipment needs should be clearly described in the disk description."

Suggested Donation: NET/ALIGN $20.00.

File Descriptions:

RESWORDS	TXT	Key word list used by NELIST
SUPERDIR	BAS	"Super directory" program (Compute Magazine April, 1984)
SUPERDIR	DOC	Documentation for SUPERDIR.BAS
DUMPSCRN	BAS	BLOADable high resolution screen dump (Softalk, July, 1983)
DUMPSCRN	MRG	Model BASIC program for using DUMPSCRN.BAS
DUMPSCRN	DOC	Documentation for DUMPSCRN
ALIGN	EXE	Disk alignment program
ALIGN	DOC	Documentation for disk alignment program
NELIST	DOC	Documentation for NELIST
NELIST	COM	Turbo Pascal source lister — underlines key words etc.
NEPRN	DAT	Printer control data for NELIST
NEINST	COM	Installation program to create NEPRN.DAT
NELIST	PAS	Source code for NELIST
NEINST	PAS	Source code for NEINST
WA-TOR	COM	Predator-prey simulation (Scientific American, Dec., 1984)
WA-TOR	000	Overlays used by WA-TOR.COM
WA-TOR	PAS	Turbo Pascal source code for WA-TOR
WA-TOR	DOC	Documentation for WA-TOR

245
Ultra-Utilities Files — Unsqueezed
v1

The Ultra-Utilities are a powerful collection of tools for the PC owner interested in getting more from his system. U-MIND is an "intelligent" database generator which allows you to produce clean, sophisticated programs very quickly. U-OPT will help clean-up BASIC code so that it will compile tighter and faster. More of these utilities are available, in squeezed format, on Disk 133.

Usage: Intermediate/advanced users and programmers.

System Requirements: 128K, 1 disk drive, monochrome monitor.

How to Start: For instructions on running BASIC programs, please refer to the GETTING STARTED section in this catalog. To read DOC or TXT files enter TYPE filename.ext and press ENTER.

● To run an EXE program type its name and press ENTER.

User Comments: "UTLRAMIND: I liked the ease of use and the documentation was very easy to follow." "Very helpful disk utility i use it sometimes to format 'rare' sectors on my disks." "Good set of utilities, although not as friendly or as useful as Norton's, despite what your catalog says."

Suggested Donation: Ultra-Utilities $30.00.

File Descriptions:

U-MIND	DOC	Documentation for U-MIND (51K)
U-OPT	DOC	Documentation for O-OPT (2K)
DOC41	TXT	Ultra-Utility documentation — Part 1 (52K)
DOC42	TXT	Ultra-Utility documentation — Part 2 (23K)
U-OPT	EXE	Ultra-Optimize program
SKELETON	BAS	Used with Ultra-Mind
U-MIND	BAS	Ultra-Mind program (Intelligent database)

LOAD-US	COM	Main program
LOAD-US	DOC	Documentation (listable)
LOAD-US	ABS	Abstract

252

ListMate/Load-US by SWFTE

v1.1

This disk contains two user-supported programs from SWFTE. ListMate is a menu driven label producer with all documentation and help displayed from the program. Load-US (tm) allows you to run Lotus 123 and Symphony directly from a hard disk without the system disk in Drive A. This saves you the aggravation of locating your System disk each time you need to run it.

Usage: Lotus and DOS aids.

System Requirements: Load-Us requires a hard disk.

Features: ListMate contains on-line help screens, internal documentation, and is compatible with MultiMate (tm) files.

How to Start: Type LISTMATE and press ENTER. To read DOC files enter TYPE LISTMATE.DOC and press ENTER. For Load-us, enter TYPE LOAD-US.DOC to read docs, and LOAD-US and press ENTER to run.

User Comments: "LOAD-US works well — have recommended it to many at the office. Only problem — when used in my AUTOEXEC.BAT file, I had to experiment with the order in which it was loaded in relation to other files." "Too limited. Needs to accept more data files." "(LISMATE) Very helpful!! Excellent label program." "I am a Multi-Mate user and found the program to be very helpful." "LOAD-US is really convenient; I don't have to look for my systems disk every time I want to start SYMPHONY."

Suggested Donation: ListMate $25.00, Load-Us $10.00.

File Descriptions:

LISTMATE	EXE	This is the main ListMate program
LISTMATE	SYS	ListMate system files
LISTMATE	TXT	ListMate text files
LISTMATE	HLP	ListMate help files
LISTMATE	DOC	ListMate documentation (not listable)
LISTMATE	ABS	ListMate abstract

277

FINDFILE

v1

FINDFILE is a utility which no hard-disk user should be without. Menudriven, it searches through subdirectories to find a file you may have lost. It includes a host of support routines to help you manage your files. Besides this support, it provides improved TREE display, single or multiple file operations.

Usage: Hard-disk users.

System Requirements: 128K, 1 floppy drive, one hard disk, ASCII printer, and 80-column display.

Features:

- Menu driven
- Improved TREE display
- Single or multiple file operations.

How to Start: Enter TYPE TYPE.ME for installation instructions.

Suggested Donation: FINDFILE $5.00

File Descriptions:

TYPE	ME	Tells you to LISTER file COVER
BUG		Bug report form, send to author
COVER		A letter to the user about installation
DOC		The documentaion
DSKLABEL		A correct disk label
ORDER		Order form for On-Disk Software
LISTER	EXE	Used to print BUG, COVER, DOC and ORDER
MOVBAS	BAT	Moves FindFile to disk — BAS version
MOVEXE	BAT	Moves FindFile to disk — EXE version
MOVLIB	BAT	Moves FindFile to disk — for people with BASRUN.EXE
MENU	BAT	Executes the menu program
FINDFILE	BAT	Finds a file
$$DOEXBA	BAT	Setup batch file
$$NEWTRE	BAT	Setup batch file
$$MENU	BAS	Gives you the menu of options
COMSEP	BAS	Makes $$TREE into $$TREE.CSV for other programs to use
FFILE	BAS	Finds any file or group of files
FFILEBIG	BAS	Use FFILE except on more than about 1,000 files

MAPTREE	BAS	Converts TREE output to something useful
SAMECHK	BAS	Checks for duplicate files
SETDRV	BAS	Resets the drive FindFile is using
*	LIB	Compiled version to be used with BASRUN.EXE (6 files)
*	EXE	Faster compiled versions of BASIC programs (6 files)
FFILEMEN	DAT	The data which defines your menu

325 Logon/Off

v2

This disk is dedicated to a special category of utilities: programs for PC user logging, timekeeping and documenting job starting/ending. For example, PC-Logger gives you a computer use log that creates a PC FILE III database for later sort/print. These types of utilities are a must for anyone who needs to document machine-time, for taxes or other reasons.

Usage: For systems usage tracking, required for IRS deductions.

System Requirements: 128k, 1 disk drive, monochrome monitor

How to Start: To read DOC files, enter TYPE filename.ext and press ENTER.

• To run an EXE or COM program, just type its name and press ENTER. For instructions on running BASIC programs, please refer to the GETTING STARTED section in this catalog.

User Comments: "This program is worthwhile for anyone who needs to document his computer activities for the IRS." "I kept getting errors while trying to install SYSLOG." "SYSLOG is the best on this disk, but the others are very useful." "Easy to use and very practical." "(LOGON/LOGOFF) a must for an office of multiple users. Allows a manager to track utilization even if not for tax purposes."

Suggested Donation: SYSLOG has a suggested donation of $25.00

File Descriptions:

— — —	— —	Time Keeper
TIMEKEEP	DOC	Documentation for TIMEKEEP
TIMEKEEP	EXE	TIMEKEEPER (Ver 3.0): produces job log report
TIMSTALL	COM	Install program for TIMEKEEP
— — —	— —	PC-Logger

DEFAULTS	COM	Defaults.com creates log file
STARTLOG	COM	Writes date & time to log
STOPLOG	COM	Reads log, calculates time
USELOG	HDR	PC-FILE III header file defining log database
USELOG	RPT	PC-FILE III report file listing database
PCUSELOG	DOC	Documentation
— — —	— —	SYSLOG
SYSLOG	EXE	SYSLOG (Ver 2.0): system use log (128K;DOS 2.0)
SYSLOG	DOC	Documentation
START	BAS	START/END: Logs start & end of jobs with comments
START	EXE	compiled version of start log program
END	BAS	BASICA version of end log program
END	EXE	compiled version of end log program

355 PC-ZAP

v1

PC-ZAP is a utility program which allows easy modification of any DOS file without the use of the DOS DEBUG command. PC-ZAP can dump a file, verify data in a file and replace data in a file. PC-ZAP functions are controlled by user created files. Several examples are included in the documentation [but not on disk]: Unprotect Lotus 123, Unprotect MemoryShift, Make /v default for FORMAT.COM and others.

Usage: Intermediate/advanced programmer tool.

System Requirements: 128K, 1 Disk drive, monochrome monitor.

How to Start: Type PC-ZAP20 and press ENTER to start program.

User Comments: "The program ran but the addresses given in the documentation were incorrect. Hence the program did me no good." "The idea of PC-ZAP is good, similar to Norton's Utilities and Ultra Utilities but it lacks their sophistication." "Good way to implement a patch program. The control file may be retained as an "audit" trail."

Suggested Donation: PC-ZAP has a suggested donation of $35.00

File Descriptions:

| PC-ZAP20 | DOC | Documentation for PC-ZAP. Only prints on IBM/EPSON or |
| PC-ZAP20 | EXE | Executable PC-ZAP program |

374
DOS Utilities
No 18
v1

A collection of handy DOS programs and utilities that can be used to improve your system. From the simple (a screen-clock routine), to the sublime (give programs access to DOS path-search capabilities. Along with display controllers, security programs, and others, this disk can become a valuable part of your everyday operations.

Usage: System enhancement tools.

System Requirements: 64k, 1 disk drive, monochrome display.

How to Start: To read DOC or TXT files, enter TYPE filename.ext and press ENTER.

• To run an EXE or COM program, just type its name and press ENTER.

User Comments: "Excellent collection of general-purpose utilities." "Very useful for hard-disk system." "Our IBM tech support man at work was even impressed with some of the utilities. He now has joined PC-SIG."

File Descriptions:

AUTORES	BAT	Batch file for AUTOMENU under DOS 2.0
AUTORES2	BAT	Same as AUTORES.BAT
BANNER2	BAT	batch file to extract all the files from BANNER.LBR
BANNER2	LBR	Library of the BANNER program files.
CAL-YR	BAS	Displays a calendar for any given year.
CGCLOCK	COM	Real time clock display for color/graphics display.
CGCLOCK	DOC	Documentation for CGCLOCK.COM
CLCK	COM	Displays clock and key status in the upper right hand
CLOKATTR	DOC	Instructions to change clock display
DPATH	COM	Gives programs a directory path search capability
DPATH	DOC	Documentation for DPATH.COM
DU	COM	Displays disk/directory information.
EQUIP	COM	Display of the equiptment installed in/on the PC/XT.
EQUIP	DOC	Documentation for EQUIP.COM
EXL	EXE	Allows extension of DOS commands.
FK20	COM	Function key handler for PC-DOS 1.0 and 1.1
FK20	DOC	Documentation for FK20.COM
FLIP	COM	Control special key status (i.e. FLIP NUM OFF).
HGC	COM	Screen Save Program for the Hercules Graphics Card

HGC	DOC	Documentation for HGC.COM
KBFIX	COM	Change DOS keyboard buffer size.
KBFIX	FIX	Patch to quiet the bell in KBFIX.COM
KEYLOC	DOC	Documentation for KEYLOC-3.EXE
KEYLOC–3	EXE	Modifies operation of the Alt, Ctrl, AND Shift keys.
KEYSTAT	COM	Displays status of CapsLock and NumLock keys.
KEYSTAT	DOC	Documentation for KEYSTAT.COM
LUE	COM	Used by BANNER2.BAT
MONOCLK2	COM	MONOCHROME Clock display.
MONOCLK2	DOC	Documentation for MONOCLK2.COM
NOBLINK	COM	Prevents blinking of displayed characters.
NOLF	EXE	Allows use of RADIO SHACK printer with the IBM PC.
NOLF	DOC	Documentation for NOLF.EXE
NPAD	COM	A windowing notepad.
NPAD	DOC	Documentation for NPAD.COM
PASSWORD	BAS	Provides password protection for you system
PASSWORD	DAT	Password file
PASSWORD	DOC	Documentation for PASSWORD.BAS
PC-WINDO	COM	Public domain attempt at SIDEKICK
RE-VIEW	COM	Screen scroll buffer program
RE-VIEW	DOC	Documentation for RE-VIEW.COM
RE-CLS	COM	Used by RE-VIEW.COM
RE-UP	COM	Used by RE-VIEW.COM
RECALL	COM	Allows retrieval of previously issued DOS commands
RECALL	DOC	Documentation for RECALL.COM
REMIND	COM	Memo keeper. Like a string around your finger.
RUN	COM	Allows execution of a file in a 'HIDDEN' directory
RUN	DOC	Documentation for RUN.COM
S-LOCK	COM	Part of RE-VIEW.COM
SCRN	COM	Shuts off display when it has not been used for a time
SCRN	DOC	Documentation for SCRN.COM
SEARCH	COM	Useful replacement for the DOS PATH command.
SEARCH	DOC	Documentation for SEARCH.COM
SNAPSHOT	COM	DOS extension saves graphics screen in a disk file.
SPEEDKEY	COM	Speeds up the PC keyboard.
SPEEDKEY	DOC	Documentation for SPEEDKEY.COM
SPOOL20	COM	Improved print spooling utility.
SPRINT	COM	Speedy PRINT replacement for IBM ROM BIOS routines.
SPRINT	DOC	Documentation for SPRINT.COM
UPDIR	COM	Utility to go back up the directory path
XTMENU	BAS	Menu and utilities program.

382
PC-CONVERT/SWEEP
v1

PC-CONVERT/SWEEP is a powerful collection of file conversion and disk utilities. PC-SWEEP is a file handling utility. Operating in either single or multi-file mode, this program lets you easily conduct file operations (copy, delete, rename, etc.) and has some very informative screen displays. This one deserves a place in everyone's collection.

Usage: File handling and system enhancement.

System Requirements: 128k, 1 disk drive, PC (not MS) DOS 2.0 or greater.

How to Start: To read DOC files, enter TYPE filename.ext and press ENTER.

- To run a BAT or COM program, just type its name and press ENTER. For instructions on running BASIC programs, please refer to the GETTING STARTED section in this catalog.

User Comments: "SWEEP is a MUST for MS-DOS users!!" "(PC-CONVERT) Still don't know what it does." "Just a slow version of WASH. Get SR if you can."

Suggested Donation: PC-SWEEP $20.00

File Descriptions:

INSTALL	BAT	Installs PC-CONVERT
PC-SWEEP	COM	Disk management utility
PC-SWEEP	DOC	Documentation for PC-SWEEP.COM
PCSWEEP	DOC	Documentation for PCSWP110.COM
PCSWP110	COM	PC-SWEEP v1.10
PCCONMNU	BAS	Main PC-CONVERT file
PCCONERS	BAS	Part of PC-CONVERT
1REFORM	BAS	Part of PC-CONVERT
2REFORM	BAS	Part of PC-CONVERT
3REFORM	BAS	Part of PC-CONVERT
PCCONPRT	BAS	Part of PC-CONVERT
PCCONREF	BAS	Part of PC-CONVERT
PCCONV	BAT	Batch file to invoke PC-CONVERT
STARTUP	BAT	Batch file to start installation of PC-CONVERT

413
DOS Utilities
v1

This disk is chock full of useful sets of utility programs and systems that enhance and simplify the sometimes obscure MS/PC-DOS operating system command structure. There are also utility programs that provide functions that are not available in 'plain vanilla' DOS. POPALARM allows you to display the clock (constant, every minute), run a stopwatch, set a clock alarm, and more.

Usage: DOS tools and system enhancements.

System Requirements: 128K, 1 disk drive, monochrome monitor.

How to Start: To read DOC or TXT files, enter TYPE filename.ext and press ENTER.

- To run an EXE or COM program, just type its name and press ENTER. For instructions on ASM listings, refer to your Assembler manual.

User Comments: "CED is a superset of DOSEDIT, which I like very much. The documentation is very good for a public domain program." "CED and PARTNERS are particulary useful and fun to run. very useful util. Lots of neat tricks!" "POPALARM is a very good resident clock and alarm system. Unfortunately, it does not get along very well with my favorite word processor (Microsoft WORD)."

Suggested Donation: PARTNER $15.00, PCPF $12.00

File Descriptions:

1DIR	COM	A sample of this 'Wonder' DOS shell program
BWVID	ASM	Source code of the BWVID.COM program
BWVID	COM	A program that stops a composite monitor from putting out
BWVID	DOC	Documentation of the BWVID.COM program
CED	COM	Command EDitor (expanded DOSEDIT) -command line editing
CED	DOC	Documentation for the CED.COM program
COMMENT	DOC	Documentation for the COMMENT.SYS device driver
COMMENT	SYS	An MS/PC-DOS 2.0(+) device driver
DW	COM	DiskWipe — totally erases a diskette
DW	DOC	Documentation for DW.COM program
FASTFMT	LBR	Fast format utility system
FASTFMT	TXT	Text file explaining how to unscramble FASTFMT.LBR
LU	EXE	A Library unscramble program — used by the FASTFMT and

MEMINIT	EXE	Sets memory switches; speed up power on
PARTNER	COM	RAM resident utility program
PARTNER	DOC	Documentation for the PARTNER.COM program
PC-STAT	COM	Diplays system status — both hardware & software
PCPF	COM	A session manager — replaces bare DOS prompt with a
PCPF	DOC	Documentation for the PCPF.COM program
POPALARM	DOC	Documentation for the POPALARM.EXE program
POPALARM	EXE	BellSoft's alarm clock program — some nice features
SCREN2	LBR	Screen Image Editor and utility; program DOS menus;
SCREN2	TXT	Text file explaining how to unscramble SCREN2.LBR
SETBW40	COM	Used with BWVID.COM-does the same thing as DOS's MODE BW40
SETBW80	COM	Used with BWVID.COM-does the same thing as DOS's MODE BW80
UNSQ	COM	Unsqeeze utility, restores squeezed files. Used by SCREN2

478

Hard Disk Utilities

v1

This is a collection of utilities for the hard disk drive user that was compiled from over 25 disks in our library. If you have a fixed disk, this excellent set of file handlers, sort routines, directory and attribute handlers, and etc. will make your system much more manageable, efficient, and just plain more enjoyable to use. Try 'em and see.

Usage: Intermediate/Advanced users.

System Requirements: 128k, monochrome monitor, fixed disk.

How to Start: To read DOC or TXT files, enter TYPE filename.ext and press ENTER.

• To run an EXE or COM program, just type its name and press ENTER. For instructions on running BASIC programs, please refer to the GETTING STARTED section in this catalog.

User Comments: "These very useful programs lack good documentation & an overall description of what they can do for your hard disk. Excellent programs once you fully understand them. Should be made easier for the novice to utilize." "Good utility! A good compilation of programs for a new

user of hard-disks" "Even if you use just one of these utilities, it is worth the price!"

Suggested Donation: SDIR5 $10.00, VIEWDISK $15.00

File Descriptions:

ALTER	COM	Utility to change file attributes (HIDDEN/READONLY/ETC)
ALTER	DOC	Documentation for ALTER.COM (4k)
BACKSTAT	EXE	Tells you which files on the hard disk haven't been backed-up
CATALOG	COM	Make a sorted directory
CDSECRET	COM	Go to a "secret" sub-directory
DD	BAT	Sort Directory by date (PART OF DNXSD.BAT)
DIR2	BAS	Basic version of a directory sorter
DISKPARK	DOC	Documentation for DISKPARK.EXE (1k)
DISKPARK	EXE	Position the hard disk drive head in a saftey zone
DISRTN	EXE	Undeletes and recovers lost first sectors
DN	BAT	Sort Directory by name (PART OF DNXSD.BAT)
DNXSD	DOC	Documentation for sorting directory
DS	BAT	Sort Directory by size (PART OF DNXSD.BAT)
DX	BAT	Sort Directory by extension (PART OF DNXSD.BAT)
DXSAVE	BAT	Sample change in BAT to save sorted directory to disk
FREE	COM	Displays amount of actual free space on hard disk
GCOPY	DOC	Documentation for GCOPY.EXE (1k)
GCOPY	EXE	Menu type selective copy program
GDEL	DOC	Documentation for GDEL.EXE (1k)
GDEL	EXE	Menu type selective delete program
MDSECRET	COM	Make a "secret" sub-directory
NDOSEDIT	COM	VM style editor for dos commands
NDOSEDIT	DOC	Documentation for NDOSEDIT.COM (5k)
POKING	TXT	Text file containing locations of information about the hard disk
RDSECRET	COM	Remove "secret" sub-directory
READONLY	COM	Make a file read-only to make it un-erasable
READONLY	DOC	Documentation for READONLY.COM
READWRIT	COM	Return a read-only file back to read/write status
READWRIT	DOC	Documentation for READWRIT.COM
SDIR5	COM	Utility to list files by specific types and different formats
SDIR5	DOC	Documentation for SDIR5.COM
SEARCH	COM	Useful replacement for DOS path command
SEARCH	DOC	Documenation for SEARCH.COM (2k)
SECRET	DOC	Documentation for RDSECRET,MDSECRET,& CDSECRET (1k)
TREED	COM	Make a directory tree
UNDEL	COM	Recovers erased files
UNDO	BAS	Allows fixed disk users to read backup diskettes
VDL	COM	File deletion utility
VDL	DOC	Documentation for VDL.COM (2k)
VIEWDISK	DOC	Documentation for VIEWDISK.EXE
VIEWDISK	EXE	Look at individual disk sectors
WHEREIS	COM	Find a file anywhere on the hard disk regardless of location
WHEREIS	DOC	Documentation for WHEREIS.COM (1k)
WRT	DOC	Documentation for WRTE.COM and WRTP.COM

| WRTE | COM | Make a read-only file copyable |
| WRTP | COM | Make a read-only file |

481
Still River Shell V1.54

V1.33

The Still River Shell provides a better working environment than DOS. It saves time by allowing the use of one key commands and at the same time lets the user do anything that DOS would normally do. It provides a much more comfortable and informative operating environment than DOS alone does, and the friendly, visible nature of the display can actually help a new user understand the operating system better.

Usage: DOS shell manager for personal or business use.

System Requirements: 128K, 1 disk drive, monochrome monitor.

How to Start: Type COPY SR.DOC PRN and press ENTER to print documentation. Type SR and press ENTER to start program.

User Comments: "Better than MicroSoft WINDOWS in my estimation!" "The main program on this disk really seems too complicated. The documentation on the disk does not tell how to program macros" "...offers an excellent environment for using DOS and utilizes many features found in individual DOS utility packages." "For those who like a DOS "Front End", this one is great. Some programs run from the shell remained in memory afterwords, though. Don't know why."

Suggested Donation: $25.00

File Descriptions:

GOODIES	DOC	Documentation for POPD, PUCHD, AND XDOS.
POPD	EXE	Pops a directory off the stack and makes it the current directory.
PUSHD	EXE	Pushes the current directory onto a stack
SR	EXE	An enhanced PC-DOS environment program
SR	DOC	Documentation for SR.EXE
SRF1	BAT	Used with SR.EXE function keys
SRF2	BAT	Used with SR.EXE function keys
XDOS	EXE	Calls another batch file from within a batch file

498
DOSamatic Version 2.0

v1

DOSamatic is an acclaimed task-switching utility that allows the loading of several programs and manipulating them with simple keystroke commands. It contains a nice menu that list available drives, directories and files on the current drive. Commands available include VIEW, SORT RENAME EDIT, PRINT, DEBUG, COPY, and DELETE. Programs can be run from memory. Now you can do two things at once!

Usage: Intermediate/Advanced System manager.

System Requirements: 128k, 1 disk drive, monochrome monitor.

How to Start: Type DOSAMATC and press ENTER.

User Comments: "Might help someone out in a pinch, or be of interest to someone with a very convoluted hard disk, but not much help otherwise." "Awkward and substantially below the other programs available for this purpose." "The program didn't work on my PCjr with 640K. It hangs up after the first screen."

Suggested Donation: DOSAMATIC $39.00.

File Descriptions:

DOSAMATC	COM	DOSamatic program
DOSAMATC	HLP	Help screen information used with DOSAMATC.COM
DOSAMATC	DOC	Documentation for DOSAMATC.COM

534
COMPUTER USER'S HANDBAG #1
V1

This disk contains several powerful DOS utilities, a background dialer, a text file lister, and a multi-tasking operating environment. It also contains a communications program, some printer utilities, and a small memory resident program to automatically disable Caps Lock when an alphabetic key is pressed. All but one of the programs are fully documented, and most have Assembly source code or BASIC listings.

Usage: MS-DOS systems managers and hackers.

System Requirements: 128k, 1 disk drive, monochrome monitor.

How to Start: To read DOC or TXT files, enter TYPE filename.ext and press ENTER.

- To run an EXE or COM program, just type its name and press ENTER. For instructions on ASM listings, refer to your Assembler manual.

Suggested Donation: SDIR50 $10.00

File Descriptions:

CAPSUNLK	ASM	ASSEMBLY Source Listing for CAPSUNLK.COM
CAPSUNLK	COM	Memory resident utility to automatically unlock the caps-lock key
DIALER95	COM	Background dialer program
DIALER95	DOC	Background dialer documentation
DISKIDX	BAS	BASIC source code listing for disk organizer utility
DISKIDX	DOC	Documentation for disk organizer
ERRMON	COM	Disk I/O Error Monitor for the AT
ERRMON	DOC	Documentation for Disk I/O Error Monitor
INT13	ASM	ASSEMBLY Source Listing for Copy Protection Breaker
INT13	COM	Copy Protection Breaker DOS Utility
INT13	DOC	Documentation for Copy Protection Breaker
LPTX	ASM	ASSEMBLY Source Listing for above
LPTX	COM	Allow interrupt handlers to capture output to printer on disk
LPTX	DOC	Documentation for above
SDIR50	COM	All purpose directory utility and command shell
SDIR50	DOC	Documentation for all purpose directory utility
TFL	BAS	ASCII File Transfer Utility — BASIC source listing
TFL	DOC	ASCII File Transfer Utility — Documentation
TFL	EXE	ASCII File Transfer Utility — Compiled
TMODEM	CNF	Configuration file for communications program
TMODEM	KEY	Auxiliary Communications utility
TMODEM32	COM	Communications program to transmit data in several protocols

535
COMPUTER USER'S HANDBAG #2
V1

This disk contains the DOS users magic bag of tools. Save or restore a screen image in a file, Rename files, subdirectories, or even volume labels easily. Other routines include a prompting mass-copy program, an easy way to catalog disks or print labels, and more. For writers, there's a utility to help with indexing chores. HANDBAG #2 has things to help make your life just a little easier.

Usage: MS-DOS systems managers and hackers.

System Requirements: 128K, 1 disk drive, monochrome monitor.

How to Start: To read DOC or TXT files, enter TYPE filename.ext and press ENTER.

- To run an EXE or COM program, just type its name and press ENTER. For instructions on ASM, PAS, or 'C' listings, please refer to your associated manual.

File Descriptions:

CED1-0B	COM	DOS Multiple Command line editor — create new DOS commands
CED1-0B	DOC	Documentation for CED1-0B.COM.
COPYQ	EXE	Wildcard selective y/n copy, such as used in VDEL.
PCDISK	COM	Disk cataloging program.
QWIKLABL	EXE	Computer-assisted typing of gummed labels
QWIKLABL	KEY	Key assignments file for QWIKLABL
LOAD	COM	Loads COM file larger than 64KB.
LOAD	ASM	ASSEMBLY Source for LOAD.COM
PUSH	COM	Save CRT image to a file.
POP	COM	Restore CRT image from a file.
PUSH-POP	DOC	Documentation for PUSH & POP.COM.
SUPEREN	COM	Renames files, subdirectories, volume labels.
SUPEREN	ASM	ASSEMBLY Source for SUPEREN.COM
TRIVIA	C	A chuckle for C programmers.
FLIP	COM	Flips between page 0 & 1 of graphics text screens.
FLIP	ASM	ASSEMBLY Source for FLIP.COM.
SHOW	COM	Like TYPE with MORE built in.
INDEXER	EXE	Computer-aid for book indexing
INDEXER	PAS	Microsoft PASCAL Source Code of INDEXER

558
PC Prompt
(DOS HELP)
v1

PC-prompt is a unique, memory resident DOS extension that automatically provides syntax prompting for DOS commands as you type. The F10 function key can be used to display additional help whenever needed. Help screens can also be invoked for EDLIN, DEBUG, BASIC(A) and Borland's Turbo Pascal editor from within these programs.

Usage: Beginning DOS users.

System Requirements: 128K, 1 disk drive, monochrome monitor.

How to Start: Type AUTOEXEC and press ENTER.

Suggested Donation: $10.00 from individuals, site licenses available.

File Descriptions:

AUTOEXEC	BAT	Batch file for automatically installing PC-prompt
HELP	DOC	User's Guide for PC-prompt
HELP	EXE	PC-prompt...Memory resident, automatic DOS Help
HELP	INV	Printable invoice for business users
HELPCMDF	NCP	Full Help mode command file
HELPCMDP	NCP	Prompts-Only mode command file
HELPF	CMP	Full Help mode compressed Help file
HELPP	CMP	Prompts-Only mode compressed Help file
HELPPOPF	CMP	Full mode Popup DOS command prompts
HELPPOPP	CMP	Prompts-Only Popup DOS command prompts
HELPTABF	NCP	Full mode decompression table
HELPTABP	NCP	Prompts-Only mode decompression table
PCPROMPT	ARC	All PC-prompt files in Archived format serves as a backup.

564
Jon Dart's DOS
Utilities
v1

This disk contains several useful utilities for the MS-DOS environment including file copy/move, cyclic redundancy check (CRC) generation, file preview, sorted directories, enable/disable file protection, and others. With these aids, you will find that many of the most frustrating aspects of file/system management will be vastly simplified. And for the programmers among you, most programs include the source files.

Usage: Intermediate/Advanced user/programmer tools.

System Requirements: 128K, 1 disk drive, monochrome monitor.

How to Start: To read DOC files, enter TYPE filename.ext and press ENTER.

● To run an EXE or COM program, just type its name and press ENTER. For instructions on ASM or 'C' listings, refer to your Assembler or 'C' language manuals.

File Descriptions:

ASM	ARC	assembly-language library source and header files
ASM	LIB	assembly-language library (linkable binary)
B	ARC	c utility library source and header files
B	LIB	c utility library (linkable binary)
CLEAN	C	program to remove control chars. from a file (source)
CLEAN	EXE	program to remove control chars. from a file (executable)
CP	AQM	file/directory copy utility (source, squeezed)
CP	EXE	file/directory copy utility (executable)
CRC	C	Cyclic Redundancy Code generator (source)
CRC	EXE	Cyclic Redundancy Code generator (executable)
DETAB	C	program to expand tabs to spaces (source)
DETAB	EXE	program to expand tabs to spaces (executable)
FDUMP	C	file dump/patch utility (source)
FDUMP	EXE	file dump/patch utility (executable)
FIXLINES	C	makes all lines in a file end with CR/LF (source)
FIXLINES	EXE	makes all lines in a file end with CR/LF (executable)
HEAD	ASM	displays first few lines of a file (source)
HEAD	EXE	displays first few lines of a file (executable)
LS-PC	EXE	directory listing program (PC executable)
LS	AQM	directory listing program (source, squeezed)
LS	EXE	directory listing program (MSDOS executable)

MODEM	C	simple communications program (source)
MODEM	EXE	simple communications program (executable)
MV	AQM	file/directory move utility (source, squeezed)
MV	EXE	file/directory move utility (executable)
RM	AQM	improved DEL function (source, squeezed)
RM	EXE	improved DEL function (executable)
RO	C	sets file to read-only status (source)
RO	EXE	sets file to read-only status (executable)
RW	C	sets file to read-write status (source)
RW	EXE	sets file to read-write status (executable)
SHOW	AQM	bidirectional file display program (source, squeezed)
SHOW	EXE	bidirectional file display program (executable)
TAIL	ASM	displays last few lines of a file (source)
TAIL	EXE	displays last few lines of a file (executable)
UNSQ	COM	program to expand squeezed (.AQM) files
UPDATE	C	makes date and time of a file current (source)
UPDATE	EXE	makes date and time of a file current (executable)
UTIL	DOC	documentation for all programs
WC	ASM	byte/word/line counting utility (source)
WC	EXE	byte/word/line counting utility (executable)

585 DOS EXTENSIONS (Disk 1 of 2)
v1

This disk contains the User Manual, Reference Manual and one of a series of extremely flexible and useful DOS Extensions. These do not necessarily replace resident DOS commands, which can still be used as is. Rather, they add more versatile and powerful supersets of these commands which greatly add to their utility. Disk 589 contains the DOS EXTENSIONS programs.

Usage: System enhancement tools.

System Requirements: DOS 2.1, 256K, 1 disk drive, monochrome monitor.

How to Start: To read DOC files, enter TYPE filename.DOC and press ENTER.

Suggested Donation: $55.00

File Descriptions:

LS	EXE	DOS Extension — Directory lister
REF	DOC	Documentation — Reference Manual for DOS Extensions
USER	DOC	Documentation — Manual for Installation and use of extensions

586 DOS EXTENSIONS (Disk 2 of 2)
v1

This disk is the second of the DOS EXTENSION series. It contains all but one of the actual DOS extensions in this package. The documentation files are on Disk No 585. Because of the sophistication of DOS Extensions, which enhance DOS comand structures, the documentation disk is strongly recommended.

Usage: System enhancement tools.

System Requirements: 128K, 1 disk drive, monochrome monitor.

How to Start: To run an EXE program type its name and press ENTER.

File Descriptions:

ATT	EXE	DOS Extension — View or change file attributes
ALARM	EXE	DOS Extension — Sound a controllable tone
CAT	EXE	DOS Extension — Concatenate files
CLK	EXE	DOS Extension — Measure elapse time of programs or commands
CMD	EXE	DOS Extension — Execute programs, commands, or batch files
CP	EXE	DOS Extension — Copy files
DIRSRT	EXE	DOS Extension — Directory sorter
GPM	EXE	DOS Extension — Find text patterns in files
INFO	EXE	DOS Extension — Display system, disk, or memory information
INP	EXE	DOS Extension — Input data to a DOS pipe
MERGE	EXE	DOS Extension — Merge text lines from multiple files
MV	EXE	DOS Extension — Move files
PRNT	EXE	DOS Extension — Output selected text lines of files
RENDIR	EXE	DOS Extension — Rename a subdirectory
RENM	EXE	DOS Extension — Rename files
RM	EXE	DOS Extension — Delete files
SED	EXE	DOS Extension — File editor
SELECT	EXE	DOS Extension — Visual selector
SLEEP	EXE	DOS Extension — Pause command
STAT	EXE	DOS Extension — Statistical text file information
TEE	EXE	DOS Extension — DOS pipe output controller
TXLAT	EXE	DOS Extension — Character translator
UNDEL	EXE	DOS Extension — Retreive a deleted file
UNIQ	EXE	DOS Extension — Duplicate text line handler
VOLM	EXE	DOS Extension — View or change volume name
WHEREIS	EXE	DOS Extension — File locator

592 TSHELL

v1

TSHELL is a powerful visual shell for the PC which provides an efficient environment for the user to manage DOS. This version is a working demonstration of a larger, more powerful version (2.0). Complete with callable help screens, installation and customization files, and a manual, this could be a solid enhancement for your system.

Usage: DOS manager utility.

System Requirements: DOS 2.0 or greater, 256K, hard disk recommended, monochrome monitor.

How to Start: Read the README.1ST and then TSH.DOC for instructions and documentation

• To run TSHELL, just type TSH and press ENTER.

Suggested Donation: Version 2.0 available for $37.50

File Descriptions:

TSH	HLP	This file contains help screens
TSH	DOC	Documentation manual
SETUP	TSH	The customizing routine for Tshell
README	1ST	Contains comments on installation and operation of Tshell
INSTALL	BAT	Batch file to install Tshell on a designated disk
TSH	EXE	The main Tshell program file.
USQ	EXE	Expands (unsqueezes) compressed Tshell files

598 Master Key V1.6c

V1

Master Key is an incredibly powerful and easy to use disk and file manipulation utility. It is comparable with, if not better than, some commercial programs like the Norton Utilities. With this program, the user can edit any part of any disk or file using a handy windowed hex and ASCII dump of the file on the screen. Editing can be from the ASCII text, or from the hex dump. Menus and excellent organization allow the user to quickly learn the package. Many other utilties are included, such as a duplicate file search, file renaming and erasing abilities, DOS directly updating, and

UNERASING. The program comes with 30+ pages of well written documentation.

Usage: Advanced — Intermediate users.

System Requirements: 128K, 1 disk drive, monochrome monitor.

How to Start: Type MK and press ENTER.

Suggested Donation: MASTERKEY : $20.00

File Descriptions:

————	——	Master Key (v1.6c)
MK	COM	Master Key program, will run from DOS directly
MK	DOC	30+ pages of documentation for Master Key
MASTRKEY	ARC	Backup of disk information

ENCODE/DECODE UTILITIES:

Protecting your data is more than not bending the floppies. You will find it a wise investment of your time to consider the data security devices found in these disks. They range from programs to encode/decode your text files for transmission over phone lines to different levels of encryption/decryption. A number of these programs are comparable in complexity to those used by the National Security Agency.

On a more down to earth scale, people who work in agencies and businesses that deal with confidential files (personnel departments, psychiatric clinics, private hospitals, etc.) can find the use of an encoding device ensures the privacy of your clients. Which, of course, increase your peace of mind, too!

112 Computer Security Package Version 1.53
v1.3

This computer security package is a set of user-supported programs for encrypting data files to prevent unauthorized access or for transmission across phone lines. If you have a need to protect sensitive or private communications, then this disk has a lot to offer you. Please read .DOC files for operating instructions.

Usage: System security aids, Intermediate to Advanced users

System Requirements: 64K, one disk drive and a monochrome display

How to Start: Consult the accompanying documentation files (.DOC and READ.ME) for directions

- To run a program with the suffix .COM, .EXE, or .BAT, such as PC-MENU.EXE, type PC-MENU and press ENTER.

User Comments: "Very easy to use and well written but not good for a beginner." "I am fairly well steeped in code/cipher theory and #112 is the only program that offers a security level that matches the computers' capability." "It is worlds better than any DES implementing program." "GOOD PROGRAM. NSA would have a ruff time breaking this program."

Suggested Donation: $25.00

File Descriptions:

COPYRIGH	T	Copyright notes — disk not for export
READ	ME	Notes from the author
AUTOEXEC	BAT	Auto execute file
PC-CODE1	EXE	Encodes/decodes files
PC-CODE2	EXE	Encodes/decodes text files
PC-HELP	EXE	Type "PC-HELP" for help
PC-MENU	EXE	Execute other programs from this one
PC-TAMP?	EXE	Checks to see if files have been altered or examined (2 files)
PC-ZERO	EXE	Writes "zeros" to file before deleting it
*	153	Program versions to use with BASRUN.EXE
DIALOG??	DOC	Sample dialogues for using programs
FILES	DOC	Documentation
I-8087	DOC	Source of 8087 BASIC compiler versions

PC-CODE?	DOC	Documentation for PC-CODE (2 files)
PC-TAMP1	DOC	Documentation for PC-TAMPx
PC-ZERO	DOC	Documentation for PC-ZERO
*	KEY	Key files (3 files)
PC-STAT2	LOG	Sample files
SAMPLE?	COD	Sample files (3 files)
SAMPLE	MSG	Sample message

230 The Confidant Version 2.0

v1

The Confidant is a user-supported program which encodes sensitive data in order to keep it confidential. The Confidant protects information transmitted by communications lines from alteration as well as from unauthorized use by anyone intercepting it or trying to change it. The Confidant gives a choice of two encryption procedures. The national Data Encryption Standard (DES) provides very high security. A faster "privacy" procedure that is somewhat less secure provides encryption for normal use, where speed is important.

Usage: Data protection

System Requirements: 128k, 2 disk drives, monochrome monitor

How to Start: Consult the voluminous documentation in the four files marked .DOC. Initiate the program by typing CONFIDE at the DOS prompt.

User Comments: "Using for patient records and it has worked great as well as allowing me to carry records home witho ut worrying about compromising these people!" "New disk, easy to use and well documentated. This is a very useful addition to any PC user who wants to have a the privacy necessary to write or use files you know won't be read by anyone who uses your system and files." "FANTASTIC! The documentation is very well written and the program performs quite well." "In my opinion, one of the best PC-SIG Disks offered."

Suggested Donation: $10.00

File Descriptions:

CONFIDE	EXE	Main program
CONFIDE	HLP	Help file
CONFIDE	CRY	Part of CONFIDE
CONFIDE	INV	Part of CONFIDE
REFCARD	DOC	A brief summary of the main commands
TUTORIAL	DOC	A step-by-step tutorial (69K)
DESCRIPT	DOC	An overall description of the program (24K)
REFER	DOC	A technical reference manual (60K)
TYPE	ME	How to list documentation

482 ENCODE/ DECODE

v1

The computer programs 'ENCODE' and 'DECODE' allow spreadsheets, programs, source code, word processor documents, data files (any file at all) to be sent via electronic mail between MS-DOS computers with perfect integrity. ENCODE/DECODE presents the user with a more efficient and less expensive way to send information via electronic mail. This progam's value is seen in that without it word processing files will regularly lose their formatting when sent via electronic mail.

Usage: Information security, Intermediate users.

System Requirements: 64K, one disk drive and a monochrome display

How to Start: Most programs are accompanied by a documentation/instructions file with the suffix .DOC (for DOCument), or .TXT (for TeXT) files.

● To run a program with the suffix .COM, .EXE, or .BAT, just type its name, i.e., for DECIPHER.COM, type DECIPHER and press ENTER.

File Descriptions:

DECIPHER	COM	Executable file for deciphering enciphered files
DECIPHER	PAS	Turbo pascal source code
DECODE	COM	Executable file for decoding encoded files
DECODE	PAS	Turbo pascal sorce code
DECRYPT	COM	Executable file for decrypting encrypted files
DECRYPT	PAS	Turbo pascal source code
ENCIPHER	65	File for enciphering files for electronic mail, short output
ENCIPER	COM	Executable file for enciphering files for electronic mail
ENCIPHER	PAS	Turbo pascal source code
ENCODE	65	File for encoding files for electronic mail, short output

ENCODE	COM	Executable file for encoding files for electronic mail
ENCODE	DOC	Documented file for encoding (28k)
ENCODE	PAS	Turbo pascal source code
ENCODE	TXT	Complete documentation and instructions for executing program
ENCRYPT	65	File for secure file encryption, short output
ENCRYPT	COM	Executable file for secure file encryption
ENCRYPT	PAS	Turbo pascal source code
MAKEKEY	COM	Executable file for preparing encryption keys
MAKEKEY	PAS	Turbo pascal source code
NORMAL	STY	Microsoft word style sheet for ENCODE.TXT
README	DOC	Documented list of files on the disk (2k)
REBOOT	ASM	Information on rebooting the system
REBOOT	COM	Executable file for rebooting the system

490
Micro-computer Data Security — by Dan Cronin
V1

This disk is a compilation of very useful utilities for data security as well as saftey when using DOS. It was compiled by Dan Cronin who refers to them in his book "Microcomputer Data Security: Issues and Strategies". Each of the files here listed has its own documentation file!!

Usage: System security tools, Intermediate-advanced users.

System Requirements: 64K RAM, one disk drive and monochrome display

How to Start: Consult the accompanying documentation files for directions

- To run a program with the suffix .COM, .EXE, or .BAT, just type its name, i.e., for BLANK.COM, type BLANK and press ENTER.

User Comments: "MC: GREAT IF NEEDED!" "(VDEL) Great improvement over DEL DOS command." "(UTILITIES) Would recommend certain programs based on asker's needs." "SYSTAT does not function properly with DOS 3.1. However, these utilities are a very useful extension of DOS for manipulating files."

File Descriptions:

ALTER	COM	Hide a file or subdirectory
ASK	COM	Allows interactive input to a batch file
BLANK	COM	Turns off the computer screen in 5 minutes
BROWSE	COM	Allows two-way scrolling of text files
CLEAN2	COM	Disk Drive head cleaning utility
DJCRONIN	DOC	A note from the autor of the book by this disk's name
GCOPY	EXE	Selective file copy utility
MOVE	COM	Hybrid of the Copy and Delete commands
NDOSEDIT	COM	DOS command editor
PC-ZERO	EXE	Security for zeroing out files before deleting the file
SDIR	COM	Sorted directory
SYSTAT	COM	Enhanced version of DOS check disk (CHKDSK)
VDEL	COM	Selective delete utility
VOLSER	COM	Alter or create volume lables on a disk
WHEREIS	COM	Find a file in any subdirectory, on floppy or hard disk
????????	DOC	Documentation files for programs by the same name

491
CRYPTANALYSIS HELPER
v1

This program is designed to aid in the decoding of simple substitution aristocrat ciphers; it suggests translations based on a comparison of letter frequencies, with the frequency of the first letters of words, all letters, last letters and one letter words in your secret message. It matches words with some letters decoded in its dictionaries which are written in 'C'.

Usage: Code translation, Intermediate to Advanced users.

System Requirements: 64K RAM, one disk drive and a monchrome display

How to Start: Read CRYPTAID.DOC thoroughly before using this program

- To run, enter CRYPTAID and press ENTER.

Suggested Donation: $10.00

File Descriptions:

CRYPTAID	EXE	Main program in Microsoft's "C" Ver 3.00
CRYPTAID	DOC	Documentation-4 pages
??	DCT	Dictionary of ?? letter words
ADDTODCT	EXE	Adds words to dictionaries

AUTOADD	EXE	Adds words to dictionaries
SORTDCT	EXE	Sorts a dictionary
SORTALL	BAT	Sorts all the dictionaries
SAMPLE	CIP	Sample message that needs decoding

569
PC-CODE3 and PC-CODE4

v1

PC-CODE3 is a simplified version of PC-CODE2 (V1.53); it is a code analysis program. PC-CODE4 is a simplified version of PC-CODE1 (V1.53) and likewise is intended for encoding files as opposed to text.

PC-STAT3 is a simple statistical program by which the user may do simple analysis of either a Plain Text FILE or a Coded FILE. Basically, it does frequency counts that were embedded features of PC-CODE1 and 2.

PC-CODE3 and PC-CODE4 are Portable Versions Specifically for Generic MS-DOS and Xenix 5. They are written in a strictly portable Microsoft FORTRAN-77 V3.30. The Object code on these diskette(s) is compatiable with both MS-DOS and Microsoft Xenix; meaning these program need NO recompiling they only needed to LINKED to the respective libraries.

Usage: File coding programs, Intermediate to Advanced users.

System Requirements: 64K RAM, two disk drives and a monochrome display; MS-DOS or Xenix 5 are operating system options.

How to Start: After loading DOS, enter PC-CODE.DOC for a review of the documentation. Note that you must run INSTALL3 before you can run either PC-CODE3 or 4.

Suggested Donation: $10.00

File Descriptions:

COPYRIGH	.T	© Copyright Notice
PC-CODE	DOC	Documentation and Notes on PC-CODE3 & PC-CODE4
PC-CODE3	EXE	Combination 8086(88) and 8087 version (works on both)
PC-CODE4	EXE	Cluster Oriented Block Semi-binary version PC-CODE3

INSTALL3	EXE	A program configurator that sets options/defaults
PC-STAT3	EXE	A Analysis program to check codes/texts
CONFIG	PC3	The Configuration file used by PC-CODE3 & INSTALL3
PC-STAT3	FOR	FORTRAN77 Source Code for PC-STAT.EXE
PC-CODE4	FOR	FORTRAN77 Source Code for PC-CODE4.EXE (8088/8087)
PC-CODE3	FOR	FORTRAN77 Source Code for PC-CODE3.EXE (8088/8087)
INSTALL3	FOR	FORTRAN77 Source Code for Installer program
PC-CODE4	OBJ	Object code for BOTH MS-DOS (PC-DOS) and XENIX V
PC-CODE3	OBJ	Object code for BOTH MS-DOS (PC-DOS) and XENIX V
INSTALL3	OBJ	Object code for BOTH MS-DOS (PC-DOS) and XENIX V
PC-STAT3	OBJ	Object code for BOTH MS-DOS (PC-DOS) and XENIX V
SECRET3	MSG	Test file for Encoding using PC-CODE3
SECRET3	COD	Test code from encoding "SECRET.MSG" using PC-CODE3
SECRET3	KEY	Test key file for encoding "SECRET.MSG" for PC-CODE3
SECRET3	TXT	Result of decoding SECRET.COD using PC-CODE3
SECRET4	MSG	Test file for Encoding using PC-CODE4
SECRET4	COD	Test code from encoding "SECRET.MSG" using PC-CODE4
SECRET4	KEY	Test key file for encoding "SECRET.MSG" for PC-CODE4
SECRET4	TXT	Result of decoding SECRET.COD using PC-CODE4
CRC	COM	Does Check Bit sums to verify NO alterations of files
CRC	TXT	This is the Check Bit Sums for the Entire Disk
EXAMPLE	DOC	This Execution Log or printout of sample run

GENERAL SYSTEM UTILITIES:

System enhancement is the goal of the General System Utilities. Be it squeezing or unsqueezing disks or files, diskette cleaning or special file management tools, the target here is your most efficient use of your computer environment. Whether you see your computer as an impersonal "general system" or your customized, down-home working environment, we believe that your computer needs to work for you, not you have to work for it.

There are many general collections here, some aimed at a specified task like file management or a collection of text processing tools, all these utilities revolve around getting your housekeeping chores firmly in hand. And keeping them that way!

52   DOS Utilities No 1
v1

An updated version of the FREE1 RAM-disk package for electronic disk fans. Use this collection of file handling utilities to insert carriage returns, strip high-order characters from a text file, and to hide a file from prying eyes. Also included is a text-search routine, and a binary to hex converter.

Usage: System enhancement.

System Requirements: 256K, some programs run under DOS 1.x ONLY!

How to Start: To run a COM or EXE program type its name and press ENTER. For instructions on running BASIC programs, please refer to the GETTING STARTED section in this catalog. To read DOC files enter TYPE filename.ext and press ENTER.

User Comments: "..I have had an easy time picking them up"

Suggested Donation: FREE4 $15.00; FREE5 $10.00

File Descriptions:

BEEP	COM	Generates beep sound — useful for match files
CRETURN	BAS	Adds carriage returns to downloaded files
DISRTN	EXE	File directory utility
DSKPGM2	BAS	Creates batch file for copying files
FILTER	BAS	Removes control and non-ASCII characters from disk files
FIXDEL	EXE	Disk file utility
FIXIT	BAS	Creates PRINTFIX.COM
FREE4	COM	160K electronic disk drive — update to FREE1
FREE4	DOC	Documentation for FREE4.COM
FREE5	COM	New reset program — update to FREE3
FREE5	DOC	Documentation for FREE5.COM
HEX	BAS	Convert binary files to and from hex format for downloading
HIDEFILE	BAS	Modifies a file's directory status
PARTCOPY	EXE	Copies files from double-sided disk to 2 single-sided disks
PATCH256	ASC	Patches various printers into PR256
POKEPEEK	DOC	Memory locations in ROM BIOS accessable from BASIC
PR256	ASM	Printer patch
SHIFTBS	COM	Converts backslash key into left shift key
SHIFTIBM	COM	Converts backslash key back to IBM standard configuration
TUNE	COM	Plays tune
UTSCAN	BAS	Scans text files for specified string and prints

56
Keyboard Utilities No 1
v2

This assortment of BASIC language programs gives you animation, word processing, a filing system, and more. This disk has good stuff for those interested in exploring the capabilities of the BASIC language. The keyboard programs serve to give the user an on-screen status display of the CAPS LOCK and NUM LOCK keys, and are meant for use with BASIC and the Volkswriter word processing program.

Usage: BASIC tools and entertainment.

System Requirements: 64K, one disk drive and monochrome display.

How to Start: To run an EXE program type its name and press ENTER. To read DOC files, enter TYPE filename.ext and press ENTER.

File Descriptions:

BASIC-KB	ASM	Assembly language source for BASIC-KB.EXE
BASIC-KB	EXE	Executable program file
BASIC-KB	DOC	Documentation for BASIC-KB.BAS
DISTAR	BAS	IPCO Computes stellar parameters
DECIDE	BAS	IPCO Decision maker
XMASCARD	BAS+	IPCO Animated Christmas card
KEYBOARD	ASM	Assembly language source for KEYBOARD.EXE
KEYBOARD	EXE	Executable program file
KEYBOARD	DOC	Documentation for KEYBOARD.BAS
MINI-WP	BAS	Mini word processor
SPEECH	BAS	IPCO Produces test of speech
ADDR-PH	BAS	IPCO Filing system for names, addresses and telephone numbers
PROVERB1	BAS	IPCO Prints proverbs

66
GINACO Programs
v2

This is a very popular disk full of useful utilities and games. Included are two word processors, printer control program, label and notepad routines, and many other handy tools. All programs may be accessed by running the main menu program.

Usage: Beginner/Intermediate system enhancement.

System Requirements: 64K, one disk drive and monochrome display; files marked with "+" require color/graphics.

How to Start: For instructions on running BASIC programs, please refer to the GETTING STARTED section in this catalog. To read DOC files enter TYPE filename.ext and press ENTER.

User Comments: "Some stuff I use almost daily, others never used. Overall easily worth the cost." "The menu program is nice, but now the utilities seem a bit outdated.."

File Descriptions:

BLUEMENU	BAS.	
ALPHAHEX	BAS	Alpha to hex reference display
BLUEBERY	BAS	Label creator, filer, record system — simular to LABELPRO.BAS
BLUEBERY	DOC	Documentation for BLUEBERY.BAS
BLUEBRY2	DOC	Documentation for BLUEBRY2.BAS
BLUEMENU	BAS	Menu for running programs on this disk
BOXINBOX	BAS	Displays border boxes on CRT — can be used as subroutine
BOXINPUT	BAS	Disables all input keys except those needed by your program
BUSCHECK	BAS	Checking or cash account reconciliation aid
CALULATE	BAS	Simple calculator
CHEKFORM	BAS	Check ledger & statement reconciliation form sheet
CHR$PRNT	BAS	Prints you printers character set
CIRCLE	GRA+	Hypnotic circle
COLORSEE	CLR+	Displays full-color range
COMPOUND	BAS	Annual compounded value of a sum at end of each year
D&CFORM	BAS	Debit/credit worksheet
EASYRITE	BAS	Word processor
EASYWORD	BAS	Simple text editor with no file storage
EPSONSET	BAS	Epson printer control and tester
ESCKEY	BAS	Converts ESC key to Continue key
FILEDATE	BAS	Date and time stamp on PC files
GASFORM	BAS	Mileage and trip log form
HEADCLN	BAS	Diskette drive head cleaning utility
HEXPRINT	BAS	Hex/decimal display printout

HEXSAY	BAS	Converts hex to decimal
IBMLABEL	BAS	Label print routine
KEYSET	BAS	BASIC function key settings
LABLFILE	BAS	Label creator, notebook, record keeper, file system
LISTSKIP	10P	10 pitch program listing
LISTSKIP	17P	17.5 pitch program listing
LPT12SET	BAS	Toggles between LPT1 and LPT2 if you have 2 printers
MENUPRNT	BAS+	Graphics print routine
NECLABEL	BAS	NEC 8023A label printer
NICELIST	BAS	Print an ASCII file with page skip and header
PC-COLOR	BAS+	Color monitor test
PCADD	GRA+	Graphics print routine
PEEKPRNT	BAS	Alpha to hex reference display
PRNTCALL	BAS	Subroutine for printer control
PROGHEAD	BAS	BASIC program heading
QUICKBOX	CLR	Part of showbox
RANDSEED	BAS	Random number generator
SAMPLE	TWD	Data for TESTWRIT.BAS
SAVINGS	BAS	Display & print savings or checking account information
SHOWBOX	BAS	BASIC subroutine — border
SIXBOXES	BAS	Program example — 6 nested boxes
STARTUP	BAS	Example of menu display
STARTUP	CLR	Example of menu display
TASKLIST	BAS	Daily phone call and to-do list
TESTWRIT	DOC	Documentation for TESTWRIT.BAS
TIMESHOW	BAS	Display, retains elapsed time
WEIGHTFM	BAS	Daily health record form
WORKFILE	BAS	General ledger — daily journal entry form
WORKFILE	DAT	Part of WORKFILE
YESORNO	BAS	Yes/no response subroutine
YOURMENU	BAS	Menu subroutine
ZIPCLEAR	BAS	Clears designated screen area

How to Start: For instructions on running BASIC programs, please refer to the GETTING STARTED section in this catalog. To read DOC files enter TYPE filename.ext and press ENTER.

User Comments: "(UNPROT is)..a good program"

File Descriptions:

GROWTH	BAS	Growth rate projections
PRINTER	BAS	Epson printer routine
UN	P	File used to unprotect a BASIC program
UNPROT	DOC	Description of how to unprotect a BASIC program
REGRESS	BAS	IPCO game — linear regression
NONLIN	BAS	Performs non-linear least squares fit
FUNC2	BAS	Part of NONLIN — Gausian function
FUNC1	BAS	Part of NONLIN — Lorentzian function
DATA		Part of NONLIN — set of test data
BIGCHAR	BAS	Displays big characters on screen
LABELS	BAS	Quick label printer
APPLECOM	BAS	Simple communication program
CLKMOD	BAS	Prints day of week
TM-BREAK	BAS	PC-TALK 2.0 modifications to add true break with ALT-B
TM-DIAL2	BAS	PC-TALK 2.0 modifications to add automatic redial function
TM-LDIR1	BAS	PC-TALK 2.0 modifications to expand directory to 4 pages
TM-TIME1	BAS	PC-TALK 2.0 modifications to leave correct system on program exit
LABELEPS	BAS	Label maker
SCISUBV1	BAS	Simple plotting program
MATHFUNC	BAS	IPCO 20 complex math functions

67
NONLIN
v1

This disk contains a variety of useful BASIC programs that will unprotect a BASIC program saved with the P switch, print labels, and control your printer. NONLIN also includes some interesting math functions. In addition, there is a simple communication program and several PC-TALK modification files.

Usage: BASIC utilities and enhancements.

System Requirements: 64K, one disk drive and monochrome display.

79
DOS Utilities
No 2
v1.1

This disk contains an assortment of utilities, and a game or two, to interest almost anyone. The selection includes the popular game of LIFE in several versions; programs to test your drives, change your keyboard, and control your printer. Other games and utilities should give something for almost anyone.

Usage: Beginner/Intermediate level system tools.

System Requirements: 64K, one disk drive and monochrome display.

How to Start: To run a COM or EXE program type its name and press ENTER. For instructions on ASM listings, refer to your Assembler manual. To read DOC or TXT files, enter TYPE filename.ext and press ENTER.

User Comments: "A little slow, but for the money, who's complaining?" "(RAMDRIVE may)..not work with other cards than Quadram" "..the LIFE game is quite good."

File Descriptions:

AD	COM	Quadram's Alphabetic Directory (Name & Extent in 5 columns.)
ADD-LF	BAS	Adds linefeeds to files that contain only carriage returns
BALL	BAS	Shoot pea into cup — simple text mode game
CONV	BAS	Converts COM/EXE to transmittable BASIC which will rewrite file
DESIGN	BAS+	Nice graphics demo program
DISPLAY	BAS	Program portion of IBM Bulletin UU-12
DISPLAY	TXT	IBM Bulletin UU-12. Faster screen writes
DRIVETST	BAS	Disk Drive Test program
DSKTST	BAS	Disk Drive Test program
KEYLOC	ASM	Source code for KEYLOC.EXE
KEYLOC	DOC	Documentation for KEYLOC.EXE
KEYLOC	EXE	Converts momentary keys (Alt,Ctrl,Shift) to toggle keys
LIFE	ASM	Source code for LIFE.EXE — bugs
LIFE	EXE	Rabbit paced version of John Conway's famous Game of Life
LUNAR	BAS+	Pick a flat spot and try to land, not too hard!
MAIL1	BAS	Mail list program. Keeps sort indexes on four fields
MAIL1	DOC	Documentation for MAIL1.BAS
MEMORY	COM	Sets memory size independent of system board switches
MEMORY	DOC	Documentation for MEMORY.COM
PEEKPOKE	TXT	Information on memory locations and their contents
QD	EXE	QUADRAM 8 sector drive 0 to 320KB
QDXT	EXE	QUADRAM 9 sector drive 0 to 360KB
QM	EXE	QUADRAM 8 sector multidrive 0 to 320KB
QMXT	EXE	QUADRAM 9 sector multidrive 0 to 360KB
QSPOOL	COM	QUADRAM print spooler
QSWAP	COM	QUADRAM printer swap, LPT1:/LPT2:
QUADRAM	DOC	Documentation for QUADRAM programs
ROD	BAS+	Draws every varying mosaic pattern
SETPRTR	C	Source for SETPRTR.EXE
SETPRTR	EXE	Setup MX-80 printer from Menu Screen
LIFE2	BAS	Another version of Life, runs on color monitors
LIFE2	EXE	Compiled super fast version of LIFE2

84 DOS Utilities No 4

v1

DOS Utilities No 4 is a selection of file tools which let you change a file's attribute byte, control BASIC program functions with a command shell, or give you a menu-driven BASIC file-deletion tool. Another program of interest is DRAWIT, a BASIC screen drawing utility, which lets you design graphic screen displays.

Usage: Text handlers and file tools.

System Requirements: 64K, one disk drive and monochrome display.

How to Start: To run a COM or EXE program type its name and press ENTER. For instructions on ASM or 'C' listings, refer to your Assembler or 'C' language manuals. For instructions on running BASIC programs, please refer to the GETTING STARTED section in this catalog. To read DOC files enter TYPE filename.ext and press ENTER.

User Comments: "(I) couldn't get (DRAWIT) to print to printer" "(QPRINT)..works well on IBM and close compatibles...does not work well on Tandy 1000"

File Descriptions:

CHMOD	C	Source for CHMOD.EXE, written in C86
CHMOD	EXE	Changes file attribute byte
DOWDIF	BAT	Batch file to print DOWDIF.DOC file
DOWDIF	COM	Converts Dow Jones date to DIF format for VISICALC & 123
DOWDIF	DOC	Documentation file for DOWDIF.COM
DOWTRY	TXT	Sample data for DOWDIF.COM
DRAWIT	BAS+	Graphics draw utility — relatively simple, but very good
FILECMD	BAS	Loads, runs, renames or deletes .BAS files (DOS 1.1 version)
FILECMD2	BAS	Loads, runs, renames or deletes .BAS files (DOS 2.0 version)
FPR	C	File print routine written in C86. Personalize and compile
KILL	BAS+	Deletes multiple files selected from a menu (Color required)
QPRINT	ASM	Source for QPRINT.BIN from Byte, July 83, page 408
QPRINT	BAS	Demo of QPRINT vs PRINT
QPRINT	BIN	BLOADable BASIC CALL for fast screen writes, color or mono
TXTPRO	DOC	Documentation for TXTPRO.EXE

| TXTPRO | EXE | Filter utility for ASCII files (Requires BASRUN.LIB) |
| UPVC | DOC | How to unprotect VISICALC |

93
PC-SIG Sampler No 5

1

An interesting assortment of utilities here, PC-SIG Sampler No 5 includes programs to give help for learning MORSE code, expand tabs into spaces in text files, and analyze a loan. And for relaxation, games abound! You can battle with tanks, play with flashcards, or even create the world. Lots of fun!

Usage: Games and text handling tools.

System Requirements: 64K, one disk drive and monochrome display

How to Start: For instructions on running BASIC programs, please refer to the GETTING STARTED section in this catalog. To read DOC files enter TYPE filename.ext and press ENTER.

User Comments: "(DETAB)Program is good, if somewhat awkward to use." "MORSCOD..fine for elementary practice."

File Descriptions:

DETAB	DOC	Documentation file for DETAB.EXE
DETAB	EXE	Expands tabs in text file to correct number of spaces
FLASHCRD		Data file for FLASHCRD.BAS
FLASHCRD	BAS	IPCO — Allows the creation and drill of flashcards
FLASHCRD	LST	Sample flashcard data file
FLIPPER	BAS	IPCO puzzle game — flip the tokens
LOANANAL	BAS	Loan analysis
MORSECOD	BAS	Morse code program
TANK	BAS	IPCO Game — tank fighting for 2 players
VW128FIX	BAT	Modifies Volkswriter to bypass title page
VW128FIX	INS	Instruction for using VW128FIX.BAT
WORLDMAP	BAS+	IPCO world map drawing game

115
DOS Utilities No 6

v1

The programs on this disk include a very handy file-compression utility, another to suppress the color signal when using a mono monitor, a very interesting wave-form drawing utility (requires an 8087 chip), and other useful programs.

Usage: System enhancement.

System Requirements: 128K, 1 disk drive, some programs require color graphics.

How to Start: To run a COM or EXE program type its name and press ENTER. For instructions on running BASIC programs, please refer to the GETTING STARTED section in this catalog. To read DOC files enter TYPE filename.ext and press ENTER.

User Comments: "NOCOLOR worked for one program but not for another. When it works it is indispensible." "This has some good utilities, however I have not had a chance to use them all."

File Descriptions:

FREE	DOC	Catalog of user-supported software
SURF87	EXE	Produces wave forms on graphics printer (Requires 8087)
SURFPR	BAS	Printer installation program for SURF87.EXE
SURF87	DOC	Documentation file for SURF87.EXE
SQUEEZE	EXE	File compression program
USQUEEZ	EXE	Uncompress program
SQUSQ	DOC	Documentation file for SQUEEZ.EXE and UNSQUZ.EXE
DSKHND	BAS	Disk handler program from October Softalk
DHDEMO	BAS	Demo program for DSKHND.BAS
123KEY	PRO	PROKEY file to enable numeric keypad with LOTUS 123
123KEY	BAT	Batch file to run LOTUS 123 with PROKEY
123KEY	DOC	Documentation file for 123KEY.PRO
NOCOLOR	ASM	Suppress color signal when using mono monitor on C/G adapter
NOCOLOR	COM	Executable program file
NOCOLOR	DOC	Documentation file for NOCOLOR.COM
SCROLL	BAS	Scroll window program from PC Magazine, October, 1983, page 650
PINUP?	PIC	Pinup picture; COPY to LPT1: (4 files)

181
Keyboard Utilities No 2
v1

For those who think that their keyboard could be made better, here is the collection for you. Programs on this disk allow you to redefine function keys, or even your whole keyboard. You can also increase the size of your keyboard buffer to eliminate the dreaded type-ahead syndrome.

Usage: Keyboard enhancement tools.

System Requirements: 64K, one disk drive and monochrome display.

How to Start: Type NEWKEY and press ENTER to start. To read DOC files enter TYPE filename.ext and press ENTER. For instructions on running BASIC programs, please refer to the GETTING STARTED section in this catalog.

User Comments: "(NEWKEY)..Keyboard macros ONLY; does not offer file ecryption, etc. like PROKEY, SUPERKEY. Very easy to use."

Suggested Donation: NEWKEY $30.00

File Descriptions:

DOSKEY1	DOC	Documentation
DOSKEYS	BAS	Redefines function keys (C. Haapala)
DOSKEYS	DOC	Documentation continued
KBBUFF	BAS	Keyboard buffer — extends buffer by 160 characters
KBBUFF	DOC	Documentation (3K)
— — — —	— —	NEWKEY
NEWKEY	EXE	NEWKEY Version 1.1 — key customization package by Frank Bell
NEWKEY1	EXE	NEWKEY — additional functions
PRINTDOC	EXE	Prints NEWKEY documentation
NEWKEY	DOC	Documentation (42K)
TEST	KEY	Part of NEWKEY.EXE — Demos of features
WS	KEY	Part of NEWKEY.EXE — WordStar
LOADNEW	BAT	Part of NEWKEY.EXE — loads NEWKEY and WordStar key definitions
ASM	KEY	Part of NEWKEY.EXE — Sample for assembler
DVORAK	KEY	Part of NEWKEY.EXE — Dvorak keyboard

196
DOS Utilities No 11
v1

These programs let you speed your file-handling chores greatly. You can copy or delete multiple files at a time, compare directory listings to find duplicates, and move or rename files easily. Also, we have included an interesting program to allow the user to prepare and show computer generated 'slides' on your color graphics monitor.

Usage: System enhancement.

System Requirements: DOS 2.0 or greater, 80-column display.

How to Start: To read DOC files enter TYPE filename.ext and press ENTER.

- To run a COM or EXE program type its name and press ENTER. For instructions on ASM listings, refer to your Assembler manual.

File Descriptions:

DIRCOMP	COM	Compares two directories and lists files found in both
EQUIP102	COM	Displays system equipment configuration
EQUIP102	DOC	Documentation for above
MV	EXE	Sophisticated file move/rename utility
MV	DOC	Documentation for above
SLIDE	COM	Prepare slides on graphics display
SLIDE	ASM	Source for above
SHOW	EXE	Show prepared slides on graphics display
SHOW	ASM	Source for above
UTIL102	COM	Copy/delete multiple files
UTIL102	DOC	Documentation for above

255

DOS Utilities
No 14

v1

This entry in our DOS utility series includes a comprehensive collection of tools for handling files, configuring some system options (NEWBELL, and SCRNCOLR), cleaning up directories (OLDER and PURGEDUP), and finding lost files (WHEREIS). Some very nice BASIC routines are included. For instance, SCREEN is an input-verify routine and DOCUFILE helps you generate custom help screens.

Usage: Intermediate to Advanced system enhancement.

System Requirements: 128K, 1 disk drive and monochrome monitor.

How to Start: To run a COM program type its name and press ENTER. For instructions on ASM or 'C' listings, refer to your Assembler or 'C' language manuals. For instructions on running BASIC programs, please refer to the GETTING STARTED section in this catalog. To read DOC files enter TYPE filename.ext and press ENTER.

User Comments: "(DOSEDIT)..Put this in your AUTOEXEC.BAT file if you work in DOS at all." "(WHEREIS)..Essential for forgetful hard disk users."

Suggested Donation: DOCUFILE $10.00

File Descriptions:

NEWBELL	COM	Run once to shorten DOS (not BASIC) bell tone
NEWBELL	ASM	Source for NEWBELL.COM
HERMREAD	ME	Notes on BATQUES, SCRNCOLR, Compaq video, and FORMAT
BATQUES	COM	Prompts for character returned as error level
BATQUES	DOC	Documents BATQUES.COM (2K)
BATQUES	ASM	Source for BATQUES.COM
SCRNCOLR	COM	Intercepts screen writes to change colors
SCRNCOLR	DOC	Documents SCRNCOLR.COM (2K)
SCRNCOLR	ASM	Source for SCRNCOLR.COM
DOS-SIZE	DOC	Reference table, size of various DOS versions
WHEREIS	COM	Searches subdirectories for filename
WHEREIS	ASM	Source for WHEREIS.COM
OLDER	COM	Returns information on relative age of two files
OLDER	ASM	Source for OLDER.COM
LABEL	EXE	Change/Create Volume Labels — command line input
LABEL	C	Source for LABEL.EXE

LABEL	DOC	Documentation for LABEL.EXE
SCREEN	BAS	Utility for data input and verification
SCREEN	DOC	Documentation for SCREEN.BAS (3.6K)
TIMER	EXE	Provides continuous time of day clock on screen
MORSE	BAS	Morse code practice program
PURGEDUP	COM	Compares DIRs & erases = fnams with <= date/time
PURGEDUP	DOC	Documentation for PURGEDUP.COM
DOSEDIT	COM	Provides re-executable history file of DOS commands
DOSEDIT	DOC	Documentation for DOSEDIT.COM (3.2K)
DOCUFILE	BAS	Generates BASIC program Help screens from text file
DOCUFILE	DOC	Documentation for DOCUFILE.BAS (3.6K)
DOCUFDOC	BAS	Sample made using DOCUFILE.BAS and DOCUFILE.DOC
BYE	BAS	Protects screen, provides date & time on idle system
SDIR	COM	Sorted Directory with numerous options — best to date
SDIR	DOC	Documentation for SDIR.COM
LIST	COM	ASCII file lister, viable alternative to TYPE/MORE
LIST	DOC	Documentation for LIST.COM (2.1K)
CRYPTO	BAS	Aids in solving cryptograms
PX	COM	Procedure Cross Referencer for ASM and MASM
PX	DOC	Documentation for PX.COM (14K)
SPEED	COM	Modifies disk parameter table
SPEED	ASM	Source for SPEED.COM, easily modified to your taste
CHN	PAS	Provides command line execution of Turbo .CHN files
L4	COM	Displays file w/ up/down paging, horz scroll, find
L4	DOC	Documentation for L4.COM (4K)
L4	ASM	Source for L4.COM
KBFIX	COM	CAPS, NUM & SCROLL flags plus a 127 byte kybd buffer
KBFIX	ASM	Source for KBFIX.COM
KBFIX	DOC	Documentation for KBFIX.COM
KBD–FIX	COM	Expands DOS typeahead buffer to 160 characters
KBD–FIX	ASM	Source for KEY–FIX.COM (See Softalk PC, November 83 & January 84
BAT-CD	COM	Changes working directory based on standard input
BAT-CD	DOC	Documents BATCD.COM
BAT-CD	ASM	Source for BATCD.COM

256

DOS and
Programmer Utilities

v1

A fine collection of handy tools for almost anyone is on this disk. The special emphasis is on file handling and management. With some, you can find free space on a floppy disk, find files lost in your subdirectories, de-fragment floppies, etc. A particularly handy tool traps the infamous "parity error" and thereby saves your work from being destroyed. For those of you who need a high-precision mathematics tool, there's BIGCALC, with 100-place or better precision.

Usage: System enhancement tools.

System Requirements: 64K, one disk drive and monochrome display.

How to Start: To run a COM or EXE program type its name and press ENTER. For instructions on ASM listings, refer to your Assembler manual. For instructions on running BASIC programs, please refer to the GETTING STARTED section in this catalog. To read DOC files enter TYPE filename.ext and press ENTER.

User Comments: "A very nice collection of useful utilities" "Most of the files were not useful to me; too advanced." "I am using Caps Lock Defeat (Wonderful!), FREE, DEFRAG, and possibly NUSQ."

File Descriptions:

SAVE	COM	Copy current screen to alternate monitor
DISPRE	COM	Displays the 8088 registers after being loaded
DISPRE	EXE	by different programs, ie: DEBUG vs COMMAND.COM
DISPRE	ASM	Source for DISPRE.COM/EXE
DISPRE	DOC	Documentation for DISPRE.COM/EXE
MONOCLOK	COM	Time in UR corner of mono display, graphics unaffected
LABEL	EXE	Diskette label program (Softalk March 84)
LABEL	ASM	Source for LABEL.EXE
FREE	COM	Reports free space on one or all drives
FREE	ASM	Source for FREE.COM
FREE	DOC	Documentation for FREE.COM
WHEREIS	COM	File searcher, upgraded with 23 line pause feature
WHEREIS	ASM	Source for WHEREIS.COM
DEFRAG	BAS	Defragments diskette space
DEFRAG	DOC	Documentation for DEFRAG.BAS

NUSQ	COM	New UnSQueeze program, small, fast, improved
NUSQ	DOC	Documentation on NUSQ.COM
DUMP	EXE	Displays a file in hex and ASCII (From May Softalk)
DUMP	ASM	Source for DUMP.EXE
PARCHK	COM	Replaces std parity routine, errors don't stop machine
PARCHK	ASM	Source for PARCHK.COM
PARCHK	DOC	Documentation for PARCHK.COM
REFCD	DOC	INT 21 reference card, DOS 2.1 version
TABS	EXE	Converts spaces to tabs (Shrinks files)
TABS	ASM	Source for TABS.EXE
TABS	DOC	Documentation for TABS.EXE
LOOK	COM	Memory display program
LOOK	ASM	Source for LOOK.COM
LOOK	DOC	Documentation for LOOK.COM
ZAPDEB	BAS	Patch DEBUG.COM to fix timer interrupt bug
ZAPDEB	DOC	Documentation for ZAPDEB.BAS
ZAPTRE	BAS	Patches TREE.COM to support a filename operand
ZAPTRE	DOC	Documentation for ZAPTRE.BAS
QS	RIO	Quick Startup patch for BIOS
QS	TXT	Documentation for QS.RIO
CLOCK	SYS	Device driver for AST and TECMAR boards with clock
CLOCK	ASM	Source for CLOCK.ASM
CAPSDEF	COM	Defeats the CapsLock key
CAPSDEF	DOC	Documentation for CAPSDEF.COM
CAPSDEF	ASM	Source for CAPSDEF.COM
BIGCALC	BAS	High precision calculator, 100 digits or better.
BIGCALC	EXE	Compiled version of BIGCALC.BAS
BIGCALC	DOC	Documentation for BIGCALC
EXPAND	BAS	Replaces tabs with appropiate number of spaces
EXPAND	DOC	Documentation for EXPAND.BAS
DIRECT	BAS	Creates BLOADable file to directly read disk directory
DIRDEM	BAS	Demonstrates DIRECTORY function created by DIRECT.BAS
WHEREIS	COM	Searches all directories for specified file
WHEREIS	BAS	Generates WHEREIS.COM
DSKTYP	EXE	Reports the format of the selected diskette
DSKTYP	ASM	Source for DSKTYP.EXE
FORMAT	VOL	Patch to DOS 2.0 FORMAT to always request VOL label
COLOR	PE	Passionate shades for the Personal Editor
PE-NOTAB	DOC	Fixes Personal Editor to save without those #@%& TABS
DCBA2	HOW	Modify DISKCOPY.COM (Version 2.10) for production copying

273
Best Utilities
V1.1

The programs on this disk comprise a collection of some of our most popular utilities — our "Greatest Hits" gathered from other disks in our library. Some of the high points include a couple of screen/type handlers, to let you pick the one you like best; a couple of selective copy and delete utilities allow you to perform mass file functions with ease and confidence; and SDIR24C, a multi-talented performer whih is much more than just a "directory display". Enjoy these and others on this disk!

Usage: Beginner-Advanced system enhancement tools.

System Requirements: 64K, one disk drive and monochrome display.

How to Start: To run a COM or EXE program type its name and press ENTER. To read DOC files enter TYPE filename.ext and press ENTER.

User Comments: "Lots of good stuff here. I had collected most of this from other sources but still found it worth the money just for NDOSEDIT." "BACKSCRL..This program is excellent on an IBM PC. It does NOT run on an IBM AT which is a shame." "BROWSE..200% Better than "Type". Easy to use. Just wish memory resident." "(SDIR24C)!! Why couldn't Microsoft have written their DIR to be this good?"

Suggested Donation: BACKSCRL $20.00; SP $15.00

File Descriptions:

MEMBRAIN	EXE	Flexible RAMdisk
MEMBRAIN	DOC	Documentation for MEMBRAIN.EXE
L4	EXE	Full screen list program with 4 way scroll and search
L4	DOC	Documentation for L4.EXE
L4	ASM	Source code for L4.EXE
SP	EXE	Super spooler program — variable size
SP	DOC	Documentation for SP.EXE
BACKSCRL	COM	Retrieve what has scrolled off top of screen — very useful
BACKSCRL	DOC	Documentation for BACKSCRL.COM
VDEL	COM	Selective delete utility — prompts to delete each file
WHEREIS	COM	Find a file in any subdirectory
WHEREIS	DOC	Documentation for WHEREIS.COM

GCOPY	EXE	Selective copy — changes date to current
GCOPY	DOC	Documentation for GCOPY.EXE
GDEL	EXE	Selective delete utility
GDEL	DOC	Documentation for GDEL.EXE
SDIR24C	COM	Flexible screen directory display — many options
SDIR24C	DOC	Documentation for SDIR24C.COM
ST	COM	Super type command — 2 way scrolling
ST	DOC	Documentation for ST.COM
MOVE	COM	Flexible copy, copy and erase utility with prompts
MOVE	DOC	Documentation for MOVE.COM

283
DOS Utilities No 15
v1

This disk contains a wide variety of different file and system tools. DTK and CWEEP13 are powerful file handlers. DOCUFILE lets you develop callable help screens for your programs, RAM is a nice RAM-disk program, installable as a device driver, (exercise caution when using with other RAM-resident software, and it will serve you well). Other utilities give Epson owners good letter-quality print, generate interrupts on demand, find files, and more.

Usage: Intermediate-Advanced file and system utilities.

System Requirements: 64K, one disk drive and monochrome display.

How to Start: To run an EXE or COM program type its name and press ENTER. To read DOC files enter TYPE filename.ext and press ENTER.

User Comments: "CWEEP..If it just supported pathnames, this would be a 10." "I became very dependent upon this program when I was working in CP/M, and I like it even better in MS-DOS." "DTK..Great little program for making disk labels, renaming a disk, putting on a different volume label, etc. etc. Use it with some frequency."

Suggested Donation: DTK $10.00

File Descriptions:

— — — —	— —	KWSEARCH by Patrick Teti
KWSEARCH	EXE	Copies text using search criteria
KWSEARCH	DOC	Documentation for KWSEARCH (13K)

————	——	3 Utilities by John White
INT	COM	Program interrupt
INT	A	Part of INT
INT	DOC	Documentation for INT
INT-PORT	DOC	Additional Documentation for INT
RAM	SYS	RAM drive installer
RAM	A	Part of RAM
RAM	DOC	Documentation for RAM
SETRAM	EXE	Sets up RAM
FFIND	EXE	Finds files by scanning for specific argument
FFIND	C	Part of FFIND
FFIND	DOC	Documentation for FFIND
MAKEINT	BAT	Batch file to install INT
MAKERAM	BAT	Batch file to install RAM
————	——	Directory Toolkit
DTK	EXE	Sort directory, change attributes, etc.
DTK	DOC	Documentation for DTK (8K)
————	——	Famous Sweep program from CPM
CWEEP13	EXE	File manipulation utility
CWEEP13	DOC	Documentation for CWEEP13 (8K)
————	——	Docufile
AUTOEXEC	BAT	Batch file to diskcopy
KILLER	EXE	Deletes files
CATALOG	EXE	Demonstration of multiple file searcher
DOCUFILE	BAS	Creates BASIC program of text file
README	TXT	Documentation for DOCUFILE
README	BAS	BASIC version of README.TXT
HELP	BAT	DOCUFILE help screen generator
DOCUFILE	BAT	Batch file to bring up DOCUFILE in BASIC
————	——	Letter Quality print routine
LQ	COM	Letter quality print on Epson MX printer
LQ	DOC	Documentation for LQ (9K)

284
PC-SIG Sampler
No 8
v2

This disk is a collection of utilities that, for the most part, are not related to one another, but are very handy things to have in your personal library. The labelmaker program lets you print labels for your disks to help avoid confusion, and is a real timesaver. DJ (as in Disk Jockey) helps you look at specific sectors and tracks. As with other programs of this type, the power carries responsibility. Use caution here, and experiment only on copies, not originals.

Usage: Programmer tools.

System Requirements: 64K, one disk drive and monochrome display.

How to Start: To run an EXE program type its name and press ENTER. For instructions on running BASIC programs, please refer to the GETTING STARTED section in this catalog. To read DOC files enter TYPE filename.ext and press ENTER.

User Comments: "I have looked for a label maker for a long time but this was worth waiting for." "DK..is an outstanding program. I learned more about disk structure in two hours..than in four months prior." "(LOAD-US)..Commercial programs of this type cost big bucks, and are probably no more effective than this one."

Suggested Donation: NUMZAP requests a donation of your choice

File Descriptions:

————	——	Disk labelmaker
DLIB	EXE	Part of Labelmaker
DSTAT	EXE	Part of Labelmaker
LBLUT1	EXE	Part of Labelmaker
LBL	BAT	Part of Labelmaker
LABELPNT	BAS	Part of Labelmaker
INFO	DOC	Documentation info about Labelmaker
LABLREAD	1ST	Startup instructions for Labelmaker
————	——	Disk Jockey
DJ	COM	Allows you to read sectors and tracks on disk
————	——	Separate user-supported programs
LOAD-US	COM	Enables you to use Lotus and Symphony on hard disk
LOAD-US	DOC	Documentation for LOAD-US
NUMZAP	EXE	Removes line numbers from BASIC programs
NUMZAP	DOC	Documentation for NUMZAP
NUMZAP	BAS	BASIC source code for NUMZAP
RENUM	EXE	Renumbers a file that has been through NUMZAP
RENUM	BAS	BASIC source code for RENUM

319
DOS Utilities
No 16
v1.1

This collection has a bit of everything. There are programs to find files lost in a hard disk subdirectory (or in a big pile of floppies) and programs that list BASIC and WordStar files without having to go into either program first. For more major computer maintainance projects there are programs to develop a visual DOS shell and disk catalog programs. This is one disk that every DOS user should have.

Usage: File and DOS handling utilities

System Requirements: 128K, one disk drive and monochrome display

How to Start: To run an EXE or COM program type its name and press ENTER. To read DOC files enter TYPE filename.ext and press ENTER.

User Comments: "Vfiler is an excellent disk manager program. It is particularly good for a hard disk system." "This disk could rival #273 for "Best Utilities". I find that I use (it) extensively.." "

Suggested Donation: SDIR50 $10.00

File Descriptions:

COVER	DOC	Documentation for cover2
COVER2	COM	Prints compressed directory for diskette envelopes
DISKORAY	EXE	Check diskette for rotation speed and seek test
DRVTEST	BAS	Simple disk test
FASTDISK	COM	Part of speedup
FDATE	COM	Change date and time stamp of a disk file
FDATE	DOC	Documentation for FDATE
HIDE	DOC	Documentation for HIDE a Simple security system
HIDE–CD	COM	Access a hidden directory
HIDE–MD	COM	Make a hidden directory
HIDE–RD	COM	Remove a hidden directory
KNEW	DOC	Documentation for KNEW.EXE
KNEW	EXE	Copy *.* but only copies files with more recent date stamp
LABEL	LBR	Part of COVER2
LIST — —	DOC	Documentation for LIST2DAY,LISTPAST,LISTARCH
LIST2DAY	COM	List all files with todays date stamp
LIST52	COM	Scroll up and down through files useing editor keys
LIST52	DOC	Dcumentation for LIST52
LIST52	HLP	Part of LIST52
LISTARCH	COM	List all archive files
LISTPAST	COM	List all files crearted before today
MOVE2	COM	Copies files to new dir verifies new copy then erases old copy
MOVE2	DOC	Documentation for MOVE2
PC-DISK	COM	Catalogs your floppy diskettes
PFM	COM	Visual shell for DOS commands
READBAS5	EXE	List a non-ASCII basic program without loading basic
RENDIR	COM	Rename directories
SCAVEN	COM	Protect blocks from being deallocated by CHKDSK
SCAVEN	DOC	Documentation for SCAVEN
SDIR26	COM	List directories in 4 columns with just file name and size
SDIR50	COM	Visual shell for executing dos programs
SDIR50	DOC	Documentation for SDIR50
SDISK2	COM	Sorts disk directory so dir will always list files in order
SDISK2	DOC	Documentation for SDISK2
SDL	COM	List directories sorted by various means
SDL	DOC	Documentation for SDL
SHOWDIR	COM	List subdirectories in a given directory
SORTF	DOC	Documentation for SORTF
SORTF	EXE	Sorts ASCII data files
SPEEDUP	COM	Make your floppy disk run faster
SPEEDUP	DOC	Documentation on SPEEDUP
ST	COM	List WORD STAR files one screen at a time
ST	DOC	Documentation for ST.COM
TD13	COM	Combines DOS TREE and DIR commands to make a more useful tree
TD13	DOC	Documentation on TD13
TREE2	COM	Tree showing only subdirectory names without file names
UNIQCOPY	BAT	Same as copy *.* but does not copy files that are already on target disk.
UNIQCOPY	DOC	Documentation for uniqcopy
VFILER	DOC	Documentation for VFILER
VFILER	EXE	Visual interface for maintaining files and subdirectories
WHEREII	COM	Finds directory path for all copies of a file on a disk
WHEREII	DOC	Documentation for WHEREII
Z	EXE	Visual shell lets you look at your directories

373 DOS Utilities No 17
v1

This collection is oriented towards general system maintenance with programs for applying self-styled, useful filename extensions and other enhancements to the DOS batch file capabilities. There is also an assortment of general purpose utilities. You can improve the security of your system by preventing 'break-out' of a boot or file operation. The SCR121F package provides full screen design and edit capabilities, and includes interfaces to DOS, dBASE, MS Cobol, and Clipper. And just for fun, the BANNER program lets you design and print large messages.

Usage: Intermediate level system programming tools.

System Requirements: 64K, one disk drive and monochrome display.

How to Start: To run a COM or BAT program type its name and press ENTER. For instructions on running BASIC programs, please refer to the GETTING STARTED section in this catalog. To read DOC files enter TYPE filename.ext and press ENTER.

User Comments: "My batch files are much cleaner because of (QUERY)" "(BATCH)..is for those who already know what batch files are all about"

Suggested Donation: SCR1 $24.00

File Descriptions:

BANNER1	COM	Prints block letters on the display/printer with options.
BANNER1	DOC	Documentation for BANNER1.COM
BANNR1	BAT	Batch file to run BANNER1.COM
BRK	COM	Causes a termination with error code return
CHECKING	COM	Allows conditional termination of batch files
CHECKING	DOC	Documentation for CHECKING.COM
CR	COM	Useful for putting 64K, one disk drive and monochrome display responses in batch files
DSIZE	COM	Determine the format of a diskette from within a batch file
DSIZE	DOC	Documentation for DSIZE.COM
FLIP	COM	Control special key states from the DOS command line
FLIP	DOC	Documentation for FLIP.COM
GETDIGIT	COM	Accepts a prompt from the command line and a one digit
GETDIGIT	DOC	Documentation for GETDIGIT.COM
INP	BAT	Sample batch file
INP-TEST	BAT	Sample batch file
INPUT	COM	Get input from console
NOBRKCOM	BAS	Patches COMMAND.COM to prevent breaking of AUTOEXEC.BAT AltDel keyboard reset sequence AltDel keyboard reset sequence
PAUSE2	COM	Improved version of DOS's PAUSE command
PAUSE2	DOC	Documentation for PAUSE2.COM
PKXARC	EXE	Unarchive utility
PRTSC	COM	Starts/stops the printer during batch file processing
PRTSC	DOC	Documentation for PRTSC.COM
QUERY	ASM	Assembly source code for QUERY.EXE
QUERY	EXE	Batch file 'Y/N' prompt routine
REMDOT	EXE	Displays keyboard buffer strings
SCR21F	ARC	Screen editor and display utilities (Archived format)
SETERROR	COM	Accepts one command line argument and sets the DOS
SETERROR	DOC	Documentation for SETERROR.COM
SIGNAL	COM	Produces a signal and waits for a keystroke
SIZER	ASM	Assembly version of SIZER
SIZER	BAS	BASIC version of SIZER
SIZER	COM	Tests the size of a file and sets an errorlevel based
SIZER	DOC	Documentation for SIZER.COM
TUNE	COM	Used in batch files to produce an audible signal of
TUNE	DOC	Documentation for TUNE.COM
WAIT	COM	Pauses a batch file for 3 seconds to allow interruption
WAIT	DOC	Documentation for WAIT.COM
WAITTIME	COM	Used in batch files to wait for a certain time to pass
WAITTIME	DOC	Documentation for WAITTIME.COM

384
Conden
v1

CONDEN as in "Condense" is the theme here! On board you'll find several handy utilities that save you a lot of the paper or disk space often required by text files by removing excess blank lines, titles, etc. Heading in the other direction is an associated program will let you produce multiple page-across listings using a wide-carriage printer. Some other useful programs allow you to set screen colors from DOS, and generate a cross-reference of your program listings.

Usage: Economizing printer usage.

System Requirements: 64K, one disk drive and monochrome display.

How to Start: To read DOC files enter TYPE filename.ext and press ENTER.

- To run an EXE program type its name and press ENTER.

File Descriptions:

CONDEN	DOC	Documentation for CONDEN.EXE
CONDEN	EXE	Remove blank lines, leading blanks, page titles, etc
DELO2	DOC	Documentation for DELO2.EXE
DELO2A	BAT	BATCH file to read disks
DELO2B	EXE	Checks for duplication
DELO2C	EXE	Slower version of DELO2B.EXE
DELO3	DOC	Documentation for DELO3.EXE
DELO3	EXE	Used to randomly set the color from DOS
THREEPAG	DOC	Documentation for THREEPAG.DOC
THREEPAG	EXE	Used with CONDEN to produce three page wide printer output
XXREF	DOC	Documentation for XXREF.EXE
XXREF	EXE	Used to cross-reference strings in line number programs

420 File Utilities
v1

System Enhancement through specially designed file handling utilities is the target of this collection. As expected, some of the files on this disk are updates of old favorites found elsewhere in the library, while some are redesigned towards new functions new. Many of these can are quite powerful and can be used to inspect individual disk sectors, protect files from overwriting or erasure, encrypt or decrypt text files, and many other important chores. You'll find many new friends and helpers here!

Usage: System enhancement.

System Requirements: 64K, one disk drive and monochrome display.

How to Start: To read DOC or TXT files enter TYPE filename.ext and press ENTER.

● To run an EXE or COM program type its name and press ENTER.

User Comments: "(L6)..I love this utility! Better than sliced bread." "This undelete is fast and works cleanly, even on my Leading Edge clone." "I use (UNDEL) at least once weekly."

Suggested Donation: ARC and TCOUNT both request donations, but do not specify an amount; SORT-IT $15.00; VIEWDISK $15.00

File Descriptions:

BACKSTAT	EXE	List files on your hard disk which are not backed up
GCOPY2	EXE	Copy files selectively
GCOPY2	TXT	Documentation file
L6	COM	Full screen file browse
LC	COM	Count lines in a file
LF	COM	List files by extension — fast
LQTYPE	COM	List squeezed library files
UNDEL	COM	Recover erased files
UNSQ	COM	Unsqueeze files
FILTERS	LBR	A collection of useful DOS filters
FILTERS	TXT	How to prepare FILTERS.LBR for use
VIEWDISK	EXE	Look at individual disk sectors
VIEWDISK	DOC	Documentation file
COPYPC	COM	A better DISKCOPY command
COPYPC	DOC	Documentation file
SORT-IT	COM	File sorter
SORT-IT	DOC	Documentation file
NIB	EXE	Unerase, patch files, create files from memory

LOCK	COM	Encrypt your files
UNLOCK	COM	De-encrypt your files
UN-LOCK	DOC	Documentation file for LOCK and UNLOCK
ARC	EXE	Combine and squeeze files in one pass
ARC	DOC	Documentation file
FCOMPARE	EXE	Good file compare program
FCOMPARE	C	C source code
FCOMPARE	DOC	Documentation file
SEARCH	COM	Search an entire disk for character or string
SEARCH	DOC	Documentation file
READONLY	COM	Make file uneraseable
READONLY	DOC	Documentation file
READWRIT	COM	Make file eraseable
READWRIT	DOC	Documentation file
DISKUNSQ	COM	Unsqueeze files
DISKSQ	COM	Squeeze all files on disk
TREED	COM	Make directory tree
TCOUNT	COM	Count characters, words, lines, pages in document
TCOUNT	DOC	Documentation file

444 Hotkey/xDOS/ EZ-Menu/CALC
v1

While not related, the four separate programs have been brought together because they all help with little needs that show up with great frequency on a personal computer. PC-Calculator is an RPN-type calculator for your computer. HOTKEY lets you easily customize your function keys. EZ-MENU gives you a quick and easy way to run programs, a shortcut around the many commands sometimes necessary. And the X-DOS package is a collection of system enhancements.

Usage: Beginner-Intermediate system enhancement tools.

System Requirements: 64K, one disk drive and monochrome display.

How to Start: To read DOC files enter TYPE filename.ext and press ENTER.

● To run a COM program type its name and press ENTER.

User Comments: "Diskfile is the answer to my mania for neatly labeled disks." "Calc is a Hewlett Packard calculator on a PC. It excels the puny calculator on Sidekick." "(HOTKEY)..makes some common commands easier to use."

Suggested Donation: XDOS $10.00; PC-CALCULATOR $30.00; HOTKEY $15.00

File Descriptions:

————	——	PC-Calculator (v1.0)
CALC	EXE	Main program for pop-up reverse Polish notation calculator
READ	ME	Shows how to start CALC. Just "TYPE READ.ME"
FINDKEY	COM	Gives 4 number code for each key on the keyboard
MANUAL		Documentation (38k)
LETTER		Program release letter
CALC	HE0	Overlay for CALC
BCALC	COM	Allows definition of "pop-up" key
————	——	HOTKEY (v1.01)
HOTKEY	EXE	HotKey is used to redefine the function keys (F1-F10)
HOTKEY	DEF	Sample key definition file
HOTKEY	DOC	Doc for HotKey. Type "COPY HOTKEY.DOC PRN" and hit return (5K)
CONFIG	SYS	Must be on boot disk. ANSI.SYS must also be present
README		Starting introductory note
————	——	xDOS
ALARM	COM	An alarm clock function
CAT	COM	An alternative to DOS's DIR command
HELP	COM	Assistance with DOS commands
LOCK	COM	Provides the ability to lock and hide files
NOPRINT	COM	Re-directs printer output to the screen
ZAP	COM	Two methods for securing sensitive files
XDOS	DOC	Reference manual for the XDOS commands
PRINTMAN	BAT	A batch file to print this manual
README	TXT	A greeting file
————	——	EZ-MENU
EZ-MENU	LST	A mini file that describes the 3 EZ-MENU files
EZ-MENU	TXT	Documentation for ez-menu (4K)
EZ-MENU	BAS	Instant, ez menu to run EXE, BAT, COM and BAS files

---

543
Utilities Ecetera
v1

Not your typical utilities disk by any means! This interesting assortment of programs includes routines to print the time on the screen, several astronomically oriented tasks, polar to rectangular conversions and vice versa, a system to help document files on a disk, another to help hide and protect files, a sample general ledger and another for a simple address book and lots, lots more !

Usage: System enhancement.

System Requirements: 128K 1 disk drive, programs marked (+) require color/graphics.

How to Start: To read DOC files enter TYPE filename.ext and press ENTER.

- To run an EXE or COM program type its name and press ENTER. For instructions on running BASIC programs, please refer to the GETTING STARTED section in this catalog.

Suggested Donation: GLV12 $50.00; SEARCH $15.00

File Descriptions:

ADDRBOOK	BAS	Simple address program
ADDRBOOK	DOC	Addressbook documentation
ARCTRIG	BAS	Inverse trig functions
AUTOMENU	BAT	Batch file to run MENU.BAS
BLATHER	DOC	Documents BLATHER
BLATHER	EXE	Communications program
CDEL	BAT	Batch file to run YN.COM erase files
CLOCK	BAS	Creates CLOCK.COM
CLOCK	COM	Digital clock in DOS upper right screen
COVER	COM	Print diskette directory for jacket
COVER	DOC	Documents COVER
DAYNUM	BAS	Calculates days since Jan 1
DOORS	BAS	Source for DOORS.COM in BASIC
DOORS	COM	Gives a window (new screen) for input
DOORS	DOC	Documentation for DOORS.COM
EASTER	BAS	Finds day of easter sunday
F	EXE	Program to hide/protect/backup files on a disk
FINDFILE	BAT	Find any file current drive
FINDFILE	DOC	Documentation for FINDFILE.BAT
GLV12	DOC	Documents GVL12
GLV12	EXE	General ledger program
HALLEY	BAS	Commet calculations for Halley's
KEPLER	BAS	Kepler's equation for astronomy
LOCSTIME	BAS	Local sidereal time calculation
LOTTO	BAS	Generates winning(?) LOTTO 649 numbers
MENU	BAS	Generates BASIC menu
MENU	DOC	Documentation for MENU.BAS
MOVDIR	EXE	Move directory around
NPAD	BAS	Source in BASIC for NPAD.COM
NPAD	COM	Displays a small window in upper right
NPAD	DOC	Documentation for NPAD.COM
PMOR	BAT	Batch file to run PORE.COM
POLRECT	BAS	Polar to rectangular coordinates
PORE	COM	Modified MORE to allow 55 line listings
PORE	DOC	Documentation for PORE.COM and PMOR.BAT
PRECESS	BAS	Astonomical precession calculation
PRTSCOFF	COM	COMPAQ ONLY — disables Shift-Prtsc key
RANDOM	BAS	Random number generating program
README	GL	Readme for GVL12
RECTPOL	BAS	Rectangular to polar coordinates
SAMPLEGL	GL1	Sample ledger for GVL12
SAMPLEGL	GL2	Sample ledger for GVL12
SEARCH	COM	Set path search

SEARCH	DOC	Documents SEARCH
SF	BAT	Starts SFX with passable parameter
SFX	EXE	Simplifile — document files on a disk
SUNNY	BAS	Sunrise...sunset... calculations
TIMEAL	BAS	Time, altitude and azimuth, julian date
TOUT	BAS	Pick the winners at the track!
WEEKDAYS	BAS	Days of the week astronomy program
WHERE	BAS	Source for WHERE.COM in BASIC
WHERE	COM	Finds files dir. & subdir. any drive
WHERE	DOC	Documentation for WHERE.COM
WHEREIS	COM	Find a file anywhere in a tree-structured directory
XYZ	BAS	Astronomical coordinates of the sun
YN	COM	Protective batch for ERASE.COM(DOS)
YN	DOC	Documentation for YN.COM

607
Text Utilities
v1

A special collection of text-processing utilities:

HEBREW uses a downloaded character set on an Epson FX series printer to print in Hebrew, after preparing the file with WordStar. The source code is provided for those who might want to change the mapping of English to Hebrew letters.

TEXT CHECKER checks a WordStar text file for two kinds of errors: certain control characters, quotes, parentheses, and brackets, that are not in pairs; extra spaces between words and inconsistent numbers of spaces between sentences.

CDIR -> DB is a cataloging program. Most of the disk cataloging programs available impose size limitations but this one creates two files on the 64K, one disk drive and monochrome display disk, VOL.LIB and DB.LIB, and keeps appending to these as long as you keep shoving in disks. CDIR is terminated after each disk read to permit you to do something else in the midst of doing all this cataloging.

SMX is a printer utility designed for an EPSON MX80 (SFX is for the FX185). It accepts a parameter (or asks for one) and then sends the translated codes to the printer.

INDEXER creates an index file, with page numbers, from a formatted text file.

Usage: Disk and file maintenance.

System Requirements: 96K, one disk drive and a monochrome display; however, many are printer-specific, so verify substitutions!

How to Start: Consult the files ending in .DOC for instructions; all can be printed out by entering COPY filename.DOC prn from the DOS prompt

● To run, type the filename and press ENTER.

Suggested Donation: TEXTCHECK: $15.00; HEBREW: $15.00

File Descriptions:

CD??????	FNC	CDIR function files (9 files)
CDCONCAT	BAT	Batch file to collect CDIR source into one file
CDIR	EXE	Disk cataloging program
CDIR	C	C source code for CDIR.EXE
CDIR	DOC	Documentation for CDIR
CDIR	H	Constants and declaration for CDIR
CDIRA	ASM	Assembly source code to get directory and freespace
CDIRA	OBJ	Assembler directory and freespace routines
HEBREW	BAS	Source code for HEBREW.EXE
HEBREW	DOC	Documentation for HEBREW.EXE
HEBREW	EXE	HEBREW characters for and EPSON printer
INDEXER	EXE	Program to genereate indexex
INDEXER	C	C source code for INDEXER.EXE
INDEXER	DOC	Documentation for INDEXER.EXE
LNK	BAT	Batch file to link CDIR
MAINLIB	DBF	Sample dBASE II file from CDIR
MC	BAT	Batch file to compide CDIR
READ	ME	Letter about HEBREW and Text Checker
SFX	ASM	Assembly source code to set up an FX 185 printer
SMX	ASM	Assembly source code to set up an MX 80 printer
SMX	COM	Printer initialization for MX 80, run file
SMX	DOC	Documentation for SMX.COM
TC	DOC	Documentation for TC.EXE
TC	EXE	Text checker program
*	LIB	Sample output files (2 files)

609

Disk Spool Version 2.06

v1

DISK SPOOL spools printed data onto a disk allowing a virtually unlimited (except by disk space) amount of information to be spooled. Even though this is a "demo" it works exactly like the full model. It includes a pop up menu and runs with virtually any application. The one major limitation: the "pop up" menu works for about 10 minutes. After, you can no longer perform any of the menu functions (unless you re-boot, and re-load DISK SPOOL to memory).

Usage: Spooling to disk.

System Requirements: Any level PC with 128K, one disk drive and a monochrome display.

Features:

- Runs with virtually any application
- Runs in the background, at the same time other programs are running
- "Pop up" menu allows the following functions: — stop or start spooling — stop or start printing — clear spool file — display spooled data on screen — reposition printing anywhere within spool file (even if data has already been printed)

How to Start: Read SP.HLP for directions on use

- To run, enter SP if you have a PC/XT; SA if you own an AT/compatible.

Suggested Donation: $39.95 gets you the full-featured version.

File Descriptions:

SA	COM	Print spooler that works with an AT
SA	WRK	Part of SA.COM
SP	COM	Print spooler that works with a PC or XT
SP	WRK	Part of SP.COM
SP	HLP	Documentation on Disk Spool programs

610

PACKDISK Version 1.2

v1

PACKDISK utilities is a handy collection for file, floppy and hard disk managment. They are:

DELDIR — Deletes a subdirectory with its files and subdirectories.
LISTFRAG — Lists all fragmented files in the drive.
NAMEDIR — Renames a subdirectory.
PACKDISK — Eliminates file fragmentation in the drive. — Eliminates unallocated spaces between files. — Reintegrates lost clusters (file allocation units) into the available space on the disk. — Packs the root directory and subdirectories and frees subdirectory trailing clusters.
TRANSDIR — Transfers a subdirectory together with its files and subdirectories into another directory in the same drive.
PARK — Parks disk(s) before power off.

NOTE: DO NOT ATTEMPT TO USE ANY OF THESE UTILITIES ON A NETWORK DRIVE.

Usage: File management

System Requirements: 128K, one floppy or hard disk and monochrome display

How to Start: Read MANUAL before using

- To run, enter program name at the DOS prompt and press ENTER.

Suggested Donation: $35.00; source code available for $65-115.00 per program

File Descriptions:

DELDIR	COM	Deletes the designated subdirectory with its files
LISTFRAG	COM	List all fragmented files
NAMEDIR	COM	Renames subdirectory
PACKDISK	COM	Disk optimizer
TRANSDIR	COM	Transfers subdirectory and its files to another subdirectory
PARK	COM	Parks hard drive head into safety zone before power down
MANUAL		Documentation READ FIRST
FILES610	TXT	This file
GO	BAT	Start up batch file

634
WAGNER UTILITIES and PCLOG
v1

PCLOG is an account logging utility which is quite complete except for documentation. However, PCLOG is probably simple enough to use with the short "help" file that is included. The set of utilities from Wagner are simple, but handy.

Usage: Time tracking for your computer's use.

System Requirements: 128K, one disk drive and monochrome display.

How to Start: To run a COM program type its name and press ENTER.

File Descriptions:

PCLOG	COM	A program to keep track of the time spent on each program
PCLOG	HLP	The help files for PCLOG
PCLOG	86	A log for 1986
PDVL	COM	Prints out labels for floppies with Vol label and directory
CALENDAR	COM	Prints out full page monthly calendars for desk or wall
LABELER	COM	Allows typing out small quantities of labels easily
MODEL	COM	Displays your computers ROM date and equipment

658
DOS Toolkit
v1

This disk contains a small but excellent collection of programs which aid in DOS utilities and collectively are called "TOOLKIT." WC.EXE is an advanced word/char/line counter, which supports command line wildcards. TC.EXE is an easy to read text compare program to find differences in a file. INPATH.EXE is a file finder program with a twist: it locates files based upon the PATH variable, and uses the same extension hierarchy (COM-EXE-BAT) that DOS does; it is similar to "whereis" in the UNIX system.

Usage: DOS Housekeeping.

System Requirements: 128K, one disk drive and monochrome display.

How to Start: To read DOC files enter TYPE filename.ext and press ENTER. Type GO and press ENTER for startup instructions.

Suggested Donation: $5.00 gets you latest version and documentation; $20.00 requested for commercial/government usage.

File Descriptions:

INPATH	EXE	DOS file finder program
TC	EXE	Text compare program
WC	EXE	Text word, character and line counter program
TOOLKIT	DOC	Documentation for above programs (17k)
IDEA	DOC	Idea request message
IDEA	FRM	Idea form
TOOLKIT	ORD	Toolkit registration form
GO	BAT	Startup information batch file

LANGUAGE UTILITIES:

This section is designed to be language-specific by disk but, as always, there is a lot of cross-communication and cross-fertilization between them. Chatty bunch, these guys!

These are basically specialized explorations of all the possibilities that each language brings. While even humble BASIC has a few disks here, the biggest representations are in C and Turbo Pascal, which has an entire series devoted to it. It is important to note how deep you wish to go with your explorations as many of them offer Assembly-level as well as DOS-level calling capacity.

130   Pascal Tools (Disk 1 of 3)

v1

This is the first of the three-disk series Pascal Tools. The series consists of routines adapted from the book "Software Tools in Pascal" which are useful for processing and extracting information from text files. This disk includes six programs for formatting output, echoing arguments to output, defining your KWIC (key-word-in-context) index, and a file archiving program.

Usage: Pascal programmers

System Requirements: 128K, one disk drive, monochrome display

How to Start: Read manual (*.MAN) files before using corresponding programs

● To run, type filename and press ENTER.

User Comments: "Flexible pattern search/replace missing from usual word processors is so worth having." "Good UNIX practice." "Saves typing in the programs from the book."

File Descriptions:

README1		Notes about using Pascal Tools
ARCHIVE	EXE	File archiving program
CHANGE	EXE	Changes patterns in text
CHARCNT	EXE	Count characters in input
ECHOARG	EXE	Echo arguments to output
FINDP	EXE	Find patterns in text
FMT	EXE	Produce formatted output
KWIC	EXE	Produce lines for KWIC index
*	FNT	Printer setup files (4 files)
*	MAN	Documentation (17 files)

131
Pascal Tools
(Disk 2 of 3)
v1

This is the second of the three-disk series Pascal Tools. The series consists of routines adapted from the book "Software Tools in Pascal" which are useful for processing and extracting information from text files. This disk's routines include text file sorting, tranliterating characters, a word counter, and TED a small line editor.

Usage: Pascal programmers, general PC users

System Requirements: 128K, one disk drive

How to start: Enter TYPE README and press ENTER for program information

User Comments: "Flexible pattern search/replace missing from usual word processors is so worth having." "Good UNIX practice." "Saves typing in the programs from the book."

File Descriptions:

README2		Notes about using Pascal tools
LINECNT	EXE	Counts number of lines in a text file
MACRO	EXE	Expands string definitions
PRINTF	EXE	Print files with headings
SORTF	EXE	Sort lines in text file
TED	EXE	Line editor for text files
TRANSLIT	EXE	Transliterate characters
UNIQUE	EXE	Deletes adjacent duplicate lines
UNROTATE	EXE	Formats lines for a KWIC index
WORDCNT	EXE	Counts words in standard inputs

132
Pascal Tools
(Disk 3 of 3)
v1

This is the third of the three-disk series Pascal Tools. The series consists of routines adapted from the book "Software Tools in Pascal" which are useful for processing and extracting information from text files. This disk includes the source code for the routines included on Disks No 130 and 131 along with batch files to create utilties, all accompanied by documentation.

Usage: Pascal programmers

System Requirements: 128K, one disk drive, monochrome display

How to Start: Enter TYPE README and press ENTER for program information

- To run Pascal routines, refer to your Pascal language manual.

User Comments: "Flexible pattern search/replace missing from usual word processors is so worth having." "Good UNIX practice." "Saves typing in the programs from the book."

File Descriptions:

README3		Notes about using Pascal tools
*	AR	Source code for Pascal tools (15 files)
GETFCB	ASM	Pascal callable routine to fill File Control Block (FCB)
GLOBCONS	INC	Include files (3 files)
CMDFILE	BAT	Batch files used to create utilities (3 files)
*	DCL	Procedure definition files
*	OBJ	Object files

149
C Utilities No 1
v1

The files on the disk contain many useful routines including LUMP which is used to join files together for BBS file transfer. Inversely the UNLUMP routine separates the files. This disk also contains a UNIX-type GREP string search function.

Usage: C programmers, general PC users

System Requirements: 128K, one drive, optional C compiler

How to Start: To read the files with the DOC extension enter TYPE filename.DOC and press ENTER.

- To run files with EXE extention, type: filename and press ENTER.
- To run the programs with the C extension, refer to your C manual for compilation and linkage.

User Comments: "Excellent set of utilities for the C programmer." "The LUMP and UNLUMP files are a must for file uploading."

File Descriptions:

LUMP	DOC	Documentation for LUMP
LUMP	C	Source code for LUMP
UNLUMP	C	Source code for UNLUMP
LUMP	EXE	Program to lump files together
UNLUMP	EXE	Program to split files apart
GREP	DOC	Documentation for GREP
GREP	EXE	Unix like grep command to find strings in files
GREP	C	Source code for LUMP
XC	DOC	Documentation for XC
XC	C	Source code for LUMP
XC	EXE	Xreference utility for c programs
CC	DOC	Documentation for CC
CC	EXE	c program checker
CC	OBJ	Object file for CC
CC	C	Source code for CC
README		Notes about the files on this disk

162
BASIC NECESSITIES
Version 1.12
v1.1

This disk contains several handy items that are highly useful to a BASIC programmer. Its files include a source code archiver, a utility to remove tabs from files, debug functions, and a structured BASIC preprocessor. This disk is must for any one doing any extensive programming in BASIC.

Usage: BASIC programmers

System Requirements: 128K, two disk drives

How to Start: To read the files with the DOC extension enter TYPE filename.DOC and press ENTER.

• To run the files with EXE extension enter the filename then press return.

User Comments: "Very useful for any amateur programmer." "A real necessity for every BASIC user." "Very good documentation."

Suggested Donation: $25.00

File Descriptions:

ED	EXE	Program editor
SB	EXE	Structured BASIC preprocessor
LLIST	EXE	Lister
XREF	EXE	Cross-reference

ARCH	EXE	Source code archiver
ENTAB	EXE	Utility to put tabs in files
DETAB	EXE	Utility to remove tabs from files
ATTRIB	SB	Sample program
CHARS	SB	Sample program
LC	SB	Sample program
DEBUG	INC	Debug functions
SCREEN	INC	Screen functions
INPUT	INC	Input functions
CLS	INC	Fast screen clear functions
SB	DOC	Preprocessor manual (30k)
ED	DOC	Editor manual (26k)
UTIL	DOC	Utilities manual (17k)
READ	ME	File to read first

167
BASIC Aids No 1
v1

This disk contains many useful routines for the BASIC programmer. Routines include a BASIC to FORTRAN converter, a BASIC program squisher, and a REMark remover.

Usage: BASIC programmers

System Requirements: 128K, one disk drive, monochrome display

How to Start: From BASIC, type in LOAD"filename, then run. To read the files with the DOC extensions, enter TYPE filename.DOC and press ENTER.

User Comments: "ANIMATE has some good tips for animation." "Some nice programming ideas and shortcuts." "Several good routines to incorporate into your own programs."

File Descriptions:

ADVANCED	BAS	Checks to see if a program requires BASICA or not
ADVANCED	DOC	Documentation
ANIMATE	BAS	Demonstrates how to use several BASICA graphics commands
BASKEYS	BAS	Sets up BASIC programming function keys
BASTODOS	BAS	Several callable Assembler routines for BASIC programs
BASTOFOR	BAS	Converts BASIC to Fortran
BASTOFOR	DOC	Documentation
CHARDISP	BAS	Displays ASCII character set
PSQUISH	BAS	BASIC program squisher
REMREM	BAS	Removes REMarks from BASIC programs
STOPGAP	BAS	Screen text editor for BASIC programming +6TRANDUMP /7BAS /8Dump utility
TRS2PC	BAS	Converts TRS80 BASIC partways to IBM PC BASIC

216 C Utilities No 2

v1

This is the second in our series of utilities and functions for the "C" programmers. Some of the time-savers included are many screen-handling routines to draw boxes, clear lines, move the cursor, etc. Some DOS interfaces to allow you to access DOS time, convert date formats, interface w/BIOS, and more. If you'd like some help, or just wish to see how others do it, be sure to check out this one!

Usage: C programmers

System Requirements: 256K, two disk drives

How to Start: Enter TYPE README and press ENTER for program information. For instructions on C listings, refer to your C language manual.

User Comments: "Excellent set of routines for C language users."

File Descriptions:

README	DOC	Notes about programs on this disk
WEEKDAY	C	Function to determine the day of the week a given Gregorian date
READS	C	Reads string from stdin
SCONTROL	H	Header file used by screen and keyboard control library
CHOSIT	C	Function to display menu, prompt for a response and validate
ELINE	C	Function to erase line of screen
JTOG	C	Function to convert Julian date to Gregorian date
DOSDATE	ASM	Returns DOS month, day, year as integers
JTOJ	C	Returns Julian day from date in form (yddd)
SCRINIT	C	Initializes screen and keyboard arrays
SCRATT	C	Toggles screen attributes (ie BOLD, blink, reverse video)
FRAME	C	Function to draw box given two corners
CURSOR	C	Function to move cursor to a specific r,c position
CURDOWN	C	Function to move curser down y relative lines
GETLINE	C	Read record from file to string
CVTDATE	C	Unpacks Gregorian date (1/1/84) to (01/01/84)
GTOJ	C	Converts Gregorian date to Julian date
CURFOR	C	Move cursor forward x columns
CURBACK	C	Move cursor back x columns
PAUSE	C	Pauses a program for period of time
CURUP	C	Mover cursor up y lines

ESCREEN	C	Function to erase line from screen
DOSTIME	ASM	Return DOS time in hours, minutes, seconds and 1/100 seconds
GETTIME	C	Gets time in form HH:MM:SS (24 hour clock)
GETDATE	C	Gets date in string form MM/DD/YY
BIOSIO	ASM	Assembly routines which interface directly with BIOS
READC	C	Function to read string from stdin
WRITES	C	Function to write string to stdout
WRITEC	C	Function to write character to screen using DOS function
MENCON	C	Function to open menu file and display it on screen
COMM	MNU	Menu for communications program
IBMTTY	C	Terminal emulation program with file upload and download capability
???	BAT	Batch files to emulate UNIX commands (9 files)

223 Assembly/Pascal Utilities

v1

This disk contains a variety of Assembly language routines for screen clearing and cursor size alteration. There is a small database management system written in Pascal which is linkable to LOCATE.ASM for cursor positioning, a text-file preview utility, a routine using ANSI.SYS to reset the keyboard, and others.

Usage: Assembly language and/or Pascal programmers

System Requirements: 128K, two disk drives, an Assembler and a Pascal compiler.

How to Start: To run the files with the C and PAS extentions, refer to your Assembler and Pascal manuals. To read DOC files, just enter TYPE filename.DOC and press ENTER.

User Comments: "Excellent cursor control and cursor sizing routines."

File Descriptions:

BEEP	ASM	Program to make "beep" on speaker
BEEP	DOC	Documentation for BEEP
CANCEL	ASM	Source for CANCEL
CANCEL	EXE	Program to cancel the setting that SETP causes
CLS	ASM	Program to clear screen
CLS	DOC	Documentation for CLS
CLS	OBJ	Object file
CONTENTS	DOC	Description of file on this disk

CONTRACT	ASM	Procedure to restore the cursor to its system size
CONTRACT	DOC	Documentation for CONTRACT
CONTRACT	OBJ	Object file
EXPAND	ASM	Procedure to expand curser to solid blinking rectangle
EXPAND	DOC	Documentation for EXPAND
EXPAND	OBJ	Object file
FILE	PAS	Pascal Program to manage a small data base type program
INFO	BAT	Batch file to list file information on screen
LOCATE	ASM	Procedure to set cursor position from Pascal
LOCATE	DOC	Documentation for LOCATE
LOCATE	OBJ	Object file
MODULE	OBJ	Object file
MODULE	PAS	Module to be linked with FILE.PAS
MORE	COM	Filter to one screen at a time
MSBFILE	EXE	Executable image of file
PREVIEW	EXE	A Pascal utility to preview a text file prior to printing
PREVIEW	PAS	Pascal source code for PREVIEW
READCHAR	ASM	Procedure to read a specified number of characters
READCHAR	DOC	Documentation for READCHAR
READCHAR	OBJ	Object file
REPLY	ASM	Source code for REPLY
REPLY	COM	Produces beep
REPLY	EXE	Produces beep
RESPOND	ASM	Produces beep
RESPOND	DOC	Documentation for RESPOND
RESPOND	OBJ	Object file
SETANSI	ASM	Source code for SETANSI
SETANSI	COM	A procedure to communicate with ANSI.SYS to reset keys
SETANSI	EXE	Executable file version of SETANSI
SETP	ASM	Source code for SETP
SETP	EXE	Program to setup Epson printer to skip perforations
SETP	OBJ	Object file

2.0 of the compiler are not compatible with earlier versions.

Usage: Complex mathematical work

System Requirements: 128K, one disk drive, monochrome display and the appropriate compiler.

How to Start: Consult COMPLEX.DOC for program documentation. Verify compatibility access through your compiler.

User Comments: "Good pattern for program listers — easily modified." "Home-brewn procedures." "Very useful." "Need this in more languages."

Suggested Donation: $25.00 includes complete documentation (40 pages) and one free update, up to one year after registering.

File Descriptions:

— — — —	— —	User-supported complex function library — version 1.2
COMPLEX	LIB	Function library 1.3
COMPLEX	DOC	Documentation (32K)
COMPLEXP	PAS	Pascal sample program
COMPLEXF	FOR	Fortran sample program
— — — —	— —	Pascal programs
LISTING	COM	Lists Turbo Pascal files with xreference and begin/end blocks
LISTING	DOC	Documentation for LISTING.COM
LISTING	PAS	Source code for LISTING.COM
PRINTER	COM	Sets Epson printer settings
PRINTER	PAS	Source code for PRINTER.COM
FUNCTION	PAS	Additional functions for Turbo Pascal
FUNCTION	DOC	Documentation for FUNCTION.PAS

248
PASCAL Math Library
v1.1

With the advent of version 2.0 of IBM Pascal and FORTRAN compilers, it has become practical to do serious numerical work with them. PASCAL Math Library contains a library of functions of complex variables. The library includes arithmetic, trigonometric and transcendental functions, in both single and double precision with example programs for using FORTRAN and Pascal.

PLEASE NOTE: All the libraries to be used with Pascal programs were compiled usimg IBM's Pascal Compiler 2.0. The changes that went into version

269
BetaTool's BASIC Development System
v1.2

This disk contains completely functional versions of BetaTool's BASIC Development System except that they are limited to programs of less than 6500 bytes. BetaTool's system works with the BASIC interpreter to add easy file editing, instant cross-reference lists, selective line renumber variable dump, program expand and

Usage: BASIC programmers

System Requirements: 128K, one disk drive, monochrome display

How to Start: Copy the file that corresponds to your computer and version of BASIC to your working disk and name it BTS.COM. Start the program by typing: BTS M BASICA then press ENTER.

User Comments: "Certainly saves time when programming in BASIC."

Suggested Donation: $99.00

File Descriptions:

BDS	DOC	Documentation text file
SAMPLE	BAS	Sample BASIC program
BCONFIG	COM	Configures the BDS.COM program file for selected options
IBMPC	2XX	Copy to BDS.COM if you are using IBM PC BASIC Version 2.??
IBMPC	3XX	Copy to BDS.COM if you are using IBM PC BASIC Version 3.??
CORONA03	112	Copy to BDS.COM if you are using CORONA BASIC Version 1.12.03
CORONA04	112	Copy to BDS.COM if you are using CORONA BASIC Version 1.12.04
CORONA05	112	Copy to BDS.COM if you are using CORONA BASIC Version 1.12.05
CORONA01	202	Copy to BDS.COM if you are using CORONA BASIC Version 2.02.01
ITTXTRA	200	Copy to BDS.COM if you are using ITT XTRA BASIC Version 2.00
ITTXTRA	311	Copy to BDS.COM if you are using ITT XTRA BASIC Version 3.11
COMPAQ	200	Copy to BDS.COM if you are using COMPAQ BASIC Version 2.00
COMPAQ	210	Copy to BDS.COM if you are using COMPAQ BASIC Version 2.10
COMPAQ	211	Copy to BDS.COM if you are using COMPAQ BASIC Version 2.11
COMPAQ	300	Copy to BDS.COM if you are using COMPAQ BASIC Version 3.00
COMPAQ	310	Copy to BDS.COM if you are using COMPAQ BASIC Version 3.10
COMPAQ	311	Copy to BDS.COM if you are using COMPAQ BASIC Version 3.11

307 Assembly Utilities No 1

v1

The programs on this disk are utilities for hackers or experienced programmers. They do many different things and most are aimed at system operations and DOS commands. Routines include on-screen calculator, and a disk drive alignment program.

Usage: Assembly language programmers, general programmers.

System Requirements: 128K, one disk drive, monochrome display, optional 8087 co-processor

How to Start: To read DOC or TXT files, enter TYPE filename.ext and press ENTER.

- To run an EXE or COM program, type its name and press ENTER. For instructions on running BASIC programs, please refer to the GETTING STARTED section in this catalog.

User Comments: "A useful set of utilities." "The routines have good potential." "Nice shortcuts."

File Descriptions:

87ERROR	ASM	Assembly source for 87ERROR
87ERROR	COM	Handles error calls from optional 8087 math coprocessor
87ERROR	DOC	Documentation for 87ERROR
87ERROR	OBJ	Part of 87ERROR
ALIGN	BAS	Head alignment program
ANSI&2K	SYS	Expands function key buffer by 2k
ANSIKEYS	DOC	Documentation for ANSI&2K
ASCII	COM	Displays ASCII table on screen
AST-TEST	COM	Memory test program
BDNCHM	TXT	A fast and dirty function accuracy test
CALC	EXE	On screen calculator
CIPHER	BAS	A simple encoding and decoding security system
CLEARRO	COM	Clears read only attribute from files
CLEARRO	DOC	Docs for CLEARRO
CORELOOK	COM	Takes snapshot of memory core
CPMDOSXR	DOC	Displays equivelent commands in DOS and CP/M
CURSOR	COM	Sets maximum size of cursor
CURSOR	DOC	Documentation for CURSOR
DEBUG	TXT	A small tutorial about the DEBUG command in DOS
DEFRAG	BAS	Unifies a file that is fragmented by repeated use

DEFRAG	DOC	Documentation for DEFRAG
DOS-BUG	4E	Reports on bug in DOS 2.1 function calls
DOS2A	TXT	Information about DOS 2.0 interrupts
ENVINUSE	COM	Sizes environment buffer
ENVIRO	PAT	Patches COMMAND.COM for larger environement area
ENVIRON	DOC	Explains some of the SET command options
ENVXPAND	DOC	Documentation for ENVXPAND
ENVXPAND	SYS	Expands environment buffer by 1k
KEYS		Optional key assignment list
LOOKMEM	COM	Another memory look program
MEMORY	COM	Allows dynamic memory switch change
MEMORY	DOC	Docs to explain MEMORY
MORERAM	ASM	Assembler source for MORERAM
MORERAM	COM	Allows PC to use more RAM then switch sets suggest
MORERAM	DOC	Docs for MORERAM
NULLKEYS		Optional key assignment list
PARINT	COM	Parity intercept
QUIKUP	COM	Faster bootup by use of software memory switches
QUIKUP	DOC	Documentation for QUIKUP
QUIKUPQD	COM	Part of QUIKUP
REBOOT	DOC	Brief apologetic note explaining lack of documentation
REBOOT	EXE	Software system reboot
SETKEY	DOC	Documentation for SETKEY
SETKEY	EXE	Allows user redefinition of keyboard
SETRO	COM	Sets read only parameter to on
SETRO	DOC	Documentation for SETRO
SETVAR	COM	Allows variables and variations to the set command
SETVAR	DOC	Documentation for SETVAR
SYSTAT	COM	Displays name and comments of each disk drive in system
SYSTAT	DOC	Documentation for SYSTAT
TEE	COM	Allows you to see what is being piped in piping commands
TEE	DOC	Documentation for TEE
TESTDRV	BAS	Performs read/write test on drives
UNDO	BAS	Allows fixed disk users to read backup diskettes
UNDOBKUP	BAS	Same as UNDO

308

Assembly Utilities No 2

v1

The files on this disk are Assembly programs that may serve to both teach and tantalize you Assembly language programmers out there. This disk is intended for the more experienced, or adventurous, among you. Not all routines have much in the way of remarks.

Usage: Assembly language programmers

System Requirements: 128K, one disk drive, monochrome monitor

How to Start: To read the files with the DOC extensions, enter TYPE filename.DOC and press ENTER.

● To run the files with the ASM extension, refer to your Assembler manual.

User Comments: "Many of the routines saved me quite a bit of time." "Good for the budding Assembly language programmer." "Extremely useful. Author responded to my bug report with a new version."

File Descriptions:

ASC–BIN	ASM	Converts a string of numbers to a signed 16 binary
ASC–BIN	OBJ	Object code for ASC–BIN
BIN–ASC	ASM	Converts signed binary to a 6 digit ASCII string
BIN–ASC	OBJ	Object code for BIN–ASC
CASE	ASM	Source code for CASE
CASE	COM	Utility changes case for comments and instructions
CASE	DOC	Documentation for CASE
CIRCLE–1	ASM	Calls circle subroutine
CIRCLE–2	ASM	Similar to CIRCLE–1.ASM
CIRCLE–3	ASM	Similar to CIRCLE–1.ASM
CLOSER	ASM	Demonstrates a bug in CLOSE routine in PC-DOS
COMPAQ	ASM	Function unknown
DEC–ADJ	ASM	Multiplies a number by ten
DEC–ADJ	OBJ	Object code for DEC–ADJ
DISP-REG	ASM	Display various registers as set by loader
DPATH	ASM	Does something with subdirectories or paths
DRAWLINE	ASM	Program to draw line
FAST–CIR	ASM	Program to draw a circle
FLIST	ASM	Sorted list of diskette files
HELLO	ASM	Assembly language demo program
IBM	ASM	Function unknown
KEYBUFF	ASM	Keyboard buffer expansion program
LOAD	ASM	Will load a .COM file larger than 64k
LOOK	ASM	Looks at memory
MACRO	ASM	A bunch of utility macros
MACRO1	ASM	More macros
OPER	ASM	Demonstrates operators:20a
PMODE	ASM	Sets up printer modes
PX	DOC	Documentation for PX
PX	EXE	Keeps track of procedure calls within a program
SETOKI	ASM	Sends control characters to Okidata Microline 92
SQ–RT	ASM	Assembly source for SQ–RT
SQ–RT	EXE	Calculates square roots
SQ–RT	OBJ	Object code for SQ–RT
STDBOOT	ASM	Define IBMBIO entry point
SWITCH–1	ASM	Fool hardware switch settings
SWITCH–2	ASM	Another version of SWITCH–1
SWPTR	ASM	Exchanges printer addresses LPT1 and LPT2
SYSINT	ASM	Indexes system interrupt function calls

SYSINT2	ASM	Variation of SYSINT.ASM " "
TESTLINE	ASM	Sample driver for DRAWLINE
TRACE02	COM	Displays current values of CS:IP registers
TRACE02	DOC	Documentation for TRACE02
UASM-LST	BAS	Removes addresses and adds labels on DEBUG output
UNDOS	ASM	UnDOS a system disk
VMODE	ASM	Sets up display mode
VW-TO-WS	ASM	Volkswriter to Wordstar conversion
WHEREIS	ASM	Find a file on a hard disk drive
WS-TO-VW	ASM	Wordstar to Volkswriter conversion

309

Assembly Utilities No 3

v1

The programs on this disk are Assembly language programs relating specifically to the IBM PC. Routines include sound effects generator, a text editor, space left on disk and how many sectors are free. Password protection is also included.

Usage: Assembly language programmers

System Requirements: 128K, one disk drive, and an Assembler.

How to Start: To read the the files with the DOC or TXT extension enter TYPE filename.ext and press ENTER. For instructions on ASM listings, refer to your Assembler manual.

User Comments: "Many of these routines saved me a great deal of time." "DISKDIRL.ASM is excellent, well written and very useful." "Extremely useful."

File Descriptions:

ASM	TXT	2 tips from Boca Raton
BEEP	ASM	Sound effect generator
CLEAR	ASM	Sample clear screen routine from CHASM
CLOCK	ASM	Print date and time on screen
CLOCK	DOC	Documentation for CLOCK
CO	DOC	Documentation for COENDP and COPRNT
COENDP	ASM	Part of program to list disk contents
COPRNT	ASM	Part of program to list disk contents
DISASM	BAS	A BASIC program that disassembles assem. progs. ?
DISKDIRL	ASM	Part of program to list disk contents
DISPTEXT	ASM	Displays a line on screen without BIOS
DOS-EDIT	ASM	Assembly language text editor
DOSERROR	DOC	Lists error return codes

DSK	ASM	Returns the number of free sectors on a disk
FREE	ASM	Shows available free space on a disk
FREE	DOC	Documentation for FREE
GETSP	ASM	Lists free space on diskp
INIT	ASM	Initialize
INITMEM	ASM	Initializes memory between 544k and 576k
LIST80	ASM	Lists the first 80 characters in a line of ASCII text
MEMDRV	ASM	Faster bootup and use ALL of your available memory
MEMDRV	DOC	Documents MEMDRV
MORERAM	ASM	Use all of available RAM
NOLF	ASM	Deletes extra linefeeds from some printer files
OBJSNOOP	COM	Displays label references in object files
OPCODE	DOC	Used by DISASM.BAS
OPCODE	TXT	Used by DISASM.BAS
PAGE	ASM	Demonstrates multiple screen pages
PARTBIOS	LIS	Partial listing of BIOS low memory
PASSWORD	ASM	Password protection of system
PRTPATH	ASM	Prints current directory path
PUT-DEC	ASM	Puts decimal point in ASCII string
PUT-DEC	OBJ	Object code for PUT-DEC
ROMBIOS	ASM	ROM BIOS information
SCRN	ASM	A variable time screen saver
SCRN	DOC	Documentation for SCRN.ASM
SCROLL10	ASM	Tests DISPTEXT
SKELETON	ASM	Skeleton of a minimal Assembly language program
SL	ASM	Tests program thst scrolls screen
SPEDUPDK	ASM	Changes some disk drive parameters
TABS	ASM	Replaces blanks with tabs in ASCII text files
TALK1	ASM	Dumb terminal for IBM PC
TEXT	DOC	Documentation for TEXT.EXE
TEXT	EXE	Several text conversion options
UPDIR	ASM	Moves the user up one directory level
UPPATCH	ASM	Patch of another program

314

C Utilities No 4

v1

This disk has an excellent Unix-type Grep function (string find) regardless of what C compiler you use. Also here is XENIX which is a very nice set of disk I/O routines that support all the DOS features, and UNLUMP to help build larger C programs.

Usage: C and Assembly language programmers

System Requirements: 128K, one disk drive; C compiler and Assembler are optional.

How to Start: To read DOC files, enter TYPE filename.ext and press ENTER.

● To run an EXE program, just type its name and press ENTER. For instructions on ASM or C listings, refer to your Assembler or C language manuals.

User Comments: "Many useful utilities." "Good routines for the budding C and Assembly language programmer." "Fun to probe around in."

File Descriptions:

C86MOD	DOC	How to make C86 programs return status to DOS 2.0 bat files
C86SAMPL	BAT	Batch file to run C86 compiler
CASYNC	ASM	C interface to serial port. Includes XON/XOFF, buffered input
CC	C	C program that does the same thing as C86SAMPL.BAT !
CC	EXE	CC.C ready to run
CLS	C	C program to clear screen
CPRGRMS1	BAT	Copies all the files on this diskette to another disk
CPRGRMS1	DOC	Short descption of the files on this disk
CPRGRMS2	DOC	Short descption of the files on this disk
CRC	C	Does CRC error checking on blocks of data
CSYSINT	ASM	Interface between Lattice C and the 8088 interrupts
GETSEG-C	ASM	Gets vaule for all the segment registors
GREP	C	GREP for Lattice C
GREP	C86	GREP for C86
GREP	DOC	GREP manual
IOS1-20	ASM	DOS disk I/O functions for Lattice C
KERMITPC	C	Reliable file transfer over unreliable I/O channels
KERMITPC	HLP	lets pc emmulate a TTY termial. Documentation on KERMIT
LEJ–LIB	C	Routines to count words etc, ASCII HEX conversion etc.
LOCATE	C	C routine to position cursor on screen
LUMP	C	Lump a group of files together
MEMCLEAN	C	Zeros memory to avoid parity checks
MEMCLEAN	DOC	Documentation on MEMCLEAN
MOVMEML	ASM	C callable function to move memory
NAMES	C	Shows how to Access disk from C
RANDOM	ASM	Random number generator for C
RANDOM	C	Test for RANDOM.ASM
SETPTR	C	Setup the parameters for EPSON printers
SQ	C86	Squeeze a text file into less space
SWITCH	C86	Change display type
SWITCH1	C	Change display mode
TPRINT	C	Prints files with page numbers headers ect.
TPRINT	DOC	Documentation for TPRINT
TYPESQ	C86	Type a squeezed file
UNLUMP	C	Seperate lumped files
USQ	C86	Unsqueeze a text file
XC	C	Cross reference utility for C programs
XC	DOC	Documtation for XC
XC	EXE	XC ready to run
XENIX	ASM	Source code for OPEN READ WRITE ect. supports full path names
XENIX	OBJ	XENIX ready to link. Lattice C

---

315 C Utilities No 5

v1

A set of C subroutines ranging from an explantion for how C does type conversion for the beginner to a menu system for application programers to a small C for serious hacker. Includes a C dump program to aid in debugging C programs also.

Usage: C and Assembly language programmers

System Requirements: 128K, two disk drives, a C compiler

How to Start: To read DOC files, enter TYPE filename.ext and press ENTER.

• To run an EXE program, just type its name and press ENTER. For instructions on C listings, refer to your C language manual.

User Comments: "Excellent dubugging aids." "A must for the C program developer." "It's very interesting to see how a C compiler might be put together."

File Descriptions:

ADDLF	C	Filter to add line feeds after carrage returns only if needed
CONIO	C	Console I/O getchar scanf ect.
CPCLIB	OBJ	Part of CPCN
CPCN	C	Small C compiler written in C
CPMFILES	C	Makes BDS C look more UNIX compatible
DUMP2	C	Debug type core dump
FRAME	C	Builds a nice frame around menus
FUNKEY	C	Program to redefine the keyboard
INKEY	C	Get a char from the keyboard
ISAMC	LBR	OBJ code for ISAM utilites
ISCHECK	C	Checks Microsofts issomthing matrix
LAR	C	CP/M LU program to combine files for uploading/downloading
LIFE	C	Another life game
PRINT	C	Print text files with page numbers, headers, etc.
RENAME	C	C program to rename a file
SNAP	C	Nice snap shot of memory for debugging C programs
SNAP	OBJ	Compiled SNAP
STRING	C	Complete set of string functions
TEXTFORM	C	Prints wordstar files even if you dont have wordstar.
TINKEY	C	Test inkey program
TOWERS	C	Towers of Hanoi
TYPECONV	C	Documentation on how C does type conversion
UNTAB4	C	Convert tabs to spaces
UNTAB4	EXE	UNTAB4 ready to run

ZAPLOAD	C	Convert Binary file to INTEL hex format
ZAPLOAD	DOC	Documentation on ZAPLOAD
ZAPLOAD	EXE	ZAPLOAD ready to run
–MAIN	C	Shell for main C program that includes command line

324
Turbo Pascal Programs No 1
v1

Useful subroutine collections, hi-resolution graphics demonstrations, a calculator and even a game or two make this collection of source programs very worthwhile. The code can be used as is in your programs, modified for your special purpose, or just used as a model for learning.

Usage: Turbo Pascal users

System Requirements: 128K, two disk drives, color graphics, Turbo Pascal

How to Start: Bring up Turbo Pascal, then load desired Pascal program into the work file area, compile and run. To view the .DOC files, enter TYPE filename.DOC and press ENTER.

User Comments: "Great for the new Turbo Pascal user." "A great teachers aid." "Great demos."

File Descriptions:

		Graphics programs
CLS	INV	Required by PLOT3D, GALEXY
LINE	INV	Required by PLOT3D, PLOTFUNC, SPIN, SPOKES, WORLDMAP
POINT	INV	Required by GALEXY, RANDDOT
PLOT3D	PAS	3D object display, rotation and scaling demo
PLOT3DD	PAS	3D object display, rotation and scaling by user
CUBE	3D	Data file for PLOT3D
DIAMOND	3D	Data file for PLOT3D
PYRAMID	3D	Data file for PLOT3D
GALEXY	PAS	Travel thru the Milky Way! Best with 8087 chip.
STARS	DAT	Data file for GALEXY
PLOTFUNC	PAS	Hi-res graphics plot of 2 functions with hidden line features
RANDDOT	PAS	Graphics screen hi-speed random dot display
SPIN	PAS	Spinning box hi-res graphics demo
SPOKES	PAS	Polyhedron ("spoke-connected wheel") hi-res graphics demo
WORLDMAP	PAS	Draws continents on hi-res graphics screen
WORLDMAP	DAT	Data file for WORLDMAP

		PASCAL tools
PTOOLDAT	INC	Routines to convert and manipulate Gregorian and Julian dates
PTOOLDAT	PAS	Demo of PTOOLDAT routines
PTOOLENT	INC	Routines to display, edit and validate data netry fields
PDEMOENT	PAS	Demo of PTOOLENT routines
PTOOLTIM	INC	Routines to read and interpret system clock
PTOOLTIM	PAS	Demo of PTOOLTIM routines
PTOOLWIN	INC	Routines to create and manipulate text windows
PTOOLWIN	PAS	Demo of PTOOLWIN routines
PTOOLWIN	DOC	How to use the windowing routines in PTOOLWIN.INC

		Miscellaneous
CALL	PAS	Garbage
CONVRT	PAS	Convert TURBO PASCAL chain files to callable COM pgms
LOADER	INC	Required by CONVRT — include in calling program
FASTPRNT	INV	TURBO PASCAL external routine
HAL-PC	DOC	HAL-PC PASCAL disk library information
HAT	PAS	Draws the "hat" mathematical function. Best with 8087 chip.
HEXDUMP	PAS	HEX/ASCII listing of any disk file — continuous display
INPUT2	PAS	Routines to display, edit and validate data entry fields
LIFE	PAS	Conway's game of LIFE — user defines cell coords
LIFETRBO	PAS	Conway's game of LIFE — optional computer defines cell coords
PFORMAT	PAS	Change case of PASCAL source code — NO INDENTINGv1.01
PFORMAT	DOC	How to use PFORMAT
SHOWCHRS	PAS	Display all 256 characters on monitor
SIEVE	PAS	Counts primes between 1 and a max number defined in program
TENKEY	PAS	4-function algebraic-notation calculator
TEST	PAS	Garbage
TSTATTR	PAS	Display combinations of color monitor display attributes
TURBOTST	PAS	Test TURBO PASCAL version 2.0 for math errors
NEW	PAS	How to do line-oriented file I/O in TURBO PASCAL
TYPEFILE	PAS	How to do line-oriented file I/O in TURBO PASCAL (same as NEW)

351
Turbo Pascal Programs No 2
v1

This disk has handy tools for Turbo Pascal programs. Routines include library files for geometric drawings, peripherals information function, make or remove subdirectories, DOS path get and set routines and more...

Usage: Turbo Pascal users

System Requirements: 128K, two disk drives, monochrome display and Turbo Pascal

How to Start: Bring up Turbo Pascal, then load desired Pascal source program into work file area, compile and run. To read the files with the DOC extension, enter TYPE filename.DOC and press ENTER.

User Comments: "Neil Rubenking has obviously put a lot of thought into these routines." "A good set of routines for the new and the experienced Pascal programmer."

Suggested Donation: $10.00

File Descriptions:

READTHIS	NOW	Documentation (9pp) and detailing of disk files
ALLFILES	LIB	Get files matching template + display, then select
CIRCLE	LIB	Circle-drawing procedure for graphics mode
CURSOR	LIB	Change or hide cursor
GETSECTR	LIB	Read a sector from disk to buffer (see DISKMOD.PAS)
DISKTYP	LIB	Get disk type (single/double/fixed, 8/9 sectors)
EQUIPMNT	LIB	Returns information about equipment attached to PC
ERRMESSG	LIB	Error messages for DOS 2.0 function calls
EXISTFIL	LIB	Test for file's existence before opening
EXTENDIO	LIB	EXTENDED I/O based on DOS 2.0 full-path commands
EXTENDIO	DAT	Specifications for the new I/O functions
FILEATTR	LIB	Read and write the attribute byte for any file
FILENAME	TYP	Filename type definition — shared by several others
GETFILE	LIB	Procedures to GET FILEs matching a template
GETFREE	LIB	Get amount of free space on disk
GETINTGR	LIB	Takes an integer in a given range
HEXFUNCT	LIB	Convert integers in range (-32,768 to 32,767)
GETKEYS	LIB	Simple procedure to catch any keystroke
KEYCHART	DAT	Chart of key codes for GETKEYS.LIB
GETSETDD	LIB	Get or set the default drive

GRFXTABL	LIB	Get the dot patterns from the ROM graphics table
TITLES	LIB	Uses ROM character patterns to create titles
GTSETDIR	LIB	Get or Set the current directory path
KAVAIL	LIB	Returns available memory in K
KEYBOARD	LIB	Another approach to catching any keystroke
SCANCODE	DAT	Chart of keyboard Scan Codes (use with KEYBOARD.LIB)
REBOOT	LIB	"Warm" system reboot (without clearing RAM)
LESSRAM	COM	Runs COMPILED only (uses REBOOT.LIB)
NUMDISKS	COM	Runs COMPILED only (uses REBOOT.LIB)
MKRMDIR	LIB	Make or remove subdirectories
MONITOR	LIB	Simple procedure to check for color or mono
MOVEFILE	LIB	DOS 2.0 file RENAME with parameter for MOVE
NEWINT9	LIB	Change the keyboard interrupt to get key release codes
PARAMETR	LIB	Pass parameters to programs from DOS command line
PARAMETR	COM	Runs COMPILED only
POPSCREN	LIB	Pop full screens into view by addressing screen memory
POPSCREN	PAS	Source code for POPSCREN
POPSCREN	DAT	Sample screen demo (uses SCREENS.TYP)
SCREENS	TYP	Type declarations for full-screen manipulation
QUEUE	LIB	A generic line-up
RECTANGL	LIB	Rectangle-drawing procedure for graphics modes
REGPACK	TYP	Contains type definition for REGPACK (Where ...? [ED.])
SAFEWRIT	LIB	Write to screen w/o control characters wrecking display
SCREEN	LIB	Direct video screen input/output
WINDOWS	LIB	Eases use of windows and window-frames
SUCCESS	DOC	Documention (about another Turbo PASCAL resource)
*	PAS	Pascal source code for *.LIB files

353
Turbo Pascal Programs No 3
v1

This disk contains Turbo Pascal programs and other programs suited both to the novice and the advanced user alike. Most of the files on this disk pertain more to visual routines. For example, the file SHOWMOVI which is a text animation program. There is an array of printer utilities, and a program that generates mazes.

Usage: Turbo Pascal users

System Requirements: 128K, two disk drives, Turbo Pascal

How to Start: To read DOC files enter TYPE filename.ext and press ENTER. For instructions on PAS listings, refer to your Pascal language manual.

File Descriptions:

AMAZING	COM	Produces a maze-like pattern (great with color)
AMAZING	PAS	TURBO PASCAL source code
DECIHEX	COM	Enter a decimal integer, receive a hexadecimal number
DECIHEX	ASM	Source code from Waite Group book — Ctrl C to exit
FONTEDIT	BAS	Create new fonts for OKIDATA 93, 92, and maybe 82
FONTEDIT	DOC	Documentation guide
NEWCHARS	BAS	Program created by FONTEDIT.BAS (Okidata fonts)
NEWCHARS	DOC	Documentation guide
KEYDEMO	COM	A demo program that reads all keystrokes
KEYDEMO	PAS	TURBO PASCAL source code
MAKAMOVI	COM	Create animation in text mode (needs 96K minimum)
MAKAMOVI	DOC	Documentation (user guide) version 1.0
MAKAMOVI	PAS	TURBO PASCAL source code
INTRO	SCN	Used by MAKAMOVI.COM (must be on same disk)
SHOWMOVI	COM	Used to "show" the "movies" created by MAKAMOVI.COM
SHOWMOVI	DOC	Documentation (user guide)
SHOWMOVI	PAS	TURBO PASCAL source code
BOUNCY	SCN	File created by MAKAMOVI.COM (used by SHOWMOVI.COM)
SQUARE	SCN	File created by MAKAMOVI.COM (used by SHOWMOVI.COM)
OKIGRAFX	COM	Create all-points-addressable graphics up to 10″ square
OKIGRAFX	DOC	Documentation guide
OKIGRAFX	PAS	TURBO PASCAL source code
ANAGRAM	OKI	File created by OKIGRAFX.COM
DICT	OKI	File created by OKIGRAFX.COM
NOISE	COM	Makes a "machine-gun" noise
NOISE	ASM	Source code from Waite Group book on IBM Assembler
PIANO	COM	PC piano (version 1.00) with record and playback
PIANO	PAS	TURBO PASCAL source code
PIANO	TXT	Short text on PIANO.COM
TURBO	DOC	Random comments about Borland's Turbo Pascal
FILES	TXT	Disk documentation

---

365 — Turbo Pascal Programs No 5

v2

Collection of routines written in Turbo Pascal for the IBM-PC. BLIST.PAS and GETDIR.PAS were written for CP/M-80. Programs include asynchronous communications routines, an excellent disk cataloging program, and window management routines.

Usage: Turbo Pascal users

System Requirements: 128K, one disk drive, Turbo Pascal

How to Start: To read DOC files, enter TYPE filename.ext and press ENTER. For instructions on PAS listings, refer to your Pascal language manual

● To run a COM program, type its name and press ENTER.

User Comments: "The tools are varied and valuable." "Nicely done set of routines." "Great label program." "PC-DISK is extremely good."

File Descriptions:

ASYNC	PAS	Asynchronous communication routines
BLIST	PAS	TURBO program lister and begin/end counter for CP/M-80
BLIST	COM	Compiled
BLIST	DOC	Brief documentation
CRFONTS	PAS	Character font creation and editing
CRFONTS	DOC	Documentation
DATETIME	INC	Date and time functions
GETDIR	PAS	Get 8-sector, DSDD disk directory — not TURBO
HEXCALC	PAS	Hexadecimal calculations
MODEM	PAS	Telecommunications program
PARAMS	PAS	Demonstrates getting command line parameters
PC-DISK	PAS	Disk Catalog program — full-featured
PC-DISK	COM	Compiled version
BYTES	PAS	Associated program
PTOOLDAT	INC	Pascal TOOLs for DATe manipulation — very complete
PTOOLDAT	PAS	Demonstration
PTOOLENT	INC	Pascal TOOls for record-oriented data ENTry
PTOOLSCR	INC	Associated file
PTOOLENT	DOC	Documentation
PTOOLENT	PAS	Demonstration
PTOOLSCR	PAS	Demonstration
PTOOL1	BOX	Combination of PTOOLDAT, PTOOLENT, and PTOOLSCR

PTOOLWIN	INC	Pascal TOOLs for WINdow management
PTOOLWIN	DOC	Documentation
PTOOLWIN	PAS	Demo/driver
RDIBMKBD	INC	Procedure to read IBM keyboard — all keys
SETCURSR	PAS	Set cursor size for monochrome monitor
TURBO	DOC	Various routines — date/time, hex math, registers

366
Turbo Pascal Programs No 6
v2

Collection of files and routines written in Turbo Pascal for the IBM-PC. The files on this disk include a good array of communication routines which include, a Hayes modem dialer, serial communication routine, and a file opener with error handling. These files can help users construct their own communications software.

Usage: Turbo Pascal users

System Requirements: 128K, one disk drive, Turbo Pascal

How to Start: To read DOC files enter TYPE filename.ext and press ENTER. For instructions on PAS listings, refer to your Pascal language manual.

User Comments: "Much more than I anticipated." "Good learning tool with many possibilities for tweaking."

File Descriptions:

2DIR	PAS	Sorted directory
ARGLIST2	PAS	Get command line parameters (argument list) — classy
CLIMB	PAS	Climb around the directory tree — compiled only
COLORDEM	PAS	Demonstrates TURBO color modes
COMMCALL	PAS	Serial communications routines
DIALER	PAS	Dials HAYES SmartModem
DIRSRCH	PAS	Directory search
FILEIO	INC	File IO routines, w/o explanation
INDEX	PAS	Index, view, delete, or print files on disk
INKEY	INC	Routine to get char from keyboard — like BASIC INKEY$
INKEYGET	PAS	Program to receive ANY keypress from keyboard
INUSE	PAS	Password demonstration
JFYDIR	PAS	Writes directory of default drive
LU	PAS	Library Utility — needs modification for IBM & TURBO
LU-1	PAS	Included file

LU-2	PAS	Included file
LU	DOC	Documentation
OPENFILE	INC	Opens a file, with protection agains error crashes
PASCAL	LIB	Various routines
PRINTUSG	INC	Print according to "mask", like BASIC PRINT USING
PRINTUSG	PAS	Demonstration
READDATE	INC	Function accepts and returns a valid data (oo/oo/oo)
SENDASCI	INC	Routine to send ASCII chars ???
STRIPTAB	PAS	Strips TABs from a file — replaces with one space
TOOLKIT	INC	Routines for interactive programs — NOT TURBO
TXREF	PAS	TURBO cross-reference & lister — needs TURBO TOOLBOX
TXREF	COM	Compiled version
UTIL	INC	Fifty-Two utility routines (!!!)
XLIST	PAS	TURBO cross-reference & lister
XREFT	PAS	TURBO cross-reference & lister — $Include files, too
— — — —	— —	The following five incomplete files are are called by other programs
BLANK	INC	Routines to create string of blanks, center string
DIR	PAS	Get directory — incomplete???
DRAWBOX	INC	Draw a box (one style) and use window inside it
FREESPAC	INC	Routine to get amount of free space on disk
SCREEN	INC	Routines to accept valid data of various types
TYPES	INC	Type declarations used by other files

371
BASIC Aids No 2
v1.1

These utilities assist the programmer in writing and debugging BASIC programs. Files include a BASIC source code compressor, a BASIC cross reference utility, and a BASIC to Fortran converter. The programs on this disk are useful to the experienced programer as well as the novice.

Usage: BASIC programmers

System Requirements: 128K, one disk drive, monochrome display

How to Start: To read the files with the DOC or TXT extensions, enter TYPE filename.DOC and press ENTER.

- To run BASIC programs, refer to the GETTING STARTED section in this catalog.

User Comments: "Good aid for every BASIC user." "BASICREF is a indispensable program." "Routines on this disk can be a lifesaver."

File Descriptions:

BASBUG	BAS	Information on BASIC screen bug
BASCONV	BAS	Fortran to BASIC conversion
BASCONV	DOC	Documentation for BASCONV.BAS
BASICDOS	BAS	Information on different commands
BASICREF	BAS	BASIC cross reference utility
BASICREF	DOC	Documentation for BASICREF.BAS
COMPILER	ERR	Info about "string space corrupt" error in a compiled program:
COMPRESS	BAS	Compresses a BASIC program by taking out extra spaces and
COMPRESS	DOC	Documentation for COMPRESS.BAS
COREFIX	BAS	Display/change memory
CR-LF	TXT	Info on Epson printers in graphics mode
DITHRING	TXT	Where instead of a solid color, you have an everyother-dot
FC	BAS	File compare utility
GS-RENUM	EXE	GS — BASIC utilities
GS-UNNUM	EXE	GS — BASIC utilities
GS-VAREN	EXE	GS — BASIC utilities
GS-XXXXX	DOC	Documentation for GS — BASIC utilities
HIRESCOL	BAS	640 X 200 B/W graphics demo program
KB–FLAG	BAS	Demo program shows BASIC access to DOS Keyboard flag
KEYIN	ASM	Source code for KEYIN.EXE
KEYIN	EXE	Places up to parameter characters into the keyboard buffer
LBAS	DOC	Documentation for LBAS.EXE
LBAS	EXE	Label BASIC translator program
LBL-BAS	BAS	BASIC source file label checker
LBL-SAMP	BAS	Sample file for LBL-BAS.BAS
LINEBUG	BAS	Utility to check BASIC source files for errors
LINEBUG	DOC	Documentation for LINEBUG.BAS
MONITOR	BAS	Series of routines that provide a user interface for
MONITOR	DQC	Documentation for MONITOR.BAS
PAL80	BAS	80 column palette prompter
POKEPEEK	TXT	Commonly used BASIC peeks, pokes and subroutines
PROFILE	BAS	Utility that logs how much time is spent executing each
PROFILE	DOC	Documentation for PROFILE.BAS
PROFILE	MEM	Part of PROFILE.BAS
READBAS	BAS	Read BASIC files save in BINARY
SAVEBAS	COM	Creates a file from a BASIC program that was "lost"
SAVEBAS	DOC	Documentation for SAVEBAS.COM
SCRN-MAP	BAS	Print a form for graphic screen layout
SQUISHER	BAS	Compresses BASIC programs
SQUISHER	DOC	Documentation for SQUISHER.BAS
STARTBAS	BAS	A BASIC file menu program
TRACE	BAS	Helps debug BASIC programs
TRACE	DOC	Documentation for TRACE.BAS
UN-COMPQ	DOC	Documentation for UN-COMPQ.EXE
UN-COMPQ	EXE	Unprotects a BASIC program on the COMPAQ computer
UN-NEW	DOC	How to recover a BASIC program after typing 'NEW'

UNP-IBM	DOC	Documentation for UNP-IBM.EXE
UNP-IBM	EXE	Unprotects a BASIC program on the IBM computer

372 BASIC Aids No 3
v1

Here is a collection of BASIC extensions and subroutines which can make BASIC much more flexible. Routines include some for enabling access to DOS command line parameters, joystick port watch program, read directory from within BASIC program, and a screen splitting routine. The programs are useful in incorporating I/O functions within your own BASIC programs.

Usage: BASIC programmers

System Requirements: 64K, one disk drive, mono display

How to Start: To read the files with the DOC extensions, enter TYPE filename.DOC and press ENTER.

- To run BASIC programs, refer to the GETTING STARTED section in this catalog.

User Comments: "This is great for programming your own BASIC programs by providing linkable object files." "Disk contains some useful BASIC utilities."

File Descriptions:

BASICSUB	DOC	Documentation of 'CALL' statement
BASPARAM	BAS	Subroutine to access DOS command line parameters
BASSUB	ASC	Test program for BASSUB.OBJ
BASSUB	OBJ	Subroutine to access DOS directory commands
CAPLOCK	BAS	Test and display the state of NUM/CAPS lock keys
CMDLIN	DOC	A routine to enable the use of command line parameters
CNTRL-BR	BAS	Defeat BASIC file protection to list a file
DAYOFWK	BAS	Calculates the day of the week given date
DAYS	BAS	Program to calculate the days between two dates
DIR4	BAS	Demonstration file for DIR4.BIN
DIR4	BIN	Binary directory routine
DISKHAND	BIN	Get drive number from within BASIC
DISKTYPE	SUB	Get media type from within BASIC
FCBREAD	BAS	Example for FCBREAD.BSV routine
FCBREAD	BSV	Binary directory search routine

FIND-DS	BAS	Finds the value of BASIC/BASICA'S data segment
GETSP	ASM	Assembly code for GETSPACE routine
GETSP	BAS	Basic source code to create BLOAD module of GETSPACE
GETSP1	BAS	Sample of getspace routine
GETSP1	EXE	Executable module for sample of getspace routine
GETSPACE		Binary LOAD module created by program
GETSPACE	DOC	Documentation for GETSPACE routine
HEAPSORT	BAS	Demo of the HEAPSORT sorting algorithm
HEAPSORT	DOC	Documentation for HEAPSORT.BAS
INKEY	BAS	Name/address data base program
INKEY2	BAS	Demo program like INKEY.BAS
JOYSTIK	BAS	Program to watch the joystick ports
JULIAN	BAS	Converts dates
JULIAN	DOC	Documentation for JULIAN.BAS
NUM2WORD	BAS	Convert numbers to words
PAK-DATE	BAS	Subroutines can pack a 6 byte date into a 2 byte integer
PRTSC	BAS	Routine to print the screen from a basic program
QCLEAR	BIN	machine code for screen-clearing routine
QPRINT	BIN	machine code for quick print routine
QPRINTC	BIN	same, but for compiled programs
QSORT	BAS	Quicksort algorithm demonstration
QUICKC	BAS	Quick printing routine
READ–DIR	BAS	Demo of READ–DIR.SUB
READ–DIR	SUB	Read directory from within BASIC program
SCRLDEMO	BAS	Screen scrolling demo
SCRN-DOC		Documentation for the next three files
SCRN-WK	BAS	Create and save screens
SCRN-GET	TWO	A BASIC program to demonstrate screen swapping
SCRNSLGR	DEM	A BASIC program that draws and swaps two screens
SCRNDUMP	BAS	Routine to print an image of the graphics screen
SCROLL	BAS	Subroutine to be used with a BASIC program to perform
SCROLL	BLD	BLOAD version of SCROLL.BAS
SCROLL	DOC	Documentation for SCROLL.BAS
SETMEM	BAS	Routine to set memory from BASIC
SHELSORT	BAS	Shell sort routine
SHORTSUB	BAS	Collection of menu driven subroutines
SPLTSCRN	BAS	Splits the screen at horizontal dividing line location
TIMER	BAS	Times invoked from the system timer to 1/100th of a second
TIMER	RTN	Routine for TIMER.BAS
UPCASE	BAS	Routine to change lowercase to uppercase

375

Turbo Pascal Programs No 7

v1

Collection of programs and utilities useful for both the Pascal Programmer and the casual Pascal user. Routines include floating point accuracy testing, sorted directory printing, file dumping in hex and ASCII, file allocation table information, and a routine to read the internal clock.

Usage: Turbo Pascal users

System Requirements: 128K, one disk drive, Turbo Pascal

How to Start: To read DOC files enter TYPE filename.ext and press ENTER. For instructions on PAS listings, refer to your Pascal language manual.

User Comments: "Routines save time, and are instructive also." "COVER works well and is helpful in organizing disks." "Great routines for screen formatting and string manipulation."

File Descriptions:

BENCHMRK	PAS	Program to test the accuracy of floating point functions.
BIOSREAD	INC	Part of PRINTDIR.PAS, READFAT.PAS
CHECKPSP	INC	Part of PRINT2.PAS
CLS	INV	Used by FRACTAL.PAS
COMBINE	BAT	Sort/Merge book index file
COVER	COM	Utility to print a sorted directory for a disk cover
COVER	DOC	Documentation for COVER.COM
DATE	INC	Part of TEST.PAS
DECBIN	INC	Part of TESTDB.PAS
DOT	PAS	Program to test the speed of Bios interupt to perform
DOWN	PAS	Looks like some kind of BASIC to Pascal file conversion?
DTA	INC	Part of PRINT2.PAS
DUMPHEX	INC	Part of READFAT.PAS
ENTER	BAT	Enter index entries for book indexing
EQUIP	INC	Performs Bios interrupt hex 11 the equipment check
FASTPRNT	INV	Used by FRACTAL.PAS
FLOAT	PAS	Test range of floating point numbers
FRACTAL	PAS	Produces fractal images on the hi-res graphics screen
FREE	INC	Part of TEST.PAS
GETDATE	INC	Part of PRINT2.PAS, PRINTDIR.PAS, READFAT.PAS
GETDIR	PAS	Get the directory by using DOS function calls
GETFREE	INC	Part of PRINTDIR.PAS, READFAT.PAS

GETSEC	ASM	Assembly source code for direct disk access
GETSEC	OBJ	Assembled version of GETSEC.ASM
HAL-PC	DOC	Information on HAL-PC library disk
HEAPTEST	PAS	This program demonstrates a bug in Turbo's version 2
HEXDUMP	PAS	Dump the specified file in hex and ascii
INDEX	BAT	Formats an book index from your data
INFO	BAT	Information on producing book indexes
LINE	INV	Used by FRACTAL.PAS
MEM	INC	Part of TEST.PAS
MEMDISP	PAS	Displays the contents of memory onto the IBM PC screen
PASCAPS	PAS	Converts identifiers in a source code file to upper case
POINT	INV	Used by FRACTAL.PAS
POINTERS	PAS	Demo on how to use pointers and dynamic memory (Heap Space)
PRINT2	PAS	Program to print an ASCII file in a nice way on the printer
PRINTDIR	PAS	Print a sorted directory listing
READFAT	PAS	Read the File Allocation Table information
READPSP1	INC	Read Program Segment Prefix information
SIDEWYTR	PAS	Print the "infile" sideways on an EPSON MX-80 Printer
START	BAT	Begins book indexing
STRPRNT	PAS	Program for testing of Dos 2.0 print string function
TEST	PAS	Test of utility funtions
TESTDB	PAS	Test of utility funtions
TIME	INC	Part of TEST.PAS
TIMESTMP	PAS	Reads the internal clock returning a string of the form
TSIN	PAS	Test range of sin function
TURBO-UT	PAS	Utilities to handle data input, validation of data
TURBO-UT	COM	Compiled version of TURBO-UT.PAS
TURBO-UT	DEM	Demo file for TURBO-UT.PAS
TURBO-UT	DOC	Documentation for TURBO-UT.PAS
TSTSOUND	COM	Part of TURBO-UT.PAS
UT-MOD??	INC	Part of TURBO-UT.PAS (6 files)

426 Turbo Pascal Routines #6
v1

This disk contains powerful Turbo Pascal routines to assist users with data format manipulation, graphics, register manipulation, and window manipulation tools. The two GRAPH programs manipulate a predefined object in a variety of ways. The PTOOLWIN routines provide window opening and closing with data saved and borders. Worth Your Attention: The TURBHERC is a collection of procedures for Hercules graphics support.

Usage: Turbo Pascal users

System Requirements: 128K, two disk drives, color or monochrome graphics, Turbo Pascal

How to Start: To read DOC files enter TYPE filename.ext and press ENTER. For instructions on PAS listings, refer to your Pascal language manual.

User Comments: "Nice package of window stuff" "The program PTOOLWI3 is excellent." "PTOOLWI3 is one of the best window management systems."

Suggested Donation: $20.00

File Descriptions:

GRAPH	PAS	Graphic manipulation of a model; demo of GRAPH2
GRAPH2	PAS	Graphic manipulation procedures
LASTRSTR	INC	Routine to restore registers
LASTSAVE	INC	Routine to save registers and restore previous contents
LASTWIN	INC	Provides further window capabilities
PIBPICT	DAT	Data for PIBPICT.PAS
PIBPICT	PAS	Demo of editing facilities of PICTFORM.PAS
PICTFORM	PAS	Edits variables or strings as in PL/1 or COBOL
PTOOLWI3	DOC	Description of PTOOLWI3.INC
PTOOLWI3	INC	Text window manipulation tools: open,close,borders
PTOOLWI3	PAS	Demo program for PTOOLWI3.INC
TURBHERC	PAS	Collection of procedures for Hercules graphics support

427 Turbo Pascal Routines #7
v1

This is a fascinating and useful assortment of Turbo Pascal routines and procedures. There are I/O routines for the joystick, PC Mouse, and asynchronous communications. Several routines provide menu capabilities, with stacked windows available. TURBORUN allows the user to issue DOS commands from within his Turbo Pascal program. The low-resolution graphics of PIBLORES is ideal for the color graphics of a user's game program. Timer interrupts, Turtle graphics, "help facility" for Pascal, and listings of source code and cross-reference on the screen or the printer are just a few of these helpful programs.

Usage: Turbo Pascal users

System Requirements: 128K, two disk drives, game port, serial port, monochrome or color graphics, Turbo Pascal

How to Start: To read DOC or TXT files, enter TYPE filename.ext and press ENTER.

- To run a COM program, just type its name and press ENTER. For instructions on PAS listings, refer to your Pascal language manual.

User Comments: "Works like a charm." "Good solid routines." "A good selection of Turbo Pascal routines."

File Descriptions:

JOYSTICK	PAS	Joystick control procedure & demo
MENUX	PAS	Generate & operate a user-defined menu
MOUSE	PAS	PC Mouse interface procedures
PIBDODOS	DOC	Description of TURBORUN.COM
PIBDODOS	PAS	Pascal routine to teach TURBORUN.COM
PLIST	COM	Output Pascal source & cross-ref to printer or screen
READENV	INC	Functions to search DOS environment area
READWKS	PAS	Print Lotus .WKS Worksheet file data
SERIAL	PAS	Routines for user to access COM1 & COM2
SERTST	PAS	Demo/test of SERIAL.PAS
THELP	COM	TURBO Pascal resident "help facility"
THELP	DOC	Description of THELP.COM
TPRO	PAS	Very fast screen output; screen handling
TPRO2	PAS	Get record fix from Borland's Turbo Toolbox
TPRO3	PAS	Draw line on screen at 13,000 pixels per second
TRBOEXT	PAS	Retrieve command line parameters
TURBLE	LBR	Turtle graphics in LBR form ... for hard disk
TURBLE	TXT	Description of TURBLE.LBR
TURBORUN	ASM	Assembler source code for TURBORUN.COM
TURBORUN	COM	Allows DOS commands from TURBO Pascal programs
XREFPAS	PAS	Cross-reference generator
POWERS	PAS	Computes an integer or real power of a real number
TIMER	PAS	Timer interrupt routine for IBM PC DOS 2.0
PIBLORES	PAS+	Low-resolution (160x100x16 colors) graphics
PIBASYNC	PAS	Asynchronous I/O for MS-DOS
PIBMENUS	PAS	Menu routines, similar to Lotus; stacked windows

---

428
Turbo Pascal Routines #8
v1

The Turbo Pascal routines on this diskette perform a wide variety of helpful functions ranging from string manipulation to playing music. GETDIR and PATHS will scan and change the MS-DOS directory and could even have options added to read system and hidden files. Included are communications support, a graphics library, a translator from 8088 Assembler source code to Pascal INLINE code, a very fast string writer to output to mono or color screens, screen scrolling and more.

Usage: Turbo Pascal users

System Requirements: 128K, two disk drives, Turbo Pascal

How to Start: To read DOC or TXT files enter TYPE filename.ext and press ENTER. For instructions on PAS listings, refer to your Pascal language manual.

User Comments: "The graphics system on this diskette is very, very good." 'A must for every civilized programer who wants structure and not 'wildlife' in his programs."

File Descriptions:

ARGLIST	PAS	Reads argument list, like argc/argv in C
COMMCALL	PAS	COM1 support; interrupt handling; one port
DIR	PAS	Outputs MS-DOS directory entries
FASTWRIT	PAS	Very fast strings to mono or color screen
GETDIR	PAS	Scan MS-DOS directory
GRAPHICS	LBR	Pascal graphics library
GRAPHICS	TXT	Installation instructions for GRAPHICS
GRAPHSRC	LBR	Pascal graphics library + demo
INLINER	PAS	Translates 8088 Assembler source to Pascal INLINE
PATHS	PAS	Get, create, delete, modify disk directories
SAMPDIR	PAS	Example of how to use GETDIR.PAS
SAMPPATH	PAS	Example of how to use PATHS.PAS
SCROLL	PAS	Scroll portion or all of screen up or down
STRNGLIB	DOC	Description of STRNGLIB.INC 6STRNGLIB /7INC /8String functions not provided in TURBO Pascal
PIBMUSIC	PAS	Play music like in BASIC PLAY statement

442
SPA:WN
Structured
Programming/Warnier
Diagram
v1

SPA:WN is an acronym for 'Structured Programming Automated: Warnier Notation'. This disk provides both a tutorial on the concepts of structured programming, and a working tool for design and documentation of the programs. Any target language is accomodated, but structured languages (Pascal, dBASE, True BASIC) work best. Design, automated code generation, and long-range documentation for maintenance are all provided for. This package is targeted at serious programmers; it may be daunting to the casual user, but the potential benefits are great.

Usage: Structured language programmers

System Requirements: 192K, two disk drives

How to Start: To read LST or READ.ME files, enter TYPE filename.ext and press ENTER.

• To run a COM program, just type its name and press ENTER.

User Comments: "Very good tutorial for structured programming." "A must for every civilized programmer who wants structure and not 'wildlife' in his programs." "Very useful but somewhat cumbersome in practice."

Suggested Donation: $50.00

File Descriptions:

DIR	DIR	Short description of the files on this disk
PWARN	COM	Executable code for Pascal Warnier program
PWARN	PAS	Turbo Pascal source for Warnier program
PWARN	WAR	SPA:WN source for Pascal Warnier program
READ	ME	Miscellaneous matters; expl'n of files
RODGERS	WAR	SPA:WN source for a FORTRAN program
SPAWN	BAT	Batch file for doing SPA:WN runs: 'SPAWN fn'
SUMMARY	USE	Brief, cryptic reminder of input requirements
WARNCMS	LST	Detailed instructions for CMS mainframe users
WARNIEEE	LST	Academically oriented paper about SPA:WN
WARNINTR	LST	Introduction for Structured Programming beginners

PRINTER UTILITIES:

Since no one presently alive will live to see "the paperless office," we all are going to have to get out some hardcopy sometime. The great frustration of most of us is that we have these extraordinary dot matrix and letter quality printers packed with features that few of us can get to without an expensive word processor or a resident computer whiz who can translate all those escape sequences. This collection can give you the benefit of thousands who have wrestled with this dilemma and have won.

Maximizing the quality and quantity of your printed output is the major thrust here. There are lots of programs designed for special applications like screen dumps, control of screen graphics, and using special print characteristics (boldface, underscore, italics, superscript and subscript). There are several text formatters, including one for large-scale document production and another to combine WordStar with Epson for technical document processing!

Admittedly, there is a heavy edge to Epson/compatibles in the specialty design packages here, but there are also whole packages for NECs, ProWriters, and TranStars! For the advanced and courageous, we have font and icon design packages to keep you up late at night.

---

48 RUNOFF

v1

RUNOFF is a simple text formatter that allows you to send form feed commands to the printer from DOS and gives you even more control of print commands from DOS. Along with EDIPAGE, FF, and PCFORM, this combination of program which allows you to "custom print" with greater control over your printout's appearance. The documentation gives you all the features and special functions that will assist you in running the program.

Usage: All PC users.

System Requirements: 128K, one disk drive, monochrome display and either a serial or parallel printer.

How to Start: Consult the .DOC and .TXT files for directions.

- To run a program with the suffix .COM, .EXE, or .BAT, just type its name, i.e., for FF.BAT, type FF and press ENTER.
- To run the BASIC programs, consult the directions in GETTING STARTED for your configuration.

Suggested Donation: $10.00

File Descriptions:

DATAFIX	BAS	Utility to add or delete line numbers from sequential files
EDIPAGE	BAS	Produces formatted listing of BASIC programs
FF	BAT	Sends formfeed to printer
FF	DOC	Description of FF.BAT
FF	TXT	Used by FF.BAT
FORTH	BAS	Implimentation of FORTH language in BASIC (From Dr Dobbs)
GROWTH2	BAS	Analysis trends and projects future growth rates
LOAN2	BAS	Calculates the missing loan amortization factor
PCFORM	BAS	Form generater example
QUADRIVE	DOC	Documentation for QUADRAM board
RUNOFF	BAS	Simple text formatter
RUNOFF	RNO	Sample text for RUNOFF text formatter
SERIAL	BAS	Allows printscreen command to work with serial printer

186

Screen and Printer Utilities

v1

Suggested Donation: $15.00

File Descriptions:

NOCOLOR	COM	Switch color graphics card to B/W mode
NOCOLOR	DOC	Documentation
SCRLKY	ASM	Assembler source
SCRLKY	COM	Better screen scrolling control
SCROLLK	COM	Another screen scrolling control utility
SCROLLK	DOC	Documentation
COMPRSOF	COM	Set compressed print off
COMPRSON	COM	Set compressed print on
CREATOR	BAS	Displays characters in dot matrix pattern
DBLHITOF	COM	Set enlarged print off
DBLHITON	COM	Set enlarged print on
DBLWDEOF	COM	Set wide print off
DBLWDEON	COM	Set wide print on
EMPHASOF	COM	Set emphasized print off
EMPHASON	COM	Set emphasized print on
EPSONCHR	ASM	Assembler source
EPSONCHR	DOC	Documentation
EPSONCHR	EXE	Permits printing all characters
ITALICOF	COM	Set italics off
ITALICON	COM	Set italics on
KYBD	BAS	Send printing directly to monochrome parallel port
PRINT20	DOC	Patch to skip LPT1: prompt from PRINT.COM
PRINTSET		Sets Epson to compressed print
PRINTSET	DOC	Documentation
PRTSCFX	COM	Graphics printing for Epson FX & RX
PRTSCFX	DOC	Documentation
MONOCG	ASM	Source code for monochrome display
PRTSCFX	ASM	Source code for PrtscFX
RESET	COM	Reset printer to power-on settings
SET-PRTR	C	Source
SET-PRTR	EXE	MX-80 printer settings
SET51LNS	COM	Set 51 lines per page
SETCW132	COM	Set 132 columns per page
SETPRF19	COM	Perforation setting
SKP6PERF	COM	Perforation setting — 6 lines/inch
SKP8PERF	COM	Perforation setting — 8 lines/inch
SP	DOC	Documentation
SP	EXE	Print spooler by Alan Jones
SPC	EXE	Print spooler for use with data communications
TOPOFORM	COM	Skip to top of form
UNDERLOF	COM	Set underline off
UNDERLON	COM	Set underline on

Here is an exceptional — in size and quality — collection of printer and spooler utilies primarily for the Epson printer.

PrtScFX is a screen dump program which prints a graphic image of a text mode display on an Epson FX or RX (not MX!) series printer. The printout looks just like a screen display, including connected line graphics, and can produce camera-ready quality hardcopy. PRINTSET provides the means of easily adding compressed print; EPSONCHR will print ALL 255 characters of the IBM character set on MX100, MX80 (IBM), or MX80 Graftrax (not Graftrax+) printers; others place color and other special features of the Epson printers at your finger tips. There are also some handy utilities, notably SCROLLK, one of public domain's favorites: this machine-language program is attached to DOS and allows much better scroll control than <Ctrl-NumLock>.

Usage: Epson printer users.

System Requirements: Epson printer, 128K, one drive, mono or color display.

How to Start: Consult the .DOC and .TXT files for directions

- To run a program with the suffix .COM, .EXE, or .BAT, just type its name, i.e., for SP.EXE, type SP and press ENTER.
- To run the BASIC programs, consult the directions in GETTING STARTED for your configuration.

User Comments: "Many of these little programs (e.g. TOPOFORM) are quite handy and take up little space." "PRTSCFX is an excellent printscreen utility. It is part of my system. I appreciate that it is compatible with the IBM graphics dump." "Good programs. Programs gives good instructions, but is limited on the use by way of changes in the spooler. Needs ability to change the buffer size from keyboard." "Everyone that owns an Epson printer should have this disk." "Everyone could use some of these utilities. I particularly like the program PRTSCFX. Now I can print the graphics from my screen to my RX100 printer also works well with the STAR SG-10 printer."

211 JUSTIFY and Speed Reader Demo
v1

JUSTIFY is a proportional spacing device for text printed on IBM, Epson or STAR Micronics printers. The Speed Reading Demo gives you a solid overview of this commercial program's style and exercises. LINEBUG is a very useful BASIC utility to verify line numbering.

Usage: Proportional spacing

System Requirements: Monochrome/graphics display, 64K, two drives

How to Start: After loading BASICA from DOS, switch disks to drive A: and type SR.BAS or LINEBUG.BAS. Run JUSTIFY.EXE directly from DOS.

File Descriptions:

ART	TXT	Part of Speed Reading demo
EYE	TXT	Part of Speed Reading demo
JUSTIFY	ASM	Assembler source code
JUSTIFY	EXE	Right/left micro-justifies text (COMFAX)
LINEBUG	BAS	Part of JUSTIFY.EXE
SR	BAS	Speed Reading demo (BBP)
TIMED	TXT	Part of Speed Reading demo
TUTOR2		Part of JUSTIFY.EXE
TUTORIAL		Part of JUSTIFY.EXE

220 Printer Utilities No 1
v1

This disk contains a copy of the SOFT and EASY Utilities for the PROWRITER I and II. In addition to the three main program procedures, there are ASCII files which contain copies of both the user's manual and the appendicies for that manual (together totaling 100+ pages!) Each of these ASCII files will produce a formatted manual, (or appendix), on your PROWRITER I or II dot matrix printer.

DO NOT ATTEMPT TO PRINT THESE FILES ON ANY OTHER PRINTERS. IT JUST WON'T WORK...

Usage: Prowriter users.

System Requirements: Prowriter printer, 128K memory, one drive, either monochrome or color display and graphics card.

How to Start: Consult the MANUAL.DOC and APPENDIX.DOC files for directions

- To run a program with the suffix .COM, .EXE, or .BAT, just type its name, i.e., for PRNT-SCN.COM, type PRNTSCN and press ENTER.
- To run the BASIC programs, consult the directions in GETTING STARTED for your configuration.

User Comments: "The documentation with this disk helped clarify many of the printer's functions that are described in the manual that comes with the printer. The programs on the disk had my printer performing tasks I didn't know it was capable of." "Very helpful with my Prowriter."

Suggested Donation: $30.00

File Descriptions:

PRNT-SCN	COM	Print screen utility
PRNT-CHR	COM	Allows italics and extended ASCII characters to be printed
PRNT-SET	COM	Program to allow printer to be setup easily
SCN-DEMO	BAS	Demonstration program for PRNT-SCN
CHR-DEMO	BAS	Demonstration program for PRNT-CHR
USMAP	PIC	Graphic test image of USA for use with SCN-DEMO
PRN-MAN	BAT	Batch file to print manual
MANUAL	DOC	Formatted manual (Use Prowriter I or II only
PRN-APX	BAT	Batch file to print appendix
APPENDIX	DOC	Appendix (Use Prowriter I or II only — 65K)
NOTICE		Message to those who print manual and/or appendix
README		Instruction for printing documentation

221
Printer Utilities No 2
v1

This disk contains a copy of the SOFT and EASY Utilities for the NEC 8023A. In addition to the three main program procedures, there are ASCII files which contain copies of both the user's manual and the appendicies for that manual (together totaling 100+ pages!) Each of these ASCII files will produce a formatted manual, (or appendix), on your NEC 8023A.

DO NOT ATTEMPT TO PRINT THESE FILES ON ANY OTHER PRINTERS. JUST WON'T WORK...

Usage: NEC 8023A owners

System Requirements: 8023A NEC printer, 128K, one disk drive and either a color or monochrome display.

How to Start: Consult the MANUAL.DOC and APPENDIX.DOC files for directions and documentation

- To run the BASIC programs, consult the directions in GETTING STARTED for your configuration
- To run a program with the suffix .COM, or .EXE, just type its name, i.e., for PRNT-SET.COM, type PRNT-SET and press ENTER.

User Comments: "This is a utility that really does what it is supposed to do." "Does nice screen dumps. Reasonable IBM printer emulation, but can be slow: try a PrtSc on PC-WRITE's No.1 helpscreen. Will work well for normal use." "Excellent explanations of codes and workings of NEC8023."

Suggested Donation: $10.00

File Descriptions:

PRNT-SCN	COM	Print screen utility
PRNT-CHR	COM	Allows italics and extended ASCII characters to be printed
PRNT-SET	COM	Program to allow printer to be setup easily
SCN-DEMO	BAS	Demonstration program for PRNT-SCN
CHR-DEMO	BAS	Demonstration program for PRNT-CHR
USMAP	PIC	Graphic test image of USA for use with SCN-DEMO
PRN-MAN	BAT	Batch file to print manual
MANUAL	DOC	Formatted manual (Use NEC 8023A only — takes 50 minutes — 124K)
PRN-APX	BAT	Batch file to print appendix
APPENDIX	DOC	Appendix (Use NEC 8023A only — takes 20 minutes — 61K)
NOTICE		Message to those who print manual and/or appendix
README		Instruction for printing documentation

222
Printer Utilities No 3
v1

This disk contains a copy of the SOFT and EASY Utilities for the TranStar printers. In addition to the three main program procedures, there are ASCII files which contain copies of both the user's manual and the appendicies for that manual (together totaling 60+ pages!) Each of these ASCII files will produce a formatted manual, (or appendix), on your TranStar 315 printer.

DO NOT ATTEMPT TO PRINT THESE FILES ON ANY OTHER PRINTERS. JUST WON'T WORK...

Usage: TranStar printer owners.

System Requirements: TranStar printer, 128K memory, one drive and either a monochrome or color display.

How to Start: Consult the MANUAL.DOC and APPENDIX.DOC files for directions and documentation

- To run the BASIC programs, consult the directions in GETTING STARTED for your configuration
- To run a program with the suffix .COM, or .EXE, just type its name, i.e., for PRNT-CHR.COM, type PRNT-CHR and press ENTER.

Suggested Donation: $10.00

File Descriptions:

PRNT-SCN	COM	Print screen utility
PRNT-CHR	COM	Allows italics and extended ASCII characters to be printed
SCN-DEMO	BAS	Demonstration program for PRNT-SCN
CHR-DEMO	BAS	Demonstration program for PRNT-CHR
USMAP	PIC	Graphic test image of USA for use with SCN-DEMO
PRN-MAN	BAT	Batch file to print manual
MANUAL	DOC	Formatted manual (Use TranStar 315 only — takes 50 minutes — 48K)

PRN-APX	BAT	Batch file to print appendix
APPENDIX	DOC	Appendix (Use TranStar 315 — takes 30 minutes — 36K)
NOTICE		Message to those who print manual and/or appendix
README		Instruction for printing documentation

225 PC-FONT
v1

PC-FONT enables an Epson MX (with Graftrax), RX, or FX printer to print 243 of the 256 ASCII characters. These characters include those applicable for engineering/scientific/financial, foreign language characters, and miscellaneous characters. Other capabilities include performing block graphic fonts and calling up one of 13 different fonts from the command line. Command line font selection allows the casual user a wide variety of output styles without having to research esoteric printer control codes.

Usage: Epson printer owners.

System Requirements: 96K, one disk drive, monochrome or color display, and one of the following printers: Epson MX (with Graftrax), RX, or FX printer or the IBM Graphics Printer.

How to Start: At the prompt enter TYPE PC-FONT2.PRN and press ENTER, this will print the on disk manual for the program

• To run it, enter PC-FONT2 and press ENTER.

User Comments: "I have an Epson FX-85 and this disk causes my printer to flex every muscle. A great disk to have, and really nice documentation. author has earned user support." "A very useful program to those who need to customize their printout. I found it easy to understand the instructions and am pleased with the program. Nearly a must for everybody who needs to print all 243 characters in good quality." "Does help make attractive printouts; it's great to get a manual with a piece of software." "Great printer control utility."

Suggested Donation: $20.00

File Descriptions:

PC-FONT2	EXE	Program to print 243 of PC's 256 characters
PC-FONT2	TST	Test file
DESCRIPT	TXT	Brief program description
PC-FONT2	PRN	Manual (70K bytes)
README		How to print manual

236 Printer Utilities No 4
v1.1

FPRINT's purpose is to print ASCII files, but with certain safeguards built-in for your convenience. For instance, a check will be made to see if it is indeed an ASCII file. If the program thinks you are trying to print a non-ASCII file, it will pause and tell you so. You then have the option to cancel your print request, or continue anyway. FPRINT also has a printer setup menu which can be useful for regular print jobs when you want specific printer settings. This can be very useful with the accompanying set of tables for using the Toshiba printer with Volkswriter Deluxe. The program converts the IBM codes into Toshiba codes and allows the user to use the various types of printer programs with ease.

Usage: Toshiba and Volkswriter printer users.

System Requirements: Toshiba printer with Volkswriter, 128K, one disk drive, and either a color or mono display.

How to Start: Consult the .DOC and README files for directions

• To run the BASIC programs, consult the directions in GETTING STARTED for your configuration
• To run a program suffixed .COM or .EXE, just type its name, i.e., for FPRINTF.EXE, type FRPINT and press ENTER.

Suggested Donation: $15.00 to $25.00 for Volkswriter to Toshiba

File Descriptions:

— — — —	— —	BPRINT (BASIC program lister) Version 1.05
BPRINT	EXE	List BASIC programs
FPRINT	EXE	List ASCII files
FPRINT	DOC	Documentation for FPRINT.EXE
FPRINT	HLP	Help file for FPRINT.EXE
FPRINT	TRY	Sample file for FPRINT.EXE

— — — —	— —	Toshiba/Volkswriter printer tables
README	— —	How to use the Toshiba printer/Volkswriter tables
INSTVXPT	RCE	Part of Toshiba printer/Volkswriter tables
IN12	FMT	Part of Toshiba printer/Volkswriter tables (5 files)
COPYPRTR	BAT	Copy file utilities for Toshiba/Volkswriter tables (3 files)
VXPRINT*	TBL	Part of Toshiba printer/Volkswriter tables

SIDEWAYS	EXE	Prints text file sideways on Epson printer
SIDEWAYS	PAS	Source for SIDEWAYS.EXE
OKICHAR	LBR	Library used for Okidata printers
OKICHAR	TXT	Explanatory text
OKIMENU	BAS	Menu based program for OKIDATA printer setup
OKIMENUC	BAS	Compressed (by BetaTools BDS) version of OKIMENU.BAS
OKIMENU	DOC	Documentation for OKIDATA.BAS (17K)
OKITALIC	BAS	Downloadable italics font for OKIDATA printer
PRINT1	EXE	XON/XOFF Serial printer driver Diable 630 and ?.
PRINT2	EXE	Same as PRINT1.EXE except drives COMM2 port
PRINT	DOC	Documentation for PRINT1.EXE and PRINT2.EXE

265
Printer and Graphics Utilities
v2

Three well-done and very different graphics utilites: GRAF displays mathematical functions; SPIRO simulates a spirograph; and DEFINE allows BASIC programmers use of PUT statements in graphics. The best of the printer utilites is OKIMENU.BAS which allows Okidata printer users a menu-driven approach to formatting their output. NOTE: OKIMENU.BAS will function properly on a printer with the Okidata-IBM Plug'n'Play ROMs installed.

Usage: Graphics users and Okidata printer owners.

System Requirements: 128K, one disk drive, color graphics card, graphics printer.

How to Start: Consult the .DOC and README files for directions

- To run the BASIC programs, consult the directions in GETTING STARTED for your configuration
- To run a program with the suffix .COM, or .EXE, just type its name, i.e., for SPIRO.EXE, type SPIRO and press ENTER.

Suggested Donation: $10.00

File Descriptions:

— — — —	— —	Graphics Utilities
SPIRO	EXE +	Simulates a Spirograph, you enter the parameters, it draws
SPIRO	DOC	Documentation for SPIRO.EXE (9K)
SPIRO	BAS	Source for SPIRO.EXE
SPIRO1	EXE +	Demonstration of SPIRO
GRAF	BAS +	Plots mathematical function on graphics screen
DEFINE	BAS +	Defines graphics characters for use with PUT statements
DEFINE	INS	Instruction file for DEFINE.BAS
THING	PLT	Sample data file for DEFINE.BAS
— — — —	— —	Printer Utilities

276
COLLIST 2.0
v1

The programs on this disk work together to list column type files on your printer in a superior format. The distribution disk is coded and needs to be decoded with the "START" command before normal use. The program features page-layout controls and program- or user-specified formatting. NOTE: User-specified settings become defaults until changed again.

Usage: Heavy printer users.

System Requirements: Printer, one drive, 128K memory and either a color or mono display.

How to Start: At the prompt type in START ENTER. The printout will give you the necessary directions on how to print the manual and all the other documentation that is on the disk to make it faster and easier for you to use these programs.

User Comments: "I think the documentation is not good for a novice user." "The program works but is very complicated and convoluted. Only the experienced need apply." "Very powerful but complex."

Suggested Donation: $10.00

File Descriptions:

RELSE-2	0	Displays title in directory
COLLST	PRE	" "
INSTALL	ED	" "
DISK		" "
START	TXT	Part of COLLIST
START	EXE	This is the program to start the decoding, type "start"
*	*	Part of COLLIST (17 more files)

326
Printer Utilities No 5

v1

A super collection of printer utilities for the popular Epson series, this one especially good for the setup and applications of the Epson FX-80 printer. You can get special, italics, doublestrike and compressed characters, print mailing labels and much more!

Worthy of your Attention: The DISKMASTER utility prints disk labels on 5" x 1 7/16" label stock. This size label just fits on the top of a standard 5 1/4 inch disk. The program supports EPSON, IBM and OKIDATA printers with plug'n'play. Many options are provided. Also, for those of you into banners, SIDEWAYS and POSTER are certainly worth playing with!

Usage: Epson FX-80 (and compatible) printer users.

System Requirements: Epson FX-80 printer, 128K memory, one drive and either a color or mono display.

How to Start: Consult the .DOC and README files for documentation

- To run the BASIC programs, consult the directions in GETTING STARTED for your configuration
- To run a program with the suffix .COM, or .EXE, just type its name, i.e., for DMASTER.EXE, type DMASTER and press ENTER.

User Comments: "(GRAF) Simple, and just what the doctor ordered. Much better than the IBM GRAPHIX, and more flexible. Produces two different sizes at your choice." "Helpful Epson print initialization programs." "It serves my needs quite well and the price is right. Would like to get more out of my Epson, this did it." "THE LABEL PROGRAM WAS GOOD AND I LIKED THE SETPRINT PROGRAM." "A must for everyone who owns a Epson-printer or compatible, as I do"

Suggested Donation: $10.00

File Descriptions:

BUZOFF	COM	? checks for printer
COLRVIEW	EXE	Print & display text file in color
EMBEDDED	BAS	Basic prog to demonstrate embedded print attributes
FASTPRT	COM	Resident speed up for PrtSc utility
FASTPRT	DOC	Documentation for FASTPRT.COM
FORMFEED	COM	Set prnter to top of form from DOS, batch file, Wordstar, etc.
FORMFEED	DOC	Documentation for FORMFEED.COM
FSPOOL	COM	Resident prog to redirect parallel prntr output to disk
FSPOOL	DOC	Documentation for FSPOOL.COM
FXPR4	DOC	Epson FX-80 utility to change print font sizes & styles
FXPR4	EXE	Documentation for FXPR4
GRAF	COM	print IBMPC graphics on bit-plot printers
GRAF	DOC	Documentation for GRAF.COM
JUST-LQ	EXE	Micro-justification file printer for EPSON LQ-1500
JUSTIFY	DOC	Documentation for JUSTIFY.EXE
JUSTIFY	EXE	Print justified copy on low priced printers with graphics cap.
DMASTER	CMT	Part of DiskMaster
DMASTER	CTL	Part of DiskMaster
DMASTER	EXE	DiskMaster program file
DMASTER	HLP	Help file for DiskMaster
LABEL	EXE	Prints n 5 line labels
P	COM	Powerful prntr utility — compress, double, italics,
PERFSKIP	COM	IBM or MX-80 printer utility to skip n lines over perforation
PERFSKIP	DOC	Documentation for PERFSKIP.COM
PLOTTER	BAS	Basic prog to plot graphs — linear, parabolic, trig., comb.
POSTER	BAS	Large poster maker. Puts your message on printer sideways.
PRINTES1	BAS	Printer test returns printer speed char/sec lines/min
PRINTFIX	COM	Possible fix for bad print — character/lines dropped
PRINTFIX	DOC	Documentation for PRINTFIX.COM
PRTPAGE	DOC	Documentation for PRTPAGE.EXE
PRTPAGE	EXE	Print with pagination — spool to disk, line numbering, etc.
SCNMAP	BAS	produces paper chart of 40 or 80 col screen Epson MX-80
SCNMAP	DOC	Documentation for SCNMAP.BAS
SETPRN	COM	Printer utility for IBMPC-set prn param from DOS or batch
SETPRN	DOC	Documentation for SETPRN.COM
SIDEWAYS	EXE	Prints a disk file sideways on printer
SWPTR	COM	Swaps printer LPT1: with printer LPT2:.
SWPTR	DOC	Documentation for SWPTR.COM

377
Printer Utilities No 6
v1

While this disk is packed with an amazing variety of printer utilities for printers from Gemini to Prowriter to NEC to LaserJets, the outstanding program is the PRINTER.COM, a program which allows you to use special print functions with ease on ANY make of printer. PRINTER.COM sets up your printer to make use of its special print functions (compressed print, double strike print, italics print, etc.). Whatever your printer has the capability to do, you can easily do it with PRINTER.COM.

But don't overlook BANNERIFIC! BANNERIFIC is a program which lets you produce large banners on your computer printer. All IBM PC keyboard characters may be used. The size of the characters produced on the printer is variable, and may be as large as the width of your computer paper.

Usage: Creative printer users.

System Requirements: 128K, one drive and either a color or monochrome display with the appropriate printer.

How to Start: Consult the .TXT and .DOC files for directions and documentation

- To run the BASIC programs, consult the directions in GETTING STARTED for your configuration
- To run any file marked .EXE or .COM, type its filename and press ENTER.

User Comments: "Wonderful!" "BANNER program is fun and actually somewhat useful. Would be nice to have a speicific list of the printers for which this disk applies."

Suggested Donation: $15.00

File Descriptions:

BANNERIF	DOC	Documentation for BANNERIF.EXE
BANNERIF	EXE	Print any size characters on your printer
CITOHSET	BAS	Sample file
COVER–TB	COM	Doesn't work
DIABLO	DOC	Documentation for DIABLO.EXE
DIABLO	EXE	Support a serial printer with ETX/ACK handshaking

EPSN-OKI	COM	Convert a "print" file from IBM/Epson format to Oki format
EPSN-OKI	DOC	Documentation for EPSN-OKI.COM
EW-PROWR	EWF	Use Prowriter or NEC 8023 printer with Easy Writer 1.1
EW-PROWR	TXT	Sample print file
GDUMP	BAS	Medium resolution graphic dump of C.ITOH 8510 and NEC 8023
GDUMP	EXE	Executable file of GDUMP.EXE
GEMINI	EXE	Configuration program for Gemini printer
GEMSET	EXE	Set up program for Gemini printer
GRCITOH	COM	Graphics dump for C.ITOH printer
HP7470A	BAS	Example of function for generating HP7470A plots
IDSPRISM	BAS	Initialize IDS Prism Color Printer
LASERJET	EXE	Configuration for Laserjet printer
NECGRAF	COM	Graphic screen dump for NEC printer
NECPLOT7	BAS	Demo plot for NEC 8023 printer
NECPRINT	BAS	Text editor for NEC PC-8023A
NECPRINT	TXT	Sample file for NECPRINT.BAS
NECPRTSC	COM	Driver for the NEC 8023 for the Shft-PrtSc screen print sequence
NECPRTSC	DOC	Documentation for NECPRTSC.COM
NECSCRN	COM	Graphics and text screen dump for NEC 8023A printer
NECSCRN	DOC	Documentation for NECSCRN.COM
NECSET	COM	Set the C Itoh 8510A or NEC 8023A-C printer parameters
NECSET	DOC	Documentation for NECSET.COM
OK84ASET	BAS	Okidata 82A configuration program
OKIDATA	EXE	Executable version of OK84ASSET.BAS
OKIDUMP	COM	Allow graphic screens to be printed on the line printer
OKIDUMP	DOC	Documentation for OKIDUMP.COM
OKIGRAF	COM	Graphic dump program for Okidata printers
OKISET	COM	Sends control characters to OkiData Microline 92 connected
OKISET	DOC	Documentation for OKISET.COM
PRINTER	COM	Allows use of special print functions on any make of printer
PRINTER	DAT	Part of PRINTER.COM
PRINTER	DOC	Documentation for PRINTER.COM
PROWRITE	EXE	Configuration set up for Prowriter printers
PROWRTER	DOC	Switch settings for Prowriter/NEC 8023 printer
SETOKI	COM	Set up program for Okidata printers

386
Banner
v1

BANNER makes long and large-letter banners on your printer from keyboard and console input. The program will do graphics as well as text. Included is the MS-FORTRAN source code so it can be customized to suit your needs. All together, one of the better programs of it's type available, and a good addition to anyone's collection.

Usage: Graphics users.

System Requirements: Graphics printer, 128K, one drive and either a color or monochrome display; Fortran complier optional

How to Start: Consult the README for directions

• To run it, use either BANV1 for DOS 1.0 or BANV2 for DOS 2.0 and above.

User Comments: "GOOD for printing out banners for birthdays, sales, etc. Some special characters other than the alphabet would have been nice." "Very impressive, although I would like to be able to control the size of the letters, the spacing between the lines of print, and the margins from the program. I would also like to be able to put more than one line of text on a banner." "Works very well. Had some wrinkles getting it to work with my Toshiba 1340 printer, but got it working."

Suggested Donation: $5.00

File Descriptions:

ACHN	FOR	Prints the second part of lower-case 'H' and 'N'
ACHN	OBJ	Compiled ACHN.FOR module
BANLNK	INP	Links input files for DOS V2 Banner
BANNER	FOR	Main program of BANNER
BANNER	OBJ	Compiled BANNER.FOR module
BANV1	EXE	Executable BANNER for PCDOS/MSDOS V1.x
BANV2	EXE	Executable BANNER for PCDOS/MSDOS V2.x
BAXX	FOR	Puts background symbols in the output lines
BAXX	OBJ	Compiled BAXX.FOR module
BLKDAT	FOR	Contains character data for output
BLKDAT	OBJ	Compiled BLKDAT.FOR module
FILES	SUM	Additional information about the files on this disk
FRNT	FOR	Puts foreground symbols in the output lines
FRNT	OBJ	Compiled FRNT.FOR module
LEGL	FOR	Prints the initial part of lower-case 'H', 'K', 'L', 'M',
LEGL	OBJ	Compiled LEGL.FOR module
LEGU	FOR	Prints the initial part of upper-case 'B', 'D', 'E', 'F',
LEGU	OBJ	Compiled LEGU.FOR module
MINMAX	FOR	Part of BANNER
MINMAX	OBJ	Compiled MINMAX.FOR module
OHAF	FOR	Prints the left or right part of upper-case 'O' for
OHAF	OBJ	Compiled OHAF.FOR module
OHAV	FOR	Prints the left or right half of lower-case 'O' for
OHAV	OBJ	Compiled OHAV.FOR module
PRNT	FOR	Manages the printing of each character
PRNT	OBJ	Compiled PRNT.FOR module
RASSIG	FOR	Assigns filename for the read routine
RASSIG	OBJ	Compiled RASSIG.FOR module
README	DOC	Documentation file
WASSIG	FOR	Assigns filename for write routine
WASSIG	OBJ	Compiled WASSIG.FOR module
BANV1	EXE	BANNER for PCDOS/MSDOS V1.x +
TECO	ARC	Editor w/docs useful for post-processing print files
PKARC	ARC	Archiver program and doc
PKXARC	ARC	Dearchiver program and doc

411
Printer Utilities
v1

This disk contains a set of utility programs that are useful in many printer applications. There are programs to print banners; to print data sideways for wide documents; to use print spoolers; to do graphic screen dumps to a wide variety of printers; to permit output that would normally go to the printer to be redirected to a disk file; to change printer settings; and the ever-popular SIDEWAYS program rounds out the disk.

Usage: Graphics users.

System Requirements: Graphics printer, 128K, one floppy drive, and either a color or monochrome display.

How to Start: Consult the .DOC and README files for documentation

• To run the BASIC programs, consult the directions in GETTING STARTED for your configuration
• To run a program with the suffix .COM or .EXE, just type its name, i.e., for BANNER85.EXE, type BANNER85 and press ENTER.

User Comments: "(EPSTAR)...Good program for beginners, good documentation, and supplies some basic printer utilities which can be very useful." "(LQ) This may be the most useful public domain program I have." "LQ is excellent, but needs improvement; it should have a pagination feature, for those word processors which need a separate formatter to paginate." "Banner85, LQ, Sideways, and all the gang on this disk seem to be in use constantly and I guess that is the best compliment of all." "Many useful printer aids. I especially like SPOOL and FPRINT." "Much of the documentation is not clear enough, but I think it is worth getting merely for the BANNER program."

Suggested Donation: $15.00 BANNER85

File Descriptions:

BANNER85	DOC	Documentation for BANNER85.EXE program
BANNER85	EXE	Makes sideways banners on any printer
EPSTAR	COM	Menu control of Epson/IBM/Star printers
EPSTAR	DOC	Documentation for EPSTAR.COM program
FPRINT	COM	Enhanced print spooler for PC/MS-DOS — prints a queue of
FPRINT	DOC	Documentation for FPRINT.COM program
FX	COM	Replacement for GRAPHICS.COM (graphics screen printer) for
GEMGRAPH	COM	Replacement for GRAPHICS.COM for Gemini 10X printer
GEMGRAPH	DOC	Documentation for GEMGRAPH.COM program
GRAFTRAX	COM	Replacement for GRAPHICS.COM for Epson MX80 printers
LASERFON	EXE	Laser printer settings
LPR	EXE	Line printer utility
LPTPORT	COM	Printer port switcher
LPTSWAP	COM	Printer port swapper
LQ	COM	Produce letter quality & proportional spacing on an Epson
LQ	DOC	Documentation for LQ.COM program
LU	EXE	Library file manager (menu driven)
OKIDUMP	COM	Downloading of all ASCII or italic characters to an
PERFSKIP	COM	Skip designated number of lines over perforations of fan-
PERFSKIP	DOC	Documentation for PERFSKIP.COM
PM	DOC	Documentation for PM.EXE program
PM	EXE	Print-Master program — modifies printer settings
PMCONFIG	PRT	Printer configuration file for C.Itoh Prowriter — used by
REDIRPRN	EXE	Redirects printer output to a disk file
REDIRPRN	TXT	Documentation for REDIRPRN.EXE program
SFTPRTSC	COM	Produce Shft/PrtSc (screen -> printer) from a batch file
SIDEWAYS	EXE	Sideways printing of text to Epson printers
SPOOL	DOC	Documentation for SPOOL.EXE program
SPOOL	EXE	Print spooler
TOF	COM	Advance printer to Top-of-Form from batch file or DOS
TOSHDUMP	EXE	Replacement for GRAPHICS.COM for Toshiba printers
TPRINT	COM	Replacement for PRINT.COM — start at any page
TPRINT	DOC	Documentation for TPRINT.COM program
VPRINT	COM	Redirect printer output to a disk file
VPRINT	DOC	Documentation for VPRINT.COM program

438 Printer Utilities

v1

A set of printer utility programs to ease setup for the Panasonic KX-1091, STAR MICRONICS, Gemini and Epson printers to take advantage of their special printing characteristics and options. Two programs of note:

The SET group is an Epson printer setup utility. It comes ready for the Epson FX80 (SETE) and LQ (SETLQ) versions. It gives you a menu to select commands sent to the printer to select or deselect: Elite, Pica, italics, emphasized, expanded, double strike and several others.

LISTASC.EXE (version 3.0) is designed to list BASIC files saved with an .ASC extension using the A (ASCII) parameter. The program formats the BASIC statements in the file to "paragraph" form using either standard or compressed font; line overflow is indented to provide easy reading. LISTASC supports the C.Itoh (8510), Epson (MX-80), Okidata (92), and IBM Proprinter (default setting).

Usage: Star, Gemini, Epson and Panasonic KX-1091 printer users.

System Requirements: Star, Gemini or Panasonic printer, 128K, one drive, graphics card and either a color or mono display.

How to Start: Consult the .DOC and README files for directions and documentation

- To run the BASIC programs, consult the directions in GETTING STARTED for your configuration.

User Comments: "EXCELLENT for specified printers." "Superceeded by RAM-based utilities." "Very good banner program; I using the printer utilities for my Star printer very useful program." "SIDEWAYS program does not work and no .doc file for it." "Very good printer utilities. Handy for setting printer from DOS."

Suggested Donation: $13.00

File Descriptions:

————	——	PANASONIC PRINTER SETUP UTILITIES
CR8CMD	EXE	Create a Mode & Options Command Sequence to program a
CR8CMD	DOC	User documentation for the above program
CR8READ	ME	Explanation of how to use the program
————	——	STAR MICRONICS GEMINI PRINTER UTILITIES
GEM'PRTR	BAS	Program to provide keyboard control
README	DOC	Detailed instructions
FILE1	TMP	This file is the command line for use when the Basic
INSTALL	BAT	This program selects one of the files FILE1.TMP or FILE2.TMP
README	BAT	This file simply issues a TYPE command with the |MORE
FILE2	TMP	This file is the command line for use when the Basic call
FILE3	TMP	This file is the command line for use when the Basic call
————	——	EPSON & STAR PRINTER SETUP UTILITIES
SETE	COM	Epson printer setup utility
SETE	ASM	Assembly source for SETE
SETLQ	COM	Epson Letter Quality printer setup utility
SETLQ	ASM	Assembly source for 2SETLQ
SET	DOC	Help file for SETLQ and SETE
————	—	BANNER PROGRAM
BANNER	EXE	A program for printing wide banners on your printer
————	——	BASIC PROGRAM LISTER
LISTASC	EXE	Lists Basic programs — compiled program executable code
LISTASC	DOC	Program instructions and user notes

485 Icon Maker & FX Matrix

v1

Icon Maker is a well structured, menu-driven character generator that allows you to create, save, and print graphical icons and cross stitch graphics interactively in any of three graphical modes supported by the IBM PC family. These three modes include the high resolution 640 X 200 two color, the 320 X 200 four color, and the 160 X 100 sixteen color.

The combination of files listed as the FX programs also allow you special design opportunities on Epson's FX and JX printers. The most important are: FXMATRIX.COM, the main program, is a matrix program that permits design of your own characters, store them in a file, and download them to the Epson FX and JX dot matrix printers;

FX.COM which automatically downloads a designated character file; and FXPRINT.COM is a simple print driver that will print an ASCII file that makes use of the flip from ROM to RAM of the FX and JX printers. The rest are special features and implementation files that the documentation will assist you in using.

Usage: Epson printer users

System Requirements: 192K, Epson/compatible printer, graphics card, two disk drives and monochrome or color display.

How to Start: To read the documentation type TYPE IM.DOC or FXEDIT.DOC and press ENTER.

● To run, enter program name and press ENTER.

User Comments: "Really a fun program to use for drawing real looking pictures on a printer." "Lots of different colors to use and easy to run." "Very impressive for user-supported software; makes me want to upgrade my system again!"

Suggested Donation: FXMATRIX $18.00; ICON MAKER $10.00

File Descriptions:

————	——	Icon Maker (v1.0)
IM	EXE	Create graphic icons and cross stitch graphics
IM	DOC	Documentation for Icon Maker program
DOTGRAPH	TXT	Text about 16 color dot graphics on the PC
————	——	Fx Matrix (v1.0)
FXMATRIX	COM	Character designer for use with FX-programs
FX	COM	Downloads character files
FXPRINT	COM	Prints ASCII files
COMMAND	COM	Command file
GRID	COM	Utility for printing 16 x 22 character grids
ANSI	SYS	System file
COMFILE	SYS	System command file
CONFIG	SYS	System configure file
ALPHA	FAC	Default ASCII characters
ALPHA	FXF	Default ASCII characters
AUTO	FXF	Automatic download file
BIG	FXF	Test file for big characters
BIGALPHA	FXF	Large CAPS
BLOCK	FXF	Block letters
TEST	TXT	Test file for use with FXPRINT.COM
FXEDIT	DOC	Documentation on FX-programs

F	DAT	Data file for FONTDEMO.BAT
IMPTUTR1	TXT	Simple ImagePrint demonstration
IMPTUTR2	TXT	Detailed ImagePrint demonstration
FTABLE	TXT	Font ASCII table.
NATIONAL	COM	Redefine ImagePrint to ten international character sets,
PCWRT24	HLP	Patch for PC-Write 2.4-2.55 help file HELPE.DEF
PCWRT26	HLP	Patch for PC-Write 2.6 help file ED.HLP
PC-WRITE	DEF	PC-Write definition file

517
ImagePrint Version 1.4
V1.1

ImagePrint is a program which allows you to produce high quality characters on a dot matrix printer. ImagePrint produces the IBM Graphics Printer's character set, which matches the IBM PC's character set, in letter quality. Text input to ImagePrint can come either directly from the keyboard (typewriter mode) or from a disk file. The text input can contain embedded backslash "/" commands, which select bold, underlining, double width, italics, superscript, subscript, half high, ten or twelve characters per inch, compressed, proportional spacing, etc. Text can be formatted (left and right micro-justification, hard and soft hyphens, margins, headers and footers, etc.) with ImagePrint's built-in formatting capabilities.

Usage: IBM/Epson printer users.

System Requirements: IBM/Epson printer, graphics card, DOS, 128K one drivem, color/mono display.

Features:

- Controlled by simple backslash commands, e.g., "/B" = bold
- Four print qualities: draft, fast quality, laser
- Text formatting, including micro-justification!
- Print using bold, underline, proportional spacing, italics, etc.
- Each font has full extended IBM graphics Printer character set
- Compatible with DOS 1.0 and above

How to Start: Consult the README and MANUAL.DOC files for directions and documentation.

- To run the main program, enter IMP80 and press ENTER.

Suggested Donation: $10.00 for basic registration level; $20.00 for an additional six fonts.

File Descriptions:

README		Introduction, directions
IMP80	EXE	ImagePrint program
FONT1		Cubic font
MANUAL	DOC	ImagePrint User Manual
FONTDEMO	BAT	Demonstration of all Image Computer Systems fonts

523
SIDE WRITER
V1

Sidewriter is a program that allows printers to output sideways on paper. This allows the printing of reports and other materials that do not fit in the number of columns allowed across a page, because it prints down the length of the sheet instead of across the width. The program is written in Pascal and the source code is provided with the package. Side Writer prints existing text sideways, allowing unlimited print width. Spreadsheet columns can be printed on one continuous page. The function keys and menus make it easy to learn and use.

Usage: Spreadsheet users.

System Requirements: 128K, one or more disk drives, and either a color or monochrome display and an IBM/Epson or ThinkJet printer.

How to Start: Consult the .DOC files for directions and documentation.

- To run any program with the suffix .COM or .EXE, just type its name, e.g., for SWC.COM, type "SWC" and press ENTER.

Suggested Donation: $15.00

File Descriptions:

SAMPLE	PRN	Sample 123 print file
SAMPLE	WKS	Sample 123 worksheet
SIDE	SET	Sidewriter configuration file
SIDEWRIT	ARC	Sidewriter program backup in archive format
SW	DOC	System documentation for SIDEWAYS.EXE
SWC	COM	Sidewriter for color screen
SWM	COM	Sidewriter for monochrome screen
SIDEWAYS	EXE	Sidewriter executable program
SIDEWAYS	PAS	Sidewriter Pascal source code

526 WSMX80 Version 4.1

v1

Designed to be used with Epson MX/RX/FX dot matrix and "Epson-compatible" printers, this product provides an impressive variety of enhancements for WordStar documents. It should be especially useful to users of WordStar involved with mathematical and scientific notation. Character density, size and style are all subject to a wide range of variation. Any part of the document can be printed in italics, boldface, "doublewide" or compressed type. Sub-scripts and superscripts are included. WSMX80 prints a variety of underline styles and strikeovers. WSMX80 can insert alternate character sets, such as the Greek alphabet included in the product, or custom character sets designed by the user. There are also features for Table of Contents and Indexes of the document being printed.

Usage: WordStar and Epson users.

System Requirements: WordStar 3.0 or better. Epson printer or compatable, 256K memory, one drive and either a color or mono display.

How to Start: Consult the .TXT and .DOC files for documentation.

● To run a program marked .EXE or .COM, just type its name, i.e., for WSMX.EXE, type WSMX and press ENTER.

Suggested Donation: $25.00

File Descriptions:

README	TXT	Notes on how to print documentation (TYPE "GO" to Display)
WSMX	EXE	Main program
CHRCOM	EXE	Character look-up program
WPATCH	EXE	WORDSTAR patch
DBL	TXT	Text file with examples of Double high text
DBL	CHR	Double high character code file
GREEK	TXT	Text file with examples of Greek text
GREEK	CHR	Greek character code file
GREEKD	TXT	Text file with examples of Greek text for the Diablo printer
GREEKD	CHR	Greek character code file for the Diablo printer
WSMXDOC	TXT	Instruction Manual
OMSG	TXT	Licence information; how to register
HAPPY	PRN	Disc Backup and Manual instructions can be printed with WSMX

640 LIST

v1

LIST is a printer-related utility program designed to aid programmers and others with simple document printing requirements. The program controls printing of documents, providing automatic pagination, page numbering, titling, printing of headers and footers, and a number of other similar features. Most significantly, the program easily handles printing multiple documents, such as might occur when a programmer wishes to print out all program source code files used on a project.

Usage: Document printing

System Requirements: 256K, one floppy drive and a monochrome, black & white, or color monitor.

How to Start: After consulting the documentation in LIST.DOC, initiate the program by running INSTALL and then LIST.

Suggested Donation: $10.00

File Descriptions:

README	DOC	Contents, installation and execution of LIST
INSTALL	BAT	Batch file to install LIST for display type
LINSTALL	COM	Program run by the BAT file
LIST	COM	Main program
LIST	DOC	Documentation file

PROGRAMMER UTILITIES:

Here are the goodies for all you aspiring and perspiring programmers! The range is large: collections of BASIC aids for structuring, listing and subroutines; Assembly language tutorials and callable subroutines; business application routines for dBASE II and III programmers; Turbo Pascal collections for scientists and engineers; and of course, miscellaneous groupings of utilities, such as: Logo programs, Lisp in Pascal, Assembly code, C code, and graphics code.

Among the unique and fascinating tools available is the public domain version of a powerful parser and an ever-growing library of Turbo Pascal tools, presently twelve disks packed with everything from subroutines to full utilities and programs. A great example of the power and fun Turbo Pascal can be are the graphics design package and its companion sprites design package.

The emphasis here is definitely towards applications-oriented programming. And while working within the language and data structures is the design of the Languages Utilities section, we urge you to search each section for pertinent programs.

---

7 — EXPLIST
v1

Here are four of our earliest user-supported programming aids. EXPLIST (for Expanding Lister) is the most powerful, giving a structured code look to BASIC listings. It does this by adding blank lines between specific keywords (GOTO, NEXT, etc); FOR...NEXTs and WHILE...WENDs are indented; and nested loops are indented even more. REMarks are highlighted in several ways. PRINT works with EXPLIST to print the listings with title headings and page numbers.

BIHEX converts any file to ASCII (7 bit) for modem transfer or printing. LF prints a directory alphabetically with the post script on the right of the list, and all names associated with that post script grouped to the left of the list.

Usage: EXPLIST is for BASIC programers; rest are general.

System Requirements: 64K, one disk drive and monochrome display.

How to Start: Consult the .DOC and README files for directions and documentation

- To run the BASIC programs, consult the directions in GETTING STARTED for your configuration
- To run a program with the suffix .COM or .EXE, just type its name, i.e., for LF.EXE, type LF and press ENTER.

User Comments: "Brings much better readability to most BASIC programms I use. No problems running on my "clone" COPAM PC-501AT under MS-DOS v3.1" "Documentation is needed to make this program run better." "Excellent value. Nice, clean, simple stuff. Very straight forward."

Suggested Donation: EXPLIST $15.00

File Descriptions:

EXPLIST	EXE	Expanding lister for BASIC programs
EXPLISTR	EXE	Expanding lister requiring compiler runtime library
EXPLIST	DOC	Documentation file for Expanding Lister
EXPOPT		Options file — EXPLIST.EXE
EXPMAIL	EXE	Generates a reply/contribution letter to author
PRINT	BAS	Prints ASCII files with title banner and page #'s

PRINTNEC	BAS	Same as "print" for NEC 8023/C.Itoh 8510 printers
BIHEX	BAS	Converts binary files to ASCII hex and back again
LF	COM	Directory list sorted alphabetically by extent & name

8 CROSSREF
v1

Here are two excellent user-supported BASIC programming tools. CROSSREF produces a cross-reference listing of variables referenced in a BASIC program, with line numbers. MONITOR provides a user interface for any BASIC application, by creating a "library" of small BASIC modules which set up the screen, display menus, ask questions and more. They give a uniform, professional look to your programs and, more importantly, relieve the programmer from "re-inventing the wheel" for each application.

Usage: Intermediate to advanced BASIC programers.

System Requirements: 64K, one disk drive and monochrome display.

How to Start: Read and then print the file CROSSREF.DOC. The directions to run the programs are on that file.

User Comments: "CROSSREF is nice if you need something like it." "Easy to use and bug free. Sound package. Helpful utility for BASIC programmers." "Great for small programs but locks up for large programs or for programs with a lot of variables, GOSUB, etc."

Suggested Donation: CROSSREF and MONITOR $15.00

File Descriptions:

CROSSREF	EXE	Extensive cross-reference generator for BASIC programs
CROSSREF	DOC	Documentation file
CRMAIL	EXE	Generates a reply/contribution letter to the author
CROSSOPT		Options file
CROSSWDS	DAT	Data file
MONITOR	BAS	BASIC subroutines for formatted screen displays
MONITOR	DOC	Documentation file

9 SQUISH
v1

This disk is half BASIC subprograms and the rest are DOS file-handling programs. The BASIC programs are all modules to be used in other programs for both programming ease and consistency. These are nice, reuseable general purpose modules, like NUMVERT.BAS which displays numbers in ASCII, dec, oct, hex and binary.

The other programs help with day to day computer activities. LOOK and FIND search memory for certain bytes and strings. SQUISH saves space by removing unwanted extra bytes from BASIC programs. Other goodies include an autostart device, programs to shift you from monochrome to color graphics and back, and even a miniature modem package with file transfer capacity (MDM7I).

Usage: Intermediate to advanced

System Requirements: 64K, one disk drive and monochrome display.

How to Start: Consult the .DOC and README files for directions and documentation

- To run the BASIC programs, consult the directions in GETTING STARTED for your configuration
- To run a program with the suffix .COM or .EXE, just type its name, i.e., for FF.BAT, type FF and press ENTER.

File Descriptions:

ACATALOG	BAS	A catalog of the programs on this disk (Items 1-31)
ASCICHAR	BAS	Display or Prints primary and alternate character sets
ASCII	BAS	A chart of ASCII Characters (Decimal)
AUTOINST	BAS	Prints Autostart Program Instructions (AUTOST.BAS)
AUTOPEEK	BAS	Displays 10 locations of memory in dec or hex
AUTOST	BAS	Sets date and time, displays files and runs program
CHECKOUT	BAS	Checks Serial and Parallel equipment & handshake
COLORSET	BAS	Displays color options on a color monitor
KEYSBAS	BAS	Programs Function keys for BASIC and prints OVERLAY
KEYSMP	BAS	Prints a Function Key OVERLAY for Multiplan programs

LONGZONE	BAS	Computes GMT (UCT) and local time for any longitude
MENU	BAS	Runs AUTOST.BAS program
MINIPROG	BAS	A Skeleton BASIC program used to start a new program
MODULO	BAS	Demonstrates Modulo Arithmetic
MONOSET	BAS	Displays screen options for the monochrome monitor
NUMVERT	BAS	Displays numbers in ASCII, dec, oct, hex and binary
OPKEYS	BAS	Programs the Function Keys for BASIC programming
PAYMENT	BAS	Computes payment for a fully amortized loan
PEEK	BAS	Peeks at a location in memory
Q	BAS	Returns to DOS with a clear screen and keys reset
REAL$	BAS	Displays and prints a table of Real Estate Appreciation
SYS	BAS	Returns to DOS with a clear screen and keys reset
TIME	BAS	Displays system date and time on the screen
!	BAT	Boots up BASICA and AUTOST from DOS
AUTOEXEC	BAT	Boots up BASICA and AUTOST from power ON Startup
STARTUP	BAT	Transfers DOS and BASICA from DOS Disk in B to Disk in A
2COLOR	COM	Transfers to Color Graphics Adapter and Monitor from DOS
2MONO	COM	Transfers to Monochrome Adaptor and Monitor from DOS
DISKID	REV	Contains Disk ID Label and Year for AUTOST program
2COLOR	SYS+	Transfers to Color Graphics Adapt and Monitor from BASICA
2MONO	SYS	Transfers to Monochrome Adaptor and Monitor from BASICA
INDEX	DOC	This contains details on files on this disk
MDM7I	COM	This is a MODEM and TERMINAL file transfer program
MDMIBM	ASM	Part of MDM7I above
MDM7	DOC	This describes how the modem program is to be used
CRCK4	COM	This a file checksum program
CRCK4	CPM	Part of CRCK4.COM
LOOK	COM	This is a memory byte search program
FIND	COM	This is a disk file string search program
WASH	COM	This is a disk maintenance program
WASH	DOC	This documents WASH.COM
SQUISH	BAS	This program removes spaces, REM's and condenses lines
SQUISH	DOC	Documentation for SQUISH program

60

UTIL 1.2/MAKE/BASREF

v1

BASREF produces a listing of variables in a BASIC program. The cross reference produced lists for every variable and line number as referenced by a line-numbered GOTO, GOSUB, THEN, ON... that appears in your BASIC program. The program will read any type of file, ASCII or tokenized. The listing can be sent to the screen, printer, or disk file. An interactive menu guides the user through the program, with help menus available. A formatted listing of the program can also be printed.

The other two programs are designed for doing housekeeping chores: UTIL is a flexible ASCII text file manipulator and appender; MAKE converts Easywriter 1.1 files to DOS files.

Usage: BASREF is for BASIC programmers, MAKE is for Easywriter users and UTIL is for everybody.

System Requirements: 64K, one disk drive and monochrome display.

How to Start: From the DOS prompt enter TYPE MAKEDOC1.DOC for MAKE, and TYPE BASREF.DOC for BASREF. UTIL's help file is called UTIL.HLP

Suggested Donation: UTIL $3.00; BASREF $15.00

File Descriptions:

— — —	— —	UTIL 1.2 for text file manipulation
UTIL	EXE	Main program
UTIL	HLP	Documentation for UTIL program (15K)
DEMO?	BAT	Demonstration files for UTIL.EXE (8 files)
TF1		UTIL dummy text file
TF2		UTIL dummy text file
— — —	— —	BASREF, a BASIC cross-reference lister
BASREF	DOC	Documentation for BASREF
BASREF	EXE	Produces cross-reference list of variables in BASIC program
— — —	— —	MAKE, Easywriter to DOS file conversion
MAKE	COM	Main program to convert EASYWRITER (1.1) files to DOS files
MAKE????	DOC	Documentation for MAKE (4 files)

110
Programmer Utilities No 2
v1

A Programmers Toolbag! This disk holds lots of little tools, such as AUTOFILE, PRINTER, DEFINE, SCRN, and DOSCOLOR, which are all BASIC utilities. HC, SIZER, UPPER, and WHEREIS are all tools which perform some function on files from the DOS prompt. The rest are miscellaneous utilities.

Usage: Half for BASIC programmers; rest are general

System Requirements: 64K, one disk drive and monochrome display.

How to Start: After loading DOS type DIR *.DOC for all the text files on this disk. Each one describes its own utility and are well documented that way.

User Comments: "Fine as far as it goes. Needs enhancement to support my new LQ1000. People with older equipment may not need the help. I bought for this one util & am ambivalent about it." "Can use alone but not with software. I use only Ramdisk. It is nice to specify the size of the ramdisk I want via the CONFIG.SYS file, and I use the ramdisk with PC-Write and PC-Calc."

Suggested Donation: Generally $3.00 to $15.00

File Descriptions:

AUTOFILE	BAS	Free format filer/indexer with keyed lookup
AUTOFILE	BAT	Batch file for invoking AUTOFILE
AUTOFILE	DOC	Documentation for AUTOFILE
DEFINE	BAS	Create pictures your BASIC programs can GET/PUT
DEFINE	DOC	Documentation for DEFINE
DOSCOLOR	BAS	Program to set colors used by DOS 2.0
DOSCOLOR	BAT	Batch/documentation file for DOSCOLOR
HC	COM	Fast, assembly coded hex-binary file converter
HC	DOC	Documentation for the above
PRINTER	COM	Menu-driven printer mode setup program
PRINTER	DAT	File to customize the above for your printer
PRINTER	DOC	Documentation for PRINTER program
PRINTER	ASM	Source for PRINTER program
RAMDISK	SYS	DOS 2.0 RAM disk sized by parameter in CONFIG.SYS
RAMDISK	DOC	Documentation for RAM disk program
ROMBIOS	ASM	Source include file for ROM BIOS data areas

SCRN	ASM	BASIC-callable routines for display windowing
SCRN	DOC	Documentation for the above
SIZER	COM	Checks the size of a file and sets ERRORLEVEL
SIZER	DOC	Documentation for SIZER program
SIZER	ASM	Source for SIZER program
STEEPDES	APL	Steepest descent equation solution in APL
TABLET	BAS	Interactive graphics editor
UPPER	COM	Filter program to convert file to upper case
UPPER	DOC	Documentation for UPPER program
UPPER	ASM	Source for UPPER program
WHEREIS	COM	Names all the subdirectories containing a given file
WHEREIS	DOC	Documentation for WHEREIS
XT370	DOC	Insider information on the new PC XT/370

126
dBASE II Programs
v1

Here are seven routines that will enhance your overall business use of dBASE II. Included are mini-programs for such tasks as: form letter generator, mailing label manager, a back-up routine, a library routine, a state-zip code checker, and a conversion program.

Usage: dBASE II programmers

System Requirements: 64K, one disk drive and monochrome display, 192K needed for dBASEII software.

How to Start: Copy the programs marked *.prg to your DBASE II disk, then from the DOS prompt enter TYPE DOC.TXT for instructions on how to run the programs from inside DBASE II.

User Comments: "Not complete. Missing several format files in the mailing list program." "Parts only of value inside US." "This collection of dbase II programs has been very useful to me. I have used several of the programs in applications and find that they work wonderfully. Keep up the good work."

Suggested Donation: $10.00 per

File Descriptions:

BACKUP	PRG	dBASE II backup routine
SUPERBAK	PRG	dBASE II backup routine
STATEX	NDX	dBASE II state & zipcode checker
STATEZIP	DBF	Part of dBASE II state & zipcode checker

STATEZIP	PRG	Part of dBASE II state & zipcode checker
DOC	TXT	Documentation
————	——	dBASE II form letter generator
MAIL	PRG	dBASE II form letter generator
MAIL	DBF	Part of dBASE II form letter generator
MAILENTR	PRG	Part of dBASE II form letter generator
MAILFMT	FMT	Part of dBASE II form letter generator
MAILINFO	PRG	Part of dBASE II form letter generator
MAILLAB	PRG	Part of dBASE II form letter generator
MAILLTTR	PRG	Part of dBASE II form letter generator
MIS	DBF	Part of dBASE II form letter generator
PRINT	TXT	Part of dBASE II form letter generator
————	——	dBASE II mailing label manager
ML2	PRG	dBASE II mailing label manager
ML2	DOC	Documentation for dBASE II mailing label manager
ML2	DBF	Part of dBASE II mailing label manager
ML2*	PRG	Mailing label manager program files (16)
MLABEL5	PRG	Part of dBASE II mailing label manager
*	PRG	dBASE II library routine (16 files)

File Descriptions:

ANIMAL	BAS	Guess the animal game
ANIMAL	GME	Sample data file of animals for ANIMAL.BAS
BANNER	BAS	Make large banners on the screen
LBANNER	BAS	Make large banners on the printer
BARIC	BAS	Two person Tron like game
HAMURABI	BAS	Be king for a ten year term
PICTURE	BAS+	3-D graphic demo (Requires color graphics)
PINWHEEL	BAS	Animated program listing
KBD–FIX	BAS	Creates KBD–FIX.COM
KBD–FIX	COM	Increase keyboard buffer to 159 characters
DAY	PRG	dBASE II program to find day of week
DATE	PRG	dBASE II program to set date from system date
TIME	PRG	dBASE II program to get system time
COMSTRIP	PRG	dBASE II program to strip comments from other dBASE II programs
GEMINI	ABS	Fix to use DOS 2.0 graphic dump on Gemini printer
CATALOG	TXT	List of files on this disk
DBS	EXE	Program to generate dBASE II & III screens

128 PC-SIG Sampler No 6

v1

This disk is split. Half are dBASE II utilities and half are miscellaneous programs. The dBASE II files make day to day use of DBASE II easier (automatically set date and time, set up initial conditions, ect.) The other half consists of games, presentations, and DOS utilities. There's even a fix for GEMINI printers.

Usage: BASIC & DBASE II and III programmers.

System Requirements: 64K, one disk drive and monochrome display; 192K needed for dBASE II software.

How to Start: To use DBASE II programs make sure the *.PRG programs are on your DBASE work disk, then type DO filename from the DBASE dot prompt.

User Comments: "Not particularly useful, as I have DBASE III, and most of the BASIC programs from other sources." "DBSCREEN makes this disk worth purchasing. This program makes dBASE much more practical to use." "This program certainly makes input screen setup easy compared to entering screen coordinates."

140 DOS Utilities No 7

v1

This disk has several file maintanence programs. LU, GDEL, GCOPY, SQ-USQ, and EJLUTIL's all concern themselves with mass file storage and handling. FREE works like CPM's STAT, by locating free room on the disk. The 8087 files are routines to easily incorporate the Intel 8087 math chip into high level languages.

Usage: All but most helpful for large capacity hard disks.

System Requirements: 64K, one disk drive and monochrome display.

How to Start: From DOS prompt enter TYPE EJLUTIL.DOC for information about EJLUTIL. then enter LU EJLUTIL to unsqueeze EJLUTIL. GDEL, GCOPY, LU, and SQ-USQ all have .DOC files to explain them.

User Comments: "(FREE) I use it often." "(GDEL) just a little slow. I use them often." "SQUEEZE/UNSQU" Not quite versatile enough (you cannot choose the name you want a file to unsqueeze to), and confusing to use. But very useful and great for archiving." "Squeeze is slow; I use the NUSQ (disk #139) version of unsqueeze, and it is not slow."

File Descriptions:

EJLUTIL	LBR	A library of useful utilities. Unpack with LU.EXE
EJLUTIL	DOC	Documentation for the utility library
FLCHART	WKS	1-2-3 worksheet macros for drawing flowcharts
FREE	COM	Reports free space on hard or floppy disk
GCOPY	EXE	Choose multiple files to copy from full-screen menu
GCOPY	DOC	Documentation for GCOPY.EXE
GDEL	EXE	Choose multiple files to delete from full-screen menu
GDEL	DOC	Documentation for GDEL.EXE
INTOOLS	PAS	A set of interactive keyboard I/O procedures and functions
LU	EXE	The latest and best library maintainer
LU	DOC	Documentation for LU.EXE
M8087	MAC	Macros for issuing 8087 instructions
PAS87	ASM	Assembler subroutines for using 8087 from Pascal
P87–INT		Pascal interface to PAS87.ASM routines
SQPC161	EXE	The latest file squeeze utility
USQLC10	COM	The latest file unsqueeze utility
SQ-USQ	DOC	Documentation for SQPC161.EXE and USQLC10.COM
X2COLOR	COM	Copies the monochrome screen to the color display

141
Programmer Utilities No 5
v1

This disk contains 2 BASIC utilities, a LOTUS 1-2-3 utility, and a DOS tool. 123PREP allows you to quickly create a properly formatted input file for 1-2-3's IMPORT feature. AID will reduce or eliminate repetitive steps which are usually required in the creating, editing, and using of BASIC programs. SCREENIN provides the BASIC programmer with a customizable, generalized screen input program which will reduce duplication of BASIC code from program to program (very useful if all your programs require some input from the user). W20 is a mini-DOS manager which presents the user with a menu of standard DOS file functions (copy, delete, print, etc.) and each file in the directory (sorted alphabetically).

Usage: BASIC programmers, 1-2-3 users who input text files, and DOS users who like menus and don't like DOS commands.

System Requirements: 64K, one disk drive and monochrome display; For 1-2-3 uses, system software required.

How to Start: Consult the .DOC and README files for directions and documentation

- To run the BASIC programs, consult the directions in GETTING STARTED for your configuration
- To run a program with the suffix .COM or .EXE, just type its name, i.e., for 123PREP.EXE, type 123PREP and press ENTER.

File Descriptions:

123PREP	EXE	Converts a simple text file to a 1-2-3 form
123PREP	DOC	Documentation for 123PREP.EXE
AID	BAS	A BASIC programming development aid
AID	EXE	Compiled version of AID.BAS
AID	BAT	Batch file for invoking AID
AID	DOC	Documentation for the AID system
SCREENIN	BAS	Full-screen formatted input subroutine for BASIC
SCREENIN	DOC	Documentation for SCREENIN.BAS
W20	COM	Directory "wash" program — list/copy/view/delete multiple files

142
Programmer Utilities No 6
v1

A disk for advanced and advancing programmers! This disk holds quite a varied list of utilities. It contains Logo programs, BASIC code, Lisp in Pascal, Assembly code, C code, and graphics code. BASSUB calls DOS 2.x functions from BASIC programs. KVUTIL provides a screen management function for DOS. AFT8087 and TRAN both support math functions in ASM and C respectively. LDIR and LTYPE add screen display and printing of files squeezed by LAR. The other files fill out the disk and are "icing on the disk".

Usage: Advanced programmers.

System Requirements: 64K, one disk drive and monochrome display; C compiler and assembler software also.

How to Start: Consult the .DOC and README files for documentation

- To run the BASIC programs, consult the directions in GETTING STARTED for your configuration
- To run a program with the suffix .COM or .EXE, just type its name, i.e., for LTYPE.EXE, type LTYPE and press ENTER.

File Descriptions:

AFT8087	MAC	Assembly macros and interface for Fortran access to 8087
BASSUB	BAS	Call DOS 2.0 functions from BASIC
BASSUB	OBJ	Part of BASSUB.BAS
BIOS	MAC	Assembly macros for accessing all BIOS functions
CLINK	COM	Program to load text fonts for graphics display
CLINK	ASM	Source for CLINK.COM
DOS	MAC	Assembly macros for accessing all DOS 2.0 functions
GRDRAW	LF	Logo program for interactive graphics drawing
HP	C	HP-style RPN calculator in c (Requires TRAN.C — see below)
KVUTIL	COM	Display control functions (Auto screen blank, scroll lock...)
KVSET	COM	Part of KVUTIL.COM
KVUTIL	DOC	Documentation for KVUTIL.COM
LDIR	EXE	List the table of contents of library files made by LAR and LU
LDIR	DOC	Documentation for LDIR.EXE
LDIR	C	Source for LDIR.EXE
LTYPE	EXE	Type a library file without extracting it — very useful
LTYPE	C	Source for LTYPE.EXE
LISP	PAS	A simple LISP interpreter in Pascal
PCUTIL	COM	Several screen and keyboard utility functions
PCUTIL	DOC	Documentation for PCUTIL.DOC
TRAN	C	Transcendental functions in c
UTILITES	MAC	A set of utility macros and subroutines for IBM Assembler
VUE	EXE	View file in hex and ASCII
XENIX	ASM	Xenix-like subroutines for accessing DOS 2.0 functions in c

143
Programmer Utilities No 7

v1

This disk contains many different kinds and flavors of utilities. CMP compares files (either ASCII or binary) of different lengths and reports differences, good for archiving or updating text files. COPYFLD is a dBASE II tool to cut and paste from different dBASE files. D and PC-ZAP both work on individual disk sectors, tracks, and sides for low level disk data manipulation and display. RUSQ performs the inverse function of SQ, whichs squeezes files, but it does it in a different way than the public domain version of UNSQ, helpful if UNSQ doesnt work. Lastly, SCRIPT is a XTALK utility used to set up a menu driven environment within XTALK.

Usage: Intermediate; D, PC-ZAP, and SCRIPT are Advanced.

System Requirements: 64K, one disk drive and monochrome display.

How to Start: The instructions for running the programs are in their respective text files.

File Descriptions:

CMP	COM	Intelligent file compare — works on binary files of different sizes
CMP	DOC	Documentation for CMP.COM
COPYFLD	PRG	dBASE II program to copy fields from one file to another
COPYFLD	DOC	Documentation for COPYFLD.PRG
D	EXE	Display selected disk sides/sectors/tracks
D	DOC	Documentation for D.EXE
PC-ZAP	EXE	Apply patches to disk(ette) — supports auto-patch files
PC-ZAP	DOC	Documentation for PC-ZAP.EXE
PROJECTS	BAS	Home projects database manager
PROJECTS	DAT	Sample database for PROJECTS.BAS
RUSQ	EXE	Another (different) file unsqueezer — try this if others fail!
SCRIPT	DOC	A Crosstalk script for menu-driven operation

206 BASIC Aids and Math
v1

A collection of programs for working in and with BASIC programming tasks. For instance, FACTOR, when run with BASIC, calculates factorials of integers, but does the math done so speedily there is no effective upper limit on number size. SORT is a FAST sort module to be used in BASIC programs to speed up doing sorts in BASIC.

For mathematical assistance, we have PUNYCALC which is a good "old math" representation of math functions. MULTREG does multiple regression analysis specifically, for the beginner on up.

Specialized and general helpers: CMP compares ALL types of files ASCII or binary. PERTCHT is PERT version 1.1 written in BASIC to generate a critical path analysis of any project. KEYPUNCH and VISICOM perform specialised functions.

Usage: Intermediate programmers and math enthusiasts.

System Requirements: 64K, one disk drive and monochrome display.

How to Start: From the DOS prompt (A>) enter PRINT *.DOC, ready your printer and print the document files for the files (there are 4 of them); they will then explain how to run the programs.

File Descriptions:

CMP	COM	File compare utility Version 1.0
CMP	DOC	Documentation
FACTOR	BAS	Calculates factorials
KEYPUNCH	BAS	Programmable keypunching
MULTREG	EXE	Outstanding multiple regression analysis program
PERT	DAT	Part of PERTCHT.BAS
PERTCHT	BAS	PERT schedule Version 1.1
PROFILE	MEM	Helps optimize BASIC programs — load co-resident with BASIC
PUNYCALC	BAS	Four function simple calculator
PUNYCALC	DOC	Documentation
SORT	BLD	Machine language subroutine for BASIC programs
SORT	DOC	Documentation
SORTEST	BAS	Demo of SORT.BLD
VISICOM	DOC	Convert VISICALC to standard COM file

358 BASICXREF Version 1.05
v1.1

The BASIC Cross Reference Utility is a programming aid for the serious programmer using the BASIC language on the IBM PC. Its use will facilitate the programming and debugging of BASIC source language programs.

The utility provides the following output:

1. A complete listing of all program line numbers, showing all references by other statements in the program. 2. An alphabetic listing of all reserved words showing the line numbers in which they appear. 3. An alphabetic listing of all program variables and I/O related variables that are neither reserved words nor program variables. 4. A listing of the BASIC source program may be produced, with top and bottom page margins, page headings, and formatting of program statements for improvement in program readability.

SPECIAL NOTE ON ALL BASICREF VERSIONS: BASICREF does not recognize path filenames, since the backslash character will be interpreted as a delimiter preceding program option characters. Therefore, all files referenced by BASICREF should reside in the root directory. Sub-directories will be treated in future versions.

Usage: All BASIC programmers

Features:

- The BASIC source program may include both numbered and un-numbered statements.
- The BASIC program may be processed as either BASIC Version 1.1, 2.0 or 3.0.
- Cross reference output is stored on a disk file, for listing to the screen and/or printer when desired.
- Last, but certainly not least, this utility will produce a cross reference listing for any size BASIC program, without exception.

System Requirements: 128K, one disk drive and monochrome/color display.

How to Start: Consult BASICREF.DOC.

- To run, enter BASICREF from the DOS prompt and follow directions.

User Comments: "Excellent resource for tracking my BASIC work." "A real gem. It keeps track of the details while I concentrate on writing my BASIC programs, and I write big ones." "I would recommend it to anyone writing in BASIC. However, please note: program is intolerant of keystroke errors."

Suggested Donation: $25.00 gets you the enhanced program and documentation; updates, corrections, modifications, etc., at nominal cost; and free consultation by mail/phone.

File Descriptions:

BASICREF	EXE	Program to generate BASIC Cross Reference file
BASICRF1	EXE	Program to produce printer and/or screen listings
BASICREF	DOC	Documentation file
BASICREF	TXT	Documentation
TESTPROG	BAS	Sample BASIC source file
UPDATES	TXT	Update information about Basic Xref

419 QPARSER Public Domain Version 2.61
v2.1

Here is the public domain version of QPARSER, a tool for writing translators, compilers, assemblers, and other language parsing programs. This disk contains the full QPARSER software but it is limited in that it has a top limit of 25 production/parsing rules.

Usage: Advanced programmers.

System Requirements: 64K, one disk drive and monochrome display.

How to Start: Enter SHOWQP for the tutorial. Read QPARSER.DOC for directions.

User Comments: "An excellent way to experiment with language design and compiler development. Very useful for computer science students." "incomplete...but very interesting!" "It's especially gratifying that a software producer (who sells the full QPARSER system for around $500) is willing to provide a useful demonstration of the system to potential purchasers and users." "It should be mentioned in the directory that this program, not the documentation, will not run without a hard

disk." "As a student in computer science I find this program to be helpful in understanding of compiler design. The documentation serves as an excellent introduction to the LR parser."

Suggested Donation: $10.00

File Descriptions:

CALC	COM	Executable calculator file
CALC	GRM	Grammar definition file for calculator
CALCDBUG	PAS	Skeleton source files
CALCSKEL	PAS	Skeleton file customized for calculator
CALCSEM	PAS	Calculator-specific semantics
CALCUTIL	PAS	Calculator-specific semantics
LR1	COM	The parser generator program
LR1P	COM	The program generator program
LR1SKEL	PAS	A general parser "skeleton" file
PMACS	TXT	Pascal form amcro file
QPARSER	BAT	Bat file to run the parser program
SHOWQP	COM	Automated tutorial program
QPARSER	DOC	Documentation for the parser program
QPDEMO	TXT	Data file for SHOWQP.COM
READ	ME	Note on where to get full QPARSER SYSTEM
SHOWQP	COM	Automated tutorial program
SKELNUM	PAS	Skeleton source files
SKELRTBL	PAS	Skeleton source files
SKELSYMS	PAS	Skeleton source files
SKELDTBL	PAS	Skeleton source files

435 Turbo Pascal Statistics, Trig, Utilities
v1

This disk contains three separate sets of Turbo Pascal routines. All but the last three entries pertain to the package of statistical distribution functions. The distributions include the Beta, Log Gamma, Incomplete Gamma, F, T, Chi-square, and Normal distributions; both the forward and inverse functions are provided. TRIGFUNC contains Pascal procedures for the common trigonometric functions. UTIL features more than 50 Turbo Pascal utility routines for such diverse functions as screen output, frames, windows, menus, serial communications, string manipulation, loan calculations, file I/O, and even a siren for intruder alert.

Usage: Intermediate Pascal programmers.

System Requirements: 64K, one disk drive and monochrome display; Borland's Turbo Pascal.

How to Start: Enter TYPE README.DOC from the DOS prompt and follow the directions in that file.

User Comments: "Excellent documentation — very steady on screen easy to print." "Very powerful statistical procedures. It would be helpful if your catalog mentioned that Turbo-87 is required by these procedures for optimum accuracy." "The probability functions are of great benefit in my work. Seeing them implemented in Pascal gives me a better feel for the language's capabilities."

File Descriptions:

README	DOC	Description of statistical distribution procedures
NINV	PAS	Find percentage point of normal distribution
TESTSIGF	PAS	Demo of F-significance routine
SIGF	PAS	Significance of F distribution
ERF	PAS	Error function
SIGCONST	PAS	Global constants for significance routines
ALGAMA	PAS	Logarithm (base E) of Gamma distribution
CDBETA	PAS	Cumulative Beta distribution
SIGCHI	PAS	Significance of Chi-square distribution
CDNORM	PAS	Cumulative normal distribution probability
TESTSIGC	PAS	Demo of Chi-square distribution routine
POWTEN	PAS	Calculate power of ten (integer powers only)
GAMMAIN	PAS	Evaluate incomplete Gamma integral
CINV	PAS	Inverse Chi-square (percentage point)
SIGT	PAS	Significance of T distribution
TESTINVF	PAS	Demo of inverse F routine
TESTSIGT	PAS	Demo of T-significance routine
TESTINVC	PAS	Demo of inverse Chi-square routine
TESTINVN	PAS	Demo of inverse normal routine
SIGNORM	PAS	Significance of normal distribution
TESTSIGN	PAS	Demo of significance of normal distribution
APINVB	PAS	Inverse Beta distribution
FINV	PAS	Inverse central F distribution
SIGALL	PAS	List of statistical routines on this disk
BETAINV	PAS	Inverse Beta distribution
LOGTEN	PAS	Base 10 logarithm
NINV2	PAS	Percentage point of normal distribution
POWER	PAS	Exponentiation of real to real power
TESTINVT	PAS	Demo of inverse central T distribution
POWERI	PAS	Exponentiation of real to integer power
TINV	PAS	Inverse central T distribution
TRIGFUNC	PAS	Description of TRIGFUNC.PAS
TRIGFUNC	PAS	Pascal procedures for trigonometric functions
UTIL	PAS	More than 50 utility routines

---

511 Turbo Sprites and Animation

v1

Turbo Sprites and Animation is a series of utilities, library files and demo programs to create, maintain and animate sprites (user-defined graphics images) in the Turbo Pascal environment. Both multi-page animation and xor animation are supported. Three main parts:

DESIGNER.COM is a sprite-designing utility which has an editor-like environment for creating sprites. It also allows you to store them in tables of up to 24 sprites. The utility will also generate code allowing you to incorporate sprites in your programs as typed constants.

COMPOSER.COM is a screen and animation composing utility that will help in positioning the sprites for display.

SPRITES.LIB is a library of display routines for sprites. A number of demo programs have been included to be sure you understand how to use the sprite files. Along with the demo programs, there are a number of sprite tables that have already been created.

Usage: Turbo Pascal users.

System Requirements: 256K, one disk drive and monochrome/graphics display; Turbo Pascal compiler.

How to Start: From the DOS prompt enter TYPE READTHIS.NOW and follow directions.

Suggested Donation: $20.00

File Descriptions:

DESIGNER	COM	Sprite design utility
DESIGNER	—1	Screen file for DESIGNER.COM
DESIGNER	—2	Screen file for DESIGNER.COM
DESIGNER	DOC	Documentation for DESIGNER.COM (formatted for printer)
COMPOSER	COM	Programming utility to load screen file and sprite tables
COMPOSER	DOC	Documentation for COMPOSER.COM (formatted for printer)
SPRITES	LIB	Sprite definitions and driver routines
DEMO?	PAS	Turbo Pascal source code of demo program (8 Files)
DEMO?	TAB	Sprite table for DEMO.PAS programs (5 Files)

??????	SPR	Individual sprite for demo programs
SANTA	INC	Individual sprite converted to typed constant array
DRAGON	INC	Individual sprite converted to typed constant array
SAVESCRN	COM	Utility to import PC Paint screens to Turbo Pascal programs
SAVESCRN	LIB	Library routines to save and load Turbo Pascal screens
READTHIS	NOW	Program overview

513

BMenu and Others

v1

BMENU and MENUGET comprise a menu development and use system that provides a simplified means for any user to build command menus using a text editor. This way the user can make the computer as "user friendly" as he wants. The two main sections of BMENU are:

BMENU.EXE is a menu program which reads its menu file and presents you with a menu. You can edit the menu with any text editor. Once the menu is displayed you can choose menu items by pressing the up and down arrow keys or pressing a letter key.

MENUGET.EXE Build menus into your batch files! Menuget waits and accepts a single ASCII character then creates a small file that you can test for in your batch file.

A variety of others — games, graphics demos and a Fortune Cookie program — constitutes the remainder of the disk.

Usage: Users wishing to create their own menus

System Requirements: 64K, one disk drive and monochrome/graphics display.

How to Start: Print the documentation in file READ.ME.

Suggested Donation: $10.00

File Descriptions:

AUTOEXEC	BAT	Autoexecute batch file to start menu program
BMENU	EXE	Executable program to display menus
BMENU	MNU	Sample menu
COOKIE	DAT	Data file for COOKIE.EXE

COOKIE	EXE	Fortune cookie program
DATIME	EXE	Day & time program to display on 1 line
DOMENU	BAT	Batch file to demonstrate menu system
EGGS	EXE	Graphics demonstration program
ESCAPE	EXE	Program to detect the ESC key in a batch file
GRAPH	MNU	Submenu used with demonstration programs
HANGMAN	EXE	Guess the words before it's too late program
INFO		Data file used with MENUGET.EXE
LINES	EXE	Graphics demonstration program
LISAJOU	EXE	Graphics demonstration program
MAIN	MNU	Main menu for demonstration programs
MENU	BAT	Batch program to start demo program
MENUGET	EXE	Executable program to build menus into a batch file
NOTICE	TXT	Program legal notices and list of files
READ	ME	Program documentation
WORDS		Data file for HANGMAN.EXE

536

PC-Tools

V1

This disk contains an assortment of useful utility programs with the source code for most being provided as well. They range from programs to browse through a file and print files to others that merge sorted files and even overstrike a files for a darker print. These constitute a public domain offering of some of the tools found in the packages "WildCard" and "Ace" marketed by Prickly Pear Software in Tucson Arizona (602-749-2864), $34.95 each.

NOTE: 100% IBM compatible users will need to boot up with ANSI.SYS.

Usage: Batch file users and C programmers

System Requirements: 128K, one drive, color or mono display.

How to Start: Consult READ.ME for documentation. All programs executable from DOS or using your C compiler.

Suggested Donation: $35.00

File Descriptions:

BROWSE	C	File browse utility with 4 way scrolling
XDIR	C	Read directory from/to a certain point |
DUMP	C	Provides an ASCII/HEX dump of any file | Each one
PAGE	C	View files one screen at a time | of these
SUBST	C	Oldstring newstring file | programs

MERGE	C	Merge sorted files into one sorted file | has an
FCOMP	C	File comparator program | executable
DARKEN	C	Overstrikes text file for darker print | version
WC	C	A fast word count program | with the
RM	C	Deletes files with or without verify | same name
PR	C	File printer program. |
ROFF	C	Readable source code for a text formater |
GREP	C	Improved version of GREP utility |
CASE	C	Contains string lower/upper utility /
FTRIM	C	Contains Trim–fspec
READ	ME	Brief description of programs on this disk
MAKEARG	H	Command line parser for quoted arguments

PTOOLDAT	PAS	Demo of PTOOLDAT routines
PTOOLENT	DOC	Documentation of the PTOOLENT routines
PTOOLENT	INC	Routines to display, edit and validate data entry fields
PTOOLENT	PAS	Demo of the PTOOLENT routines
PTOOLSCR	INC	Routines to manipulate screen functions
PTOOLSCR	PAS	Demo for the PTOOLSCR routines
PTOOLTIM	PAS	Demo for the PTOOLTIM routines
PTOOLTIM	INC	Routines to read and interpret system clock
PTOOLWIN	DOC	Documentation of the PTOOLWIN routines
PTOOLWIN	PAS	Demo for the PTOOLWIN routines
PTOOLWIN	INC	Routines to create and manipulate text windows
PTOOLWI3	DOC	Documentation of the PTOOLWI3 routines
PTOOLWI3	INC	Routines to create and manipulate text windows

589 PTOOLS

v1

PTOOLS will prove to be an aid to the Turbo Pascal programmer at every level. Included on the disk are the source code files for each of the routines, which will be included in your programs when compiled. Also included is a documentation file with complete rules for use and a description of the routine itself. Included for your convenience is a demonstration program of each of the routines.

These are complete stand-alone programs which can be compiled and run. They will give the user a good feel for exactly what the routine does and how to best utilize it. Included on this disk are routines which will create a window of any size and color which can overlay a text screen and later be removed (PTOOLWIN), a routine to change date types and manipulate them, many routines to allow program controlled data entry and editing.

Usage: Turbo Pascal programmers.

System Requirements: 64K, one disk drive and monochrome/graphics display.

How to Start: Check the .DOC files for each program. Since these are all Turbo Pascal routines to incorporate into other PASCAL programs, the document files provide all instructions.

Suggested Donation: $20.00

File Descriptions:

PTOOL1	BOX	Combination of PTOOLDAT, PTOOLENT, PTOOLSCR programs
PTOOLDAT	INC	Routines to convert and manipulate Gregorian & Julian dates

SCREEN UTILITIES:

Sometimes great code just isn't enough. Good style enhances your program's effectiveness. This collection of screen-design utilities gives you the tools and insights for designing the best possible user interface.

For BASIC programmers, there are several to give you lean, mean screen design while offering the challenge of designing for different languages. This screen-driver collection offers you a multitude of ways to speed up your calls and even redesign your console driver with some fancy programming structures. Finally, for Turbo Pascal and dBASE III programmers, you can unleash some of that power through our sleek forms generation packages.

163 Programmer Utilities No 8

v1

This collection of text and screen filters has many valuable pieces. The biggest and best is Dbscreen (DBS.EXE) which allows you to easily create dBASE II and III screens; instead of entering row and number designations into a format file, you simply 'paint' your screen fields on the terminal in a full-screen edit mode. You can see exactly what your screen is going to look like. Dbscreen will also let you modify and print dBASEII and III screen formats. Other programs allow you to modify character strings, change tabs into spaces, and encrypt/decrypt your files.

Usage: Programming and program modification

System Requirements: 64K, one disk drive and monochrome display.

How to Start: Read the .DOC files for documenation and instructions.

● To run a program with the suffix .COM or .EXE, just type its filename, i.e., for DBS.COM, type DBS and press ENTER.

File Descriptions:

CRYPT	DOC	CRYPT.EXE documentation
CRYPT	EXE	Encryption/decryption filter — uses a key to encode files
DBS	EXE	Screen generator for dBASEII & III
DETAB	DOC	Documentation for DETAB.EXE
DETAB	EXE	Replaces tabs with appropriate number of spaces
*	C	Source for C subroutines (15 files)
SPSCN	DOC	Documentation for SPSCN.EXE
SPSCN	EXE	Removes spaces at the ends of lines in a text file
TRANSLIT	DOC	Documentation for TRANSLIT.EXE
TRANSLIT	EXE	Translates a character string into a different string
WC	DOC	Documentation for WC.EXE
WC	EXE	Counts characters, words and lines in a text file

285
WHIZZARD
Screen

v1

The WHIZZARD Screen I/O Routines are designed to allow maximum performance on the IBM PC. They can be called from BASIC to increase the speed at which text goes to the screen. Some of the routines will NOT work properly on non-IBM PCs. In particular, the pieces that increase print speed for the BASIC Interpreter (See Item 3, below) will not operate properly with non-IBM versions of BASIC. Try the software. If it works on your configuration, great. If not, the source code is here.

The software on this disk can be divided:

(1) WHIZZARD Screen I/O Subroutines. These can be called from BASIC to increase the speed at which text gets to the screen.
(2) A rational approach to calling assembly routines in BASIC code. This approach allows one source version for both interpreter and compiler input. The example uses Whizzard Screen I/O Subroutines, but any useful assembly routines can be added.
(3) Software to accelerate the PRINT statement for interpreted BASIC WITHOUT changing the BASIC source code.
(4) Software to accelerate the PRINT statement for compiled BASIC that uses BASRUN.EXE. Source code is NOT changed.
(5) Software to accelerate the PRINT statement for BASIC compiled /O. Source code is NOT changed.
(6) Software to demonstrate BASPRINT, COMPRINT, PRSLASHO and ASMBASIC
(7) Patch to DOS 2.0 DEBUG TRACE command to prevent collision between external interrupts)(like the timer) and the TRACE command
(8) Software to allow editing or printing of the source and text files shown above despite the presence of tab characters

Usage: Screen editing and programming

System Requirements: 64K, one disk drive and monochrome display

How to Start: Consult the .DOC and .TXT files for directions and documentation

● To run the BASIC programs, consult the directions in GETTING STARTED for your configuration.

User Comments: "PRSLASHNO:Fantastic !!!!! By simply running prior to executing a compiled BASIC program, my displays almost "pop" onto the screen. Could be on a diskette all by itself!!"

Suggested Donation: $5.00

File Descriptions:

XREP	ASM	Repeat some character along the x axis
YREP	ASM	Repeat some character down the y axis
BASPRINT	ASM	Source to primary module
PRSLASHO	ASM	Source to primary module
COMPRINT	ASM	Source to primary module
SCRLUP	ASM	Compiled version
ASMBASIC	ASM	Source to primary module
SCRLUP	ASM	Scroll some portion of the screen up
ZPRINT	ASM	Print a string using the color/attribute given
QPRINT	ASM	Quickly print a string at the current location
CLREOS	ASM	Clear from the current position to the end of the screen
CLREOL	ASM	Clear from the current position to the end of the line
SCRLDN	ASM	Scroll some portion of the screen down
DETAB	BAS	Interpreted BASIC program to remove tabs
TIMEDEMO	BAS	Source to timing program demonstrating improvement
BANDDEMO	BAS	Source to graphic demonstration program showing the enhancement
SUBDEMO	BAS	Interpreted BASIC program demonstrating ASMBASIC
LONGDEMO	BAT	BAT file demonstrating all three modules and QPRINT from ASMBASIC
EASYDEMO	BAT	BAT file demonstrating compiled routines using PRSLOASHO
SETABS	EPS	File which can be printed to set the tab positions
PRSLASHO	EXE	Module to be executed after booting the system
BANDDEMO	EXE	BASIC graphic demonstration program compiled with the I/O option
SUBDEMO	EXE	Compiled program
COMPRINT	EXE	Module to be executed after booting the system
BASPRINT	EXE	Module to be executed after booting the system
ASMBASIC	EXE	Sample executable linked with the I/O subroutines
DEBUG20	FIX	PIPELINE input file which can be used to apply the
*	OBJ	Object code for .BAS files of the same name (9 files)
ASMBASIC	TXT	How to call assembly routines in BASIC
SCRNIO	TXT	Explanation of acceleratiing the PRINT statement
README	TXT	Description of programs
SCRNIO	TXT	Explanation of accelerating the PRINT statement
DEBUGFIX	TXT	Explanation of the patch to DOS 2.0 DEBUG TRACE command

312
Screen Design Aid and Forms
v1

The two programs here are for designing your screen and your output.

Screen Design Aid (SDA) designs display screens for data input use in other programs; these screens will be callable from Assembler, BASIC, or other high-level programs. SDA includes specifications for blinking, high-intensity, underscoring, and reverse-video options, as well as a full range of color foreground and background options. It permits the definition of a "screen" utilizing any combination of the 254 displayable characters and saves it in a highly compressed form.

The second program is the FORMS program for forms generation and management. It allows you to generate and edit master forms tailored to your individual application which can then be recalled, filled out, and stored as completed forms. FORMS supports IBM/Epson-compatible dot matrix as well as Daisy wheel printers.

Usage: Screen and forms design

System Requirements: 64K, one disk drive, monochrome/color graphics; FORMS requires 256K

How to Start: Consult the FORMS.DOC, BASSCR.DOC and SDA.DOC for documentation and instructions

● To run either, enter the program name and press ENTER.

User Comments: "FORMS is simple to use...I created my first form within 30 minutes after reading the documentation which is clear." (SCREEN DESIGN) "Excellent for screen painting, and Forms generation. I found this disk very useful as an administrator and systems manager. With this set of programs you can make things friendly." "Screen Design works as advertised with blinking characters, reverse video etc."

Suggested Donation: $25.00 SDA; $30.00 FORMS (includes full manual, latest updates and program revisions)

File Descriptions:

————	——	Screen Design Aid
SDA	COM	Screen Design Aid, Version 3.0
$SDA	OBJ	Screen Design Aid, object code
$FIELD	MAC	Macros for Screen Design Aid
BASSCR	OBJ	BASIC Interface for SDA, object code
BASSCR	ASM	BASIC Interface for SDA, Assembler
BASSCR	DOC	Documentation for BASSCR
BASMEN	OBJ	Object file for BASSCR
DEMO	EXE	SDA demo program, color monitor, 1 screen
DEMO	BAS	ASCII description of DEMO.EXE source code
SDA	DOC	Screen Design Aid manual (32 pages)
BASSCR	DOC	BASIC-SDA Interface manual (2 pages)
ANSISCR	EXE	Screen driver
————	——	Form Generator
FORMS	COM	Forms generation and management program
FORMS	DOC	Forms program documentation (10 pages)
REGISTER	FRM	Registration form for FORMS users
BUGREPT	FRM	Bug report form to report FORMS problems

356
Fansi-Console Disk 1 of 2
v3.0

Fansi-Console is a sophisticated memory-resident program which replaces the standard IBM PC console drivers, extends the ROM BIOS, processes ANSI X3.64 control sequences, provides keyboard macro capabilities, and much more. You have two versions of Fansi-Console here: FCONSOLE.DEV is the commercial version and is usually the more stable more bugfree version of FansiConsole. It is the version which most closely matches the current printed user manual and is the version which you have purchased. The version of Fansi-Console in the file called FCONBETA.DEV is the beta test version. HAVE FUN COMPARING THEM!

NOTE: This is a two disk set, the second part being Disk No 650.

Usage: Some Fansi programming of and from your keyboard!

System Requirements: 128K, two disk drives and a monochrome display

How to Start: There is an on-disk abbreviated user manual for FANSI-CONSOLE in the file FCONSOLE.DQC. To unsqueeze it, use the UNSQZ program. Once unsqueezed, it is much bigger so put it on a separate disk!

User Comments: "At last, a full ANSI device driver for the IBM-PC." "I have a lot of utility programs which do each function of this program. The virtue of this program is integration of all of them" "EXCELLENT, AGAIN! "I think this a great program. The best of its type that I've seen, but half the documentation is missing..." "Great program, but runs into other memory resident programs rather frequently. The screen writing speed is especially helpful." "This program is very interesting as it has shown me how differ drivers effect the operation of the computer."

Suggested Donation: Use license $25; $75 will get you the manual and the latest update.

File Descriptions:

-README—	NOW	Short instructions for printing the abbreviated user manual
123V2	PCH	Patch for Lotus 1-2-3 Version 2
ANSI80	TXT	Test data for 80 column screen displays
AT	LAY	AT keyboard layout file
CHARSETS	TXT	Demonstrates how to generate the entire IBM-PC character set
DEJAVU	EXE	Writes the lines from the scroll recall buffer to a file
DIZZY	C	Source for C program which generated part of ANSI80.TXT
DVORAK	TXT	Test data to set up a quasi-Dvorak keyboard layout
DVORAK2	TXT	Test data to set up a quasi-Dvorak keyboard layout (part 2)
EGALGCHR	COM	Decreases the number of lines of characters on the EGA
EGASMCHR	COM	Increases the number of lines of characters on the EGA
EXPAND	COM	Expands tab characters into spaces
FANSICAP	TXT	Termcap file for FANSI-CONSOLE when FANSI-VT100 is reset
FANSISET	EXE	Menu driven program for changing options at run-time
FANSISET	TXT	Example set-up file
FCONBBS	LST	List of Bulliten Board Systems
FCONBETA	DEV	"Beta Test" version of FANSI-CONSOLE
FCONSOLE	DEV	FANSI-CONSOLE itself
FCONSOLE	HST	Revision history
FLAYOUT	EXE	Program to rearrange your keyboard keys to your liking
LOGO	PCH	Patch for Logo
RAWMODE	MAC	Source for sub-routines useful to programmer's
SEND	EXE	Sends control sequences to the console or printer
SK111	PCH	Patch for Sidekick Version 1.11A
SNOW	COM	Test program for setting hardware options
SPIT	EXE	Program to slowly try test data
STANDARD	LAY	Standard keyboard layout file
STKSTRAW	COM	FANSI-CONSOLE utility program
TRAP	COM	Traps INT calls for problem reporting purposes
UNSQZ	COM	Unsqueeze utility
WATZITBE	COM	Displays the scan codes for each key pressed
WATZITDO	COM	Displays the effects of pressing keys
WORDSTAR	PCH	Patch for Wordstar 3.3
Z200	LAY	Sample keyboard layout file

363 PC-INPUT
v1

The PCINPUT and PCIGEN programs here give you a straightforward and lean BASIC screen generation capacity. With them you can design alphanumeric, numeric, selected character set and keyword screen input layouts for your software. Study of these programs can also be instructive towards developing modifications, especially of BASIC programs.

Usage: Screen generation

System Requirements: 64K, one disk drive and a monochrome display

How to Start: Consult the INPUT.DOC and then run the DEMO to see how the PCINPUT program functions. Check your BASIC setup for running these programs in the GETTING STARTED section.

User Comments: "I have found PCINPUT invaluable in developing screen software. PCIGEN is not really needed by an experienced programmer." "The documentation was so bad I could not get the programs to run." "Not what I expected — which was full screen input."

File Descriptions:

DEMO	BAS	PCINPUT Demonstration
PCIGEN	BAS	Screen generator for BASIC programs
PCIGEN	EXE	Compiled version of PCIGEN
PCINPUT	BAS	Data entry generator for BASIC programs
PCINPUT	DOC	File listing for PCINPUT
SKELETON	BAS	Generated BASIC statements
SKELETON	DAT	Screen Generator data files
SKELETON	MNU	Screen Generator skeleton names

| M–BB | COM | Mouse system compiled menu file |
| FORM | TXT | Order form for becoming a registered user |

611 BlackBeard Version 6.1
v1

BlackBeard is a programmer's editor that performs just about every task that a programmer needs. This is probably due to its windowing capacity (13!), excellent text formatter, macro capabilites and integral mouse driver to name a few features. Also, it works real well for source code editing in structured languages such as Pascal, C, Fortran, etc.

While its primary use is for source code editing, it also has some word processing features (reformats, centers, cut & paste, etc.) to ease up on your housekeeping and documentation chores. How can it do all this? There are four major parts to BlackBeard:

- BB The Programmer's editor
- BB132 The Programmer's editor that works in 25 by 132 columns
- BB44 The Editor for 44 by 132 columns (Requires an Everex card)
- BBF A Text formatter

Usage: Source code editing

System Requirements: 128K, one disk drive, color/monochrome display

How to Start: Consult the various .DOC and .TXT files for instructions. Each part of BB can be started from DOS.

Suggested Donation: $15.00 covers: a distinctive "BlackBeard" collectable, a registration sticker, and a copy of the latest version of BlackBeard.

File Descriptions:

BB	EXE	Programmer's editor
BB132	EXE	Programmer's editor that is 25 by 132 columns
BB44	EXE	Editor that is 44 by 132 columns (Requires an Everex card)
BBC	EXE	Blackbeard key binding compiler
BBF	EXE	Text formatter
BB	CFG	Configuration file
BB	KEY	Binding file
READ	ME	Release notes from the author
BB	DOC	Documentation for BB.EXE
BBKEYS	TXT	Key binding files ready for compilation
M–BB	MSC	Mouse system button and movement files

650 Fansi-Console (Disk 2 of 2)
V3.0

This is the second of the two disk set for Fansi-Console, a highly sophisticated memory-resident program which replaces the standard IBM PC console drivers, extends the ROM BIOS, processes ANSI X3.64 control sequences, provides keyboard macro capabilities, and much more.

NOTE: This is a two disk set, the FIRST part being Disk No 356.

Usage: Some Fansi programming of and from your keyboard!

System Requirements: 128K, two disk drives and a monochrome display

How to Start: There is an on-disk abbreviated user manual for FANSI-CONSOLE in the file FCONSOLE.DQC.

User Comments: "At last, a full ANSI device driver for the IBM-PC." "I have a lot of utility programs which do each function of this program. The virtue of this program is integration of all of them" "EXCELLENT, AGAIN! "I think this a great program. The best of its type that I've seen, but half the documentation is missing..." "Great program, but runs into other memory resident programs rather frequently. The screen writing speed is especially helpful." "This program is very interesting as it has shown me how differ drivers effect the operation of the computer."

Suggested Donation: Use license $25; $75 will get you the manual and the latest update.

File Descriptions:

-README—	NOW	Introductory text file
FCONSOLE	BQO	Squeezed advertisement for FANSI-CONSOLE
FCONSOLE	DQC	Squeezed documentation file for FANSI-CONSOLE

680 FORGE VERSION 2.0

v1.0

FORGE is a Turbo Pascal and dBASE III programmer's aid. It allows the programmer to design data input forms or help screens; it then generates the Turbo Pascal or dBASE III source code for those forms. FORGE was written entirely in Turbo Pascal, but only the .COM file is provided. Turbo Pascal and dBASE III are not required to use FORGE, but are required in order to make use of the files produced by FORGE. The source code produced by FORGE can then be compiled and used as is for data entry, or it can be included as a procedure within a larger more comprehensive program. Since this is a utility for Turbo Pascal and dBASE III, a working knowledge of these programming languages is assumed.

FORGE is noteworthy in that it allows you to do the with the forms for data input form or information screen what most wordprocessors do with text. Some of the outstanding features of FORGE are that you can: fill an area on the screen with color, without affecting the characters that are already on the screen, insert or delete lines from the screen, define areas on the form for entering data, define data entry areas as "String", "Integer", or "Real" data types, use IBM graphics characters to "draw" boxes, etc., and use blinking characters.

Usage: Data input design for Turbo Pascal and dBASE III

System Requirements: 128K, on disk drive, color/monochrome display

How to Start: Full documentation in FORGE.DOC and README.TXT files

● To run, enter FORGE and press ENTER.

Suggested Donation: $20.00

File Descriptions:

CONTENTS	TXT	Text file describing the contents of this disk
DEMO	DTA	Practice form
DEMO	FMT	dBase III code generated from DEMO.DTA
DEMO	PAS	Turbo Pascal code generated from DEMO.DTA
EXTPROC1	PAS	Turbo Pascal include files
EXTPROC2	PAS	Turbo Pascal include files
EXTPROC3	PAS	Turbo Pascal include files
EXTPROC4	PAS	Turbo Pascal include files
FORGE	COM	Main program for large memory systems
FORGE	DOC	Documentation file
FORGE2	000	Overlay files for small memory systems
FORGE2	COM	Main program for small memory systems
README	TXT	Overview of FORGE & explanation how to print documentation

5.0 INDEXES

BY DISK NUMBER

Disk #	Title	Pg #
1	GAME SERIES NO 1	149
3	RATBAS	205
5	PC-FILE III	74
7	EXPLIST	375
8	CROSSREF	376
9	SQUISH	376
10	CHASM	206
13	PDRAW	172
14	BARGRAPH	139
16	GAME SERIES NO 2	150
17	GAME SERIES NO 3	150
18	IQBUILD	106
19	ARCHIE	68
20	DRAW	173
21	PCMAN	151
23	BOWLING SECRETARY	241
24	GAME SERIES NO 4	151
25	FINANCE	140
26	INDEX BUILDER	75
28	DISKMODF	299
30	PASCAL I/O	206
31	MVP-FORTH	207
33	DOS AND PRINTER UTILITIES	300
34	SORTED DIRECTORY	300
35	GAME SERIES NO 5	152
36	PASCAL COLLECTION NO 1	207
37	GAME SERIES NO 6	152
38	BASIC DRAWING	173
40	STOCK MARKET ANALYSER	140
41	KERMIT (1 OF 2)	55
42	KERMIT (2 OF 2)	56
45	GAMES SERIES NO 8	153
46	SCREEN UTILITIES NO 1	301
47	PC-SIG SAMPLER NO 1	153
48	RUNOFF	362
49	PC-SIG SAMPLER NO 2	154
51	HYPERDRIVE	302
52	DOS UTILITIES NO 1	327
54	XMODEM	56
55	GAME SERIES NO 9	154
56	KEYBOARD UTIL NO 1	328
60	UTIL 1.2/MAKE/BASREF	377
62	INVENTORY	29
64	DESKTOP (1 OF 2)	262

Disk #	Title	Pg #
65	DESKTOP (2 OF 2)	262
66	GINACO PROGRAMS	328
67	NONLIN	329
69	DESIGNER	174
70	DISKCAT	302
71	GAME SERIES NO 10	155
72	GAME SERIES NO 11	155
73	3D	174
76	HISTORY EDUCATION	107
78	PC-WRITE (2.7/4) (1 OF 2)	278
79	DOS UTILITIES NO 2	329
80	DOS UTILITIES NO 3	303
81	COMMUNICATION PROGRAMS NO 1	57
83	WORMCITY	156
84	DOS UTILITIES NO 4	330
86	SCREEN TEXT EDITOR	279
87	PROGRAMMER'S CALCULATOR	95
88	EPISTAT STATISTICS	222
89	PC-SIG SAMPLER NO 3	304
90	GENEALOGY ON DISPLAY	190
91	PC-SIG SAMPLER NO 4	156
92	MUSIC	121
93	PC-SIG SAMPLER NO 5	331
95	MATH TUTOR	107
100	JUKEBOX	122
101	THE PORTWORTH PACKAGE	141
105	PC PROFESSOR BASIC TUTORIAL	69
106	DISKCAT 4.3F	75
107	HOME FINANCE	191
108	PROGRAMMER'S UTILITIES NO 1	208
109	DOS UTILITIES NO 5	304
110	PROGRAMMER UTILITIES NO 2	378
111	FILE UTILITIES NO 1	305
112	COMPUTER SECURITY	323
113	THREE USER-SUPPORTED PROGRAMS	96
114	ASSEMBLY TUTORIAL	208
115	DOS UTILITIES NO 6	331
116	MICROGOURMET (1 OF 2)	191
117	MICROGOURMET (2 OF 2)	192
118	QSYS DOS MENU (1 OF 2)	96
119	ABC DATABASE	76

Disk #	Title	Pg #
120	PC-CHESS	157
121	LETUS A-B-C VOL. 1	232
122	LETUS A-B-C VOL. 2	233
123	LETUS A-B-C VOL. 3	233
124	EXTENDED BATCH LANGUAGE BY SEAWARE	307
125	HOST-III PUBLIC BULLETIN BOARD PACKAGE V1.1G	25
126	DBASE II PROGRAMS	378
127	PC-MUSICIAN	122
128	PC-SIG SAMPLER NO 6	379
129	PC-DIAL	57
130	PASCAL TOOLS (1 OF 3)	344
131	PASCAL TOOLS (2 OF 3)	345
132	PASCAL TOOLS (3 OF 3)	345
133	ULTRA-UTILITIES 4.0	307
135	PROGRAMMER/ COMMUNICATIONS UTILITIES	58
136	PC-PICTURE GRAPHICS BY E. YING	175
138	PROGRAMMER UTILITIES NO 4	305
139	SCREEN UTILITIES NO 2	306
140	DOS UTILITIES NO 7	379
141	PROGRAMMER UTILITIES NO 5	380
142	PROGRAMMER UTILITIES NO 6	380
143	PROGRAMMER UTILITIES NO 7	381
144	FABULA 1 (1 OF 2)	308
145	FABULA 2 (2 OF 2)	308
146	EASYRITE/ LABLFILE FROM GINACO	280
147	SDB	76
148	XLISP	22
149	C UTILITIES NO 1	345
150	IBM BBS BY GENE PLANTZ	26
151	FINANCE MANAGER	141
152	RBBS FOR THE IBM PC	26
153	NORLAND SOFTWARE HANGMAN	107
154	PRINTER ART	175
155	BUDGET/ TASKPLAN/LOAN	30
159	PC FIRING LINE/PC UNDERGROUND ISSUE #1	234
160	PC FIRING LINE ISSUE #2 (1 OF 2)	234

Disk #	Title	Pg #
161	PC FIRING LINE ISSUE #2 (2 OF 2)	235
162	BASIC NECESSITIES	346
163	PROGRAMMER UTILITIES NO 8	387
164	TELEWARE CASHTRAC	142
165	PERSONAL GENERAL LEDGER	30
167	BASIC AIDS NO 1	346
168	MUSIC AND EDUCATIONAL PROGRAMS	108
169	MAILING LIST	31
170	SPREADSHEETS	263
171	FINANCE AND INVENTORY	142
172	STEVE'S UTILITIES	309
173	EXTRA SENSORY PERCEPTION	123
174	GAME SERIES NO 12	157
175	SIMULATION & BOARD GAMES	158
177	ARCADE SERIES NO 1	158
178	GAME SERIES NO 13	159
179	PIZZA & CHECK REGISTER	31
180	MATH AND STATISTICS	223
181	KEYBOARD UTILITIES NO 2	332
182	AUTOFILE, EASYFILE AND TIME, DATE UTILITIES	309
183	DOS UTILITIES NO 8	310
184	DOS UTILITIES NO 9	294
185	DOS UTILITIES NO 10	310
186	SCREEN AND PRINTER UTILITIES	363
187	COMMUNICATION PROGRAMS NO 1	59
188	MINITEL	59
190	TEXT EDITORS	280
191	BASIC PAINT: EASEL AND EASYGRAF	176
192	HEALTH RISK	242
193	FREEWILL	192
194	ROFF AND PC-READ	281
195	PC-GRAF	177
196	DOS UTILITIES NO 11	332
197	TWO TREKS	159
199	PC-CALC	263
203	GAME SERIES NO 14	160
204	DOS UTILITIES NO 12	295
205	DOS UTILITIES NO 13	311
206	BASIC AIDS & MATH	382
207	WORKSHEETS NO 1	264
208	PC-SIG SAMPLER NO 7	160
209	ARCADE SERIES NO 2	161
210	GAME SERIES NO 15	161
211	JUSTIFY AND SPEED READER DEMO	364
212	RBBS (1 OF 4)	27
214	DATA BASE OF STEEL (1 OF 4)	77
215	DATA BASE OF STEEL (2 OF 4)	78
216	C UTILITIES NO 2	347
217	NELIST AND DISK ALIGNMENT	312
218	ADDRESS MANAGER	78
219	MAPMAKER	177
220	PRINTER UTIL NO 1	364
221	PRINTER UTIL NO 2	365
222	PRINTER UTIL NO 3	365
223	ASSEMBLY/PASCAL UTILITIES	347
224	GORDON'S PC-CALC	264
225	PC-FONT	366
227	FINANCIAL PROGRAMS	143
228	GAME SERIES NO 16	162
229	FUNNELS & BUCKETS	109
229	FUNNELS & BUCKETS	162
230	THE CONFIDANT	324
231	REFLIST	242
232	SPPC SYSTEM DEMO (1 OF 2)	224
233	NEWBASE	79
234	TPNCALC	224
235	PARTS INVENTORY CONTROL	32
236	PRINTER UTIL NO 4	366
237	PC-GENERAL LEDGER	32
238	SPRITE GRAPHICS	178
240	FAMILY-TREE, ETC	193
241	PCJR EDUCATIONAL	109
242	SAGE TRADER	143
243	SAGE CALENDAR/TAG	33
244	SLIDE GENERATION	179
245	ULTRA-UTILITIES	312
246	STOCK CHARTING SYSTEM V1.7	144
247	BOBCAT — BUSINESS DATABASE	235
248	PASCAL MATH LIBRARY	348
249	EQUATOR/ PC-TOUCH EDUCATIONAL PROGRAMS	110
251	TIME AND MONEY	33
252	LISTMATE/LOAD-US	313
253	3X5 CARD	79
254	PC-DOS HELP	69
255	DOS UTILITIES NO 14	333
256	DOS AND PROGRAMMER UTILITIES	334
257	UTILITY 1-2-3	265
258	COMMUNICATION PROGRAMS NO 2	60
259	C ADVENTURE	123
260	GAME SERIES NO 17	163
261	PC-SIG BUSINESS SAMPLER NO 1	34
262	PC-GOLF	243
263	LAXON & PERRY FORTH (1 OF 2)	209
264	LAXON & PERRY FORTH (2 OF 2)	210
265	PRINTER AND GRAPHICS UTILITIES	367
266	NAEPIRS	111
267	DATA BASE OF STEEL (3 OF 4)	80
268	DATA BASE OF STEEL (4 OF 4)	81
269	BETATOOL'S BASIC DEVELOPMENT SYSTEM	348
273	BEST UTILITIES	335
274	BEST GAMES	163
275	PC-CHECK	193
276	COLLIST 2.0	367
277	FINDFILE	313
278	QSYS DOS DOCUMENTATION (2 OF 2)	97
279	PIANOMAN	124
280	MAGAZINE BIBLIOGRAPHIES	236
281	RECIPE INDEX	236
282	PC-SIG BUSINESS SAMPLER NO 2	35
283	DOS UTILITIES NO 15	335
284	PC-SIG SAMPLER NO 8	336
285	WHIZZARD SCREEN	388
286	PC-VT	60
287	FILE EXPRESS (1 OF 2)	81
288	FILE EXPRESS (2 OF 2)	82
289	POWER- WORKSHEETS	265
290	FITT LOTUS 1-2-3 TAX WORKSHEETS	266
292	SPACEWAR	164
293	ARCADE SERIES NO 3	165
294	EDIT (1.16)	281
295	TAX-FILE	194
296	EAMON MASTER (1 OF 2)	125
297	EAMON DESIGNER & UTILITIES (2 OF 2)	125
298	PLANETS/WATOR/ LEYGREF'S CASTLE	243
301	WORKSHEETS NO 2	266
302	WORKSHEETS NO 3	267
303	WORKSHEETS NO 4	267
304	WORKSHEETS NO 5	268
305	SYMPHONY NO 1	268
306	SYMPHONY NO 2	269
307	ASSEMBLY UTIL NO 1	349
308	ASSEMBLY UTIL NO 2	350
309	ASSEMBLY UTIL NO 3	351
310	QMODEM	61
311	MOVIE DATABASE	82

Disk #	Title	Pg #
312	SCREEN DESIGN AID AND FORMS	389
313	PC-SIG BUSINESS SAMPLER NO 3	35
314	C UTILITIES NO 4	351
315	C UTILITIES NO 5	352
316	COMMUNICATIONS UTILITIES NO 3	62
317	DATABASE PROGRAMS	83
319	DOS UTILITIES NO 16	336
320	TOUCHTYPE	111
321	HOME APPLICATIONS	195
322	MUSIC COLLECTION	126
323	TRANSTOCK	144
324	TURBO PASCAL NO 1	353
325	LOGON/OFF	314
326	PRINTER UTILITIES NO 5	368
327	TRIVIA (1 OF 2)	126
328	TRIVIA (2 OF 2)	127
329	TRIVIA & OTHERS	127
330	PC-SIG BUSINESS SAMPLER NO 4	36
331	PC-GL	37
332	KLP/DTA/MUA	37
334	RBBS (2 OF 4)	27
336	ABC DESIGN (1 OF 2)	179
337	ABC DESIGN (2 OF 2)	180
338	SYSCOMM	62
339	CREATOR	83
340	INFOBASE	84
341	C UTILITIES NO 5	210
342	GOLF SCORECARD	244
343	WORD PROCESSING	282
344	PC-KEY DRAW NO 1 (1 OF 2)	180
345	PC-KEY DRAW NO 2 (2 OF 2)	181
347	PC-FOIL	244
348	LETUS A-B-C VOL. 4	237
349	LETUS A-B-C VOL. 5	237
350	LETUS A-B-C VOL. 6	237
351	TURBO PASCAL NO 2	354
352	TWO FORTHS	210
353	TURBO PASCAL NO 3	354
354	PCJR GAMES	165
355	PC-ZAP	314
356	FANSI-CONSOLE (1 OF 2)	97
356	FANSI-CONSOLE (1 OF 2)	389
358	BASICXREF	382
359	MOONBEAM	112
360	PFROI	145
361	FAMILY HISTORY (1 OF 2)	196
362	SIMTERM	63
363	PC-INPUT	390
365	TURBO PASCAL NO 5	355
366	TURBO PASCAL NO 6	356
367	FLASH CARDS: VOCABULARY & SPELLING (1 OF 4)	112

Disk #	Title	Pg #
368	FLASH CARDS: VOCABULARY & SPELLING (2 OF 4)	112
369	FLASH CARDS: VOCABULARY & SPELLING (3 OF 4)	113
370	FLASH CARDS: VOCABULARY & SPELLING (4 OF 4)	113
371	BASIC AIDS NO 2	356
372	BASIC AIDS NO 3	357
373	DOS UTILITIES NO 17	337
374	DOS UTILITIES NO 18	315
375	TURBO PASCAL NO 7	358
376	PATCHES	295
377	PRINTER UTIL NO 6	369
379	WORDSTAR AIDS	282
380	GLUDRAW	181
381	BASIC AIDS NO 4	211
382	PC-CONVERT/SWEEP	316
383	PC-DBMS	85
384	CONDEN	338
385	PHRASE CRAZE	128
386	BANNER	370
387	KEEP IN TOUCH	98
388	FORM LETTERS	38
389	HOME BUDGET FOR LOTUS 1-2-3	269
390	GAME SERIES NO 18	166
391	NMR SPECTROSCOPY AND STATISTICS	224
392	COMPILED PASCAL ROUTINES LIBRARY	211
393	CHECKBOOK MANAGEMENT	39
394	MATH PAK	113
394	MATH PAK	225
395	HOME INVENTORY	197
396	PDS*BASE DATABASE	85
397	CHECKBOOK SYSTEM	197
398	ESIE EXPERT SYSTEM	23
399	LOAN AMORTIZATION AND PROSPECTS	39
401	THE ADDRESS BOOK	86
402	CROSS ASSEMBLER FOR THE IBM 370	212
403	TUTOR.COM	70
404	EZ-FORMS PACKAGE	40
405	PC-DESKTEAM	99
406	FINANCIAL PROGRAMS & LOTUS WORKSHEETS	145
407	VIDEOCHEM	114
408	ORIGAMI	128
409	SNOCREST BASIC #1	212
410	SNOCREST BASIC #2	213
411	PRINTER UTILITIES	370
412	PERSONAL UTILITIES	99
413	DOS UTILITIES	316

Disk #	Title	Pg #
414	COPY PROTECTION/ UNPROTECTION	297
415	W-ED, WORD PROCESSING PREVIEWER	283
416	ROFF4	284
417	A.D.A. PROLOG V1.91P	23
418	PC-GRAPH	182
419	QPARSER	383
420	FILE UTILITIES	339
422	SCREENWRITER	284
423	PROJECT MANAGER	41
424	PASCAL COMPILER	213
425	ENGINEERING PASCAL	213
426	TURBO PASCAL #6	359
427	TURBO PASCAL #7	359
428	TURBO PASCAL #8	360
429	ELEMENTARY C	214
430	ANALYTICALC (1 OF 3)	41
431	ANALYTICALC (2 OF 3)	42
432	ANALYTICALC (3 OF 3)	43
433	KERMIT-MS COMPATIBLES, ASM MODULES	64
434	KERMIT-MS COMPATIBLES, ASM MODULES II	64
435	TURBO PASCAL STATISTICS, TRIG, UTILITIES	383
436	HAM RADIO #1	115
437	HAM RADIO #2	115
438	PRINTER UTILITIES	371
439	COMMUNICATIONS PROGRAMS	65
440	MISCELLANEOUS APPLICATIONS	44
441	TEKTRONIX 4010 EMULATOR	65
442	SPA:WN STRUCTURED PROGRAMMING/ WARNIER DIAGRAM	361
442	SPA:WN STRUCTURED PROGRAMMING/ WARNIER DIAGRAM	215
443	T-SCORE/ EDUCATION	116
444	HOTKEY/ XDOS/ EZ-MENU/ CALC	339
445	WILLY THE WORM	167
446	ZORK UTILITIES	129
447	THE SKY	245
448	ASSORTED GAMES	167
450	ASSORTED BASIC GAMES	168
451	CAVEQUEST	129
452	THE AMULET OF YENDOR	130
453	ADVENTUREWARE	130
454	UNIFORTH	215

Disk #	Title	Pg #
455	PC-TYPE+ BY JIM BUTTON (1 OF 3)	285
456	ASSORTED GAMES	168
457	GREATEST ARCADE GAMES	169
458	INCTAX (1.1)	198
459	ASSORTED AGRICULTURAL PROGRAMS	245
460	ALBERTA AGRICULTURAL PROGRAMS	246
461	RIDGETOWN COLLEGE PROGRAMS	246
462	CK SYSTEM (1 OF 2)	198
463	CK SYSTEM (2 OF 2)	199
464	PBASE	87
465	FAMILY TIES	199
466	CPA-LEDGER PROGRAM (1 OF 2)	44
468	CPA-LEDGER USER'S MANUAL (2 OF 2)	45
469	MR. BILL (1 OF 2)	45
470	MR. BILL (2 OF 2)	46
471	PRESENT (5.1)	182
472	SIMPLIFIED BUSINESS BOOKKEEPING	46
473	TRIVIAL TOWERS (1 OF 2)	131
474	TRIVIAL TOWERS (2 OF 2)	131
475	MONOPOLY P.C. / TUNE TRIVIA	131
476	PATRICK'S BEST GAMES	169
477	NAME GRAM / BREAK DOWN / FONE WORD	132
478	HARD DISK UTILITIES	317
479	AM-TAX 1986	200
480	PC-OUTLINE	285
481	STILL RIVER SHELL	318
482	ENCODE/ DECODE	324
483	MAIL MONSTER	87
484	GRAPHICS FONT DESIGN UTILITY	183
485	ICON MAKER & FX MATRIX	372
486	TELISOLAR	201
487	REFLEX POINT	170
490	MICROCOMPUTER DATA SECURITY	325
491	CRYPTANALYSIS	325
492	NUTRIENT	247
493	VCRDBASE	88
494	WORLD DIGITIZED (1 OF 3)	248
495	WORLD DIGITIZED (2 OF 3)	248
496	WORLD DIGITIZED (3 OF 3)	248
497	HOMEWARE (1 OF 2)	201
498	DOSAMATIC	318
499	PROCOMM	66
500	SOFT-TOUCH	100
501	SALESEYE (2.3) PROGRAM (1 OF 2)	47
502	SALESEYE (2.3) TUTORIAL (2 OF 2)	47
503	RELIANCE MAILING	48
505	PC-STYLE	286
506	BIBLIOGRAPHY OF BUSINESS ETHICS AND MORAL VALUES	117
507	PC-SPRINT	249
508	STAT TOOLS (1 OF 2)	226
509	STAT TOOLS (2 OF 2)	226
510	VISIBLE-PASCAL	216
511	TURBO SPRITES AND ANIMATION	183
511	TURBO SPRITES AND ANIMATION	384
512	PROGRAMS FROM "THE COMPLETE TURBO PASCAL"	216
513	BMENU AND OTHERS	385
514	FOLLIES	170
515	THE DRAFTSMAN	184
517	IMAGEPRINT	373
519	BUDGETRAK (1 OF 2)	146
520	BUDGETRAK (2 OF 2)	146
521	FREEFILE	88
522	INSTANT RECALL	89
523	SIDE WRITER	373
524	EXPRESSCALC (1 OF 2)	270
525	EXPRESSCALC (2 OF 2)	270
526	WSMX80	374
527	B-WINDOW TOOLBOX, C-WINDOW	217
528	NEW YORK WORD	287
530	FREEWORD	287
531	ALAN'S TEXT EDITOR & SPREADSHEET	270
532	PC-MONEY	147
533	PDS*QUOTE	48
534	COMPUTER USER'S HANDBAG #1	319
535	COMPUTER USER'S HANDBAG #2	319
536	PC-TOOLS	385
537	DBS-KAT	89
538	ASTRONOMY #1	249
539	ADVENTURE SOLUTIONS	133
540	TINY PASCAL COMPILER BUILDER	218
542	POLYGLOT & LETTERFALL	118
543	UTILITIES ECETERA	340
544	LETUS A-B-C VOL. 7	238
545	LETUS A-B-C VOL. 8	238
546	LETUS A-B-C VOL. 9	238
547	LETUS A-B-C VOL. 10	238
548	LETUS A-B-C VOL. 11	239
549	LETUS A-B-C VOL. 12	239
550	LETUS A-B-C VOL. 13	239
551	LETUS A-B-C VOL. 14	239
552	PC-SELL	49
553	LLSQ (FORTRAN PROGRAMS)	218
554	LINPACK LIBRARY (FORTRAN PROGRAMS)	227
555	LINPACK DRIVERS	228
556	FORTRAN & ASSEMBLY	219
557	PINBALL RALLY	171
558	PC PROMPT	320
559	PC ACCOUNTING (1 OF 2)	49
560	PC ACCOUNTING (2 OF 2)	50
562	PC-HAM	250
563	MAX — FREEWARE EDITOR	288
564	JON DART'S DOS UTILITIES	320
565	PC-PAYROLL	50
566	SURVEYSOFT	90
567	DND	133
568	LOTUS UTILITIES	271
569	PC-CODE3 AND PC-CODE4	326
571	WORKSHEETS NO 7	271
572	FEDERAL BUILDING LIFE COST COMPARISON	240
573	XASM CROSS ASSEMBLER	219
574	FREECALC	272
575	PC-STOCK	147
576	PC TICKLE	100
577	C TUTOR (1 OF 2)	70
578	C TUTOR (2 OF 2)	71
579	PASCAL TUTOR (1 OF 2)	71
580	PASCAL TUTOR (2 OF 2)	72
581	WORDWORKER (1 OF 2)	250
582	WORDWORKER (2 OF 2)	251
583	LOTUS 1-2-3 — THE WHITEROCK ALTERNATIVE	272
584	COLLECTED LOTUS 1-2-3 WORKSHEETS	273
585	DOS EXTENSIONS (1 OF 2)	321
586	DOS EXTENSIONS (2 OF 2)	321
587	SYMPHONY WORD PROCESSING TIPS & MACROS	273

Disk #	Title	Pg #
588	SYMPHONY BANK/INSURANCE/ MEDICAL APPLICATIONS	274
589	PTOOLS	386
590	NUCLEAR MAGNETIC RESONANCE (NMR)	228
591	GENESIS	133
592	TSHELL	322
593	GANTT	51
594	NOTES ON DISPLAY	202
595	BASIC GAMES & PROGRAMMING INTRO	72
596	SYMPHONY NO 3	275
597	SYMPHONY NO 4	275
598	MASTER KEY V1.6C	322
599	DREAM (1 OF 3)	90
600	DREAM (2 OF 3)	91
601	DREAM (3 OF 3)	92
604	LANDING PARTY	134
606	POLYMATH	220
607	TEXT UTILITIES	341
608	AUTOMENU	101
609	DISK SPOOL	342
610	PACKDISK	342
611	BLACKBEARD	391
612	LANGUAGES	118
613	MANAGING MONEY WITH IBM PC	202
614	NEW YORK	134
615	ORACLE	251
616	CORBIN HANDBOOK (1 OF 2)	251
617	CORBIN HANDBOOK (2 OF 2)	252
618	MAKEMYDAY	101
619	HOTBOOT/INSULTS	252
620	DANAL (1.0)	184
621	RBBS (3 OF 4)	27
622	RBBS (4 OF 4)	28
623	SPPC SYSTEM DEMO (3.0) (2 OF 2)	229
624	PC-FILE III JR	93
625	PC-CALC JR	275
626	PC-DIAL	66
627	PC-WRITE (2 OF 2)	289
628	BIBLEQ	135
629	PC-ART	185
630	HOMEWARE (3.0) (2 OF 2)	203
631	HARD DISK MENU	102
632	FAMILY HISTORY (2 OF 2)	203
633	DRAWPLUS & SECRET QUEST	186
634	WAGNER UTILITIES AND PCLOG	343
635	MUSE (1 OF 2)	253

Disk #	Title	Pg #
636	MUSE (2 OF 2)	253
637	UNCLE	51
638	SST (1 OF 2)	229
639	SST (2 OF 2)	230
640	LIST	289
640	LIST	374
641	MAHJONG	135
642	MENU-MASTER	102
643	TASM	220
644	THE STOCK TRADER	148
646	AMY'S FIRST PRIMER PC,XT,AT VERSION	119
647	AMY'S FIRST PRIMER PC-JR	119
648	WALMYR PROGRAMS (1 OF 2)	254
649	WALMYR PROGRAMS (2 OF 2)	254
650	FANSI-CONSOLE (2 OF 2)	103
650	FANSI-CONSOLE (2 OF 2)	391
651	TURBO CALC / ASEASYAS SPREADSHEETS	276
652	HI-RES RAINBOW	186
654	KWIKSTAT (1 OF 2)	230
655	KWIKSTAT (2 OF 2)	230
656	REAL ESTATE SYSTEMS	148
657	ZURI EDITOR	289
658	DOS TOOLKIT	343
659	VIANSOFT® CHURCH CONTRIBUTIONS	255
660	MAROONED AGAIN & EMS	255
661	RESICALC	103
662	DATABOSS (1 OF 2)	93
663	DATABOSS (2 OF 2)	94
664	TEACHER'S SPECIAL	120
665	PC DEMONSTRATION SYSTEM	256
666	STRUCTURED PROGRAMMING LANGUAGE	221
667	THE WRITER'S TOOLKIT	290
668	WORLD	94
669	GRAPHTIME II (2.5A) (1 OF 2)	187
670	GRAPHTIME II (2.5A) (2 OF 2)	187
671	FREEWAY PAYROLL (1 OF 3)	52
672	FREEWAY PAYROLL (2 OF 3)	52
673	FREEWAY PAYROLL (3 OF 3)	53
674	ENABLE READER SPEECH SYSTEM (3.0) (1 OF 4)	256
675	ENABLE READER SPEECH SYSTEM (3.0) (2 OF 4)	257

Disk #	Title	Pg #
676	THE VOTRAX WORD PROCESSING PROGRAM	258
677	DECTALK WORD PROCESSING PROGRAMS.	258
678	THE GOLDEN WOMBAT OF DESTINY	136
679	IT (IDEAL TERMINAL)	67
680	FORGE	392
681	PC-TYPE+ BY JIM BUTTON (2 OF 3)	291
682	PC-TYPE+ BY JIM BUTTON (3 OF 3)	291
683	BUTTONWARE ADVENTURES	136
684	PAGEONE	292
685	NEW FIG FORTH	221
686	HELPDOS	72
687	IN-CONTROL (1 OF 3)	104
688	IN-CONTROL (2 OF 3)	104
689	IN-CONTROL (3 OF 3)	105
690	BEST-PLAN PLANNING SYSTEM (1 OF 2)	258
691	BEST-PLAN PLANNING SYSTEM (2 OF 2)	259
692	ASTROSOFT EPHEMERIS(ACE) (1 OF 2)	260
693	ASTROSOFT EPHEMERIS(ACE) (2 OF 2)	260
694	SLEUTH	137
695	EZ-SPREADSHEET	276
696	QUBECALC	277
697	THE FRONT OFFICE (1 OF 3)	53
698	THE FRONT OFFICE (2 OF 3)	54
699	THE FRONT OFFICE (3 OF 3)	54
700	MEALMATE	261
700	MEALMATE	204
701	DANCAD3D (1 OF 4)	188
702	DANCAD3D — DEMO EXAMPLES (2 OF 4)	188
703	DANCAD3D — DEMO EXAMPLES (3 OF 4)	189
704	DANCAD3D — DEMO EXAMPLES (4 OF 4)	189
705	KIDGAMES	137
705	KIDGAMES	171

BY DISK TITLE

NON-ALPHA

Title	Disk	Pg #
WORKSHEETS NO 7	571	271
3D	73	174
3X5 CARD	253	79

A

Title	Disk	Pg #
A.D.A. PROLOG V1.91P	417	23
ABC DATABASE	119	76
ABC DESIGN (1 OF 2)	336	179
ABC DESIGN (2 OF 2)	337	180
ADDRESS BOOK	401	86
AM-TAX 1986	479	200
AMULET OF YENDOR	452	130
AMY'S FIRST PRIMER PC,XT,AT VERSION	646	119
AMY'S FIRST PRIMER PC-JR VERSION	647	119
ARCHIE	19	68
AUTOMENU	608	101
ADDRESS MANAGER	218	78
ADVENTURE SOLUTIONS	539	133
ADVENTUREWARE	453	130
ALAN'S TEXT EDITOR & SPREADSHEET	531	270
ALBERTA AGRICULTURAL PROGRAMS	460	246
ANALYTICALC (1 OF 3)	430	41
ANALYTICALC (2 OF 3)	431	42
ANALYTICALC (3 OF 3)	432	43
ARCADE SERIES NO 1	177	158
ARCADE SERIES NO 2	209	161
ARCADE SERIES NO 3	293	165
ASSEMBLY LANGUAGE TUTORIAL	114	208
ASSEMBLY UTIL NO 1	307	349
ASSEMBLY UTIL NO 2	308	350
ASSEMBLY UTIL NO 3	309	351
ASSEMBLY/PASCAL UTILITIES	223	347
ASSORTED AGRICULTURAL PROGRAMS	459	245

Title	Disk	Pg #
ASSORTED BASIC GAMES	450	168
ASSORTED GAMES	448	167
ASSORTED GAMES	456	168
ASTRONOMY COLLECTION #1	538	249
ASTROSOFT EPHEMERIS(ACE) (1 OF 2)	692	260
ASTROSOFT EPHEMERIS(ACE) (2 OF 2)	693	260
AUTOFILE, EASYFILE AND TIME, DATE UTILITIES	182	309

B

Title	Disk	Pg #
B-WINDOW TOOLBOX, C-WINDOW	527	217
BARGRAPH	14	139
BASIC AIDS NO 1	167	346
BASIC AIDS NO 2	371	356
BASIC AIDS NO 3	372	357
BASIC AIDS NO 4	381	211
BASIC AIDS AND MATH	206	382
BASIC DRAWING	38	173
BASIC GAMES & PROGRAMMING INTRO	595	72
BASIC NECESSITIES	162	346
BASIC PAINT: EASEL AND EASYGRAF	191	176
BASICXREF	358	382
BIBLIOGRAPHY OF BUSINESS ETHICS AND MORAL VALUES	506	117
BMENU AND OTHERS	513	385
BOBCAT — BUSINESS DATABASE	247	235
BUDGETRAK (1 OF 2)	519	146
BUDGETRAK (2 OF 2)	520	146
BANNER	386	370
BEST GAMES	274	163
BEST UTILITIES	273	335
BEST-PLAN PLANNING SYSTEM (1 OF 2)	690	258
BEST-PLAN PLANNING SYSTEM (2 OF 2)	691	259
BETATOOL'S BASIC DEVELOPMENT SYSTEM	269	348
BIBLEQ	628	135

Title	Disk	Pg #
BLACKBEARD	611	391
INDEX BUILDER	26	75
BOWLING SECRETARY	23	241
BUDGET/ TASKPLAN/LOAN	155	30
BUTTONWARE ADVENTURES	683	136

C

Title	Disk	Pg #
C ADVENTURE	259	123
C TUTOR (1 OF 2)	577	70
C TUTOR (2 OF 2)	578	71
C UTILITIES NO 1	149	345
C UTILITIES NO 2	216	347
C UTILITIES NO 4	314	351
C UTILITIES NO 5	341	210
C UTILITIES NO 5	315	352
CHASM	10	206
CK SYSTEM (1 OF 2)	462	198
CK SYSTEM (2 OF 2)	463	199
COLLECTED LOTUS 1-2-3 WORKSHEETS	584	273
COLLIST 2.0	276	367
COMMUNICATIONS UTILITIES NO 3	316	62
COMPUTER USER'S HANDBAG #1	534	319
COMPUTER USER'S HANDBAG #2	535	319
CPA-LEDGER PROGRAM (1 OF 2)	466	44
CPA-LEDGER USER'S MANUAL (2 OF 2)	468	45
CROSSREF	8	376
CRYPTANALYSIS HELPER	491	325
CAVEQUEST	451	129
CHECKBOOK MANAGEMENT	393	39
CHECKBOOK SYSTEM	397	197
COMMUNICATION PROGRAMS NO 1	81	57
COMMUNICATION PROGRAMS NO 1	187	59
COMMUNICATION PROGRAMS NO 2	258	60
COMMUNICATIONS PROGRAMS	439	65
COMPILED PASCAL ROUTINES LIBRARY	392	211
COMPUTER SECURITY PACKAGE	112	323
CONDEN	384	338
ADDRESS BOOK	401	86
CONFIDANT	230	324

Title	Disk	Pg #
COPY PROTECTION/ UNPROTECT	414	297
CORBIN HANDBOOK (1 OF 2)	616	251
CORBIN HANDBOOK (2 OF 2)	617	252
CREATOR	339	83
CROSS ASSEMBLER FOR THE IBM 370	402	212

D

Title	Disk	Pg #
DANCAD3D (1 OF 4)	701	188
DANCAD3D — DEMO EXAMPLES (2 OF 4)	702	188
DANCAD3D — DEMO EXAMPLES (3 OF 4)	703	189
DANCAD3D — DEMO EXAMPLES (4 OF 4)	704	189
DATABOSS (1 OF 2)	662	93
DATABOSS (2 OF 2)	663	94
DBASE II PROGRAMS	126	378
DBS-KAT	537	89
DECTALK WORD PROCESSING PROGRAMS.	677	258
DESIGNER	69	174
DESKTOP (1 OF 2)	64	262
DESKTOP (2 OF 2)	65	262
DISKCAT	70	302
DISKCAT 4.3F	106	75
DISKMODF	28	299
DND	567	133
DOS EXTENSIONS (1 OF 2)	585	321
DOS EXTENSIONS (2 OF 2)	586	321
DOS TOOLKIT	658	343
DOS UTILITIES	413	316
DOS UTILITIES NO 1	52	327
DOS UTILITIES NO 2	79	329
DOS UTILITIES NO 3	80	303
DOS UTILITIES NO 4	84	330
DOS UTILITIES NO 5	109	304
DOS UTILITIES NO 6	115	331
DOS UTILITIES NO 7	140	379
DOS UTILITIES NO 8	183	310
DOS UTILITIES NO 9	184	294
DOS UTILITIES NO 10	185	310
DOS UTILITIES NO 11	196	332
DOS UTILITIES NO 12	204	295
DOS UTILITIES NO 13	205	311
DOS UTILITIES NO 14	255	333
DOS UTILITIES NO 15	283	335
DOS UTILITIES NO 16	319	336
DOS UTILITIES NO 17	373	337
DOS UTILITIES NO 18	374	315

Title	Disk	Pg #
DOS AND PRINTER UTILITIES	33	300
DOS AND PROGRAMMER UTILITIES	256	334
DOSAMATIC	498	318
DRAWPLUS & SECRET QUEST	633	186
DREAM (1 OF 3)	599	90
DREAM (2 OF 3)	600	91
DREAM (3 OF 3)	601	92
DANAL	620	184
DATA BASE OF STEEL (1 OF 4)	214	77
DATA BASE OF STEEL (2 OF 4)	215	78
DATA BASE OF STEEL (3 OF 4)	267	80
DATA BASE OF STEEL (4 OF 4)	268	81
DATABASE PROGRAMS	317	83
DISK SPOOL	609	342
DRAFTSMAN	515	184
DRAW	20	173

E

Title	Disk	Pg #
EAMON MASTER (1 OF 2)	296	125
EAMON DESIGNER & UTILITIES (2 OF 2)	297	125
EDIT (1.16)	294	281
ENCODE/ DECODE	482	324
EPISTAT STATISTICS PACKAGE (3.0)	88	222
ESIE EXPERT SYSTEM SHELL	398	23
EXPLIST	7	375
EZ-FORMS PACKAGE	404	40
EZ-SPREADSHEET	695	276
EASYRITE/ LABLFILE FROM GINACO	146	280
ELEMENTARY C	429	214
ENABLE READER SPEECH SYSTEM (1 OF 4)	674	256
ENABLE READER SPEECH SYSTEM (2 OF 4)	675	257
ENGINEERING PASCAL	425	213
EQUATOR/ PC-TOUCH EDUCATIONAL PROGRAMS	249	110
EXPRESSCALC (1 OF 2)	524	270

Title	Disk	Pg #
EXPRESSCALC (2 OF 2)	525	270
EXTENDED BATCH LANGUAGE VER. 2.04A BY SEAWARE	124	307
EXTRA SENSORY PERCEPTION	173	123

F

Title	Disk	Pg #
FAMILY HISTORY (1 OF 2)	361	196
FAMILY HISTORY (2 OF 2)	632	203
FINANCE	25	140
FINANCIAL PROGRAMS & LOTUS WORKSHEETS	406	145
FINDFILE	277	313
FITT LOTUS 1-2-3 TAX WORKSHEETS	290	266
FOLLIES	514	170
FORGE	680	392
FORTRAN & A LITTLE ASSEMBLY	556	219
FREEWAY PAYROLL (1 OF 3)	671	52
FREEWAY PAYROLL (2 OF 3)	672	52
FREEWAY PAYROLL (3 OF 3)	673	53
FREEWILL	193	192
FABULA 1 (1 OF 2)	144	308
FABULA 2 (2 OF 2)	145	308
FAMILY TIES	465	199
FAMILY-TREE, ETC GENEALOGY	240	193
FANSI-CONSOLE (1 OF 2)	356	389
FANSI-CONSOLE (1 OF 2)	356	97
FANSI-CONSOLE (2 OF 2)	650	391
FANSI-CONSOLE (2 OF 2)	650	103
FEDERAL BUILDING LIFE COST COMPARISON	572	240
FILE EXPRESS (1 OF 2)	287	81
FILE EXPRESS (2 OF 2)	288	82
FILE UTILITIES	420	339
FILE UTILITIES NO 1	111	305
FINANCE MANAGER BY HOOPER INTERNATIONAL	151	141
FINANCE AND INVENTORY	171	142

Title	Disk	Pg #
FINANCIAL PROGRAMS	227	143
FLASH CARDS: VOCABULARY & SPELLING (1 OF 4)	367	112
FLASH CARDS: VOCABULARY & SPELLING (2 OF 4)	368	112
FLASH CARDS: VOCABULARY & SPELLING (3 OF 4)	369	113
FLASH CARDS: VOCABULARY & SPELLING (4 OF 4)	370	113
FORM LETTERS	388	38
FREECALC	574	272
FREEFILE	521	88
FREEWORD	530	287
FRONT OFFICE (1 OF 3)	697	53
FRONT OFFICE (2 OF 3)	698	54
FRONT OFFICE (3 OF 3)	699	54
FUNNELS & BUCKETS	229	162
FUNNELS & BUCKETS	229	109

G

Title	Disk	Pg #
GANTT	593	51
GENESIS	591	133
GINACO PROGRAMS	66	328
GLUDRAW	380	181
GRAPHTIME II (2.5A) (1 OF 2)	669	187
GRAPHTIME II (2.5A) (2 OF 2)	670	187
GAME SERIES NO 1	1	149
GAME SERIES NO 2	16	150
GAME SERIES NO 3	17	150
GAME SERIES NO 4	24	151
GAME SERIES NO 5	35	152
GAME SERIES NO 6	37	152
GAMES SERIES NO 8	45	153
GAME SERIES NO 9	55	154
GAME SERIES NO 10	71	155
GAME SERIES NO 11	72	155
GAME SERIES NO 12	174	157
GAME SERIES NO 13	178	159
GAME SERIES NO 14	203	160
GAME SERIES NO 15	210	161
GAME SERIES NO 16	228	162
GAME SERIES NO 17	260	163
GAME SERIES NO 18	390	166
GENEALOGY ON DISPLAY	90	190
GOLDEN WOMBAT OF DESTINY	678	136

Title	Disk	Pg #
GOLF SCORECARD	342	244
GRAPHICS FONT DESIGN UTILITY	484	183
GORDON'S PC-CALC	224	264
GREATEST ARCADE GAMES	457	169

H

Title	Disk	Pg #
HARD DISK MENU	631	102
HI-RES RAINBOW	652	186
HOMEWARE (3.2) (1 OF 2)	497	201
HOMEWARE (3.0) (2 OF 2)	630	203
HOST-III PUBLIC BULLETIN BOARD PACKAGE V1.1G	125	25
HYPERDRIVE	51	302
HAM RADIO #1	436	115
HAM RADIO #2	437	115
HARD DISK UTILITIES	478	317
HEALTH RISK	192	242
HELPDOS	686	72
HISTORY EDUCATION	76	107
HOME APPLICATIONS	321	195
HOME BUDGET TEMPLATE FOR LOTUS 1-2-3	389	269
HOME FINANCE	107	191
HOME INVENTORY SYSTEM	395	197
HOTBOOT/INSULTS	619	252
HOTKEY/ XDOS/ EZ-MENU/ CALC	444	339

I

Title	Disk	Pg #
IBM BBS BY GENE PLANTZ	150	26
IN-CONTROL (1 OF 3)	687	104
IN-CONTROL (2 OF 3)	688	104
IN-CONTROL (3 OF 3)	689	105
INCTAX (1.1)	458	198
INSTANT RECALL	522	89
IQBUILD	18	106
IT (IDEAL TERMINAL)	679	67
ICON MAKER & FX MATRIX	485	372
IMAGEPRINT	517	373
INFOBASE	340	84
INVENTORY	62	29

J

Title	Disk	Pg #
JUSTIFY AND SPEED READER DEMO	211	364
JON DART'S DOS UTILITIES	564	320
JUKEBOX	100	122

K

Title	Disk	Pg #
KERMIT-MS COMPATIBLES, ASM MODULES	433	64
KERMIT-MS COMPATIBLES, ASM MODULES II	434	64
KIDGAMES	705	171
KIDGAMES	705	137
KLP/DTA/MUA	332	37
KWIKSTAT (1 OF 2)	654	230
KWIKSTAT (2 OF 2)	655	230
KEEP IN TOUCH	387	98
KERMIT (1 OF 2)	41	55
KERMIT (2 OF 2)	42	56
KEYBOARD UTILITIES NO 1	56	328
KEYBOARD UTILITIES NO 2	181	332

L

Title	Disk	Pg #
LETUS A-B-C VOL. 1	121	232
LETUS A-B-C VOL. 2	122	233
LETUS A-B-C VOL. 3	123	233
LETUS A-B-C VOL. 4	348	237
LETUS A-B-C VOL. 5	349	237
LETUS A-B-C VOL. 6	350	237
LETUS A-B-C VOL. 7	544	238
LETUS A-B-C VOL. 8	545	238
LETUS A-B-C VOL. 9	546	238
LETUS A-B-C VOL. 10	547	238
LETUS A-B-C VOL. 11	548	239
LETUS A-B-C VOL. 12	549	239
LETUS A-B-C VOL. 13	550	239
LETUS A-B-C VOL. 14	551	239
LINPACK DRIVERS	555	228
LINPACK LIBRARY (FORTRAN PROGRAMS)	554	227
LIST	640	374
LIST	640	289

Title	Disk	Pg #
LLSQ (FORTRAN PROGRAMS)	553	218
LOTUS 1-2-3 — THE WHITEROCK ALTERNATIVE	583	272
LOTUS UTILITIES	568	271
LOTUS WORKSHEETS NO 1	207	264
LANDING PARTY	604	134
LANGUAGES	612	118
LAXON & PERRY FORTH (1 OF 2)	263	209
LAXON & PERRY FORTH (2 OF 2)	264	210
LISTMATE/LOAD-US BY SWFTE	252	313
LOAN AMORTIZATION AND PROSPECT LIST	399	39
LOGON/OFF	325	314
LOTUS WORKSHEETS NO 2	301	266
LOTUS WORKSHEETS NO 3	302	267
LOTUS WORKSHEETS NO 4	303	267
LOTUS WORKSHEETS NO 5	304	268

M

Title	Disk	Pg #
MAHJONG	641	135
MAIL MONSTER	483	87
MAROONED AGAIN & EMS	660	255
MAX — FREEWARE EDITOR	563	288
MEALMATE AND OTHERS	700	204
MEALMATE AND OTHERS	700	261
MENU-MASTER	642	102
MINITEL COMMUNICATIONS	188	59
MUSE (1 OF 2)	635	253
MUSE (2 OF 2)	636	253
MUSIC	92	121
MVP-FORTH	31	207
MAGAZINE BIBLIOGRAPHIES	280	236
MAILING LIST PROGRAMS	169	31
MAKEMYDAY	618	101
MANAGING MONEY WITH IBM PC	613	202
MAPMAKER	219	177
MASTER KEY V1.6C	598	322

Title	Disk	Pg #
MATH PAK	394	113
MATH PAK	394	225
MATH TUTOR	95	107
MATH AND STATISTICS ROUTINES	180	223
MICROCOMPUTER DATA SECURITY — BY DAN CRONIN	490	325
MICROGOURMET (1 OF 2)	116	191
MICROGOURMET (2 OF 2)	117	192
MISCELLANEOUS APPLICATIONS	440	44
MONOPOLY P.C. / TUNE TRIVIA	475	131
MOONBEAM	359	112
MOVIE DATABASE	311	82
MR. BILL (1 OF 2)	469	45
MR. BILL (2 OF 2)	470	46
MUSIC COLLECTION	322	126
MUSIC AND EDUCATIONAL PROGRAMS	168	108

N

Title	Disk	Pg #
NAEPIRS	266	111
NEWBASE	233	79
NELIST AND DISK ALIGNMENT	217	312
NEW YORK WORD	528	287
NMR SPECTROSCOPY AND STATISTICS	391	224
NONLIN	67	329
NOTES ON DISPLAY	594	202
NUTRIENT	492	247
NAME GRAM / BREAK DOWN / FONE WORD	477	132
NEW FIG FORTH	685	221
NEW YORK	614	134
NORLAND SOFTWARE HANGMAN	153	107
NUCLEAR MAGNETIC RESONANCE (NMR)	590	228

O

Title	Disk	Pg #
ORIGAMI	408	128
ORACLE	615	251

P

Title	Disk	Pg #
PACKDISK	610	342
PAGEONE	684	292
PASCAL COLLECTION NO 1	36	207
PASCAL MATH LIBRARY	248	348
PASCAL TUTOR (1 OF 2)	579	71
PASCAL TUTOR (2 OF 2)	580	72
PC ACCOUNTING SYSTEM (1 OF 2)	559	49
PC ACCOUNTING SYSTEM (2 OF 2)	560	50
PC DEMONSTRATION SYSTEM	665	256
PC FIRING LINE ISSUE #2 (1 OF 2)	160	234
PC FIRING LINE ISSUE #2 (2 OF 2)	161	235
PC FIRING LINE/PC UNDERGROUND ISSUE #1	159	234
PC PROFESSOR BASIC TUTORIAL	105	69
PC PROMPT (DOS HELP)	558	320
PC TICKLE	576	100
PC-ART	629	185
PC-CALC	199	263
PC-CHECK	275	193
PC-CHESS	120	157
PC-CODE3 AND PC-CODE4	569	326
PC-CONVERT/SWEEP	382	316
PC-CALC JR	625	275
PC-DBMS	383	85
PC-DESKTEAM	405	99
PC-DIAL	129	57
PC-DOS HELP	254	69
PC-DIAL	626	66
PC-FILE III	5	74
PC-FOIL	347	244
PC-FONT	225	366
PC-FILE III JR	624	93
PC-GL	331	37
PC-GOLF	262	243
PC-GRAF	195	177
PC-GRAPH	418	182
PC-GENERAL LEDGER	237	32
PC-HAM	562	250
PC-INPUT	363	390
PC-KEY DRAW NO 1 (1 OF 2)	344	180

Title	Disk	Pg #
PC-KEY DRAW NO 2 (2 OF 2)	345	181
PC-MONEY	532	147
PC-MUSICIAN	127	122
PC-OUTLINE	480	285
PC-PAYROLL	565	50
PC-PICTURE GRAPHICS BY E. YING	136	175
PC-SELL	552	49
PC-SIG BUSINESS SAMPLER NO 1	261	34
PC-SIG BUSINESS SAMPLER NO 2	282	35
PC-SIG BUSINESS SAMPLER NO 3	313	35
PC-SIG BUSINESS SAMPLER NO 4	330	36
PC-SIG SAMPLER NO 1	47	153
PC-SIG SAMPLER NO 2	49	154
PC-SIG SAMPLER NO 3	89	304
PC-SIG SAMPLER NO 4	91	156
PC-SIG SAMPLER NO 5	93	331
PC-SIG SAMPLER NO 6	128	379
PC-SIG SAMPLER NO 7	208	160
PC-SIG SAMPLER NO 8	284	336
PC-SPRINT	507	249
PC-STOCK	575	147
PC-STYLE	505	286
PC-TYPE+ BY JIM BUTTON (1 OF 3)	455	285
PC-TYPE+ BY JIM BUTTON (2 OF 3)	681	291
PC-TYPE+ BY JIM BUTTON (3 OF 3)	682	291
PC-TOOLS	536	385
PC-VT	286	60
PC-WRITE (2.7/4) (1 OF 2)	78	278
PC-WRITE (2.7/4) (2 OF 2)	627	289
PC-ZAP	355	314
PCMAN	21	151
PCJR EDUCATIONAL GAMES	241	109
PCJR GAMES	354	165
PDRAW	13	172
PDS*BASE DATABASE SYSTEM	396	85
PDS*QUOTE	533	48
PFROI	360	145
PIANOMAN	279	124
PINBALL RALLY	557	171
PROJECT MANAGEMENT	423	41
PTOOLS	589	386
PARTS INVENTORY CONTROL	235	32
PASCAL COMPILER	424	213
PASCAL I/O	30	206
PASCAL TOOLS (1 OF 3)	130	344
PASCAL TOOLS (2 OF 3)	131	345
PASCAL TOOLS (3 OF 3)	132	345
PATCHES	376	295
PATRICK'S BEST GAMES	476	169
PBASE	464	87
PERSONAL GENERAL LEDGER	165	30
PERSONAL UTILITIES	412	99
PHRASE CRAZE	385	128
PIZZA & CHECK REGISTER SYSTEMS	179	31
PLANETS/WATOR/ LEYGREF'S CASTLE	298	243
POLYGLOT & LETTERFALL	542	118
POLYMATH	606	220
PORTWORTH PACKAGE	101	141
POWER-WORKSHEETS	289	265
PRESENT (5.1)	471	182
PRINTER ART	154	175
PRINTER UTILITIES	411	370
PRINTER UTILITIES	438	371
PRINTER UTIL NO 1	220	364
PRINTER UTIL NO 2	221	365
PRINTER UTIL NO 3	222	365
PRINTER UTIL NO 4	236	366
PRINTER UTIL NO 5	326	368
PRINTER UTIL NO 6	377	369
PRINTER AND GRAPHICS UTILITIES	265	367
PROCOMM	499	66
PROGRAMMER'S UTILITIES NO 1	108	208
PROGRAMMER UTILITIES NO 2	110	378
PROGRAMMER UTILITIES NO 4	138	305
PROGRAMMER UTILITIES NO 5	141	380
PROGRAMMER UTILITIES NO 6	142	380
PROGRAMMER UTILITIES NO 7	143	381
PROGRAMMER UTILITIES NO 8	163	387
PROGRAMMER'S CALCULATOR	87	95
PROGRAMMER/ COMMUNICATIONS UTILITIES	135	58
PROGRAMS FROM "THE COMPLETE TURBO PASCAL"	512	216

Q

Title	Disk	Pg #
QMODEM COMMUNICATIONS	310	61
QPARSER	419	383
QSYS DOS MENU (1 OF 2)	118	96
QSYS DOS (3.0) DOCUMENTATION (2 OF 2)	278	97
QUBECALC	696	277

R

Title	Disk	Pg #
RATBAS	3	205
RBBS (1 OF 4)	212	27
RBBS (2 OF 4)	334	27
RBBS (3 OF 4)	621	27
RBBS (4 OF 4)	622	28
RBBS FOR THE IBM PC	152	26
REFLEX POINT	487	170
REFLIST	231	242
RESICALC	661	103
ROFF AND PC-READ	194	281
ROFF4	416	284
RUNOFF	48	362
REAL ESTATE SYSTEMS	656	148
RECIPE INDEX	281	236
RELIANCE MAILING	503	48
RIDGETOWN COLLEGE PROGRAMS	461	246

S

Title	Disk	Pg #
SALESEYE (2.3) PROGRAM (1 OF 2)	501	47
SALESEYE (2.3) TUTORIAL (2 OF 2)	502	47
SCREEN TEXT EDITOR	86	279
SDB — A SIMPLE DATABASE SYSTEM	147	76
SIDE WRITER	523	373
SIMTERM	362	63
SNOCREST BASIC #1	409	212
SNOCREST BASIC #2	410	213
SPA:WN STRUCTURED PROGRAMMING/ WARNIER DIAGRAM	442	215

Title	Disk	Pg #
SPA:WN STRUCTURED PROGRAMMING/ WARNIER DIAGRAM	442	361
SPACEWAR	292	164
SPPC SYSTEM DEMO (3.0) (1 OF 2)	232	224
SPPC SYSTEM DEMO (3.0) (2 OF 2)	623	229
SPRITE GRAPHICS	238	178
SQUISH	9	376
SST (1 OF 2)	638	229
SST (2 OF 2)	639	230
SYMPHONY BANK/INSURANCE/ MEDICAL APPLICATIONS	588	274
SYMPHONY WORD PROCESSING TIPS & MACROS	587	273
SYSCOMM	338	62
SAGE CALENDAR/TAG	243	33
SAGE TRADER	242	143
SCREEN DESIGN AID AND FORMS	312	389
SCREEN UTILITIES NO 1	46	301
SCREEN UTILITIES NO 2	139	306
SCREEN AND PRINTER UTILITIES	186	363
SCREENWRITER	422	284
SIMPLIFIED BUSINESS BOOKKEEPING	472	46
SIMULATION & BOARD GAMES	175	158
SKY	447	245
SLEUTH	694	137
SLIDE GENERATION	244	179
SOFT-TOUCH	500	100
SORTED DIRECTORY	34	300
SPREADSHEETS	170	263
STAT TOOLS (1 OF 2)	508	226
STAT TOOLS (2 OF 2)	509	226
STEVE'S UTILITIES	172	309
STILL RIVER SHELL	481	318
STOCK CHARTING	246	144
STOCK MARKET ANALYSER	40	140
STOCK TRADER	644	148
STRUCTURED PROGRAMMING LANGUAGE	666	221
SURVEYSOFT	566	90
SYMPHONY NO 1	305	268
SYMPHONY NO 2	306	269
SYMPHONY NO 3	596	275
SYMPHONY NO 4	597	275

T

Title	Disk	Pg #
T-SCORE/ EDUCATION	443	116
TASM	643	220
TAX-FILE	295	194
TEACHER'S SPECIAL	664	120
TEKTRONIX 4010 EMULATOR	441	65
TELISOLAR	486	201
TPNCALC	234	224
TRANSTOCK	323	144
TSHELL	592	322
TUTOR.COM	403	70
TELEWARE CASHTRAC	164	142
TEXT EDITORS AND MISC	190	280
TEXT UTILITIES	607	341
THREE USER-SUPPORTED PROGRAMS	113	96
TIME AND MONEY	251	33
TINY PASCAL COMPILER BUILDER	540	218
TOUCHTYPE	320	111
TRIVIA (1 OF 2)	327	126
TRIVIA (2 OF 2)	328	127
TRIVIA & OTHERS	329	127
TRIVIAL TOWERS (1 OF 2)	473	131
TRIVIAL TOWERS (2 OF 2)	474	131
TURBO CALC / ASEASYAS SPREADSHEETS	651	276
TURBO PASCAL PROGRAMS NO 1	324	353
TURBO PASCAL PROGRAMS NO 2	351	354
TURBO PASCAL PROGRAMS NO 3	353	354
TURBO PASCAL PROGRAMS NO 5	365	355
TURBO PASCAL PROGRAMS NO 6	366	356
TURBO PASCAL PROGRAMS NO 7	375	358
TURBO PASCAL ROUTINES #6	426	359
TURBO PASCAL ROUTINES #7	427	359
TURBO PASCAL ROUTINES #8	428	360
TURBO PASCAL STATISTICS, TRIG, UTILITIES	435	383

Title	Disk	Pg #
TURBO SPRITES AND ANIMATION	511	384
TURBO SPRITES AND ANIMATION	511	183
TWO FORTHS	352	210
TWO TREKS	197	159

U

Title	Disk	Pg #
UNCLE	637	51
UNIFORTH	454	215
UTIL 1.2/MAKE/BASREF	60	377
ULTRA-UTILITIES 4.0	133	307
ULTRA-UTILITIES FILES — UNSQUEEZED	245	312
UTILITIES ECETERA	543	340
UTILITY 1-2-3	257	265

V

Title	Disk	Pg #
VCRDBASE	493	88
VIANSOFT® CHURCH CONTRIBUTIONS	659	255
VISIBLE-PASCAL	510	216
VIDEOCHEM EDUCATIONAL GAME	407	114
VOTRAX WORD PROCESSING PROGRAM	676	258

W

Title	Disk	Pg #
W-ED, WORD PROCESSING PREVIEWER	415	283
WAGNER UTILITIES AND PCLOG	634	343
WALMYR PROGRAMS (1 OF 2)	648	254
WALMYR PROGRAMS (2 OF 2)	649	254
WHIZZARD SCREEN	285	388
WORDWORKER (2 OF 2)	582	251
WORLD	668	94
WORLD DIGITIZED (1 OF 3)	494	248
WORLD DIGITIZED (2 OF 3)	495	248

Title	Disk	Pg #
WORLD DIGITIZED		
(3 OF 3)	496	248
WRITER'S TOOLKIT	667	290
WSMX80	526	374
WILLY THE WORM &		
MORE	445	167
WORD PROCESSING	343	282
WORDSTAR AIDS	379	282
WORDWORKER		
(1 OF 2)	581	250
WORMCITY	83	156

X

XASM CROSS		
ASSEMBLER	573	219
XLISP	148	22
XMODEM	54	56

Z

ZORK UTILITIES	446	129
ZURI EDITOR	657	289

BY SUBJECT

Disk number(s) in bold, followed by page number

NON-ALPHA

123-from-text converter, 123PREP, **141**, 380

A

Accounting, PC-GL, **331**, 37
Accounting, TELEWARE CASHTRAC, **164**, 142
Accounting and budgets, BUDGETRAK, **519,520**, 146
Accounting and finance, FINANCE MANAGER, **151**, 141
Accounting, European, FREEWAY, **671-673**, 52
Address list manager, MAIL MONSTER, **483**, 87
Address list manager, The Address Book, **401**, 86
Address manager, LetterWriter, **415**, 283
Adventure game, CASTLE, **210**, 161
Adventure game compiler, ADVENT, **91**, 156
Adventure solutions, HINTS, **539**, 133
Agricultural programs and information, Agricultural, **459**, 245
Agricultural programs and information, Alberta Ag., **460**, 246
Agricultural programs and information, Ridgetown College, **461**, 246
AI programming language, A.D.A PROLOG, **417**, 23
AI programming language, XLISP, **148**, 22
Aircraft Flight Log, The Sky, **447**, 245
Animation, Pascal, DESIGNER, **511**, 183
Animation, wire-frame CAD, DANCAD3D, **701-704**, 188
ANSI device driver, FANSI-CONSOLE, **356,650**, 97
Appointment book, DDCAL, **412**, 99
Appointment util, PC-TICKLE, **576**, 100
Archive utility, ARC, **420**, 339
Aristocrat ciphers, CRYPT. AID, **491**, 325
Assembler & tutorial, CHASM, **10**, 206
Assembler tutorial, text, ASM, **114**, 208
Assembly transfer device, TASM Version 2.2, **643**, 220
Astronomy, The Sky, **447**, 245

Astronomy — Ephemeris, ACE, **692,693**, 260
Astronomy — Solar & Lunar, Astronomy #1, **538**, 249
Astronomy calculations, PRECESS, **543**, 340

B

Banner making program, BANNER, **386**, 370
BASIC condense utility, SQUISH, **9**, 376
BASIC cross-ref generator, BASICREF, **358**, 382
BASIC databases, Database programs, **317**, 83
BASIC file lister, LISTASC.EXE, **438**, 371
BASIC line number remove/insert, NUMZAP, **284**, 336
BASIC programming language, BASIC Games & Prog., **595**, 72
BASIC programming routines, ED, **162**, 346
BASIC programming tools, BASICAID, **381**, 211
BASIC routines and helps, BASIC Aids No 1, **167**, 346
BASIC screen I/O subroutines, WHIZZARD, **285**, 388
BASIC text editing, Text Editors, **190**, 280
BASIC tools, AID, **141**, 380
BASIC tutorial, BASIC Games & Prog., **595**, 72
BASIC tutorial, PC Professor, **105**, 69
BASIC variable lister, BASREF, **60**, 377
BASIC, DOS I/O & port watch, BASICSUB, **372**, 357
BASIC, read from DOS, READBAS5, **319**, 336
BASIC, x-ref, un/re-num & compress, GS-VAREN, **371**, 356
Batch language, enhanced, BAT, **124**, 307
Batch utility, WAIT, **373**, 337
BBS (BASIC), IBM BBS, **150**, 26
BBS (BASIC), RBBS for the PC, **152**, 26
Bell tone change, NEWBELL, **255**, 333
Bible reference, WORDWORKER, **581,582**, 250
Bible trivia game, BibleQ, **628**, 135
Bibliographies, Magazine/Papers, Magazine Biblio., **247**, 235
Billing system (itemize), MR. BILL, **469,470**, 45
Biorhythm program, BIO, **55**, 154
Blind users — talking software, ENABLE, **674**, 256
Book indexer program, Book Index Builder, **26**, 75

Bowling database, Bowling Secretary, **23**, 241
Breakpoint utility, DOS Utils 5, **109**, 304
Budget management report, FINANCE, **25**, 140
Budget recordkeeping, Time & Money, **251**, 33
Budget tracking device, BUDGETRK, **155**, 30
Business — bibliography of bus. ethics & values, BIBLIO. OF BUSINESS, **506**, 117
Business analysis, THE FRONT OFFICE, **697-699**, 53
Business bar graphs, BARGRAPH, **14**, 139
Business bookkeeping system (BASIC), BKPG, **472**, 46
Business database, DB of Steel, **214,215,267,268**, 77
Business Database, Reference, BOBCAT, **280**, 236
Business Demo system, PC-DEMO, **665**, 256
Business Desktop, IN-CONTROL, **687-689**, 104
Business graphics, GRAPHTIME, **669**, 187
Business manager, KeepInTouch, **387**, 98

C

C language tutorial, C TUTOR, **577,578**, 70
C programming utilities, XC, **149**, 345
C programming utils, C Utilities No 5, **315**, 352
C routines, ABOUT-C, **429**, 214
C routines, CPRGRMS1, **314**, 351
C-to-DOS routines, WRITEC, **216**, 347
CAD system, DANCAD3D, **701**, 188
Calculator — memory resident, matrix, RESICALC, **661**, 103
Calculator, high precision, BIGCALC, **256**, 334
Calculator, programmers, Prog. Calc., **87**, 95
Calculator, RPN, CALC, **444**, 339
Calculator, RPN, HP, **142**, 380
Calender, printed, CALENDER, **634**, 343
Cash flow accounting, CASH/HARDCASH, **261**, 34
Castaway, Buttonware, **683**, 136
Catalog diskettes, CDIR, **607**, 341
Catalog diskettes, DIR, **33**, 300
Character counting tool, WC, **658**, 343
Character design (Epson), FX MATRIX, **485**, 372
Character generator, ICON MAKER, **485**, 372

Check register system,
CA.EXE, **179**, 31

Check register system, Micro
Account., **330**, 36

Checkbook management,
PC-CHECK, **282**, 35

Checkbook register system, Checkbook
Mang., **393**, 39

Checkbook tracking system,
CDBS, **282**, 35

Checkbook, Home finances, Chckbk
System v3.31, **397**, 197

Chess program, PCCHESS, **120**, 157

Children's word processor,
WPK, **343**, 282

Childrens educational games,
KIDGAMES, **705**, 137

Church — Contributions bookkeepping,
VIANSOFT, **659**, 255

Ciphers (aristocrat) CRYPT.
AID, **491**, 325

Clock, on-screen, CLOCK, **46**, 301

Clock, on-screen, CLOCK, **543**, 340

Clock, with alarm, TCLOCK, **182**, 309

Code analysis, PC-CODE3&4, **569**, 326

Coded file analysis,
PC-STAT3, **569**, 326

Color graphics, 16-color,
LORES, **139**, 306

Columnar print jobs,
COLLIST, **276**, 367

Command line editor,
NDOSEDIT, **205**, 311

Communications, Kermit, **41,42**, 55

Communications (general asynch),
Ideal Terminal, **679**, 67

Communications (general asynch),
IT, **439**, 65

Communications (general asynch),
MINITEL, **188**, 59

Communications (general asynch),
MODEM86, **439**, 65

Communications (general asynch),
PC-DIAL, **129**, 57

Communications (general asynch),
PC-DIAL, **626**, 66

Communications (general asynch),
ProComm, **499**, 66

Communications (general asynch),
QMODEM, **310**, 61

Communications (general asynch),
SYSCOMM, **338**, 62

Communications (H-P to UNIX),
SIMTERM, **362**, 63

Communications (non-IBM to
IBM/mainframe),
KERMIT,ASM, **434**, 64

Communications (PC to
mini/mainframe),
KERMIT,ASM, **433**, 64

Communications (UNIX),
PC-VT, **286**, 60

Communications (utilities), Commun.
No 1, **81**, 57

Communications (utilities), Commun.
Utils, **187**, 59

Communications (utilities), Commun.
Utils, **258**, 60

Communications (utilities), Commun.
Utils, **316**, 62

Communications (utilities), Modeming
Utils, **135**, 58

Communications (VAX),
PC-VT, **286**, 60

Compare files, PC-COMPARE, **113**, 96

Compiler design, Pascal, TU, **540**, 218

Compiler, Pascal, FACILIS, **424**, 213

Compression of input screens,
SDA, **312**, 389

Computer art utilities, DRAW, **38**, 173

Computer art utilities (animation),
DESIGNER, **69**, 174

Computer art utilities (for EPSON
printer), ABC Design, **336**, 179

Computer art utilities (for EPSON
printer), ABC Design, **337**, 180

Computer art, animation, SPRITE
Graphics, **238**, 178

Computer Graphics — PASCAL
programming aids, Turbo
Sprites, **511**, 183

Computer literacy,
TUTOR.COM, **403**, 70

Computer map creation,
MapMaker, **219**, 177

Computer security, THE
CONFIDANT, **112**, 323

Computer use log device,
USERLOG, **313**, 35

Console drivers,
FANSI-CONSOLE, **356,650**, 97

Copy/Delete by batch, GCOPY, **140**, 379

Critical Path Method, GANTT, **593**, 51

Critical Path Method, PCPM, **423**, 41

Cronin,D.J., Micro Data Secur, **490**, 325

Cross reference utility, BASIC,
CROSSREF, **8**, 376

Cross-assembler, XASM, **573**, 219

Cross-reference utility,
XXREF, **384**, 338

Curve fitting, EIGHTCRV, **261**, 34

D

Data encoding, The Confidant
v2.0, **230**, 324

Data security, Micro Data
Secur, **490**, 325

Database, U-MIND, **245**, 312

Database w/Report Generator,
FileExpress, **287,288**, 81

Database with Expert System, DB of
Steel, **268**, 81

Database with report generator,
Creator, **339**, 83

Database with report generator,
Infobase, **340**, 84

Database with screen editor,
PC-DBMS, **383**, 85

Database with Spreadsheet, DB of
Steel, **267**, 80

Database with word processor,
INSTANT RECALL, **522**, 89

Database (addresses), MAIL
MONSTER, **483**, 87

Database (addresses), The Address
Book, **401**, 86

Database (BASIC),
DATABOSS, **662,663**, 93

Database (BASIC), DB of
Steel, **214,215,267,268**, 77

Database (BASIC), PDS*BASE, **396**, 85

Database (C), SDB, **147**, 76

Database (diskette cataloging),
DBS-KAT, **537**, 89

Database (disks), DISKCAT, **106**, 75

Database (filing), ABC
Database, **119**, 76

Database (forms-driven),
Infobase, **340**, 84

Database (free-text), 3X5
CARD, **253**, 79

Database (free-text), FreeFile, **521**, 88

Database (hierarchical),
PDS*BASE, **396**, 85

Database (indexing), 3X5
CARD, **253**, 79

Database (mailings), Address
Manager, **218**, 78

Database (mailings), newBASE, **233**, 79

Database (memory resident), INSTANT
RECALL, **522**, 89

Database (menu-driven),
newBASE, **233**, 79

Database (movies), The Movie
DB, **311**, 82

Database (PCjr), PC-FILE III, **624**, 93

Database (programmable),
pBASE, **464**, 87

Database (relational),
DATABOSS, **662,663**, 93

Database (relational),
DREAM, **599-601**, 90

Database (relational), pBASE, **464**, 87

Database (relational),
PC-DBMS, **383**, 85

Database (relational), PC-FILE
III, **5**, 74

Database (surveying),
Surveysoft, **566**, 90

Database (technical),
DATABOSS, **662,663**, 93

Database (technical),
DREAM, **599-601**, 90

Database (VCR), VCRDBASE, **493**, 88

DBASE II screen design, DBS, **128**, 379

DBASE II utilities, DOC, **126**, 378

Decision tree analysis, DT, **332**, 37

Demonstration system,
PC-DEMO, **665**, 256

Design of data input screens,
SDA, **312**, 389

Desktop manager,
KeepInTouch, **387**, 98

Desktop manager, MakeMyDay, **618**, 101

Desktop manager, PC-DESKTEAM, **405**, 99

Desktop manager, PC-TICKLER, **576**, 100

Desktop manager, QSYS, **118,278**, 96

Desktop manager (business), KeepInTouch, **387**, 98

Desktop manager (business), SAGE Calendar, **243**, 33

Desktop manager, Business applications, IN-CONTROL, **687-689**, 104

Diabetic foods database, Mealmate & others, **700**, 204

Directory attribute change, HIDE, **319**, 336

Directory delete, DELDIR, **610**, 342

Directory management, DTK, **283**, 335

Directory rename, RENDIR, **319**, 336

Directory sort, DNXSD, **144**, 308

Directory sort utility, LF, **28**, 299

Directory sort utility, SDL, **319**, 336

Directory utility, SDIR, **255**, 333

Directory utility, SDIR24C, **185**, 310

Directory utility, SDIR24C, **273**, 335

Directory utility, XDIR, **80**, 303

Disbursement recordkeeping, Time & Money, **251**, 33

Disk database, DISKCAT, **106**, 75

Disk sector examine, U-ZAP, **133**, 307

Diskette catalog, DIR201, **139**, 306

Diskette cataloging database, DBS-KAT, **537**, 89

Diskette label, COVER, **277**, 313

Diskette label maker, DMASTER, **326**, 368

Diskette label utility, LISTMATE, **252**, 313

Diskette labelmaker, DiskFile, **440**, 44

Diskette Volume label utility, VOLSER, **89**, 304

Diskette, defragment, PACKDISK, **610**, 342

Document printing (multiple), LIST, **640**, 289

Documents and references, REFLIST, **231**, 242

DOS 1.1 fix, DOS utils #9, **184**, 294

DOS command buffer, DOSEDIT, **255**, 333

DOS command buffer/editor, NDOSEDIT, **205**, 311

DOS extension helps, PC Prompt (DOS HELP), **558**, 320

DOS extension system/helps, DOS EXTENSIONS, **585,586**, 321

DOS managing utility, DOS Utils 5, **109**, 304

DOS shell, SDIR50, **319**, 336

DOS Shell system, Still River Shell, **481**, 318

DOS shell (hard disk), HDM-II, **631**, 102

DOS shell (hard disk), MENU-MASTER, **642**, 102

DOS system commands (V2.0), HelpDOS, **686**, 72

DOS tutorial, PC-DOS HELP, **254**, 69

DOS tutorial, TUTOR.COM, **403**, 70

DOS visual shell system, TSHELL, **592**, 322

Dot matrix print enhancement, IMAGEPRINT, **517**, 373

Double entry bookkeeping, CPA-LEDGER, **466,468**, 44

Drawing and computer art, 3D, **73**, 174

Drawing and computer art, DRAW, **38**, 173

Drawing and computer art, DRAWPLUS, **633**, 186

Drawing and computer art, GLUDRAW, **380**, 181

Drawing and computer art, HI-RES Rainbow, **652**, 186

Drawing and computer art, PC-Art, **629**, 185

Drawing and computer art, PC-Draw #1, **344**, 180

Drawing and computer art, PC-Draw #2, **345**, 181

Drawing and computer art, PC-Picture Graphics, **136**, 175

Drawing and computer art, PDRAW, **13**, 172

Dvorak keyboard, DVORAK, **181**, 332

E

Easywriter to DOS convert, MAKE, **60**, 377

Education — American history, History Education, **76**, 107

Education — astronomy, Moonbeam, **359**, 112

Education — checmistry, VideoChem, **407**, 114

Education — educational games for PC-jr, PCjr Educat. Games, **241**, 109

Education — Flash cards: vocab/spelling, Flash Cards: Vocab., **367-370**, 112

Education — IQ exercises, IQBUILD, **18**, 106

Education — lang. Hebrew, French, German, Spanish, Languages, **612**, 118

Education — math tutor (grades 1-6), Math Tutor, **95**, 107

Education — math tutorial (basics to intermed), Math Pak, **394**, 113

Education — math, finance, science tutorial, Equator/PC-TOUCH, **249**, 110

Education — misc calculators, circuits, etc., Ham Radio #2, **437**, 115

Education — misc terms, Polyglot/Letterfall, **542**, 118

Education — Morse code, ham radio tutorial, info, Ham Radio #1, **436**, 115

Education — music and misc educ. (grades 8+), Music and Ed., **168**, 108

Education — national teaching statistics, NAEPIRS, **266**, 111

Education — pre-school games for PC, XT, AT, AMY'S FIRST PRIMER, **646,647**, 119

Education — teacher assessment & grade analysis, T-Score/Education, **443**, 116

Education — teacher's grade manager (demo), TEACHER'S SPECIAL, **664**, 120

Education — touch typing tutorial, Equator/PC-TOUCH, **249**, 110

Education — touch typing tutorial, Polyglot/Letterfall, **542**, 118

Education — touch typing tutorial (for PC kybd), Touchtype, **320**, 111

Educational math game, FUNNELS, **229**, 109

Educational, alphabet, ABC, **390**, 166

Electronic disk, HYPERDRV, **51**, 302

Electronic mail encoding, ENCODE/DECODE, **482**, 324

Employee Management, EMS, **660**, 255

Encode/decode files, PC-CODE3&4, **569**, 326

Encode/decode (electronic mail), ENCODE/DECODE, **482**, 324

Encrypt/Decrypt system, PC-CODE, **112**, 323

Encrypt/decrypt system, THE CONFIDANT, **112**, 323

Engineering routines, Pascal, MATHPACK, **425**, 213

Enhanced DOS COPY utility, GCOPY, **204**, 295

Enhanced DOS DEL utiltiy, GDEL, **204**, 295

Entertainment, NAMESMAL, **477**, 132

Ephemeris calculations, ACE, **692**, 260

Epson print enhancement (WordStar), WSMX80, **526**, 374

Epson printer utilities, Print Utils 5, **326**, 368

ESP test, ESP, **173**, 123

Estimation (business), PDS*QUOTE, **533**, 48

European accounting, FREEWAY, **671-673**, 52

European payroll, FREEWAY, **671-673**, 52

Expanded ASCII char sets, PC-FONT, **225**, 366

Expert Systems, A.D.A PROLOG, **417**, 23

Expert Systems, ESIE, **398**, 23

Federal income taxes, UNCLE, **637**, 51

File archive, ARC, **420**, 339
File attribute byte modifier, CHMOD, **84**, 330
File attribute byte modifier, HIDEFILE, **52**, 327
File attributes, change, ALTER, **80**, 303
File compare, CMP, **143**, 381
File copy, selective, GCOPY2, **420**, 339
File delete utility, GDEL, **273**, 335
File finder, FFILE, **277**, 313
File finder, INPATH, **658**, 343
File management, CWEEP13, **283**, 335
File management, SDIR, **255**, 333
File management, SDIR50, **319**, 336
File management system, Master Key V1.6c, **598**, 322
File management utility, SDIR24C, **273**, 335
File manager, LablFile, **146**, 280
File manager, PC-FILE III, **5**, 74
File manipulation utilities, U-FILE, **133**, 307
File mass copy/delete, UTIL102, **196**, 332
File move, MOVE, **80**, 303
File move utility, MOVE, **183**, 310
File move utility, MOVE, **273**, 335
File move utility, MV, **196**, 332
File search utility, WHEREIS, **256**, 334
File squeeze utility, SQUEEZE, **115**, 331
File squeeze/unsqueeze, SQIBM, **144**, 308
File squeeze/unsqueeze, ZSQ-ZUSQ, **185**, 310
File system, AUTOFILE, **182**, 309
File typer, BROWSE, **205**, 311
File typer, VTYPE, **183**, 310
File unsqueeze, NUSQ, **139**, 306
File utility, EZ-MENU, **444**, 339
Files, defragment, PACKDISK, **610**, 342
Financial aids, FINPAK, **47**, 153
Financial planning (taxes), UNCLE, **637**, 51
Financial programs (collection 1), FINANCE, **25**, 140
Financial programs (collection 2), FINANCE, **25**, 140
Financial programs (collection), BARGRAPH, **14**, 139
Financial programs (collection), FINANCE & INVENTORY, **171**, 142
Financial programs (collection), FINANCIAL PROGRAMS, **227**, 143
Financial programs (collection), FINANCIAL PROGRAMS, **406**, 145
Financial statement, CPA-LEDGER, **466,468**, 44
Flash cards, FLASHCRD, **93**, 331
Flight planning, FLITPLAN, **261**, 34
Font design utility, NEWFONTS, **484**, 183

Foreign lang. French, German, Hebrew, Spanish, Languages, **612**, 118
Form letters, Form Letters, **388**, 38
Forms design, EZ-FORMS PACKAGE, **404**, 40
Forms design & generation (Epson), FORMS, **312**, 389
Forms generator (PC-FILE), FORMGEN, **125**, 25
FORTH programming lanuage, New Fig Forth, **685**, 221
FORTRAN programs, LINPACK Drivers, **555**, 228
FORTRAN programs, LINPACK Library, **554**, 227
Fortune Telling — Iching, Oracle, **615**, 251
Fortune Telling — Tarot, Oracle, **615**, 251
Free form database, FreeFile, **521**, 88
Free form database, INSTANT RECALL, **522**, 89
French, learning a foreign language, Languages, **612**, 118
Full charge accounting, PC-GL, **331**, 37
Function key, redefine, HOTKEY, **444**, 339

G

Game, HANGMAN, **153**, 107
Game, LIFE2, **274**, 163
Game, MONOPOLY, **475**, 131
Game, PHRASE, **385**, 128
Game, PINBALL, **448**, 167
Game, STARTREK, **178**, 159
Game — Adventure, WOMBAT!, Golden Wombat, **678**, 136
Game — Marooned Again, Marooned Again, **660**, 255
Game, Startrek, PDRAW, **13**, 172
Game, adventure, CASTLE, **210**, 161
Game, adventure, DND, **567**, 133
Game, adventure, EAMON, **296**, 125
Game, adventure, HACK, **452**, 130
Game, adventure, LPARTY, **604**, 134
Game, adventure, QUEST, **451**, 129
Game, arcade, ASTEROID, **203**, 160
Game, arcade, BREAKOUT, **17**, 150
Game, arcade, BRICK, **390**, 166
Game, arcade, BUGS, **177**, 158
Game, arcade, BUGS, **274**, 163
Game, arcade, DATNOIDS, **209**, 161
Game, arcade, FROG, **174**, 157
Game, arcade, PAC-GAL, **228**, 162
Game, arcade, PACKMAN, **24**, 151
Game, arcade, Q-BERT, **446**, 129
Game, arcade, REFLEX, **487**, 170
Game, arcade, STRIKER, **457**, 169
Game, arcade, WILLY, **445**, 167

Game, arcade (Hercules or color), SWH, **292**, 164
Game, BASIC, HANGMAN, **20**, 173
Game, board-type, ACEY-DUE, **175**, 158
Game, chess, PCCHESS, **120**, 157
Game, design utility, GENESIS, **591**, 133
Game, graphic-strategy, FIRE, **456**, 168
Game, Leygref's Castle, LEYGREF, **298**, 243
Game, musical trivia, TUNETRIV, **475**, 131
Game, non-graphics, SEAWOLF, **174**, 157
Game, Planets, PLANETS, **298**, 243
Game, Secret Quest, Secret Quest, **633**, 186
Game, StarTrek, MS-TREK, **197**, 159
Game, strategy, AWARI, **178**, 159
Game, strategy, CRIBBAGE, **260**, 163
Game, strategy, ENTRAP, **329**, 127
Game, strategy, MASTER2, **208**, 160
Game, strategy-adventure, NEWYORK, **614**, 134
Game, text adventure, ADVEN1, **203**, 160
Game, text adventure, ADVENT, **259**, 123
Game, text adventure, TERROR, **453**, 130
Game, trivia, TRIVMACH, **327**, 126
Game, trivia, TTOWERS, **473,474**, 131
Game, Wator, WATOR, **298**, 243
Games, arcade (Jr. compatible), 3-DEMON, **293**, 165
Games, BASIC, STAR2001, **450**, 168
Games, casino and board type, PCOTHELL, **514**, 170
Games, monochrome, BOOGERS!, **476**, 169
Games, PC-Jr., DUN, **354**, 165
Games, pinball, TWILZON2, **557**, 171
GANTT charts, GANTT, **593**, 51
GEMINI, Print Utils 6, **377**, 369
Genealogy, Family Ties, **465**, 199
Genealogy, Family Tree, Etc, **240**, 193
Genealogy, Genealogy on Display, **90**, 190
Genealogy (also see #361), Family History Sys, **632**, 203
Genealogy (also see #632), Family History, **361**, 196
Genealogy (companion to Disk 90), Notes On Display, **594**, 202
General ledger system, CPA-LEDGER, **466,468**, 44
General ledger system (business), PC-GL, **237**, 32
General ledger (Lotus 1-2-3), Personal G-L, **165**, 30
General ledger (personal), Personal G-L, **165**, 30
Geographical database, WORLD, **668**, 94

German, learning a foreign language, Languages, **612**, 118

Golf, Golf Scorecard, **342**, 244

Golf, PC-Golf, **262**, 243

Graphics and overhead transparencies, PC-FOIL, **347**, 244

Graphics slides presentation, SLIDE, **196**, 332

Graphics, 3-d and fonts, DANCAD3D, **701**, 188

Graphics, business, GRAPHTIME, **669**, 187

Graphics, Pascal, PLOT3D, **324**, 353

Graphs and data plotting, Danal, **620**, 184

Graphs and slide shows for databases, The Draftsman, **515**, 184

Graphs for databases, PC-GRAPH, **418**, 182

Graphs, computer art, PC-GRAF, **195**, 177

Gunning Fog index, PC-READ, **194**, 281

H

Ham Radio, PC-HAM, **562**, 250

Hangman, KIDGAMES, **705**, 137

Hard disk head park, PARK, **610**, 342

Hard disk menu, HDM-II, **631**, 102

Hard disk menu, MENU-MASTER, **642**, 102

Hard Disk Utilities, Hard Disk Utils, **478**, 317

Hebrew character set, Hebrew.chr, **62**, 29

Hebrew, learning a foreign language, Languages, **612**, 118

Help screen design (dBASE III), FORMGEN, **680**, 392

Help screen design (Pascal), FORMGEN, **680**, 392

Hiding files/directories, ALTER.COM, **490**, 325

Home — checkbook program, Chckbk System v3.31, **397**, 197

Home — checkbook program, CK SYSTEM, **462,463**, 198

Home — checkbook program, PC-CHECK, **275**, 193

Home — Federal income tax, 1986, AM-TAX 1986, **479**, 200

Home — finance, Home Finance, **107**, 191

Home — inventory system, Home Inventory, **395**, 197

Home — misc assorted programs, Home Applications, **321**, 195

Home — misc assorted programs (also see #497), HOMEWARE V1.0, **630**, 203

Home — misc assorted programs (also see #630), HOMEWARE V1.0, **497**, 201

Home — personal finance, Managing Money, **613**, 202

Home — recipes, microGOURMET, **116,117**, 191

Home — solar energy, TELISOLAR, **486**, 201

Home — tax record management, TAX-FILE, **295**, 194

I

Index card system (BASIC), INDX.BAS, **317**, 83

Indexer, Book, Book Index Builder, **26**, 75

Input screen forms (dBASE III), FORMGEN, **680**, 392

Input screen forms (Pascal), FORMGEN, **680**, 392

Integrated spreadsheet/database, AnalytiCalc, **430-432**, 41

Integrated utilities, PC-DESKTEAM, **405**, 99

Inventory control, PC-SELL, **552**, 49

Inventory control system, Parts Invent., **235**, 32

Inventory for home, INVENTRY, **62**, 29

Inventory program, INVEN, **37**, 152

Inventory programs (Point-of-Sale), FINANCE & INVENTORY, **171**, 142

Itemized billing system, MR. BILL, **469,470**, 45

Itemized invoice system, MR. BILL, **469,470**, 45

J

Job scheduler, MakeMyDay, **618**, 101

Jokes and insults, Hotboot/Insults, **619**, 252

Jon Darts Utils, Jon Dart's DOS Utils, **564**, 320

K

Keyboard buffer expansion, KBBUFF, **181**, 332

Keyboard buffer expansion, KBDFIX, **255**, 333

Keyboard macro device, Soft-Touch, **500**, 100

Keyboard macro, redesign, FANSI-CONSOLE, **356,650**, 97

Keyboard reassignment, DEFKEY, **113**, 96

Keyboard redefinition, NEWKEY, **181**, 332

Keyboard toggle utility, KEYLOC, **79**, 329

Keyboard utility, HOTKEY, **444**, 339

Knowledge bases, ESIE, **398**, 23

Knowledge of Bible, BibleQ, **628**, 135

L

Label diskettes, LISTMATE, **252**, 313

Label maker, IBMLABEL, **66**, 328

Label maker, LABEL, **256**, 334

Label maker, LABLREAD, **284**, 336

Label maker for diskettes, DMASTER, **326**, 368

Label printer (Epson), LLABELEPS, **67**, 329

Label printer, directory, COVER, **543**, 340

Label printer, diskette, PDVL, **634**, 343

Label printer, diskette directory, LABELPRT, **111**, 305

Label printer, directory, COVER2, **319**, 336

Language, MVP-FORTH, **31**, 207

Language parser, QPARSER, **419**, 383

Language, FORTH, F83, **263**, 209

Large font screen display, BIGTYPE, **28**, 299

LASERJET, Print Utils 6, **377**, 369

Learning DOS (V2.0), HelpDOS, **686**, 72

Least squares curve fitting, CURVEFIT, **191**, 176

Legal — California wills, FREEWILL, **193**, 192

Library utility, LU, **140**, 379

Linear programming, KLP, **332**, 37

LISP programming language, XLISP, **148**, 22

Loan Amortization, AMORTIZE, **399**, 39

Loan calculations, LOAN.BAS, **155**, 30

LOTUS — 1985 Federal Taxes, FITT Tax, **290**, 266

LOTUS — Desktop programs, DESKTOP, **64**, 262

LOTUS — Desktop programs, DESKTOP, **65**, 262

LOTUS — Home budget, Budget Template, **389**, 269

LOTUS — misc business. financial worksheets, 1-2-3 Worksheets #7, **571**, 271

LOTUS — misc financial and math worksheets, Worksheets No 4, **303**, 267

LOTUS — misc financial worksheets, Worksheets No 3, **302**, 267

LOTUS — misc math, finance worksheets, utilities, MISC 123 Worksheets, **584**, 273

LOTUS — misc small business/financial worksheets, Worksheets No 5, **304**, 268

LOTUS — misc utilities, LOTUS Utilities, **568**, 271

LOTUS — misc utilities, worksheets, tech notes, Worksheets No 2, **301**, 266

LOTUS — misc. utilities, Utility 1-2-3, **257**, 265

LOTUS — misc. worksheets, Power-Worksheets, **289**, 265

LOTUS — Misc. worksheets, Worksheets No 1, **207**, 264

LOTUS — Template for accounting and finance, Whiterock, **583**, 272

Lotus worksheets (collection), FINANCIAL PROGRAMS, **406**, 145

M

Magazine Indexes, Personal Computer, LETUS A-B-C #1, **121**, 232

Magazine Indexes, Personal Computer, LETUS A-B-C #10, **547**, 238

Magazine Indexes, Personal Computer, LETUS A-B-C #11, **548**, 239

Magazine Indexes, Personal Computer, LETUS A-B-C #12, **549**, 239

Magazine Indexes, Personal Computer, LETUS A-B-C #13, **550**, 239

Magazine Indexes, Personal Computer, LETUS A-B-C #14, **551**, 239

Magazine Indexes, Personal Computer, LETUS A-B-C #2, **122**, 233

Magazine Indexes, Personal Computer, LETUS A-B-C #3, **123**, 233

Magazine Indexes, Personal Computer, LETUS A-B-C #4, **348**, 237

Magazine Indexes, Personal Computer, LETUS A-B-C #5, **349**, 237

Magazine Indexes, Personal Computer, LETUS A-B-C #6, **350**, 237

Magazine Indexes, Personal Computer, LETUS A-B-C #7, **544**, 238

Magazine Indexes, Personal Computer, LETUS A-B-C #8, **545**, 238

Magazine Indexes, Personal Computer, LETUS A-B-C #9, **546**, 238

Magazines, Personal Computers, PC Firing Line, **159**, 234

Magazines, Personal Computers, PC Firing Line, **160**, 234

Magazines, Personal Computers, PC Firing Line, **161**, 235

Magazines, Personal Computers, PC Firing Line, **247**, 235

Mahjong, MAHJONG, **641**, 135

Mail list database, Address Manager, **218**, 78

Mailing label system, EASYMAIL, **169**, 31

Mailing list system, Reliance Mailing, **503**, 48

Mailing progam, MAILLIST, **169**, 31

Manuscript control for authors and agents, MUSE, **635**, 253

Manuscript control for authors and agents, MUSE, **636**, 253

Map of World, The World Digitized, **494-496**, 248

Math routines, FACTOR, **206**, 382

Math routines, Math and Statistics, **180**, 223

Math routines, FORTRAN, LLSQ, **553**, 218

Math tutorials, MATH PAK, **394**, 113

Mathematical graphing, GRAF, **265**, 367

Mathematical modeling, Best-Plan, **690,691**, 258

Medical risk appraisal, Health Risk, **192**, 242

Membership list program, MEMBERS, **169**, 31

Memory expansion for older PC's, MEM640, **183**, 310

Memory resident calculator, RESICALC, **661**, 103

Memory resident keybd macro, Soft-Touch, **500**, 100

Menu design, BMENU, **513**, 385

Menu system, EZ-MENU, **444**, 339

Menu system, QSYS, **118,278**, 96

Menu system (customizable), AUTOMENU, **608**, 101

Meteorology, Astronomy #1, **538**, 249

Miscellaneous comversion programs, 3D, **73**, 174

Morse code practice, MORSE, **255,93**, 333

Mosaic building, KIDGAMES, **705**, 137

Movie database, The Movie DB, **311**, 82

Multiple prints, LIST, **640**, 289

Multiple prints, LIST, **640**, 289

Multitasking enviroment, DOSamatic Ver 2.0, **498**, 318

Multiuser programming, SNOBASIC, **409**, 212

Music play/record/edit, PIANOMAN, **279**, 124

Music player, SONGS, **292**, 164

Music score, MUSIC, **92**, 121

Music write/play, PC-MUSICIAN, **127**, 122

Music, Bach Sonata, JSB, **208**, 160

Musical tunes, JUKEBOX, **100**, 122

Mystery text adventure, Sleuth Ver 4.1, **694**, 137

N

NEC 8023A printer utils, Print. Utils No 2, **221**, 365

NEC 8023A, print enhancement utilities, Print. Utils No 2, **221**, 365

NLQ print utility, IMAGEPRINT, **517**, 373

Nuclear Magnetic Resonance (NMR), NMR, **590**, 228

Numbers to words, FONEWORD, **477**, 132

Nutrition and diet, Nutrient, **492**, 247

Nutritional planningDisk, Mealmate & others, **700**, 204

O

On-line DOS help, PC-DOS HELP, **254**, 69

Origami patterns, ORIGAMI, **408**, 128

Outline program, memory resident, PC-OUTLINE, **480**, 285

P

Page compostion sytem, PAGEONE, **684**, 292

Page layout preview, WPPS, **415**, 283

Paint program (BASIC), EASEL, **191**, 176

Paint program (BASIC), EASYGRAF, **191**, 176

Panasonic printer utils, Printer utils, **438**, 371

Paperfolding projects, ORIGAMI, **408**, 128

Parity error trapping, PARCHK, **256**, 334

Parts inventory system, Parts Invent., **235**, 32

Pascal compiler, FACILIS, **424**, 213

Pascal compiler, VISPAS, **510**, 216

Pascal language tutorial, PASCAL TUTOR, **579,580**, 71

Pascal listing enhancement, NELIST, **217**, 312

Pascal math routines, UTIL, **435**, 383

Pascal procedures, ALLFILE, **392**, 211

Pascal programming aids, PTOOLDAT, **589**, 386

Pascal programming language, PASCAL TUTOR, **579,580**, 71

Pascal programming routines, PASCAL TOOLS, **130-132**, 344

Pascal routines, PASCAL, **512**, 216

Pascal routines, animation & sound, SHOWMOVI, **353**, 354

Pascal routines, calculator, screen utils, PTOOLWIN, **324**, 353

Pascal routines, communications, COMMCALL, **366**, 356

Pascal routines, disk I/O, IOSTUFF, **30**, 206

Pascal routines, DOS & CP/M, MODEM, **365**, 355

Pascal routines, DOS access & graphics, ALLFILES, **351**, 354

Pascal, file & math routines, BENCHMRK, **375**, 358

Pascal, graphics & Hercules, GRAPH, **426**, 359

Pascal, IBM, PASCAL, **36**, 207

Pascal, I/O, DOS, & menus, MENUX, **427**, 359

Patch (miscellaneous), COPY PROTECT, **414**, 297

Patch (miscellaneous), PATCHES, **376**, 295

Payroll accounting system, FREEWAY, **671-673**, 52

Payroll system, PC-PAYROLL, **565**, 50

Payroll, European, FREEWAY, **671-673**, 52

PC-based BBS, IBM BBS, **150**, 26

PC-based BBS, RBBS for the PC, **152**, 26

PCjr communications package, PC-DIAL, **626**, 66

PCjr database, PC-FILE III, **624**, 93

Periodic events database (BASIC), PMB15.BAS, **317**, 83

Pharmaceutical routine, TPNCALC, **234**, 224

Pizza recipies, PIZZA, **179**, 31

Point-of-sale system (retail), PC-SELL, **552**, 49

Print enhancement, LQ, **283**, 335

Print enhancement utility, IMAGEPRINT, **517**, 373

Print spooler, SP, **609**, 342

Print utilites (Epson), Screen/Printer, **186**, 363

Printed Circuit Board estimating, PCBD.BAS, **440**, 44

Printer art, Printer Art, **154**, 175

Printer Control Device, Print Utils 6, **377**, 369

Printer control for MX, SETPRTR, **79**, 329

Printer control utility, EPSONSET, **66**, 328

Printer Fonts — PASCAL programming aids, Graphic Font Design, **484**, 183

Printer paper saver, CONDEN, **384**, 338

Printer setup utility, PRINTER, **110**, 378

Printer Utilites, Printer Utils.4, **236**, 366

Printer utility, Hebrew for Epson, HEBREW, **607**, 341

Printer utils (general), Print Utils, **411**, 370

Printer utils (NEC 8023A), Print. Utils No 2, **221**, 365

Printer utils (Prowriter), Print. Utils No 1, **220**, 364

Printer utils (TranStar), Print. Utils No 3, **222**, 365

Programmer tools, PC-TOOLS, **536**, 385

Programmer utilities, BASIC & C, B-WINDOW, **527**, 217

Programmer utilities, C, CC, **341**, 210

Programmer's cross-ref tool, XREF, **384**, 338

Programmer's editor, BlackBeard, **611**, 391

Programmers calculator, Prog. Calc., **87**, 95

Programming — BASIC screen editor (RV-EDIT), ARCHIE, **19**, 68

Programming — math library for Pascal & FORTRAN, PASCAL Math Library, **248**, 348

Programming — talking software, ENABLE, **674**, 256

Programming aid, SPA:WN, **442**, 215

Programming aids, BASIC, BDS, **269**, 348

Programming language, MVP-FORTH, **31**, 207

Programming language, POLYMATH, **606**, 220

Programming language, SNOBASIC, **409**, 212

Programming language, TBASIC, **381**, 211

Programming language (BASIC), BASIC Games & Prog., **595**, 72

Programming language (BASIC), PC Professor, **105**, 69

Programming language (Pascal), PASCAL TUTOR, **579,580**, 71

Programming language, FORTH, F83, **263**, 209

Programming language, FORTH, FORTH-H, **352**, 210

Programming language, FORTH, UNIFORTH, **454**, 215

Programming routines, assembly, Assembly Utils 1-3, **307-309**, 349

Programming routines, C, ABOUT-C, **429**, 214

Programming utilities, APL, UTILITY, **108**, 208

Programming utilities, FORTRAN, FORTRAN, **556**, 219

Programming, cross-assembler, XASM, **573**, 219

Programming, structured BASIC, RATBAS, **3**, 205

Programming, VM370, A370, **402**, 212

Project management tool, GANTT, **593**, 51

Project management (CPM), PCPM, **423**, 41

Project manager, TASKPLAN, **155**, 30

Project planning, Best-Plan, **690,691**, 258

Project scheduler, IPM.COM, **313**, 35

PROLOG programming language, A.D.A PROLOG, **417**, 23

Proportional spacing utility, JUSTIFY, **211**, 364

Prospect List Programs, PROSPECT, **399**, 39

Prospecting (business), THE FRONT OFFICE, **697-699**, 53

ProWriter printer utils, Print. Utils No 1, **220**, 364

Prowriter, print enhancement utilities, Print. Utils No 1, **220**, 364

Psychology — Clinical assessment, WALMYR Programs, **648**, 254

Q

Quotations (business), PDS*QUOTE, **533**, 48

R

Ram disk, FREE4, **52**, 327

Ram disk, HYPERDRV, **51**, 302

Ram disk, MEMBRAIN, **273**, 335

RAM disk, VDISK2, **34**, 300

RAM disk programs, DOS utils #9, **184**, 294

RBBS Bulletin Board System, RBBS, **212,334,621,622**, 27

Read-only file utility, WRTE, **204**, 295

Readability analyzer, PC-STYLE, **505**, 286

Real estate evaluation, HOME.EXE, **282**, 35

Real estate office management, Real Estate Systems, **656**, 148

Recipe Indexes, Recipe Index, **281**, 236

Recipie book, PC-RECIPIE, **412**, 99

Recipies, home, microGOURMET, **116,117**, 191

Remote-to-host communications, HOST-III, **125**, 25

Replaces strings, TRANSLIT, **163**, 387

Reset disable, NORESET, **373**, 337

Restaurant billing system, GBILL, **440**, 44

Retail point-of-sale system, PC-SELL, **552**, 49

Rolodex (DBASE II), ROLODEX, **412**, 99

ROM BIOS extension, FANSI-CONSOLE, **356,650**, 97

S

Sales management, SALESEYE, **501,502**, 47

Sales management, THE FRONT OFFICE, **697-699**, 53

Sales order processing, THE FRONT OFFICE, **697-699**, 53

Sales tracking, SALESEYE, **501,502**, 47

Screen color set, COLOR, **80**, 303

Screen control, DATAMORPHICS, **113**, 96

Screen designer, SCR21F, **373**, 337

Screen dump program, PrtScFX, **186**, 363

Screen forms generator (dBASE III & Pascal), FORMGEN, **680**, 392

Screen generator for data entry (BASIC), PCIGEN, **363**, 390

Screen generator (dBASE II), DBS.COM, **163**, 387

Screen handlers, assembler, CLS, **223**, 347

Screen handlers, C, SCRINIT, **216**, 347

Screen I/O subroutines (BASIC), WHIZZARD, **285**, 388

Screen split, PC-TALK III, PC3SC, **34**, 300

Screen type buffer, ST, **111**, 305

Screen type utility, VTYPE, **138**, 305

Screen, keyboard utilities, PCUTIL, **142**, 380

Screen-oriented text editor, DVED, **191**, 176

Screenplay word processor, ScreenWright, **422**, 284

Scrolling control device, SCROLLK, **186**, 363

Shipwrecked game, Buttonware, **683**, 136

Sideways print util, SIDEWAYS, **411**, 370

Sideways print utility, SIDE WRITER, **523**, 373

Sign maker, BANNER1, **373**, 337

Sign maker, POSTER, **33**, 300

Single entry accouting system, PC Account.Sys, **559,560**, 49

Slide presentation graphs and graphics, Slide Generation, **244**, 179

Slide show graphs and graphics, Present, **471**, 182

Small business accounting, PC Account.Sys, **559,560**, 49

Small business accounting, PC-PAYROLL, **365**, 355

Software demonstrration system, PC-DEMO, **665**, 256

Song write/play, PC-MUSICIAN, **127**, 122

Songs, assortment, TUNE, **322**, 126

Sound effects, SOUNDEMO, **92**, 121

Source code editor, BlackBeard, **611**, 391

Spanish, learning a foreign language, Languages, **612**, 118

Spectroscopy and statistical anlysis, NMR Spectroscopy, **391**, 224

Speech synthesis, ENABLE, **674**, 256

Speed reading demonstration, SREADER, **211**, 364

Speed-up, PC-SPRINT, **507**, 249

Spirograph emulation, SPIRO, **265**, 367

Spreadsheet — beginner level, EZ, **695**, 276

Spreadsheet — three dimensional, QUBECALC, **696**, 277

Spreadsheet print utilty, SIDE WRITER, **523**, 373

Spreadsheet program, PC-CALC, **199**, 263

Spreadsheet program — AsEasyAs spreadsheet, AsEasyAs, **651**, 276

Spreadsheet program — Expresscalc v3.09, Expresscalc V 3.09, **524**, 270

Spreadsheet program — Expresscalc v3.09, Expresscalc V 3.09, **525**, 270

Spreadsheet program — FreeCalc v 2.0, FREECALC, **574**, 272

Spreadsheet program — FreeCalc v1.01, Spreadsheets, **170**, 263

Spreadsheet program — Gordon's PC-CALC, PC-CALC, **224**, 264

Spreadsheet program — PC-Calc by Jim Button, PC-CALC, **625**, 275

Spreadsheet program — Turbo Calc, Turbo Calc, **651**, 276

Spreadsheet program with ASCII editor, Alan's Text Editor, **531**, 270

Spreadsheet with database (BASIC), DB of Steel, **267**, 80

Squeeze/unsqueeze files, SQIBM, **144**, 308

Squeeze/unsqueeze files, ZSQ-UZSQ, **185**, 310

Star Micronics printer utils, Printer utils, **438**, 371

Statistical analysis, EPISTAT, **88**, 222

Statistical analysis, KWIKSTAT, **654**, 230

Statistical analysis, KWIKSTAT, **655**, 230

Statistical analysis, Math and Statistics, **180**, 223

Statistical analysis, SPPC System Demo, **232**, 224

Statistical analysis, SPPC System Demo, **623**, 229

Statistical analysis, SST Version 1.0, **638**, 229

Statistical analysis, SST Version 1.0, **639**, 230

Statistical analysis, Stat Tools, **508**, 226

Statistical analysis, Stat Tools, **509**, 226

Stock market analysis, The Stock Trader, **644**, 148

Stocks and bonds, PC-STOCK, **575**, 147

Stocks and bonds, SAGE TRADER, **242**, 143

Stocks and bonds, STOCK MRKT ANALYSER, **40**, 140

Stocks and bonds, THE PORTWORTH PACK, **101**, 141

Stocks and bonds (database via THE SOURCE), TRANSTOCK, **323**, 144

Stocks and bonds (family management), PC-MONEY, **532**, 147

Stocks and bonds (graphs), PC-STOCK, **375**, 358

Stocks and bonds (graphs), STOCK CHARTING SYS, **246**, 144

Stocks and bonds (ROI), PFROI, **360**, 145

Structured lister for BASIC, EXPLIST, **7**, 375

Structured programming, POLYMATH, **606**, 220

Structured programming, SPA:WN, **442**, 215

Structured programming, BASIC, RATBAS, **3**, 205

Supertyper, ST, **379**, 282

Surveying database, Surveysoft, **566**, 90

SYMPHONY — misc banking, insurance, medical, SYMPHONY Bank/Ins, **588**, 274

SYMPHONY — misc macros, wordprocessing utilities, SYMPHONY, **587**, 273

SYMPHONY — misc utilities, worksheets, technotes, SYMPHONY Wks No 1, **305**, 268

SYMPHONY — misc. utilities, worksheets, technotes, SYMPHONY Wks No 2, **306**, 269

SYMPHONY — misc worksheets, Symphony Wks #3, **596**, 275

SYMPHONY — misc worksheets, Symphony Wks #3, **597**, 275

T

Tag making system, TAG, **243**, 33

Task switching enviroment, DOSamatic Ver 2.0, **498**, 318

Tax, Federal, AM-TAX 1986, **479**, 200

Teaching skills, WALMYR Programs, **648**, 254

Teaching skills, WALMYR Programs, **649**, 254

Technical database, ABC Database, **119**, 76

Technical print util., PC-FONT, **225**, 366

Terminal emulation, PC-VT, **286**, 60

Terminal emulation, SIMTERM, **362**, 63

Terminal emulation (DEC 52/100), Ideal Terminal, **679**, 67

Terminal emulation (IBM 3101), ProComm, **499**, 66

Terminal emulation (TEKTRON 4010), TEKTRONIX 4010, **441**, 65

Terminal emulation (TeleVide 912/920), ProComm, **499**, 66

Terminal emulation (TeleVide 925/950), ProComm, **499**, 66

Terminal emulation (VT 100),
TEKTRONIX 4010, **441**, 65

Terminal emulation (VT 52 and 100),
ProComm, **499**, 66

Terminal emulation (VT-52),
IT, **439**, 65

Text editor, W-ED, **415**, 283

Text editor (BASIC),
FULLSCREEN, **190**, 280

Text editor, full featured,
MAX, **563**, 288

Text editor, full featured, ZURI
Editor, **657**, 289

Text editor, screen oriented,
SCREEN, **86**, 279

Text editor, (DEC), MAX, **563**, 288

Text editor, (UNIX), MAX, **563**, 288

Text file analysis, PC-STAT3, **569**, 326

Text file manipulation, UTIL, **60**, 377

Text formatter, BlackBeard, **611**, 391

Text formatter, ROFF, **194**, 281

Text formatter, RUNOFF, **48**, 362

Text formatter (multiple prints),
LIST, **640**, 289

Text formatter, advanced,
ROFF4, **416**, 284

Theatrical word processor,
ScreenWright, **422**, 284

Tickler system, MakeMyDay, **618**, 101

Tickler system, PC-TICKLE, **576**, 100

Time logger, PCLOG, **634**, 343

TranStar printer utils, Print. Utils
No 3, **222**, 365

TranStar, print enhancement utilities,
Print. Utils No 3, **222**, 365

U

Un-archive utility, PKXARC, **373**, 337

Unattended file transfers,
HOST-III, **125**, 25

Unprotect, VISIPROT, **204**, 295

Unprotect BASIC programs,
UNPROT, **67**, 329

Unprotect (miscellaneous), COPY
PROTECT, **414**, 297

Unprotect (miscellaneous), DOS utils
#9, **184**, 294

Unprotect (miscellaneous),
PATCHES, **376**, 295

Unsqueeze files, NUSQ, **139**, 306

Utility — Processor speed,
PC-SPRINT, **507**, 249

V

VCR database, VCRDBASE, **493**, 88

Visicalc breakeven analysis,
BARGRAPH, **14**, 139

Visicalc home budget,
BARGRAPH, **14**, 139

Visually impaired — talking software,
ENABLE, **674**, 256

Volume label create/change,
LABEL, **255**, 333

Volume labels, create/alter,
VOLSER, **89**, 304

W

Wave form analysis, SURF87, **115**, 331

Weapons technology — Bullet swaging,
Corbin Handbook, **616**, 251

Weapons technology — Bullet swaging,
Corbin Handbook, **617**, 252

Windowing, B-WINDOW, **527**, 217

WOMBAT!, Golden Wombat, **678**, 136

Word counter, WC.EXE, **163**, 387

Word counting tool, WC, **658**, 343

Word processor for children,
WPK, **343**, 282

Word processor (screenplays),
ScreenWright, **422**, 284

Word processor, full featured,
FreeWord, **530**, 287

Word processor, full featured, NEW
YORK WORD, **528**, 287

Word processor, full featured,
PC-TYPE+, **455,681,682**, 285

Word processor, full featured,
PC-WRITE, **78,627**, 278

Word processor, menu-driven,
FreeWord, **530**, 287

Word processor, spelling checker, NEW
YORK WORD, **528**, 287

Word processor, spelling checker,
PC-TYPE+, **455,681,682**, 285

Word processor, general,
EDIT, **294**, 281

Word processor, typewriter style,
EasyRite, **146**, 280

WordStar print enhancement (Epson),
WSMX80, **526**, 374

WordStar to ASCII conversion,
WS-ASCII, **46**, 301

WordStar utilities, WordStar
Aids, **379**, 282

World, Map of, The World
Digitized, **494-496**, 248

Writing analysis, PC-STYLE, **505**, 286

Writing analysis (complexity),
PC-READ, **194**, 281

X

Xmodem protocol, XMODEM,
QMODEM, **54,310,499**, 56

Y

Ymodem protocol, QMODEM, **310**, 61

Z

Zork aids, ZT16, **446**, 129

6.0 APPENDIX

GLOSSARY

ADA	A powerful development language. Other program languages, compilers and interpreters can be created with ADA.
AI	Artificial intelligence. A program that gives a computer some degree of thinking ability.
Algorithm	A series of instructions or formulas designed to solve a specific problem.
Alphanumeric	Composed of both letters and numbers.
APL source file	A program written in the APL language.
Application program	A program designed to perform a specific task.
ARC	A file extension name denoting an archived file. See "Filename extension," "Archive."
Archive	One or more files that have been compressed to take up less space on a diskette. An archive can also be a backup for an original program.
ASCII	("ass-key") American Standard Code for Information Interchange. A code that is understood by most computers.
Assembly code	A code that translates English (or other) words into a machine language that the computer can understand.
BASIC	Beginner's All Purpose Symbolic Instruction Code. The most widely-used programming language.
BAT	This filename extension denotes a batch file. See "Filename extension," "Batch file."
Batch file	A collection of DOS commands placed into a separate text file with the extension .BAT attached to their filename. When this filename is typed into DOS, each command stored in the file will execute sequentially until the file ends.
Baud	(or baud rate) Transmission rate of information in bits per second. Common rates are 300 and 1200 baud over telephone lines.
Binary	A base-two number system, using only the digits 0 and 1.
BIOS	Basic Input-Output System. A fundamental part of the DOS system.

Bit	From BInary digiT. The fundamental unit of information used by digital computers to represent 0 or 1, off or on, no or yes.
Boot	Initial loading of the operating system into a computer. Starting (hardboot) or restarting (softboot) a computer.
Browse	To search a text data file for a particular reference.
Buffer	A memory that stores data on a temporary basis and provides a holding space, or intermediate stage, between two parts of a computer. Buffers are typically between a computer and a printer.
Bug	A program error.
Bulletin board	An information service through which computer users can communicate, via telephone lines, with each other and with a central information file.
Bus	The main electrical connection lines between parts of a computer or between a computer and peripherals. Buses may be in the form of circuit boards, cables or webbing.
Byte	A basic unit of computer information where 1 byte = 8 bits. Memory capacity is normally expressed in bytes, such as 64K, 256K, etc. l byte of storage accomodates l ASCII character.
C	A structured, high-level computer language. See "High-level language."
CAD	Computer-Aided Drafting. A type of program that creates and displays a wide variety of drawings, schematics, etc., as a design tool.
CAM	Computer-Aided Manufacturing. A type of program that stores engineering specifications, product requirements, process control data, etc., as a manufacturing aid.
CD ROM	Compact Disk, Read-Only Memory. An optical, laser-read disk which can store more than one-half gigabyte of data on a single 4.75" disk and which is read by a laser drive.
Character printer	A device that allows computer text to be printed on paper.
Clone	A computer that is similar to and highly compatible with another computer. Commonly refers to computers that are IBM-compatible.
COBOL	A high-level programming language for information storage and retrieval, typically used in business applications. See "High-level language."
Code	Instructions for a particular program, usually in a form that can be read by humans.
CGA (Color Graphics Adaptor)	A peripheral device inserted into one of a computer's expansion ports to enable the computer to process and display color. See "Peripheral," "Expansion port."
COM file	A command file.
Communications program	A program used to transmit and receive information through a modem over telephone lines. See "Modem."
Compatible	A computer that will operate with another computer's software. Usually refers to a non-IBM computer that will run software designed for an IBM computer. High compatibility refers to a non-IBM computer that will run most or all IBM software.

Compiler	A program that translates a high-level language into a machine code that is understood by the computer.
Computer	A device that manipulates information to provide useful, desired results. Although computers can be made in many forms, almost all modern computers are electronic and use a digital, binary number system. See "Binary."
Computer language	A language that a computer can understand.
Condor	A database manager program.
Console	A keyboard and display screen for a computer. See "Keyboard," "CRT."
Copy protect	A software or hardware system placed on a program to prevent its being copied.
CP/M	An operating system used on 8-bit computers.
CPU	Central Processing Unit. The primary functional unit of a computer through which all information passes.
CRT	Cathode Ray Tube. The television-type screen on which computer information is displayed. Also referred to as a "monitor."
Cursor	The position indicator on a CRT. Usually in the shape of a dash or rectangle, the cursor shows where the next text character or graphics input will appear.
Daisy wheel printer	A slow-speed computer printer that prints typewriter-quality letters on paper. Also see "Dot matrix printer."
Data	The information stored in a computer.
Database	An organized body of data that is stored in a computer, such as a mailing list.
Database manager	A program which can be custom-tailored to manage a set of vital data for personal or business purposes.
dBase II and dBase III	Popular database managers for the IBM-PC.
Default drive	The drive that the disk operating system will search for the presence of a program, if no specific drive has been selected.
DIR	The DOS command that invokes the in-use disk drive to display its directory on the CRT. A directory is a list of each file on a diskette. See "DOS," "CRT."
Disk	The circular medium on which data is stored in minute, magnetic charges. A rotating disk allows magnetic heads in a computer to write onto and read from the disk. Used interchangeably with "diskette." See "floppy disk," "Hard disk."
Disk drive	The system within a computer that spins a specific disk and allows data to be written onto and read from that disk.
Diskette	A small disk used in microcomputers.
Documentation	The printed instructions that accompany computer hardware or software.

APPENDIX

DOS	Disk Operating System. An essential program that controls how all information is stored on and retrieved from a disk.
DOS reserved word	A filename extension that is only used for DOS system commands. See "Filename extension," "DOS."
Dot matrix printer	A high-speed printing device whose characters or graphic shapes are formed by patterns of tiny dots. Also see "Daisy wheel printer."
Editor	A program that allows revision, repositioning and general editing of computer text.
Electronic mail	Messages exchanged through linked (or networked) computers via bulletin boards or commercial services. See "Bulletin board."
Embedded command	A command that is placed between letters or words of text in an ASCII file in order to invoke a special command. For example, embedded commands are placed within computer text to signify type face changes for typesetting. See "ASCII."
Emulate	Software that enables a computer to imitate another computer.
EXE	The command that tells a computer to execute a specific program or a part of a program.
Expansion slot	(Or card slot) One or more spaces in a computer that hold circuit boards ("cards") that enhance computer operation.
File	An organized collection of related information on one or more disks. A file may be of several types, such as a command file, an execute file or a text file.
Filename	The string of characters used to identify a file. An example of a filename in the PC-DOS system is "NAME.EXT."
Filename extension	The last part of a filename that indicates the type of file. Common filename extensions are ".BAS" for BASIC files, ".ASM" for assembly code files and ".TXT" for text files.
Firmware	A program that is permanently stored in PROM or ROM. See "PROM," "ROM."
Floppy disk	A flexible magnetic disk. Standard sizes are 8", 5 & 1/4" and 3 & 1/2". See "Disk."
Flowchart	A diagram that graphically portrays a sequence of events, usually time-related, that lead to a conclusion or to a solution of a problem.
Format	To magnetically arrange a disk into areas, or sectors, so that it is able to receive and store data from the operating system that formatted the disk.
FORTH	A structured, high-level programming language. See "High-level language."
FORTRAN	From "FORmula TRANslator." FORTRAN is a high-level language used mostly in mathematics. See "High-level language."
Freeware	Software that is distributed by its author without charge. Also see "Open software."

Graphics	Any pictorial representation, such as drawings, graphs, bar charts, borders, etc.
Graphics card	Either of two peripheral devices that allow a computer to process and display graphics. A monochrome graphics card allows only a single color display. A color graphics card enables a color display.
Hard copy	Computer text or graphics that is printed on paper.
Hardware	The physical components of a computer. Also see "Software."
Hercules Graphics card	A circuit board card that enables enhanced graphics in a computer with a monochrome display.
Hexadecimal	A base-16 number system that is sometimes used for computer functions.
High-level language	Any computer language whose commands are written in English (or other) words. These word commands are then translated by a compiler into an assembly code that the computer understands. See "Assembly code."
Host computer	A central computer that is the primary information source for other linked computers. See "Terminal."
Input	Information entered into a computer.
Interactive	Two-way, immediate communication between a computer and a human user.
Interface	A physical or functional connection between two or more devices, systems or persons.
Interpreter	A program which converts human input into data that is understood and usable by a computer. BASIC is an example of an interpreter language. instructions written in a language such as BASIC. See "BASIC."
I/O	Input/Output. Information that is exchanged between a computer and peripheral equipment. See "Peripheral."
Joystick	A device that enters positional information to a computer. Also see "Mouse."
K	Computer shorthand for kilobyte.
Keyboard	A group of keys, similar to a typewriter, that are manually pressed to enter information into a computer.
Kilobyte	1024 bytes of data. For example, 64 kilobytes (or 64K) = 64 x 1024 = 65,536 bytes of data.
Language	A set of characters and/or symbols combined under specific rules for computer use. See "High-level language," "Compiler."
Laser printer	High-resolution printer that uses laser optics to produce images on photosensitive paper.
Linker	Part of a program that links together object files that have been created by a compiler so that they form a single program. See "Object file," "Compiler."

LISP	From LISt Processing. LISP is a high-level language designed to teach programming, now used for artificial intelligence applications. See "High-level language," "Artificial intelligence."
Loop	A set of instructions to a computer that are repeated. Loops can be endless or designed to end after a certain number of repetitions.
Lotus 1-2-3	A popular spreadsheet program. See "Spreadsheet."
Machine code	The internal language of a computer by which its hardware is able to function.
Machine readable	Data stored in such a way that it can be retrieved by a computer but not necessarily by an operator.
Macro	User-definable computer instructions that group functions so that the entire group (macro) can be activated when needed.
Mainframe	A large-capacity computer that is also usually of large physical size and which is connected, or networked, to multiple users.
Megabyte	(Mg) One million bytes of data.
Memory	The ability of a computer to store data. The two kinds of memory within a computer are RAM (random access memory) and ROM (read-only memory). See "RAM," "ROM."
Menu	A list of program options, displayed on the CRT, for selection by an operator.
Merge	To combine program files or other sets of information.
Microcomputer	The smallest type of computer in use. Personal computers are most typical of this category.
Microprocessor	A CPU (central processing unit) that is contained on a silicon chip. See "CPU."
Minicomputer	Originally, a small computer. Now, a medium-size computer with capabilities between that of a mainframe and a microcomputer. See "Mainframe," "Microcomputer."
Modem	From MOdulator/DEModulator, which is the technical way of describing how this device transmits computer information over telephone lines.
Modular construction	The special positioning of modules, or groups, of information within a program. See "Structured language."
Monitor	The television-like screen that displays computer information. Also referred to as a CRT.
Motherboard	The primary hardware circuitboard of a computer.
Mouse	A hand-held, movable device that enters positional information into a computer. Also see "Joystick."
MS-DOS	A general-purpose disk operating system that is used with IBM PC and compatible computers.
Multi-user	A computer that can simultaneously support more than one terminal. See "Terminal."

Network	A number of computers capable of transmitting and receiving computer data to and from each other.
NUL	A testing device of a disk operating system. See "DOS."
Object file	A set of information created by a compiler from language source code. An object file must be linked before it can be executed. Object files have .OBJ as their filename extension. See "Compiler," "Linker," "Source code."
Off-line	Not in operation; not under control of a CPU. See "CPU."
On-line	In operation; under control of a CPU. See "CPU."
Open software	A general term for software that is made available to users on terms other than conventional sales. See "Freeware," "Shareware," "User-supported."
Operating system	The fundamental instructions by which a computer can store, process and retrieve information. See "CP/M" and "DOS" for examples of operating systems.
Output	Information generated by a computer and transmitted to one of its peripheral devices, such as a CRT or a printer. See "CRT," "Printer."
Parallel	To transmit more than one bit of information simultaneously. Also see "Serial."
Pascal	A structured, high-level language used in many applications. See "Structured language," "High-level language," "Turbo Pascal."
PC	Personal computer. Although a general term, PC usually refers to the IBM PC computer.
PCB or PC board	From Printed Circuit Board; an integrated circuit board.
PC-DOS	A disk operating system for the IBM PC computer.
Peripheral	An auxiliary device that is connected to a computer. For examples of peripherals, see "Modem," "Plotter," "Printer," "Tape memory."
Pixel	The smallest dot that can be displayed on a CRT. Large numbers of pixels, in combination, generate images on a CRT. See "CRT." Also see "Resolution."
Plotter	An output device that receives data from the computer and prints graphs, bar charts, drawings, etc. on paper.
Port	An electronic door through which information is transferred between sections of a computer and between separate computers.
Printer	Any device that accepts computer information and prints it on paper.
Program	A series of computer instructions that are designed to perform a task or solve a specific problem. See "Software."
Programmer	A person who creates computer programs. See "Program."
Prolog	A specialized language developed for artificial intelligence applications and for decision-making processes. See "Language," "Artificial intelligence."

A
P
P
E
N
D
I
X

PROM	From Programmable Read-Only Memory. PROM is changeable read-only memory. See "ROM," "RAM."
Protocol	Rules or conventions for communicating between devices. Also see "Syntax."
Public domain	The condition of being free of copyright or patent. Public domain software is free of charge and anyone who wants to may use it. Also see "Freeware," "Open software," "Shareware," "User-supported."
RAM	From Random Access Memory. Memory that is lost when a computer is turned off or loses power. Computer memory capability (64K, 640K, etc. is typically rated in RAM. Also see "Byte," "Memory."
RAM disk	Use of a computer's RAM to simulate a disk drive. RAM disk access is faster than a magnetic disk but its memory is lost when the computer is turned off. See "RAM."
Resolution	The clarity or fineness of detail that can be displayed on a CRT or printed out by a plotter or printer.
ROM	From Read-Only Memory. Non-changeable computer memory that is retained when the computer is turned off or loses power. Also see "PROM," "RAM."
Routine	A part of a program that does a limited, specific task. Many routines together make up a program. See "Program."
Run	To start the operation of a program.
Screen	The television-like display of a computer. Also called CRT, Monitor. To screen computer information is to display it on a CRT.
Serial	To transmit information sequentially, unit by unit. Also see "Parallel."
Shareware	Software that is sold with the intention that the user will pay a fee to the program author if the user is satisfied with the program. Also called User-Supported Software.
Software	Any system of instructions that directs computer operation. Software is usually imprinted on a disk. Also see "Disk," "Program," "Hardware."
Sort	To arrange information into a prescribed order.
Source code	An original program as written by the programmer.
Source file	The file created from a source code. The actual program text of a progam. See "Source code."
Spooler	A buffer between a computer and a printer which allows the computer to continue processing data while the printer is printing. See "Buffer."
Spreadsheet	An electronic accounting worksheet in which numbers, letters or symbols are placed in columns and rows. Spreadsheets, linked together, form accounting ledgers, balance sheets, etc. Also see "Template."
Storage device	Any device that stores information, such as on a disk or tape.
Structured language	Any programming language that permits repositioning of information within a program in the order selected. Also see "Modular construction."

Subroutine	A definable section within a routine.
Symphony	A multi-purpose, integrated applications program.
Syntax	The grammar rules of a computer language.
Tape memory	A device that stores information on a reel or cassette of magnetic recording tape.
Template	An electronic form, previously developed for specific applications.
Terminal	A keyboard and a CRT that are connected to a computer so that information can be entered into, and received from, a computer at the location of the terminal. See "Keyboard," "CRT."
Text file	A file of letters and/or numbers that is displayed in the form of conventional text for reading, without graphics. Text files are common in word processing. See "Word processing."
Turbo Pascal	A popular Pascal compiler for the IBM PC. See "Pascal," "Compiler."
User-supported	Any software that is financially supported by its users. See "Open software," "Shareware."
Utility	A specialized program that allows an operator to modify or extract data from a program.
VisiCalc	A popular spreadsheet program. See "Spreadsheet."
Wild card	A command that can represent one or more characters, numbers or symbols.
Word processor	Any one of a category of programs which allows an operator to edit or otherwise manipulate text.
WordStar	A popular word processing program for the IBM PC computer. See "Word processor."

A
P
P
E
N
D
I
X

The PC-SIG Library on CD ROM

The entire PC-SIG Library is also available on CD ROM. You access the CD ROM Disc as if it was a giant hard disk, and don't have to worry about erasing any of the files.

Currently, the CD ROM is available for a one time purchase at $295.00. A subscription service is available, which includes the first disk and the next three updates (the updates come every 3 to 4 months and contain additional disks and updates since the last release) for only $495.00

The CD ROM package, which is playable on the Sony, Hitachi or Philips laser-drive player, includes the CD ROM disk, the access software on floppy disk and users manual.

Ship To: (Please Print)   #315

_____

_____

_____

_____

Telephone: (   ) _____

☐ Single Purchase _____ @295.00_____   Method of Payment:

☐ Subscription _____ @495.00_____   ☐ Check enclosed ☐ Visa ☐ MasterCard

Subtotal _____   Card No. _____

California Residents add   Exp. Date _____ Sig. _____

7% State sales tax _____   Foreign orders should include payment in U.S. dollars by credit card, international money order, or check drawn on U.S. bank.

Shipping and handling _$5.00_

(S & H for Foreign orders is $50) _____   **PC-SIG** PC-SIG,
1030 East Duane Avenue, Suite D,
TOTAL _____   Sunnyvale, California 94086

F
O
R
M
S

Circle disk numbers desired:

1	2	3	4	5	6	7	8	9	10
11	12	13	14	15	16	17	18	19	20
21	22	23	24	25	26	27	28	29	30
31	32	33	34	35	36	37	38	39	40
41	42	43	44	45	46	47	48	49	50
51	52	53	54	55	56	57	58	59	60
61	62	63	64	65	66	67	68	69	70
81	82	83	84	85	86	87	88	89	90
91	92	93	94	95	96	97	98	99	100
101	102	103	104	105	106	107	108	109	110
111	112	113	114	115	116	117	118	119	120
121	122	123	124	125	126	127	128	129	130
131	132	133	134	135	136	137	138	139	140
141	142	143	144	145	146	147	148	149	150
151	152	153	154	155	156	157	158	159	160
161	162	163	164	165	166	167	168	169	170
171	172	173	174	175	176	177	178	179	180
181	182	183	184	185	186	187	188	189	190
191	192	193	194	195	196	197	198	199	200
201	202	203	204	205	206	207	208	209	210
211	112	213	214	215	216	217	218	219	220
221	222	223	224	225	226	227	228	229	230
231	232	233	234	235	236	237	238	239	240
241	242	243	244	245	246	247	248	249	250
251	252	253	254	255	256	257	258	259	260
261	262	263	264	265	266	267	268	269	270
271	272	273	274	275	276	277	278	279	280
281	282	283	284	285	286	287	288	289	290
291	292	293	294	295	296	297	298	299	300
301	302	303	304	305	306	307	308	309	310
311	312	313	314	315	316	317	318	319	320
321	322	323	324	325	326	327	328	329	330
331	332	333	334	335	336	337	338	339	340
341	342	343	344	345	346	347	348	349	350
351	352	353	354	355	356	357	358	359	360
361	362	363	364	365	366	367	368	369	370
371	372	373	374	375	376	377	378	379	380
381	382	383	384	385	386	387	388	389	390
391	392	393	394	395	396	397	398	399	400
401	402	403	404	405	406	407	408	409	410
411	412	413	414	415	416	417	418	419	420
421	422	423	424	425	426	427	428	429	430
431	432	433	434	435	436	437	438	439	440
441	442	443	444	445	446	447	448	449	450
451	452	453	454	455	456	457	458	459	460
461	462	463	464	465	466	467	468	469	470
471	472	473	474	475	476	477	478	479	480
481	482	483	484	485	486	487	488	489	490
491	492	493	494	495	496	497	498	499	500
501	502	503	504	505	506	507	508	509	510
511	512	513	514	515	516	517	518	519	520
521	522	523	524	525	526	527	528	529	530
531	532	533	534	535	536	537	538	539	540
541	542	543	544	545	546	547	548	549	550
551	552	553	554	555	556	557	558	559	560
561	562	563	564	565	566	567	568	569	570
571	572	573	574	575	576	577	578	579	580
581	582	583	584	585	586	587	588	589	590
591	592	593	594	595	596	597	598	599	600
601	602	603	604	605	606	607	608	609	610
611	612	613	614	615	616	617	618	619	620
621	622	623	624	625	626	627	628	629	630
631	632	633	634	635	636	637	638	639	640
641	642	643	644	645	646	647	648	649	650
651	652	653	654	655	656	657	658	659	660
661	662	663	664	665	666	667	668	669	670
671	672	673	674	675	676	677	678	679	680
681	682	683	684	685	686	687	688	689	690
691	692	693	694	695	696	697	698	699	700
701	702	703	704	705	706	707	708	709	710
711	712	713	714	715	716	717	718	719	720
721	722	723	724	725	726	727	728	729	730
731	732	733	734	735	736	737	738	739	740
741	742	743	744	745	746	747	748	749	750

Ship To: (Please Print)

_____

_____

_____

_____

_____

_____

Telephone: (   ) _____

Number of Disks
    Ordered _____ x $6 _____

☐ PC-SIG Directory $12.95 _____

☐ Other _____   _____

         Subtotal _____

California residents add
     7% State sales tax _____

    Shipping and handling $4.00
(Foreign include additional $10.) _____

         TOTAL _____

Method of Payment:

☐ Check enclosed   ☐ Visa   ☐ MasterCard

Card No. _____

Exp. Date _____ Sig. _____

Telephone Orders

USA (except California)	**(800) 245-6717**
California only	**(800) 222-2996**
or use FAX	**(408) 730-2107**

Foreign orders and/or Technical Support,
call **(408) 730-9291**.

Foreign orders should include payment in U.S.
dollars by credit card, international money
order, or check drawn on U.S. bank.

PC-SIG,
1030 East Duane Avenue, Suite D,
Sunnyvale, California 94086

Circle disk numbers desired:

1	2	3	4	5	6	7	8	9	10
11	12	13	14	15	16	17	18	19	20
21	22	23	24	25	26	27	28	29	30
31	32	33	34	35	36	37	38	39	40
41	42	43	44	45	46	47	48	49	50
51	52	53	54	55	56	57	58	59	60
61	62	63	64	65	66	67	68	69	70
81	82	83	84	85	86	87	88	89	90
91	92	93	94	95	96	97	98	99	100
101	102	103	104	105	106	107	108	109	110
111	112	113	114	115	116	117	118	119	120
121	122	123	124	125	126	127	128	129	130
131	132	133	134	135	136	137	138	139	140
141	142	143	144	145	146	147	148	149	150
151	152	153	154	155	156	157	158	159	160
161	162	163	164	165	166	167	168	169	170
171	172	173	174	175	176	177	178	179	180
181	182	183	184	185	186	187	188	189	190
191	192	193	194	195	196	197	198	199	200
201	202	203	204	205	206	207	208	209	210
211	112	213	214	215	216	217	218	219	220
221	222	223	224	225	226	227	228	229	230
231	232	233	234	235	236	237	238	239	240
241	242	243	244	245	246	247	248	249	250
251	252	253	254	255	256	257	258	259	260
261	262	263	264	265	266	267	268	269	270
271	272	273	274	275	276	277	278	279	280
281	282	283	284	285	286	287	288	289	290
291	292	293	294	295	296	297	298	299	300
301	302	303	304	305	306	307	308	309	310
311	312	313	314	315	316	317	318	319	320
321	322	323	324	325	326	327	328	329	330
331	332	333	334	335	336	337	338	339	340
341	342	343	344	345	346	347	348	349	350
351	352	353	354	355	356	357	358	359	360
361	362	363	364	365	366	367	368	369	370
371	372	373	374	375	376	377	378	379	380
381	382	383	384	385	386	387	388	389	390
391	392	393	394	395	396	397	398	399	400
401	402	403	404	405	406	407	408	409	410
411	412	413	414	415	416	417	418	419	420
421	422	423	424	425	426	427	428	429	430
431	432	433	434	435	436	437	438	439	440
441	442	443	444	445	446	447	448	449	450
451	452	453	454	455	456	457	458	459	460
461	462	463	464	465	466	467	468	469	470
471	472	473	474	475	476	477	478	479	480
481	482	483	484	485	486	487	488	489	490
491	492	493	494	495	496	497	498	499	500
501	502	503	504	505	506	507	508	509	510
511	512	513	514	515	516	517	518	519	520
521	522	523	524	525	526	527	528	529	530
531	532	533	534	535	536	537	538	539	540
541	542	543	544	545	546	547	548	549	550
551	552	553	554	555	556	557	558	559	560
561	562	563	564	565	566	567	568	569	570
571	572	573	574	575	576	577	578	579	580
581	582	583	584	585	586	587	588	589	590
591	592	593	594	595	596	597	598	599	600
601	602	603	604	605	606	607	608	609	610
611	612	613	614	615	616	617	618	619	620
621	622	623	624	625	626	627	628	629	630
631	632	633	634	635	636	637	638	639	640
641	642	643	644	645	646	647	648	649	650
651	652	653	654	655	656	657	658	659	660
661	662	663	664	665	666	667	668	669	670
671	672	673	674	675	676	677	678	679	680
681	682	683	684	685	686	687	688	689	690
691	692	693	694	695	696	697	698	699	700
701	702	703	704	705	706	707	708	709	710
711	712	713	714	715	716	717	718	719	720
721	722	723	724	725	726	727	728	729	730
731	732	733	734	735	736	737	738	739	740
741	742	743	744	745	746	747	748	749	750

Ship To: (Please Print)

_____

_____

_____

_____

_____

_____

Telephone: (   ) _____

Number of Disks
     Ordered _____ x $6 _____

☐ PC-SIG Directory $12.95 _____

☐ Other _____   _____

                  Subtotal _____

    California residents add
       7% State sales tax _____

    Shipping and handling $4.00
(Foreign include additional $10.) _____

               TOTAL _____

Method of Payment:

☐ Check enclosed   ☐ Visa   ☐ MasterCard

Card No. _____

Exp. Date _____ Sig. _____

Telephone Orders

USA (except California)	**(800) 245-6717**
California only	**(800) 222-2996**
or use FAX	**(408) 730-2107**

Foreign orders and/or Technical Support,
call **(408) 730-9291.**

Foreign orders should include payment in U.S.
dollars by credit card, international money
order, or check drawn on U.S. bank.

 PC-SIG,
1030 East Duane Avenue, Suite D,
Sunnyvale, California 94086

Circle disk numbers desired:

1	2	3	4	5	6	7	8	9	10
11	12	13	14	15	16	17	18	19	20
21	22	23	24	25	26	27	28	29	30
31	32	33	34	35	36	37	38	39	40
41	42	43	44	45	46	47	48	49	50
51	52	53	54	55	56	57	58	59	60
61	62	63	64	65	66	67	68	69	70
81	82	83	84	85	86	87	88	89	90
91	92	93	94	95	96	97	98	99	100
101	102	103	104	105	106	107	108	109	110
111	112	113	114	115	116	117	118	119	120
121	122	123	124	125	126	127	128	129	130
131	132	133	134	135	136	137	138	139	140
141	142	143	144	145	146	147	148	149	150
151	152	153	154	155	156	157	158	159	160
161	162	163	164	165	166	167	168	169	170
171	172	173	174	175	176	177	178	179	180
181	182	183	184	185	186	187	188	189	190
191	192	193	194	195	196	197	198	199	200
201	202	203	204	205	206	207	208	209	210
211	112	213	214	215	216	217	218	219	220
221	222	223	224	225	226	227	228	229	230
231	232	233	234	235	236	237	238	239	240
241	242	243	244	245	246	247	248	249	250
251	252	253	254	255	256	257	258	259	260
261	262	263	264	265	266	267	268	269	270
271	272	273	274	275	276	277	278	279	280
281	282	283	284	285	286	287	288	289	290
291	292	293	294	295	296	297	298	299	300
301	302	303	304	305	306	307	308	309	310
311	312	313	314	315	316	317	318	319	320
321	322	323	324	325	326	327	328	329	330
331	332	333	334	335	336	337	338	339	340
341	342	343	344	345	346	347	348	349	350
351	352	353	354	355	356	357	358	359	360
361	362	363	364	365	366	367	368	369	370
371	372	373	374	375	376	377	378	379	380
381	382	383	384	385	386	387	388	389	390
391	392	393	394	395	396	397	398	399	400
401	402	403	404	405	406	407	408	409	410
411	412	413	414	415	416	417	418	419	420
421	422	423	424	425	426	427	428	429	430
431	432	433	434	435	436	437	438	439	440
441	442	443	444	445	446	447	448	449	450
451	452	453	454	455	456	457	458	459	460
461	462	463	464	465	466	467	468	469	470
471	472	473	474	475	476	477	478	479	480
481	482	483	484	485	486	487	488	489	490
491	492	493	494	495	496	497	498	499	500
501	502	503	504	505	506	507	508	509	510
511	512	513	514	515	516	517	518	519	520
521	522	523	524	525	526	527	528	529	530
531	532	533	534	535	536	537	538	539	540
541	542	543	544	545	546	547	548	549	550
551	552	553	554	555	556	557	558	559	560
561	562	563	564	565	566	567	568	569	570
571	572	573	574	575	576	577	578	579	580
581	582	583	584	585	586	587	588	589	590
591	592	593	594	595	596	597	598	599	600
601	602	603	604	605	606	607	608	609	610
611	612	613	614	615	616	617	618	619	620
621	622	623	624	625	626	627	628	629	630
631	632	633	634	635	636	637	638	639	640
641	642	643	644	645	646	647	648	649	650
651	652	653	654	655	656	657	658	659	660
661	662	663	664	665	666	667	668	669	670
671	672	673	674	675	676	677	678	679	680
681	682	683	684	685	686	687	688	689	690
691	692	693	694	695	696	697	698	699	700
701	702	703	704	705	706	707	708	709	710
711	712	713	714	715	716	717	718	719	720
721	722	723	724	725	726	727	728	729	730
731	732	733	734	735	736	737	738	739	740
741	742	743	744	745	746	747	748	749	750

Ship To: (Please Print)

_____

_____

_____

_____

_____

_____

Telephone: (   ) _____

Number of Disks
Ordered _____ x $6 _____

☐ PC-SIG Directory $12.95 _____

☐ Other _____   _____

Subtotal _____

California residents add
7% State sales tax _____

Shipping and handling $4.00
(Foreign include additional $10.) _____

TOTAL _____

Method of Payment:

☐ Check enclosed   ☐ Visa   ☐ MasterCard

Card No. _____

Exp. Date _____ Sig. _____

Telephone Orders

USA (except California)	**(800) 245-6717**
California only	**(800) 222-2996**
or use FAX	**(408) 730-2107**

Foreign orders and/or Technical Support,
call **(408) 730-9291**.

Foreign orders should include payment in U.S.
dollars by credit card, international money
order, or check drawn on U.S. bank.

PC-SIG

PC-SIG,
1030 East Duane Avenue, Suite D,
Sunnyvale, California 94086

FORMS

Circle disk numbers desired:

1	2	3	4	5	6	7	8	9	10
11	12	13	14	15	16	17	18	19	20
21	22	23	24	25	26	27	28	29	30
31	32	33	34	35	36	37	38	39	40
41	42	43	44	45	46	47	48	49	50
51	52	53	54	55	56	57	58	59	60
61	62	63	64	65	66	67	68	69	70
81	82	83	84	85	86	87	88	89	90
91	92	93	94	95	96	97	98	99	100
101	102	103	104	105	106	107	108	109	110
111	112	113	114	115	116	117	118	119	120
121	122	123	124	125	126	127	128	129	130
131	132	133	134	135	136	137	138	139	140
141	142	143	144	145	146	147	148	149	150
151	152	153	154	155	156	157	158	159	160
161	162	163	164	165	166	167	168	169	170
171	172	173	174	175	176	177	178	179	180
181	182	183	184	185	186	187	188	189	190
191	192	193	194	195	196	197	198	199	200
201	202	203	204	205	206	207	208	209	210
211	112	213	214	215	216	217	218	219	220
221	222	223	224	225	226	227	228	229	230
231	232	233	234	235	236	237	238	239	240
241	242	243	244	245	246	247	248	249	250
251	252	253	254	255	256	257	258	259	260
261	262	263	264	265	266	267	268	269	270
271	272	273	274	275	276	277	278	279	280
281	282	283	284	285	286	287	288	289	290
291	292	293	294	295	296	297	298	299	300
301	302	303	304	305	306	307	308	309	310
311	312	313	314	315	316	317	318	319	320
321	322	323	324	325	326	327	328	329	330
331	332	333	334	335	336	337	338	339	340
341	342	343	344	345	346	347	348	349	350
351	352	353	354	355	356	357	358	359	360
361	362	363	364	365	366	367	368	369	370
371	372	373	374	375	376	377	378	379	380
381	382	383	384	385	386	387	388	389	390
391	392	393	394	395	396	397	398	399	400
401	402	403	404	405	406	407	408	409	410
411	412	413	414	415	416	417	418	419	420
421	422	423	424	425	426	427	428	429	430
431	432	433	434	435	436	437	438	439	440
441	442	443	444	445	446	447	448	449	450
451	452	453	454	455	456	457	458	459	460
461	462	463	464	465	466	467	468	469	470
471	472	473	474	475	476	477	478	479	480
481	482	483	484	485	486	487	488	489	490
491	492	493	494	495	496	497	498	499	500
501	502	503	504	505	506	507	508	509	510
511	512	513	514	515	516	517	518	519	520
521	522	523	524	525	526	527	528	529	530
531	532	533	534	535	536	537	538	539	540
541	542	543	544	545	546	547	548	549	550
551	552	553	554	555	556	557	558	559	560
561	562	563	564	565	566	567	568	569	570
571	572	573	574	575	576	577	578	579	580
581	582	583	584	585	586	587	588	589	590
591	592	593	594	595	596	597	598	599	600
601	602	603	604	605	606	607	608	609	610
611	612	613	614	615	616	617	618	619	620
621	622	623	624	625	626	627	628	629	630
631	632	633	634	635	636	637	638	639	640
641	642	643	644	645	646	647	648	649	650
651	652	653	654	655	656	657	658	659	660
661	662	663	664	665	666	667	668	669	670
671	672	673	674	675	676	677	678	679	680
681	682	683	684	685	686	687	688	689	690
691	692	693	694	695	696	697	698	699	700
701	702	703	704	705	706	707	708	709	710
711	712	713	714	715	716	717	718	719	720
721	722	723	724	725	726	727	728	729	730
731	732	733	734	735	736	737	738	739	740
741	742	743	744	745	746	747	748	749	750

Ship To: (Please Print)

_____

_____

_____

_____

_____

_____

Telephone: (   ) _____

Number of Disks

      Ordered _____ x $6 _____

☐ PC-SIG Directory $12.95 _____

☐ Other _____   _____

                    Subtotal _____

California residents add
       7% State sales tax _____

Shipping and handling $4.00
(Foreign include additional $10.) _____

                  TOTAL _____

Method of Payment:

☐ Check enclosed   ☐ Visa   ☐ MasterCard

Card No. _____

Exp. Date _____ Sig. _____

Telephone Orders

USA (except California)   **(800) 245-6717**
California only   **(800) 222-2996**
or use FAX   **(408) 730-2107**

Foreign orders and/or Technical Support,
call **(408) 730-9291.**

Foreign orders should include payment in U.S.
dollars by credit card, international money
order, or check drawn on U.S. bank.

PC-SIG

PC-SIG,
1030 East Duane Avenue, Suite D,
Sunnyvale, California 94086

F
O
R
M
S

PC-SIG
1030D East Duane Avenue
Sunnyvale, CA 94086

Your Name: _____

Address: _____

_____

_____

Daytime Telephone: (   ) _____

Please check
You ☐ May / ☐ May not give my address to the end user.
You ☐ May / ☐ May not may give my work telephone to the end user.

SOFTWARE SUBMISSION:

Type: ☐ New public domain program(s)
       ☐ New user-supported program – suggested donation $ _____
       ☐ Corrected/updated version of program(s) already in the library

       Disk #/filename(s) _____

Source language: ☐ BASIC ☐ Pascal ☐ Assembly ☐ C ☐ Other _____
Are you the author? ☐ Yes ☐ No – if no, please include any info
                        available.

Author Name: _____

Address: _____

_____

City: _____ State: _____ Zip: _____

Telephone: (   ) _____

Special requirements: ☐ Color ☐ Monochrome DOS Version No. _____

Memory _____ Drives _____ Other _____

Please describe each file enclosed. A text file containing a one-line description for each program file submitted and a one or two paragraph overall description would be helpful.

These programs are to the best of my knowledge in the public domain or if I wrote them I hereby place in the public domain or release them as user-supported programs. They may be freely distributed by PC-SIG for any lawful purpose.

       Signed _____ Date: _____

What library disk(s) would you like in return? _____

F
O
R
M
S

PC-SIG
1030D East Duane Avenue
Sunnyvale, CA 94086

Your Name: _____

Address: _____

_____

_____

Daytime Telephone: (   ) _____

Please check
You ☐ May / ☐ May not give my address to the end user.
You ☐ May / ☐ May not may give my work telephone to the end user.

SOFTWARE SUBMISSION:

Type: ☐ New public domain program(s)
      ☐ New user-supported program – suggested donation $ _____
      ☐ Corrected/updated version of program(s) already in the library

Disk #/filename(s) _____

Source language: ☐ BASIC ☐ Pascal ☐ Assembly ☐ C ☐ Other _____
Are you the author? ☐ Yes ☐ No – if no, please include any info
                      available.

Author Name: _____

Address: _____

_____

City: _____ State: _____ Zip: _____

Telephone: (   ) _____

Special requirements: ☐ Color ☐ Monochrome DOS Version No. _____

Memory _____ Drives _____ Other _____

_____

Please describe each file enclosed. A text file containing a one-line
description for each program file submitted and a one or two paragraph
overall description would be helpful.

These programs are to the best of my knowledge in the public domain or if I
wrote them I hereby place in the public domain or release them as user-
supported programs. They may be freely distributed by PC-SIG for any
lawful purpose.

        Signed _____ Date: _____

What library disk(s) would you like in return? _____

F
O
R
M
S